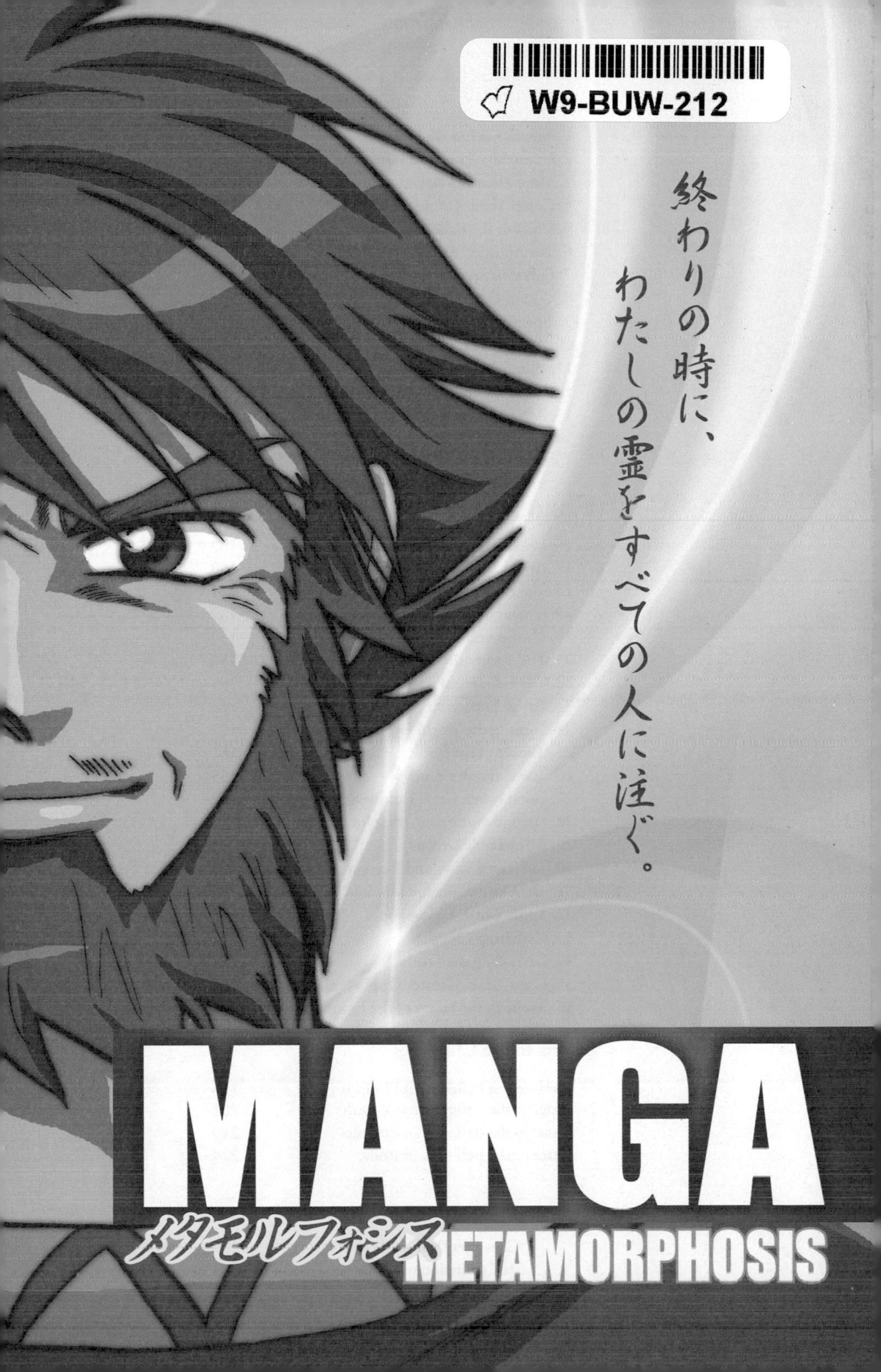

終わりの時に、
わたしの霊をすべての人に注ぐ。
MANGA
メタモルフォシス
METAMORPHOSIS

Contents

Chapter I

Chapter II

Letters to the Churches

Chapter I

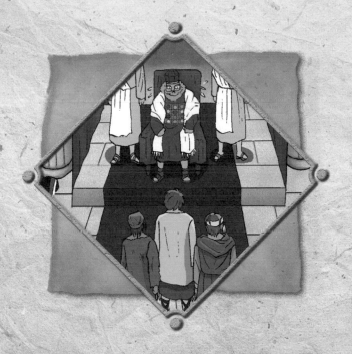

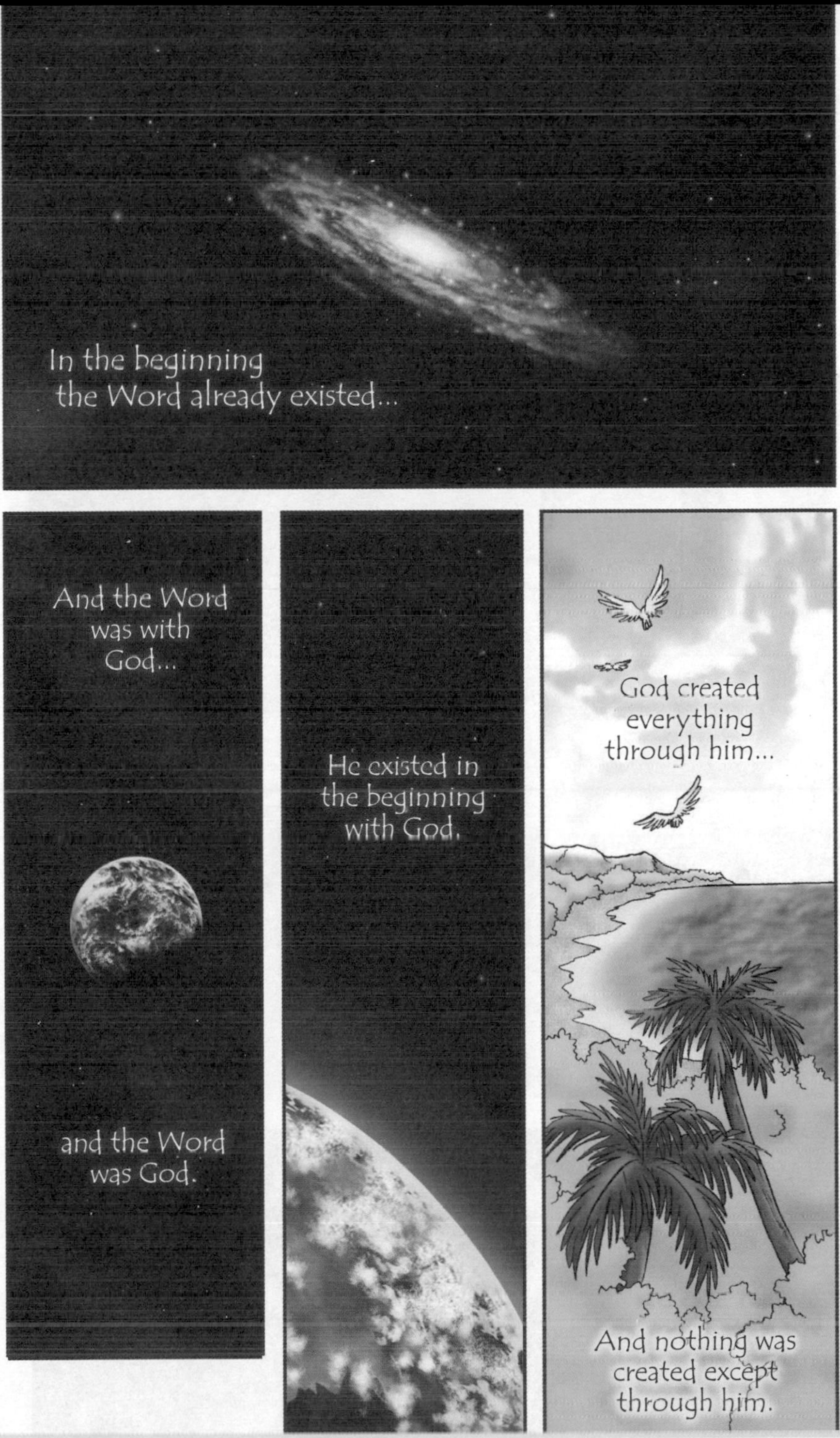
In the beginning
the Word already existed...
And the Word
was with
God...
and the Word
was God.
He existed in
the beginning
with God.
God created
everything
through him...
And nothing was
created except
through him.

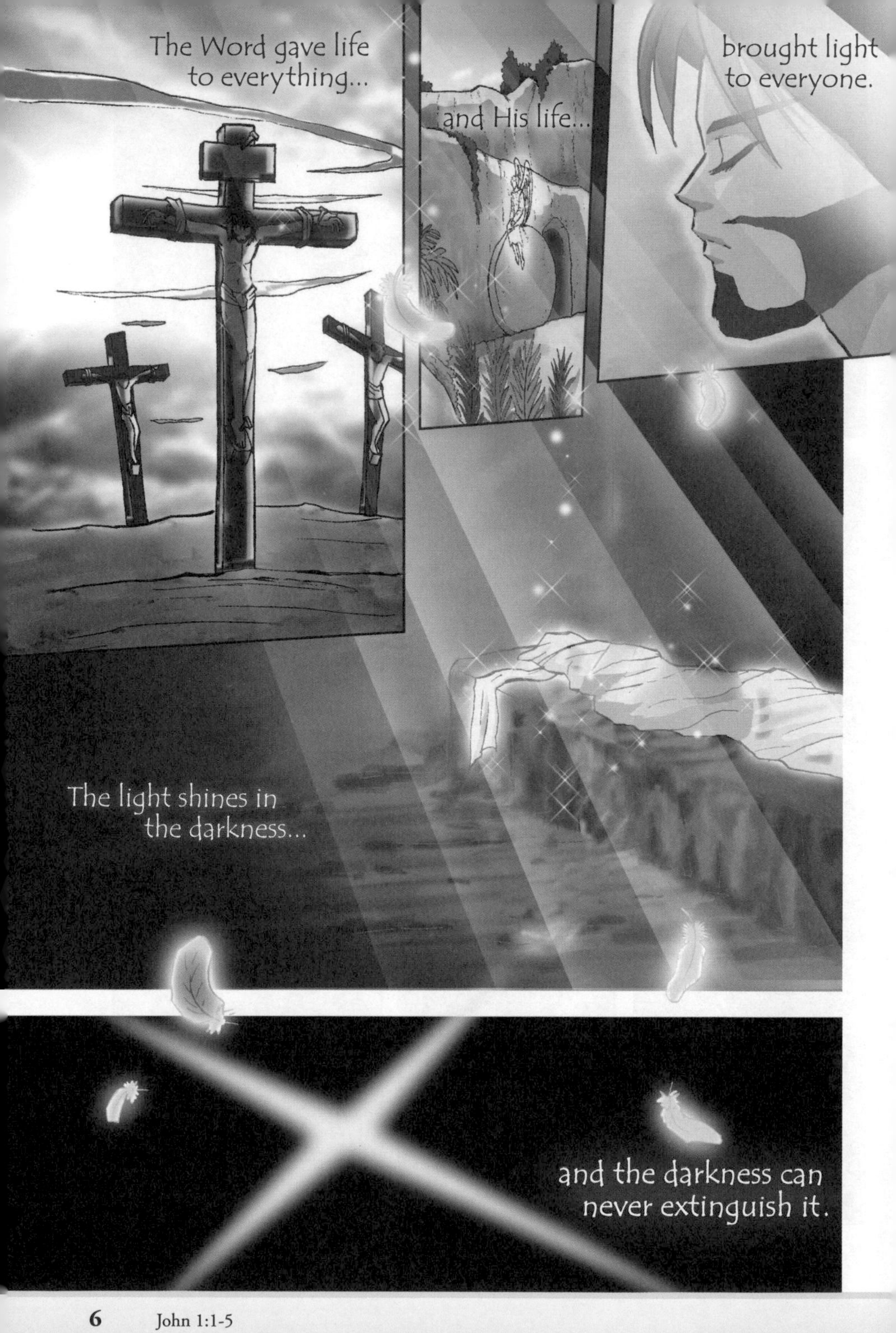

The Word gave life to everything...
and His life...
brought light to everyone.
The light shines in the darkness...
and the darkness can never extinguish it.

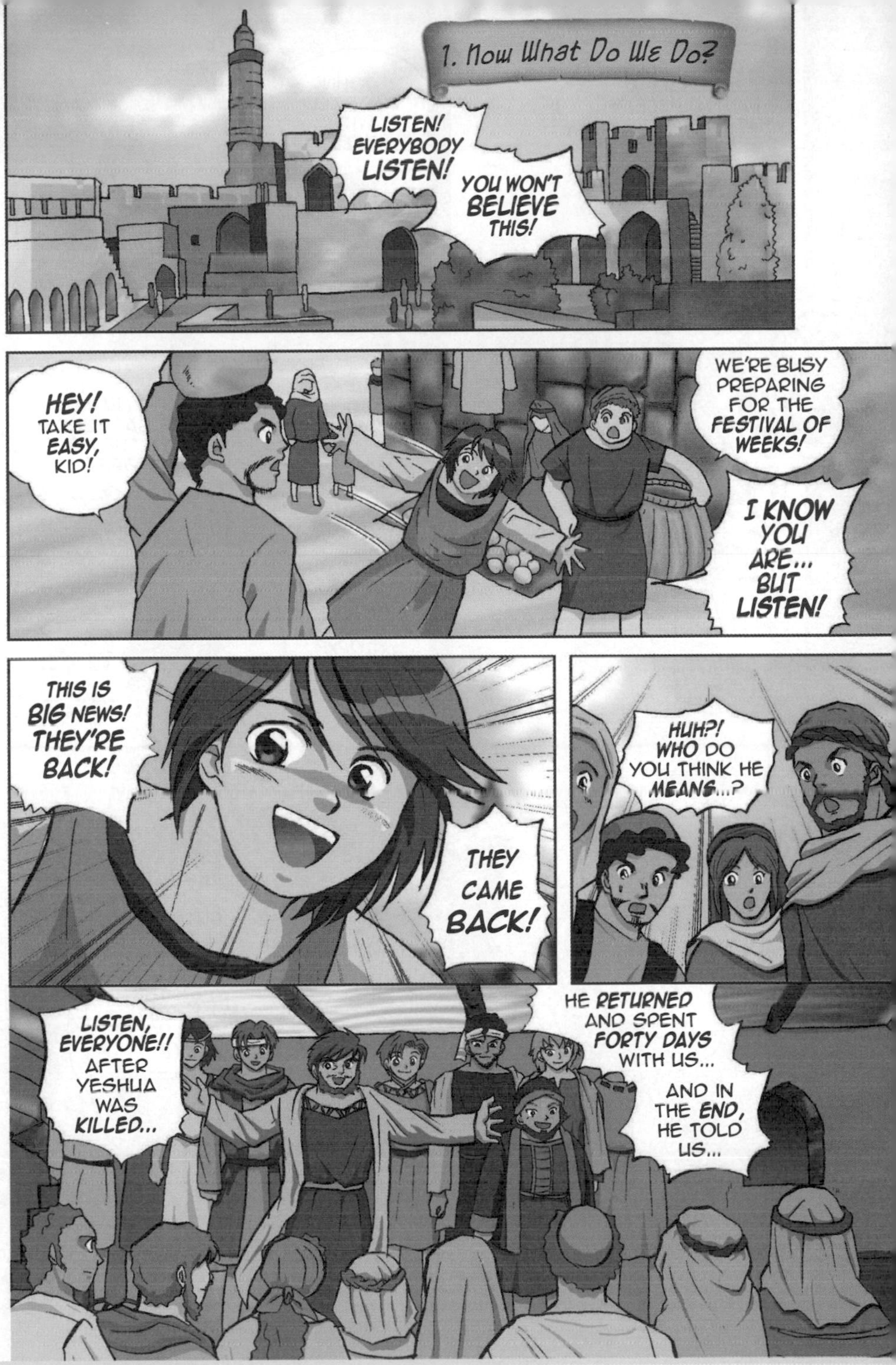
1. Now What Do We Do?
LISTEN! EVERYBODY LISTEN!
YOU WON'T BELIEVE THIS!
HEY! TAKE IT EASY, KID!
WE'RE BUSY PREPARING FOR THE FESTIVAL OF WEEKS!
I KNOW YOU ARE... BUT LISTEN!
THIS IS BIG NEWS! THEY'RE BACK!
THEY CAME BACK!
HUH?! WHO DO YOU THINK HE MEANS...?
LISTEN, EVERYONE!! AFTER YESHUA WAS KILLED...
HE RETURNED AND SPENT FORTY DAYS WITH US...
AND IN THE END, HE TOLD US...

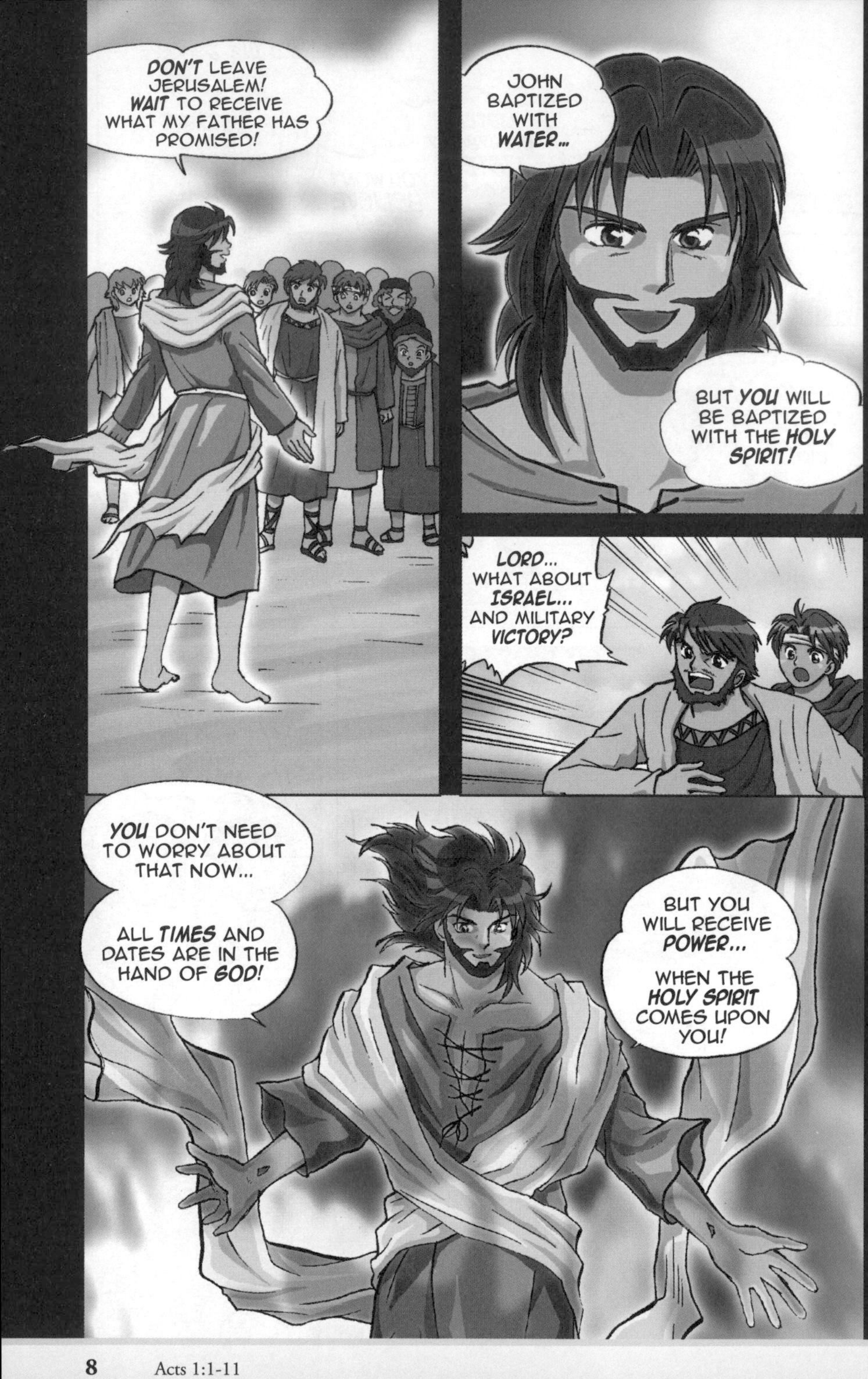
DON'T LEAVE JERUSALEM! WAIT TO RECEIVE WHAT MY FATHER HAS PROMISED!
JOHN BAPTIZED WITH WATER...
BUT YOU WILL BE BAPTIZED WITH THE HOLY SPIRIT!
LORD... WHAT ABOUT ISRAEL... AND MILITARY VICTORY?
YOU DON'T NEED TO WORRY ABOUT THAT NOW...
ALL TIMES AND DATES ARE IN THE HAND OF GOD!
BUT YOU WILL RECEIVE POWER...
WHEN THE HOLY SPIRIT COMES UPON YOU!

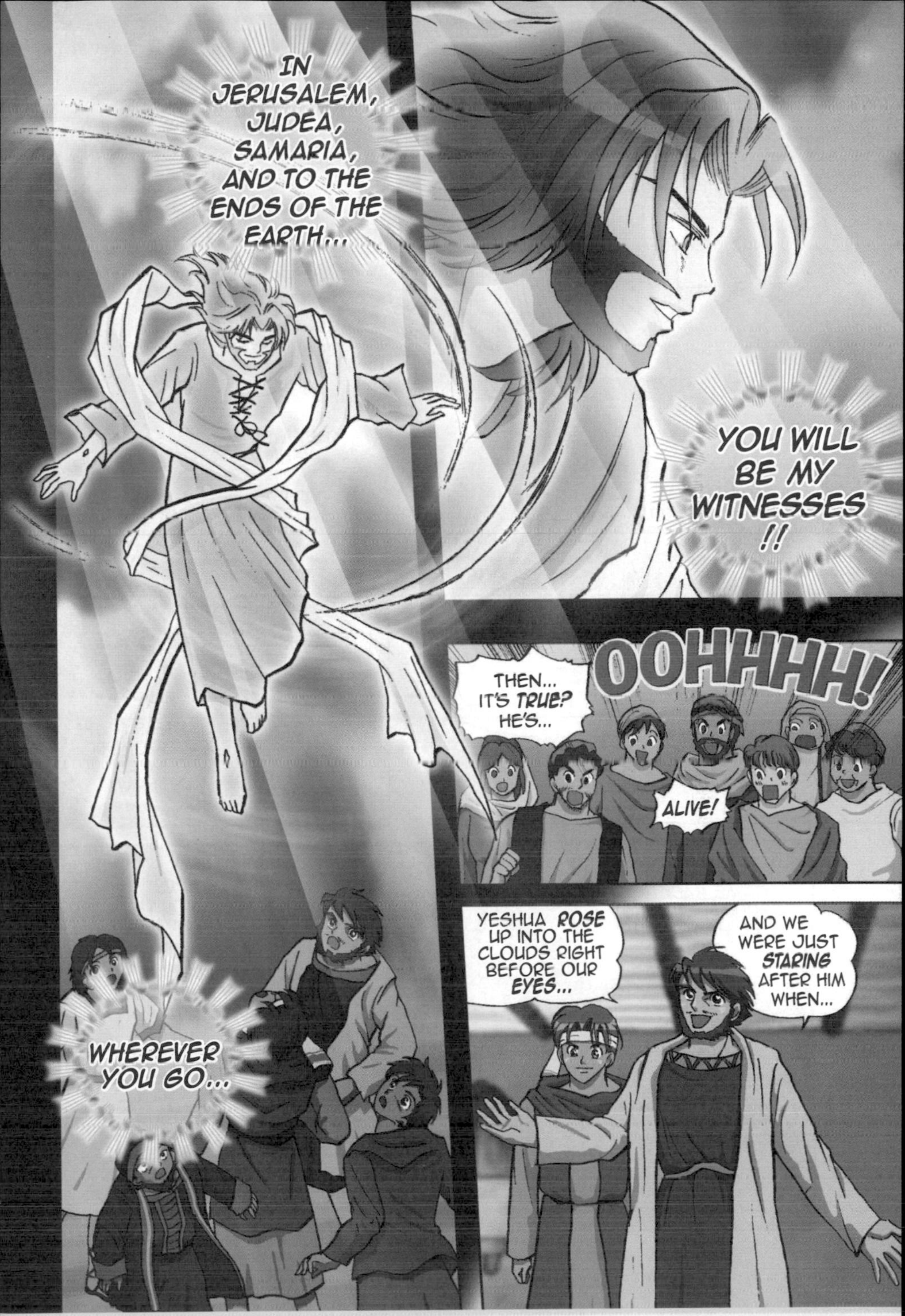
IN JERUSALEM, JUDEA, SAMARIA, AND TO THE ENDS OF THE EARTH...
YOU WILL BE MY WITNESSES !!
WHEREVER YOU GO...
OOHHHH!
THEN... IT'S TRUE? HE'S...
ALIVE!
YESHUA ROSE UP INTO THE CLOUDS RIGHT BEFORE OUR EYES...
AND WE WERE JUST STARING AFTER HIM WHEN...

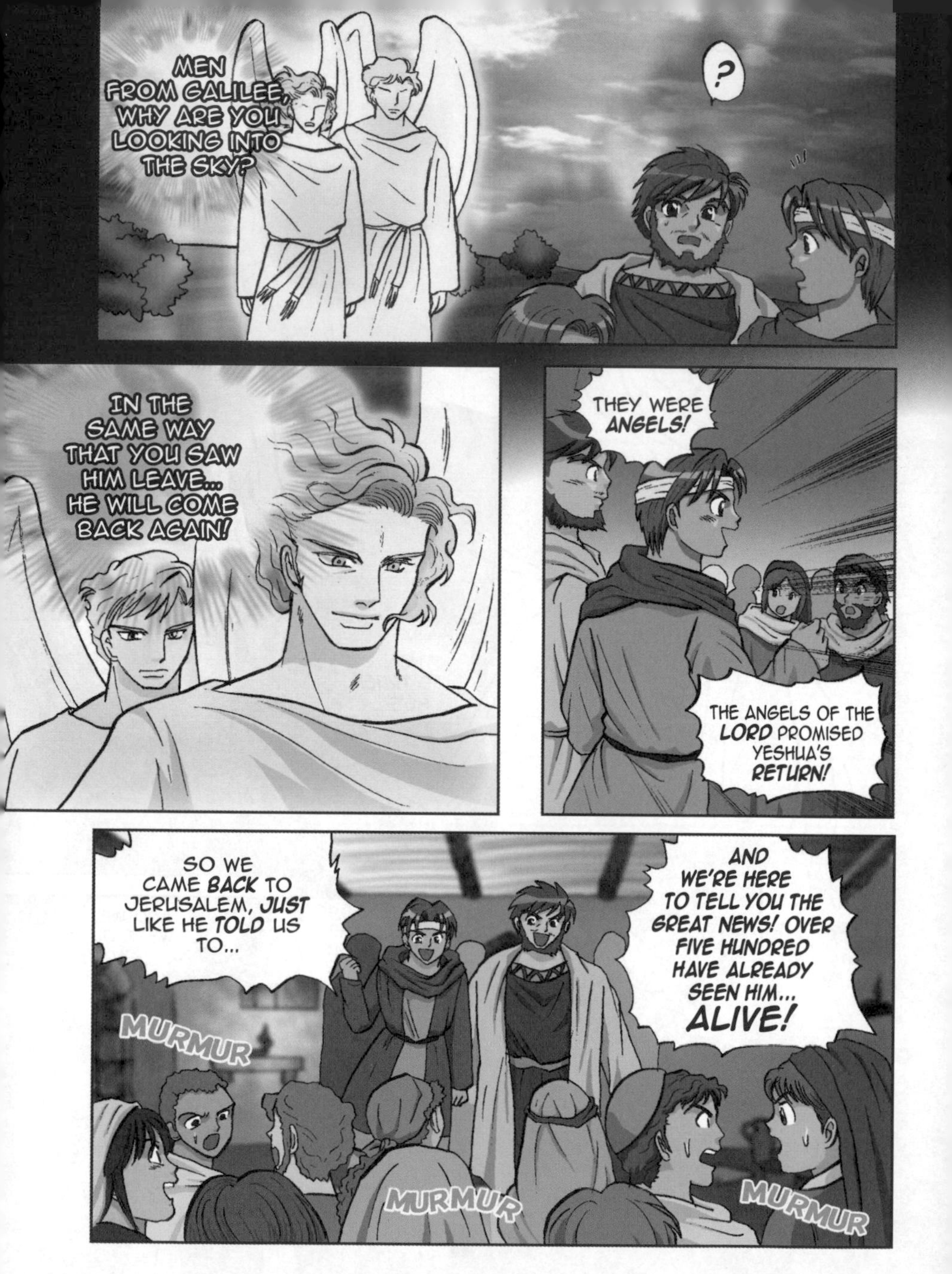
?
MEN FROM GALILEE, WHY ARE YOU LOOKING INTO THE SKY?
IN THE SAME WAY THAT YOU SAW HIM LEAVE... HE WILL COME BACK AGAIN!
THEY WERE ANGELS!
THE ANGELS OF THE LORD PROMISED YESHUA'S RETURN!
SO WE CAME BACK TO JERUSALEM, JUST LIKE HE TOLD US TO...
AND WE'RE HERE TO TELL YOU THE GREAT NEWS! OVER FIVE HUNDRED HAVE ALREADY SEEN HIM... ALIVE!
MURMUR
MURMUR
MURMUR

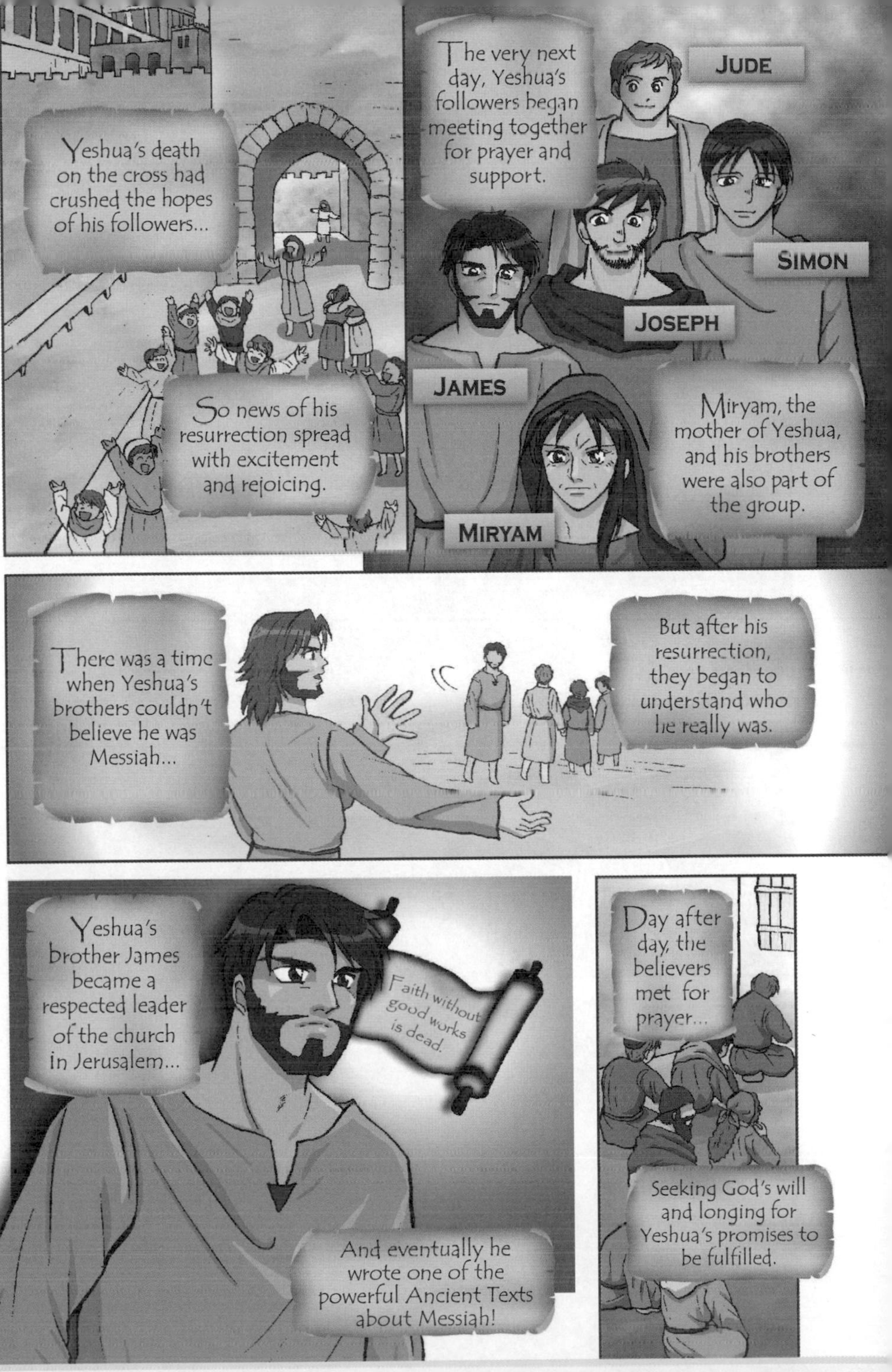
Yeshua's death on the cross had crushed the hopes of his followers...
So news of his resurrection spread with excitement and rejoicing.
The very next day, Yeshua's followers began meeting together for prayer and support.
JUDE
SIMON
JOSEPH
JAMES
MIRYAM
Miryam, the mother of Yeshua, and his brothers were also part of the group.
There was a time when Yeshua's brothers couldn't believe he was Messiah...
But after his resurrection, they began to understand who he really was.
Yeshua's brother James became a respected leader of the church in Jerusalem...
Faith without good works is dead.
And eventually he wrote one of the powerful Ancient Texts about Messiah!
Day after day, the believers met for prayer...
Seeking God's will and longing for Yeshua's promises to be fulfilled.

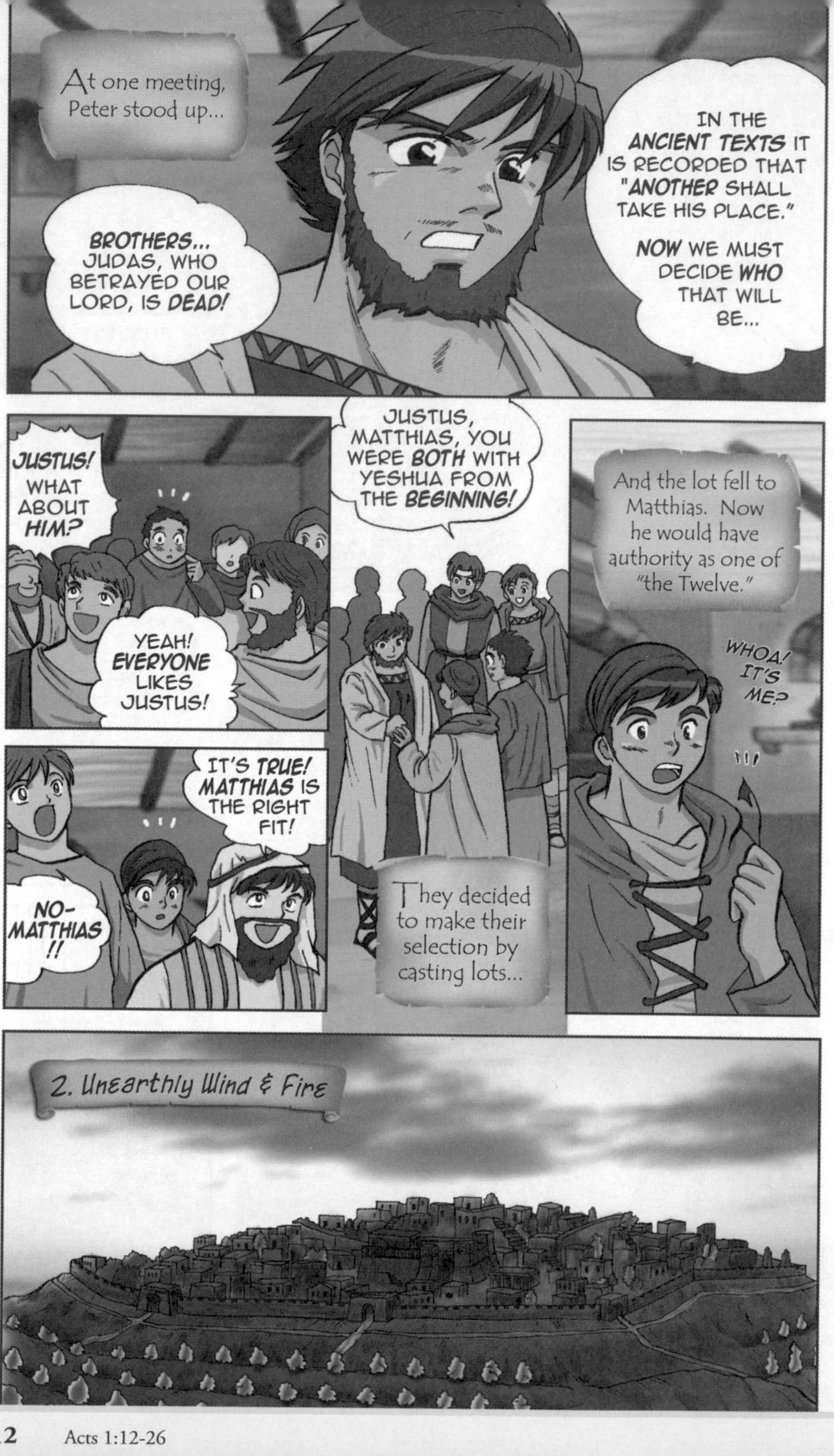
At one meeting, Peter stood up...
BROTHERS... JUDAS, WHO BETRAYED OUR LORD, IS DEAD!
IN THE ANCIENT TEXTS IT IS RECORDED THAT "ANOTHER SHALL TAKE HIS PLACE."
NOW WE MUST DECIDE WHO THAT WILL BE...
JUSTUS! WHAT ABOUT HIM?
YEAH! EVERYONE LIKES JUSTUS!
IT'S TRUE! MATTHIAS IS THE RIGHT FIT!
NO- MATTHIAS !!
JUSTUS, MATTHIAS, YOU WERE BOTH WITH YESHUA FROM THE BEGINNING!
They decided to make their selection by casting lots...
And the lot fell to Matthias. Now he would have authority as one of "the Twelve."
WHOA! IT'S ME?
2. Unearthly Wind & Fire

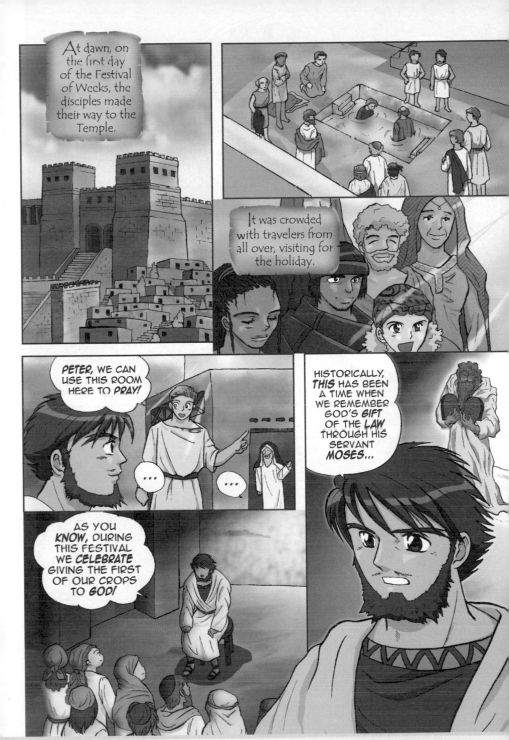

At dawn, on the first day of the Festival of Weeks, the disciples made their way to the Temple.

It was crowded with travelers from all over, visiting for the holiday.

PETER, WE CAN USE THIS ROOM HERE TO PRAY!

...

...

HISTORICALLY, **THIS** HAS BEEN A TIME WHEN WE REMEMBER GOD'S **GIFT** OF THE **LAW** THROUGH HIS SERVANT **MOSES**...

AS YOU **KNOW**, DURING THIS FESTIVAL WE **CELEBRATE** GIVING THE FIRST OF OUR CROPS TO **GOD!**

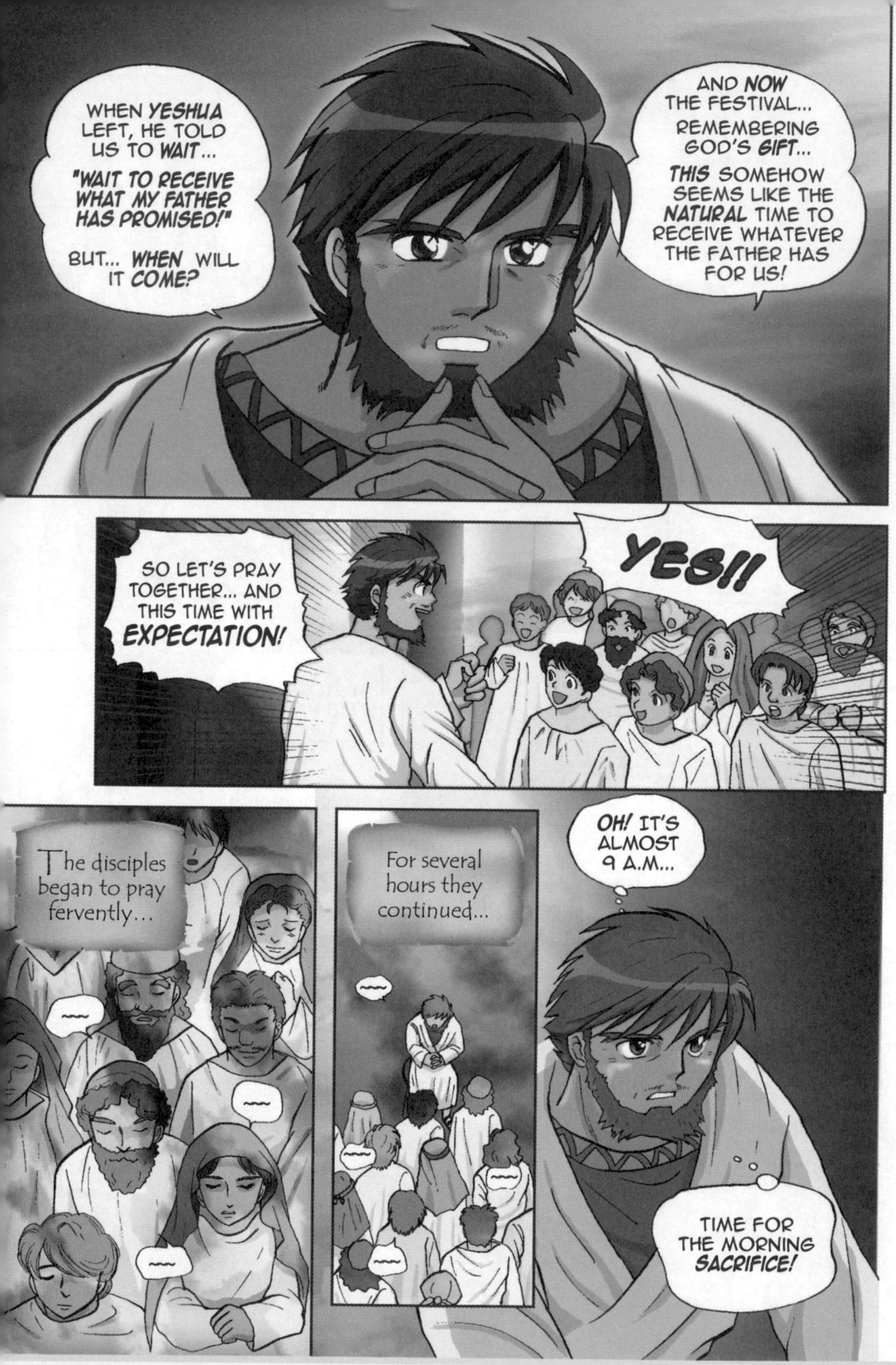
WHEN YESHUA LEFT, HE TOLD US TO WAIT... "WAIT TO RECEIVE WHAT MY FATHER HAS PROMISED!" BUT... WHEN WILL IT COME?
AND NOW THE FESTIVAL... REMEMBERING GOD'S GIFT... THIS SOMEHOW SEEMS LIKE THE NATURAL TIME TO RECEIVE WHATEVER THE FATHER HAS FOR US!
SO LET'S PRAY TOGETHER... AND THIS TIME WITH EXPECTATION!
YES!!
The disciples began to pray fervently...
For several hours they continued...
OH! IT'S ALMOST 9 A.M...
TIME FOR THE MORNING SACRIFICE!

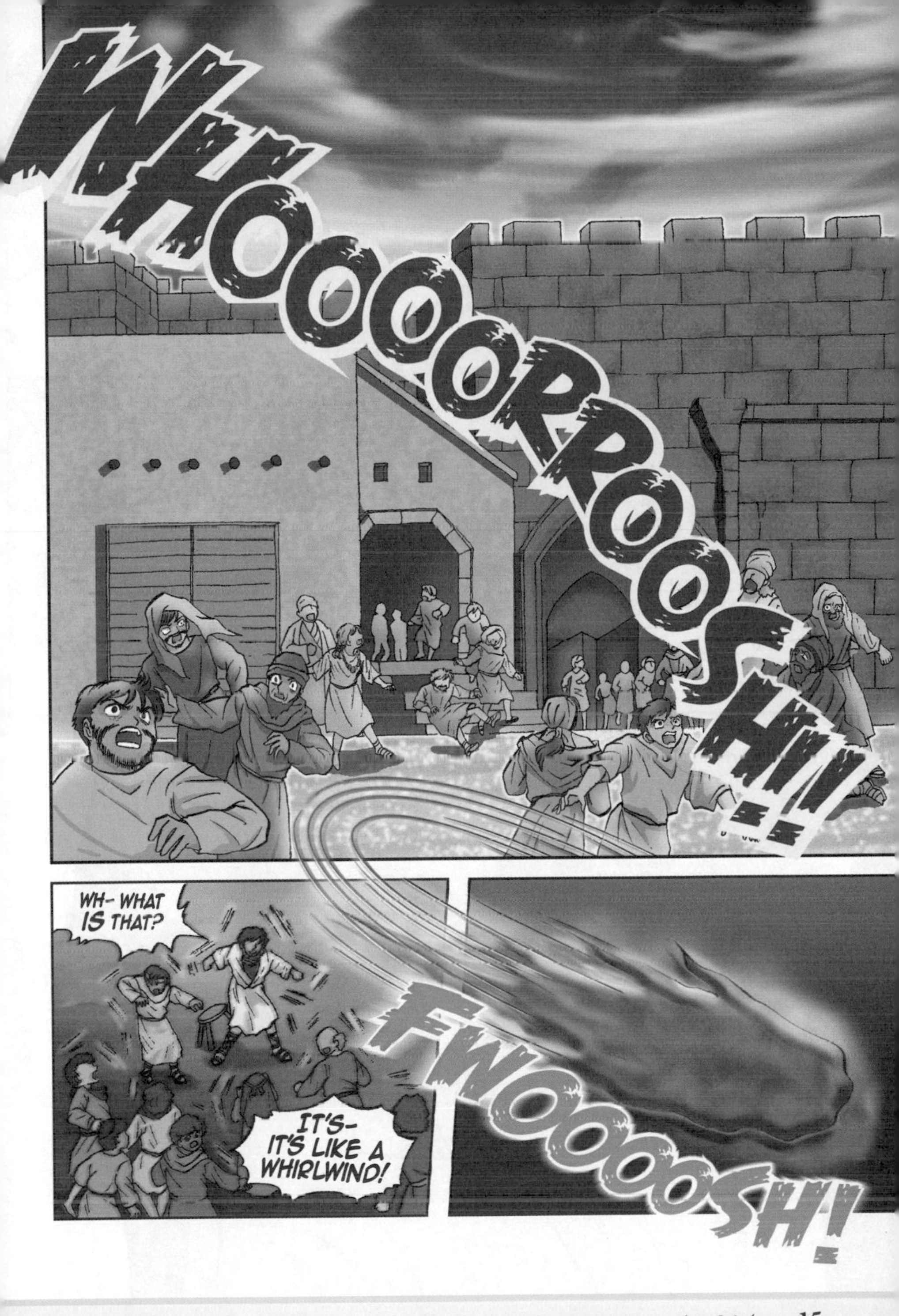
WHOOOORROOSH!!
WH- WHAT IS THAT?
IT'S- IT'S LIKE A WHIRLWIND!
FWOOOOSH!

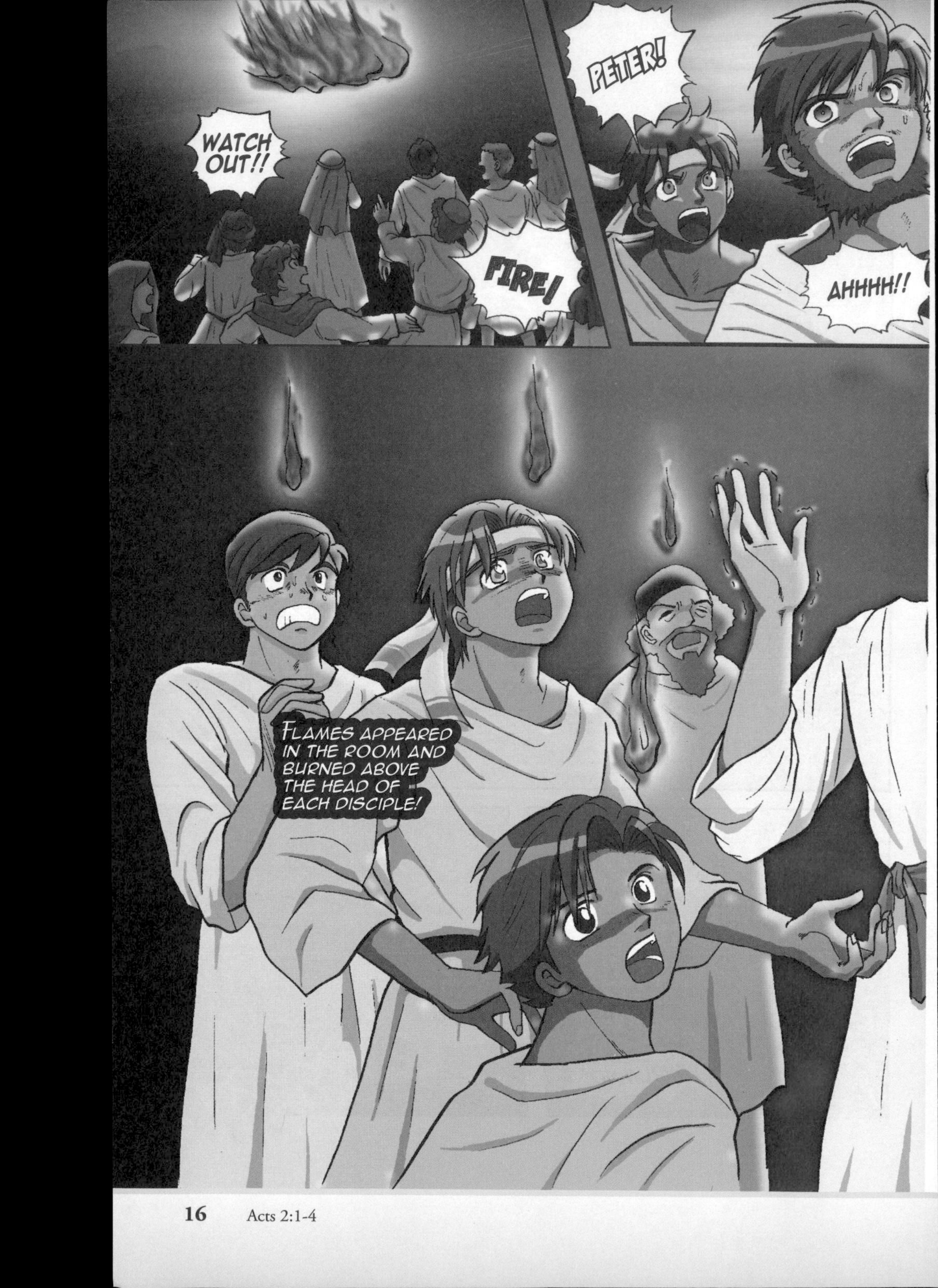
WATCH OUT!!
FIRE!
PETER!
AHHHH!!
FLAMES APPEARED IN THE ROOM AND BURNED ABOVE THE HEAD OF EACH DISCIPLE!

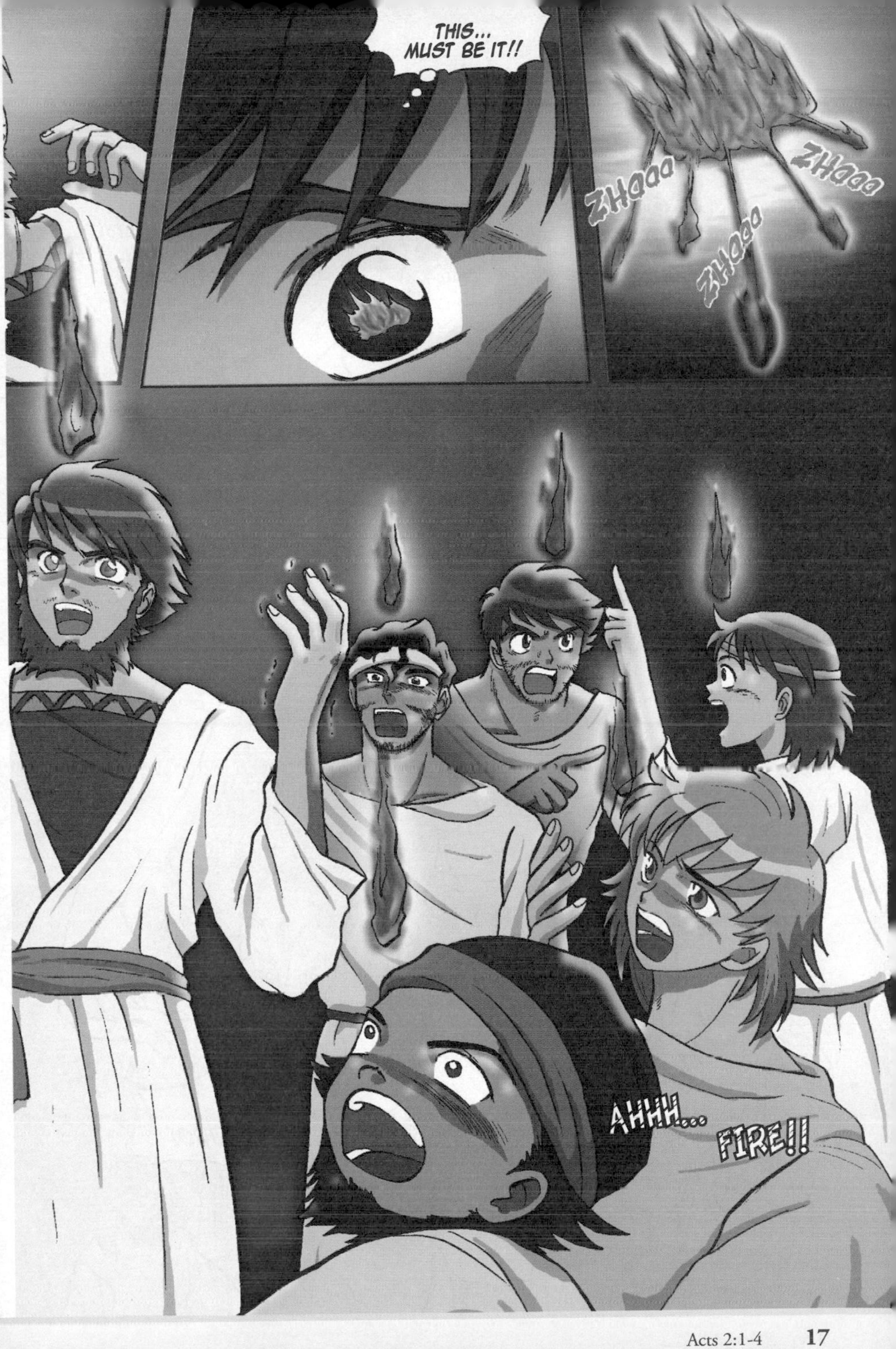
THIS... MUST BE IT!!
ZHOOO
ZHOOO
ZHOOO
AHHH... FIRE!!

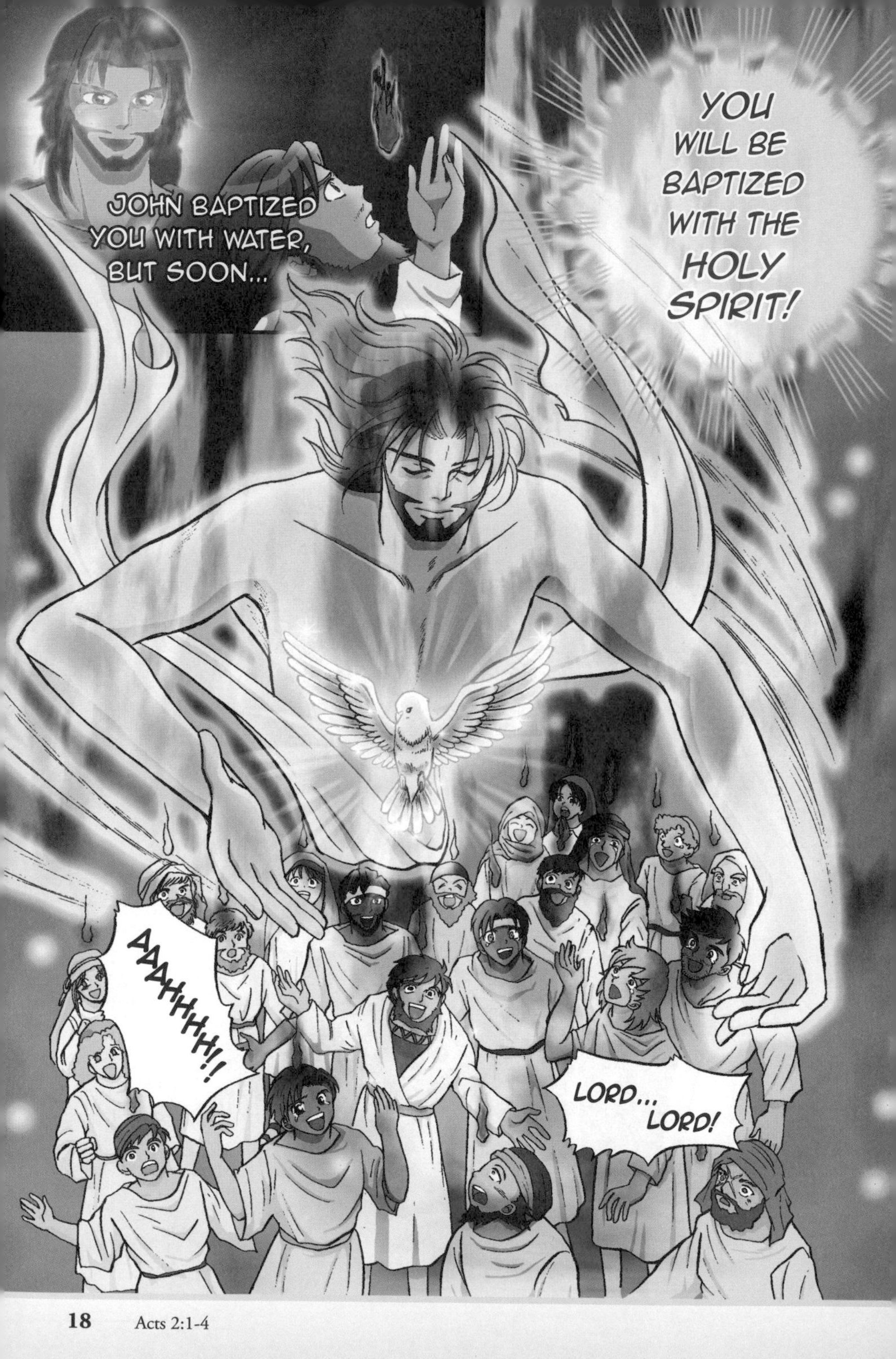
JOHN BAPTIZED YOU WITH WATER, BUT SOON...
YOU WILL BE BAPTIZED WITH THE HOLY SPIRIT!
AAAHHHH!!
LORD... LORD!

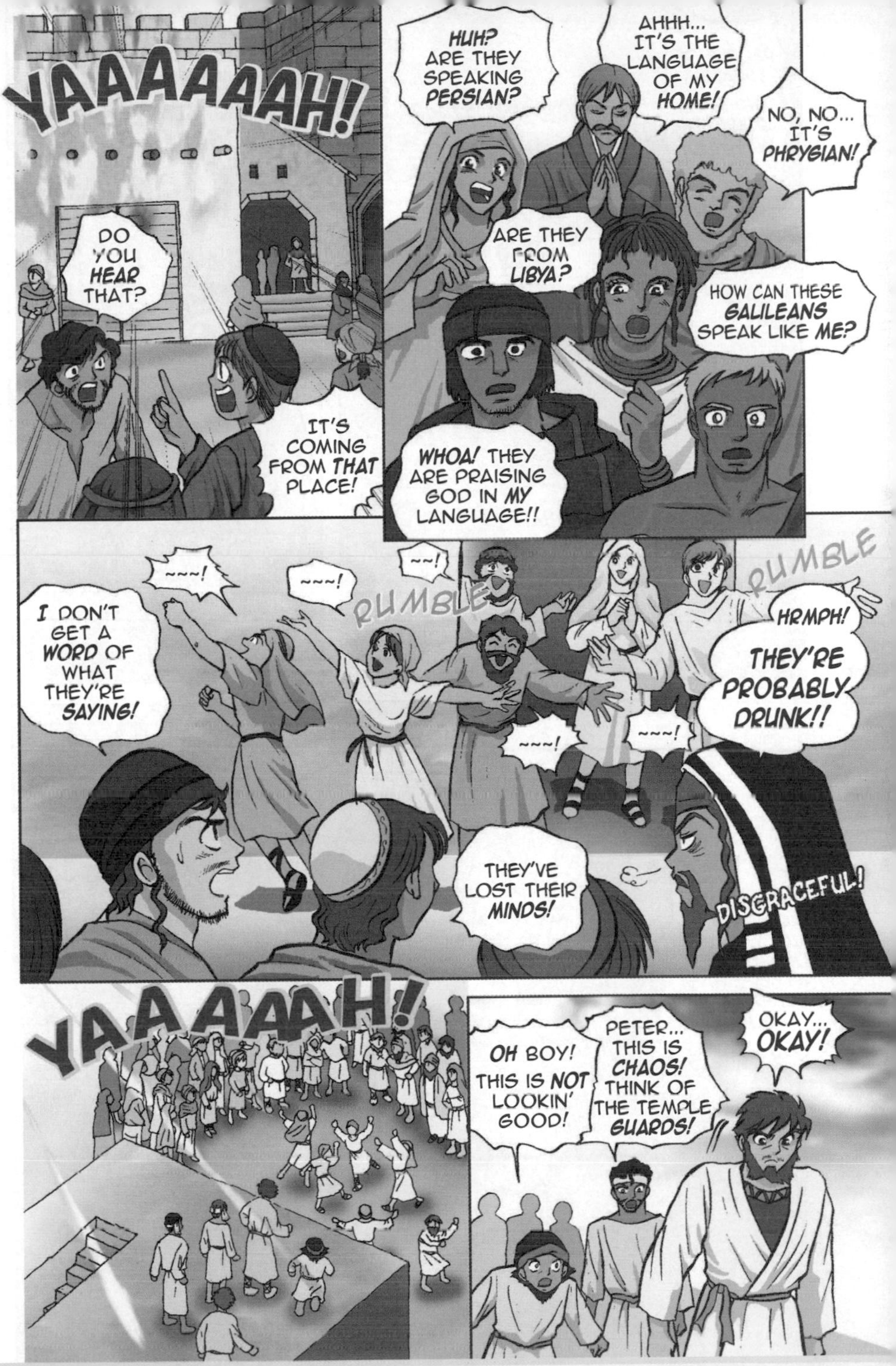
YAAAAAAH!
DO YOU HEAR THAT?
IT'S COMING FROM THAT PLACE!
HUH? ARE THEY SPEAKING PERSIAN?
AHHH... IT'S THE LANGUAGE OF MY HOME!
NO, NO... IT'S PHRYGIAN!
ARE THEY FROM LIBYA?
HOW CAN THESE GALILEANS SPEAK LIKE ME?
WHOA! THEY ARE PRAISING GOD IN MY LANGUAGE!!
~~~!
~~~!
~~!
RUMBLE
RUMBLE
I DON'T GET A WORD OF WHAT THEY'RE SAYING!
HRMPH!
THEY'RE PROBABLY DRUNK!!
~~~!
~~~!
THEY'VE LOST THEIR MINDS!
DISGRACEFUL!
YAAAAAH!
OH BOY! THIS IS NOT LOOKIN' GOOD!
PETER... THIS IS CHAOS! THINK OF THE TEMPLE GUARDS!
OKAY... OKAY!

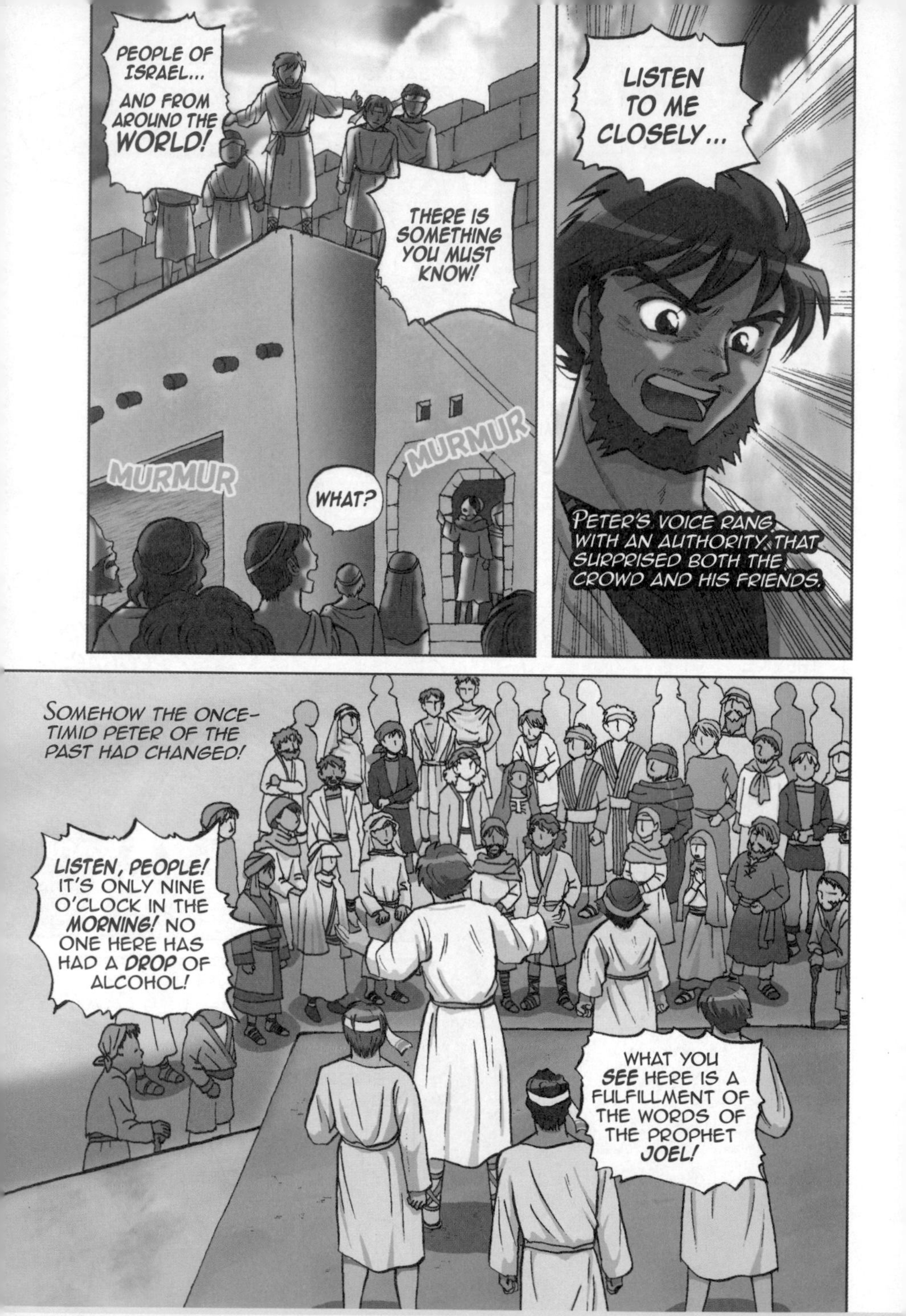
PEOPLE OF ISRAEL...
AND FROM AROUND THE WORLD!
THERE IS SOMETHING YOU MUST KNOW!
MURMUR
WHAT?
MURMUR
LISTEN TO ME CLOSELY...
PETER'S VOICE RANG WITH AN AUTHORITY THAT SURPRISED BOTH THE CROWD AND HIS FRIENDS.
SOMEHOW THE ONCE-TIMID PETER OF THE PAST HAD CHANGED!
LISTEN, PEOPLE! IT'S ONLY NINE O'CLOCK IN THE MORNING! NO ONE HERE HAS HAD A DROP OF ALCOHOL!
WHAT YOU SEE HERE IS A FULFILLMENT OF THE WORDS OF THE PROPHET JOEL!

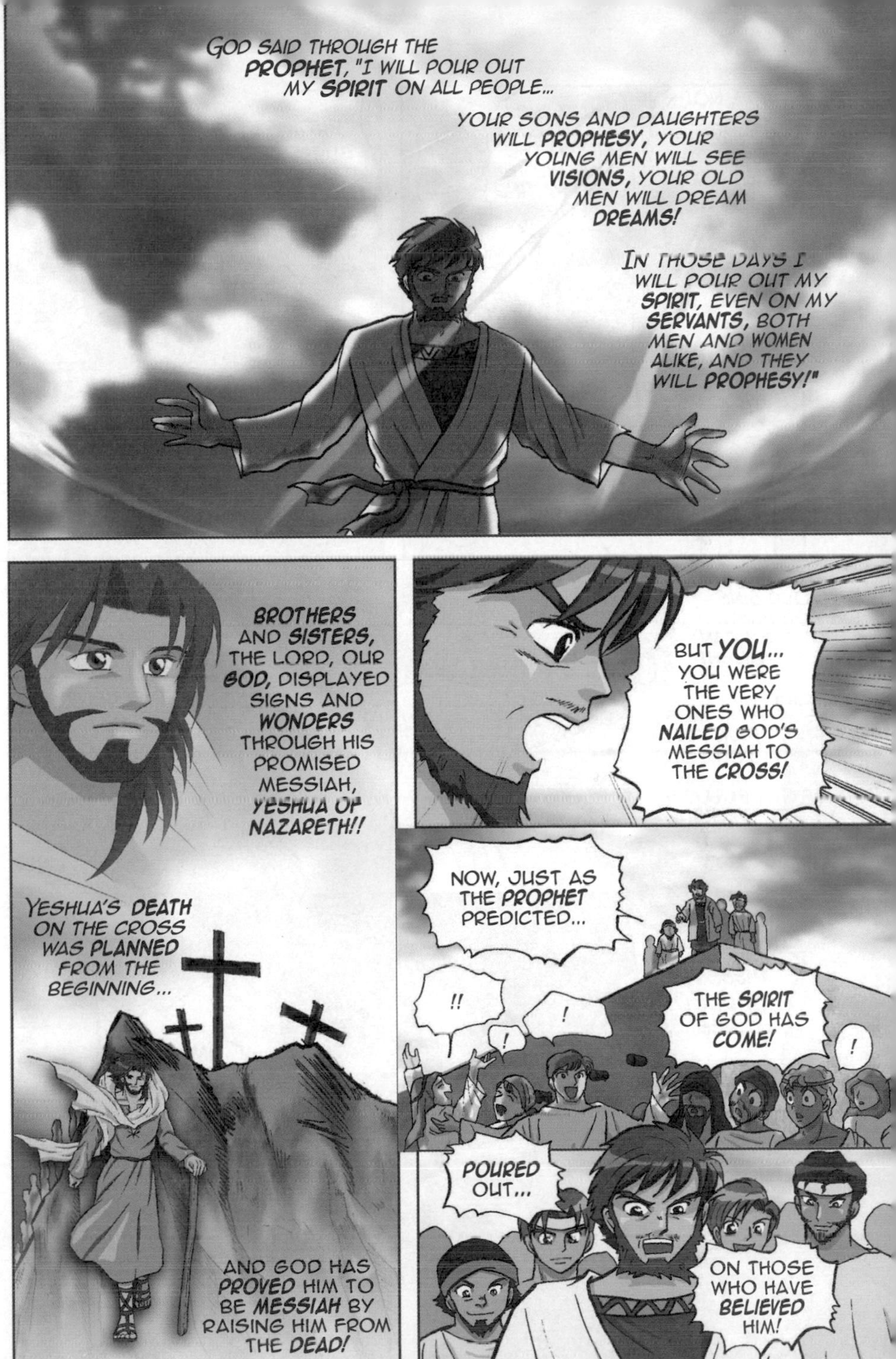
GOD SAID THROUGH THE PROPHET, "I WILL POUR OUT MY SPIRIT ON ALL PEOPLE...
YOUR SONS AND DAUGHTERS WILL PROPHESY, YOUR YOUNG MEN WILL SEE VISIONS, YOUR OLD MEN WILL DREAM DREAMS!
IN THOSE DAYS I WILL POUR OUT MY SPIRIT, EVEN ON MY SERVANTS, BOTH MEN AND WOMEN ALIKE, AND THEY WILL PROPHESY!"
BROTHERS AND SISTERS, THE LORD, OUR GOD, DISPLAYED SIGNS AND WONDERS THROUGH HIS PROMISED MESSIAH, YESHUA OF NAZARETH!!
BUT YOU... YOU WERE THE VERY ONES WHO NAILED GOD'S MESSIAH TO THE CROSS!
YESHUA'S DEATH ON THE CROSS WAS PLANNED FROM THE BEGINNING...
AND GOD HAS PROVED HIM TO BE MESSIAH BY RAISING HIM FROM THE DEAD!
NOW, JUST AS THE PROPHET PREDICTED...
!!
!
!
THE SPIRIT OF GOD HAS COME!
!
POURED OUT...
ON THOSE WHO HAVE BELIEVED HIM!

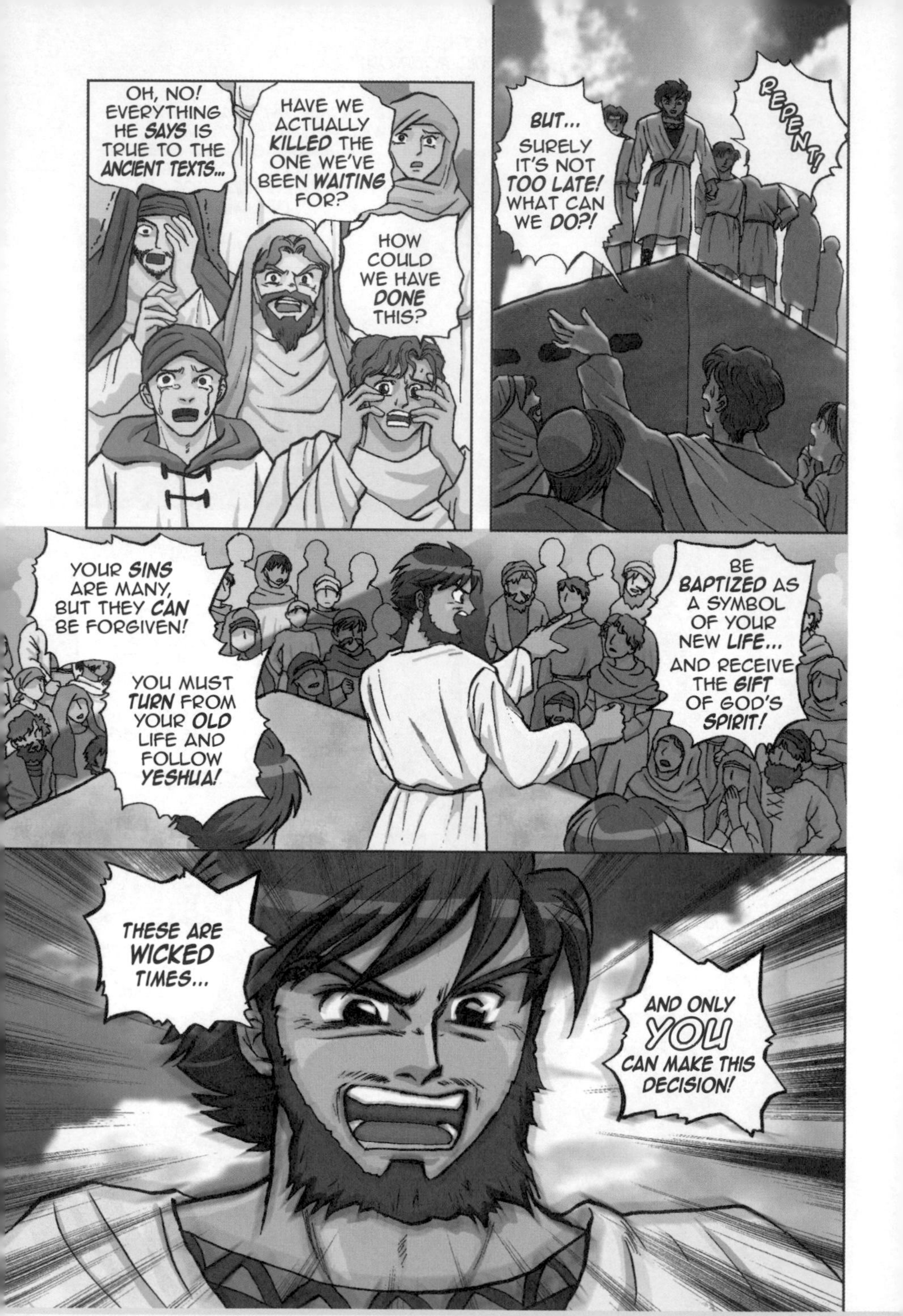
OH, NO! EVERYTHING HE SAYS IS TRUE TO THE ANCIENT TEXTS...
HAVE WE ACTUALLY KILLED THE ONE WE'VE BEEN WAITING FOR?
HOW COULD WE HAVE DONE THIS?
REPENT!
BUT... SURELY IT'S NOT TOO LATE! WHAT CAN WE DO?!
YOUR SINS ARE MANY, BUT THEY CAN BE FORGIVEN!
YOU MUST TURN FROM YOUR OLD LIFE AND FOLLOW YESHUA!
BE BAPTIZED AS A SYMBOL OF YOUR NEW LIFE...
AND RECEIVE THE GIFT OF GOD'S SPIRIT!
THESE ARE WICKED TIMES...
AND ONLY YOU CAN MAKE THIS DECISION!

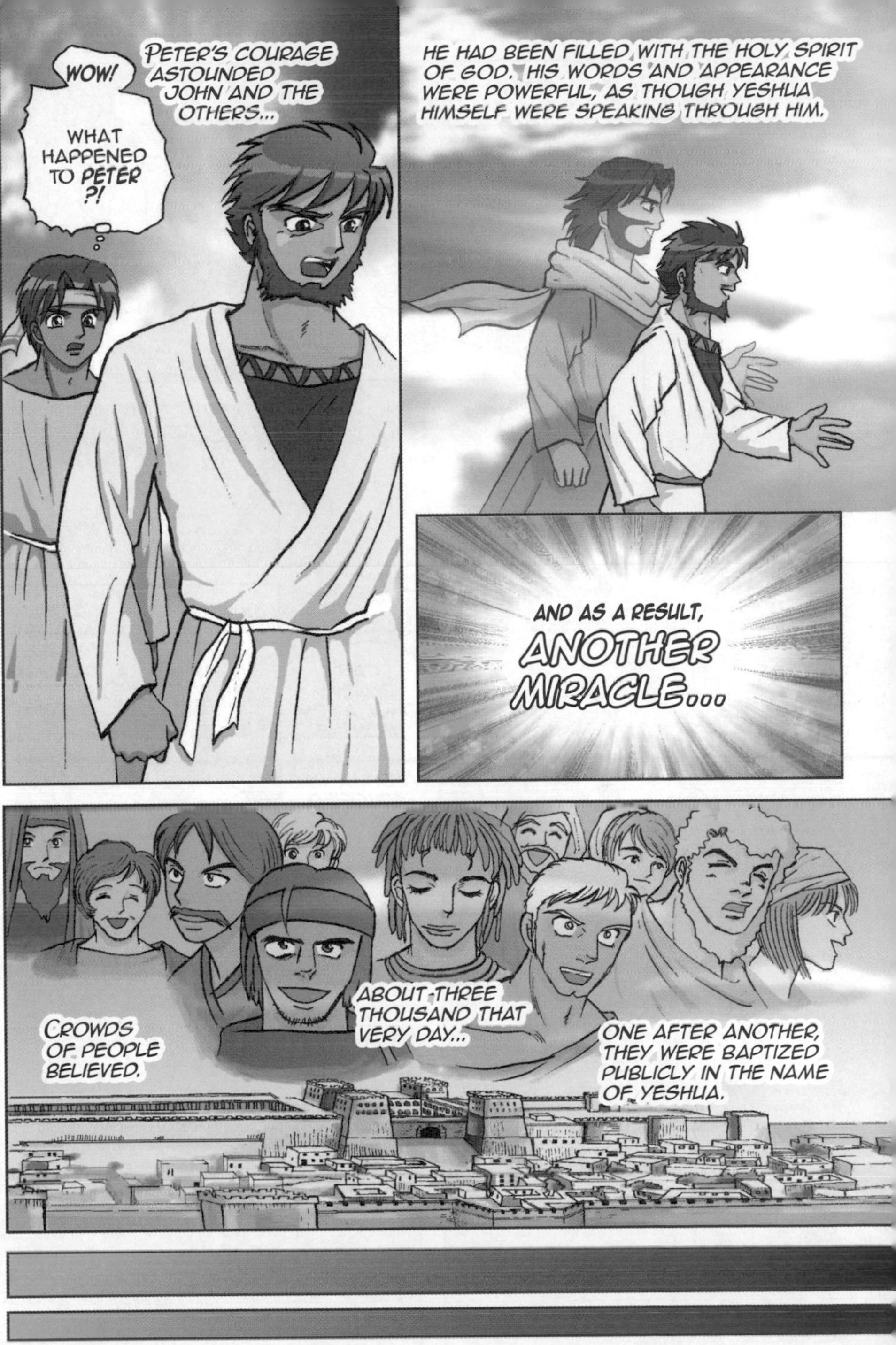
Peter's courage astounded John and the others...
WOW!
What happened to Peter ?!
He had been filled with the Holy Spirit of God. His words and appearance were powerful, as though Yeshua himself were speaking through him.
And as a result,
ANOTHER MIRACLE...
Crowds of people believed.
About three thousand that very day...
One after another, they were baptized publicly in the name of Yeshua.

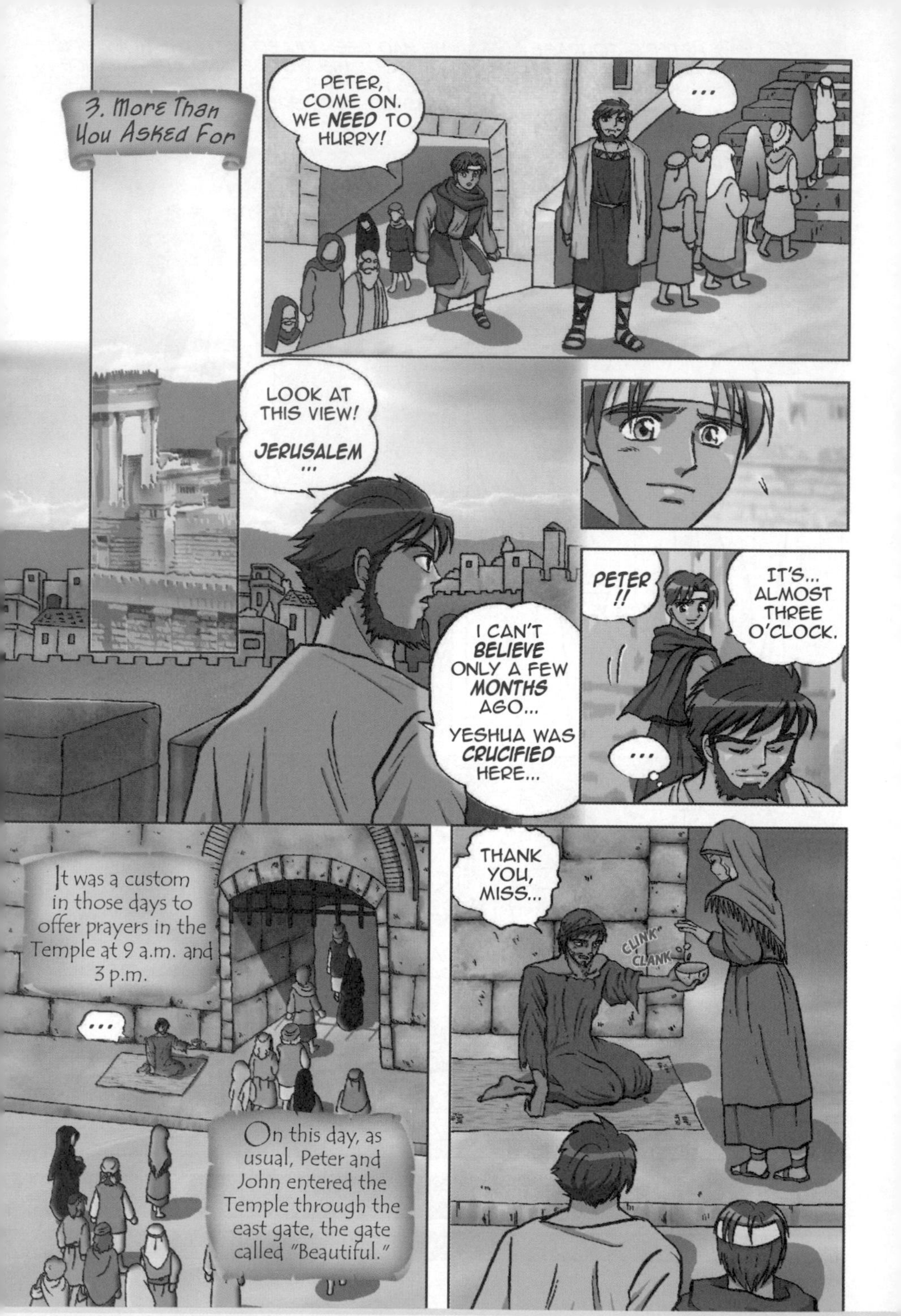
3. More Than You Asked For
PETER, COME ON. WE NEED TO HURRY!
...
LOOK AT THIS VIEW!
JERUSALEM ...
I CAN'T BELIEVE ONLY A FEW MONTHS AGO...
YESHUA WAS CRUCIFIED HERE...
PETER !!
IT'S... ALMOST THREE O'CLOCK.
...
It was a custom in those days to offer prayers in the Temple at 9 a.m. and 3 p.m.
...
On this day, as usual, Peter and John entered the Temple through the east gate, the gate called "Beautiful."
THANK YOU, MISS...
CLINK CLANK

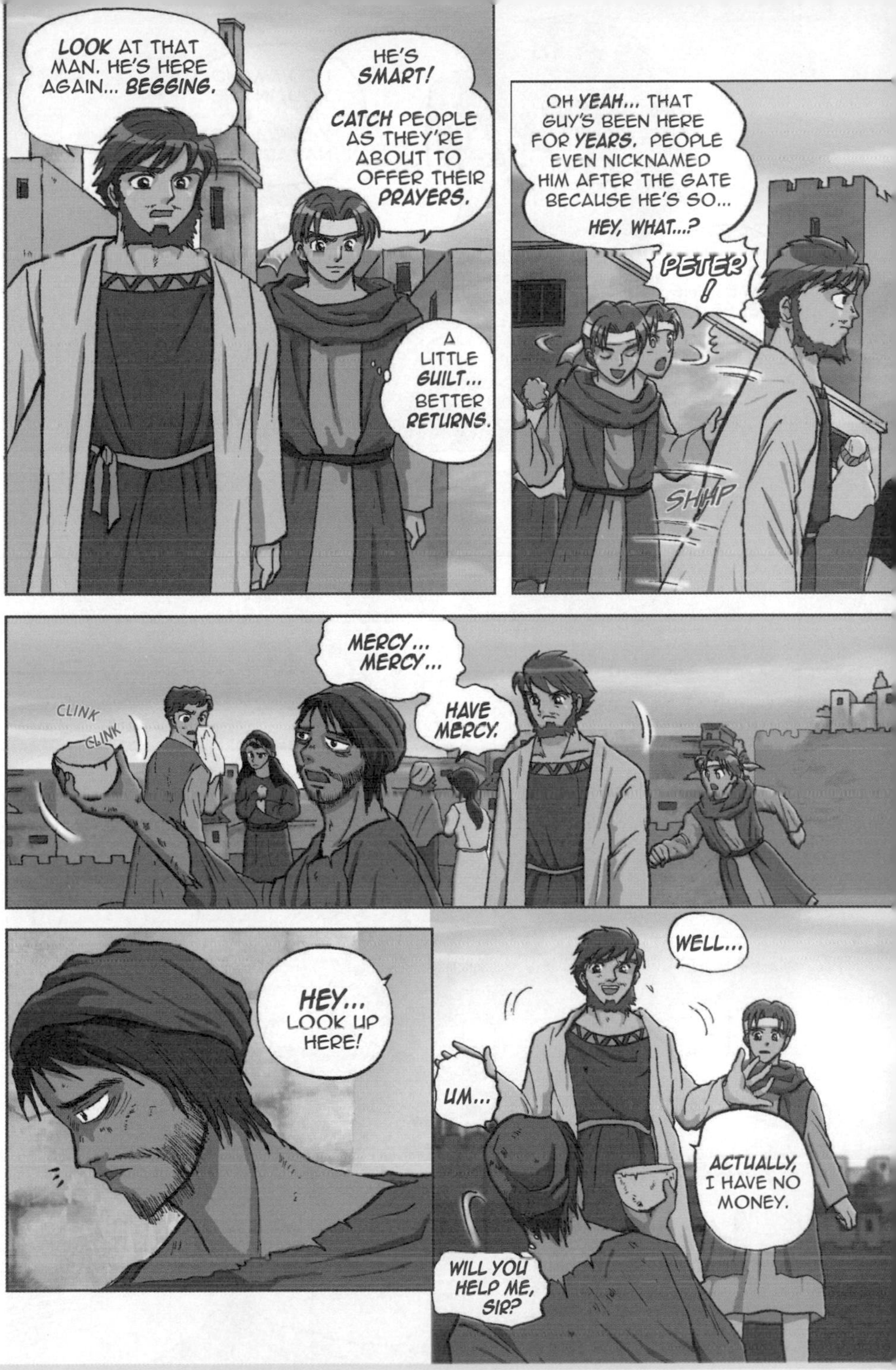
LOOK AT THAT MAN. HE'S HERE AGAIN... BEGGING.
HE'S SMART!
CATCH PEOPLE AS THEY'RE ABOUT TO OFFER THEIR PRAYERS.
A LITTLE GUILT... BETTER RETURNS.
OH YEAH... THAT GUY'S BEEN HERE FOR YEARS. PEOPLE EVEN NICKNAMED HIM AFTER THE GATE BECAUSE HE'S SO...
HEY, WHAT...?
PETER!
SHHP
MERCY... MERCY...
HAVE MERCY.
CLINK
CLINK
HEY... LOOK UP HERE!
WELL...
UM...
ACTUALLY, I HAVE NO MONEY.
WILL YOU HELP ME, SIR?

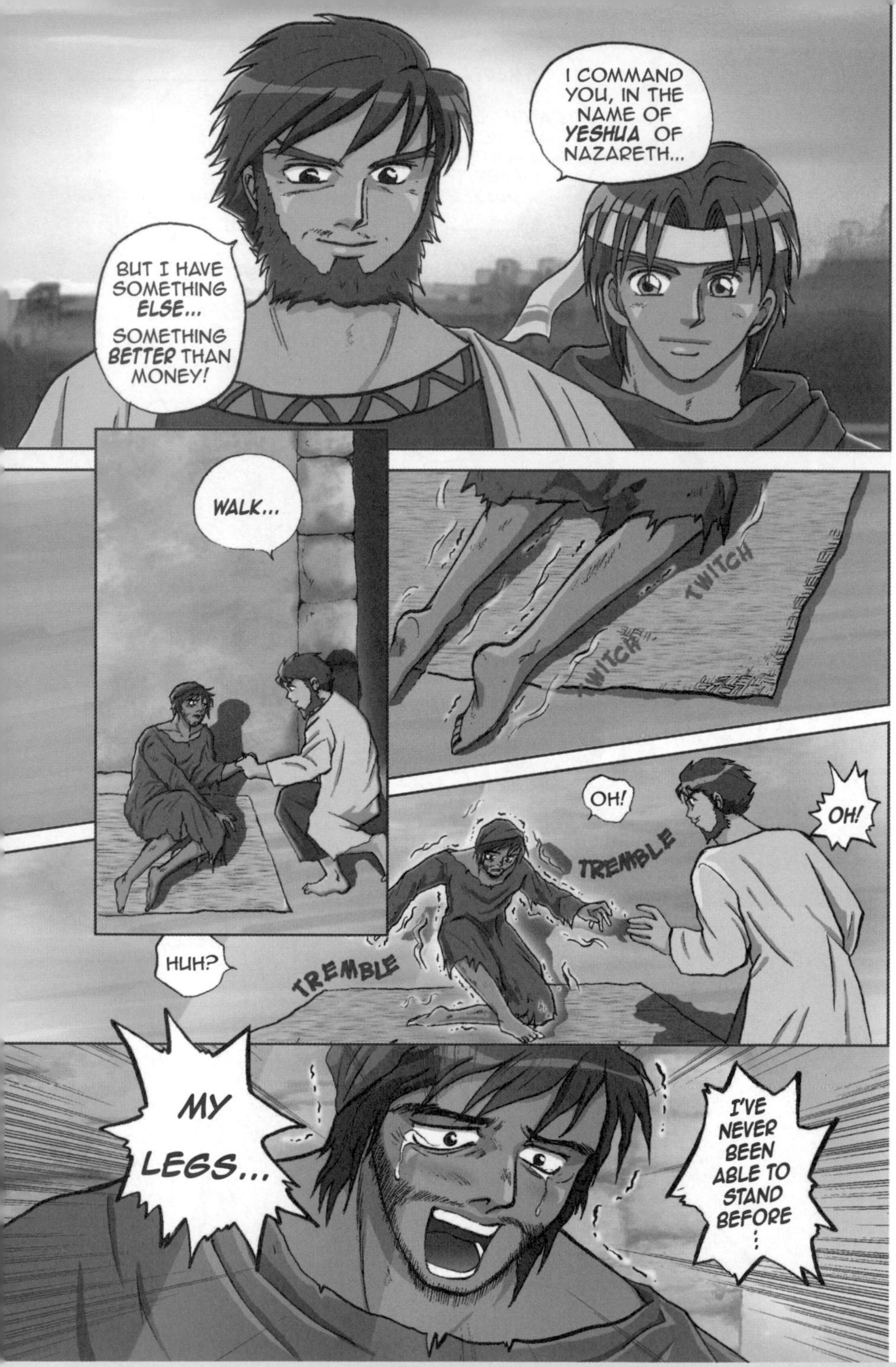
I COMMAND YOU, IN THE NAME OF YESHUA OF NAZARETH...
BUT I HAVE SOMETHING ELSE...
SOMETHING BETTER THAN MONEY!
WALK...
TWITCH
TWITCH
OH!
OH!
TREMBLE
HUH?
TREMBLE
MY LEGS...
I'VE NEVER BEEN ABLE TO STAND BEFORE
...

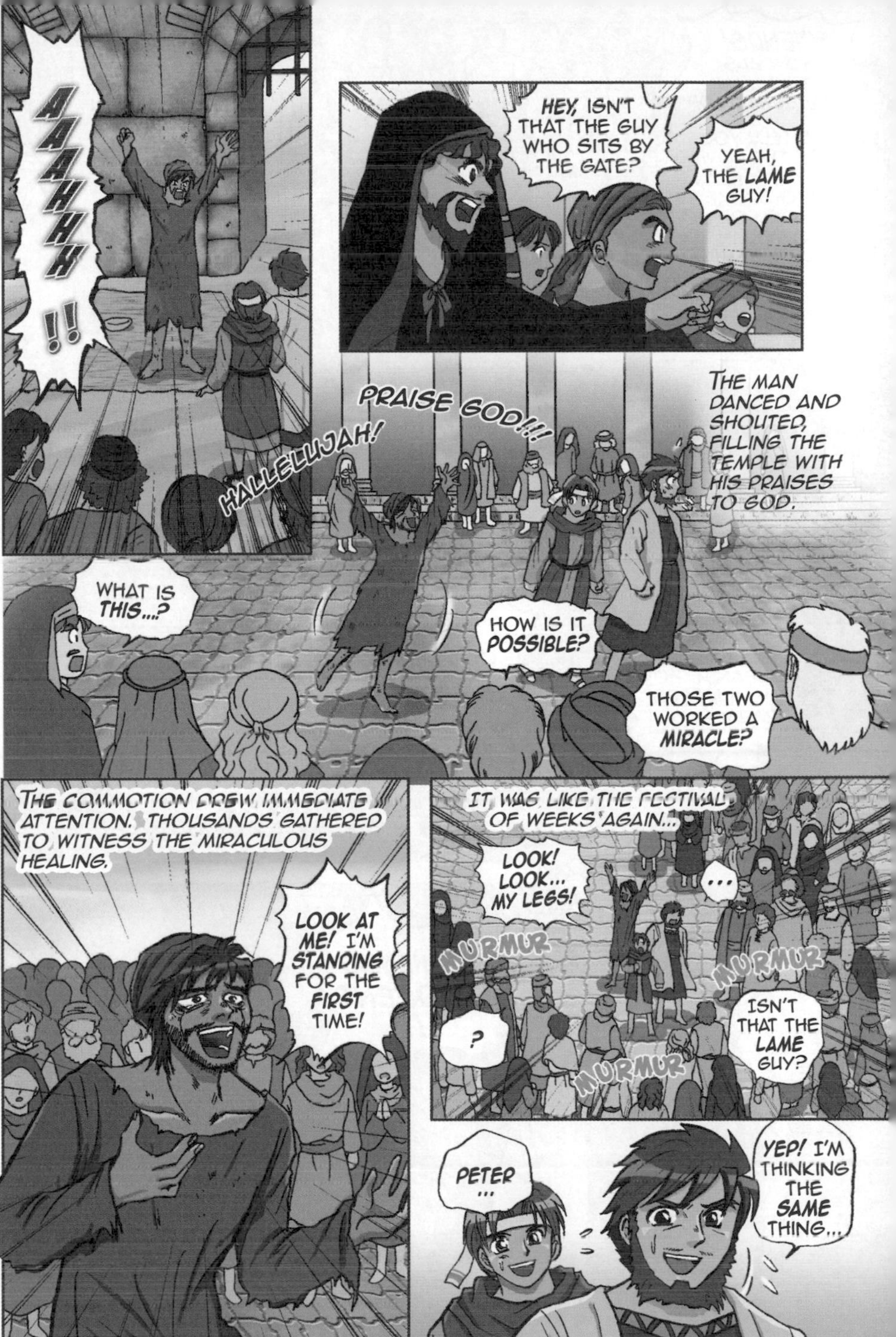
AAAAHHH!!
HEY, ISN'T THAT THE GUY WHO SITS BY THE GATE?
YEAH, THE LAME GUY!
PRAISE GOD!!!
HALLELUJAH!
THE MAN DANCED AND SHOUTED, FILLING THE TEMPLE WITH HIS PRAISES TO GOD.
WHAT IS THIS...?
HOW IS IT POSSIBLE?
THOSE TWO WORKED A MIRACLE?
THE COMMOTION DREW IMMEDIATE ATTENTION. THOUSANDS GATHERED TO WITNESS THE MIRACULOUS HEALING.
LOOK AT ME! I'M STANDING FOR THE FIRST TIME!
IT WAS LIKE THE FESTIVAL OF WEEKS AGAIN...
LOOK! LOOK... MY LEGS!
...
MURMUR
MURMUR
?
MURMUR
ISN'T THAT THE LAME GUY?
PETER ...
YEP! I'M THINKING THE SAME THING...

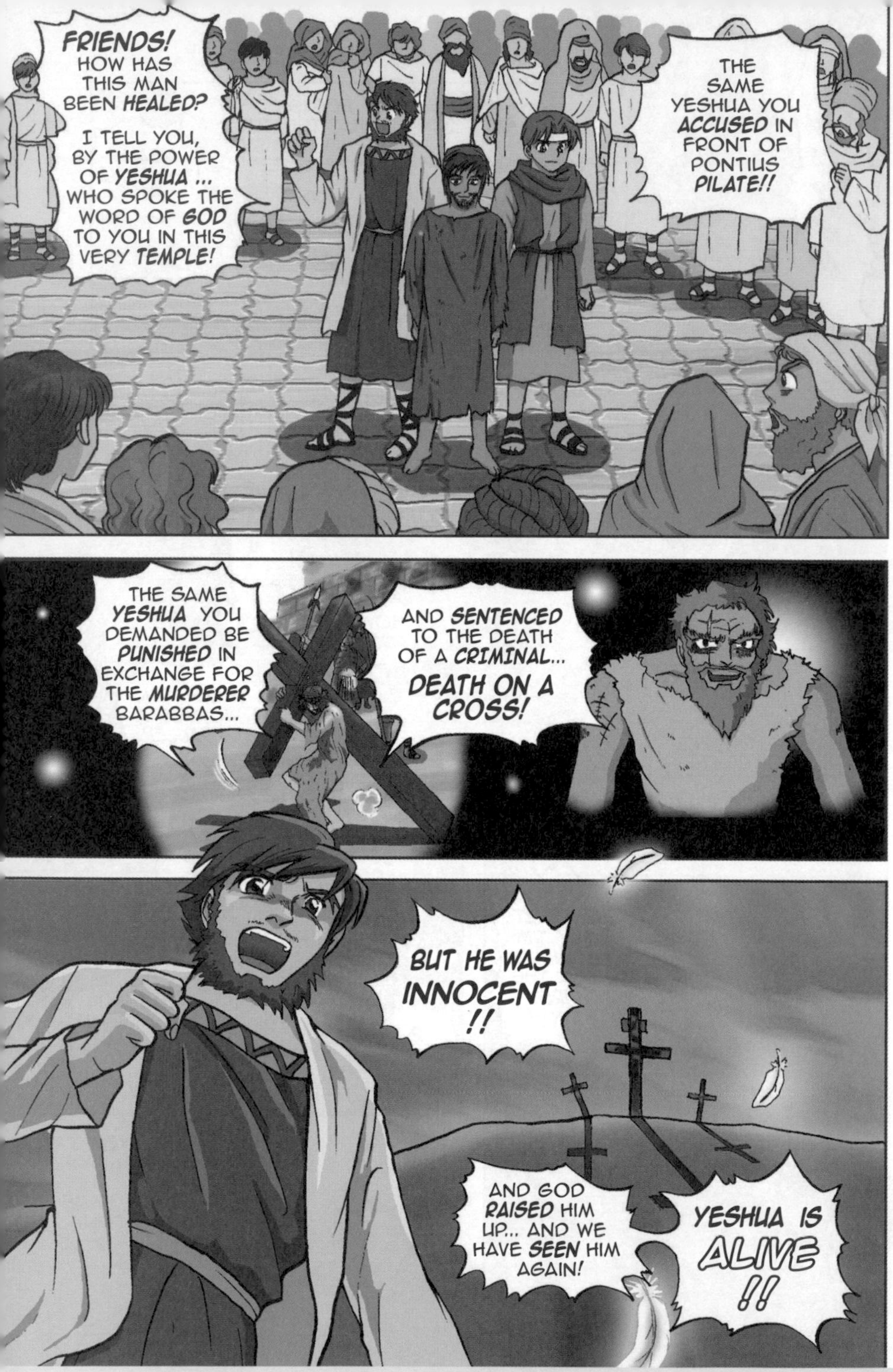
FRIENDS! HOW HAS THIS MAN BEEN HEALED?
I TELL YOU, BY THE POWER OF YESHUA ... WHO SPOKE THE WORD OF GOD TO YOU IN THIS VERY TEMPLE!
THE SAME YESHUA YOU ACCUSED IN FRONT OF PONTIUS PILATE!!
THE SAME YESHUA YOU DEMANDED BE PUNISHED IN EXCHANGE FOR THE MURDERER BARABBAS...
AND SENTENCED TO THE DEATH OF A CRIMINAL...
DEATH ON A CROSS!
BUT HE WAS INNOCENT !!
AND GOD RAISED HIM UP... AND WE HAVE SEEN HIM AGAIN!
YESHUA IS ALIVE !!

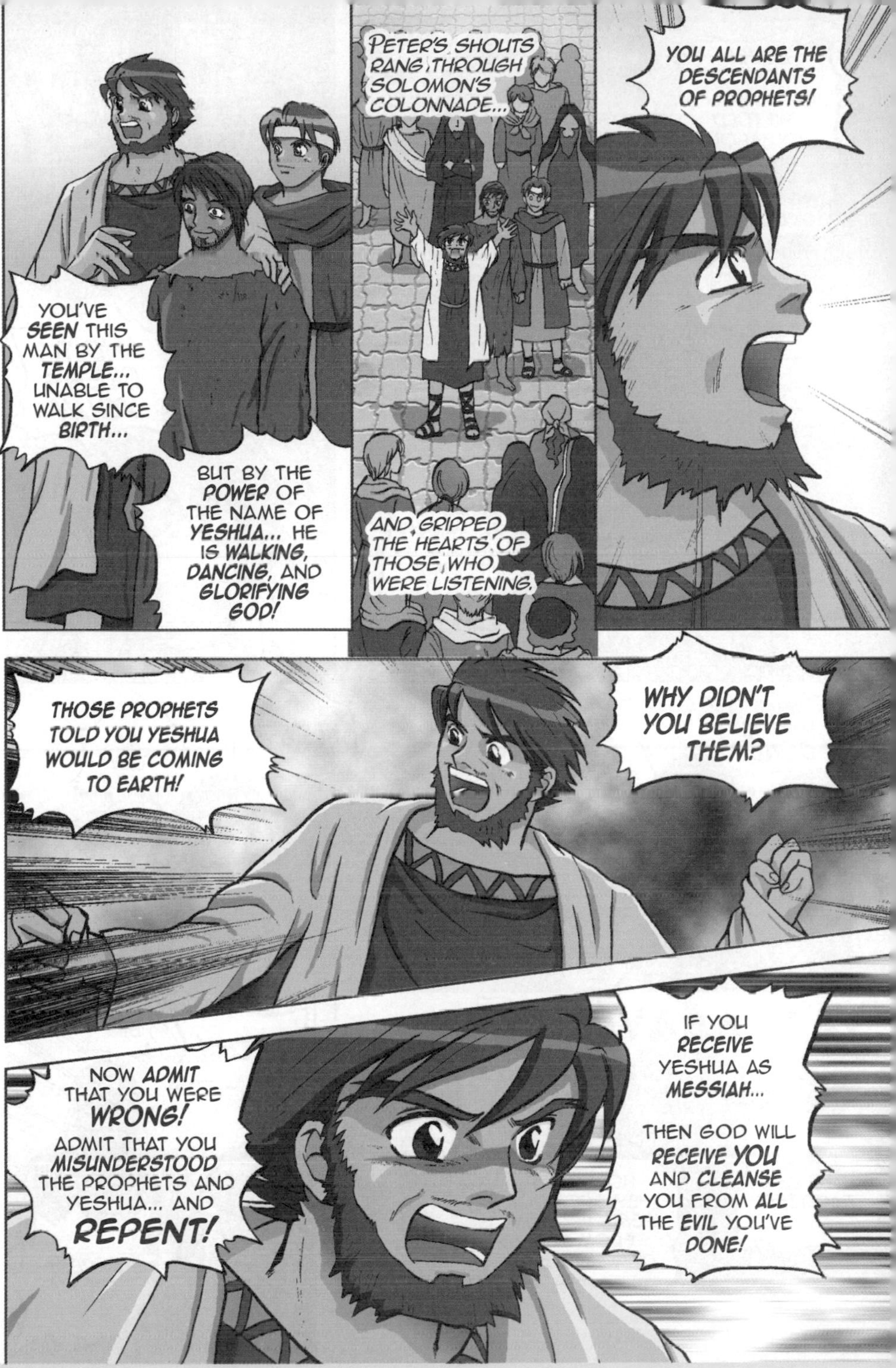
YOU'VE SEEN THIS MAN BY THE TEMPLE... UNABLE TO WALK SINCE BIRTH...
BUT BY THE POWER OF THE NAME OF YESHUA... HE IS WALKING, DANCING, AND GLORIFYING GOD!
PETER'S SHOUTS RANG THROUGH SOLOMON'S COLONNADE...
AND GRIPPED THE HEARTS OF THOSE WHO WERE LISTENING.
YOU ALL ARE THE DESCENDANTS OF PROPHETS!
THOSE PROPHETS TOLD YOU YESHUA WOULD BE COMING TO EARTH!
WHY DIDN'T YOU BELIEVE THEM?
NOW ADMIT THAT YOU WERE WRONG! ADMIT THAT YOU MISUNDERSTOOD THE PROPHETS AND YESHUA... AND REPENT!
IF YOU RECEIVE YESHUA AS MESSIAH...
THEN GOD WILL RECEIVE YOU AND CLEANSE YOU FROM ALL THE EVIL YOU'VE DONE!

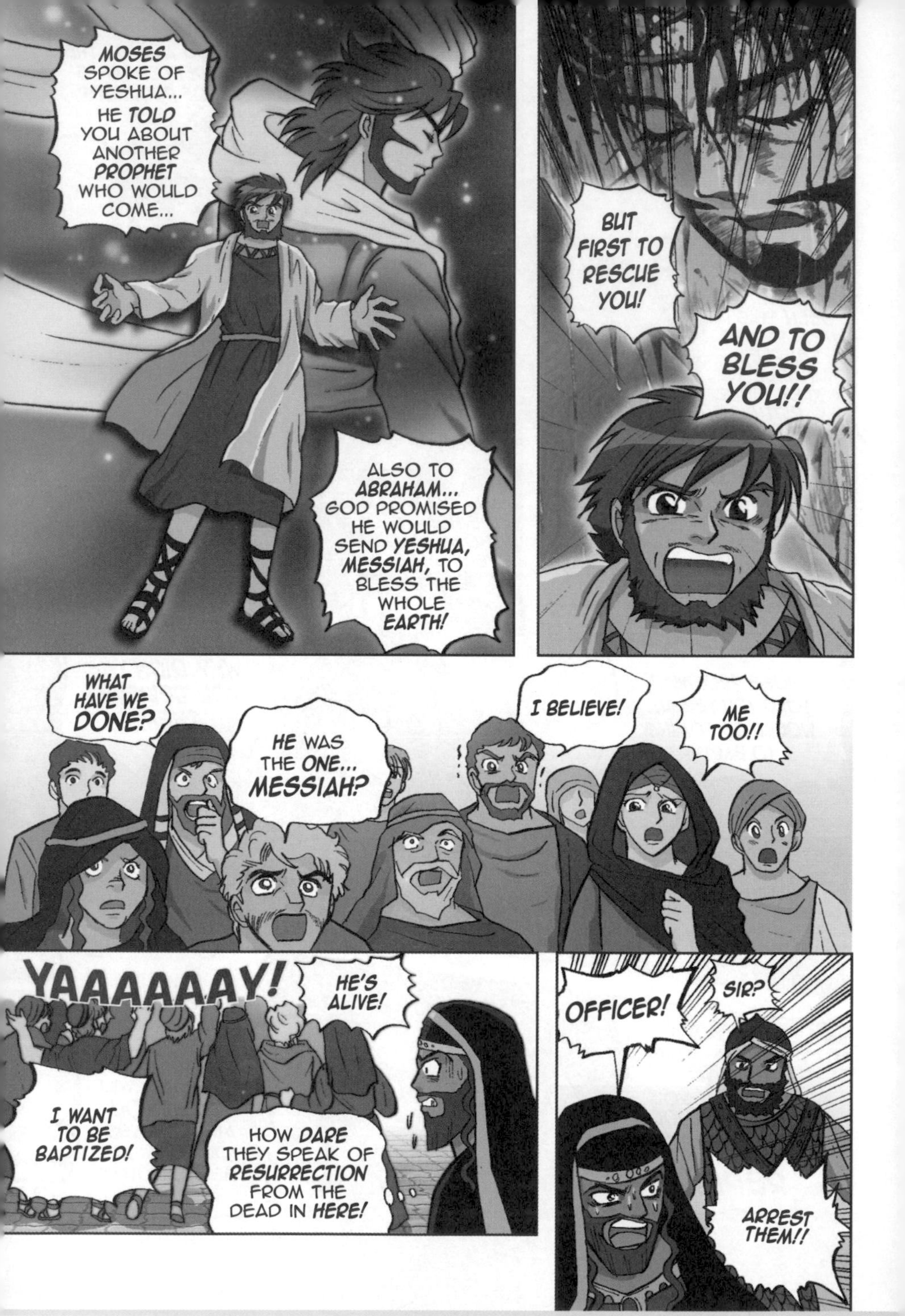
MOSES SPOKE OF YESHUA... HE TOLD YOU ABOUT ANOTHER PROPHET WHO WOULD COME...
ALSO TO ABRAHAM... GOD PROMISED HE WOULD SEND YESHUA, MESSIAH, TO BLESS THE WHOLE EARTH!
BUT FIRST TO RESCUE YOU!
AND TO BLESS YOU!!
WHAT HAVE WE DONE?
HE WAS THE ONE... MESSIAH?
I BELIEVE!
ME TOO!!
YAAAAAAY!
HE'S ALIVE!
I WANT TO BE BAPTIZED!
HOW DARE THEY SPEAK OF RESURRECTION FROM THE DEAD IN HERE!
OFFICER!
SIR?
ARREST THEM!!

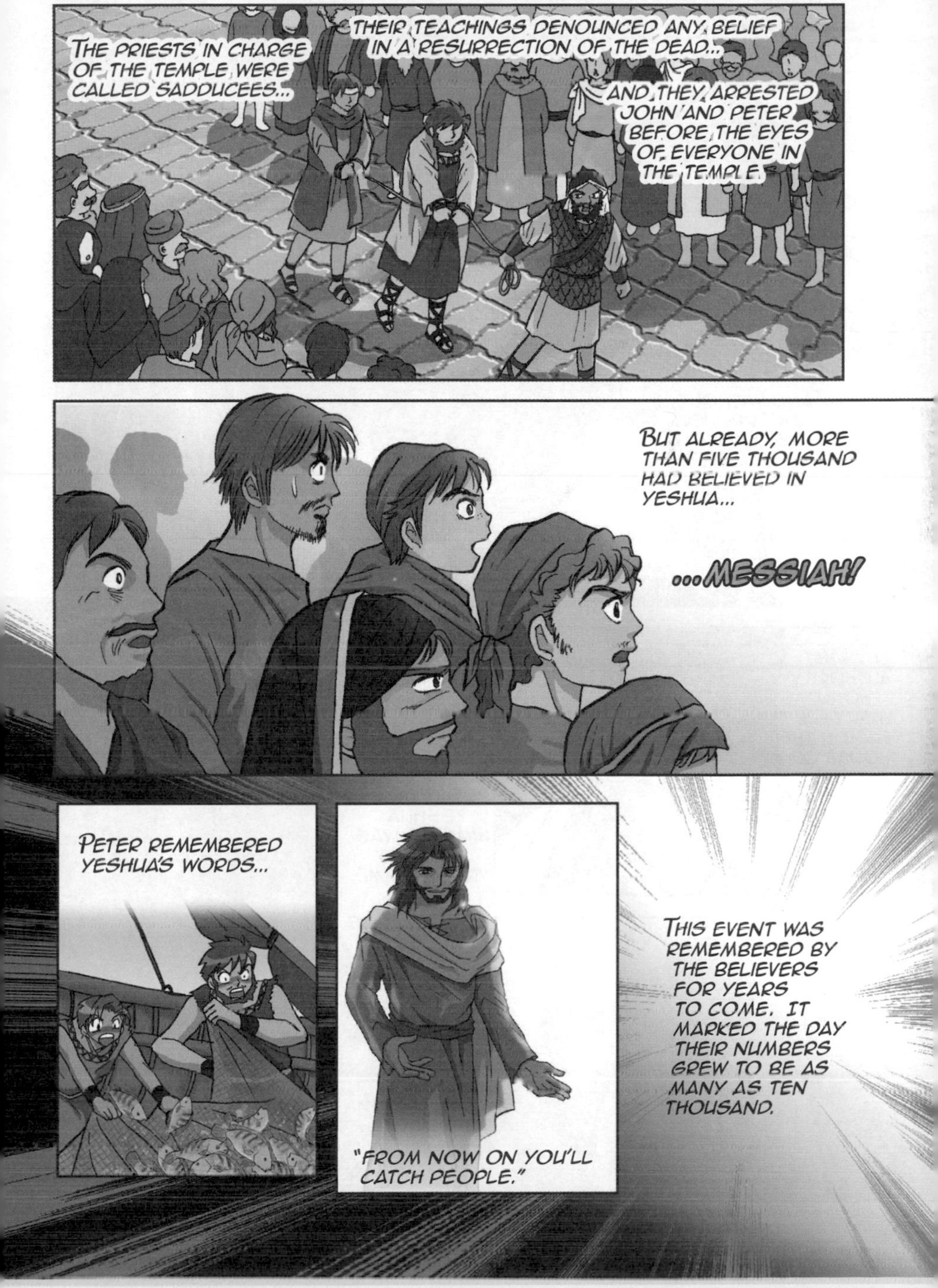
THE PRIESTS IN CHARGE OF THE TEMPLE WERE CALLED SADDUCEES...
THEIR TEACHINGS DENOUNCED ANY BELIEF IN A RESURRECTION OF THE DEAD...
AND THEY ARRESTED JOHN AND PETER BEFORE THE EYES OF EVERYONE IN THE TEMPLE.
BUT ALREADY, MORE THAN FIVE THOUSAND HAD BELIEVED IN YESHUA...
...MESSIAH!
PETER REMEMBERED YESHUA'S WORDS...
"FROM NOW ON YOU'LL CATCH PEOPLE."
THIS EVENT WAS REMEMBERED BY THE BELIEVERS FOR YEARS TO COME. IT MARKED THE DAY THEIR NUMBERS GREW TO BE AS MANY AS TEN THOUSAND.

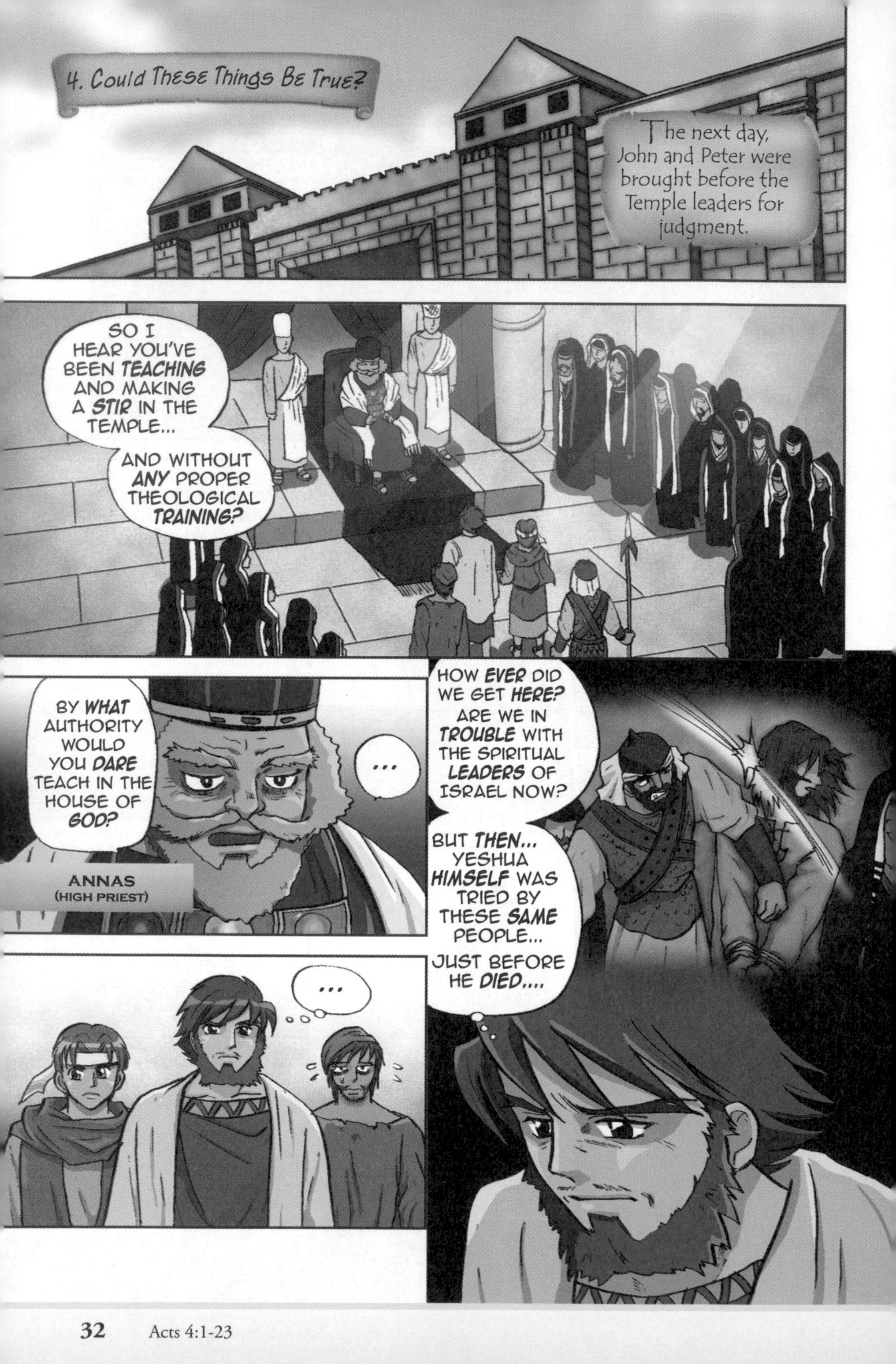
4. Could These Things Be True?
The next day, John and Peter were brought before the Temple leaders for judgment.
SO I HEAR YOU'VE BEEN TEACHING AND MAKING A STIR IN THE TEMPLE...
AND WITHOUT ANY PROPER THEOLOGICAL TRAINING?
BY WHAT AUTHORITY WOULD YOU DARE TEACH IN THE HOUSE OF GOD?
ANNAS (HIGH PRIEST)
...
...
HOW EVER DID WE GET HERE? ARE WE IN TROUBLE WITH THE SPIRITUAL LEADERS OF ISRAEL NOW?
BUT THEN... YESHUA HIMSELF WAS TRIED BY THESE SAME PEOPLE...
JUST BEFORE HE DIED....

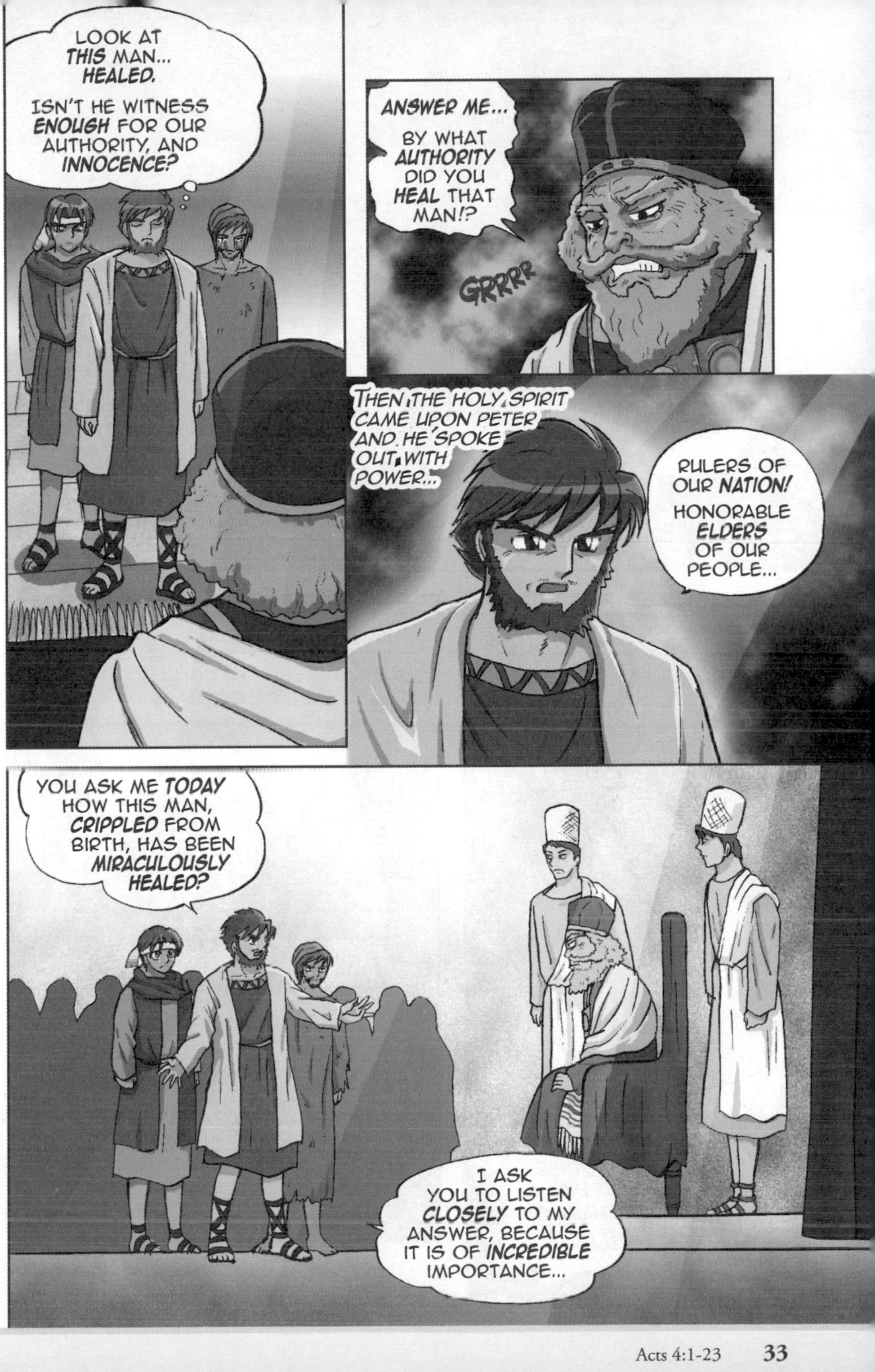
LOOK AT THIS MAN... HEALED.
ISN'T HE WITNESS ENOUGH FOR OUR AUTHORITY, AND INNOCENCE?
ANSWER ME...
BY WHAT AUTHORITY DID YOU HEAL THAT MAN!?
GRRRR
THEN THE HOLY SPIRIT CAME UPON PETER AND HE SPOKE OUT WITH POWER...
RULERS OF OUR NATION!
HONORABLE ELDERS OF OUR PEOPLE...
YOU ASK ME TODAY HOW THIS MAN, CRIPPLED FROM BIRTH, HAS BEEN MIRACULOUSLY HEALED?
I ASK YOU TO LISTEN CLOSELY TO MY ANSWER, BECAUSE IT IS OF INCREDIBLE IMPORTANCE...

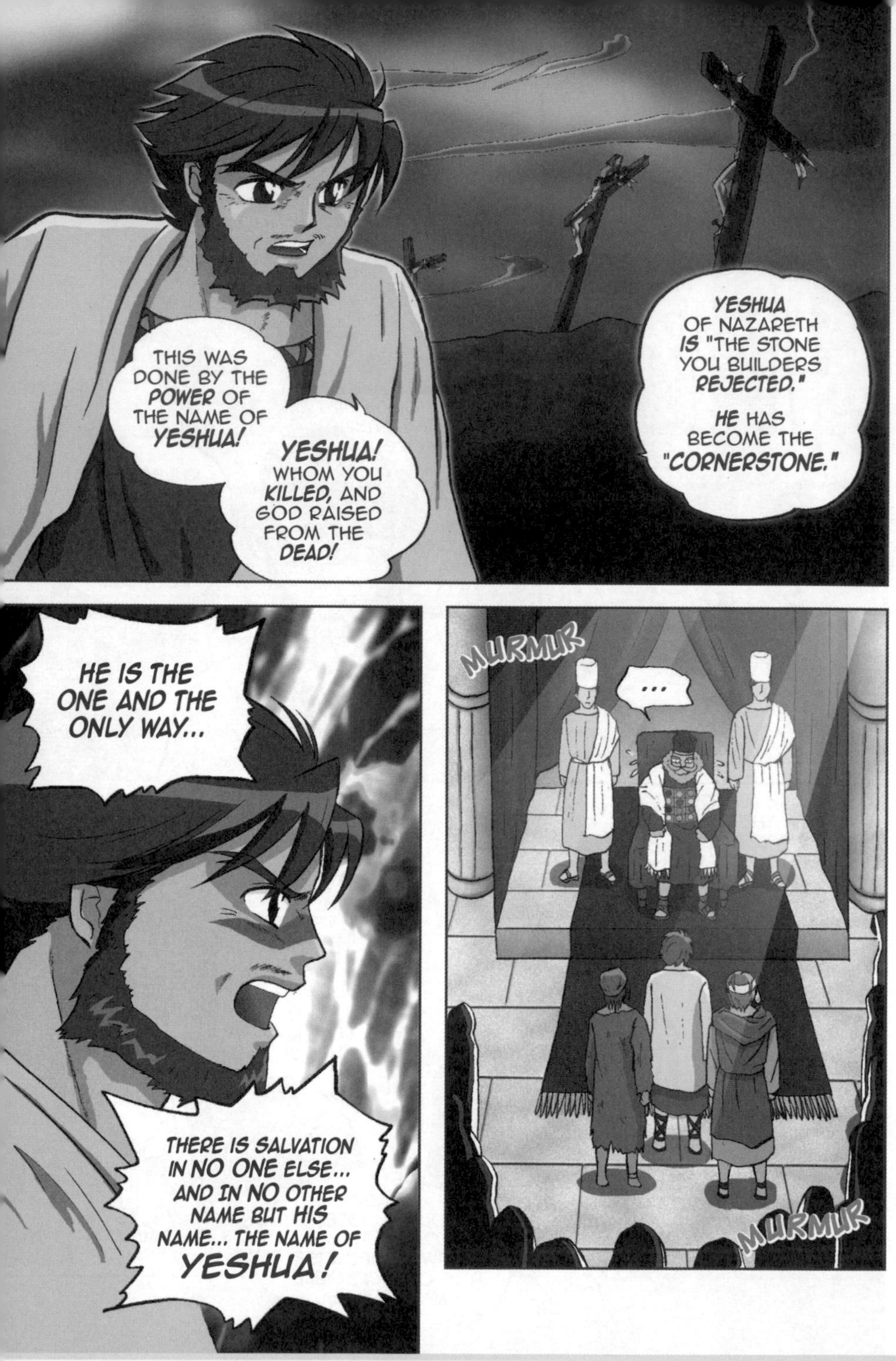
THIS WAS DONE BY THE POWER OF THE NAME OF YESHUA!
YESHUA! WHOM YOU KILLED, AND GOD RAISED FROM THE DEAD!
YESHUA OF NAZARETH IS "THE STONE YOU BUILDERS REJECTED."
HE HAS BECOME THE "CORNERSTONE."
HE IS THE ONE AND THE ONLY WAY...
THERE IS SALVATION IN NO ONE ELSE... AND IN NO OTHER NAME BUT HIS NAME... THE NAME OF YESHUA!
MURMUR
...
MURMUR

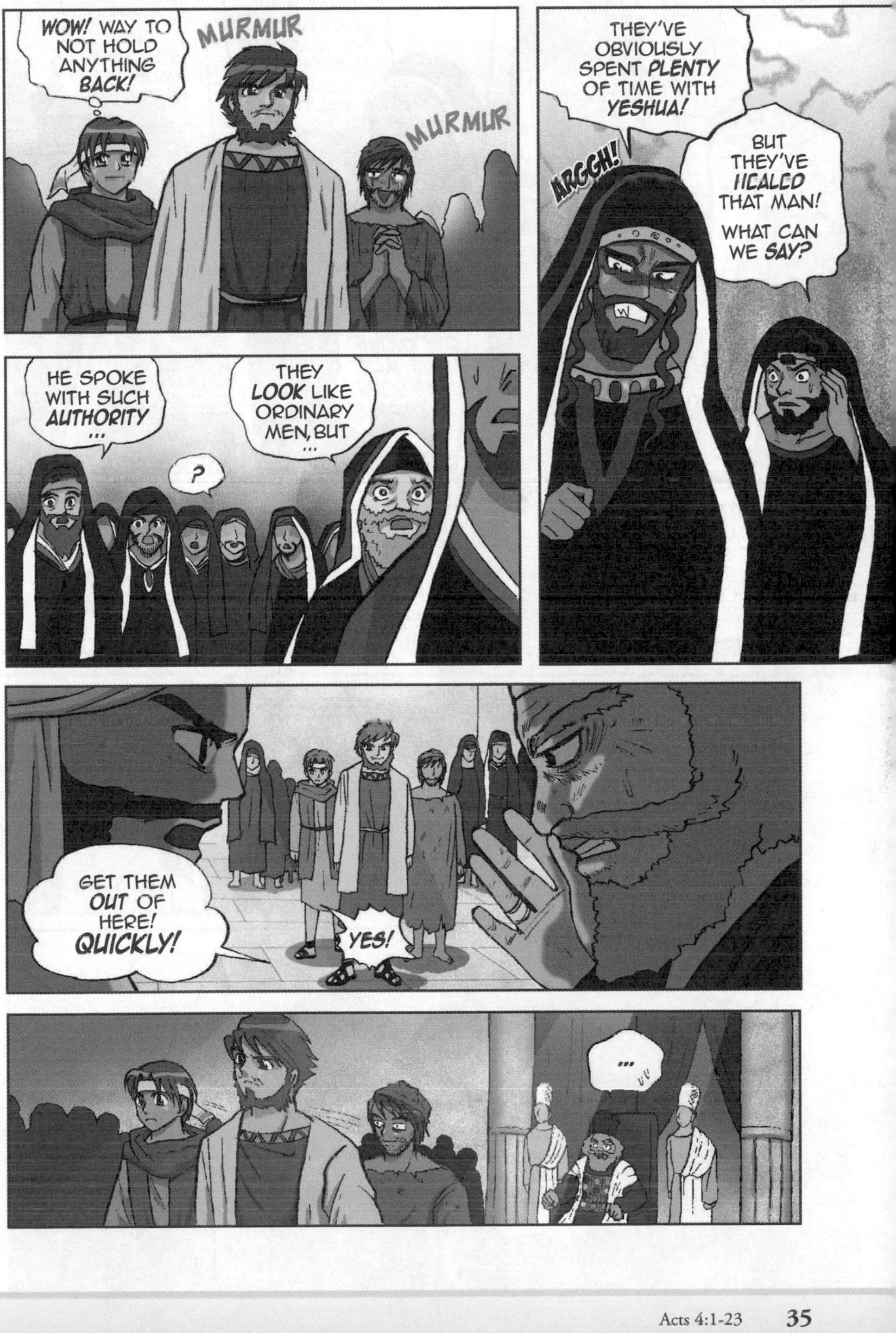
WOW! WAY TO NOT HOLD ANYTHING BACK!
MURMUR
MURMUR
THEY'VE OBVIOUSLY SPENT PLENTY OF TIME WITH YESHUA!
ARGGH!
BUT THEY'VE HEALED THAT MAN!
WHAT CAN WE SAY?
HE SPOKE WITH SUCH AUTHORITY ...
THEY LOOK LIKE ORDINARY MEN, BUT ...
?
GET THEM OUT OF HERE! QUICKLY!
YES!
...

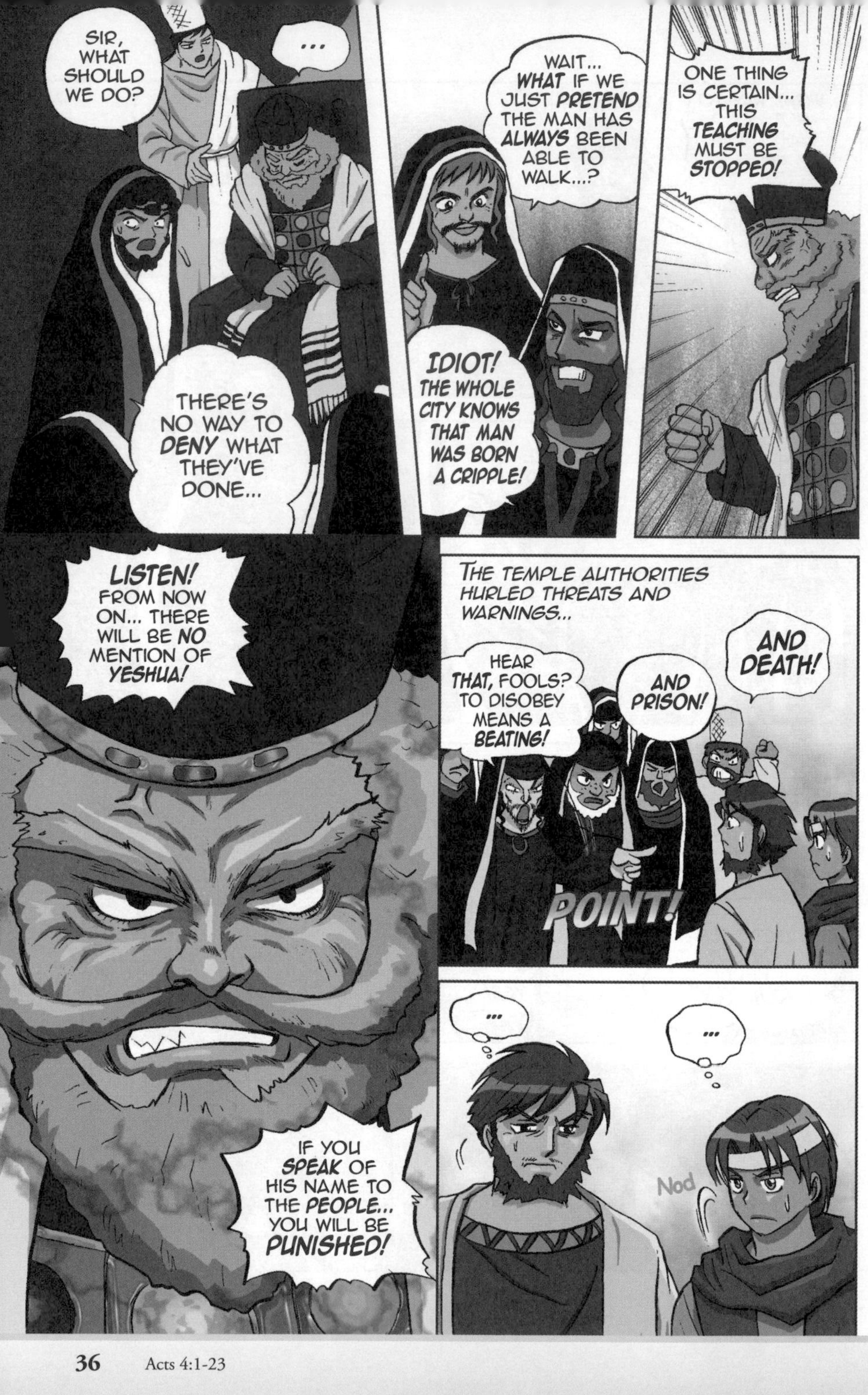
SIR, WHAT SHOULD WE DO?
...
THERE'S NO WAY TO DENY WHAT THEY'VE DONE...
WAIT... WHAT IF WE JUST PRETEND THE MAN HAS ALWAYS BEEN ABLE TO WALK...?
IDIOT! THE WHOLE CITY KNOWS THAT MAN WAS BORN A CRIPPLE!
ONE THING IS CERTAIN... THIS TEACHING MUST BE STOPPED!
LISTEN! FROM NOW ON... THERE WILL BE NO MENTION OF YESHUA!
IF YOU SPEAK OF HIS NAME TO THE PEOPLE... YOU WILL BE PUNISHED!
THE TEMPLE AUTHORITIES HURLED THREATS AND WARNINGS...
HEAR THAT, FOOLS? TO DISOBEY MEANS A BEATING!
AND PRISON!
AND DEATH!
POINT!
...
...
Nod

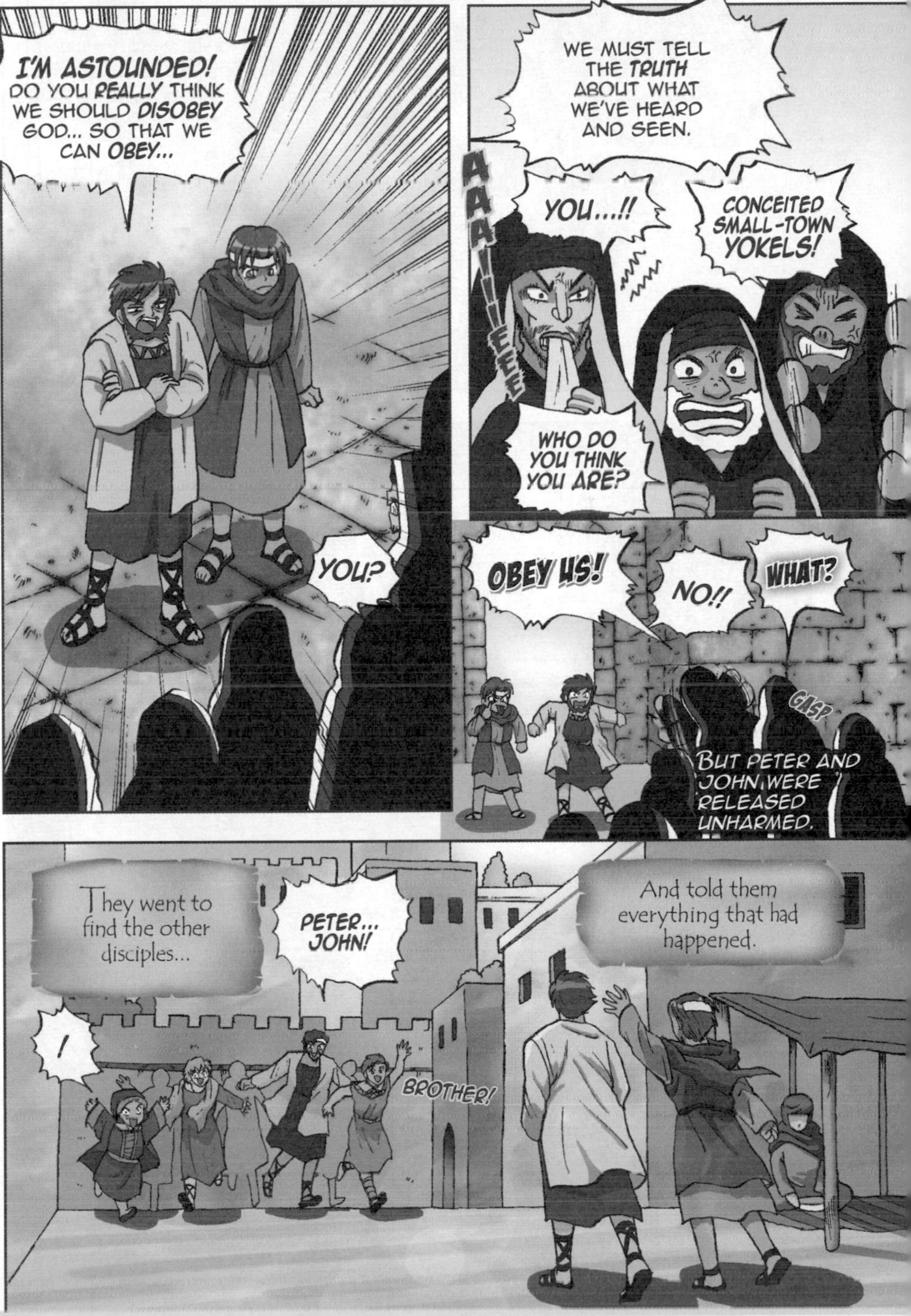
I'M ASTOUNDED! DO YOU REALLY THINK WE SHOULD DISOBEY GOD... SO THAT WE CAN OBEY...
YOU?
WE MUST TELL THE TRUTH ABOUT WHAT WE'VE HEARD AND SEEN.
AAAIIIEEE
YOU...!!
CONCEITED SMALL-TOWN YOKELS!
WHO DO YOU THINK YOU ARE?
OBEY US!
NO!!
WHAT?
GASP
BUT PETER AND JOHN WERE RELEASED UNHARMED.
They went to find the other disciples...
PETER... JOHN!
And told them everything that had happened.
!
BROTHER!

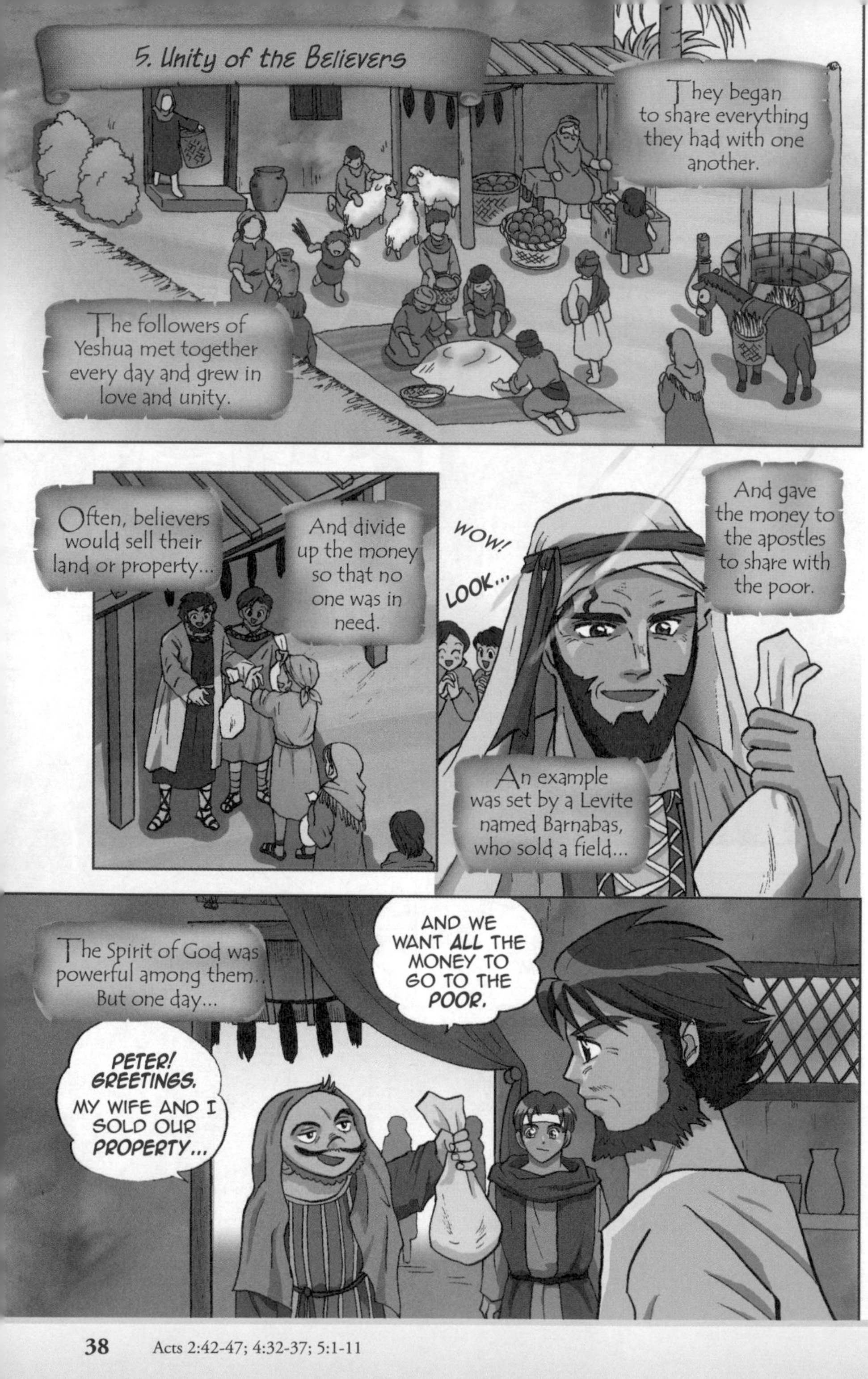
5. Unity of the Believers
They began to share everything they had with one another.
The followers of Yeshua met together every day and grew in love and unity.
Often, believers would sell their land or property...
And divide up the money so that no one was in need.
WOW!
LOOK...
And gave the money to the apostles to share with the poor.
An example was set by a Levite named Barnabas, who sold a field...
The Spirit of God was powerful among them. But one day...
PETER! GREETINGS. MY WIFE AND I SOLD OUR PROPERTY...
AND WE WANT ALL THE MONEY TO GO TO THE POOR.

 Acts 2:42-47; 4:32-37; 5:1-11

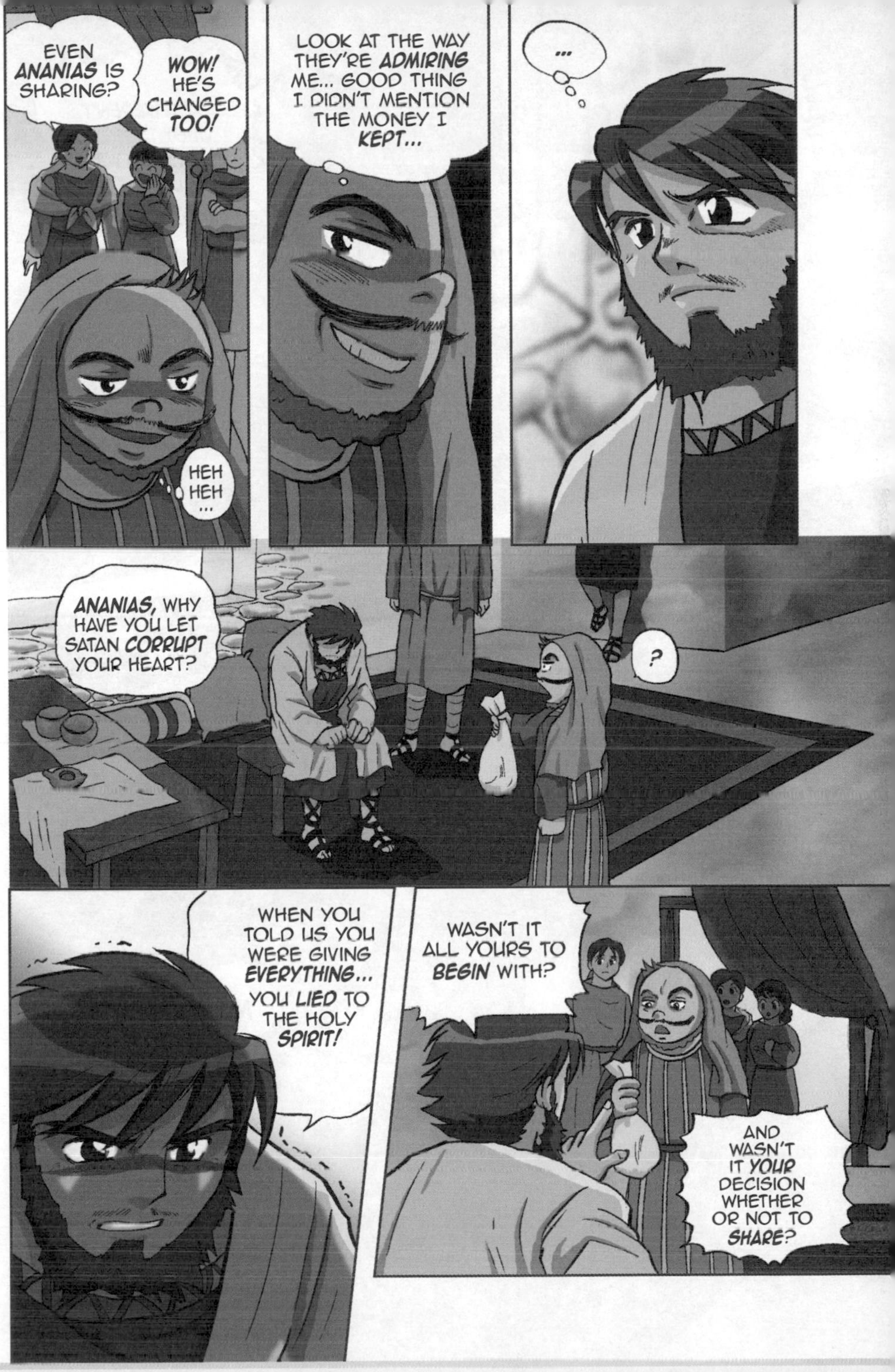

EVEN ANANIAS IS SHARING?
WOW! HE'S CHANGED TOO!
HEH HEH ...
LOOK AT THE WAY THEY'RE ADMIRING ME... GOOD THING I DIDN'T MENTION THE MONEY I KEPT...
...
ANANIAS, WHY HAVE YOU LET SATAN CORRUPT YOUR HEART?
?
WHEN YOU TOLD US YOU WERE GIVING EVERYTHING... YOU LIED TO THE HOLY SPIRIT!
WASN'T IT ALL YOURS TO BEGIN WITH?
AND WASN'T IT YOUR DECISION WHETHER OR NOT TO SHARE?

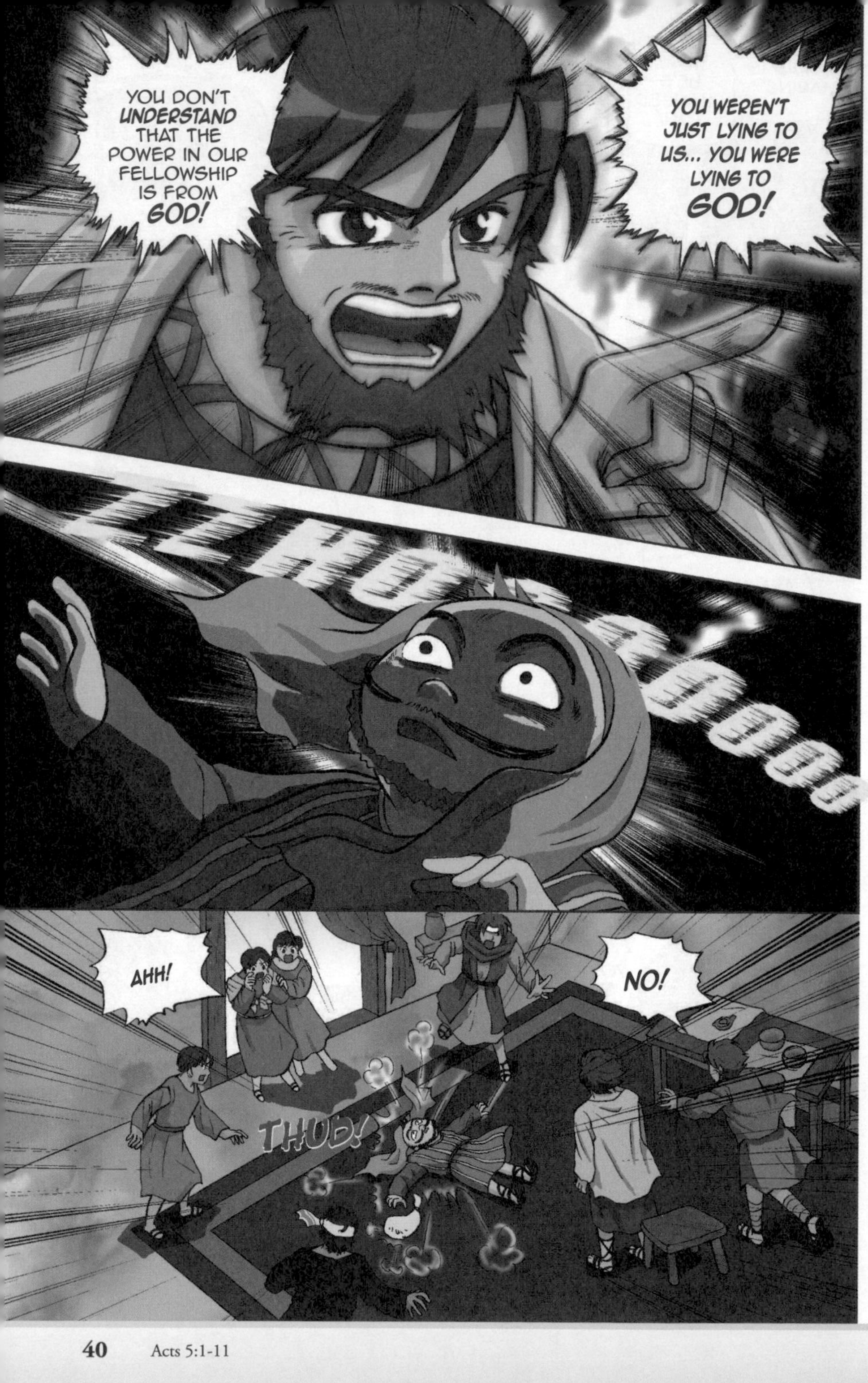

YOU DON'T UNDERSTAND THAT THE POWER IN OUR FELLOWSHIP IS FROM GOD!
YOU WEREN'T JUST LYING TO US... YOU WERE LYING TO GOD!
AHH!
NO!
THUD!

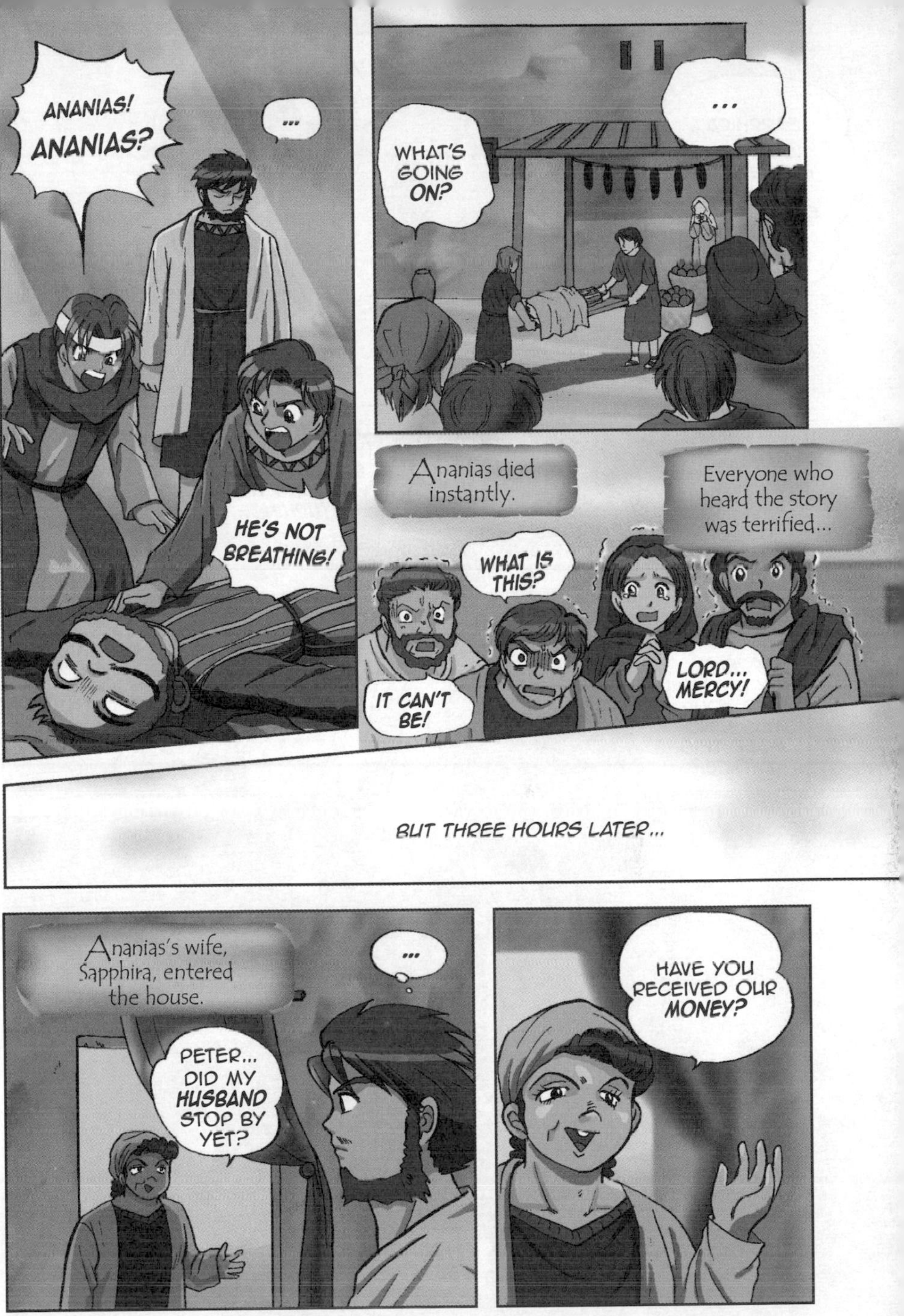
ANANIAS!
ANANIAS?
...
HE'S NOT BREATHING!
WHAT'S GOING ON?
...
Ananias died instantly.
Everyone who heard the story was terrified...
WHAT IS THIS?
IT CAN'T BE!
LORD... MERCY!
BUT THREE HOURS LATER...
Ananias's wife, Sapphira, entered the house.
...
PETER... DID MY HUSBAND STOP BY YET?
HAVE YOU RECEIVED OUR MONEY?

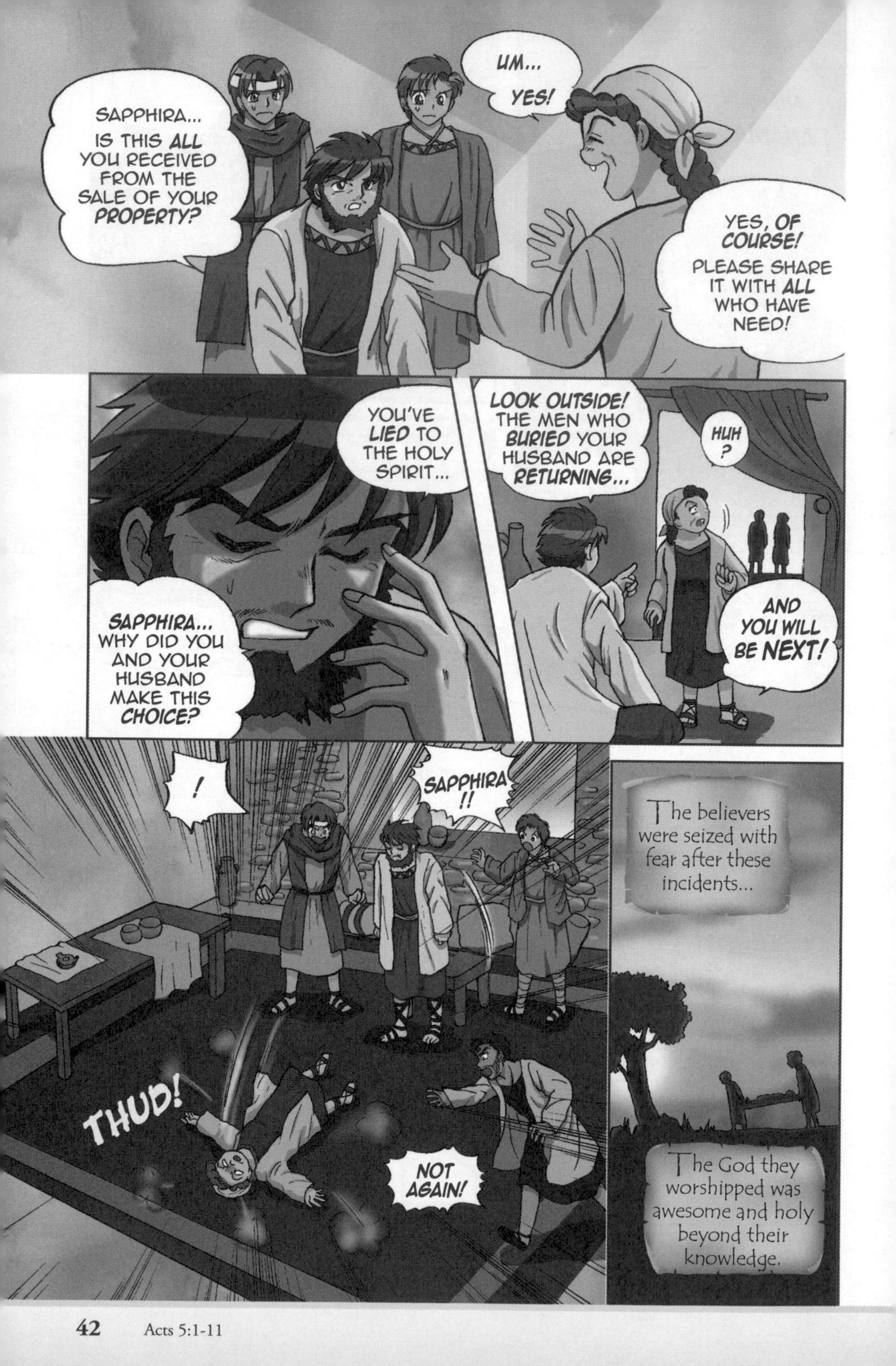
SAPPHIRA... IS THIS ALL YOU RECEIVED FROM THE SALE OF YOUR PROPERTY?
UM...
YES!
YES, OF COURSE! PLEASE SHARE IT WITH ALL WHO HAVE NEED!
YOU'VE LIED TO THE HOLY SPIRIT...
SAPPHIRA... WHY DID YOU AND YOUR HUSBAND MAKE THIS CHOICE?
LOOK OUTSIDE! THE MEN WHO BURIED YOUR HUSBAND ARE RETURNING...
HUH ?
AND YOU WILL BE NEXT!
!
SAPPHIRA !!
THUD!
NOT AGAIN!
The believers were seized with fear after these incidents...
The God they worshipped was awesome and holy beyond their knowledge.

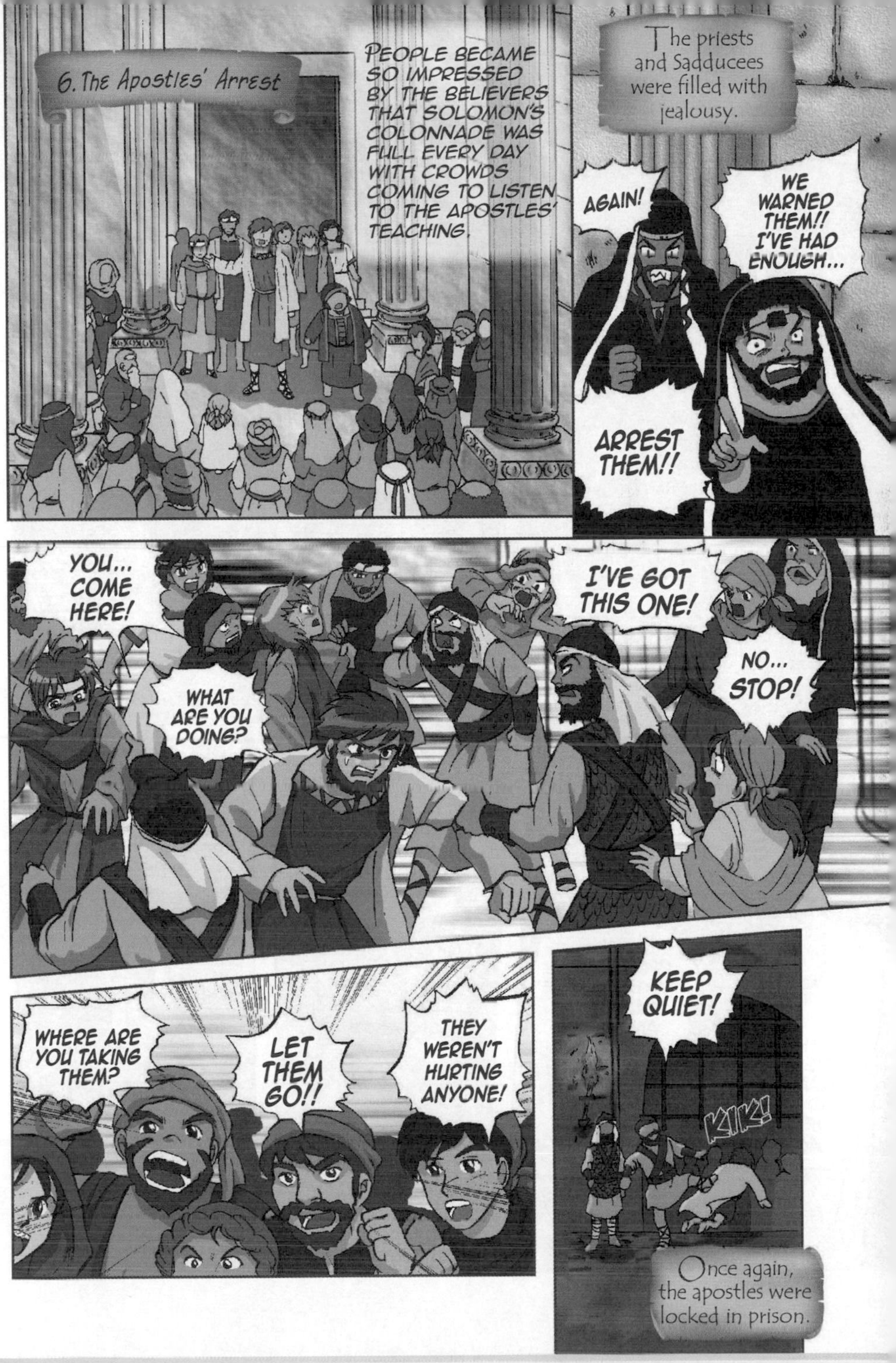
6. The Apostles' Arrest
PEOPLE BECAME SO IMPRESSED BY THE BELIEVERS THAT SOLOMON'S COLONNADE WAS FULL EVERY DAY WITH CROWDS COMING TO LISTEN TO THE APOSTLES' TEACHING.
The priests and Sadducees were filled with jealousy.
AGAIN!
WE WARNED THEM!! I'VE HAD ENOUGH...
ARREST THEM!!
YOU... COME HERE!
WHAT ARE YOU DOING?
I'VE GOT THIS ONE!
NO... STOP!
WHERE ARE YOU TAKING THEM?
LET THEM GO!!
THEY WEREN'T HURTING ANYONE!
KEEP QUIET!
KLIK!
Once again, the apostles were locked in prison.

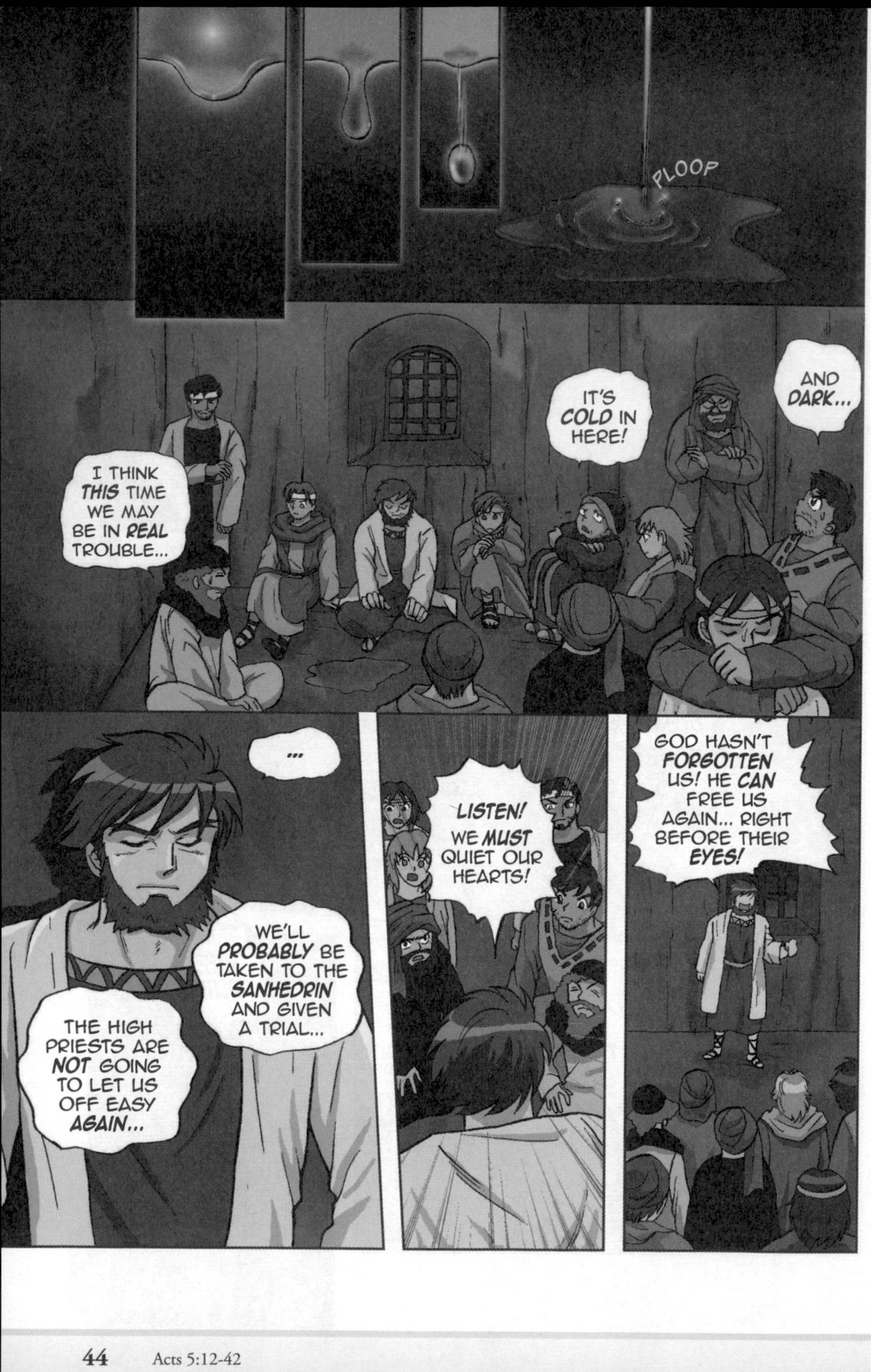
PLOOP
I THINK THIS TIME WE MAY BE IN REAL TROUBLE...
IT'S COLD IN HERE!
AND DARK...
...
THE HIGH PRIESTS ARE NOT GOING TO LET US OFF EASY AGAIN...
WE'LL PROBABLY BE TAKEN TO THE SANHEDRIN AND GIVEN A TRIAL...
LISTEN! WE MUST QUIET OUR HEARTS!
GOD HASN'T FORGOTTEN US! HE CAN FREE US AGAIN... RIGHT BEFORE THEIR EYES!

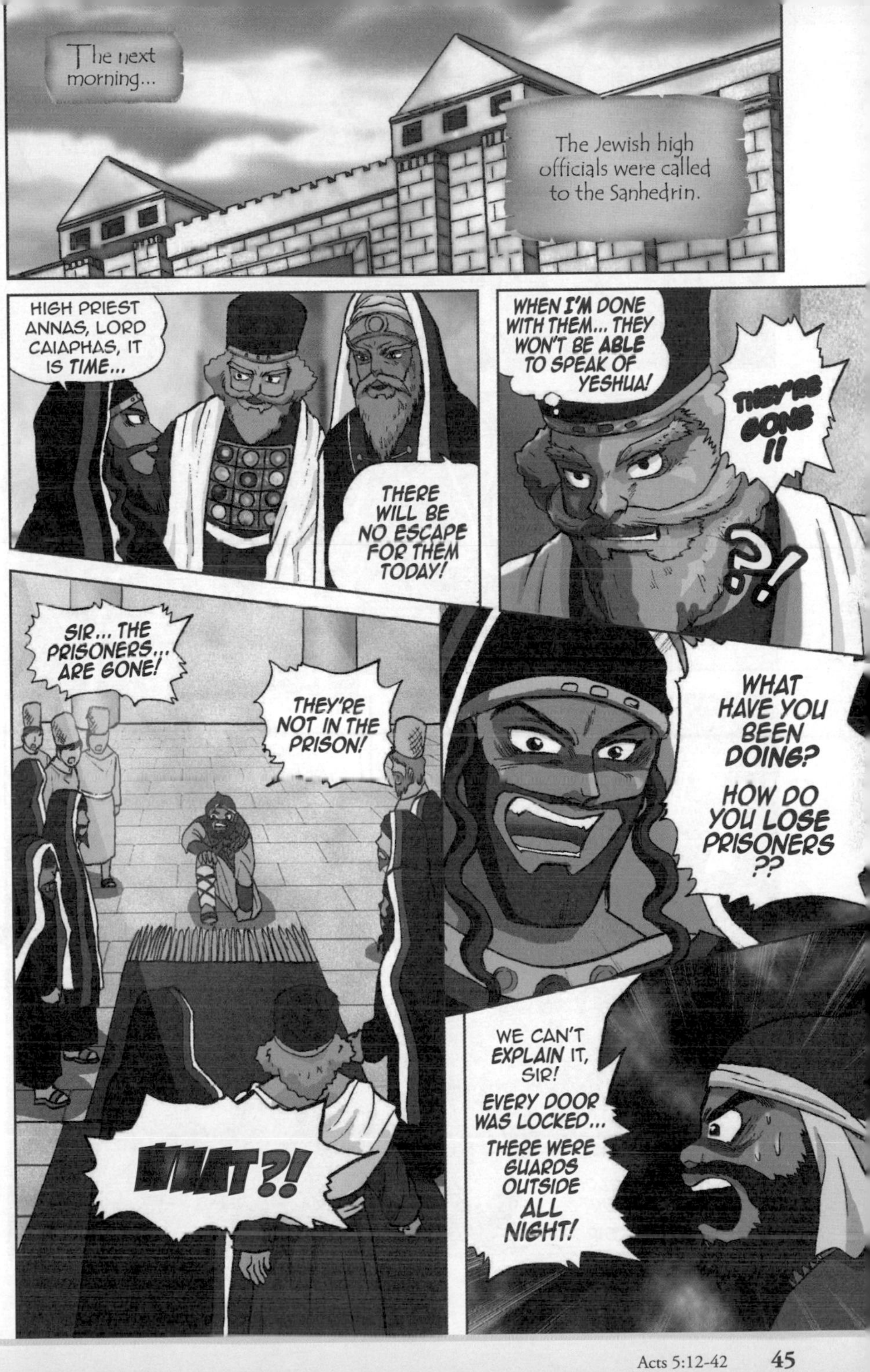
The next morning...
The Jewish high officials were called to the Sanhedrin.
HIGH PRIEST ANNAS, LORD CAIAPHAS, IT IS TIME...
THERE WILL BE NO ESCAPE FOR THEM TODAY!
WHEN I'M DONE WITH THEM... THEY WON'T BE ABLE TO SPEAK OF YESHUA!
THEY'RE GONE !!
?!
SIR... THE PRISONERS... ARE GONE!
THEY'RE NOT IN THE PRISON!
WHAT?!
WHAT HAVE YOU BEEN DOING?
HOW DO YOU LOSE PRISONERS ??
WE CAN'T EXPLAIN IT, SIR!
EVERY DOOR WAS LOCKED...
THERE WERE GUARDS OUTSIDE ALL NIGHT!

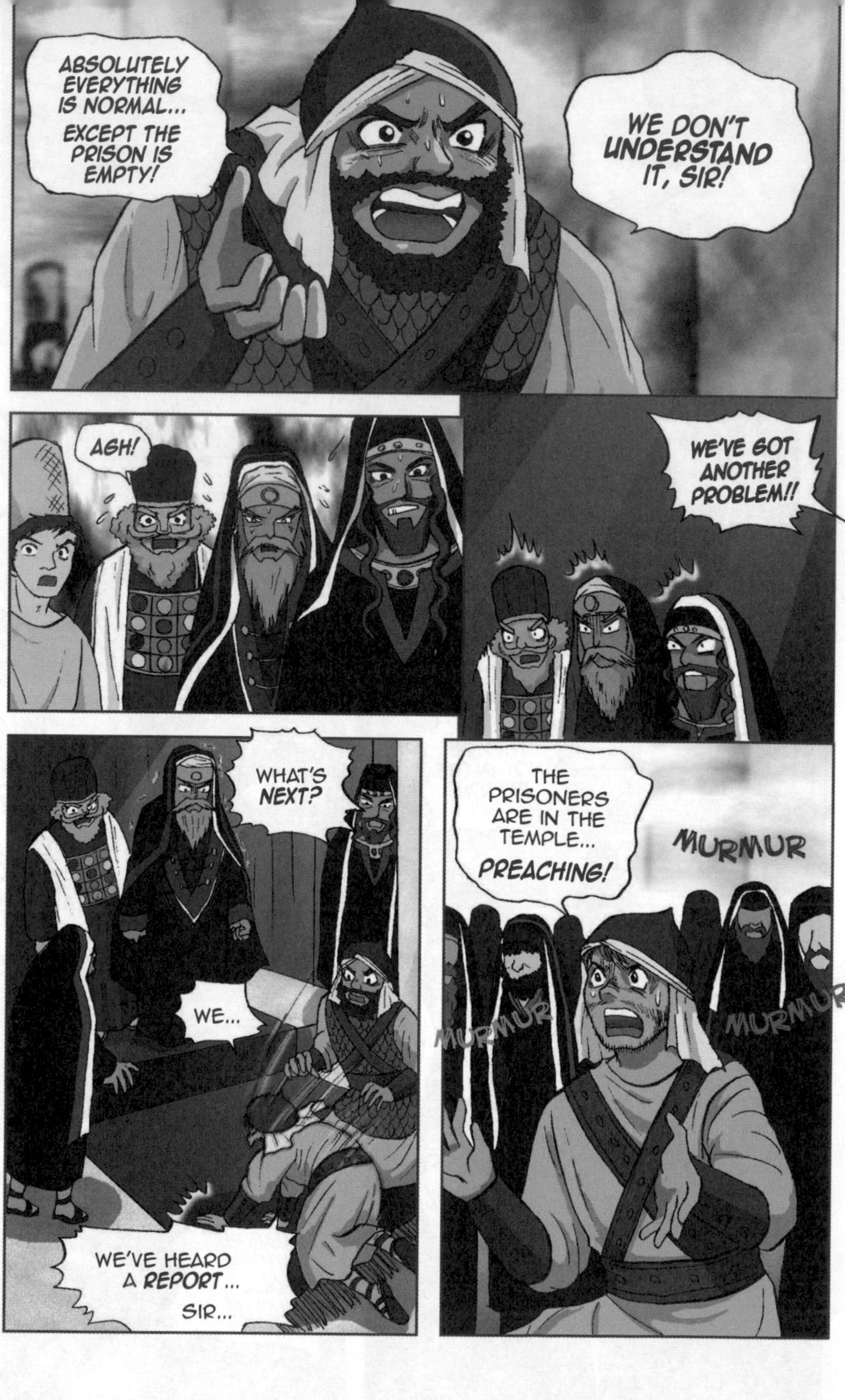
ABSOLUTELY EVERYTHING IS NORMAL... EXCEPT THE PRISON IS EMPTY!
WE DON'T UNDERSTAND IT, SIR!
AGH!
WE'VE GOT ANOTHER PROBLEM!!
WHAT'S NEXT?
WE...
WE'VE HEARD A REPORT... SIR...
THE PRISONERS ARE IN THE TEMPLE... PREACHING!
MURMUR
MURMUR
MURMUR

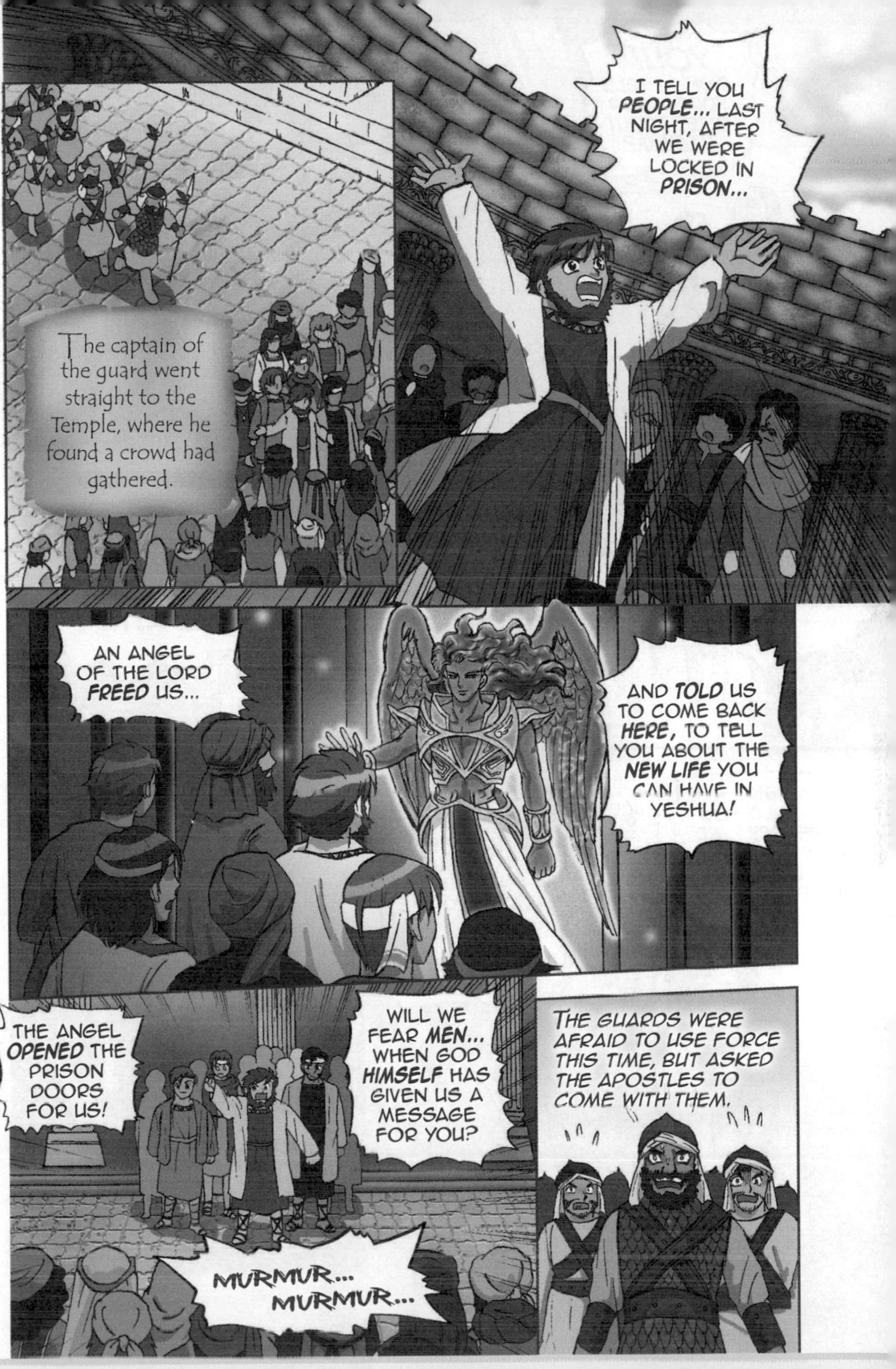
The captain of the guard went straight to the Temple, where he found a crowd had gathered.
I TELL YOU PEOPLE... LAST NIGHT, AFTER WE WERE LOCKED IN PRISON...
AN ANGEL OF THE LORD FREED US...
AND TOLD US TO COME BACK HERE, TO TELL YOU ABOUT THE NEW LIFE YOU CAN HAVE IN YESHUA!
THE ANGEL OPENED THE PRISON DOORS FOR US!
WILL WE FEAR MEN... WHEN GOD HIMSELF HAS GIVEN US A MESSAGE FOR YOU?
MURMUR... MURMUR...
THE GUARDS WERE AFRAID TO USE FORCE THIS TIME, BUT ASKED THE APOSTLES TO COME WITH THEM.

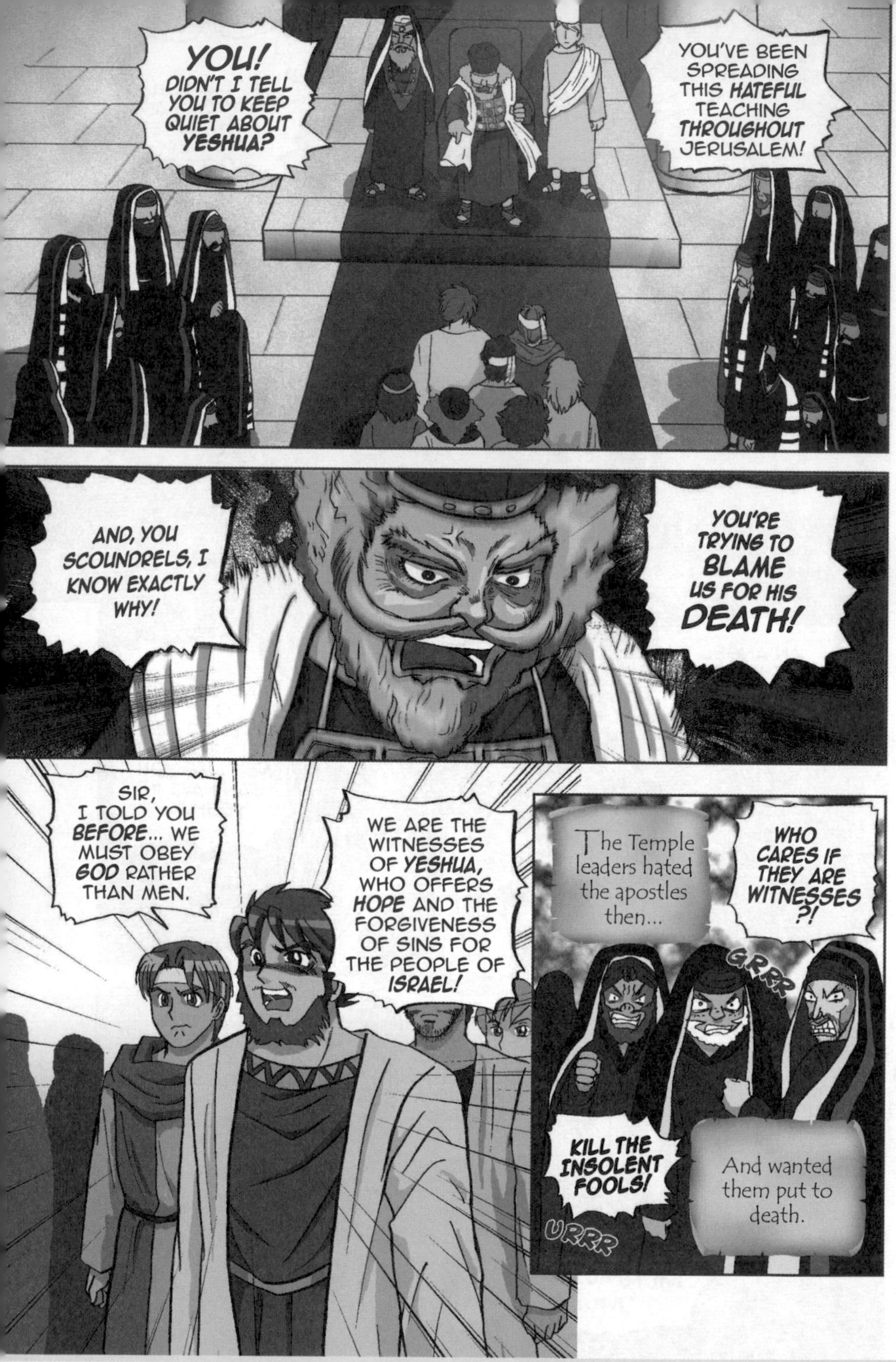
YOU! DIDN'T I TELL YOU TO KEEP QUIET ABOUT YESHUA?
YOU'VE BEEN SPREADING THIS HATEFUL TEACHING THROUGHOUT JERUSALEM!
AND, YOU SCOUNDRELS, I KNOW EXACTLY WHY!
YOU'RE TRYING TO BLAME US FOR HIS DEATH!
SIR, I TOLD YOU BEFORE... WE MUST OBEY GOD RATHER THAN MEN.
WE ARE THE WITNESSES OF YESHUA, WHO OFFERS HOPE AND THE FORGIVENESS OF SINS FOR THE PEOPLE OF ISRAEL!
The Temple leaders hated the apostles then...
WHO CARES IF THEY ARE WITNESSES ?!
GRRR
KILL THE INSOLENT FOOLS!
URRR
And wanted them put to death.

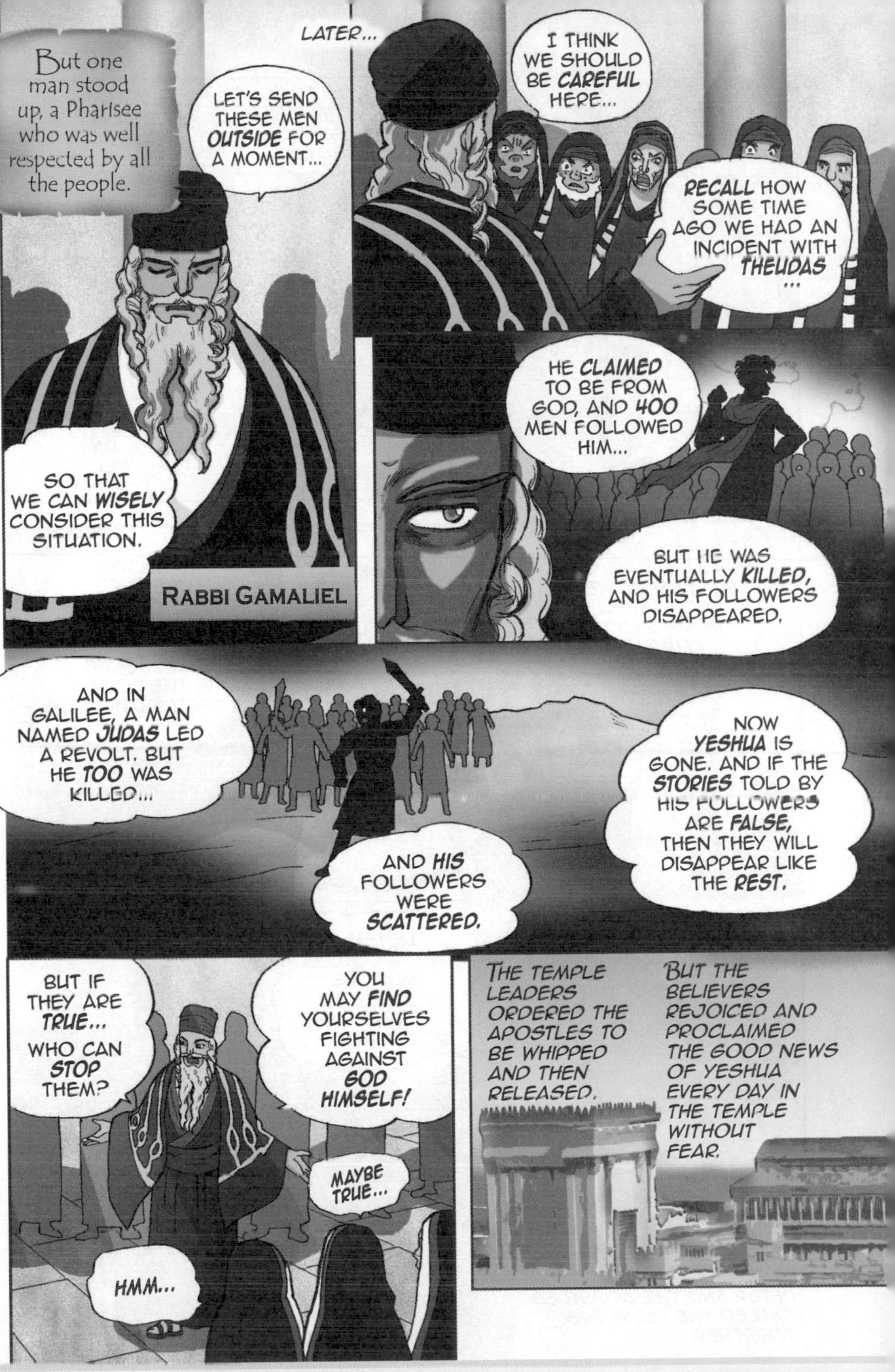
But one man stood up, a Pharisee who was well respected by all the people.
LET'S SEND THESE MEN OUTSIDE FOR A MOMENT...
SO THAT WE CAN WISELY CONSIDER THIS SITUATION.
RABBI GAMALIEL
LATER...
I THINK WE SHOULD BE CAREFUL HERE...
RECALL HOW SOME TIME AGO WE HAD AN INCIDENT WITH THEUDAS ...
HE CLAIMED TO BE FROM GOD, AND 400 MEN FOLLOWED HIM...
BUT HE WAS EVENTUALLY KILLED, AND HIS FOLLOWERS DISAPPEARED.
AND IN GALILEE, A MAN NAMED JUDAS LED A REVOLT. BUT HE TOO WAS KILLED...
AND HIS FOLLOWERS WERE SCATTERED.
NOW YESHUA IS GONE. AND IF THE STORIES TOLD BY HIS FOLLOWERS ARE FALSE, THEN THEY WILL DISAPPEAR LIKE THE REST.
BUT IF THEY ARE TRUE... WHO CAN STOP THEM?
YOU MAY FIND YOURSELVES FIGHTING AGAINST GOD HIMSELF!
MAYBE TRUE...
HMM...
THE TEMPLE LEADERS ORDERED THE APOSTLES TO BE WHIPPED AND THEN RELEASED.
BUT THE BELIEVERS REJOICED AND PROCLAIMED THE GOOD NEWS OF YESHUA EVERY DAY IN THE TEMPLE WITHOUT FEAR.

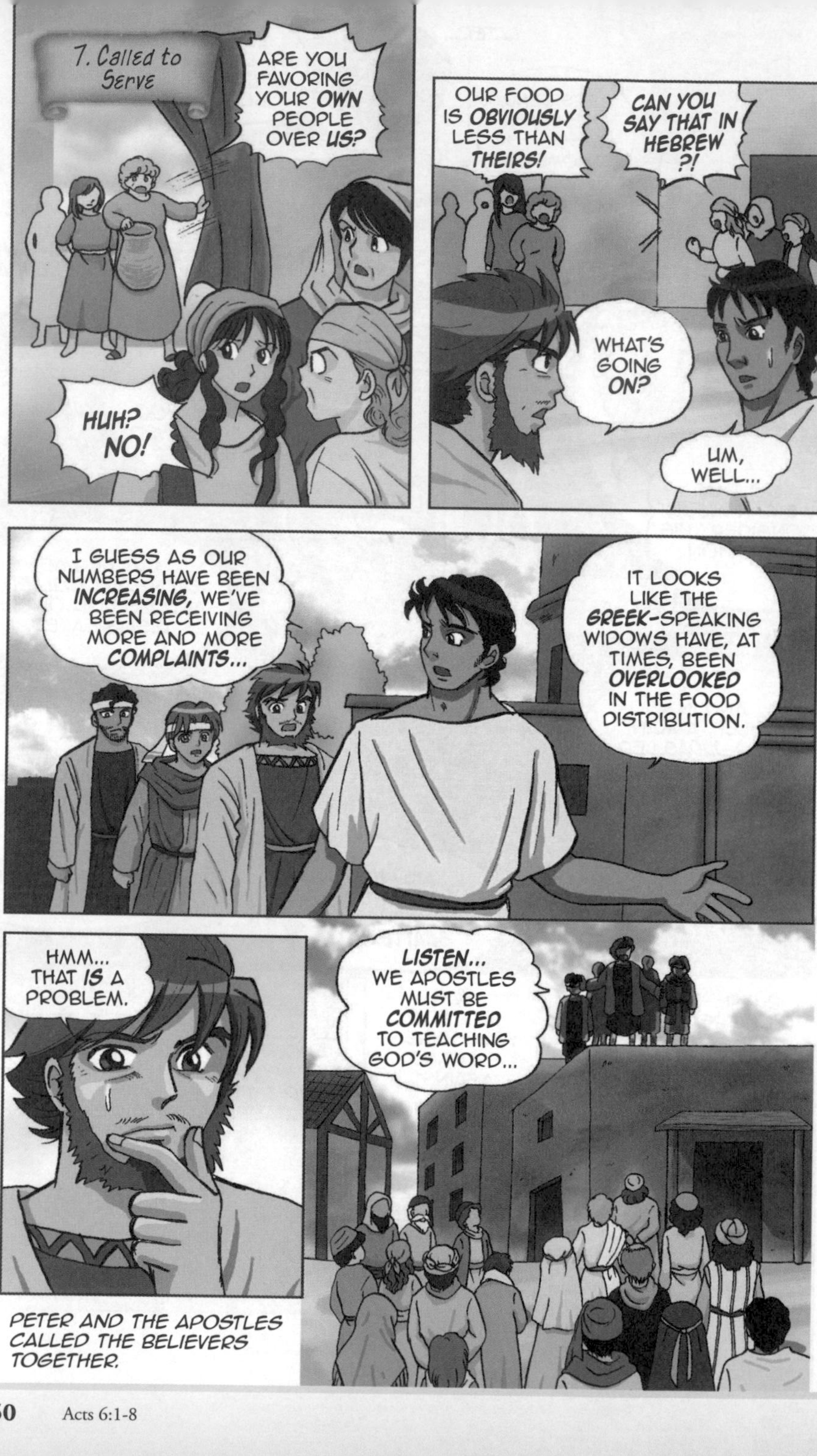
7. Called to Serve
ARE YOU FAVORING YOUR OWN PEOPLE OVER US?
HUH? NO!
OUR FOOD IS OBVIOUSLY LESS THAN THEIRS!
CAN YOU SAY THAT IN HEBREW ?!
WHAT'S GOING ON?
UM, WELL...
I GUESS AS OUR NUMBERS HAVE BEEN INCREASING, WE'VE BEEN RECEIVING MORE AND MORE COMPLAINTS...
IT LOOKS LIKE THE GREEK-SPEAKING WIDOWS HAVE, AT TIMES, BEEN OVERLOOKED IN THE FOOD DISTRIBUTION.
HMM... THAT IS A PROBLEM.
LISTEN... WE APOSTLES MUST BE COMMITTED TO TEACHING GOD'S WORD...
PETER AND THE APOSTLES CALLED THE BELIEVERS TOGETHER.

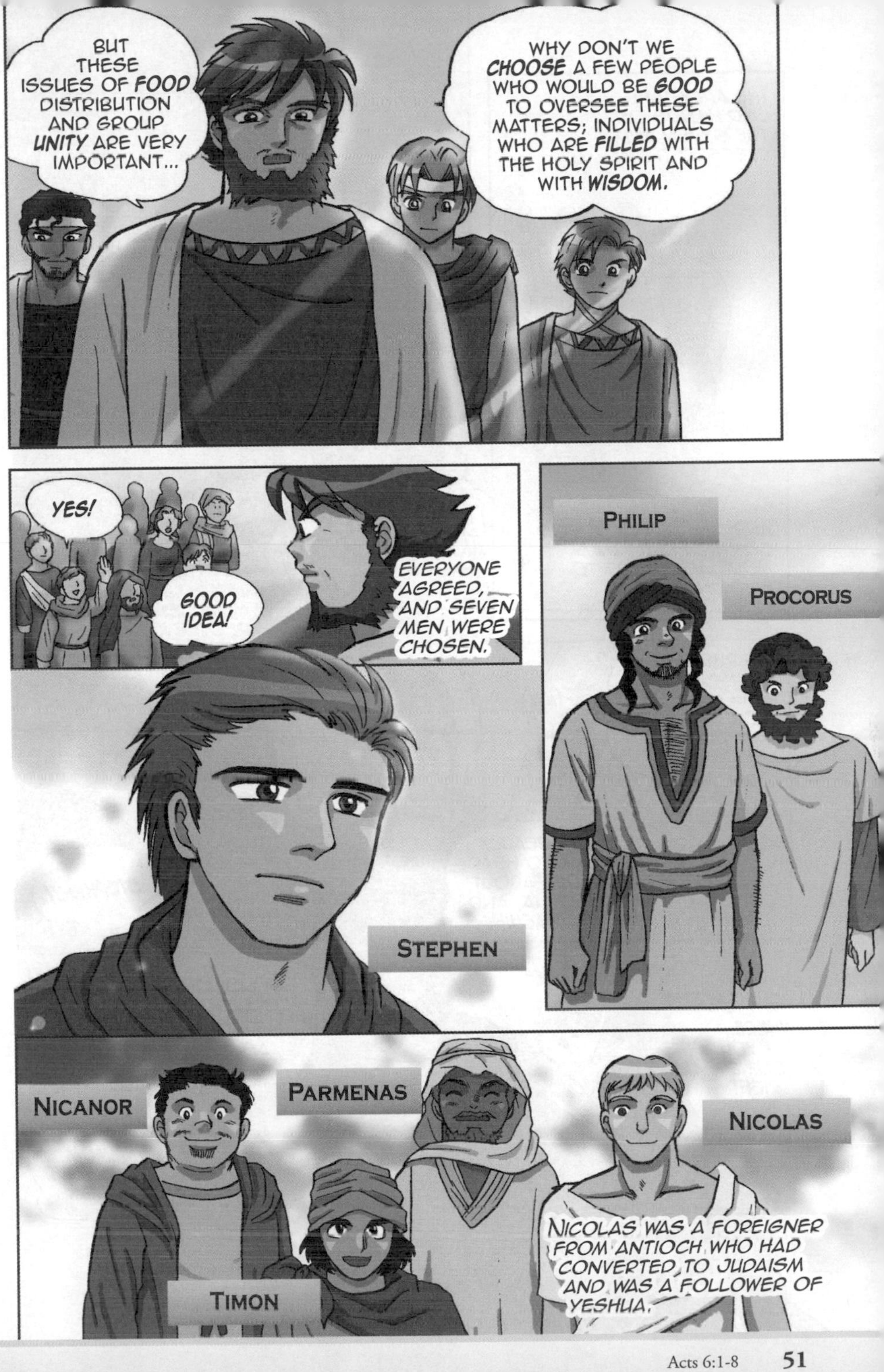

BUT THESE ISSUES OF FOOD DISTRIBUTION AND GROUP UNITY ARE VERY IMPORTANT...
WHY DON'T WE CHOOSE A FEW PEOPLE WHO WOULD BE GOOD TO OVERSEE THESE MATTERS; INDIVIDUALS WHO ARE FILLED WITH THE HOLY SPIRIT AND WITH WISDOM.
YES!
GOOD IDEA!
EVERYONE AGREED, AND SEVEN MEN WERE CHOSEN.
PHILIP
PROCORUS
STEPHEN
NICANOR
PARMENAS
NICOLAS
TIMON
NICOLAS WAS A FOREIGNER FROM ANTIOCH WHO HAD CONVERTED TO JUDAISM AND WAS A FOLLOWER OF YESHUA.

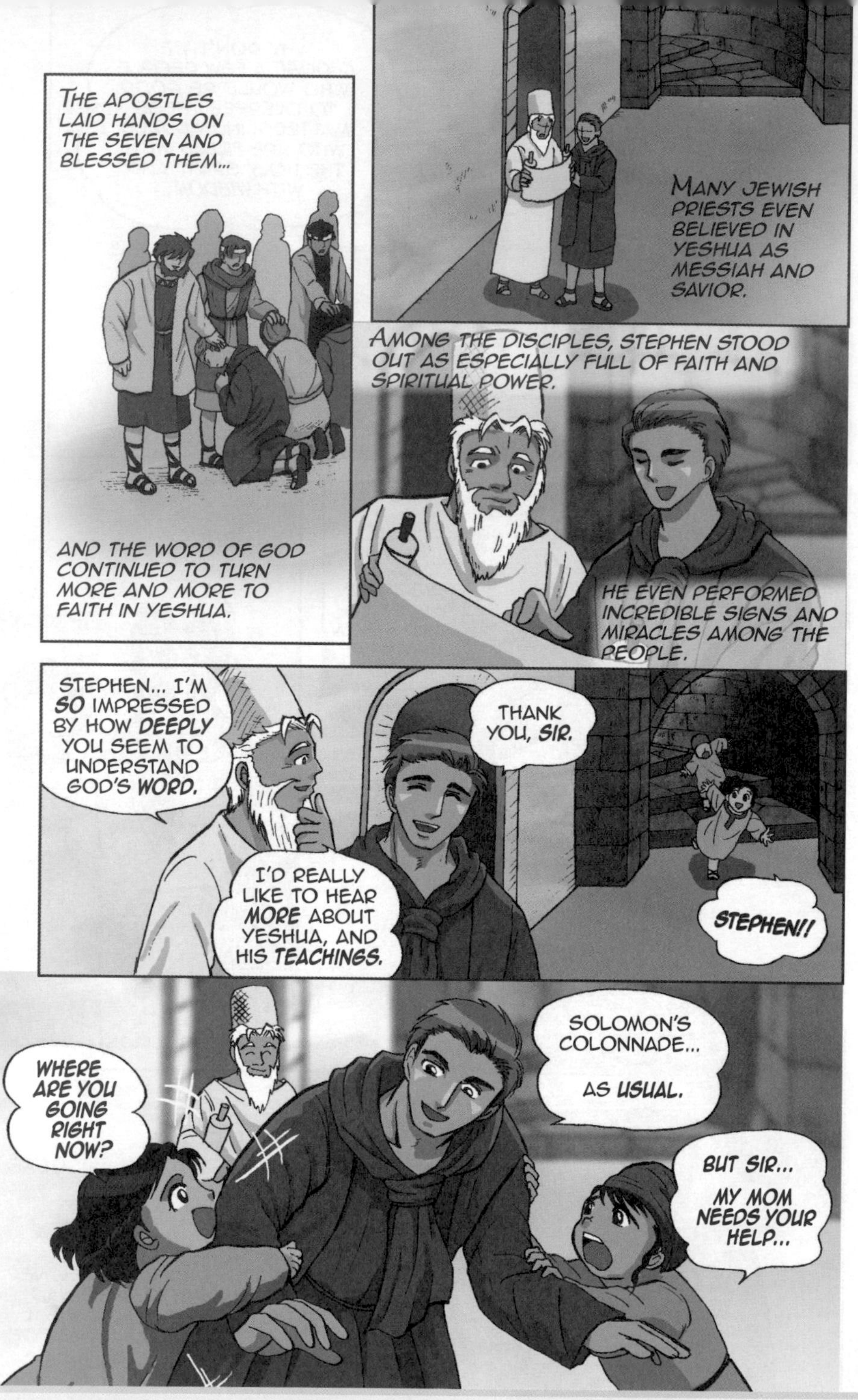
The apostles laid hands on the seven and blessed them...
Many Jewish priests even believed in Yeshua as Messiah and Savior.
And the word of God continued to turn more and more to faith in Yeshua.
Among the disciples, Stephen stood out as especially full of faith and spiritual power.
He even performed incredible signs and miracles among the people.
STEPHEN... I'M SO IMPRESSED BY HOW DEEPLY YOU SEEM TO UNDERSTAND GOD'S WORD.
THANK YOU, SIR.
I'D REALLY LIKE TO HEAR MORE ABOUT YESHUA, AND HIS TEACHINGS.
STEPHEN!!
WHERE ARE YOU GOING RIGHT NOW?
SOLOMON'S COLONNADE... AS USUAL.
BUT SIR... MY MOM NEEDS YOUR HELP...

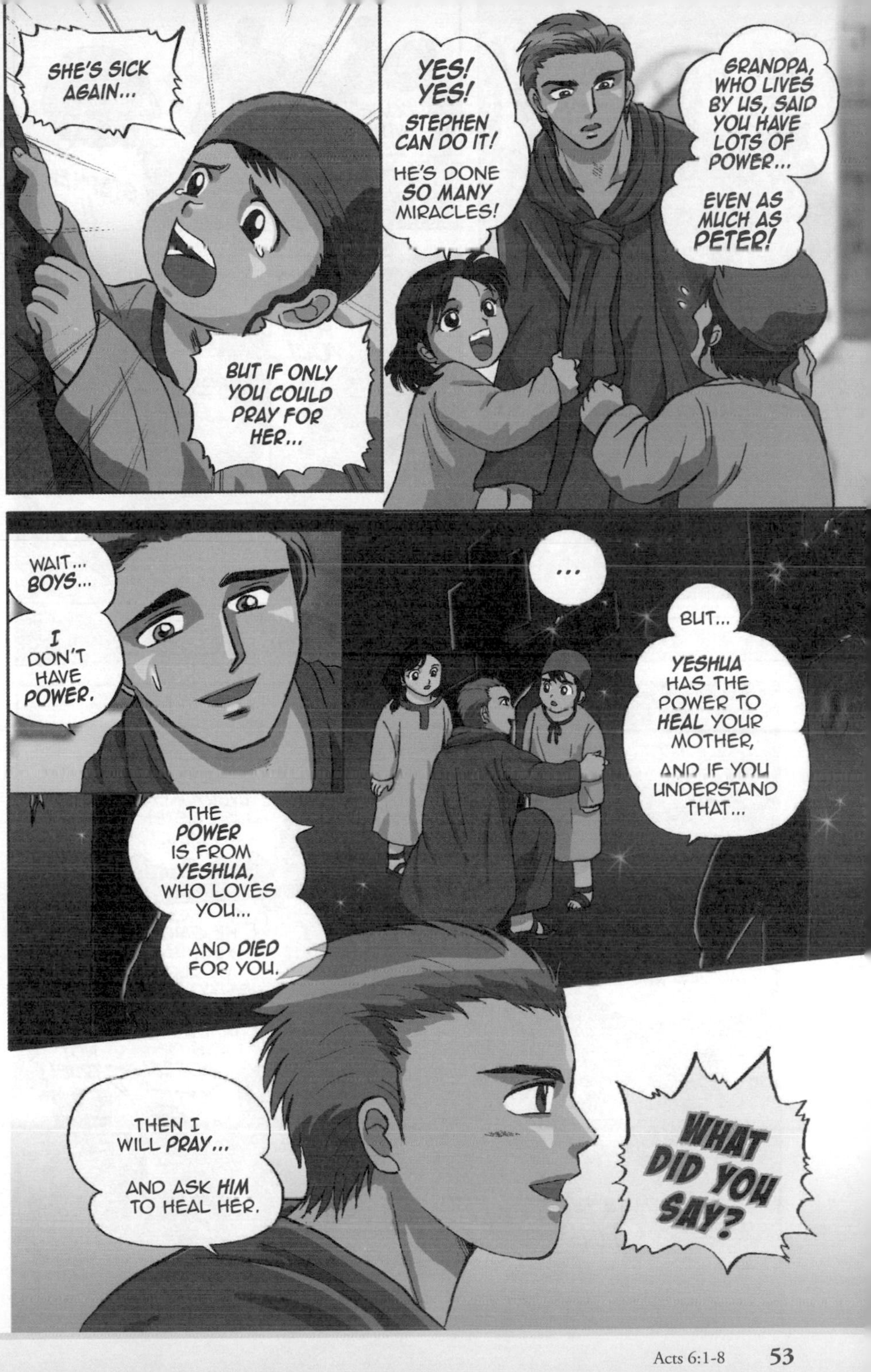
SHE'S SICK AGAIN...
BUT IF ONLY YOU COULD PRAY FOR HER...
YES! YES! STEPHEN CAN DO IT!
HE'S DONE SO MANY MIRACLES!
GRANDPA, WHO LIVES BY US, SAID YOU HAVE LOTS OF POWER...
EVEN AS MUCH AS PETER!
WAIT... BOYS...
I DON'T HAVE POWER.
...
BUT...
YESHUA HAS THE POWER TO HEAL YOUR MOTHER,
AND IF YOU UNDERSTAND THAT...
THE POWER IS FROM YESHUA, WHO LOVES YOU...
AND DIED FOR YOU.
THEN I WILL PRAY...
AND ASK HIM TO HEAL HER.
WHAT DID YOU SAY?

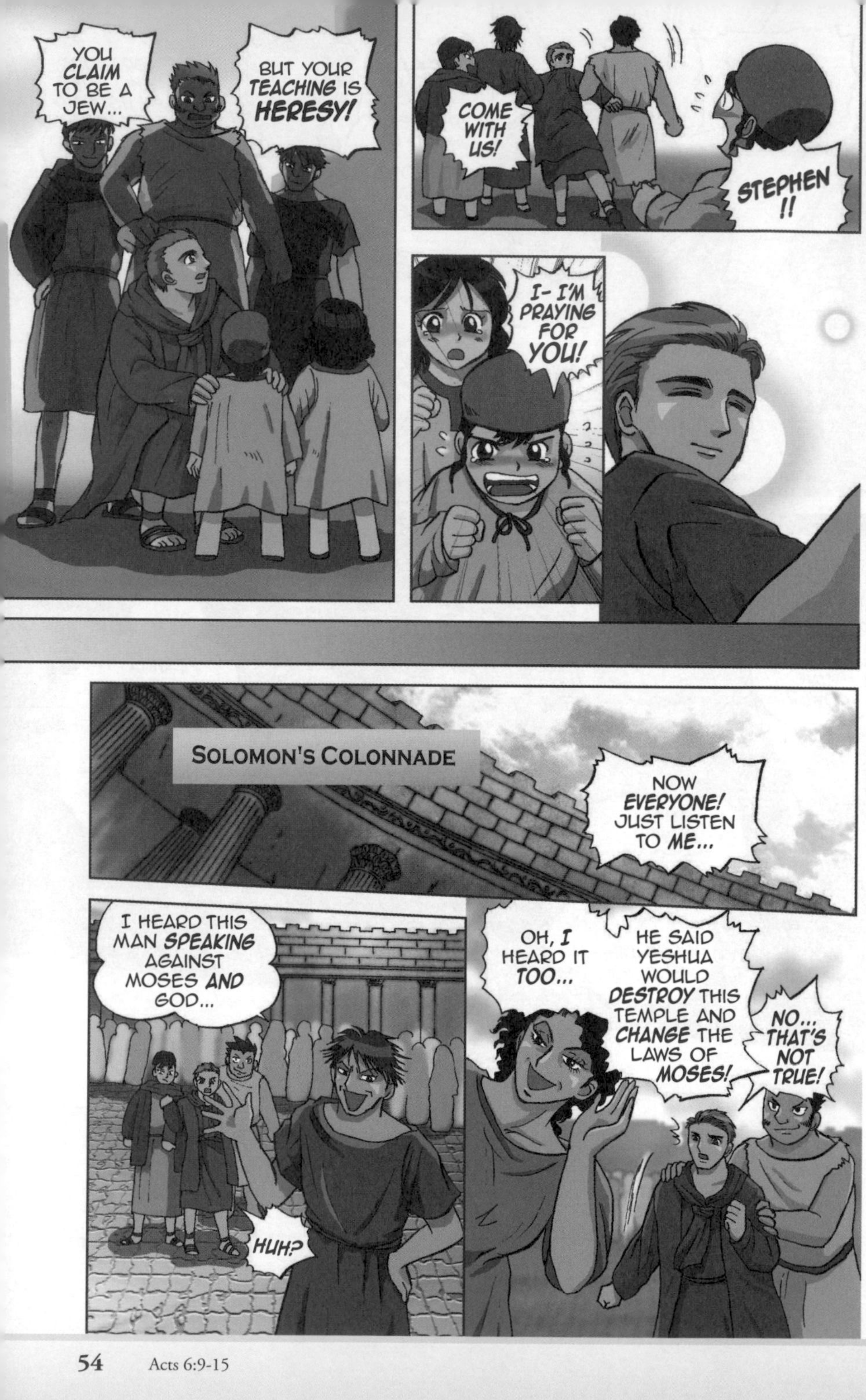
YOU CLAIM TO BE A JEW...
BUT YOUR TEACHING IS HERESY!
COME WITH US!
STEPHEN !!
I- I'M PRAYING FOR YOU!
SOLOMON'S COLONNADE
NOW EVERYONE! JUST LISTEN TO ME...
I HEARD THIS MAN SPEAKING AGAINST MOSES AND GOD...
HUH?
OH, I HEARD IT TOO...
HE SAID YESHUA WOULD DESTROY THIS TEMPLE AND CHANGE THE LAWS OF MOSES!
NO... THAT'S NOT TRUE!

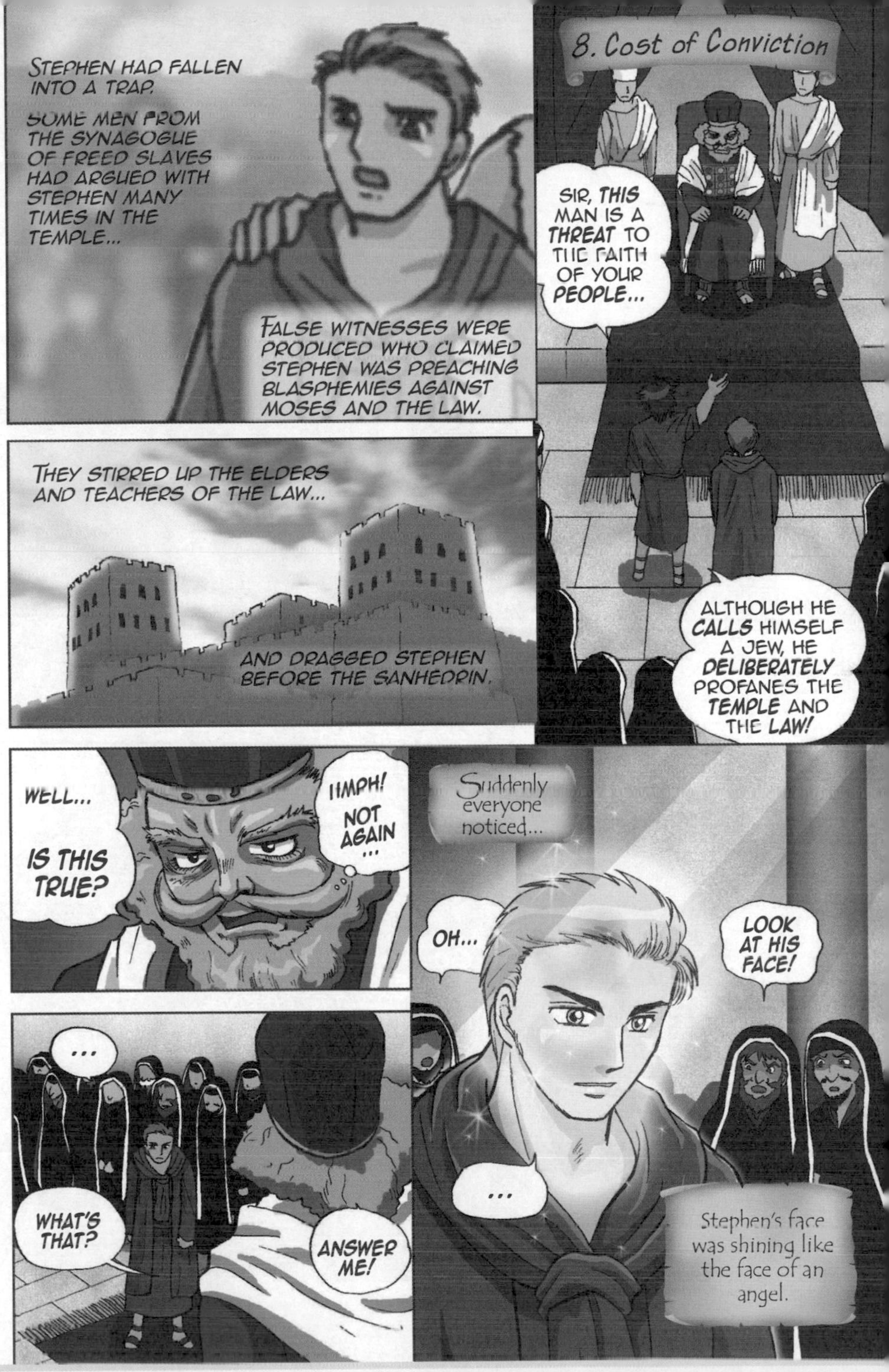
8. Cost of Conviction
STEPHEN HAD FALLEN INTO A TRAP.
SOME MEN FROM THE SYNAGOGUE OF FREED SLAVES HAD ARGUED WITH STEPHEN MANY TIMES IN THE TEMPLE...
FALSE WITNESSES WERE PRODUCED WHO CLAIMED STEPHEN WAS PREACHING BLASPHEMIES AGAINST MOSES AND THE LAW.
THEY STIRRED UP THE ELDERS AND TEACHERS OF THE LAW...
AND DRAGGED STEPHEN BEFORE THE SANHEDRIN.
SIR, THIS MAN IS A THREAT TO THE FAITH OF YOUR PEOPLE...
ALTHOUGH HE CALLS HIMSELF A JEW, HE DELIBERATELY PROFANES THE TEMPLE AND THE LAW!
WELL...
IS THIS TRUE?
HMPH! NOT AGAIN ...
...
WHAT'S THAT?
ANSWER ME!
Suddenly everyone noticed...
OH...
LOOK AT HIS FACE!
...
Stephen's face was shining like the face of an angel.

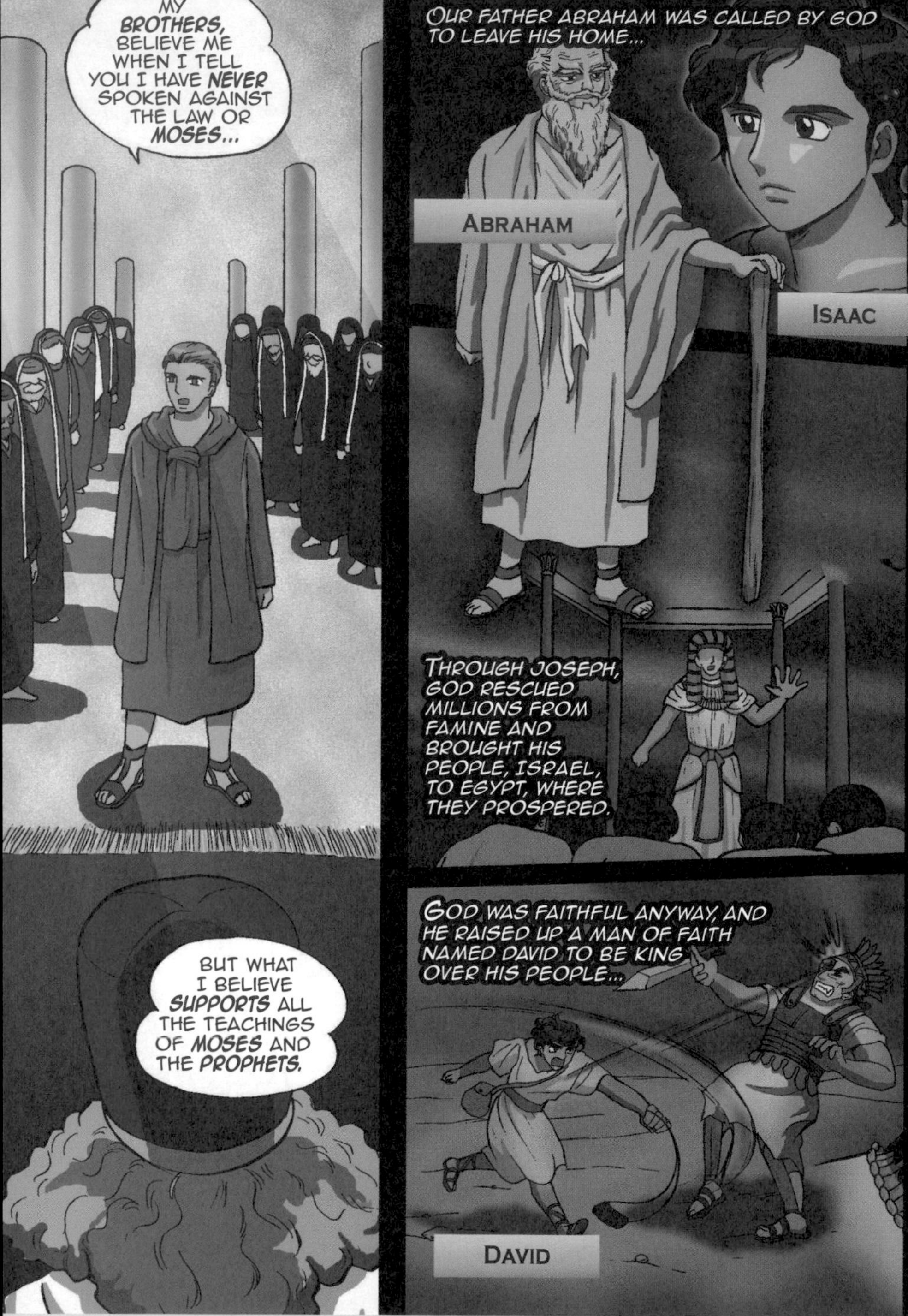

MY BROTHERS, BELIEVE ME WHEN I TELL YOU I HAVE NEVER SPOKEN AGAINST THE LAW OR MOSES...
BUT WHAT I BELIEVE SUPPORTS ALL THE TEACHINGS OF MOSES AND THE PROPHETS.
OUR FATHER ABRAHAM WAS CALLED BY GOD TO LEAVE HIS HOME...
ABRAHAM
ISAAC
THROUGH JOSEPH, GOD RESCUED MILLIONS FROM FAMINE AND BROUGHT HIS PEOPLE, ISRAEL, TO EGYPT, WHERE THEY PROSPERED.
GOD WAS FAITHFUL ANYWAY, AND HE RAISED UP A MAN OF FAITH NAMED DAVID TO BE KING OVER HIS PEOPLE...
DAVID

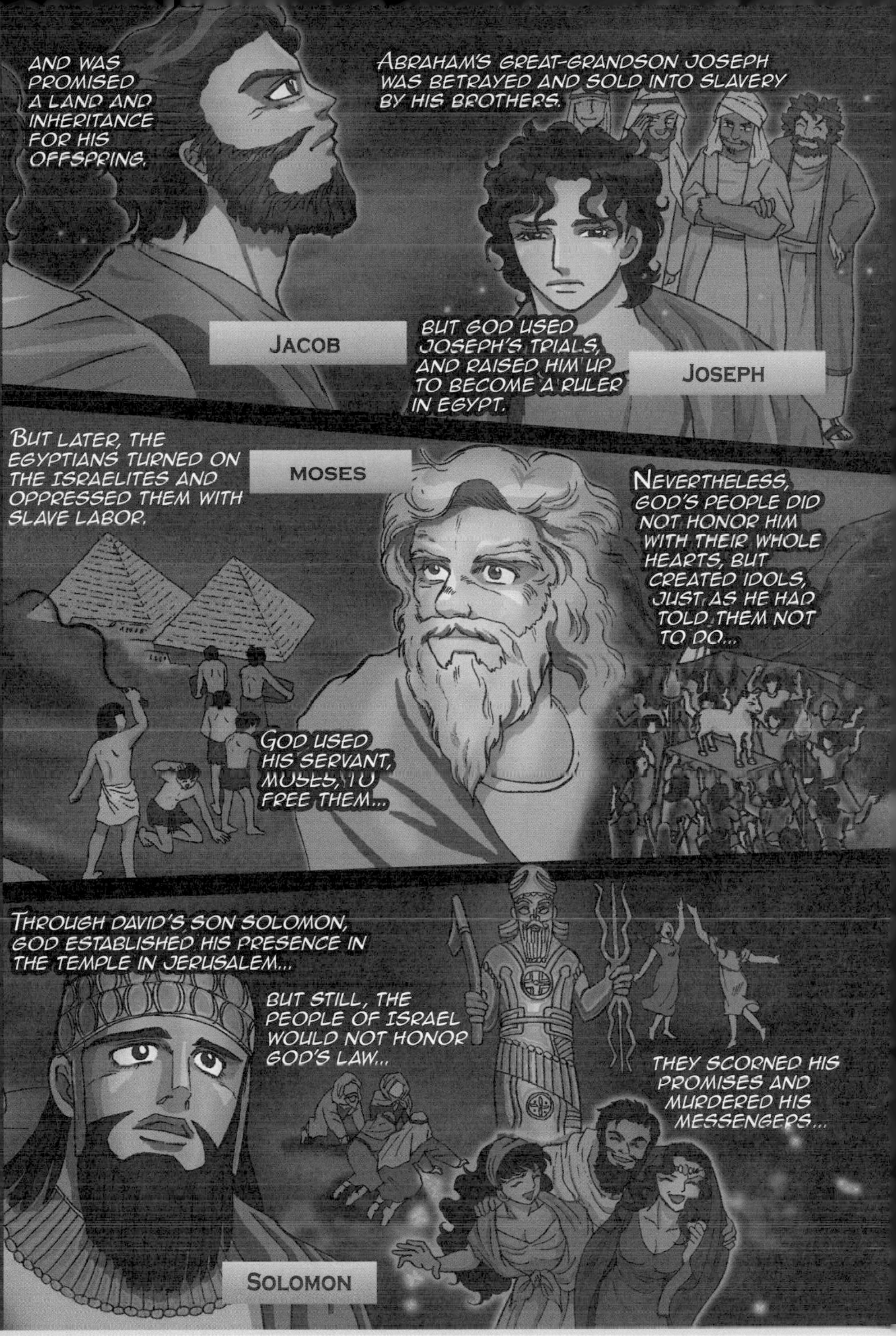
AND WAS PROMISED A LAND AND INHERITANCE FOR HIS OFFSPRING.
ABRAHAM'S GREAT-GRANDSON JOSEPH WAS BETRAYED AND SOLD INTO SLAVERY BY HIS BROTHERS.
JACOB
BUT GOD USED JOSEPH'S TRIALS, AND RAISED HIM UP TO BECOME A RULER IN EGYPT.
JOSEPH
BUT LATER, THE EGYPTIANS TURNED ON THE ISRAELITES AND OPPRESSED THEM WITH SLAVE LABOR.
MOSES
GOD USED HIS SERVANT, MOSES, TO FREE THEM...
NEVERTHELESS, GOD'S PEOPLE DID NOT HONOR HIM WITH THEIR WHOLE HEARTS, BUT CREATED IDOLS, JUST AS HE HAD TOLD THEM NOT TO DO...
THROUGH DAVID'S SON SOLOMON, GOD ESTABLISHED HIS PRESENCE IN THE TEMPLE IN JERUSALEM...
BUT STILL, THE PEOPLE OF ISRAEL WOULD NOT HONOR GOD'S LAW...
THEY SCORNED HIS PROMISES AND MURDERED HIS MESSENGERS...
SOLOMON

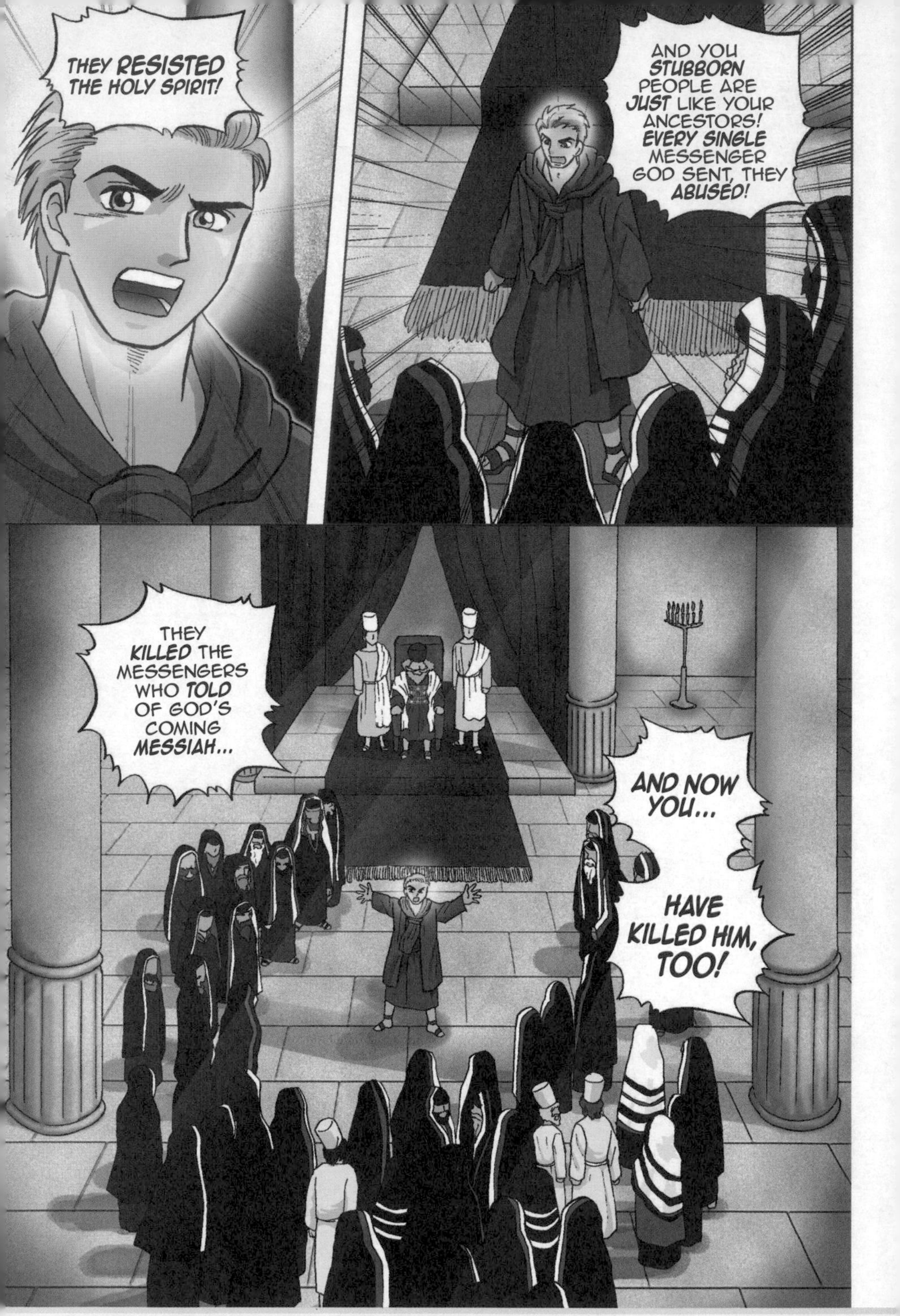
THEY RESISTED THE HOLY SPIRIT!
AND YOU STUBBORN PEOPLE ARE JUST LIKE YOUR ANCESTORS! EVERY SINGLE MESSENGER GOD SENT, THEY ABUSED!
THEY KILLED THE MESSENGERS WHO TOLD OF GOD'S COMING MESSIAH...
AND NOW YOU...
HAVE KILLED HIM, TOO!

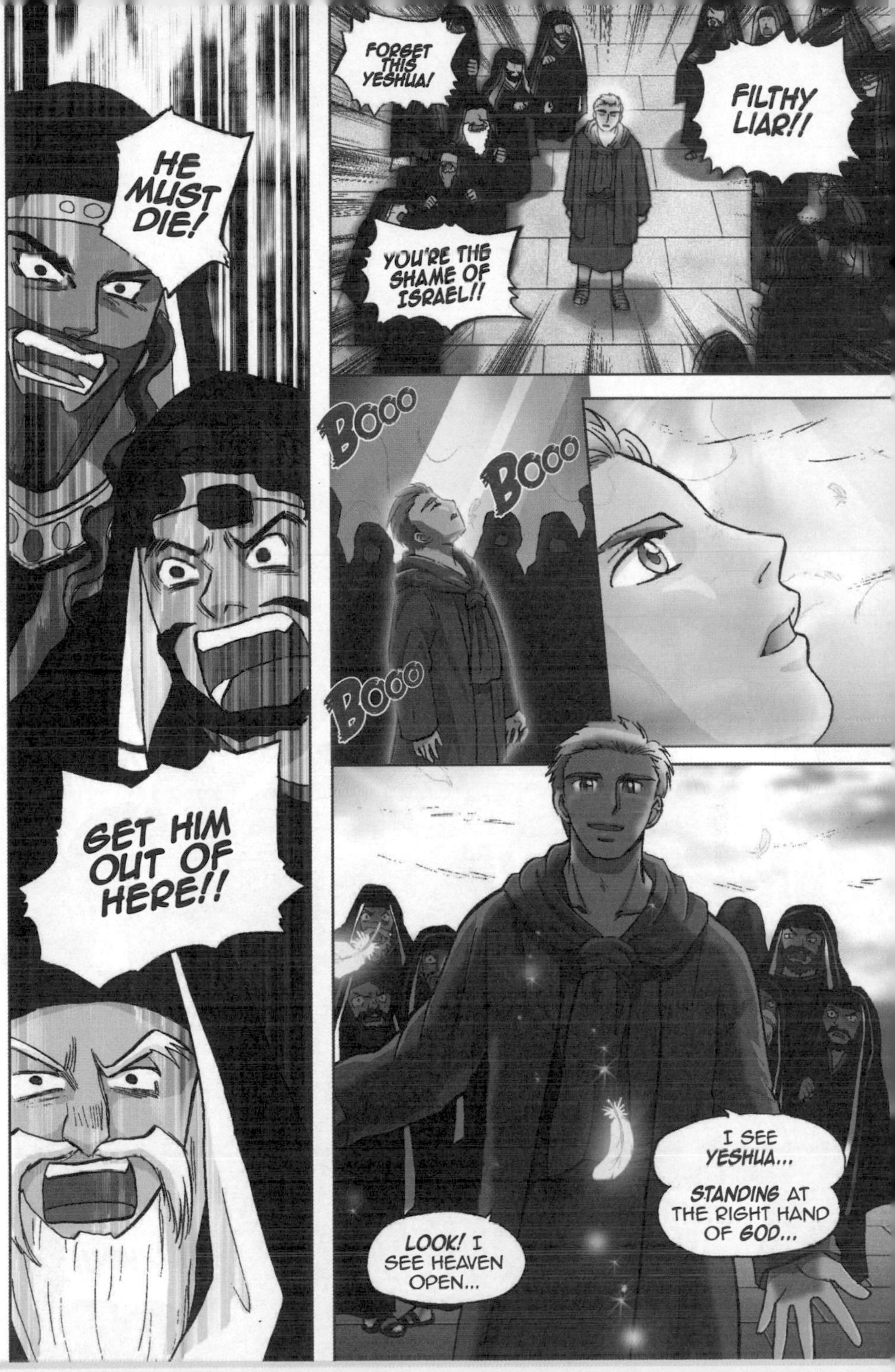
HE MUST DIE!
GET HIM OUT OF HERE!!
FORGET THIS YESHUA!
FILTHY LIAR!!
YOU'RE THE SHAME OF ISRAEL!!
BOOO
BOOO
BOOO
LOOK! I SEE HEAVEN OPEN...
I SEE YESHUA...
STANDING AT THE RIGHT HAND OF GOD...

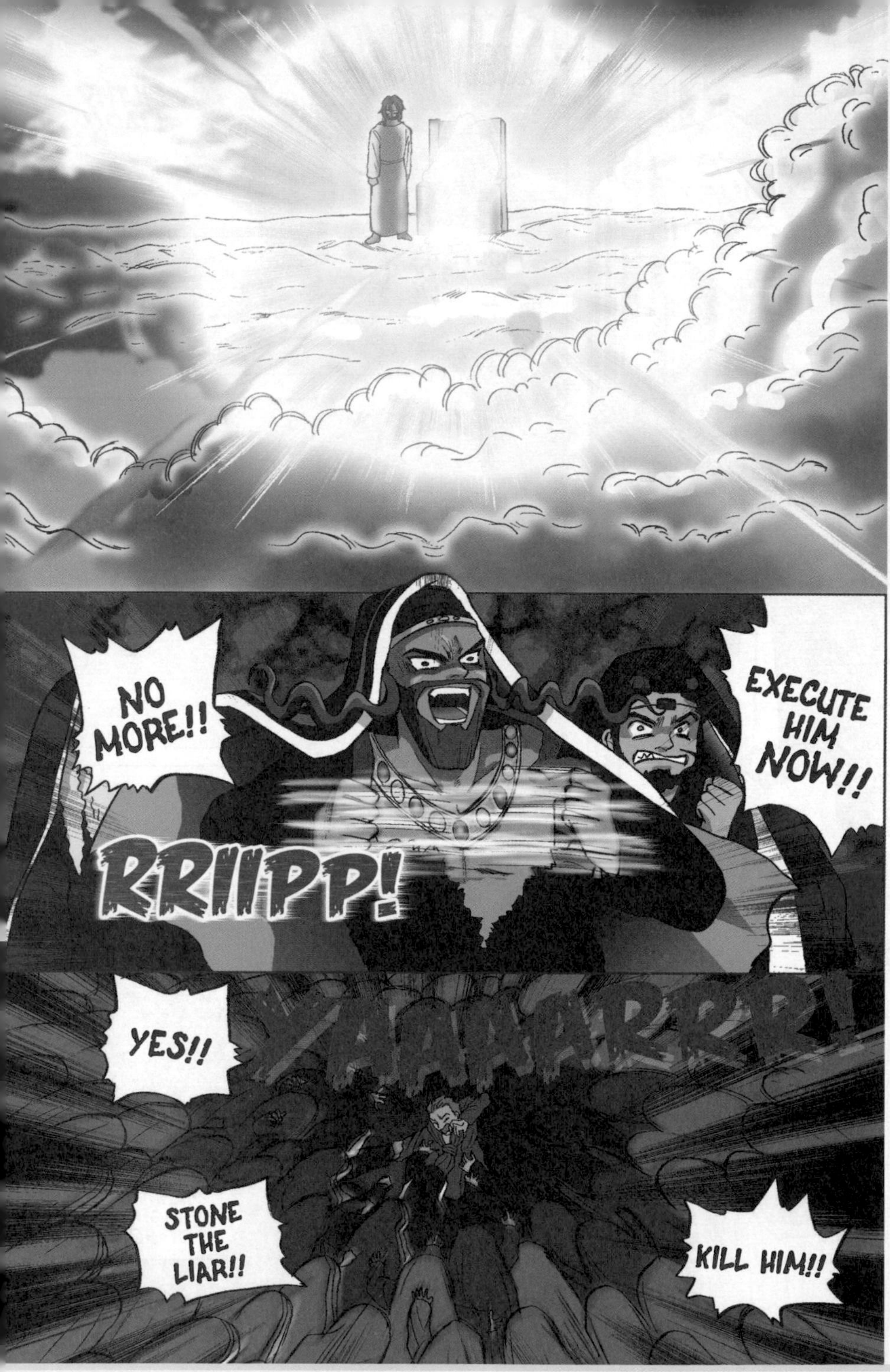
NO MORE!!
EXECUTE HIM NOW!!
RRIIPP!
YES!!
STONE THE LIAR!!
KILL HIM!!

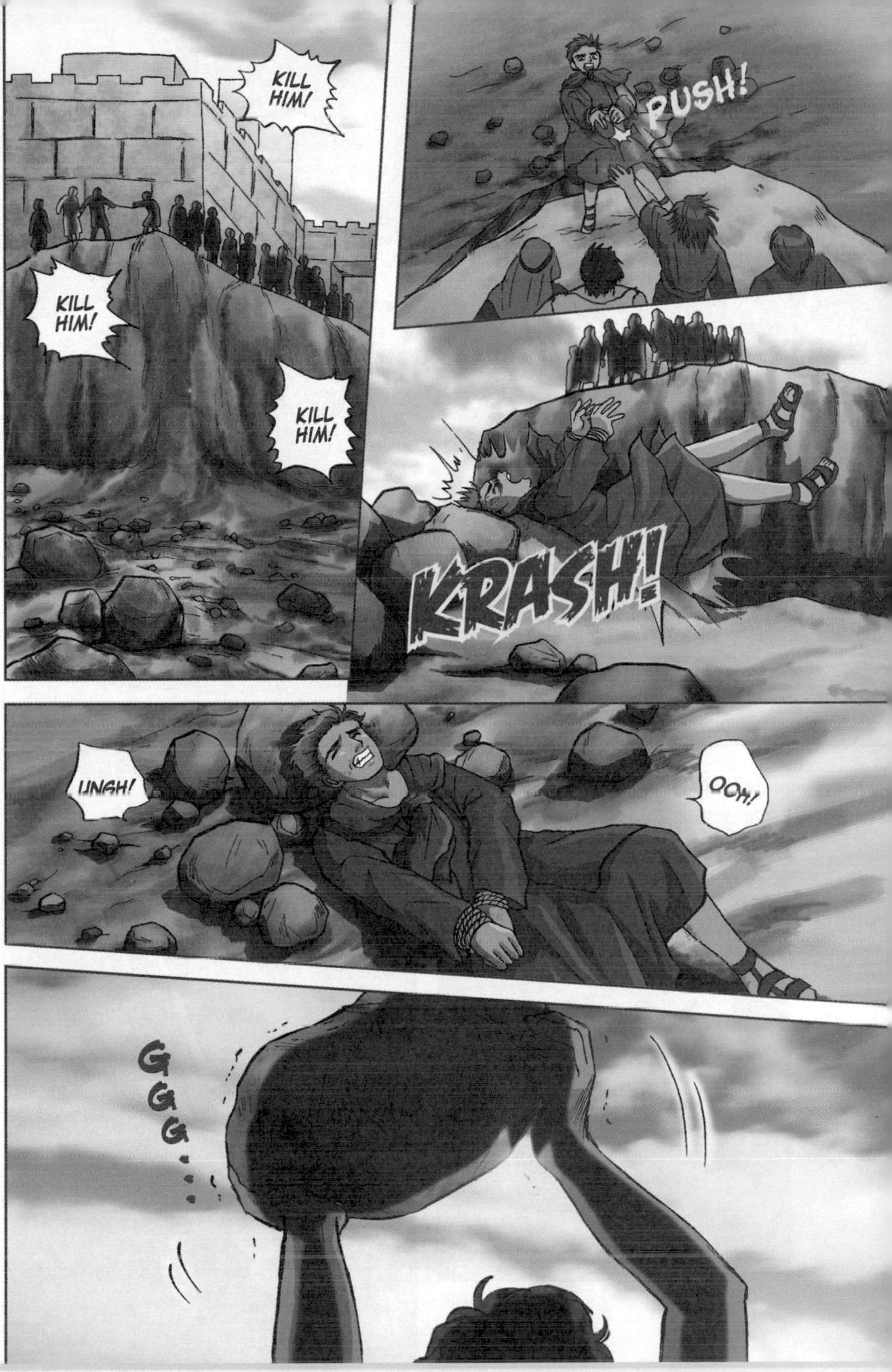
KILL HIM!
KILL HIM!
KILL HIM!
PUSH!
KRASH!
UNGH!
OOH!
GGG...

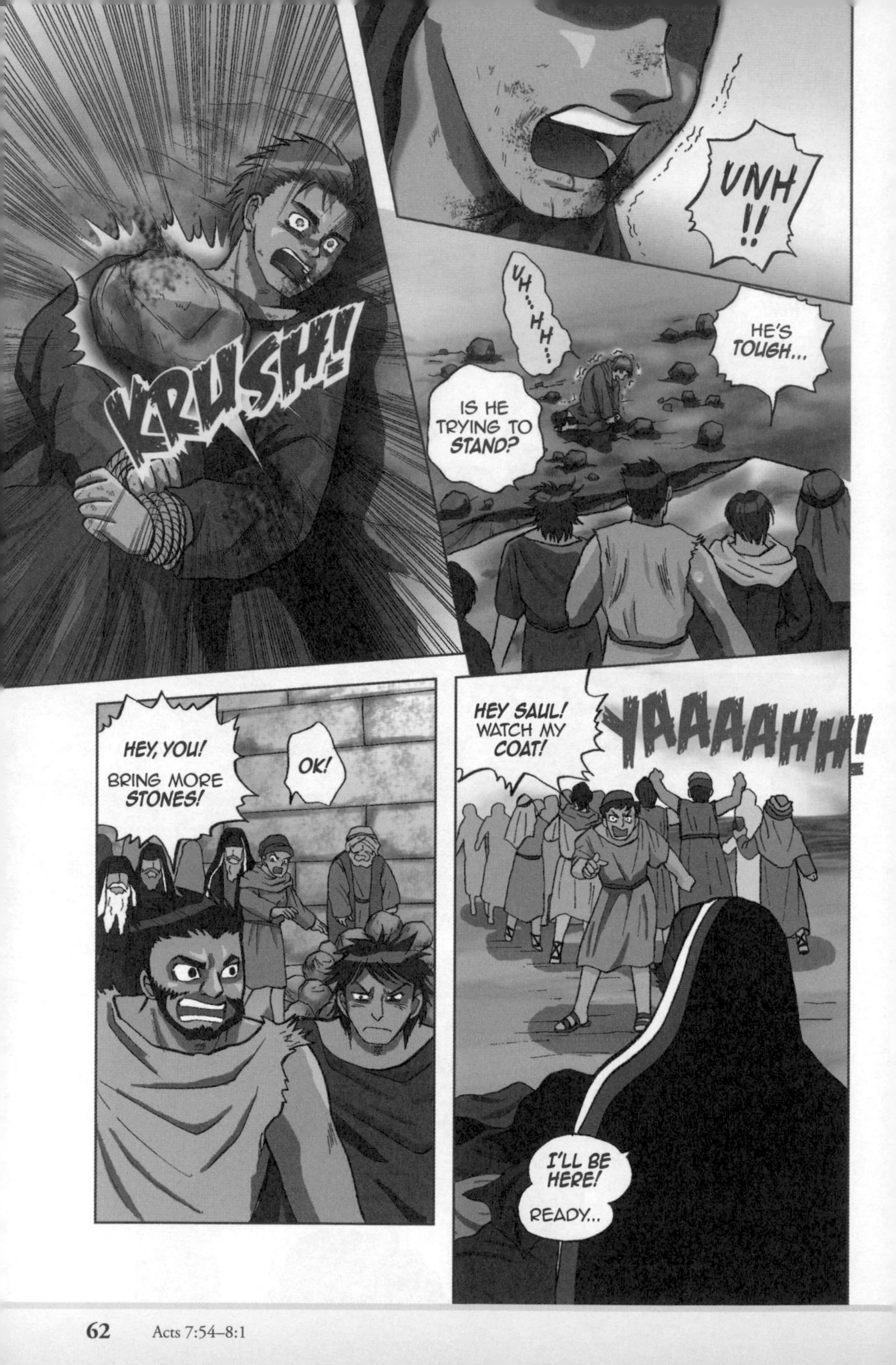
KRUSH!
UNH !!
UH...HH...
HE'S TOUGH...
IS HE TRYING TO STAND?
HEY, YOU!
BRING MORE STONES!
OK!
HEY SAUL! WATCH MY COAT!
YAAAAHH!
I'LL BE HERE!
READY...

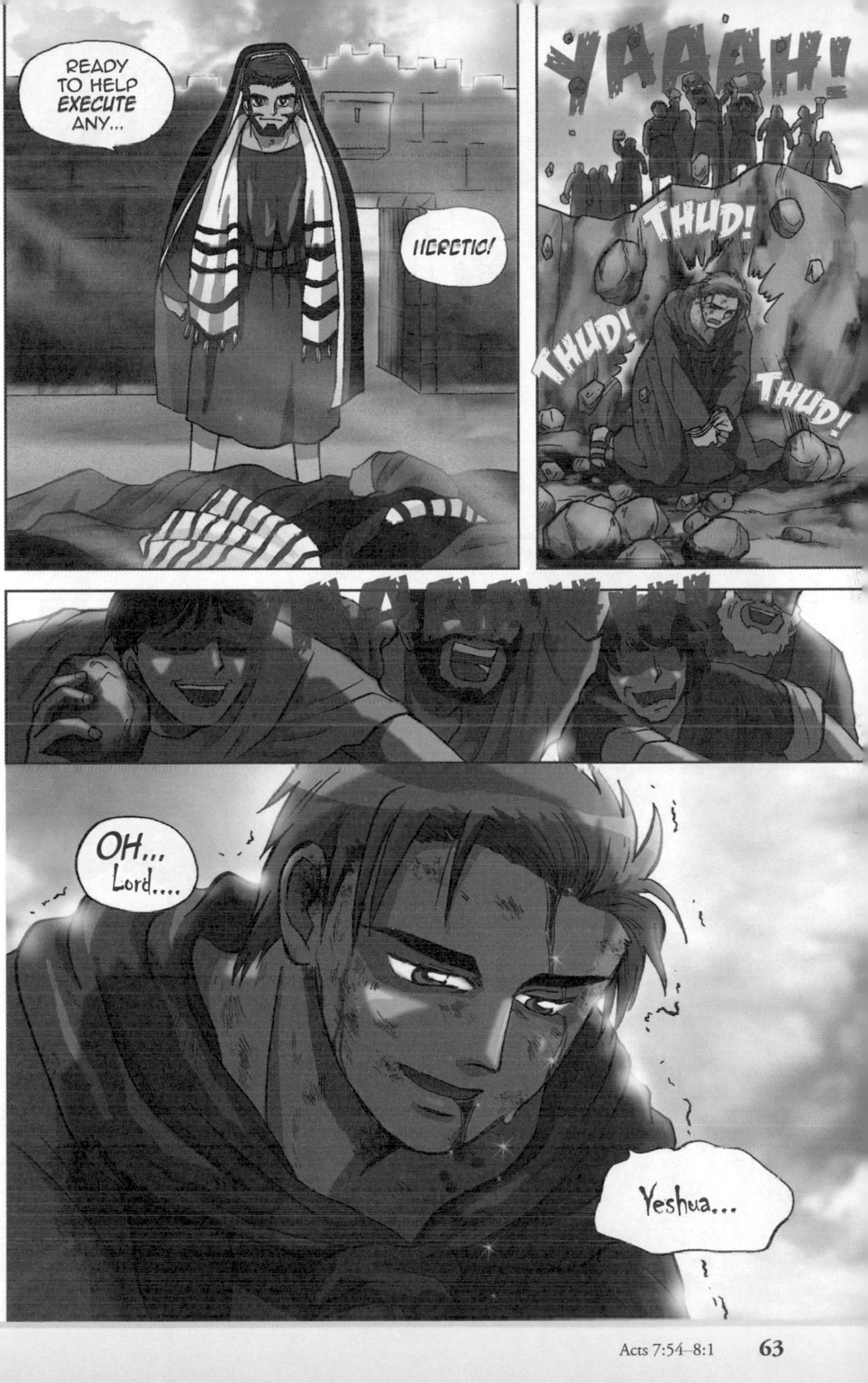
READY TO HELP EXECUTE ANY...
HERETIC!
YAAAH!
THUD!
THUD!
THUD!
OH... Lord....
Yeshua...

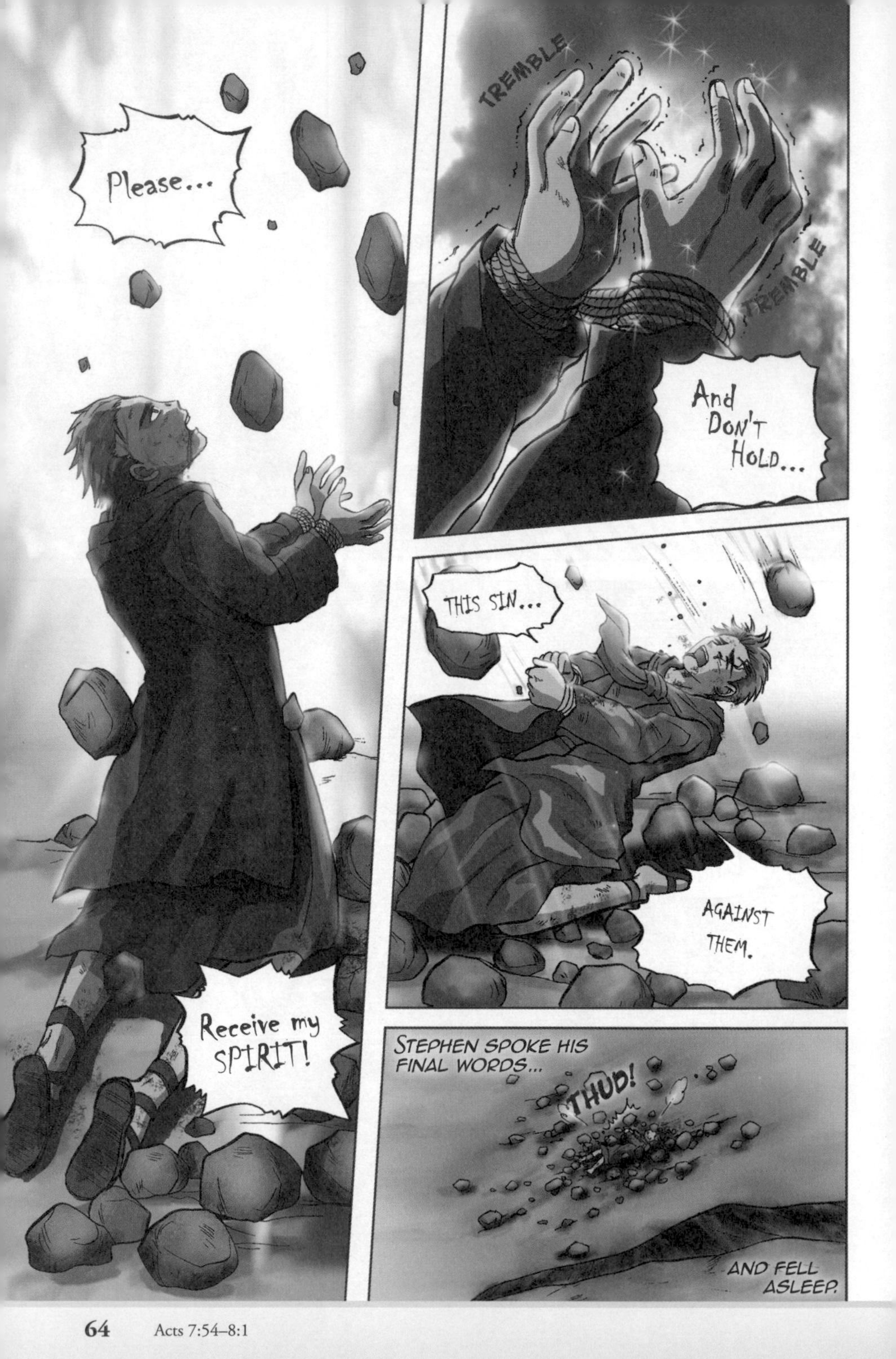
Please...
TREMBLE
TREMBLE
And DON'T HOLD...
THIS SIN...
AGAINST THEM.
Receive my SPIRIT!
STEPHEN SPOKE HIS FINAL WORDS...
THUD!
AND FELL ASLEEP.

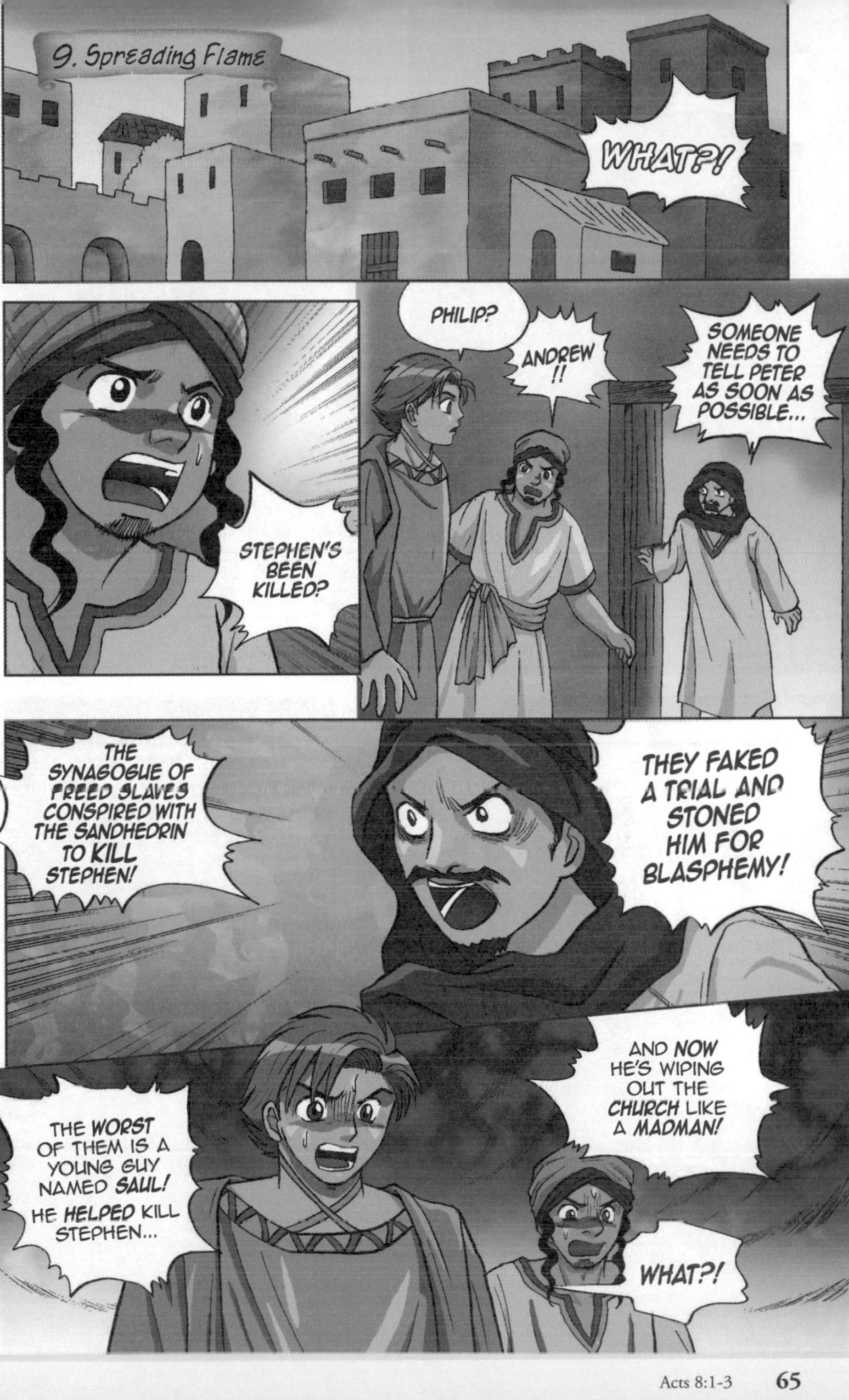
9. Spreading Flame
WHAT?!
STEPHEN'S BEEN KILLED?
PHILIP?
ANDREW !!
SOMEONE NEEDS TO TELL PETER AS SOON AS POSSIBLE...
THE SYNAGOGUE OF FREED SLAVES CONSPIRED WITH THE SANDHEDRIN TO KILL STEPHEN!
THEY FAKED A TRIAL AND STONED HIM FOR BLASPHEMY!
THE WORST OF THEM IS A YOUNG GUY NAMED SAUL!
HE HELPED KILL STEPHEN...
AND NOW HE'S WIPING OUT THE CHURCH LIKE A MADMAN!
WHAT?!

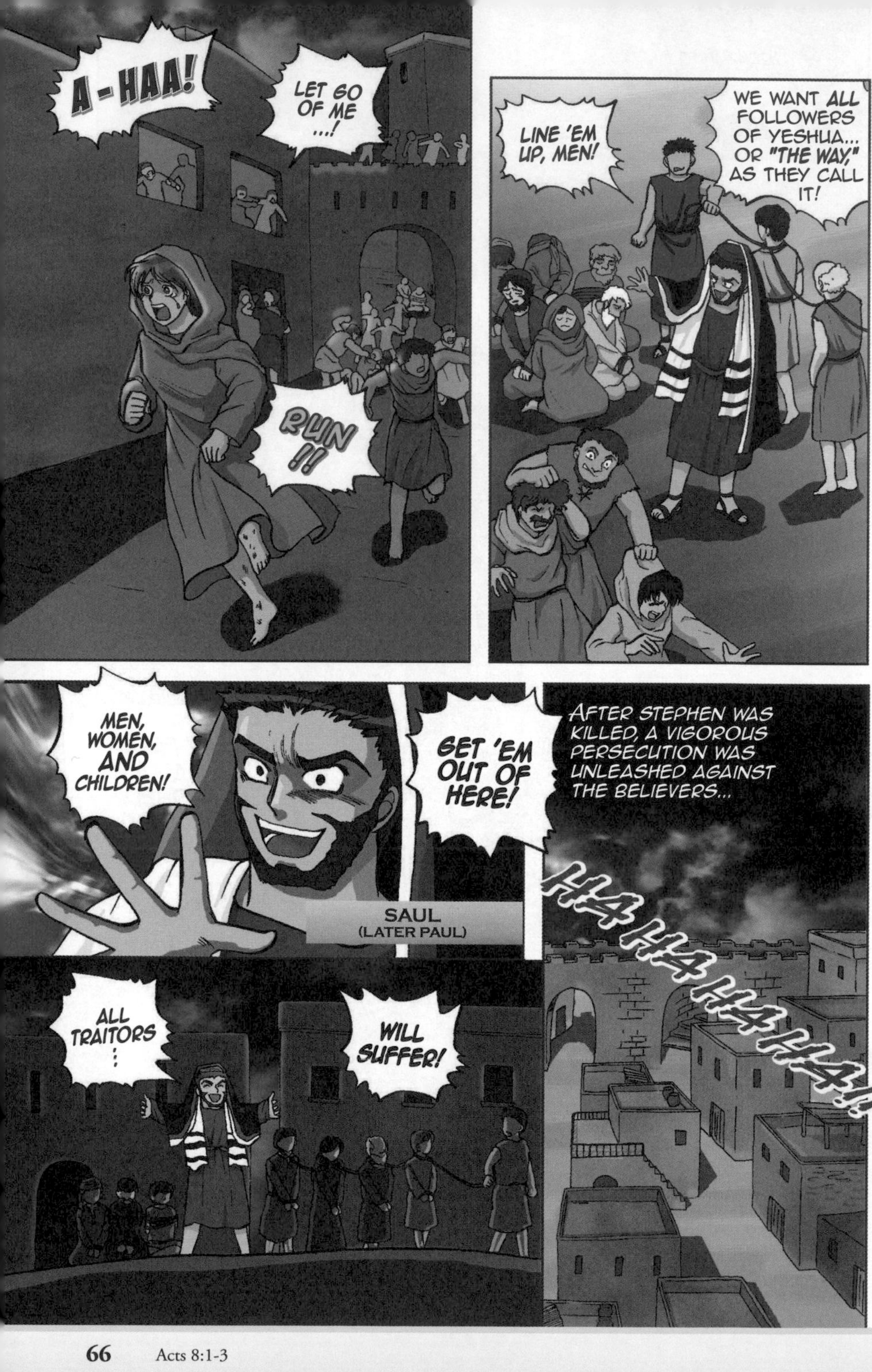
A-HAA!
LET GO OF ME ...!
RUN !!
LINE 'EM UP, MEN!
WE WANT ALL FOLLOWERS OF YESHUA... OR "THE WAY," AS THEY CALL IT!
MEN, WOMEN, AND CHILDREN!
GET 'EM OUT OF HERE!
SAUL (LATER PAUL)
AFTER STEPHEN WAS KILLED, A VIGOROUS PERSECUTION WAS UNLEASHED AGAINST THE BELIEVERS...
HA HA HA HA HA!!
ALL TRAITORS ...
WILL SUFFER!

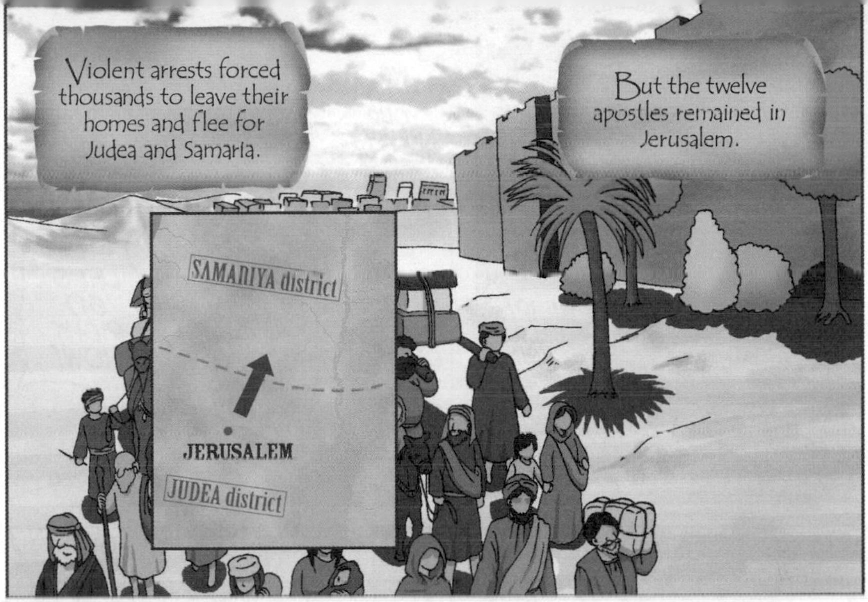
Violent arrests forced thousands to leave their homes and flee for Judea and Samaria.
But the twelve apostles remained in Jerusalem.
SAMARIYA district
JERUSALEM
JUDEA district

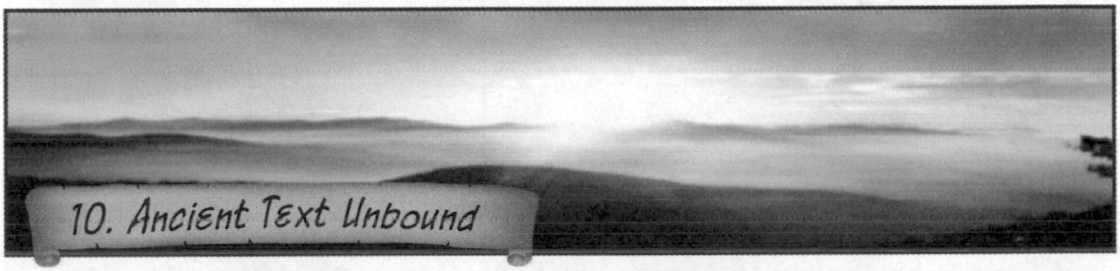

10. Ancient Text Unbound

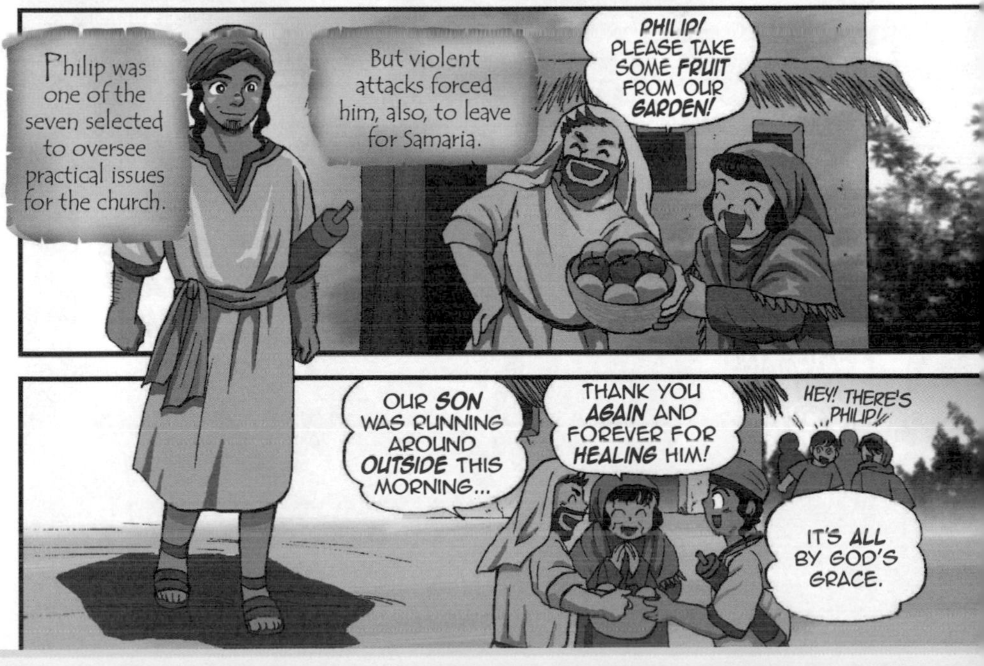
Philip was one of the seven selected to oversee practical issues for the church.
But violent attacks forced him, also, to leave for Samaria.
PHILIP! PLEASE TAKE SOME FRUIT FROM OUR GARDEN!
OUR SON WAS RUNNING AROUND OUTSIDE THIS MORNING...
THANK YOU AGAIN AND FOREVER FOR HEALING HIM!
HEY! THERE'S PHILIP!
IT'S ALL BY GOD'S GRACE.

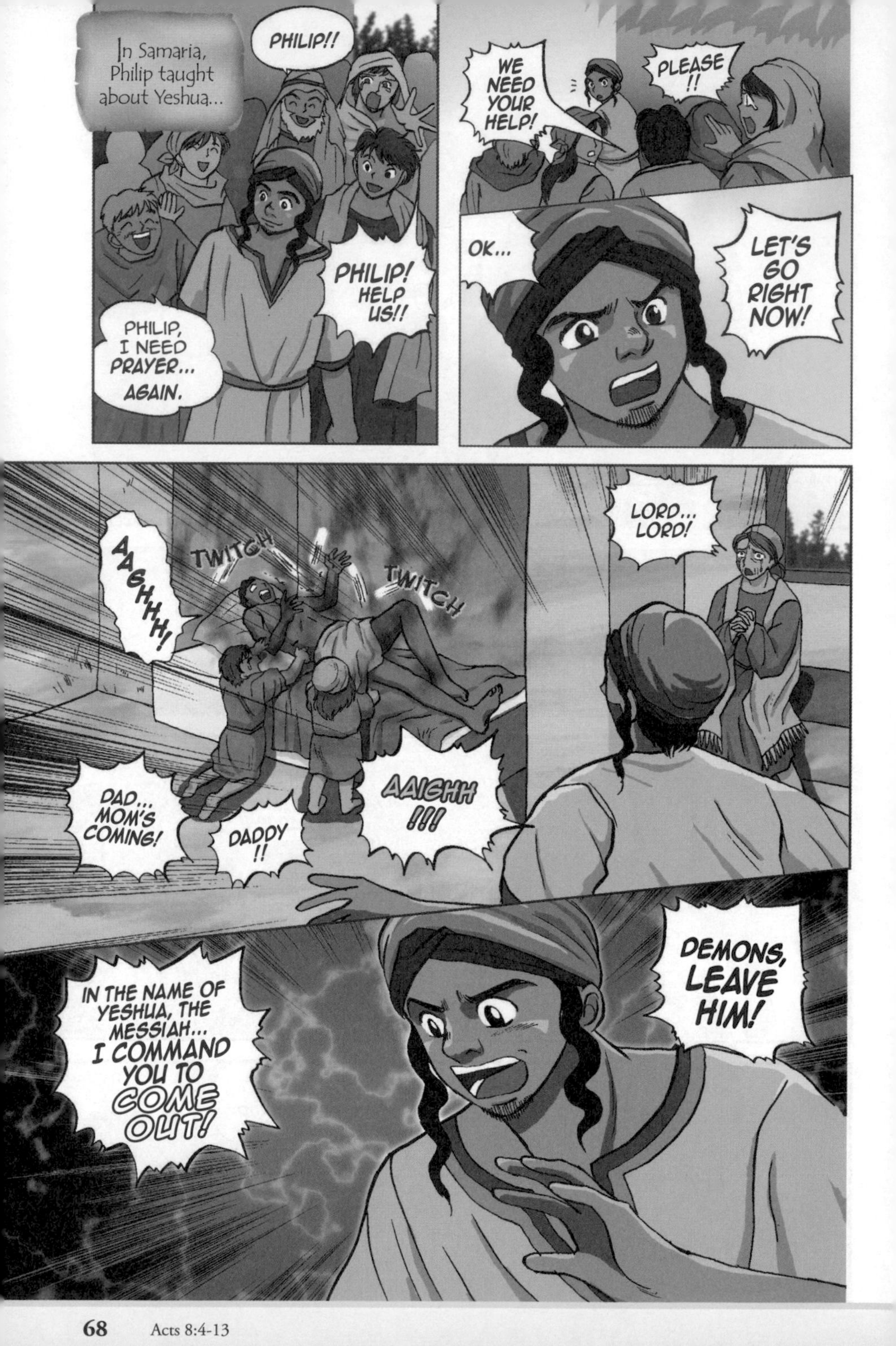

In Samaria, Philip taught about Yeshua...
PHILIP!!
PHILIP! HELP US!!
PHILIP, I NEED PRAYER... AGAIN.
WE NEED YOUR HELP!
PLEASE !!
OK...
LET'S GO RIGHT NOW!
AAGHHH!
TWITCH
TWITCH
DAD... MOM'S COMING!
DADDY !!
AAIGHH !!!
LORD... LORD!
DEMONS, LEAVE HIM!
IN THE NAME OF YESHUA, THE MESSIAH... I COMMAND YOU TO COME OUT!

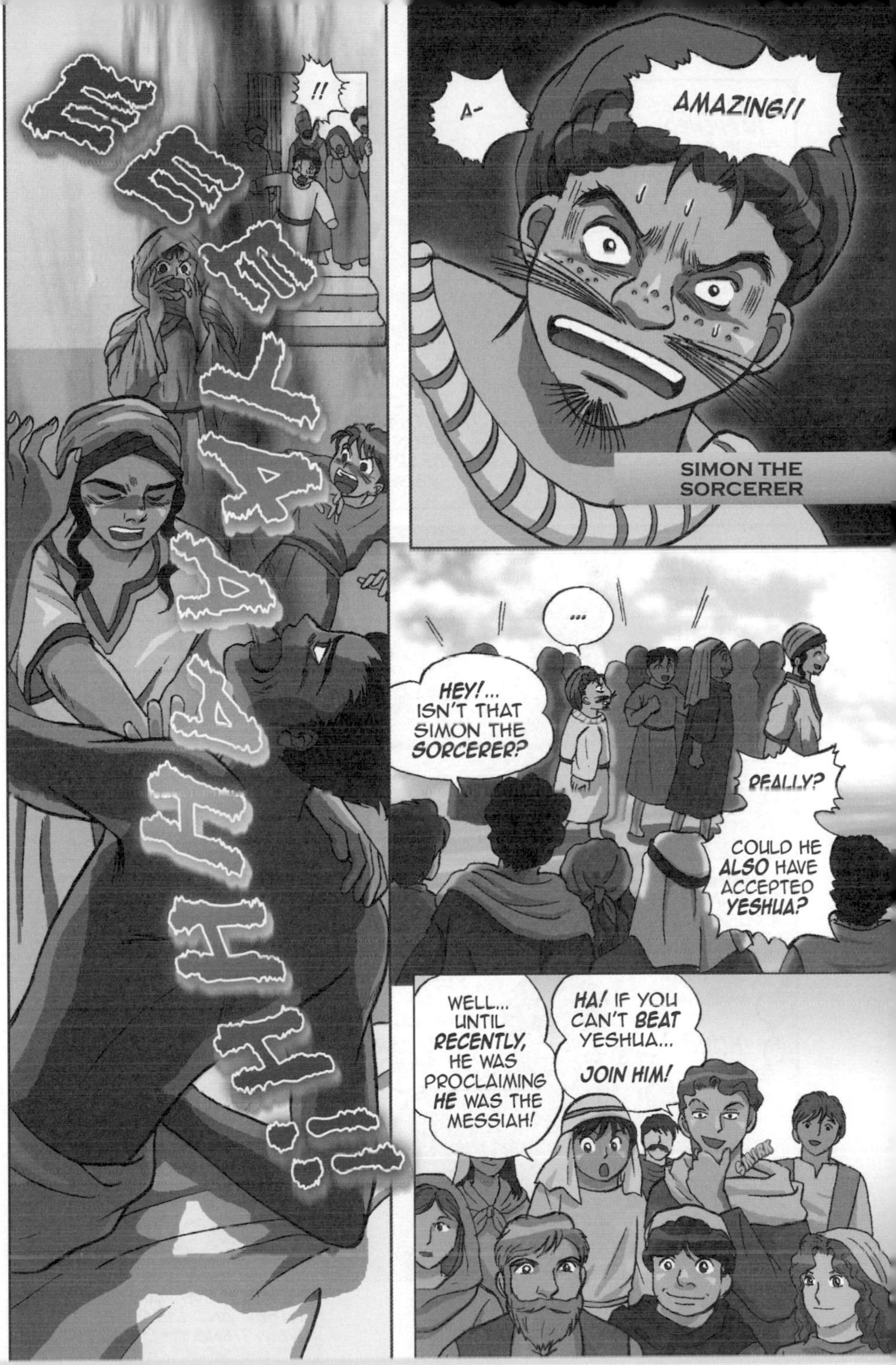

EEEEYAAAHHH!!
!!
A-
AMAZING!!
SIMON THE SORCERER
...
HEY!... ISN'T THAT SIMON THE SORCERER?
REALLY?
COULD HE ALSO HAVE ACCEPTED YESHUA?
WELL... UNTIL RECENTLY, HE WAS PROCLAIMING HE WAS THE MESSIAH!
HA! IF YOU CAN'T BEAT YESHUA...
JOIN HIM!

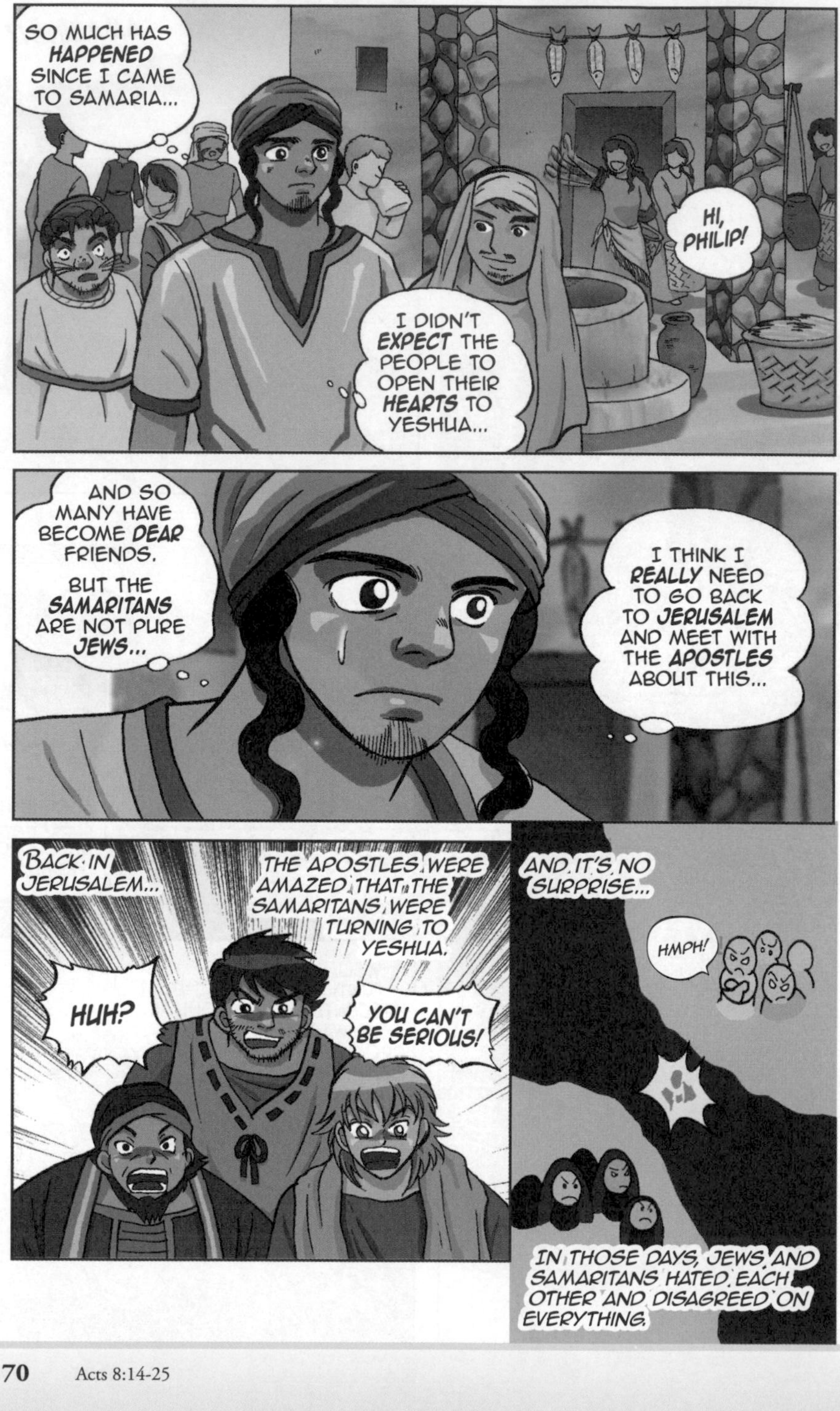
SO MUCH HAS HAPPENED SINCE I CAME TO SAMARIA...
HI, PHILIP!
I DIDN'T EXPECT THE PEOPLE TO OPEN THEIR HEARTS TO YESHUA...
AND SO MANY HAVE BECOME DEAR FRIENDS.
BUT THE SAMARITANS ARE NOT PURE JEWS...
I THINK I REALLY NEED TO GO BACK TO JERUSALEM AND MEET WITH THE APOSTLES ABOUT THIS...
BACK IN JERUSALEM...
THE APOSTLES WERE AMAZED THAT THE SAMARITANS WERE TURNING TO YESHUA.
HUH?
YOU CAN'T BE SERIOUS!
AND IT'S NO SURPRISE...
HMPH!
IN THOSE DAYS, JEWS AND SAMARITANS HATED EACH OTHER AND DISAGREED ON EVERYTHING.

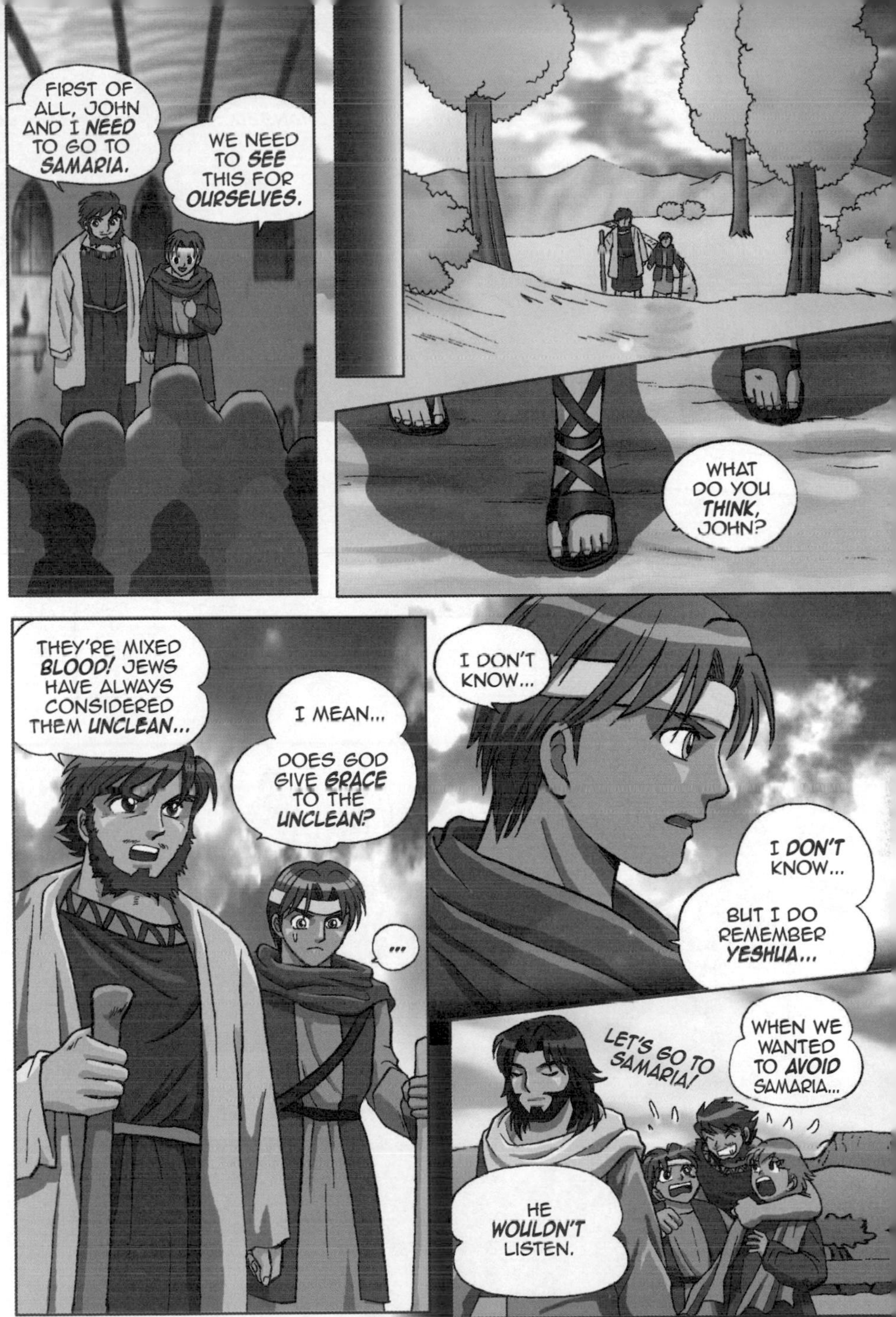
FIRST OF ALL, JOHN AND I NEED TO GO TO SAMARIA.
WE NEED TO SEE THIS FOR OURSELVES.
WHAT DO YOU THINK, JOHN?
THEY'RE MIXED BLOOD! JEWS HAVE ALWAYS CONSIDERED THEM UNCLEAN...
I MEAN...
DOES GOD GIVE GRACE TO THE UNCLEAN?
...
I DON'T KNOW...
I DON'T KNOW...
BUT I DO REMEMBER YESHUA...
WHEN WE WANTED TO AVOID SAMARIA...
LET'S GO TO SAMARIA!
HE WOULDN'T LISTEN.

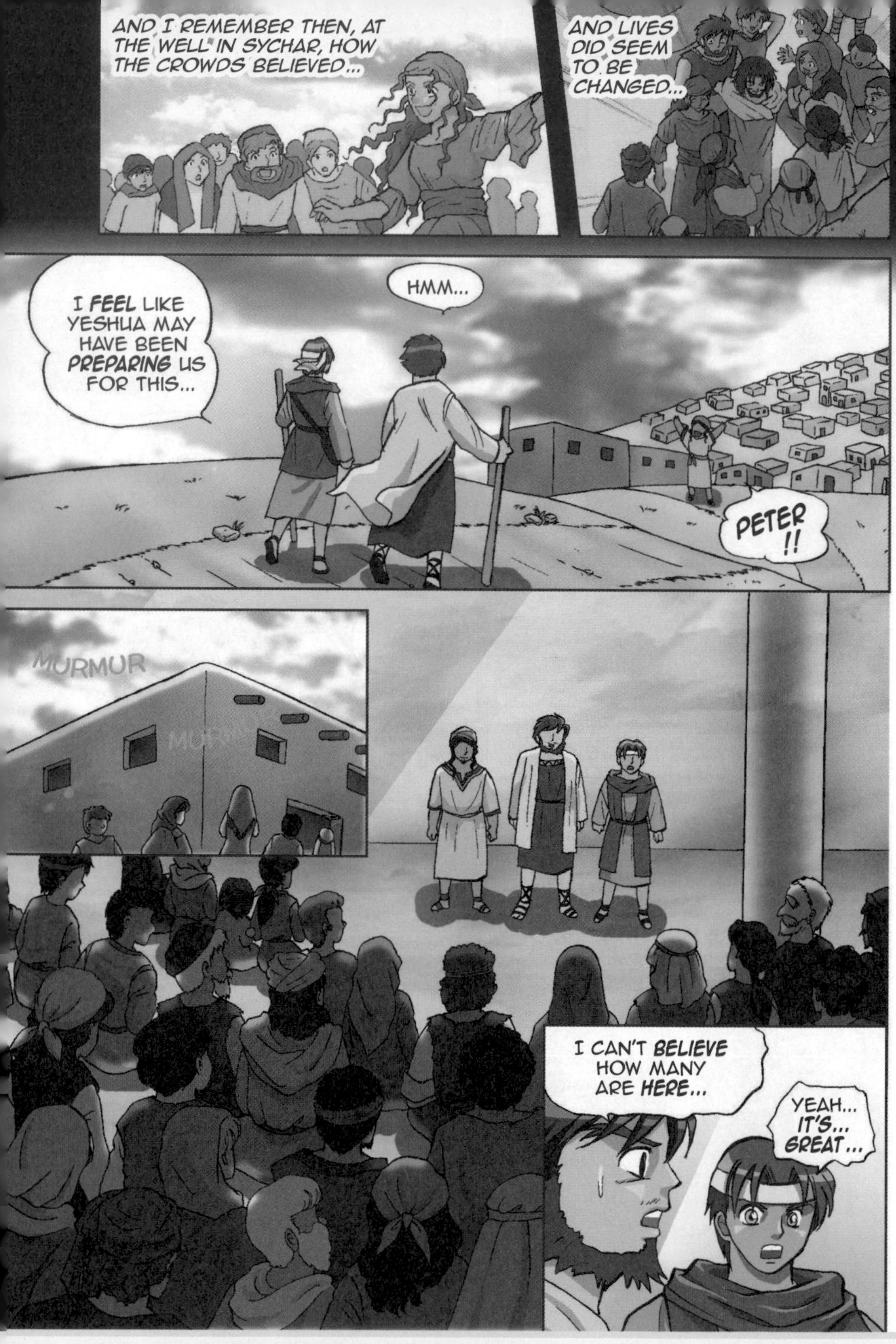
AND I REMEMBER THEN, AT THE WELL IN SYCHAR, HOW THE CROWDS BELIEVED...
AND LIVES DID SEEM TO BE CHANGED...
I FEEL LIKE YESHUA MAY HAVE BEEN PREPARING US FOR THIS...
HMM...
PETER !!
MURMUR
MURMUR
I CAN'T BELIEVE HOW MANY ARE HERE...
YEAH... IT'S... GREAT...

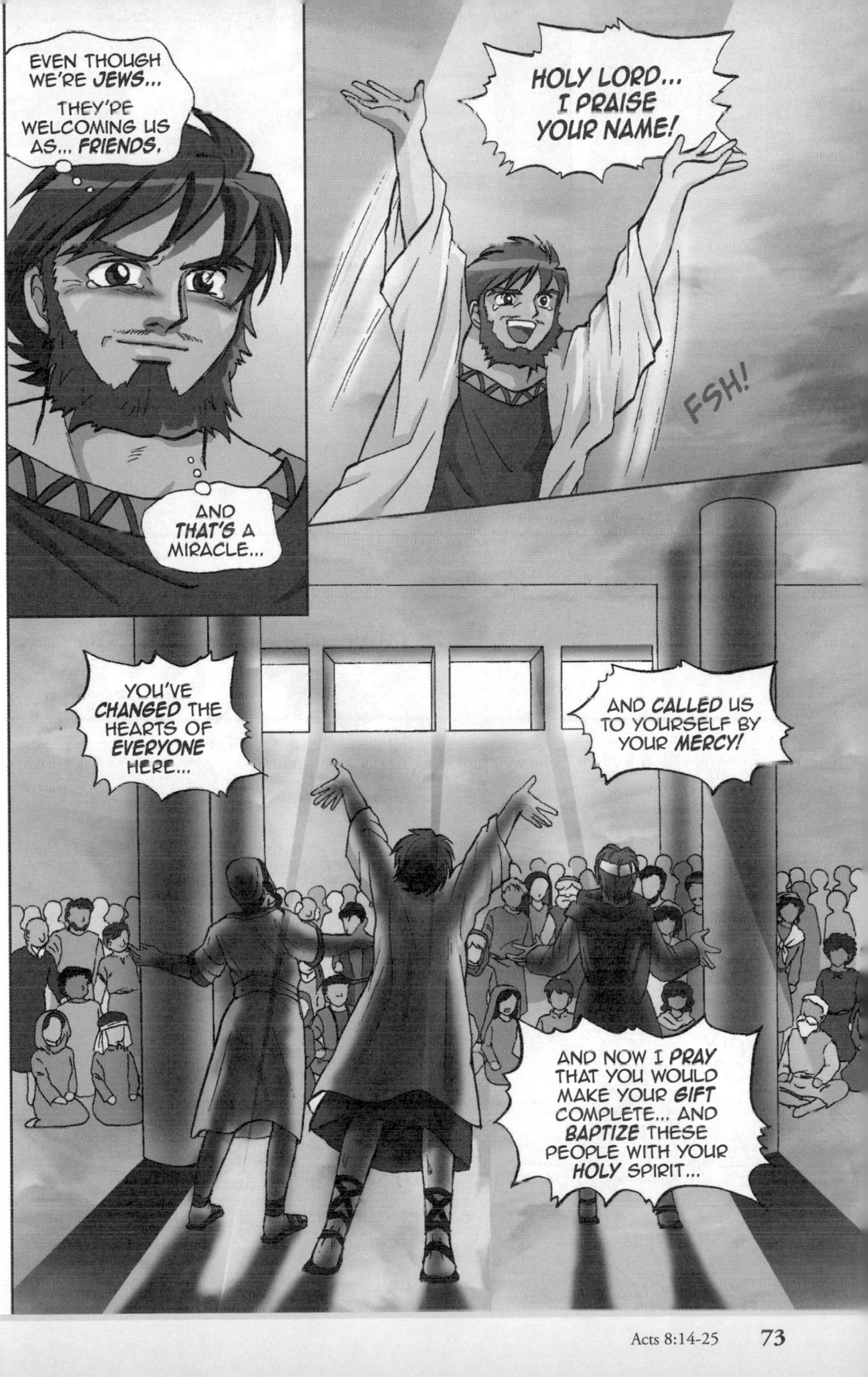
EVEN THOUGH WE'RE JEWS...
THEY'RE WELCOMING US AS... FRIENDS.
AND THAT'S A MIRACLE...
HOLY LORD... I PRAISE YOUR NAME!
FSH!
YOU'VE CHANGED THE HEARTS OF EVERYONE HERE...
AND CALLED US TO YOURSELF BY YOUR MERCY!
AND NOW I PRAY THAT YOU WOULD MAKE YOUR GIFT COMPLETE... AND BAPTIZE THESE PEOPLE WITH YOUR HOLY SPIRIT...

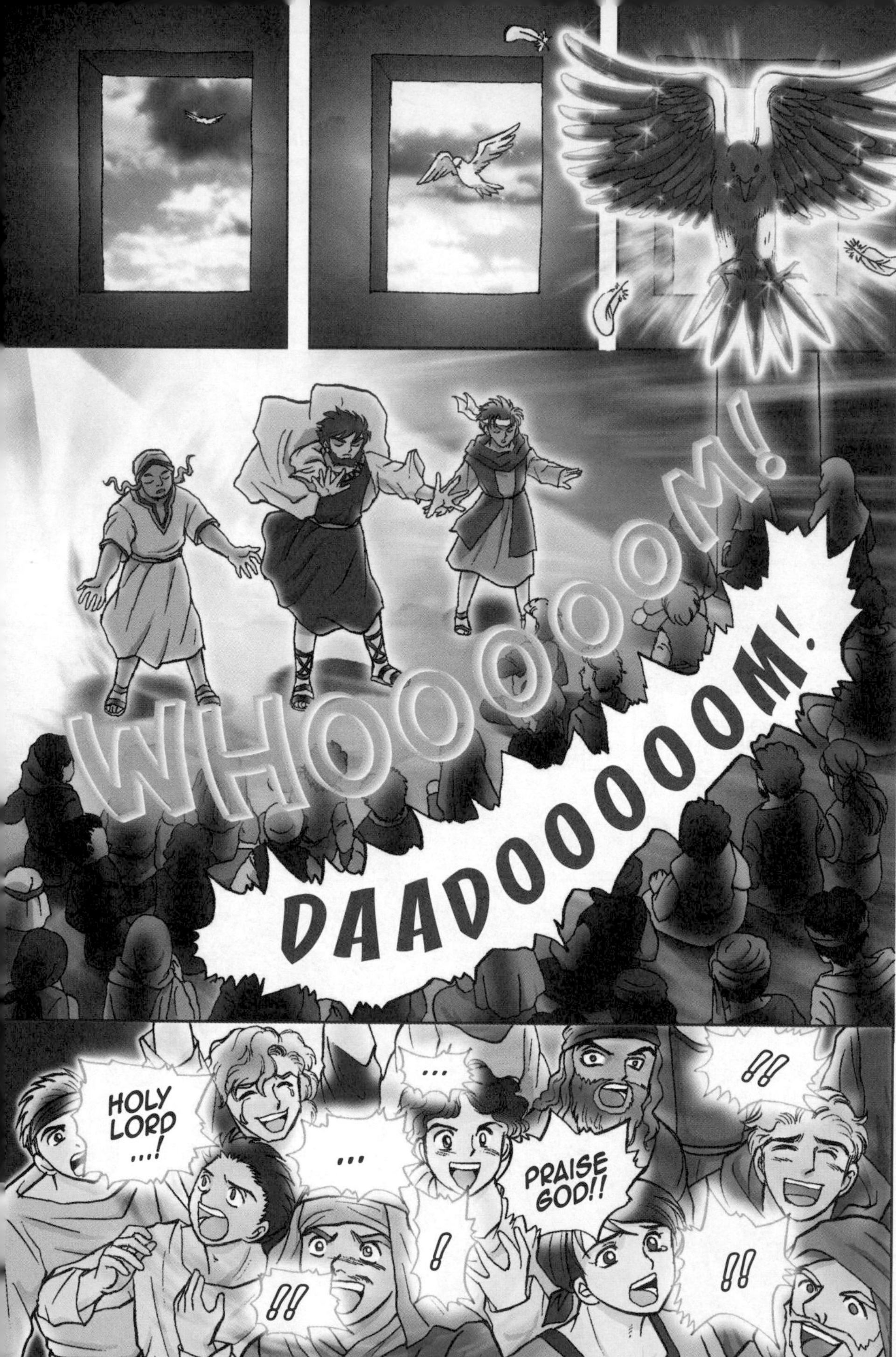
WHOOOOOOM!
DAADOOOOOM!
HOLY LORD ...!
...
...
PRAISE GOD!!
!!
!
!!
!!

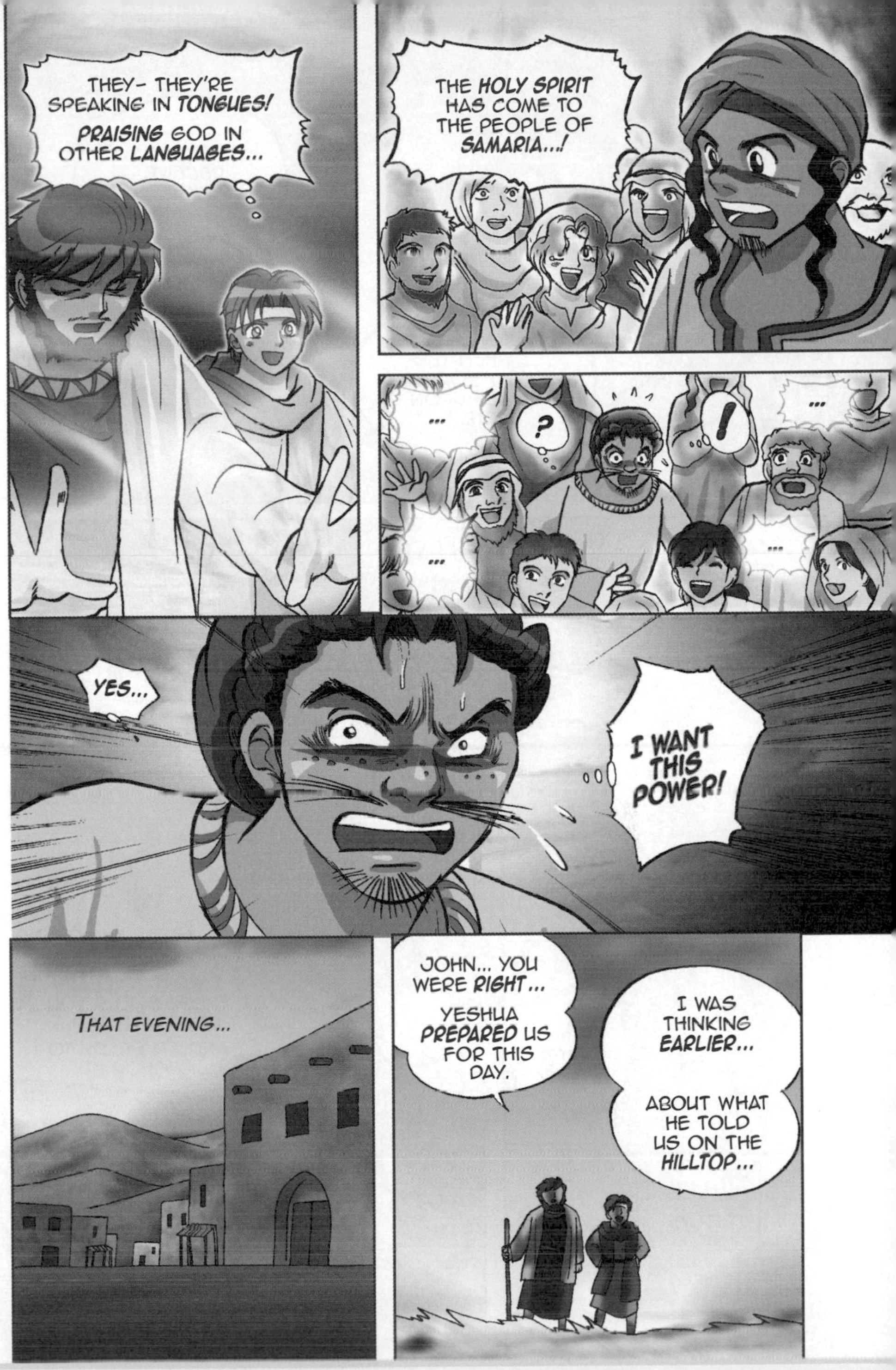
THEY- THEY'RE SPEAKING IN TONGUES! PRAISING GOD IN OTHER LANGUAGES...
THE HOLY SPIRIT HAS COME TO THE PEOPLE OF SAMARIA...!
?
!
YES...
I WANT THIS POWER!
THAT EVENING...
JOHN... YOU WERE RIGHT... YESHUA PREPARED US FOR THIS DAY.
I WAS THINKING EARLIER...
ABOUT WHAT HE TOLD US ON THE HILLTOP...

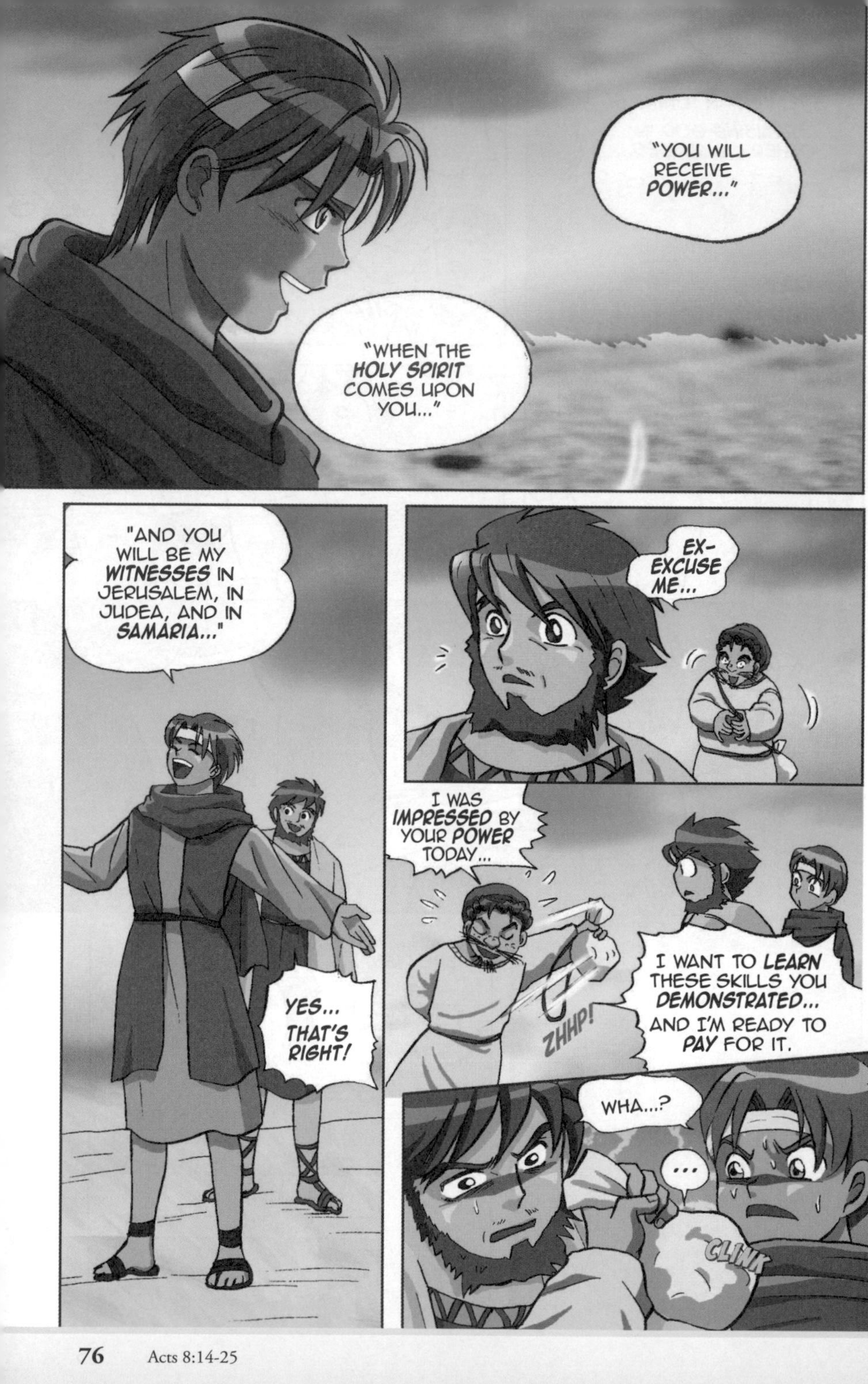
"YOU WILL RECEIVE POWER..."
"WHEN THE HOLY SPIRIT COMES UPON YOU..."
"AND YOU WILL BE MY WITNESSES IN JERUSALEM, IN JUDEA, AND IN SAMARIA..."
YES... THAT'S RIGHT!
EX- EXCUSE ME...
I WAS IMPRESSED BY YOUR POWER TODAY...
ZHHP!
I WANT TO LEARN THESE SKILLS YOU DEMONSTRATED... AND I'M READY TO PAY FOR IT.
WHA...?
...
CLINK

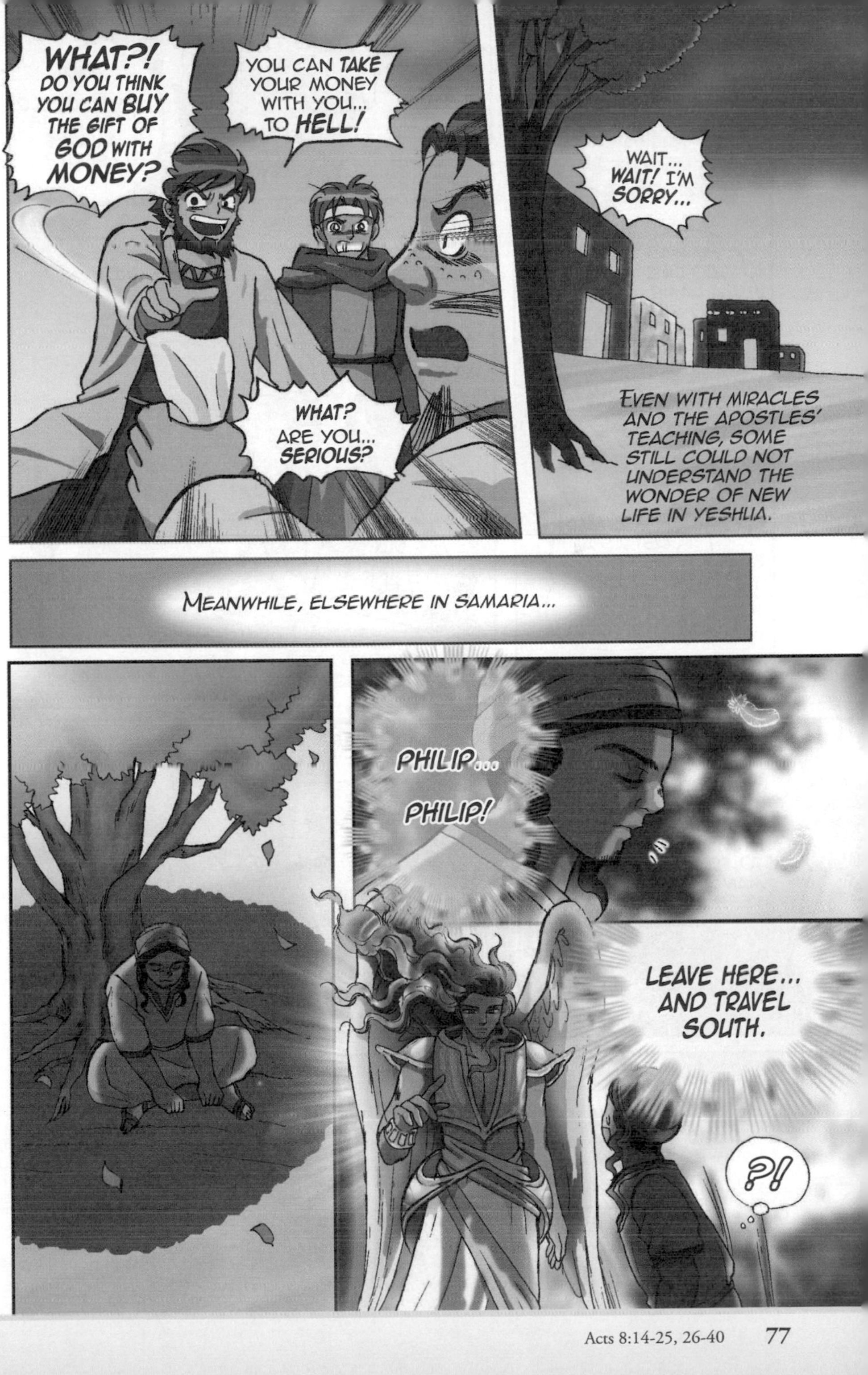
WHAT?! DO YOU THINK YOU CAN BUY THE GIFT OF GOD WITH MONEY?
YOU CAN TAKE YOUR MONEY WITH YOU... TO HELL!
WHAT? ARE YOU... SERIOUS?
WAIT... WAIT! I'M SORRY...
EVEN WITH MIRACLES AND THE APOSTLES' TEACHING, SOME STILL COULD NOT UNDERSTAND THE WONDER OF NEW LIFE IN YESHUA.
MEANWHILE, ELSEWHERE IN SAMARIA...
PHILIP...
PHILIP!
LEAVE HERE... AND TRAVEL SOUTH.
?!

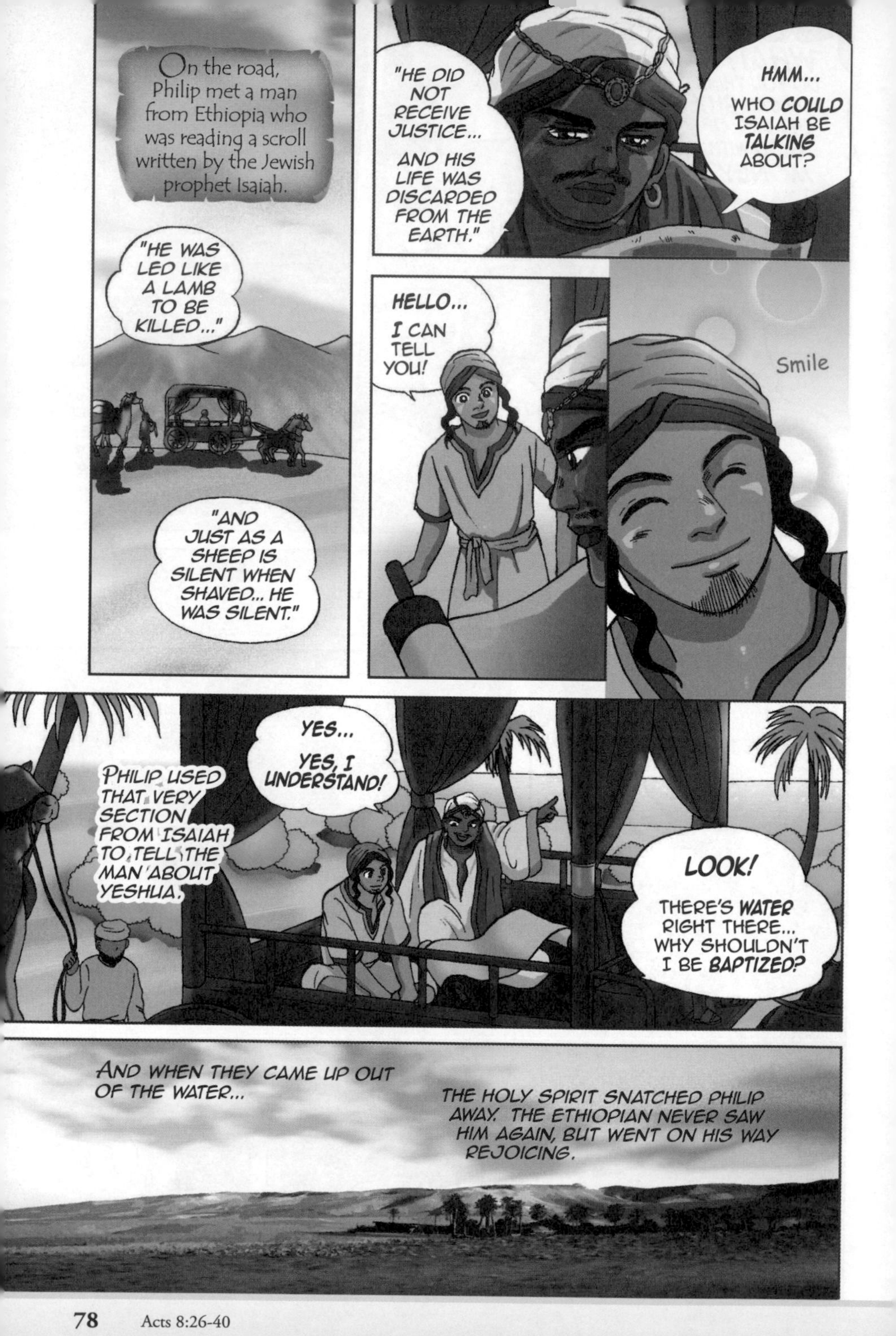
On the road, Philip met a man from Ethiopia who was reading a scroll written by the Jewish prophet Isaiah.
"HE WAS LED LIKE A LAMB TO BE KILLED..."
"AND JUST AS A SHEEP IS SILENT WHEN SHAVED... HE WAS SILENT."
"HE DID NOT RECEIVE JUSTICE... AND HIS LIFE WAS DISCARDED FROM THE EARTH."
HMM... WHO COULD ISAIAH BE TALKING ABOUT?
HELLO... I CAN TELL YOU!
Smile
PHILIP USED THAT VERY SECTION FROM ISAIAH TO TELL THE MAN ABOUT YESHUA.
YES... YES, I UNDERSTAND!
LOOK! THERE'S WATER RIGHT THERE... WHY SHOULDN'T I BE BAPTIZED?
AND WHEN THEY CAME UP OUT OF THE WATER...
THE HOLY SPIRIT SNATCHED PHILIP AWAY. THE ETHIOPIAN NEVER SAW HIM AGAIN, BUT WENT ON HIS WAY REJOICING.

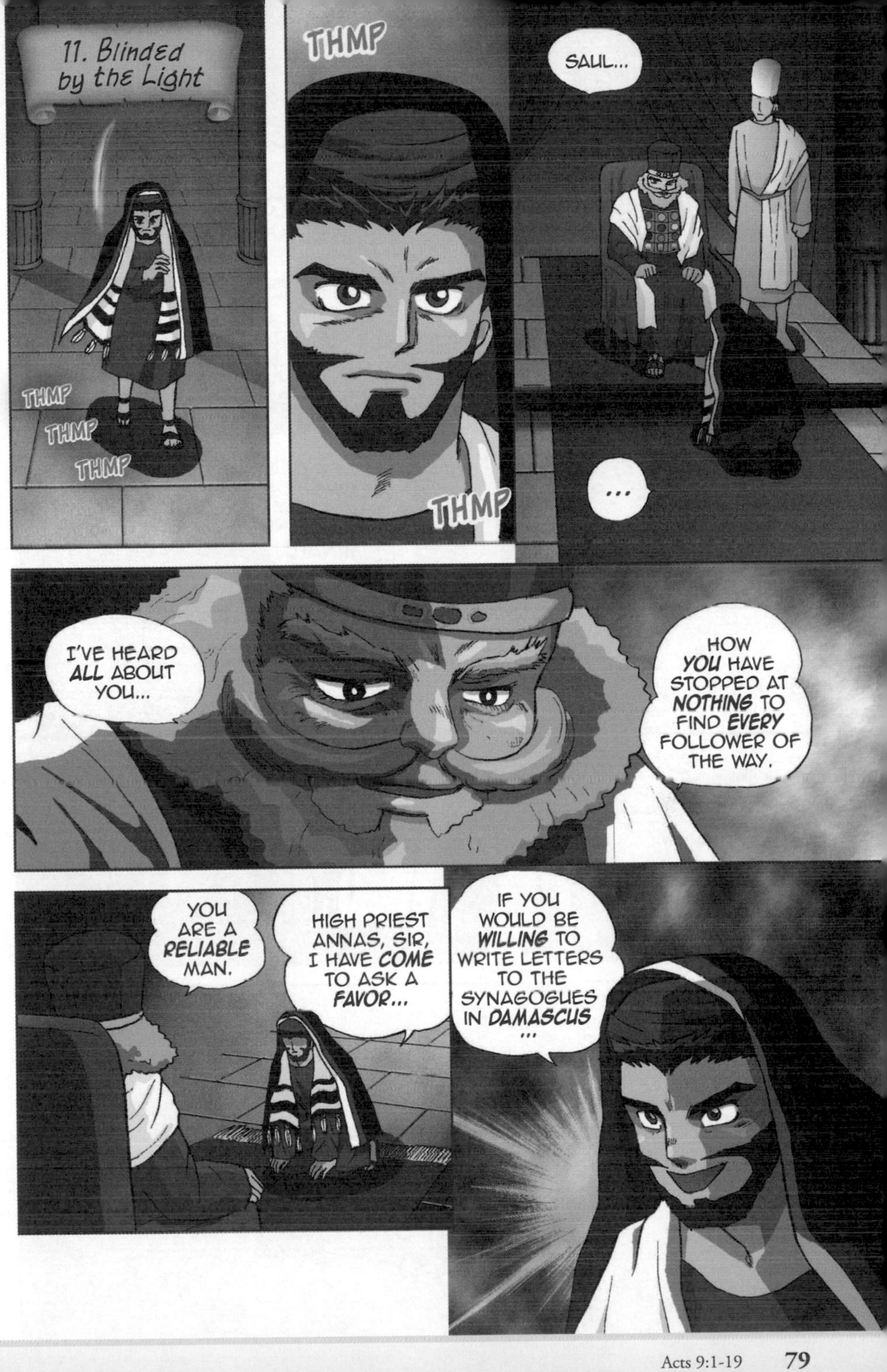
11. Blinded by the Light
THMP
THMP
THMP
THMP
THMP
SAUL...
...
I'VE HEARD ALL ABOUT YOU...
HOW YOU HAVE STOPPED AT NOTHING TO FIND EVERY FOLLOWER OF THE WAY.
YOU ARE A RELIABLE MAN.
HIGH PRIEST ANNAS, SIR, I HAVE COME TO ASK A FAVOR...
IF YOU WOULD BE WILLING TO WRITE LETTERS TO THE SYNAGOGUES IN DAMASCUS ...

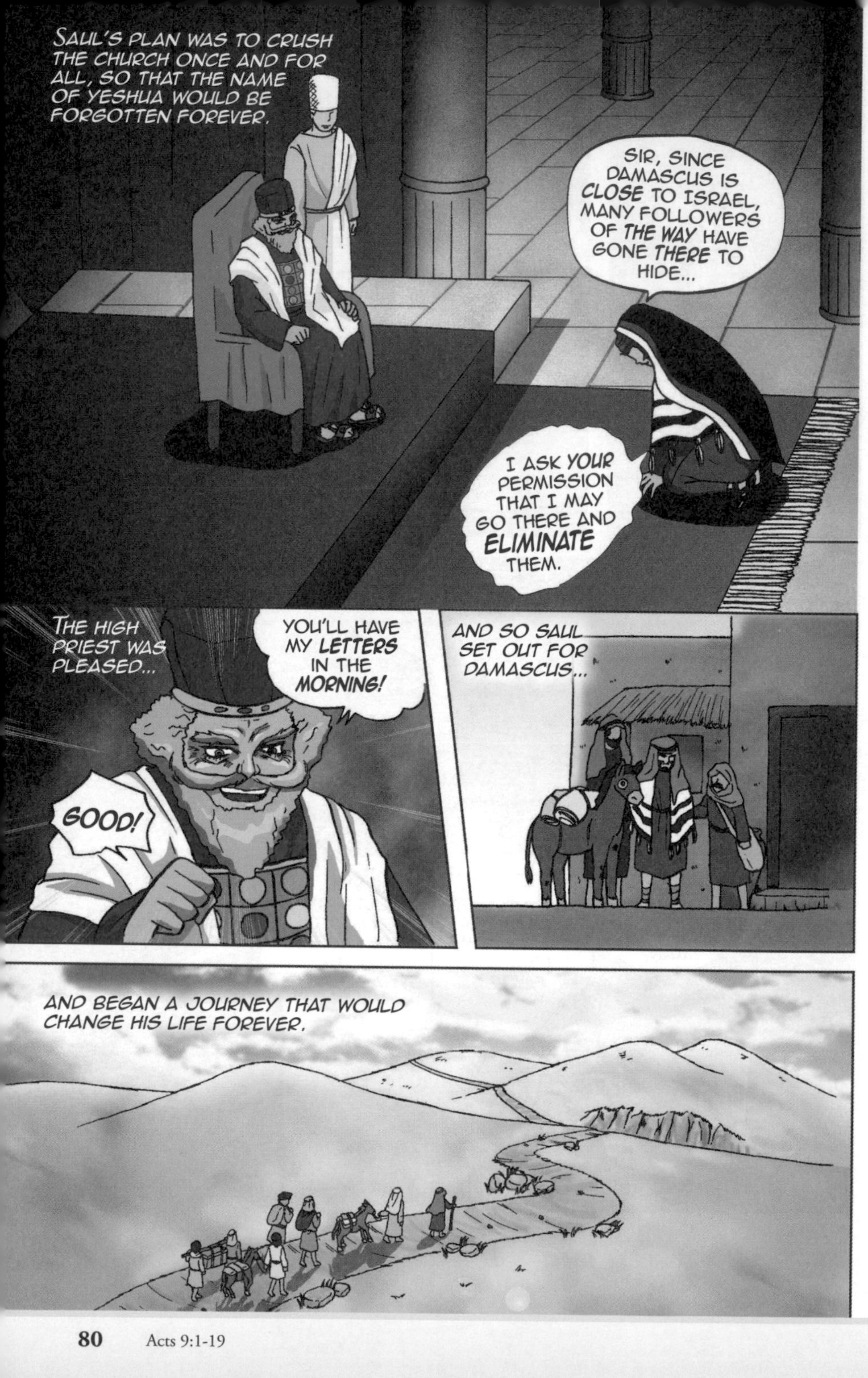
SAUL'S PLAN WAS TO CRUSH THE CHURCH ONCE AND FOR ALL, SO THAT THE NAME OF YESHUA WOULD BE FORGOTTEN FOREVER.
SIR, SINCE DAMASCUS IS CLOSE TO ISRAEL, MANY FOLLOWERS OF THE WAY HAVE GONE THERE TO HIDE...
I ASK YOUR PERMISSION THAT I MAY GO THERE AND ELIMINATE THEM.
THE HIGH PRIEST WAS PLEASED...
GOOD!
YOU'LL HAVE MY LETTERS IN THE MORNING!
AND SO SAUL SET OUT FOR DAMASCUS...
AND BEGAN A JOURNEY THAT WOULD CHANGE HIS LIFE FOREVER.

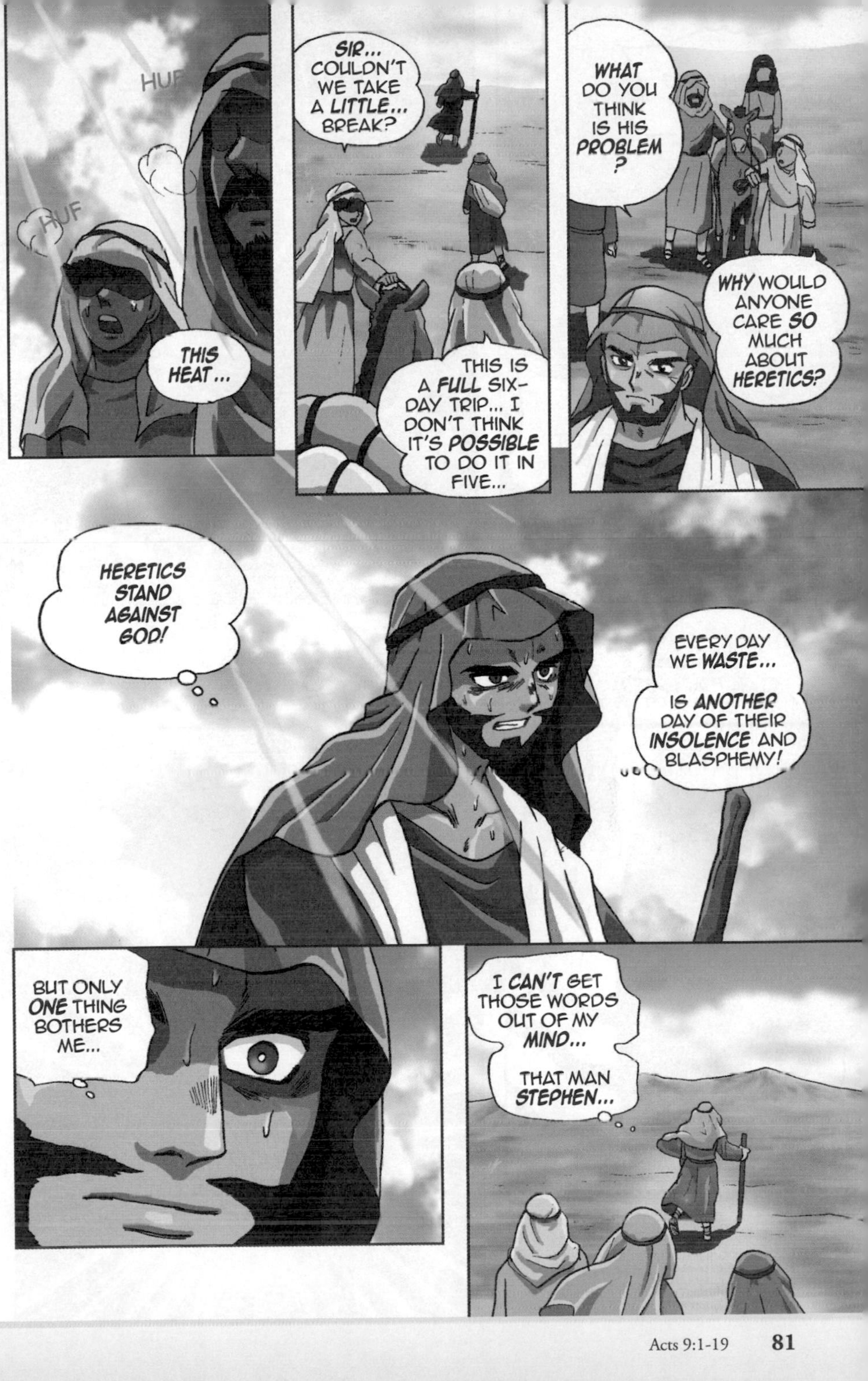
HUF
HUF
THIS HEAT...
SIR... COULDN'T WE TAKE A LITTLE... BREAK?
THIS IS A FULL SIX-DAY TRIP... I DON'T THINK IT'S POSSIBLE TO DO IT IN FIVE...
WHAT DO YOU THINK IS HIS PROBLEM?
WHY WOULD ANYONE CARE SO MUCH ABOUT HERETICS?
HERETICS STAND AGAINST GOD!
EVERY DAY WE WASTE...
IS ANOTHER DAY OF THEIR INSOLENCE AND BLASPHEMY!
BUT ONLY ONE THING BOTHERS ME...
I CAN'T GET THOSE WORDS OUT OF MY MIND...
THAT MAN STEPHEN...

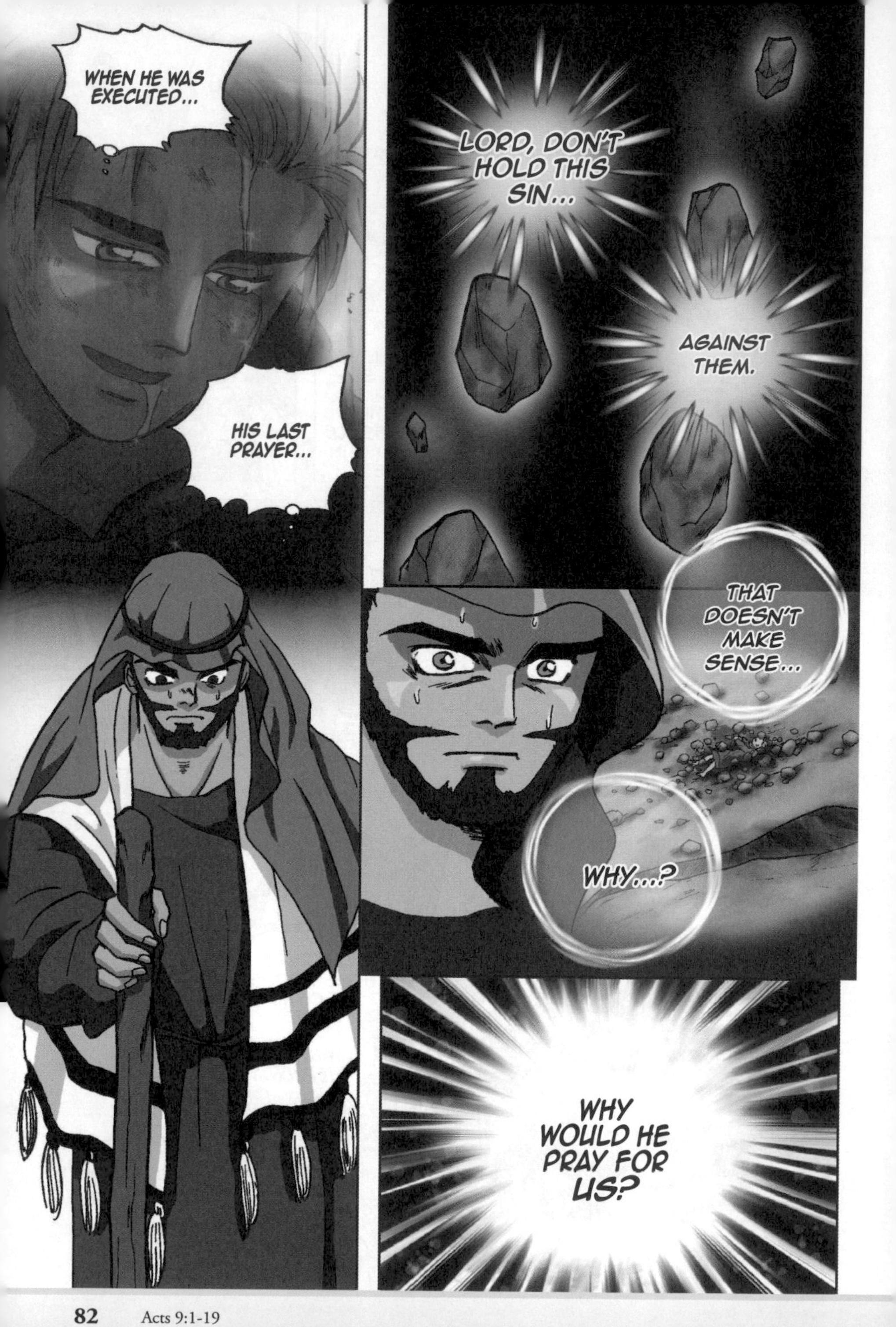
WHEN HE WAS EXECUTED...
HIS LAST PRAYER...
LORD, DON'T HOLD THIS SIN...
AGAINST THEM.
THAT DOESN'T MAKE SENSE...
WHY...?
WHY WOULD HE PRAY FOR US?

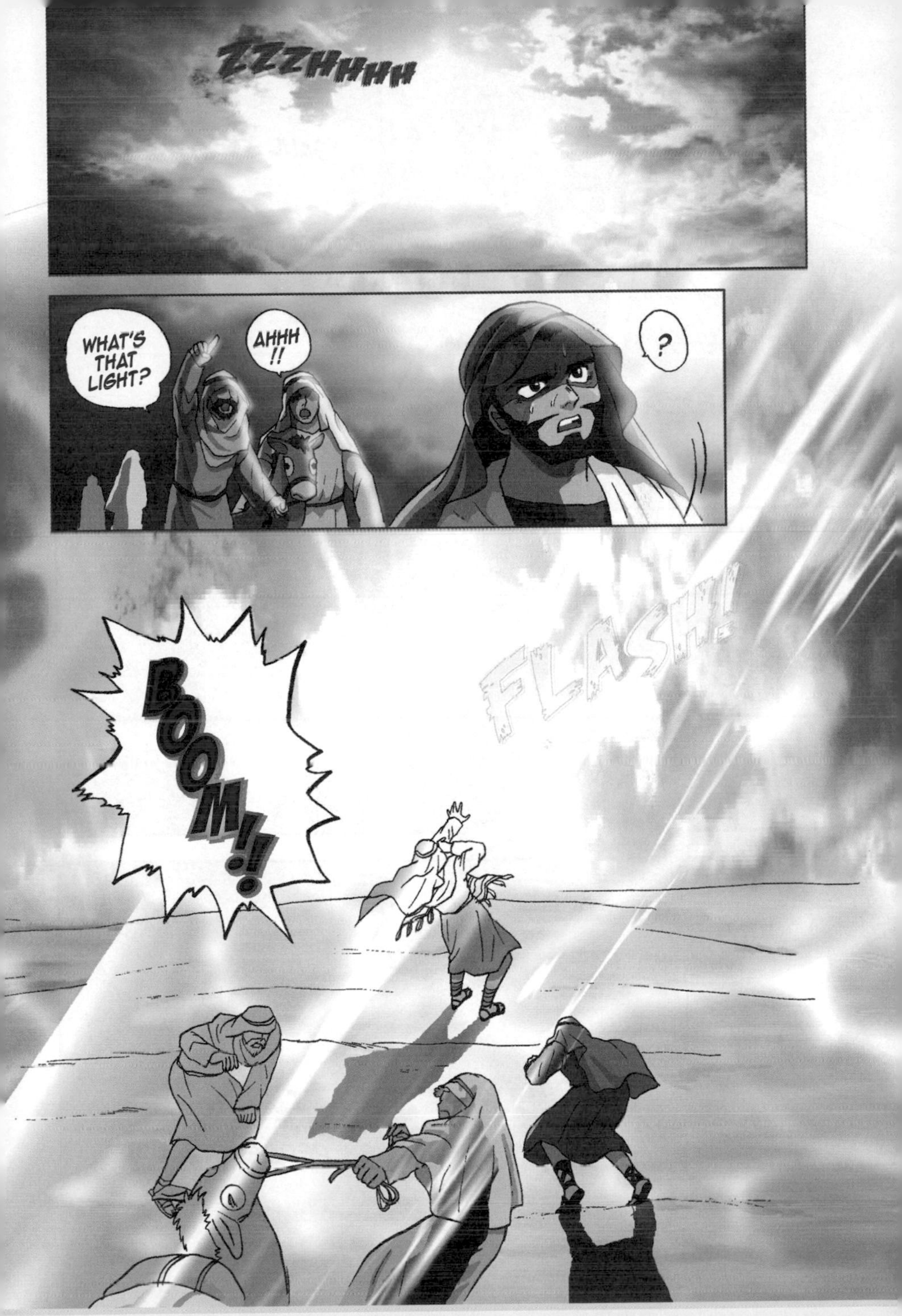
ZZZHHHHH
WHAT'S THAT LIGHT?
AHHH !!
?
BOOM!!
FLASH!!

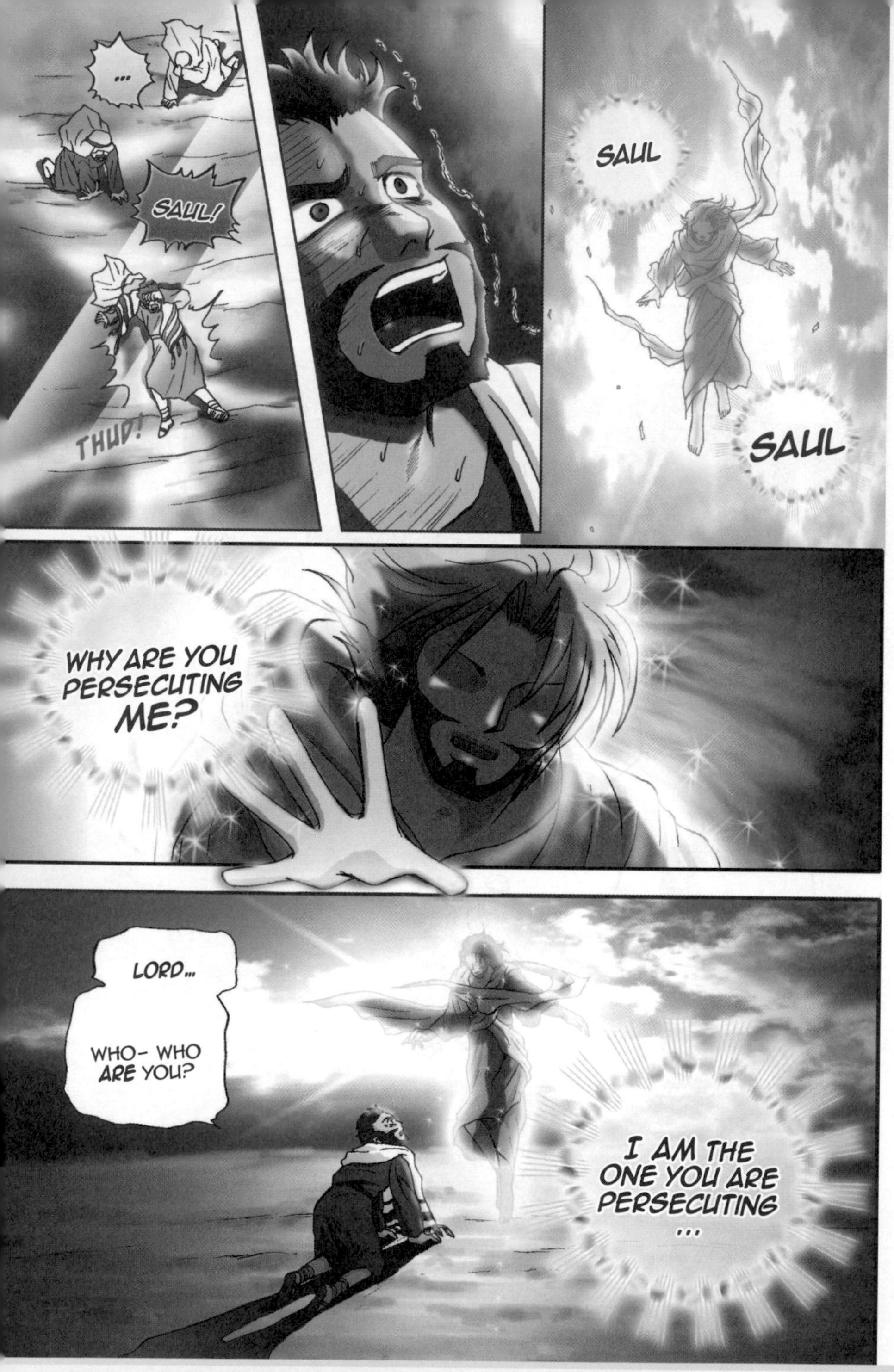
...
SAUL!
THUD!
SAUL
SAUL
WHY ARE YOU PERSECUTING ME?
LORD...
WHO- WHO ARE YOU?
I AM THE ONE YOU ARE PERSECUTING
...

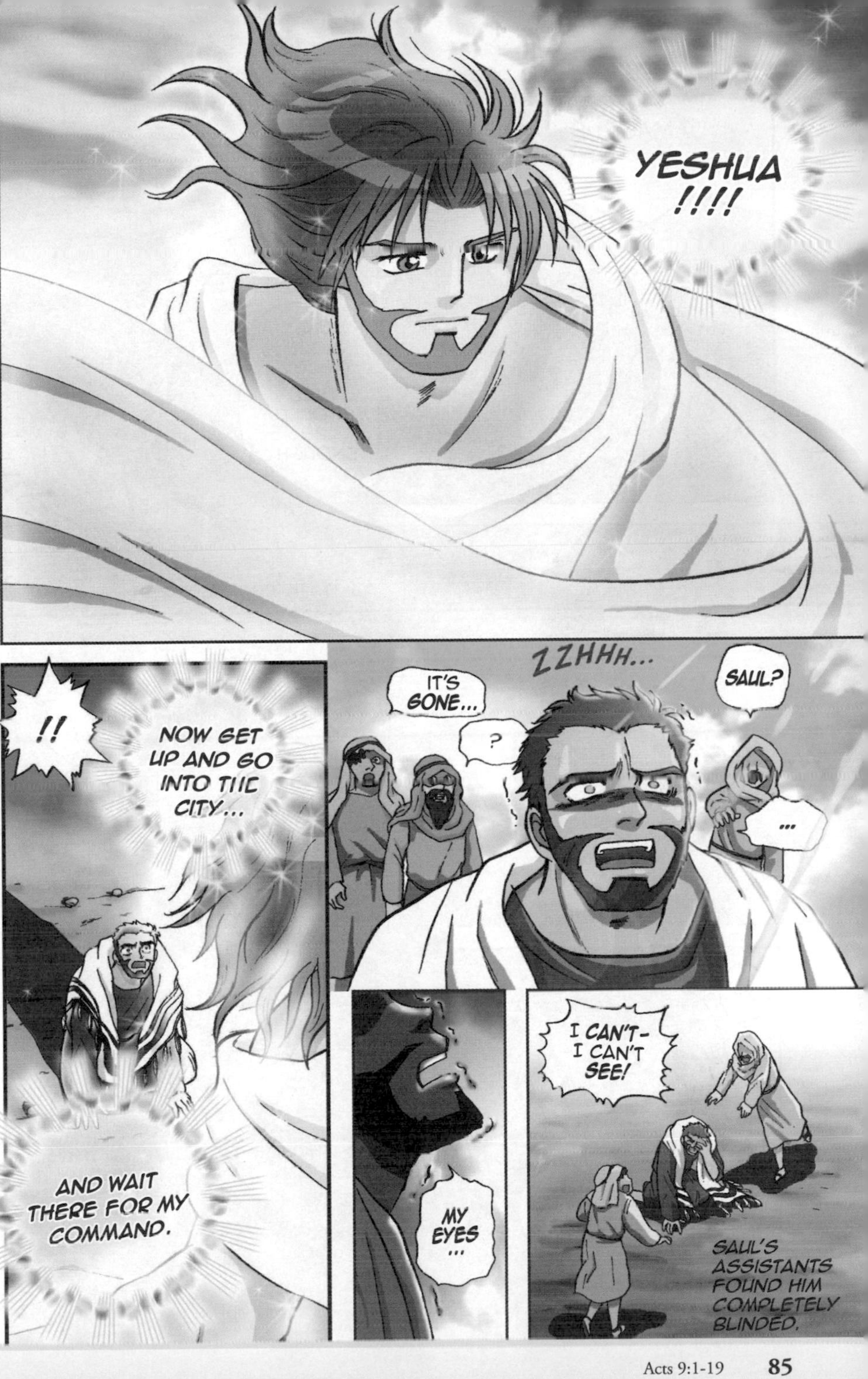
YESHUA !!!!
!!
NOW GET UP AND GO INTO THE CITY...
AND WAIT THERE FOR MY COMMAND.
ZZHHH...
IT'S GONE...
?
SAUL?
...
MY EYES ...
I CAN'T- I CAN'T SEE!
SAUL'S ASSISTANTS FOUND HIM COMPLETELY BLINDED.

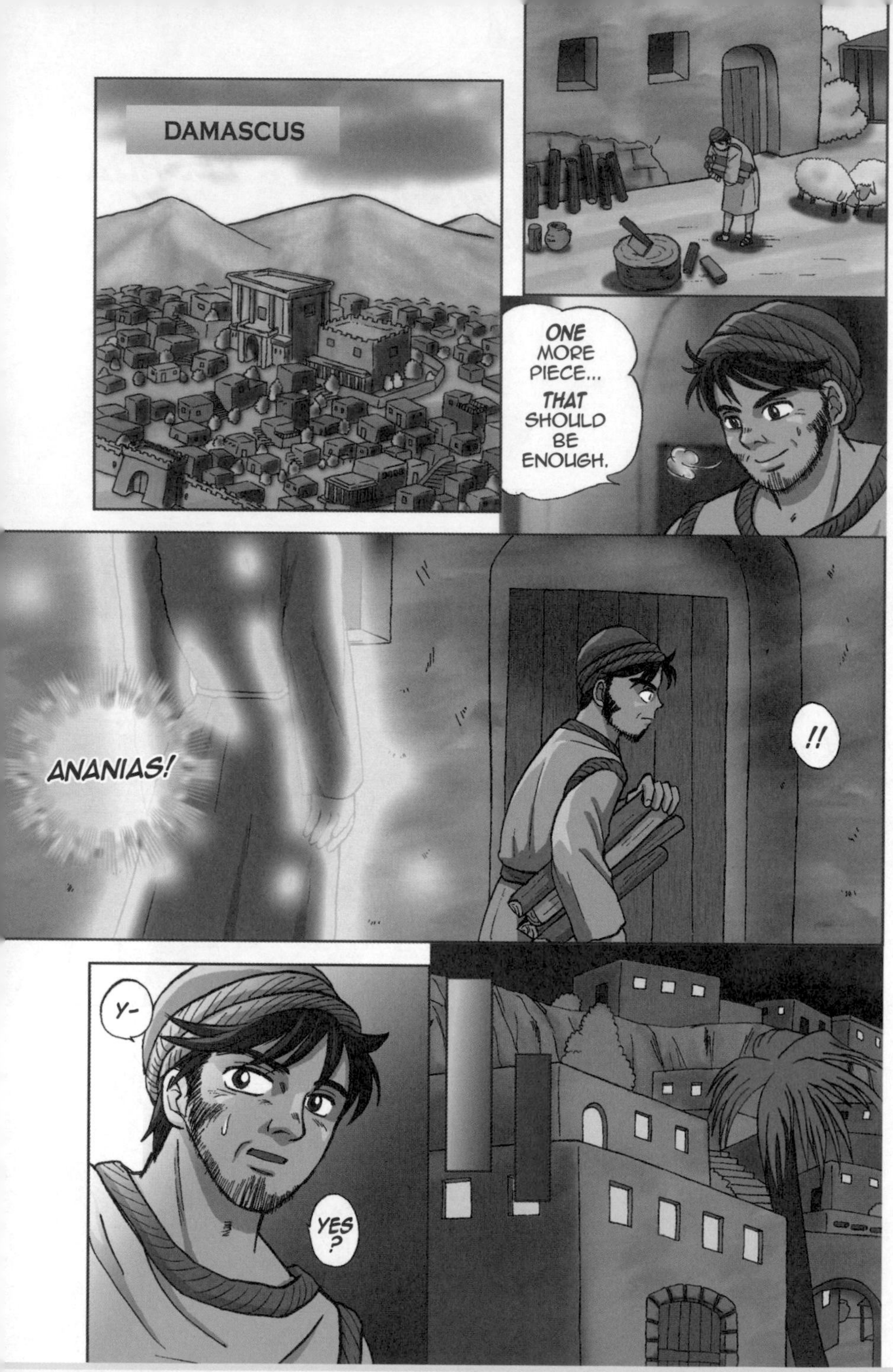
DAMASCUS
ONE MORE PIECE... THAT SHOULD BE ENOUGH.
ANANIAS!
!!
Y-
YES?

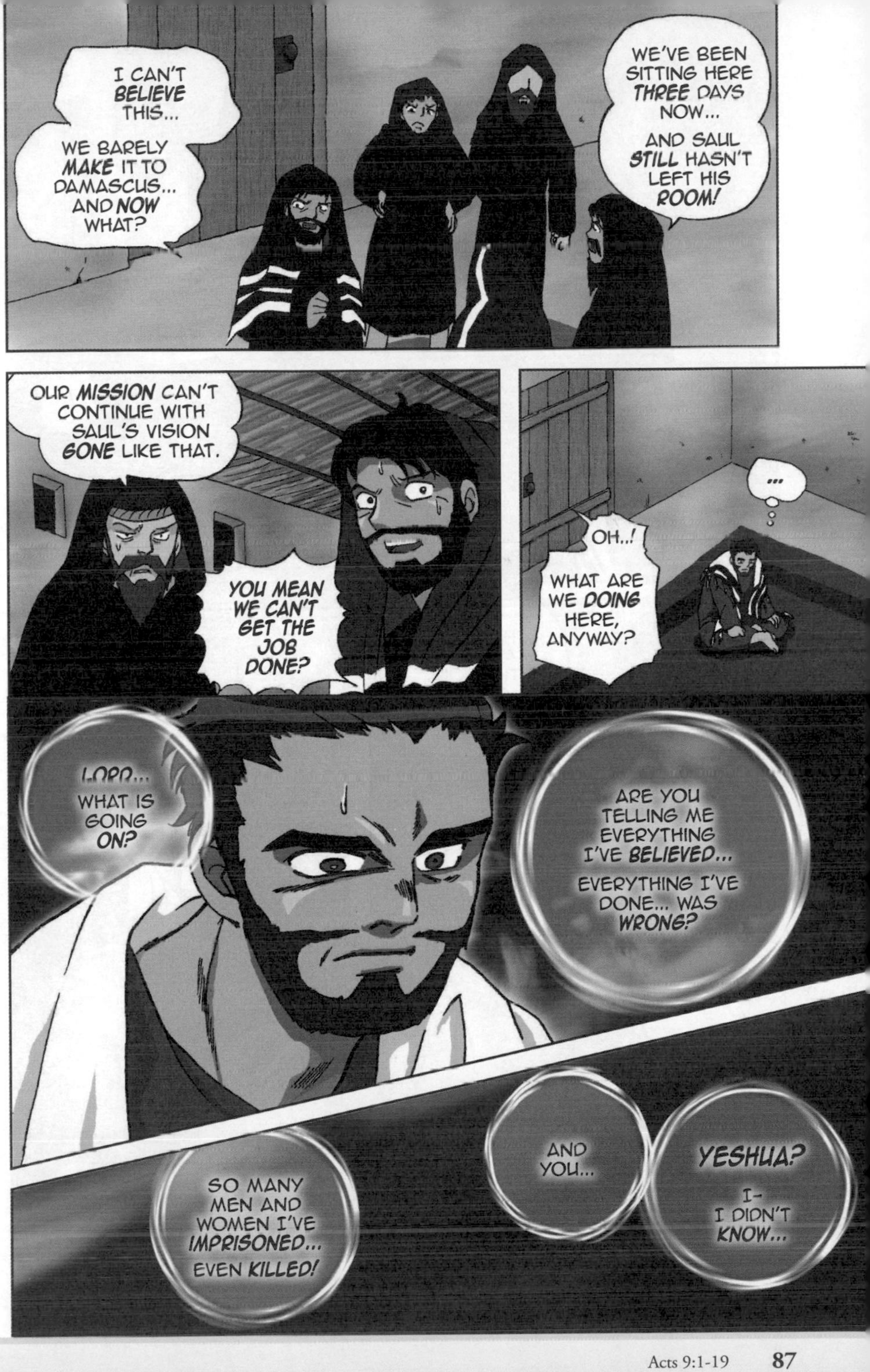
I CAN'T BELIEVE THIS...
WE BARELY MAKE IT TO DAMASCUS... AND NOW WHAT?
WE'VE BEEN SITTING HERE THREE DAYS NOW...
AND SAUL STILL HASN'T LEFT HIS ROOM!
OUR MISSION CAN'T CONTINUE WITH SAUL'S VISION GONE LIKE THAT.
YOU MEAN WE CAN'T GET THE JOB DONE?
OH..!
WHAT ARE WE DOING HERE, ANYWAY?
...
LORD... WHAT IS GOING ON?
ARE YOU TELLING ME EVERYTHING I'VE BELIEVED...
EVERYTHING I'VE DONE... WAS WRONG?
SO MANY MEN AND WOMEN I'VE IMPRISONED...
EVEN KILLED!
AND YOU...
YESHUA?
I- I DIDN'T KNOW...

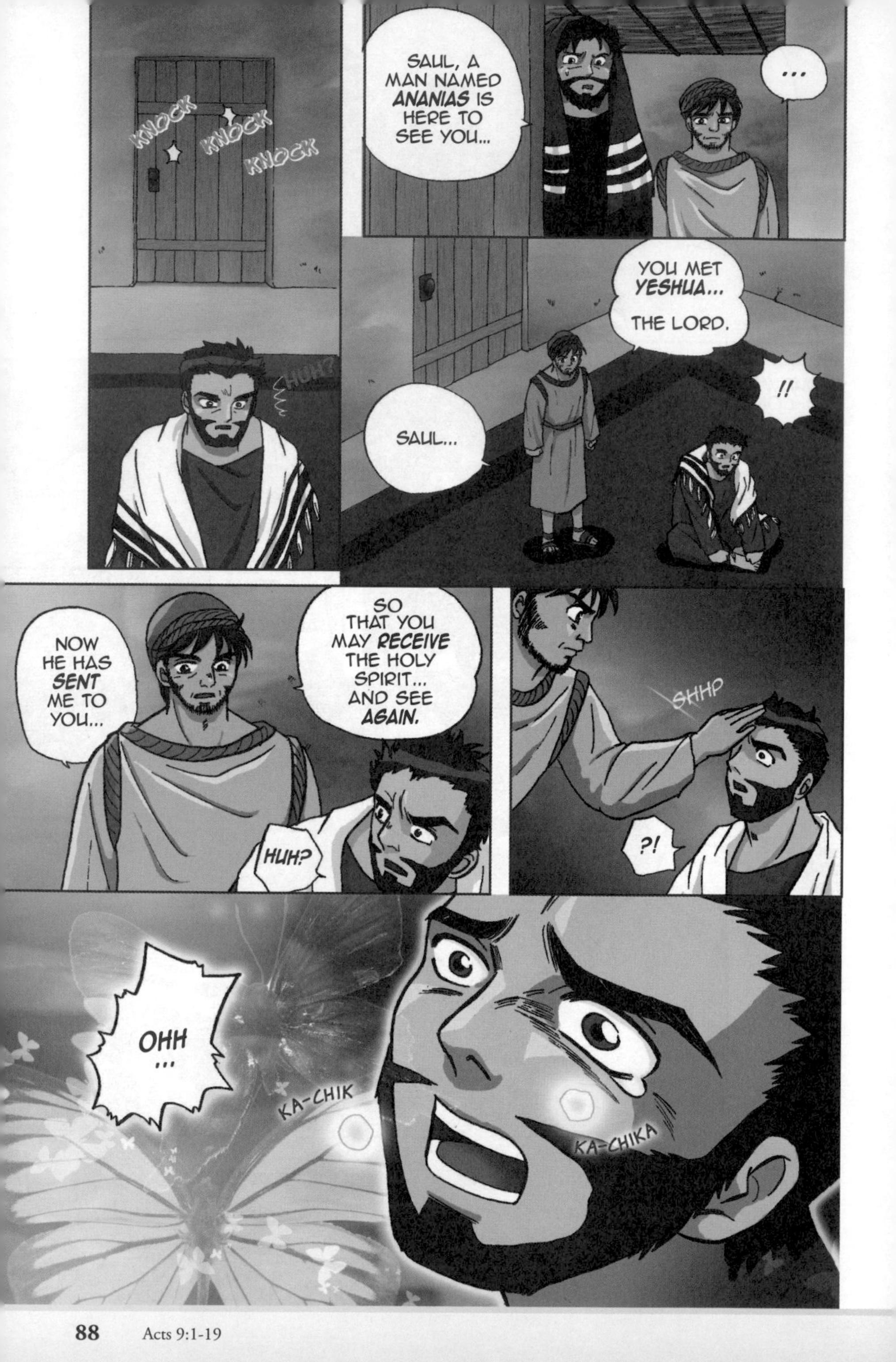
KNOCK
KNOCK
KNOCK
SAUL, A MAN NAMED ANANIAS IS HERE TO SEE YOU...
...
HUH?
YOU MET YESHUA... THE LORD.
!!
SAUL...
NOW HE HAS SENT ME TO YOU...
SO THAT YOU MAY RECEIVE THE HOLY SPIRIT... AND SEE AGAIN.
HUH?
SHHP
?!
OHH ...
KA-CHIK
KA-CHIKA

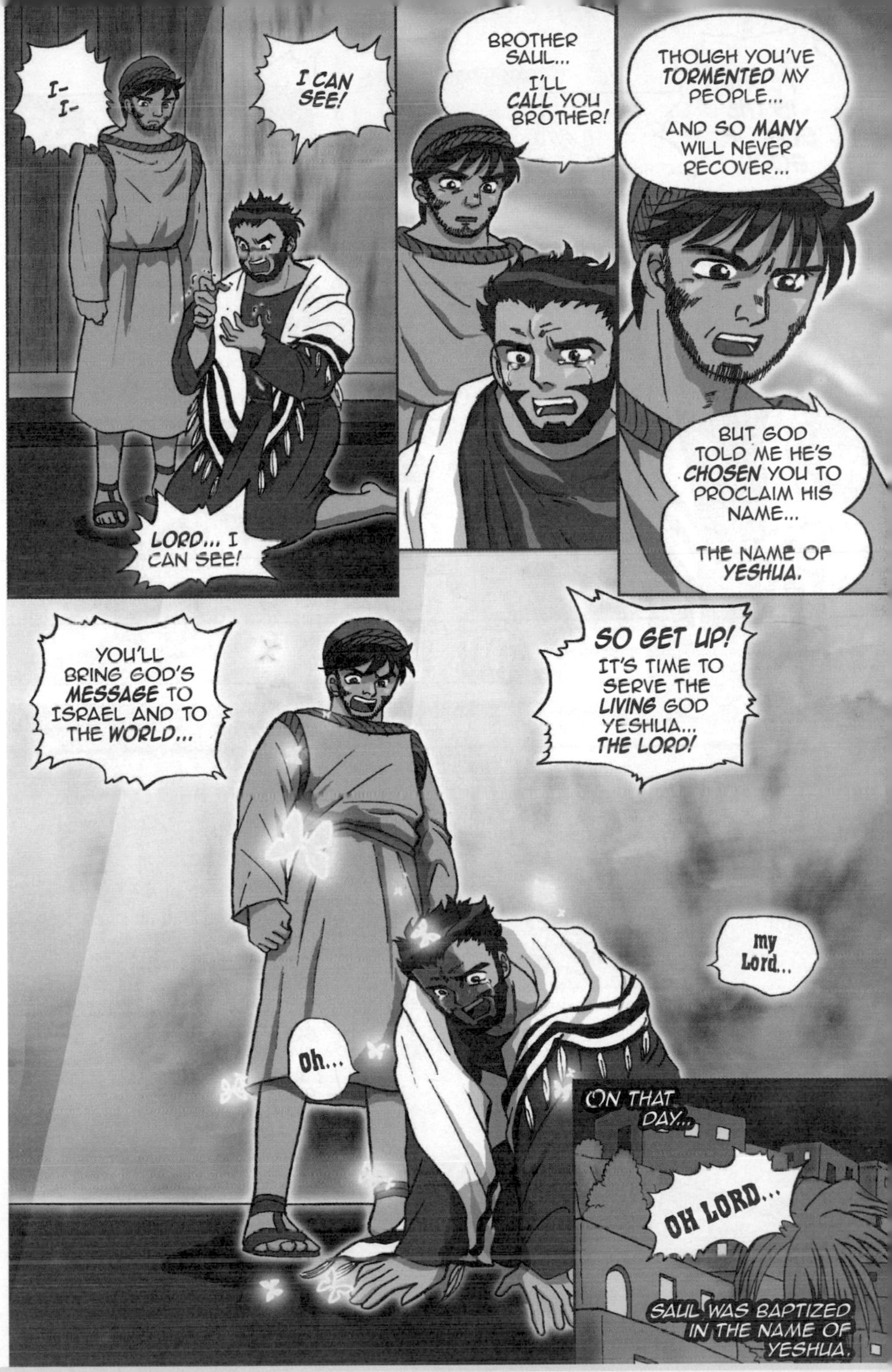
I-
I-
I CAN SEE!
LORD... I CAN SEE!
BROTHER SAUL...
I'LL CALL YOU BROTHER!
THOUGH YOU'VE TORMENTED MY PEOPLE...
AND SO MANY WILL NEVER RECOVER...
BUT GOD TOLD ME HE'S CHOSEN YOU TO PROCLAIM HIS NAME...
THE NAME OF YESHUA.
YOU'LL BRING GOD'S MESSAGE TO ISRAEL AND TO THE WORLD...
SO GET UP!
IT'S TIME TO SERVE THE LIVING GOD YESHUA... THE LORD!
my Lord...
Oh...
ON THAT DAY...
OH LORD...
SAUL WAS BAPTIZED IN THE NAME OF YESHUA.

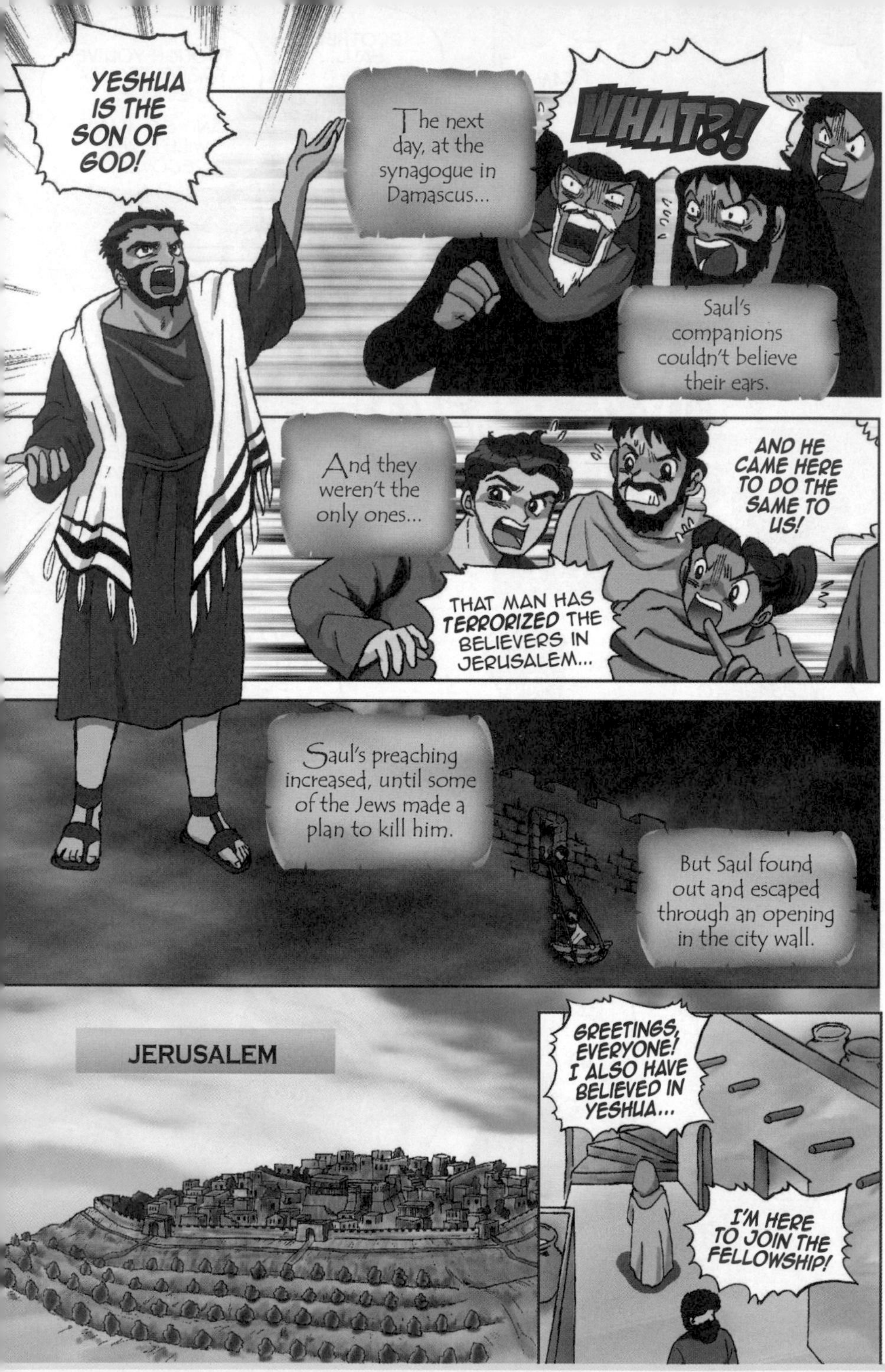
YESHUA IS THE SON OF GOD!
The next day, at the synagogue in Damascus...
WHAT?!
Saul's companions couldn't believe their ears.
And they weren't the only ones...
AND HE CAME HERE TO DO THE SAME TO US!
THAT MAN HAS TERRORIZED THE BELIEVERS IN JERUSALEM...
Saul's preaching increased, until some of the Jews made a plan to kill him.
But Saul found out and escaped through an opening in the city wall.
JERUSALEM
GREETINGS, EVERYONE! I ALSO HAVE BELIEVED IN YESHUA...
I'M HERE TO JOIN THE FELLOWSHIP!

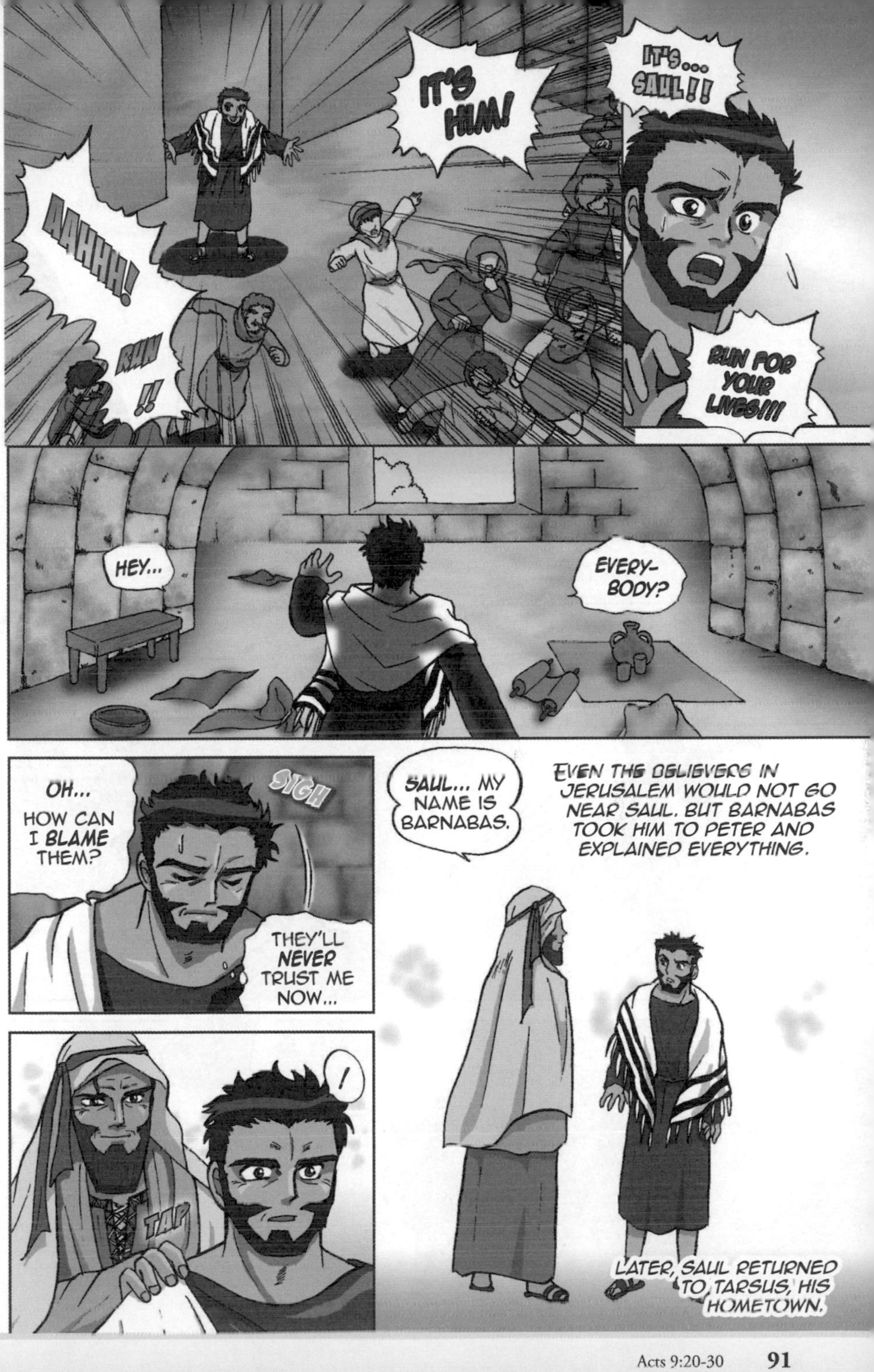
IT'S HIM!
IT'S... SAUL!!
AAHHH!
RUN !!
RUN FOR YOUR LIVES!!!
HEY...
EVERY-BODY?
OH... HOW CAN I BLAME THEM?
SIGH
THEY'LL NEVER TRUST ME NOW...
SAUL... MY NAME IS BARNABAS.
EVEN THE BELIEVERS IN JERUSALEM WOULD NOT GO NEAR SAUL. BUT BARNABAS TOOK HIM TO PETER AND EXPLAINED EVERYTHING.
!
TAP
LATER, SAUL RETURNED TO TARSUS, HIS HOMETOWN.

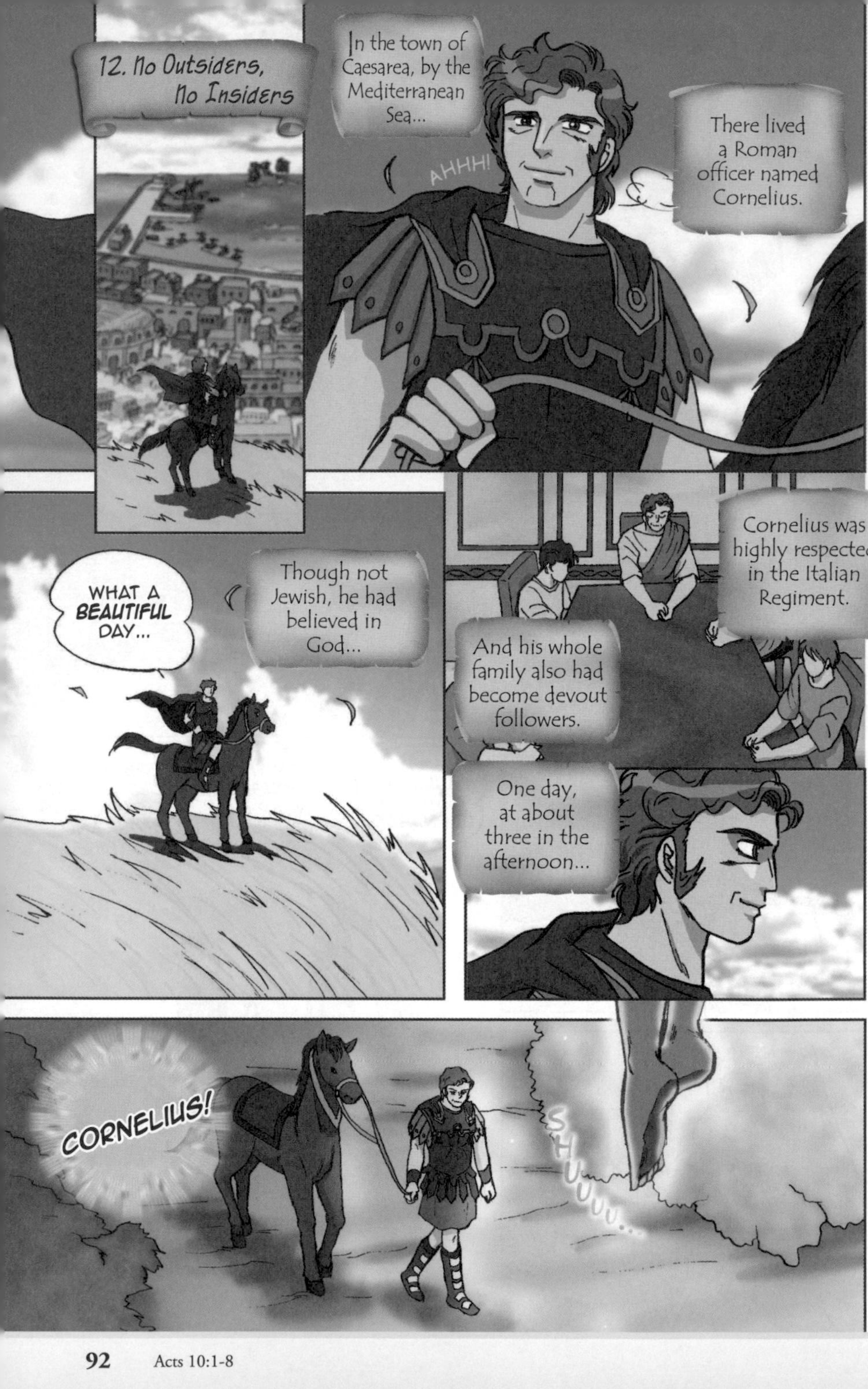
12. No Outsiders, No Insiders
In the town of Caesarea, by the Mediterranean Sea...
AHHH!
There lived a Roman officer named Cornelius.
WHAT A BEAUTIFUL DAY...
Though not Jewish, he had believed in God...
Cornelius was highly respected in the Italian Regiment.
And his whole family also had become devout followers.
One day, at about three in the afternoon...
CORNELIUS!
SHUUUU...

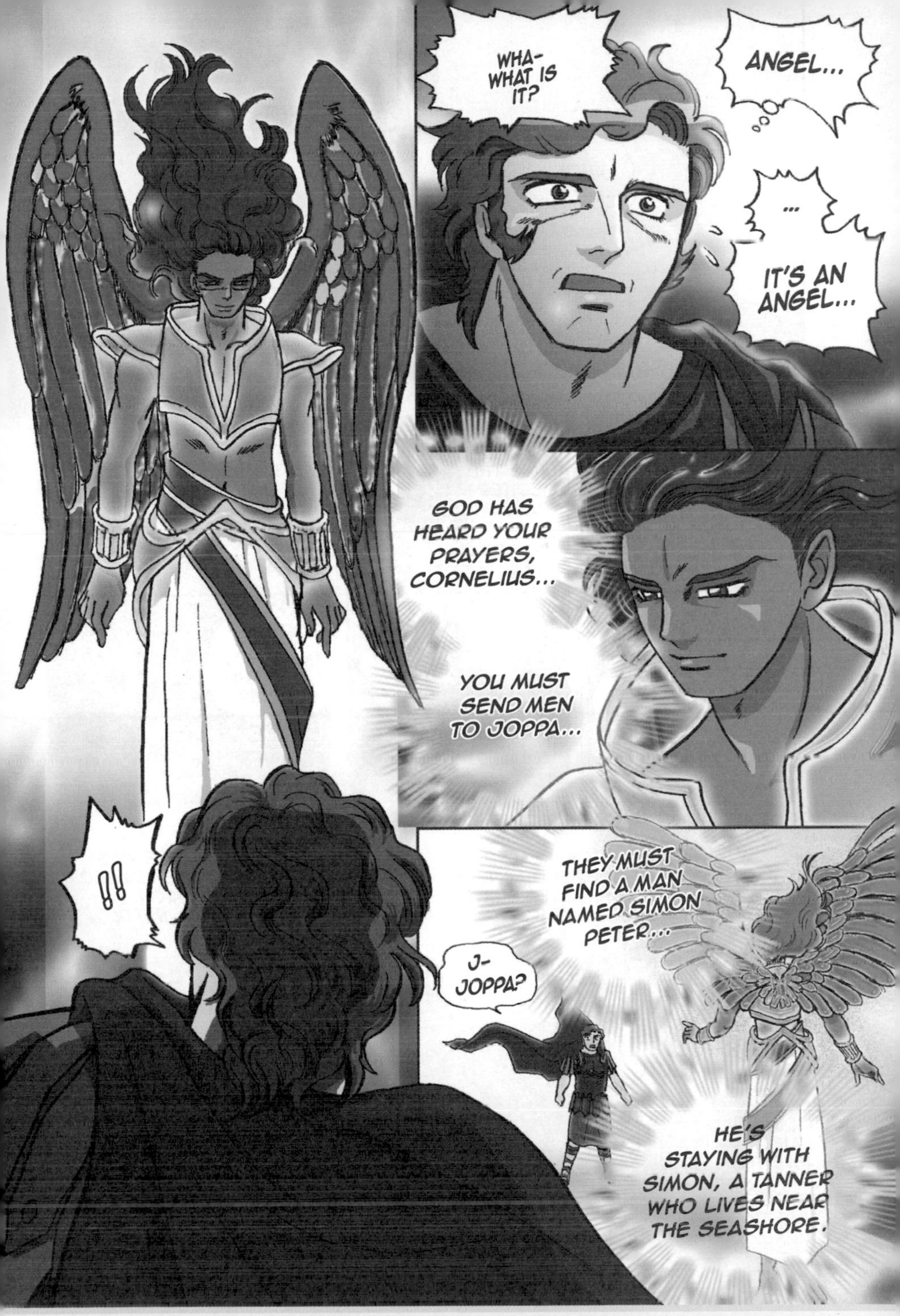
WHA-
WHAT IS
IT?
ANGEL...
...
IT'S AN
ANGEL...
GOD HAS
HEARD YOUR
PRAYERS,
CORNELIUS...
YOU MUST
SEND MEN
TO JOPPA...
!!
THEY MUST
FIND A MAN
NAMED SIMON
PETER...
J-
JOPPA?
HE'S
STAYING WITH
SIMON, A TANNER
WHO LIVES NEAR
THE SEASHORE.

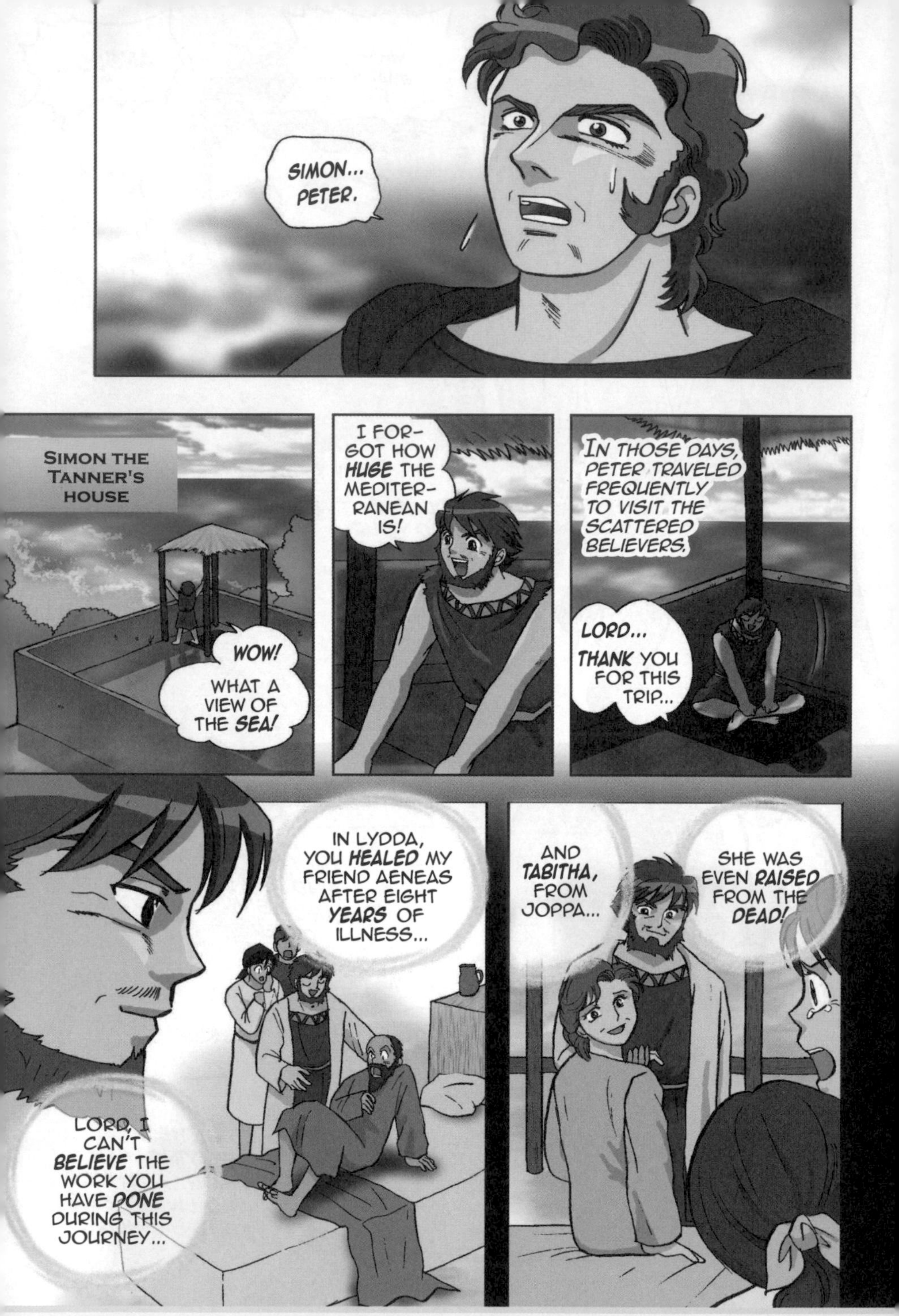
SIMON... PETER.
SIMON THE TANNER'S HOUSE
WOW! WHAT A VIEW OF THE SEA!
I FOR-GOT HOW HUGE THE MEDITER-RANEAN IS!
IN THOSE DAYS, PETER TRAVELED FREQUENTLY TO VISIT THE SCATTERED BELIEVERS.
LORD... THANK YOU FOR THIS TRIP...
LORD, I CAN'T BELIEVE THE WORK YOU HAVE DONE DURING THIS JOURNEY...
IN LYDDA, YOU HEALED MY FRIEND AENEAS AFTER EIGHT YEARS OF ILLNESS...
AND TABITHA, FROM JOPPA...
SHE WAS EVEN RAISED FROM THE DEAD!

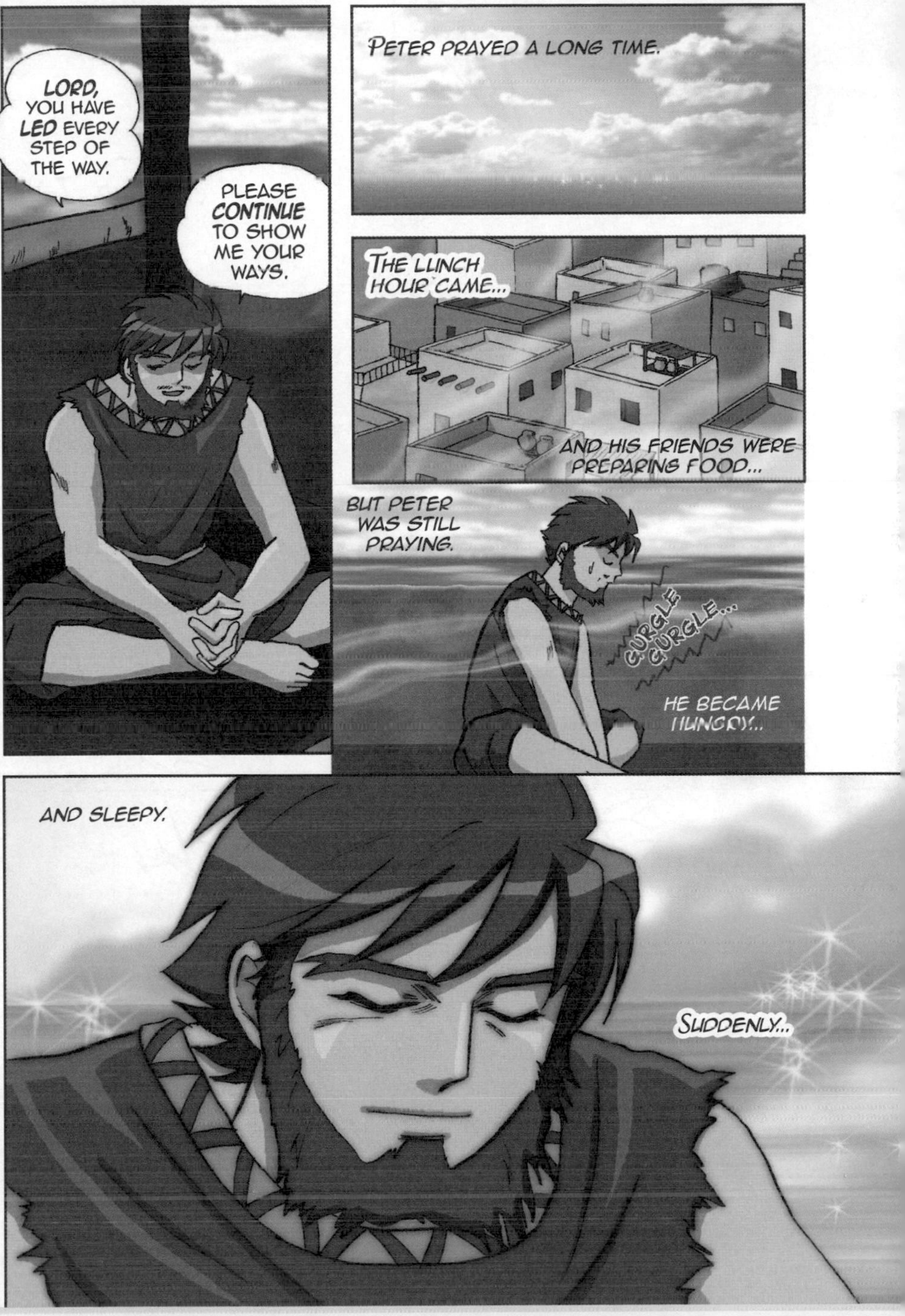
LORD, YOU HAVE LED EVERY STEP OF THE WAY.
PLEASE CONTINUE TO SHOW ME YOUR WAYS.
PETER PRAYED A LONG TIME.
THE LUNCH HOUR CAME...
AND HIS FRIENDS WERE PREPARING FOOD...
BUT PETER WAS STILL PRAYING.
GURGLE GURGLE...
HE BECAME HUNGRY...
AND SLEEPY.
SUDDENLY...

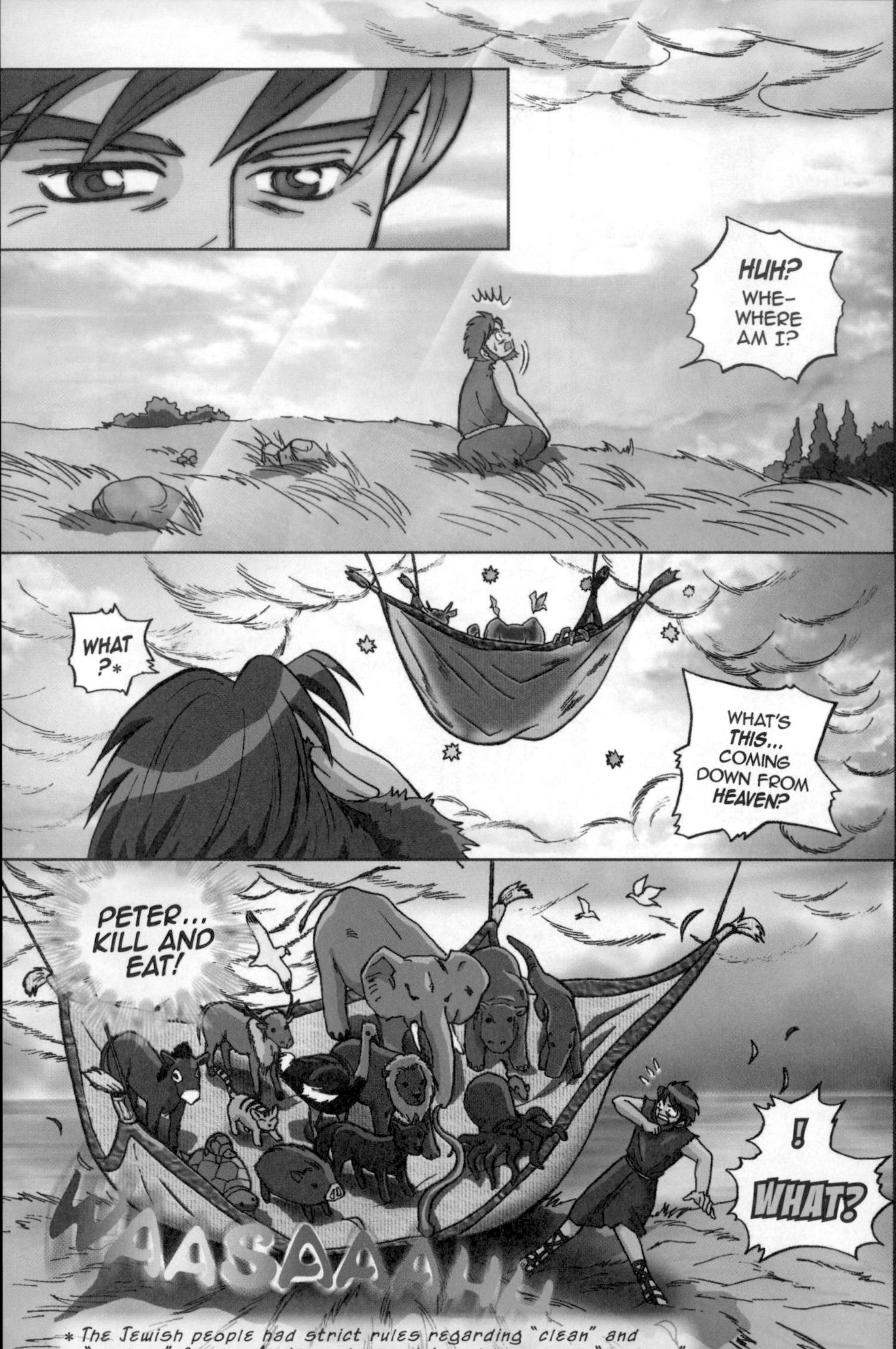
HUH? WHE- WHERE AM I?
WHAT ?*
WHAT'S THIS... COMING DOWN FROM HEAVEN?
PETER... KILL AND EAT!
!
WHAT?

* The Jewish people had strict rules regarding "clean" and "unclean" foods. All the animals pictured here were "unclean."

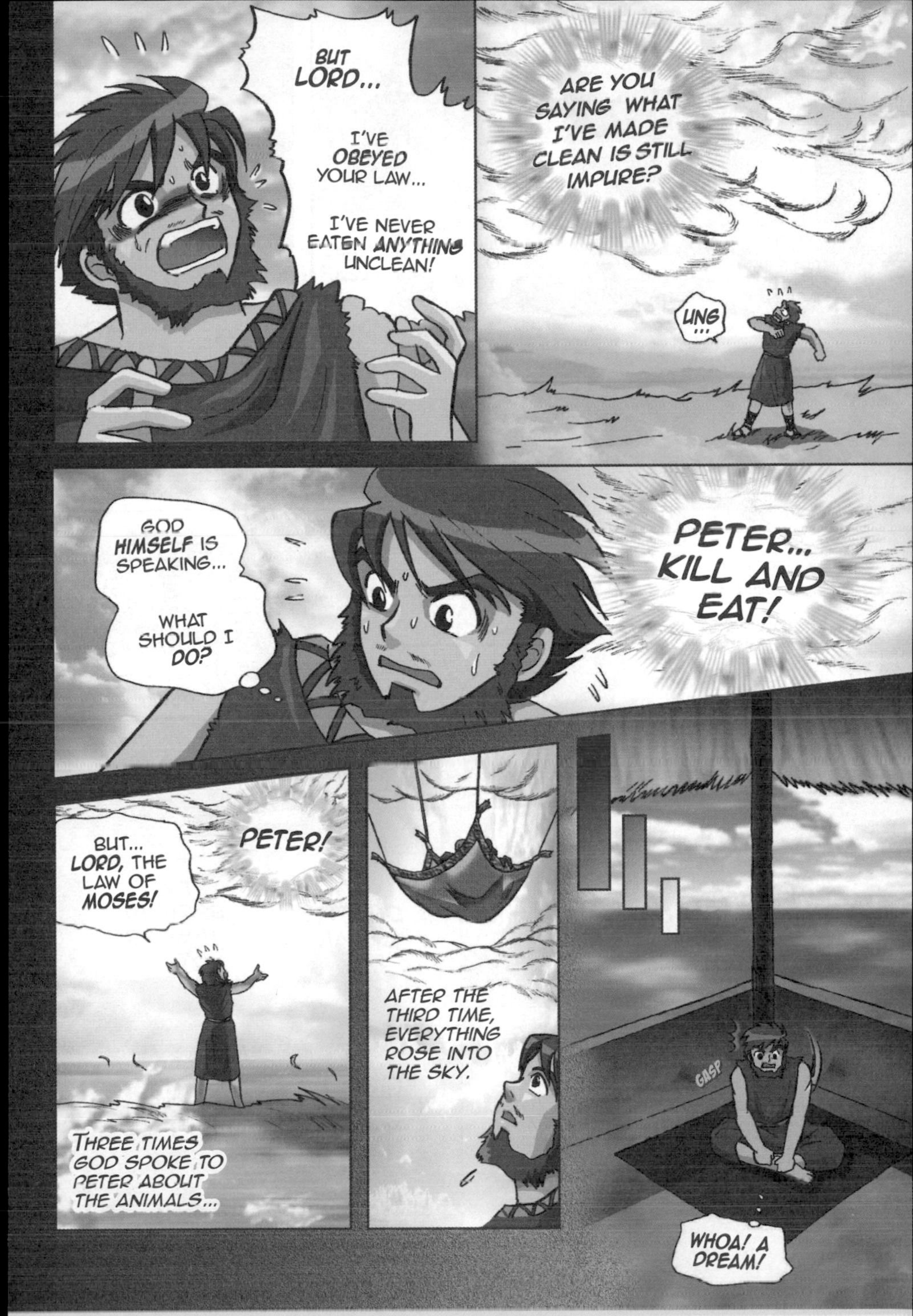
BUT LORD...
I'VE OBEYED YOUR LAW...
I'VE NEVER EATEN ANYTHING UNCLEAN!
ARE YOU SAYING WHAT I'VE MADE CLEAN IS STILL IMPURE?
UNG...
GOD HIMSELF IS SPEAKING...
WHAT SHOULD I DO?
PETER... KILL AND EAT!
BUT... LORD, THE LAW OF MOSES!
PETER!
THREE TIMES GOD SPOKE TO PETER ABOUT THE ANIMALS...
AFTER THE THIRD TIME, EVERYTHING ROSE INTO THE SKY.
GASP
WHOA! A DREAM!

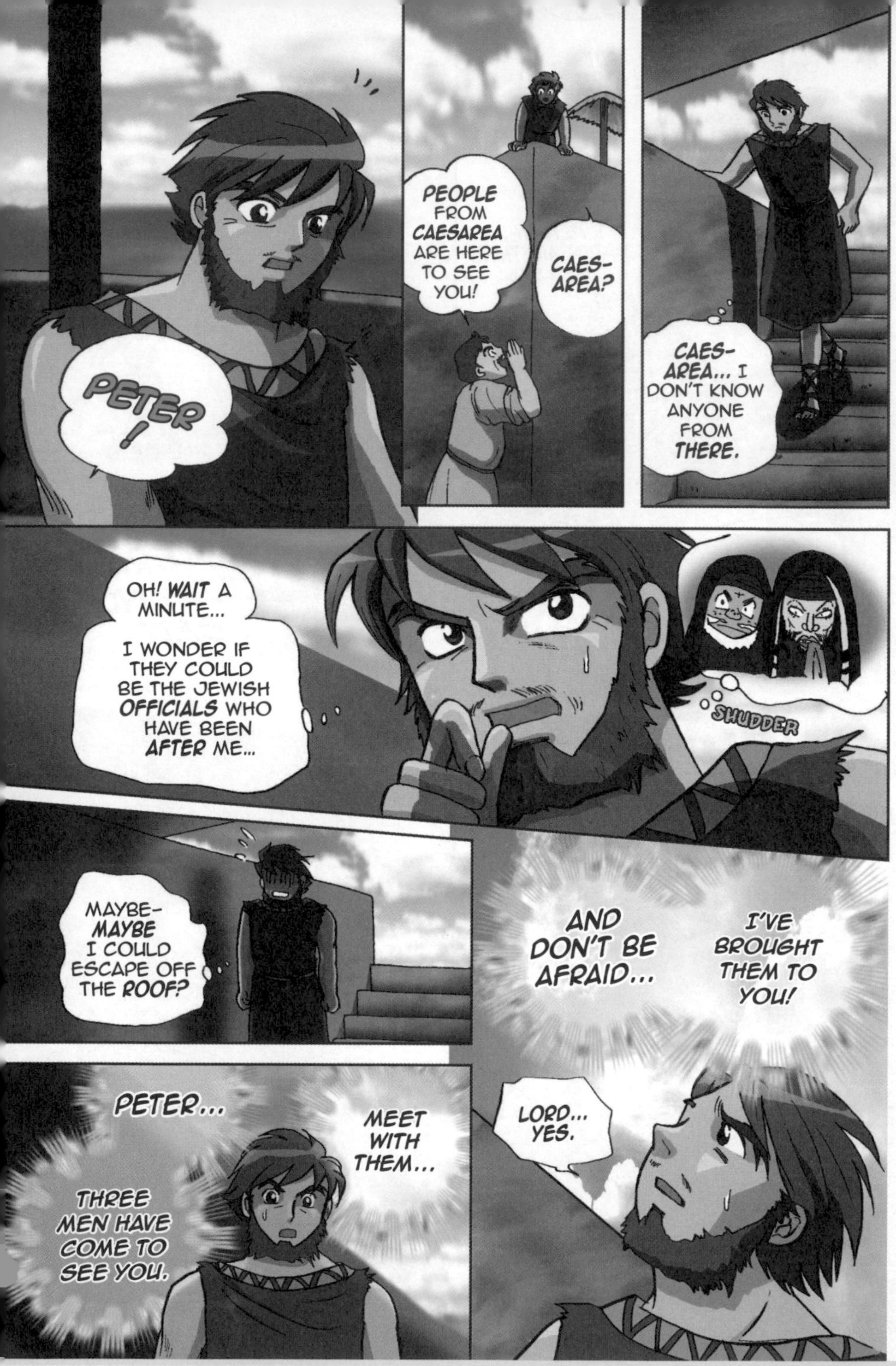
PETER!
PEOPLE FROM CAESAREA ARE HERE TO SEE YOU!
CAES-AREA?
CAES-AREA... I DON'T KNOW ANYONE FROM THERE.
OH! WAIT A MINUTE...
I WONDER IF THEY COULD BE THE JEWISH OFFICIALS WHO HAVE BEEN AFTER ME...
SHUDDER
MAYBE-MAYBE I COULD ESCAPE OFF THE ROOF?
AND DON'T BE AFRAID...
I'VE BROUGHT THEM TO YOU!
PETER...
MEET WITH THEM...
THREE MEN HAVE COME TO SEE YOU.
LORD... YES.

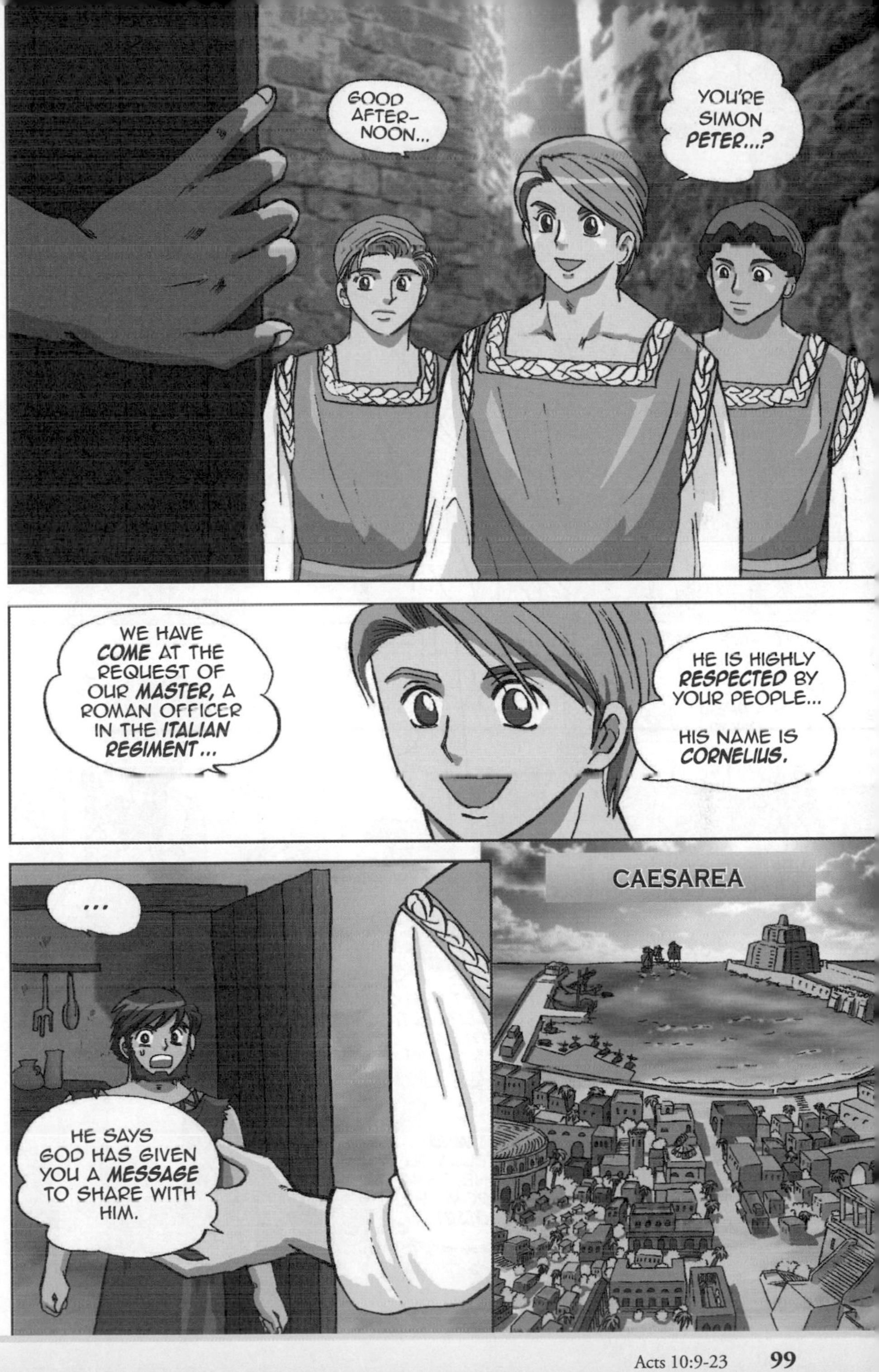
GOOD AFTER-NOON...
YOU'RE SIMON PETER...?
WE HAVE COME AT THE REQUEST OF OUR MASTER, A ROMAN OFFICER IN THE ITALIAN REGIMENT...
HE IS HIGHLY RESPECTED BY YOUR PEOPLE...
HIS NAME IS CORNELIUS.
...
HE SAYS GOD HAS GIVEN YOU A MESSAGE TO SHARE WITH HIM.
CAESAREA

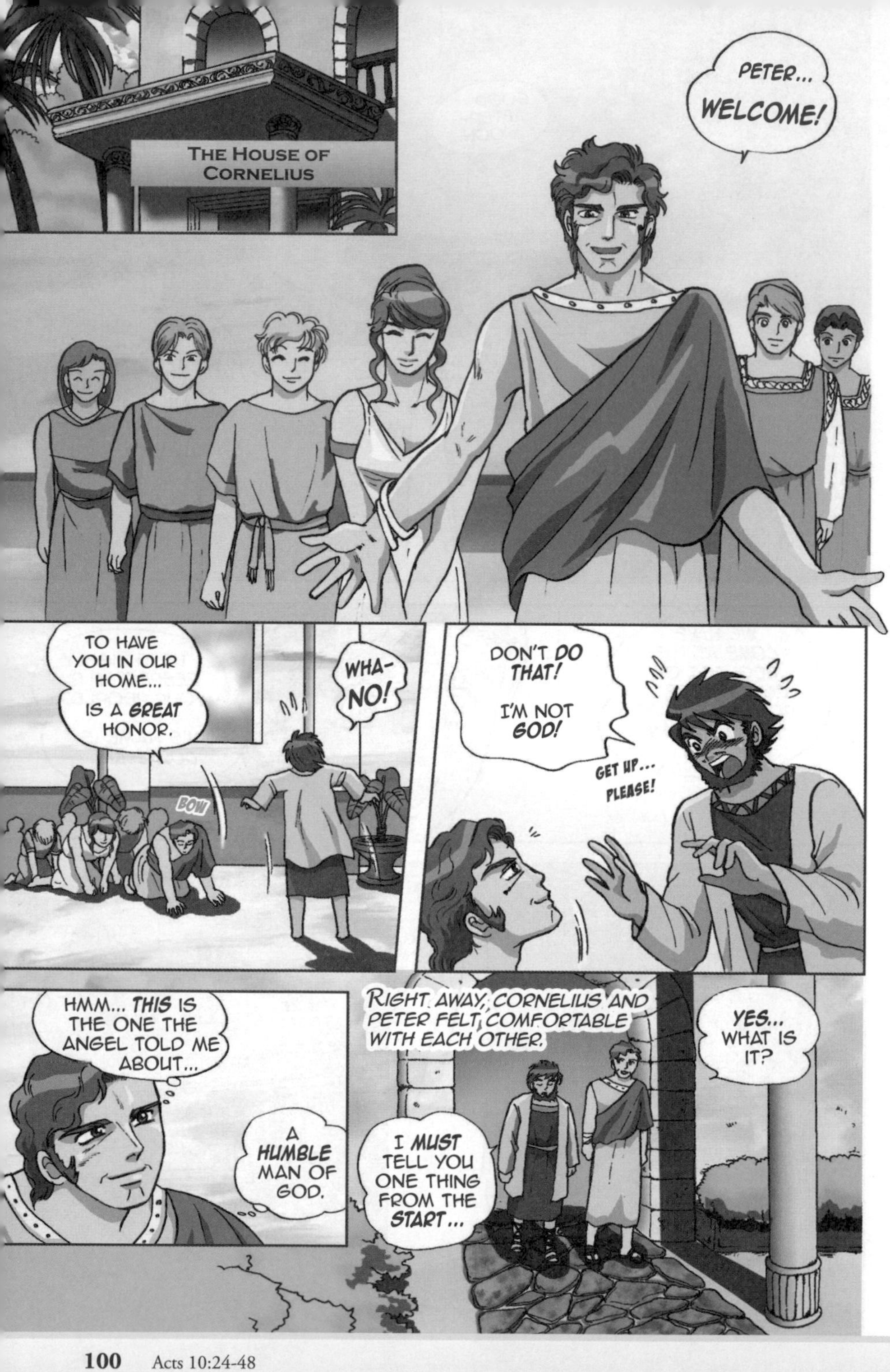
The House of Cornelius
PETER... WELCOME!
TO HAVE YOU IN OUR HOME... IS A GREAT HONOR.
BOW
WHA- NO!
DON'T DO THAT! I'M NOT GOD!
GET UP... PLEASE!
HMM... THIS IS THE ONE THE ANGEL TOLD ME ABOUT...
A HUMBLE MAN OF GOD.
RIGHT AWAY, CORNELIUS AND PETER FELT COMFORTABLE WITH EACH OTHER.
I MUST TELL YOU ONE THING FROM THE START...
YES... WHAT IS IT?

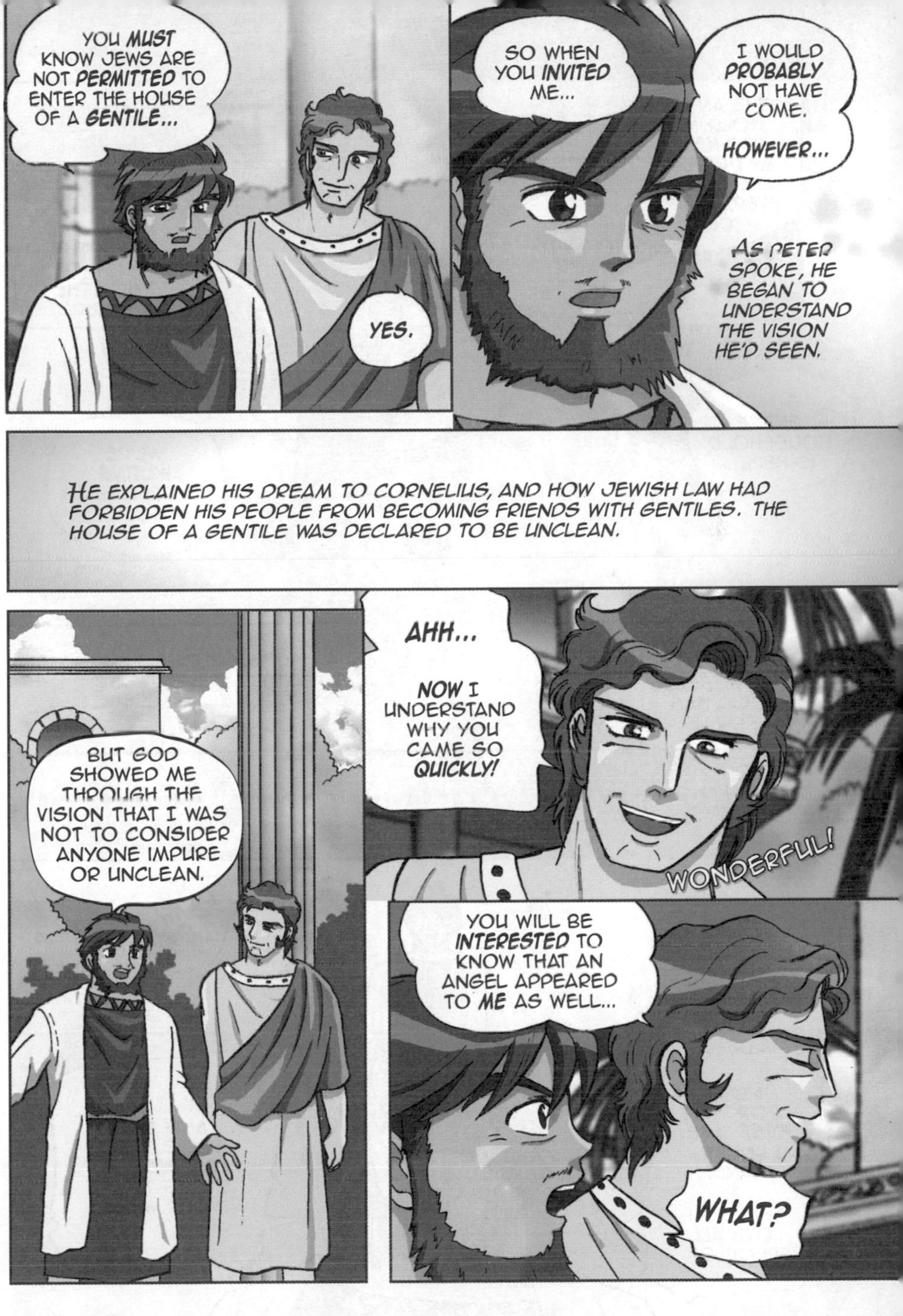
YOU MUST KNOW JEWS ARE NOT PERMITTED TO ENTER THE HOUSE OF A GENTILE...
YES.
SO WHEN YOU INVITED ME...
I WOULD PROBABLY NOT HAVE COME.
HOWEVER...
AS PETER SPOKE, HE BEGAN TO UNDERSTAND THE VISION HE'D SEEN.
HE EXPLAINED HIS DREAM TO CORNELIUS, AND HOW JEWISH LAW HAD FORBIDDEN HIS PEOPLE FROM BECOMING FRIENDS WITH GENTILES. THE HOUSE OF A GENTILE WAS DECLARED TO BE UNCLEAN.
BUT GOD SHOWED ME THROUGH THE VISION THAT I WAS NOT TO CONSIDER ANYONE IMPURE OR UNCLEAN.
AHH...
NOW I UNDERSTAND WHY YOU CAME SO QUICKLY!
WONDERFUL!
YOU WILL BE INTERESTED TO KNOW THAT AN ANGEL APPEARED TO ME AS WELL...
WHAT?

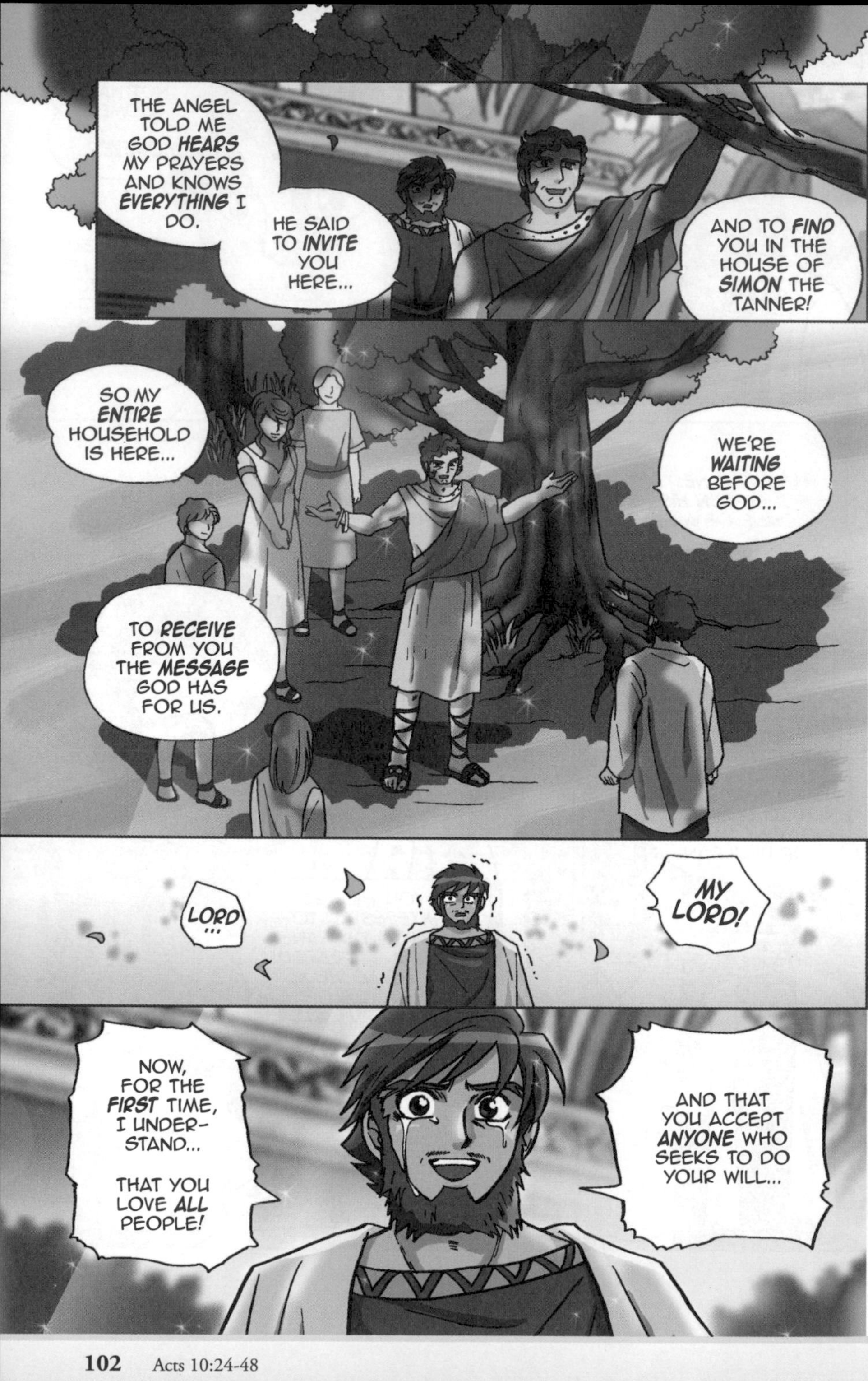
THE ANGEL TOLD ME GOD HEARS MY PRAYERS AND KNOWS EVERYTHING I DO.
HE SAID TO INVITE YOU HERE...
AND TO FIND YOU IN THE HOUSE OF SIMON THE TANNER!
SO MY ENTIRE HOUSEHOLD IS HERE...
WE'RE WAITING BEFORE GOD...
TO RECEIVE FROM YOU THE MESSAGE GOD HAS FOR US.
MY LORD!
LORD...
NOW, FOR THE FIRST TIME, I UNDER-STAND...
THAT YOU LOVE ALL PEOPLE!
AND THAT YOU ACCEPT ANYONE WHO SEEKS TO DO YOUR WILL...

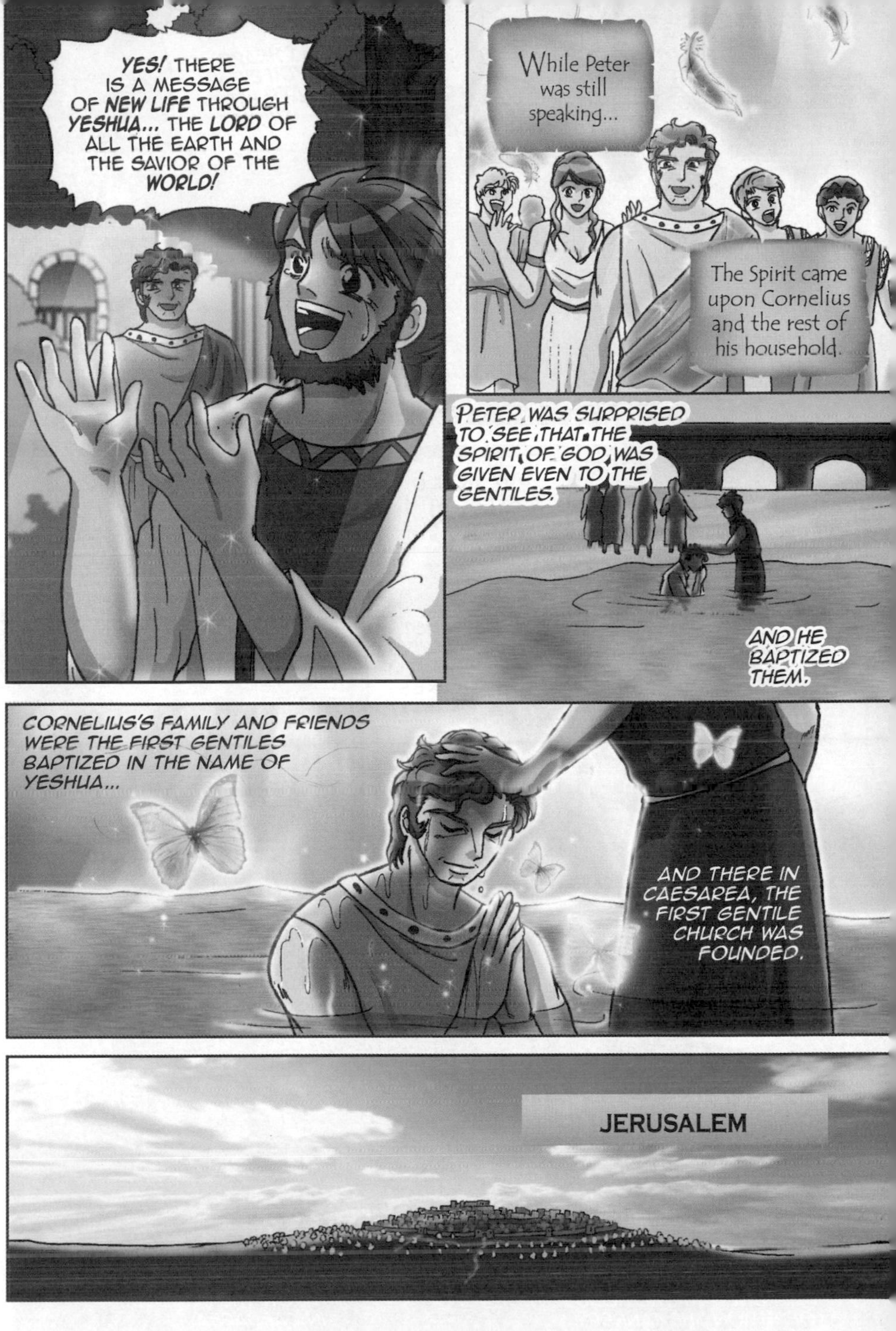
YES! THERE IS A MESSAGE OF NEW LIFE THROUGH YESHUA... THE LORD OF ALL THE EARTH AND THE SAVIOR OF THE WORLD!
While Peter was still speaking...
The Spirit came upon Cornelius and the rest of his household.
PETER WAS SURPRISED TO SEE THAT THE SPIRIT OF GOD WAS GIVEN EVEN TO THE GENTILES.
AND HE BAPTIZED THEM.
CORNELIUS'S FAMILY AND FRIENDS WERE THE FIRST GENTILES BAPTIZED IN THE NAME OF YESHUA...
AND THERE IN CAESAREA, THE FIRST GENTILE CHURCH WAS FOUNDED.
JERUSALEM

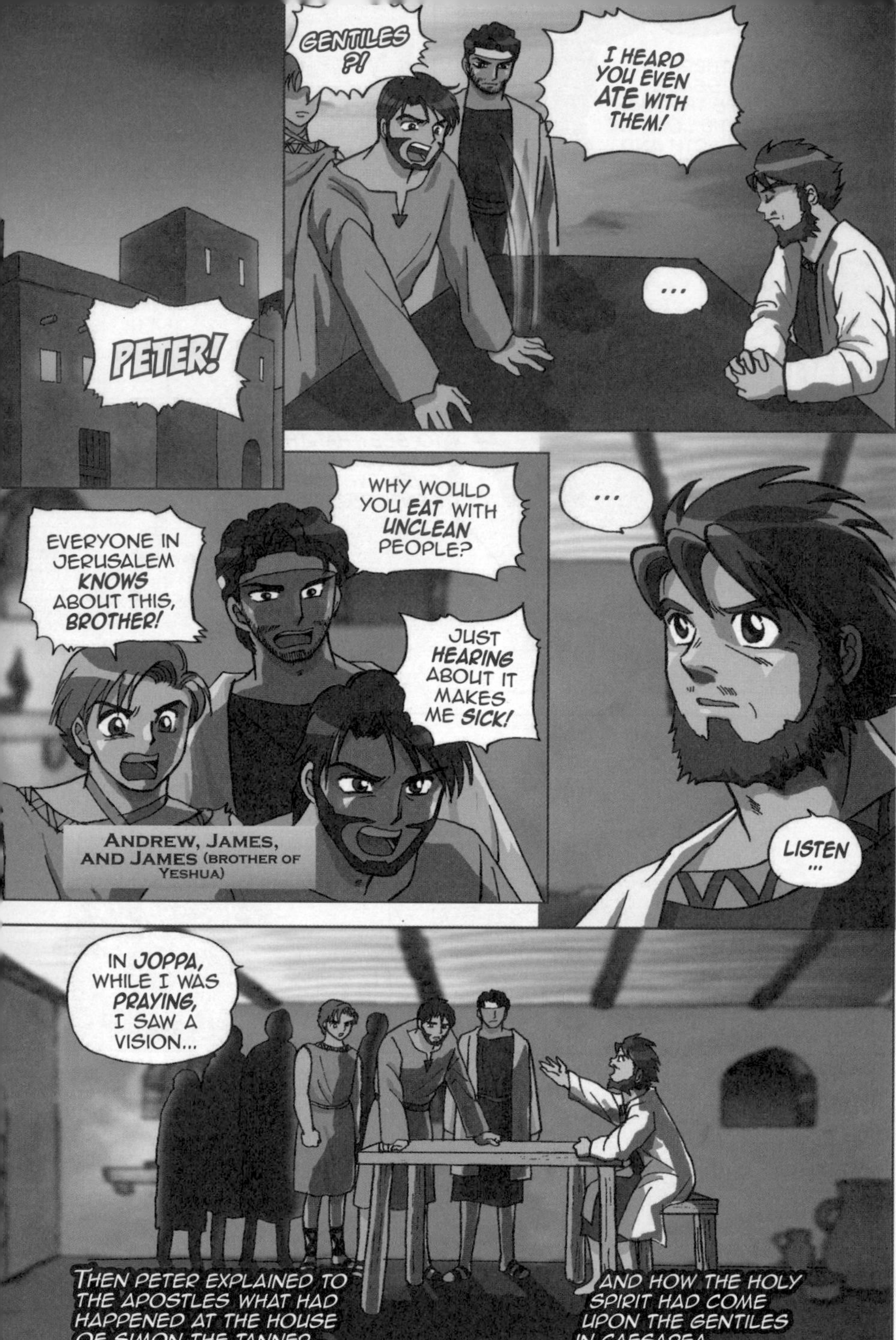

PETER!
GENTILES ?!
I HEARD YOU EVEN ATE WITH THEM!
...
EVERYONE IN JERUSALEM KNOWS ABOUT THIS, BROTHER!
WHY WOULD YOU EAT WITH UNCLEAN PEOPLE?
JUST HEARING ABOUT IT MAKES ME SICK!
ANDREW, JAMES, AND JAMES (BROTHER OF YESHUA)
...
LISTEN ...
IN JOPPA, WHILE I WAS PRAYING, I SAW A VISION...
THEN PETER EXPLAINED TO THE APOSTLES WHAT HAD HAPPENED AT THE HOUSE OF SIMON THE TANNER...
AND HOW THE HOLY SPIRIT HAD COME UPON THE GENTILES IN CAESAREA.

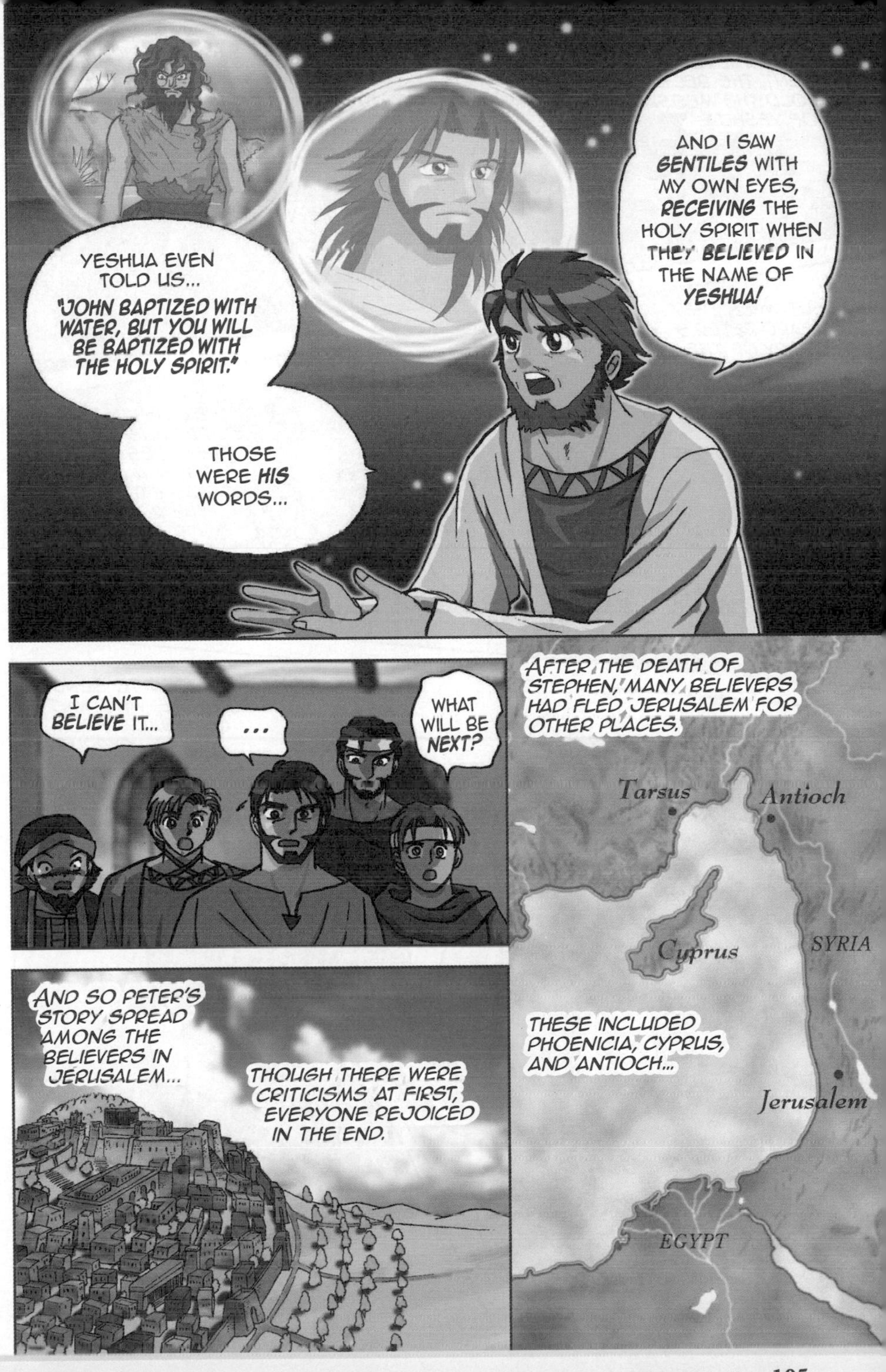
YESHUA EVEN TOLD US... "JOHN BAPTIZED WITH WATER, BUT YOU WILL BE BAPTIZED WITH THE HOLY SPIRIT."
THOSE WERE HIS WORDS...
AND I SAW GENTILES WITH MY OWN EYES, RECEIVING THE HOLY SPIRIT WHEN THEY BELIEVED IN THE NAME OF YESHUA!
I CAN'T BELIEVE IT...
...
WHAT WILL BE NEXT?
AFTER THE DEATH OF STEPHEN, MANY BELIEVERS HAD FLED JERUSALEM FOR OTHER PLACES.
Tarsus
Antioch
Cyprus
SYRIA
Jerusalem
EGYPT
THESE INCLUDED PHOENICIA, CYPRUS, AND ANTIOCH...
AND SO PETER'S STORY SPREAD AMONG THE BELIEVERS IN JERUSALEM...
THOUGH THERE WERE CRITICISMS AT FIRST, EVERYONE REJOICED IN THE END.

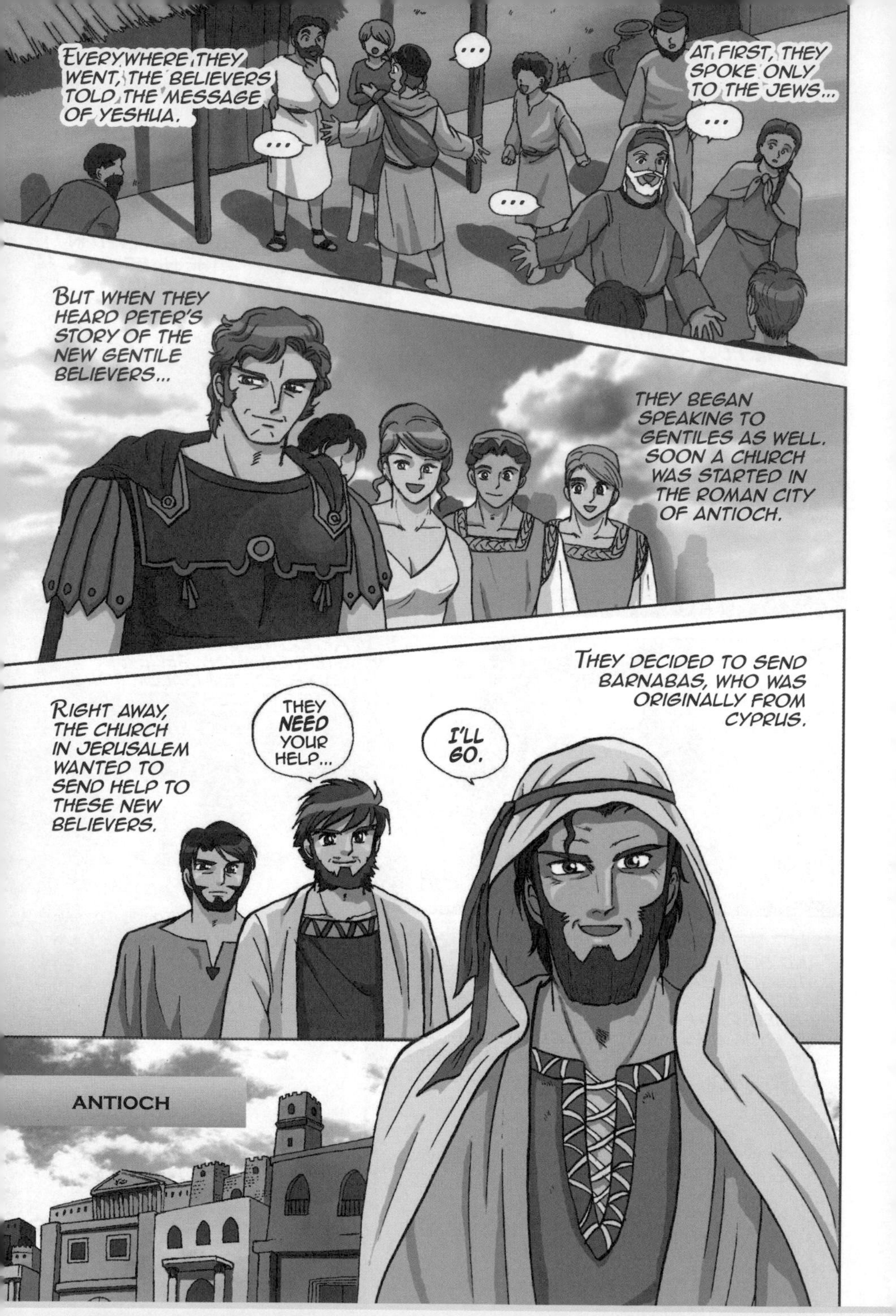

EVERYWHERE THEY WENT, THE BELIEVERS TOLD THE MESSAGE OF YESHUA.
...
...
...
AT FIRST, THEY SPOKE ONLY TO THE JEWS...
...
BUT WHEN THEY HEARD PETER'S STORY OF THE NEW GENTILE BELIEVERS...
THEY BEGAN SPEAKING TO GENTILES AS WELL. SOON A CHURCH WAS STARTED IN THE ROMAN CITY OF ANTIOCH.
RIGHT AWAY, THE CHURCH IN JERUSALEM WANTED TO SEND HELP TO THESE NEW BELIEVERS.
THEY NEED YOUR HELP...
I'LL GO.
THEY DECIDED TO SEND BARNABAS, WHO WAS ORIGINALLY FROM CYPRUS.
ANTIOCH

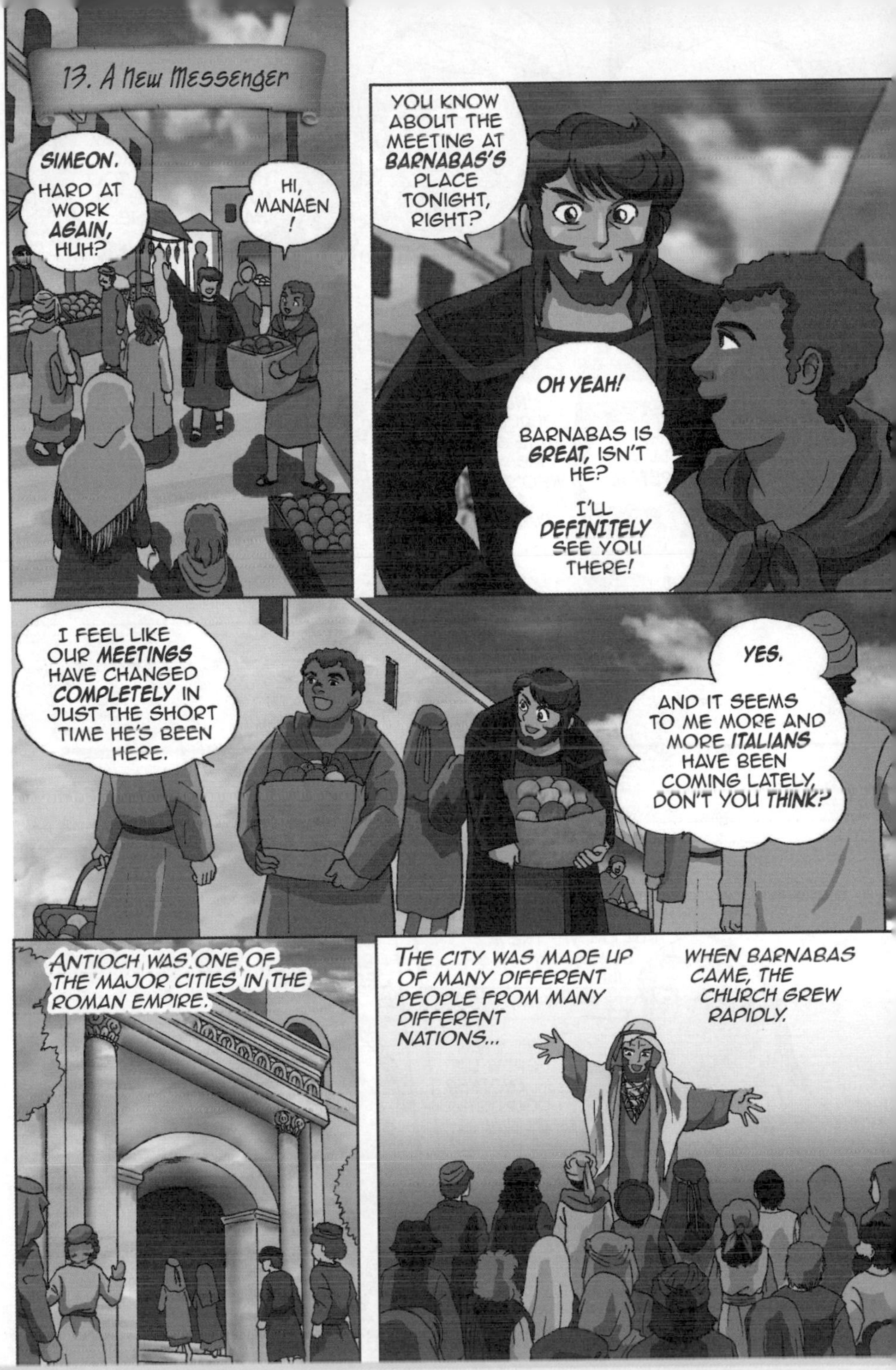
13. A New Messenger
SIMEON. HARD AT WORK AGAIN, HUH?
HI, MANAEN!
YOU KNOW ABOUT THE MEETING AT BARNABAS'S PLACE TONIGHT, RIGHT?
OH YEAH! BARNABAS IS GREAT, ISN'T HE? I'LL DEFINITELY SEE YOU THERE!
I FEEL LIKE OUR MEETINGS HAVE CHANGED COMPLETELY IN JUST THE SHORT TIME HE'S BEEN HERE.
YES. AND IT SEEMS TO ME MORE AND MORE ITALIANS HAVE BEEN COMING LATELY, DON'T YOU THINK?
ANTIOCH WAS ONE OF THE MAJOR CITIES IN THE ROMAN EMPIRE.
THE CITY WAS MADE UP OF MANY DIFFERENT PEOPLE FROM MANY DIFFERENT NATIONS...
WHEN BARNABAS CAME, THE CHURCH GREW RAPIDLY.

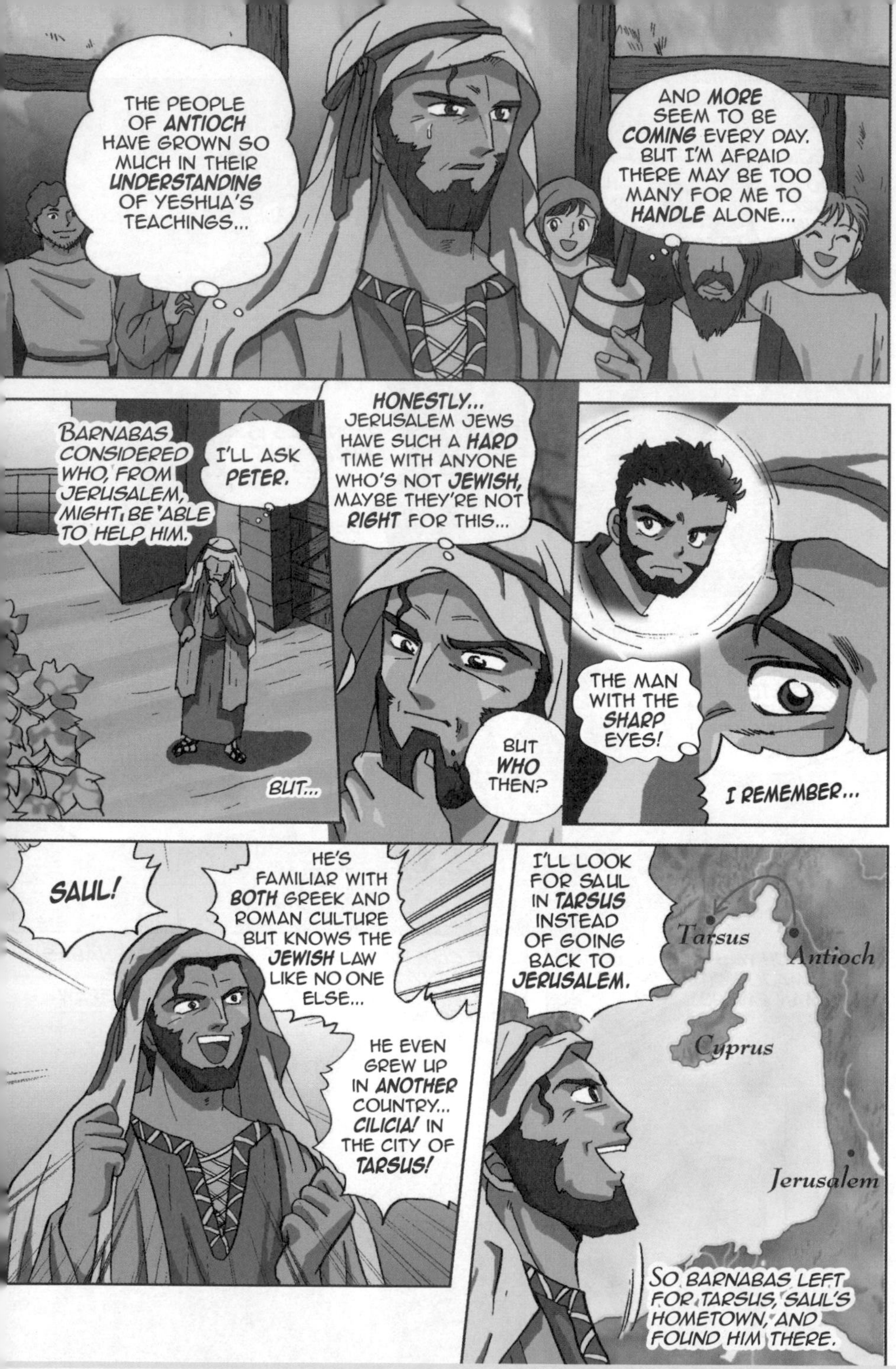
THE PEOPLE OF ANTIOCH HAVE GROWN SO MUCH IN THEIR UNDERSTANDING OF YESHUA'S TEACHINGS...
AND MORE SEEM TO BE COMING EVERY DAY. BUT I'M AFRAID THERE MAY BE TOO MANY FOR ME TO HANDLE ALONE...
BARNABAS CONSIDERED WHO, FROM JERUSALEM, MIGHT BE ABLE TO HELP HIM.
I'LL ASK PETER.
BUT...
HONESTLY... JERUSALEM JEWS HAVE SUCH A HARD TIME WITH ANYONE WHO'S NOT JEWISH, MAYBE THEY'RE NOT RIGHT FOR THIS...
BUT WHO THEN?
THE MAN WITH THE SHARP EYES!
I REMEMBER...
SAUL!
HE'S FAMILIAR WITH BOTH GREEK AND ROMAN CULTURE BUT KNOWS THE JEWISH LAW LIKE NO ONE ELSE...
HE EVEN GREW UP IN ANOTHER COUNTRY... CILICIA! IN THE CITY OF TARSUS!
I'LL LOOK FOR SAUL IN TARSUS INSTEAD OF GOING BACK TO JERUSALEM.
Tarsus
Antioch
Cyprus
Jerusalem
SO BARNABAS LEFT FOR TARSUS, SAUL'S HOMETOWN, AND FOUND HIM THERE.

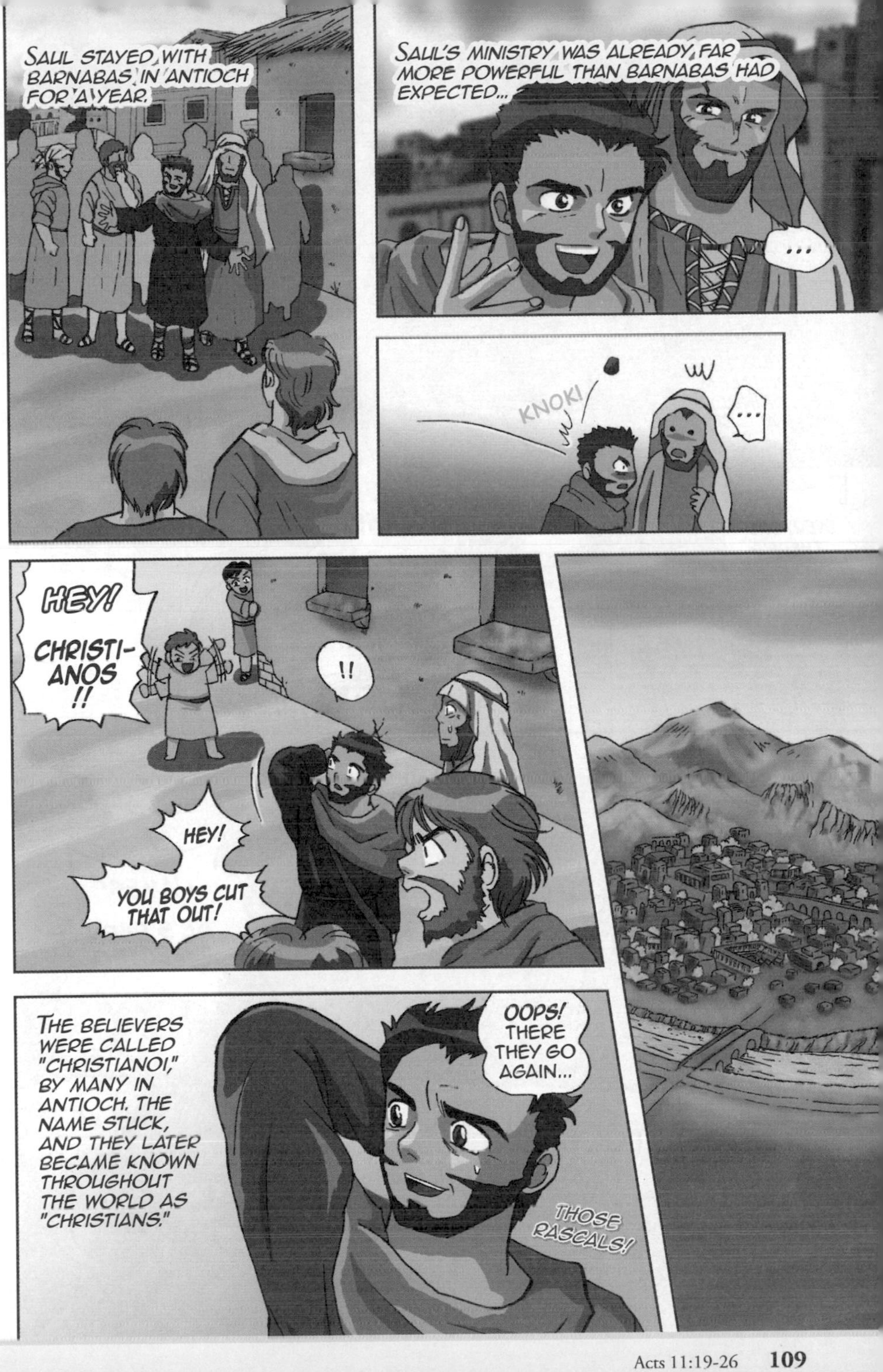

Saul stayed with Barnabas in Antioch for a year.
Saul's ministry was already far more powerful than Barnabas had expected...
...
KNOK!
...
HEY!
CHRISTI-ANOS !!
!!
HEY!
YOU BOYS CUT THAT OUT!
The believers were called "Christianoi," by many in Antioch. The name stuck, and they later became known throughout the world as "Christians."
OOPS! THERE THEY GO AGAIN...
THOSE RASCALS!

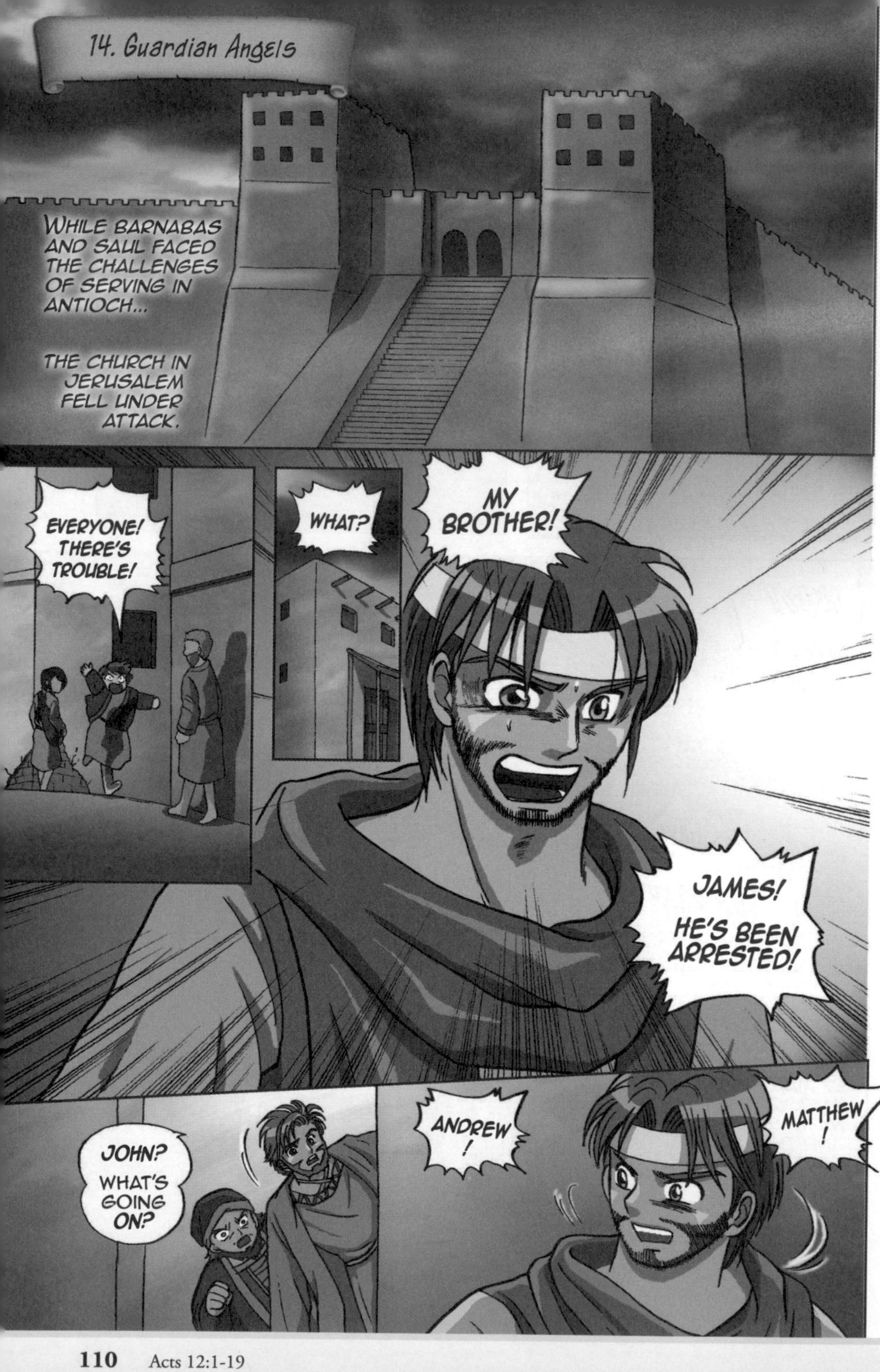
14. Guardian Angels
WHILE BARNABAS AND SAUL FACED THE CHALLENGES OF SERVING IN ANTIOCH...
THE CHURCH IN JERUSALEM FELL UNDER ATTACK.
EVERYONE! THERE'S TROUBLE!
WHAT?
MY BROTHER!
JAMES!
HE'S BEEN ARRESTED!
JOHN? WHAT'S GOING ON?
ANDREW!
MATTHEW!

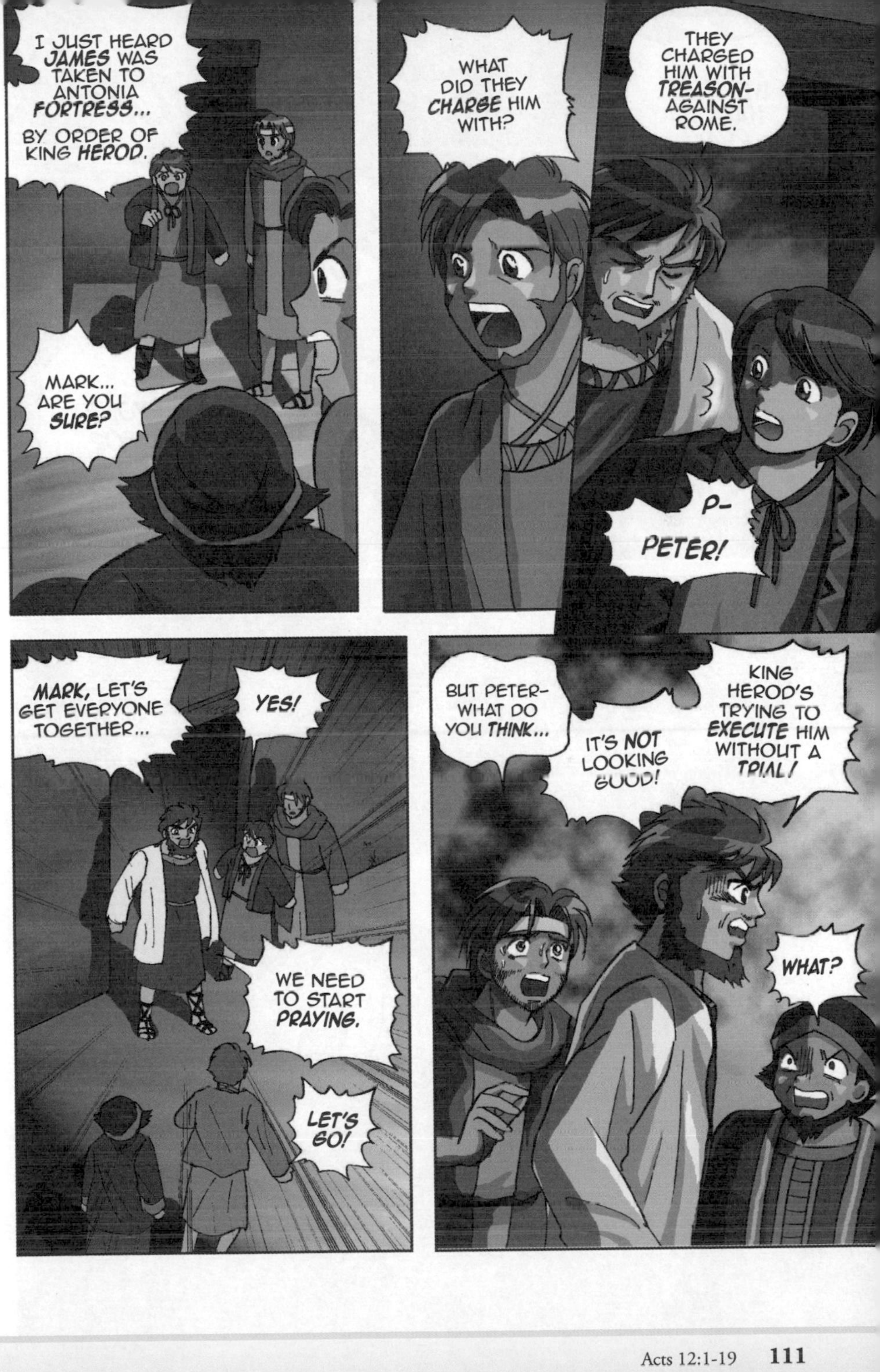
I JUST HEARD JAMES WAS TAKEN TO ANTONIA FORTRESS...
BY ORDER OF KING HEROD.
MARK... ARE YOU SURE?
WHAT DID THEY CHARGE HIM WITH?
THEY CHARGED HIM WITH TREASON-AGAINST ROME.
P-PETER!
MARK, LET'S GET EVERYONE TOGETHER...
YES!
WE NEED TO START PRAYING.
LET'S GO!
BUT PETER-WHAT DO YOU THINK...
IT'S NOT LOOKING GOOD!
KING HEROD'S TRYING TO EXECUTE HIM WITHOUT A TRIAL!
WHAT?

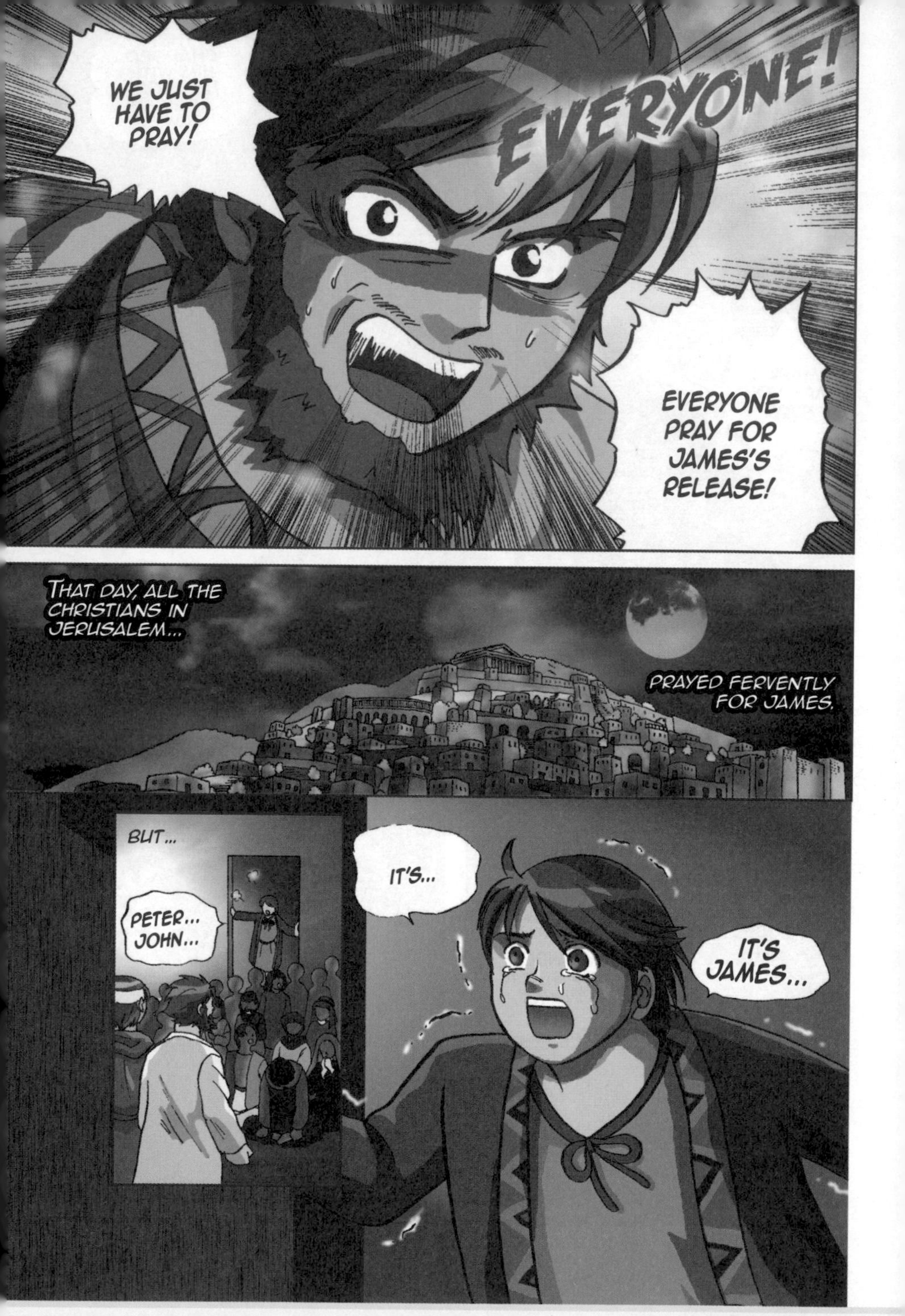
WE JUST HAVE TO PRAY!
EVERYONE!
EVERYONE PRAY FOR JAMES'S RELEASE!
THAT DAY, ALL THE CHRISTIANS IN JERUSALEM...
PRAYED FERVENTLY FOR JAMES.
BUT...
PETER... JOHN...
IT'S...
IT'S JAMES...

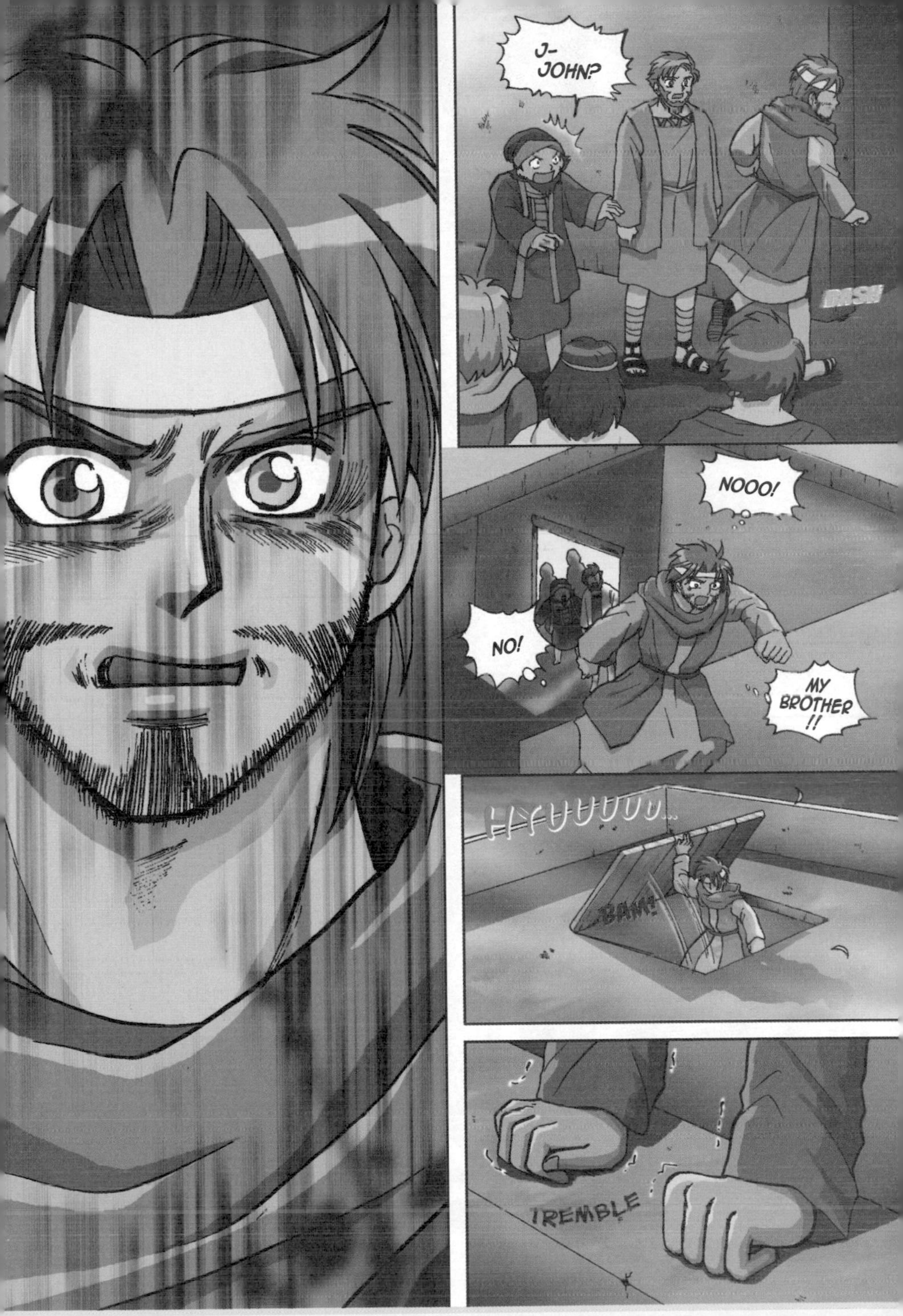
J-
JOHN?
NOOO!
NO!
MY BROTHER !!
HYUUUUU...
BAM!
TREMBLE

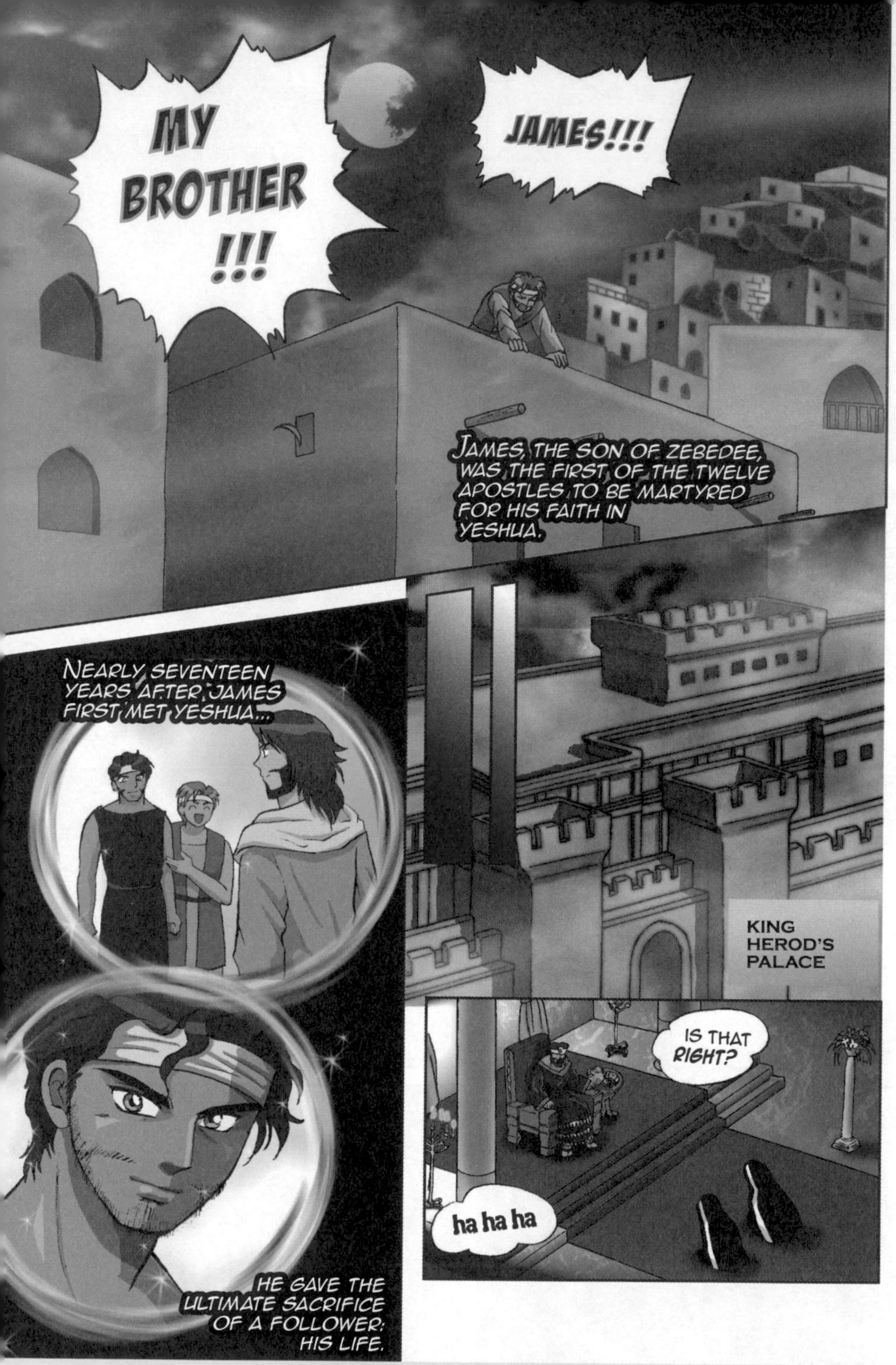
MY BROTHER !!!
JAMES!!!
JAMES, THE SON OF ZEBEDEE, WAS THE FIRST OF THE TWELVE APOSTLES TO BE MARTYRED FOR HIS FAITH IN YESHUA.
NEARLY SEVENTEEN YEARS AFTER JAMES FIRST MET YESHUA...
HE GAVE THE ULTIMATE SACRIFICE OF A FOLLOWER: HIS LIFE.
KING HEROD'S PALACE
IS THAT RIGHT?
ha ha ha

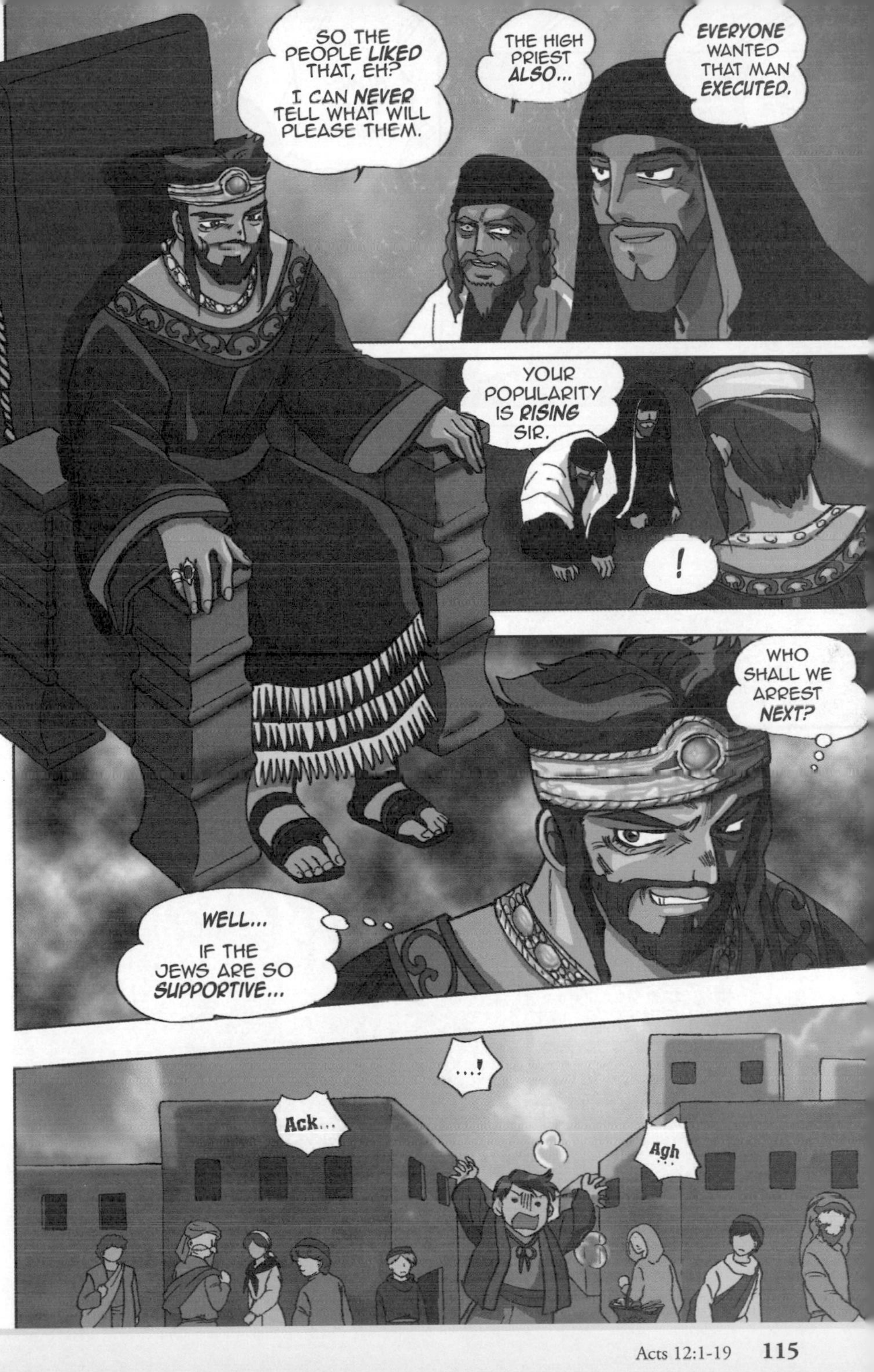
SO THE PEOPLE LIKED THAT, EH?
I CAN NEVER TELL WHAT WILL PLEASE THEM.
THE HIGH PRIEST ALSO...
EVERYONE WANTED THAT MAN EXECUTED.
YOUR POPULARITY IS RISING SIR.
!
WHO SHALL WE ARREST NEXT?
WELL...
IF THE JEWS ARE SO SUPPORTIVE...
...!
Ack...
Agh...

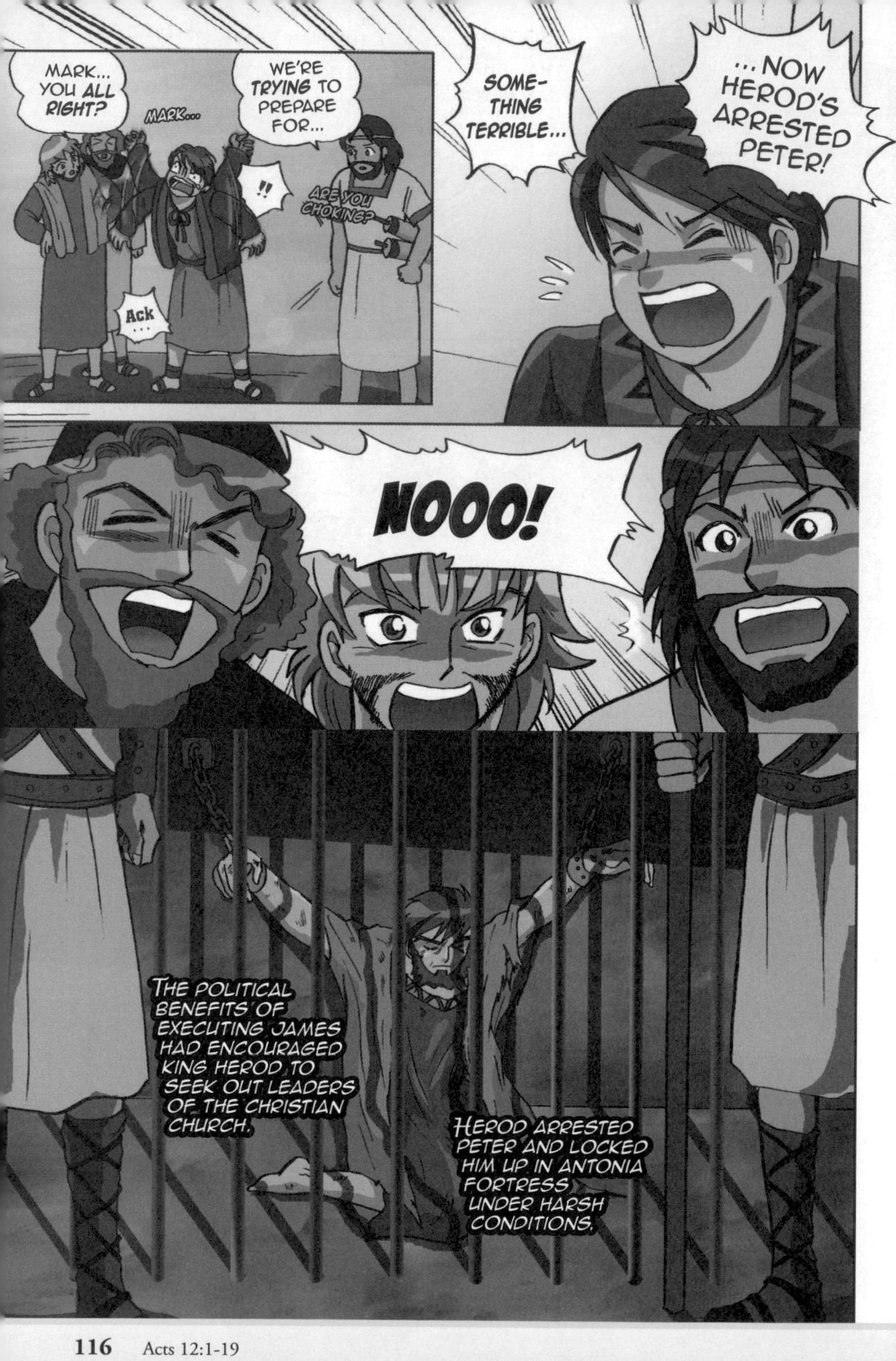
MARK... YOU ALL RIGHT?
MARK...
WE'RE TRYING TO PREPARE FOR...
!!
ARE YOU CHOKING?
Ack...
SOME-THING TERRIBLE...
...NOW HEROD'S ARRESTED PETER!
NOOO!
THE POLITICAL BENEFITS OF EXECUTING JAMES HAD ENCOURAGED KING HEROD TO SEEK OUT LEADERS OF THE CHRISTIAN CHURCH.
HEROD ARRESTED PETER AND LOCKED HIM UP IN ANTONIA FORTRESS UNDER HARSH CONDITIONS.

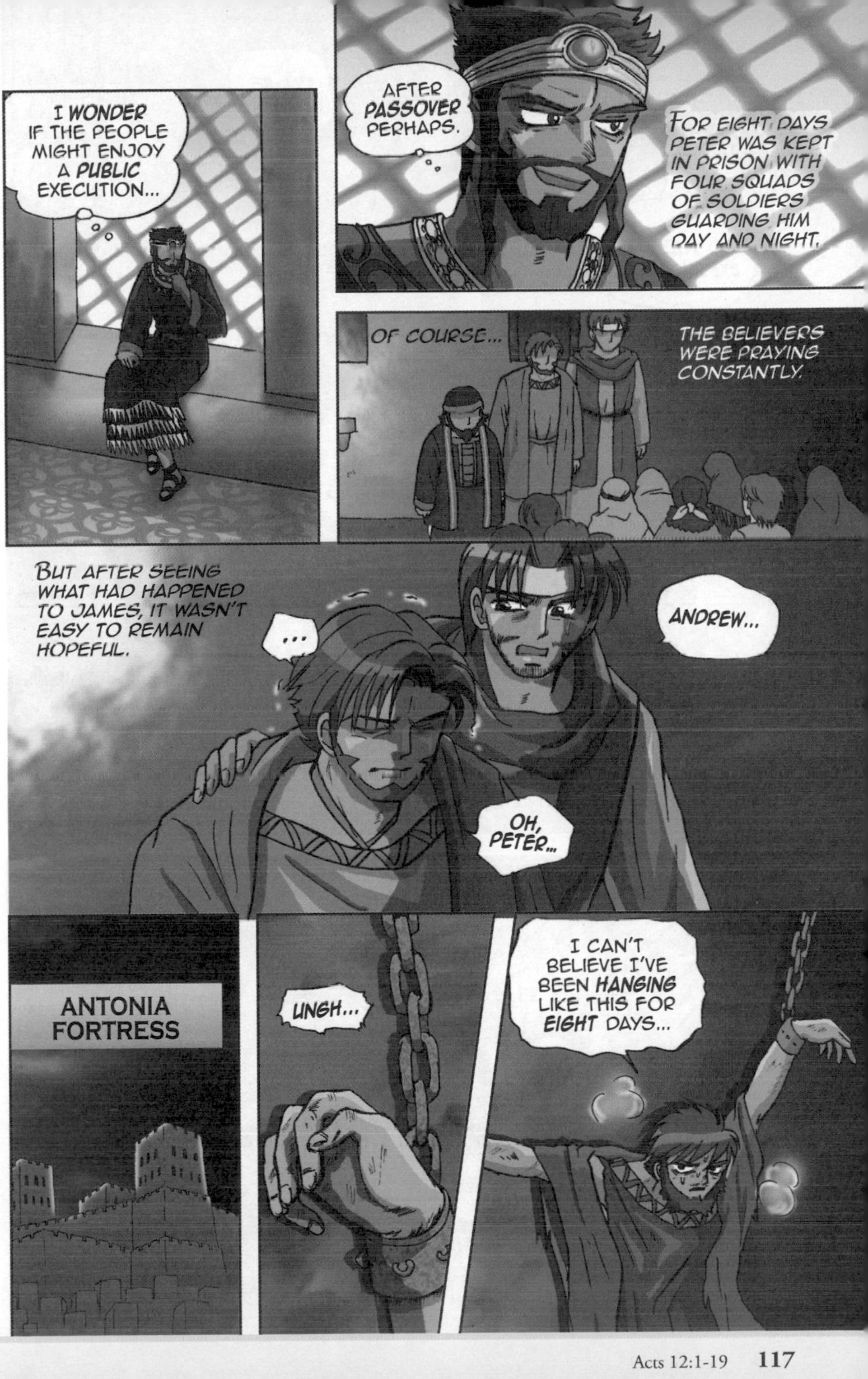
I WONDER IF THE PEOPLE MIGHT ENJOY A PUBLIC EXECUTION...
AFTER PASSOVER PERHAPS.
FOR EIGHT DAYS PETER WAS KEPT IN PRISON WITH FOUR SQUADS OF SOLDIERS GUARDING HIM DAY AND NIGHT.
OF COURSE...
THE BELIEVERS WERE PRAYING CONSTANTLY.
BUT AFTER SEEING WHAT HAD HAPPENED TO JAMES, IT WASN'T EASY TO REMAIN HOPEFUL.
...
ANDREW...
OH, PETER...
ANTONIA FORTRESS
UNGH...
I CAN'T BELIEVE I'VE BEEN HANGING LIKE THIS FOR EIGHT DAYS...

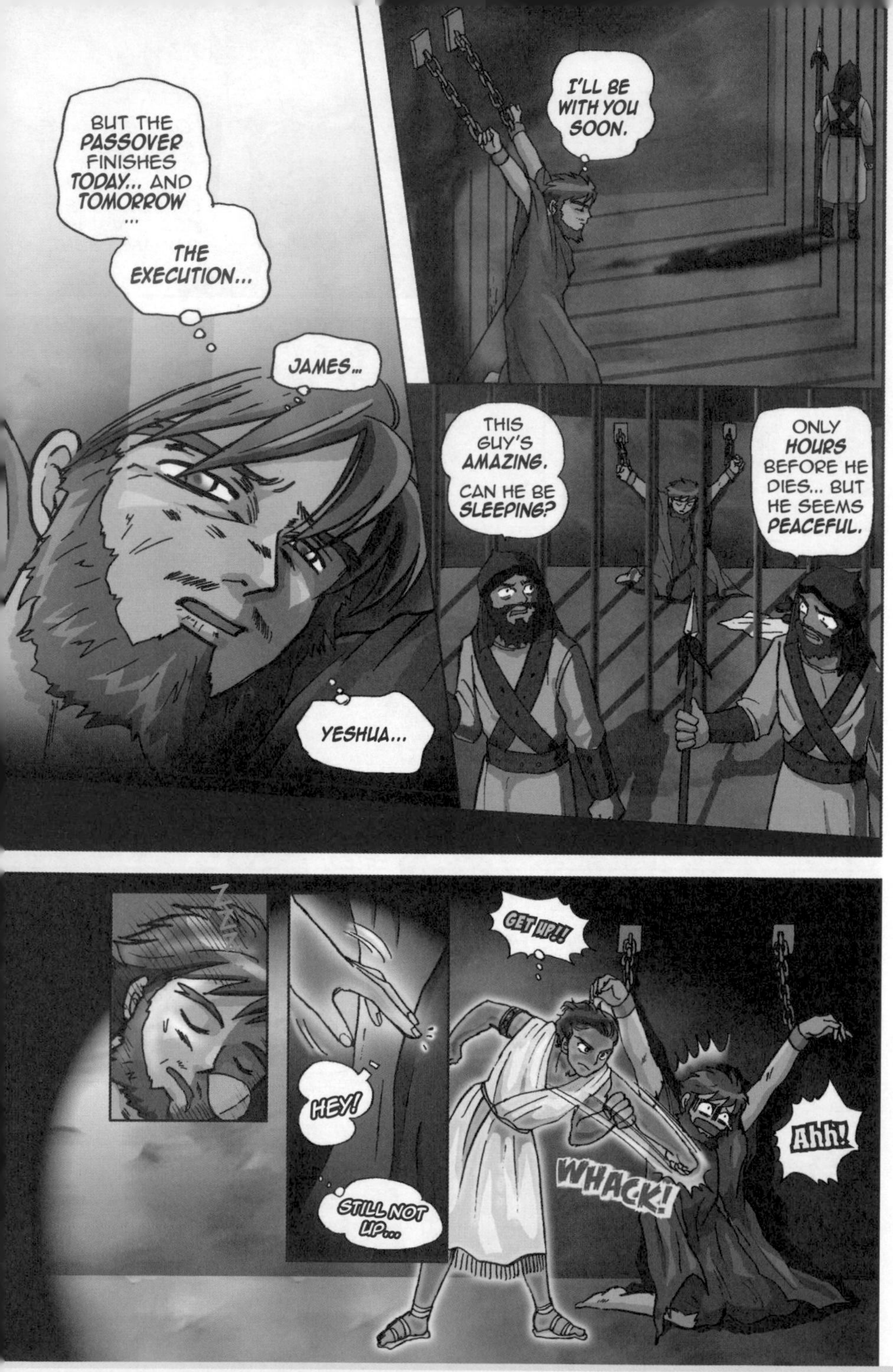
BUT THE PASSOVER FINISHES TODAY... AND TOMORROW ...
THE EXECUTION...
I'LL BE WITH YOU SOON.
JAMES...
YESHUA...
THIS GUY'S AMAZING.
CAN HE BE SLEEPING?
ONLY HOURS BEFORE HE DIES... BUT HE SEEMS PEACEFUL.
HEY!
STILL NOT UP...
GET UP!!
WHACK!
Ahh!

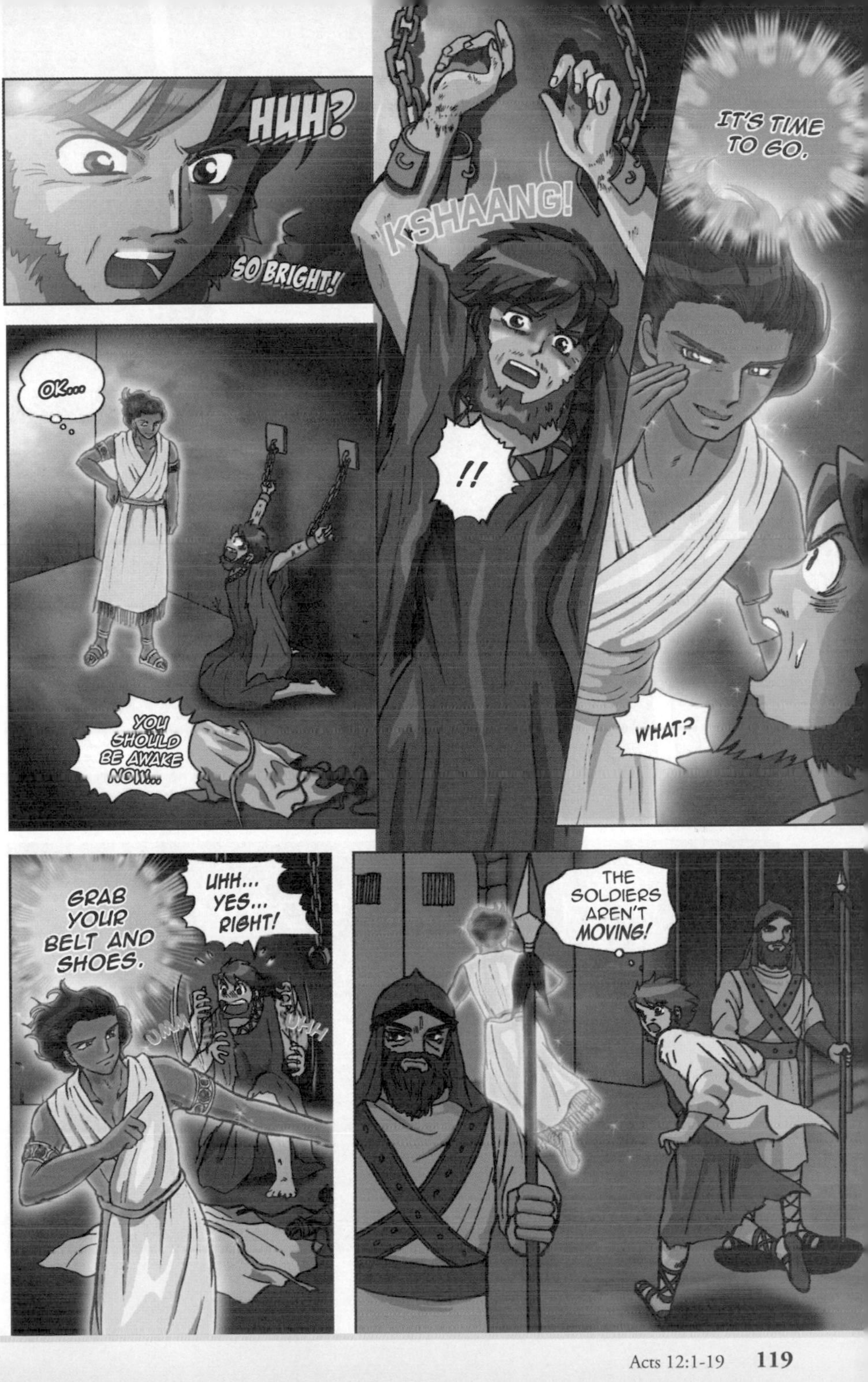
HUH?
SO BRIGHT!
KSHAANG!
IT'S TIME TO GO.
!!
OK...
WHAT?
YOU SHOULD BE AWAKE NOW...
GRAB YOUR BELT AND SHOES.
UHH... YES... RIGHT!
THE SOLDIERS AREN'T MOVING!

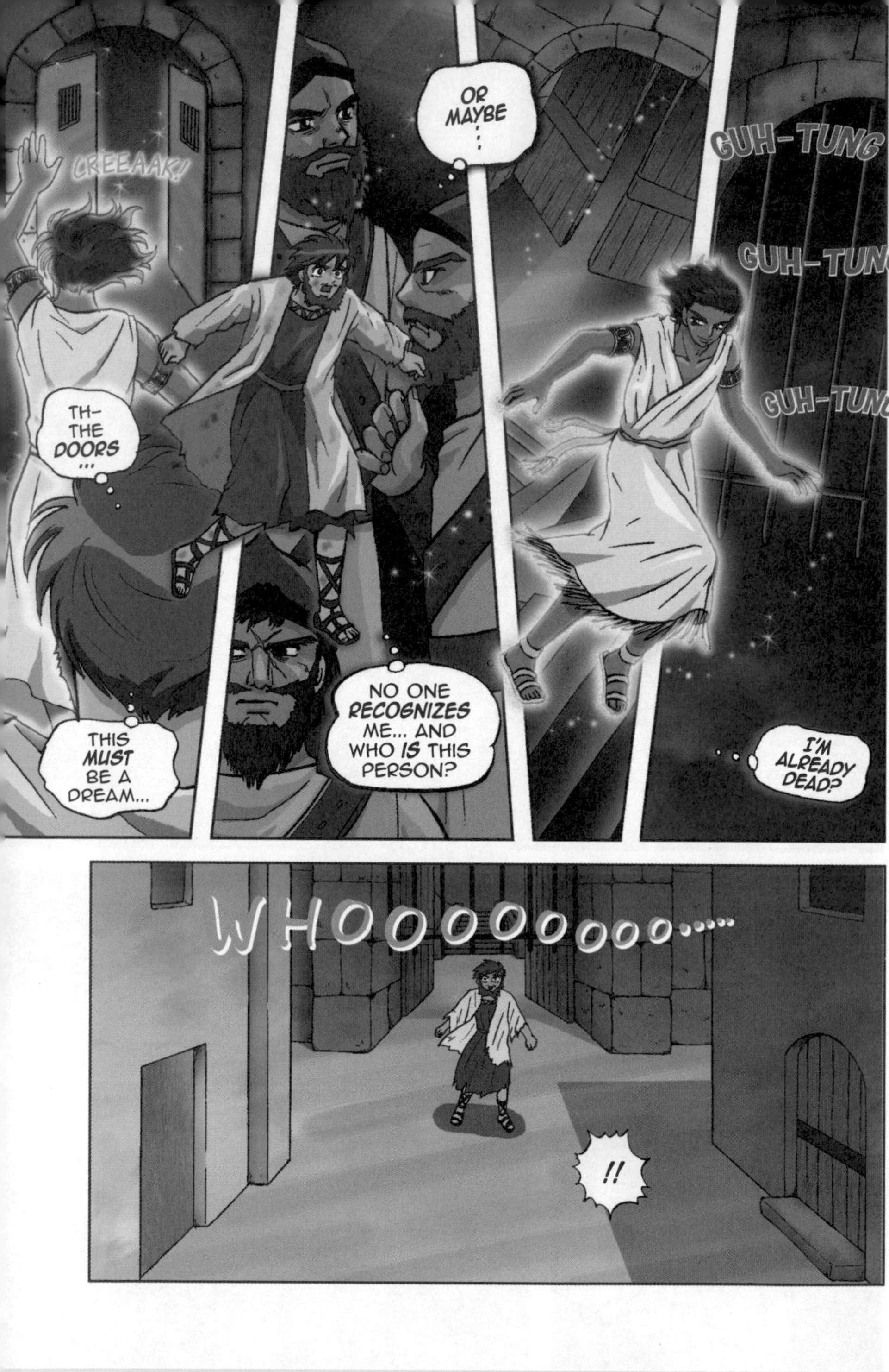
CREEAAK!
TH- THE DOORS ...
THIS MUST BE A DREAM...
NO ONE RECOGNIZES ME... AND WHO IS THIS PERSON?
OR MAYBE ...
GUH-TUNG
GUH-TUNG
GUH-TUNG
I'M ALREADY DEAD?
WHOOOOOOOOO.....
!!

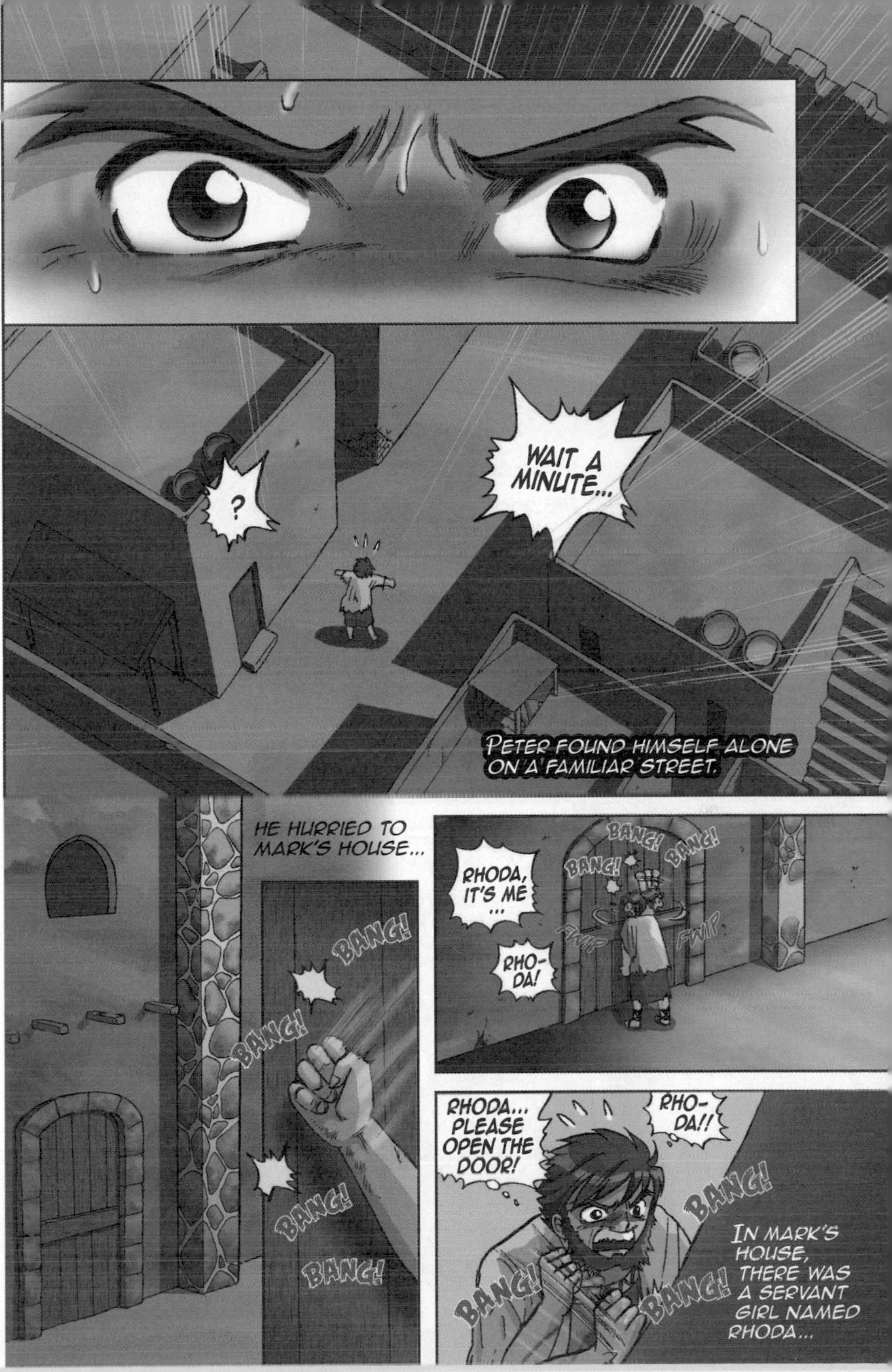
WAIT A MINUTE...
?
PETER FOUND HIMSELF ALONE ON A FAMILIAR STREET.
HE HURRIED TO MARK'S HOUSE...
BANG!
BANG!
BANG!
BANG!
BANG!
BANG!
BANG!
RHODA, IT'S ME ...
FWIP
FWIP
RHODA!
RHODA... PLEASE OPEN THE DOOR!
RHO- DA!!
BANG!
BANG!
BANG!
IN MARK'S HOUSE, THERE WAS A SERVANT GIRL NAMED RHODA...

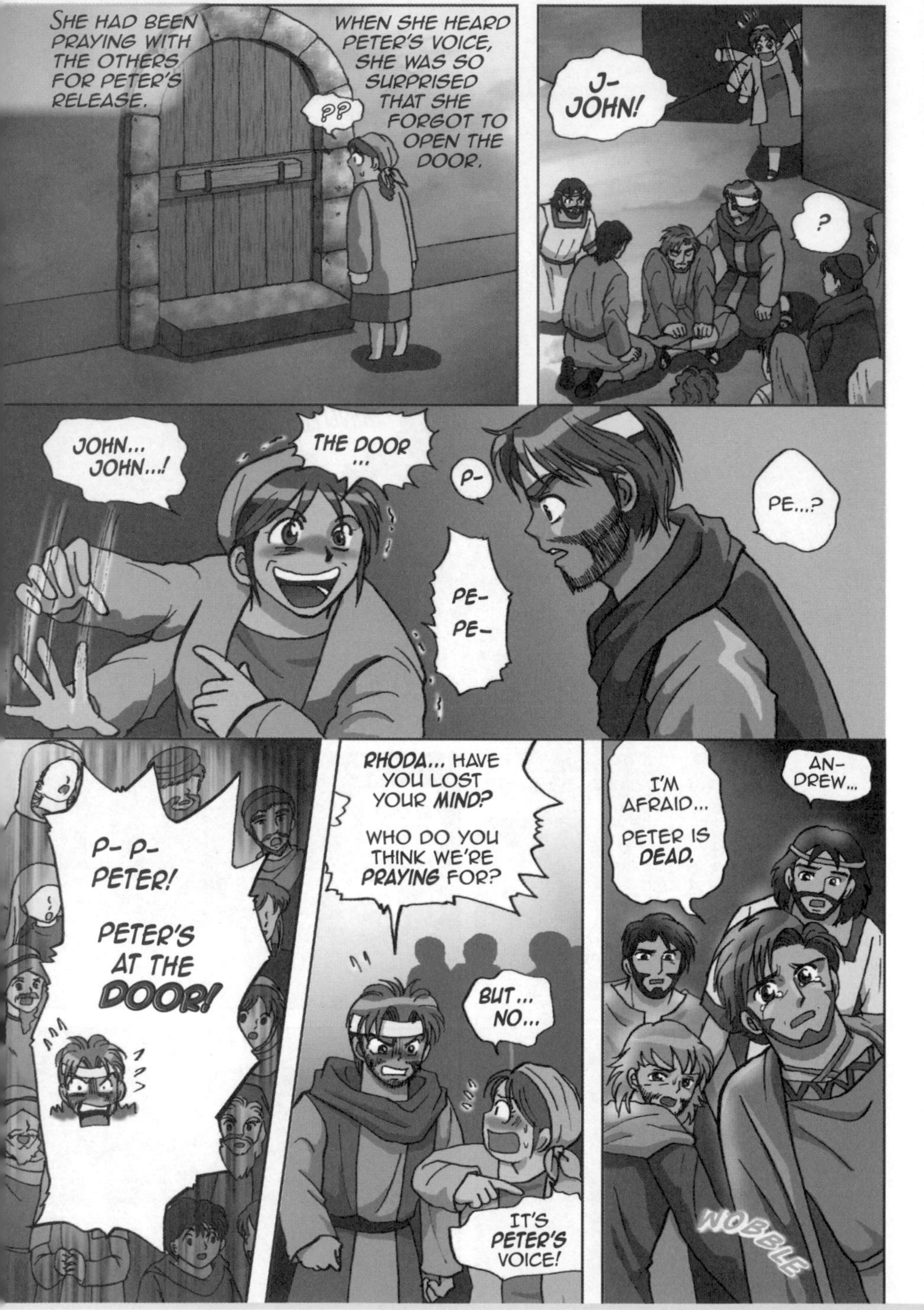
SHE HAD BEEN PRAYING WITH THE OTHERS FOR PETER'S RELEASE.
WHEN SHE HEARD PETER'S VOICE, SHE WAS SO SURPRISED THAT SHE FORGOT TO OPEN THE DOOR.
??
J- JOHN!
?
JOHN... JOHN...!
THE DOOR ...
P-
PE- PE-
PE...?
P- P- PETER!
PETER'S AT THE DOOR!
RHODA... HAVE YOU LOST YOUR MIND?
WHO DO YOU THINK WE'RE PRAYING FOR?
BUT... NO...
IT'S PETER'S VOICE!
I'M AFRAID...
PETER IS DEAD.
AN- DREW...
WOBBLE

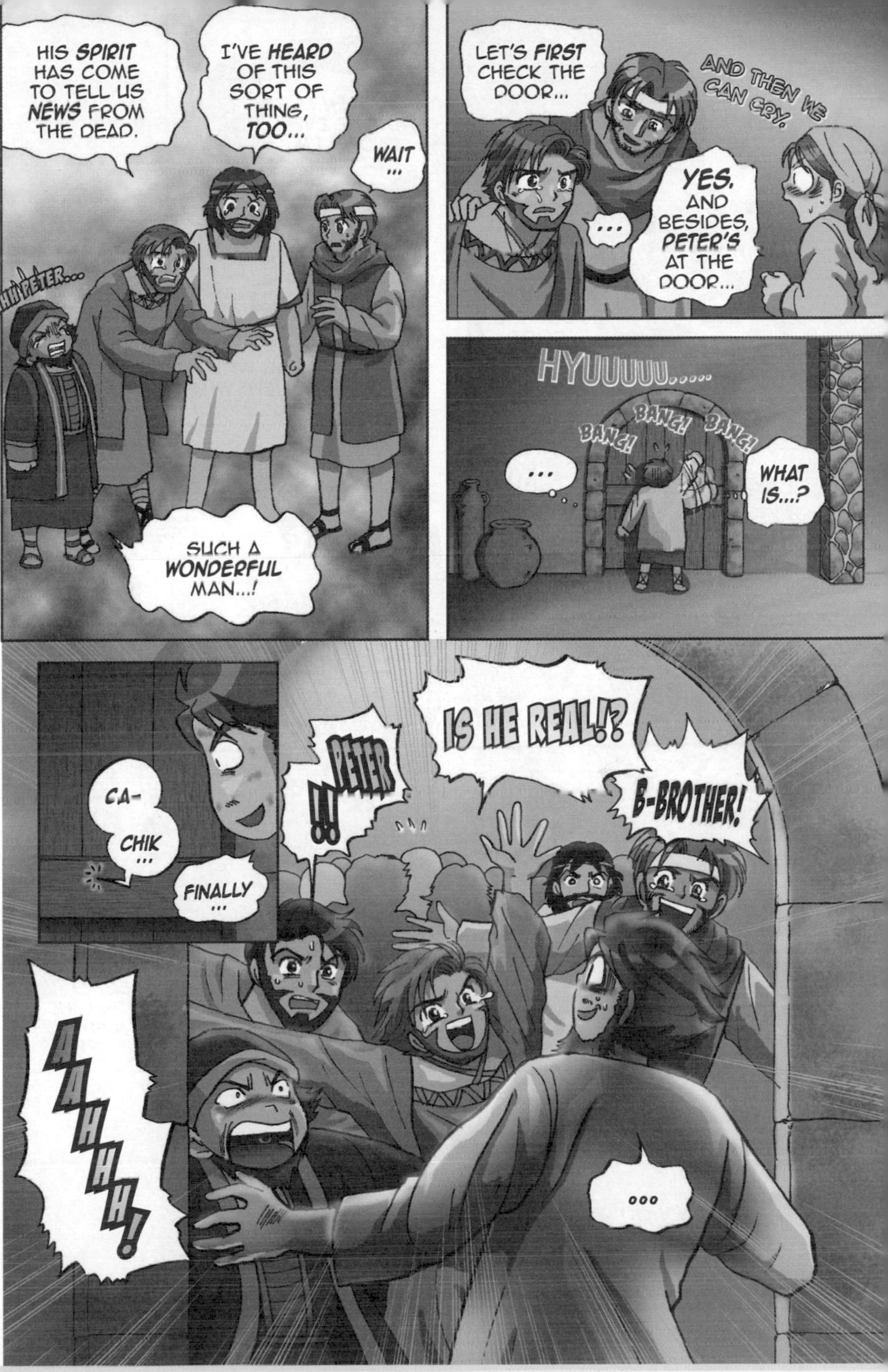

HIS SPIRIT HAS COME TO TELL US NEWS FROM THE DEAD.
I'VE HEARD OF THIS SORT OF THING, TOO...
WAIT ...
OHHH PETER...
SUCH A WONDERFUL MAN...!
LET'S FIRST CHECK THE DOOR...
AND THEN WE CAN CRY.
...
YES. AND BESIDES, PETER'S AT THE DOOR...
HYUUUUU.....
BANG! BANG! BANG!
...
WHAT IS...?
CA-
CHIK ...
FINALLY ...
!! PETER
IS HE REAL!?
B-BROTHER!
AAHHHH!
...

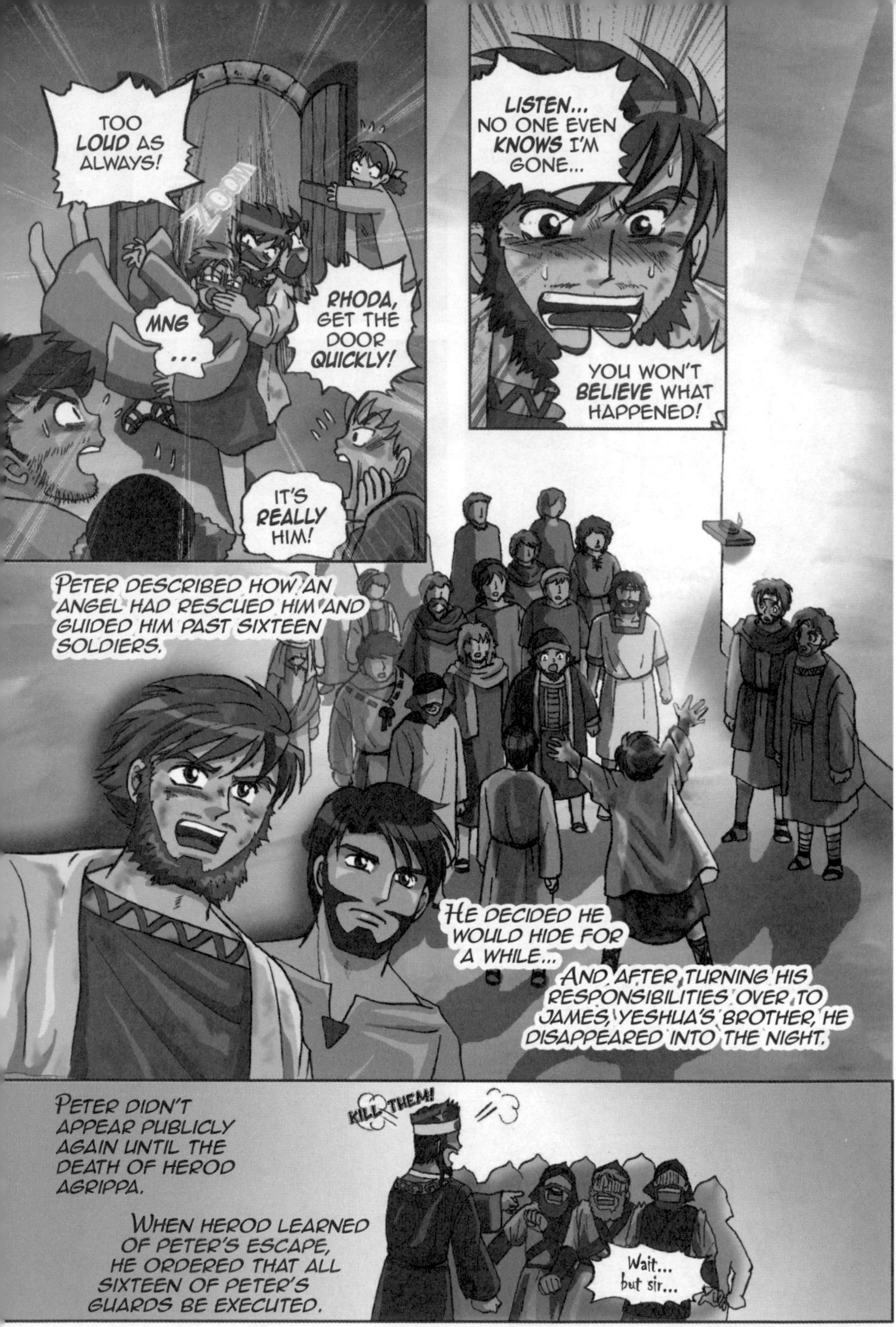
TOO LOUD AS ALWAYS!
ZOOM
MNG ...
RHODA, GET THE DOOR QUICKLY!
IT'S REALLY HIM!
LISTEN... NO ONE EVEN KNOWS I'M GONE...
YOU WON'T BELIEVE WHAT HAPPENED!
PETER DESCRIBED HOW AN ANGEL HAD RESCUED HIM AND GUIDED HIM PAST SIXTEEN SOLDIERS.
HE DECIDED HE WOULD HIDE FOR A WHILE...
AND AFTER TURNING HIS RESPONSIBILITIES OVER TO JAMES, YESHUA'S BROTHER, HE DISAPPEARED INTO THE NIGHT.
PETER DIDN'T APPEAR PUBLICLY AGAIN UNTIL THE DEATH OF HEROD AGRIPPA.
KILL THEM!
WHEN HEROD LEARNED OF PETER'S ESCAPE, HE ORDERED THAT ALL SIXTEEN OF PETER'S GUARDS BE EXECUTED.
Wait... but sir...

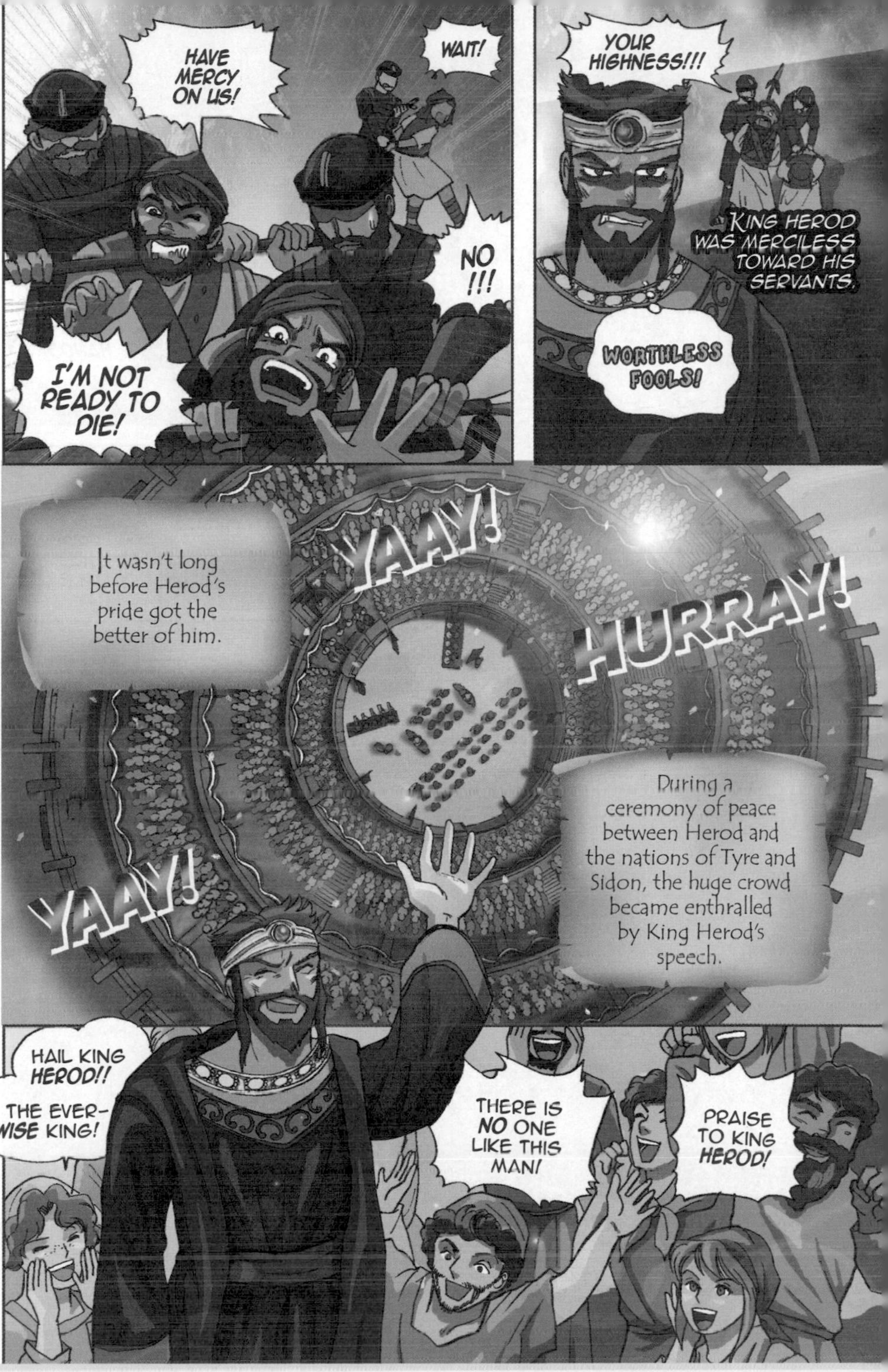
HAVE MERCY ON US!
WAIT!
NO !!!
I'M NOT READY TO DIE!
YOUR HIGHNESS!!!
KING HEROD WAS MERCILESS TOWARD HIS SERVANTS.
WORTHLESS FOOLS!
It wasn't long before Herod's pride got the better of him.
YAAY!
HURRAY!
YAAY!
During a ceremony of peace between Herod and the nations of Tyre and Sidon, the huge crowd became enthralled by King Herod's speech.
HAIL KING HEROD!!
THE EVER-WISE KING!
THERE IS NO ONE LIKE THIS MAN!
PRAISE TO KING HEROD!

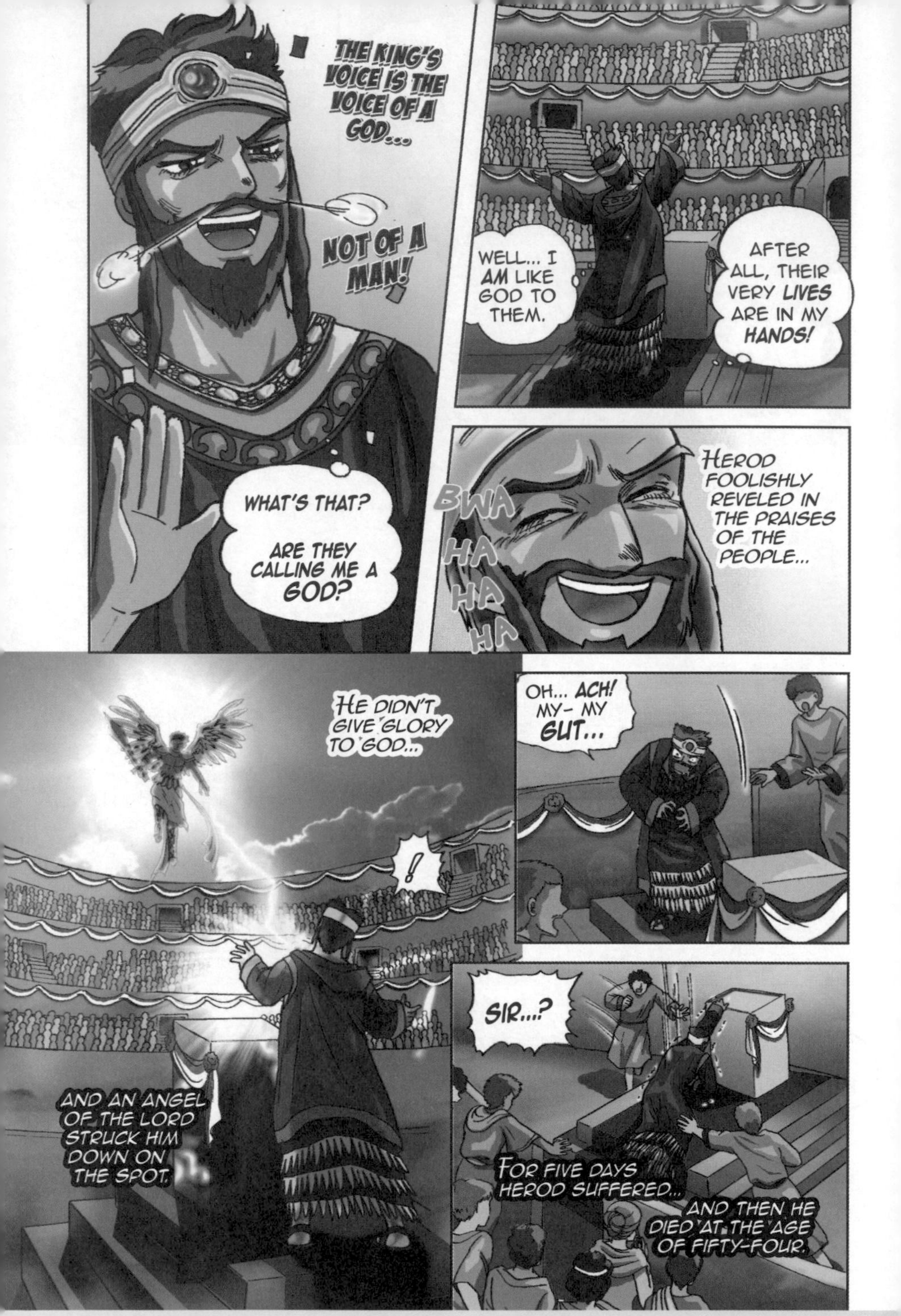
THE KING'S VOICE IS THE VOICE OF A GOD...
NOT OF A MAN!
WHAT'S THAT?
ARE THEY CALLING ME A GOD?
WELL... I AM LIKE GOD TO THEM.
AFTER ALL, THEIR VERY LIVES ARE IN MY HANDS!
HEROD FOOLISHLY REVELED IN THE PRAISES OF THE PEOPLE...
BWA HA HA HA
HE DIDN'T GIVE GLORY TO GOD...
!
AND AN ANGEL OF THE LORD STRUCK HIM DOWN ON THE SPOT.
OH... ACH! MY- MY GUT...
SIR...?
FOR FIVE DAYS HEROD SUFFERED...
AND THEN HE DIED AT THE AGE OF FIFTY-FOUR.

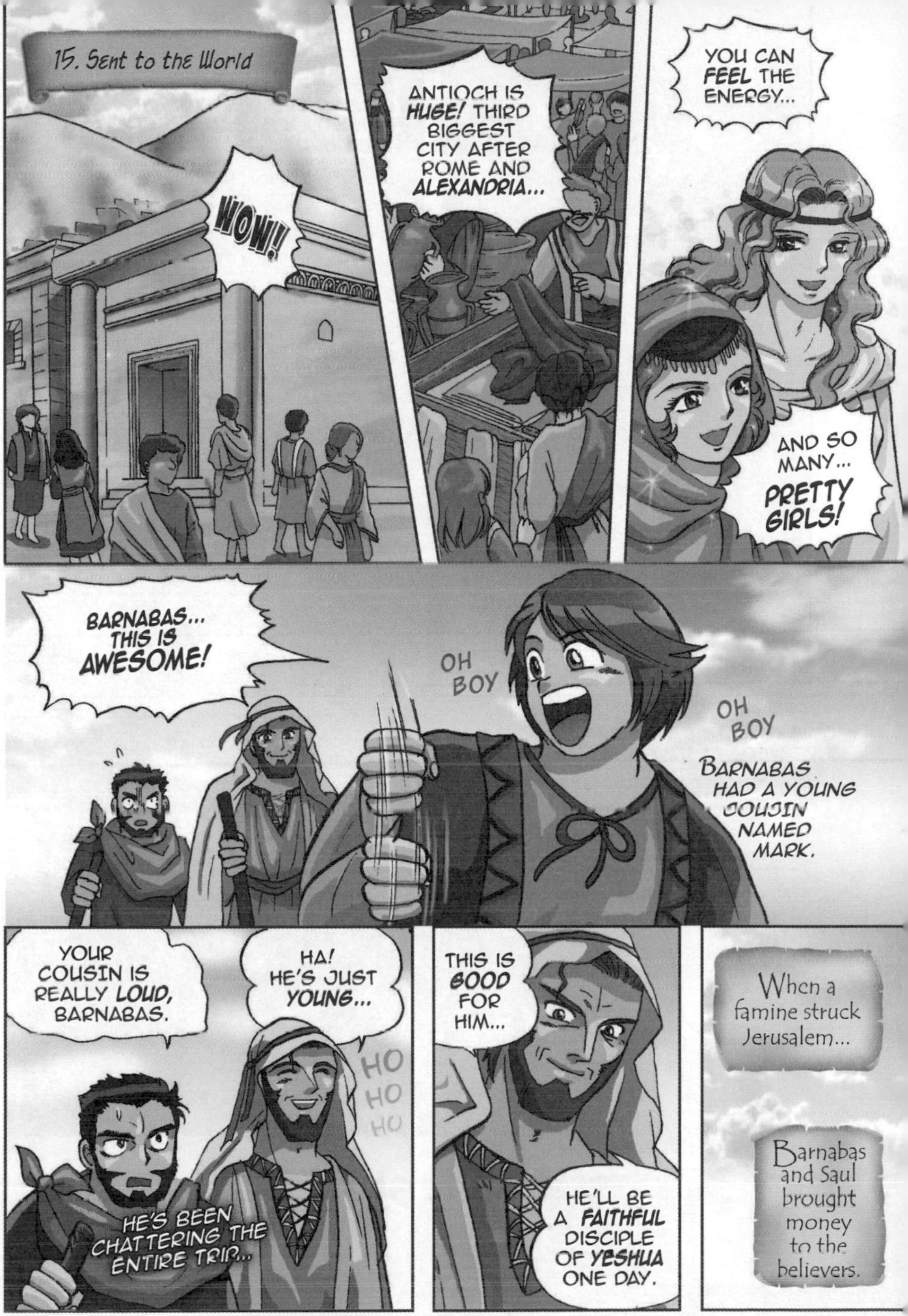
15. Sent to the World
WOW!
ANTIOCH IS HUGE! THIRD BIGGEST CITY AFTER ROME AND ALEXANDRIA...
YOU CAN FEEL THE ENERGY...
AND SO MANY... PRETTY GIRLS!
BARNABAS... THIS IS AWESOME!
OH BOY
OH BOY
BARNABAS HAD A YOUNG COUSIN NAMED MARK.
YOUR COUSIN IS REALLY LOUD, BARNABAS.
HA! HE'S JUST YOUNG...
HO HO HO
HE'S BEEN CHATTERING THE ENTIRE TRIP...
THIS IS GOOD FOR HIM...
HE'LL BE A FAITHFUL DISCIPLE OF YESHUA ONE DAY.
When a famine struck Jerusalem...
Barnabas and Saul brought money to the believers.

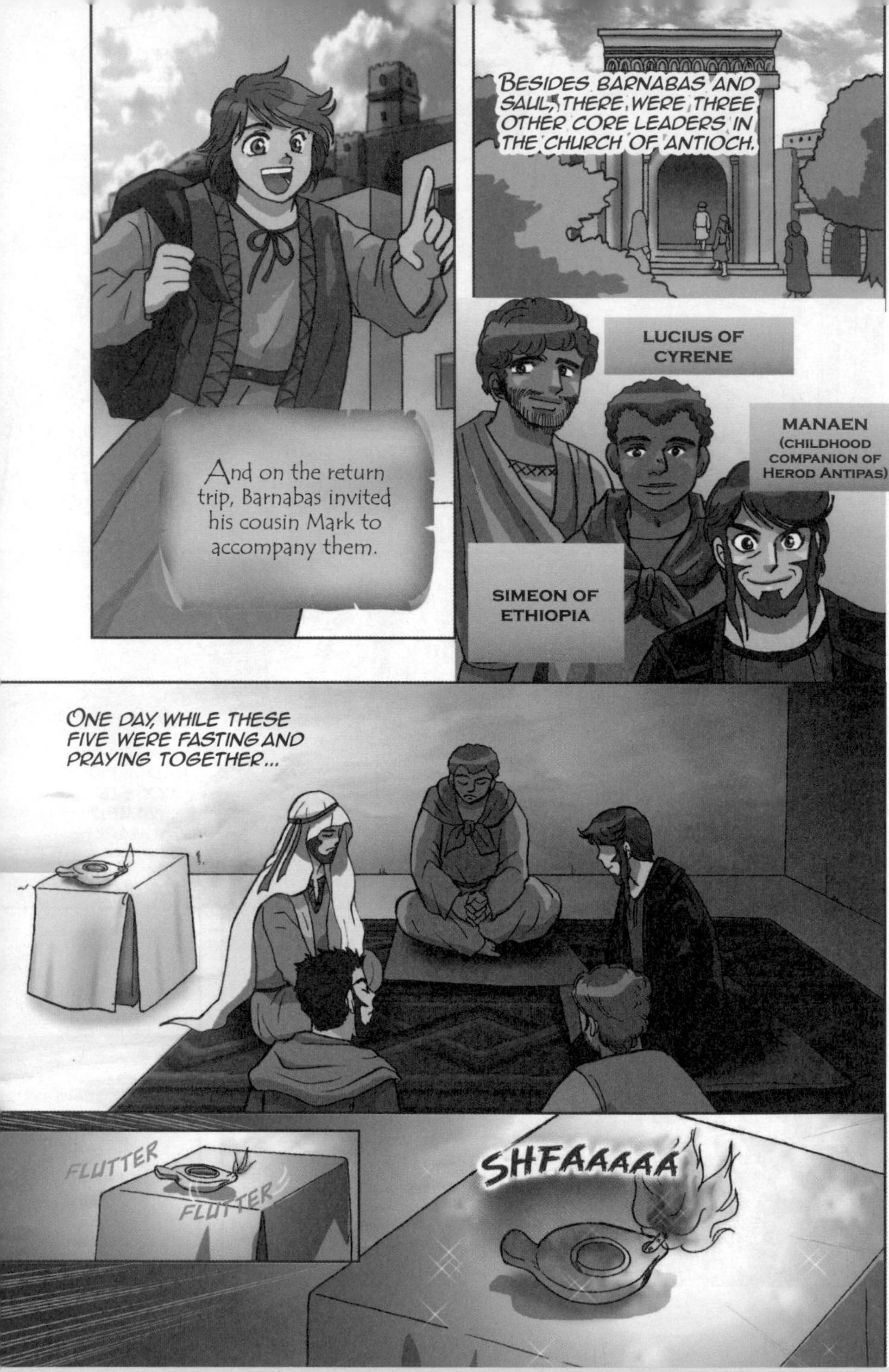
And on the return trip, Barnabas invited his cousin Mark to accompany them.
BESIDES BARNABAS AND SAUL, THERE WERE THREE OTHER CORE LEADERS IN THE CHURCH OF ANTIOCH.
LUCIUS OF CYRENE
MANAEN (CHILDHOOD COMPANION OF HEROD ANTIPAS)
SIMEON OF ETHIOPIA
ONE DAY, WHILE THESE FIVE WERE FASTING AND PRAYING TOGETHER...
FLUTTER
FLUTTER
SHFAAAAA

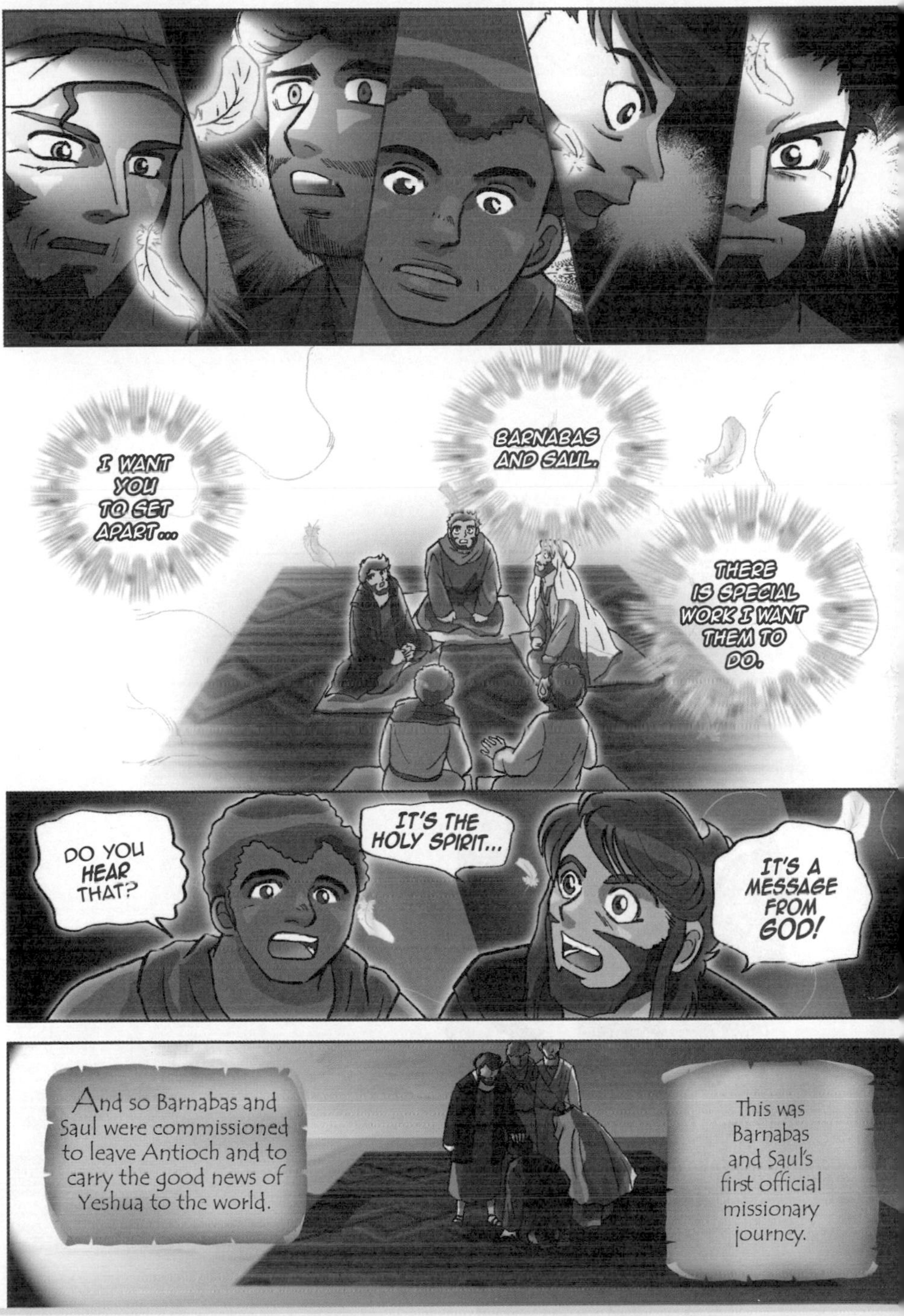
I WANT YOU TO SET APART...
BARNABAS AND SAUL.
THERE IS SPECIAL WORK I WANT THEM TO DO.
DO YOU HEAR THAT?
IT'S THE HOLY SPIRIT...
IT'S A MESSAGE FROM GOD!
And so Barnabas and Saul were commissioned to leave Antioch and to carry the good news of Yeshua to the world.
This was Barnabas and Saul's first official missionary journey.

Chapter II

16. Unstoppable Good News

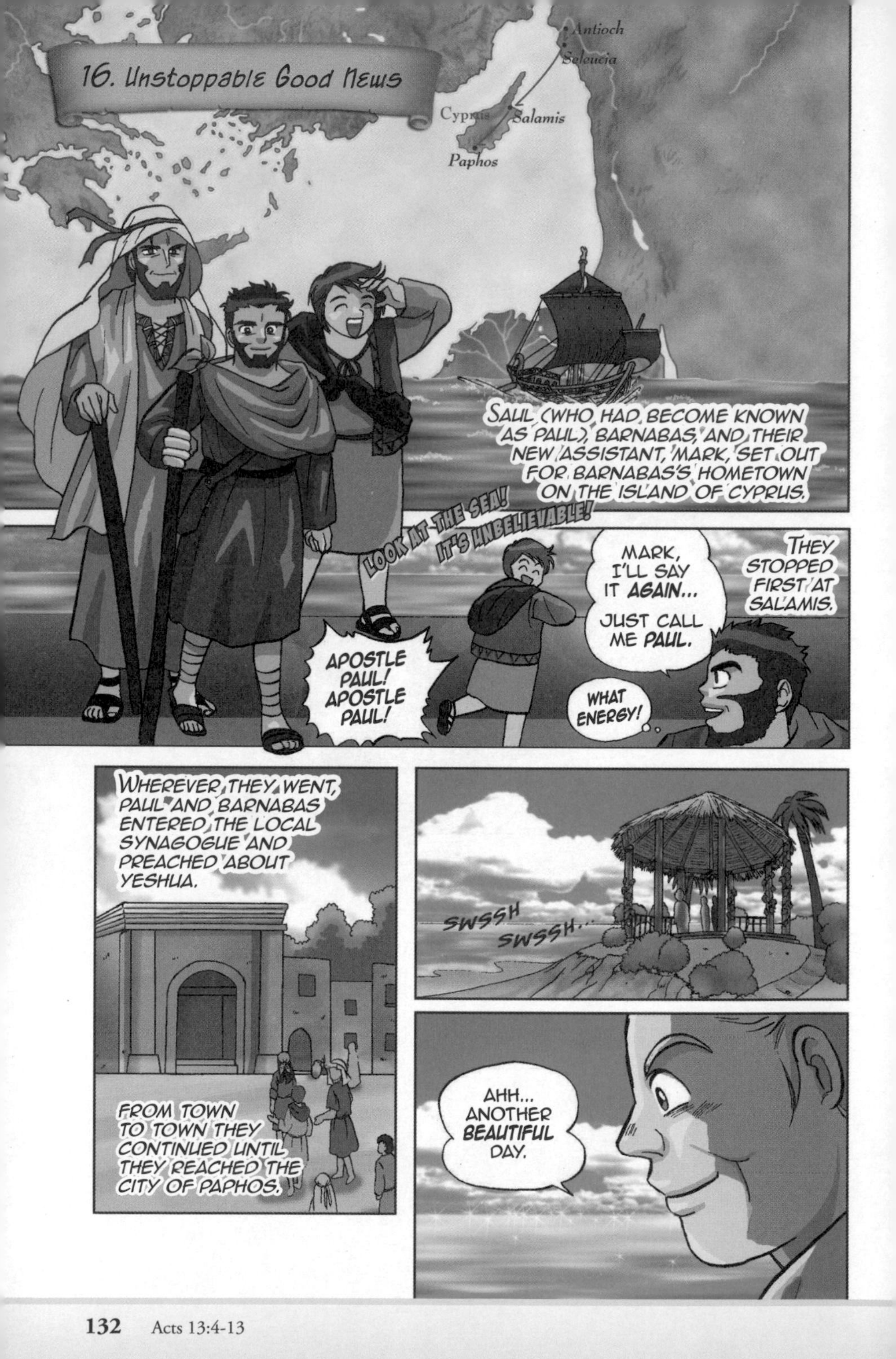

Antioch
Seleucia
Cyprus
Salamis
Paphos
Saul (who had become known as Paul), Barnabas, and their new assistant, Mark, set out for Barnabas's hometown on the island of Cyprus.
They stopped first at Salamis.
Look at the sea! It's unbelievable!
Mark, I'll say it again... Just call me Paul.
Apostle Paul! Apostle Paul!
What energy!
Wherever they went, Paul and Barnabas entered the local synagogue and preached about Yeshua.
From town to town they continued until they reached the city of Paphos.
Swssh swssh...
Ahh... another beautiful day.

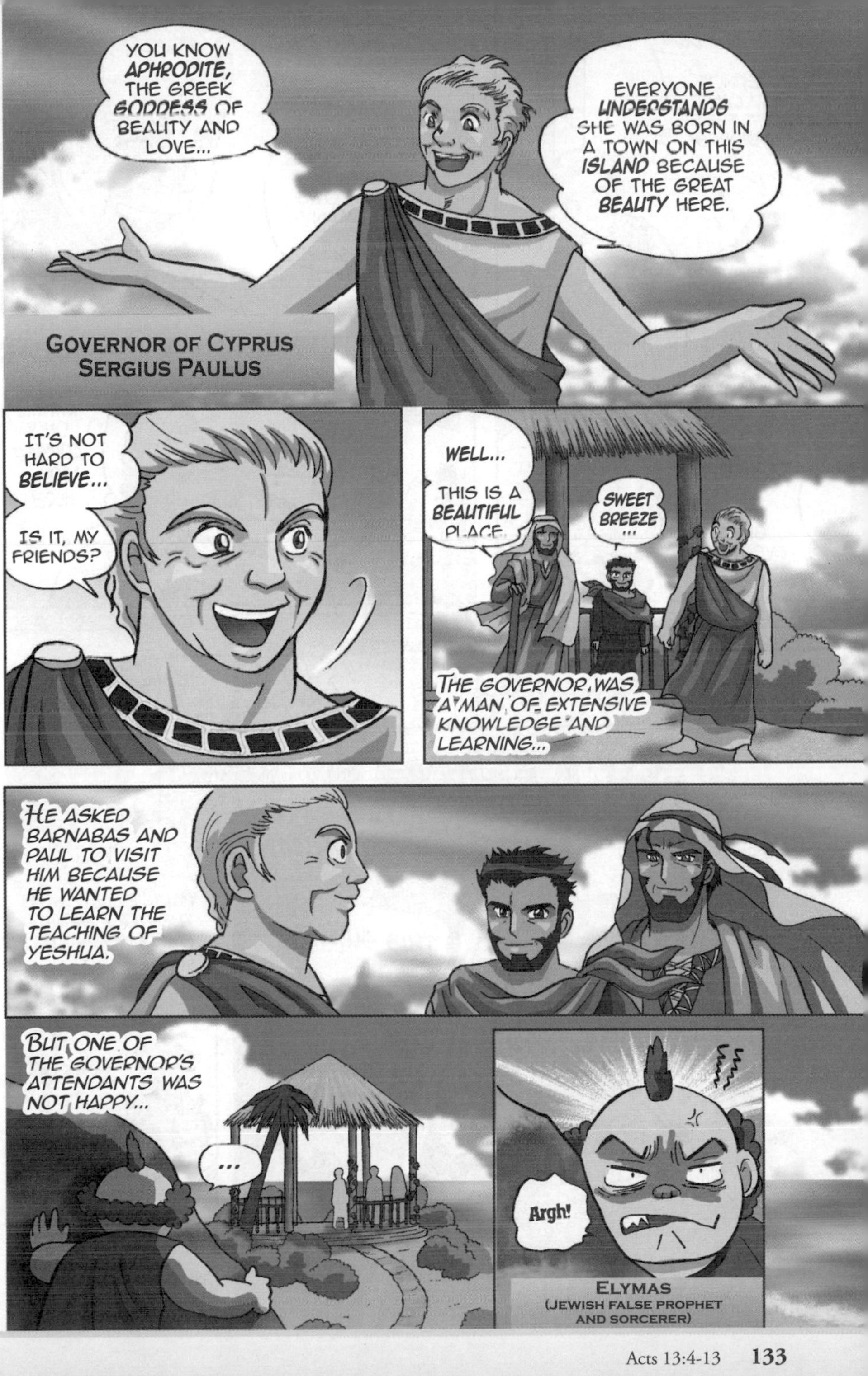
YOU KNOW APHRODITE, THE GREEK GODDESS OF BEAUTY AND LOVE...
EVERYONE UNDERSTANDS SHE WAS BORN IN A TOWN ON THIS ISLAND BECAUSE OF THE GREAT BEAUTY HERE.
GOVERNOR OF CYPRUS SERGIUS PAULUS
IT'S NOT HARD TO BELIEVE...
IS IT, MY FRIENDS?
WELL...
THIS IS A BEAUTIFUL PLACE.
SWEET BREEZE ...
THE GOVERNOR WAS A MAN OF EXTENSIVE KNOWLEDGE AND LEARNING...
HE ASKED BARNABAS AND PAUL TO VISIT HIM BECAUSE HE WANTED TO LEARN THE TEACHING OF YESHUA.
BUT ONE OF THE GOVERNOR'S ATTENDANTS WAS NOT HAPPY...
...
Argh!
ELYMAS (JEWISH FALSE PROPHET AND SORCERER)

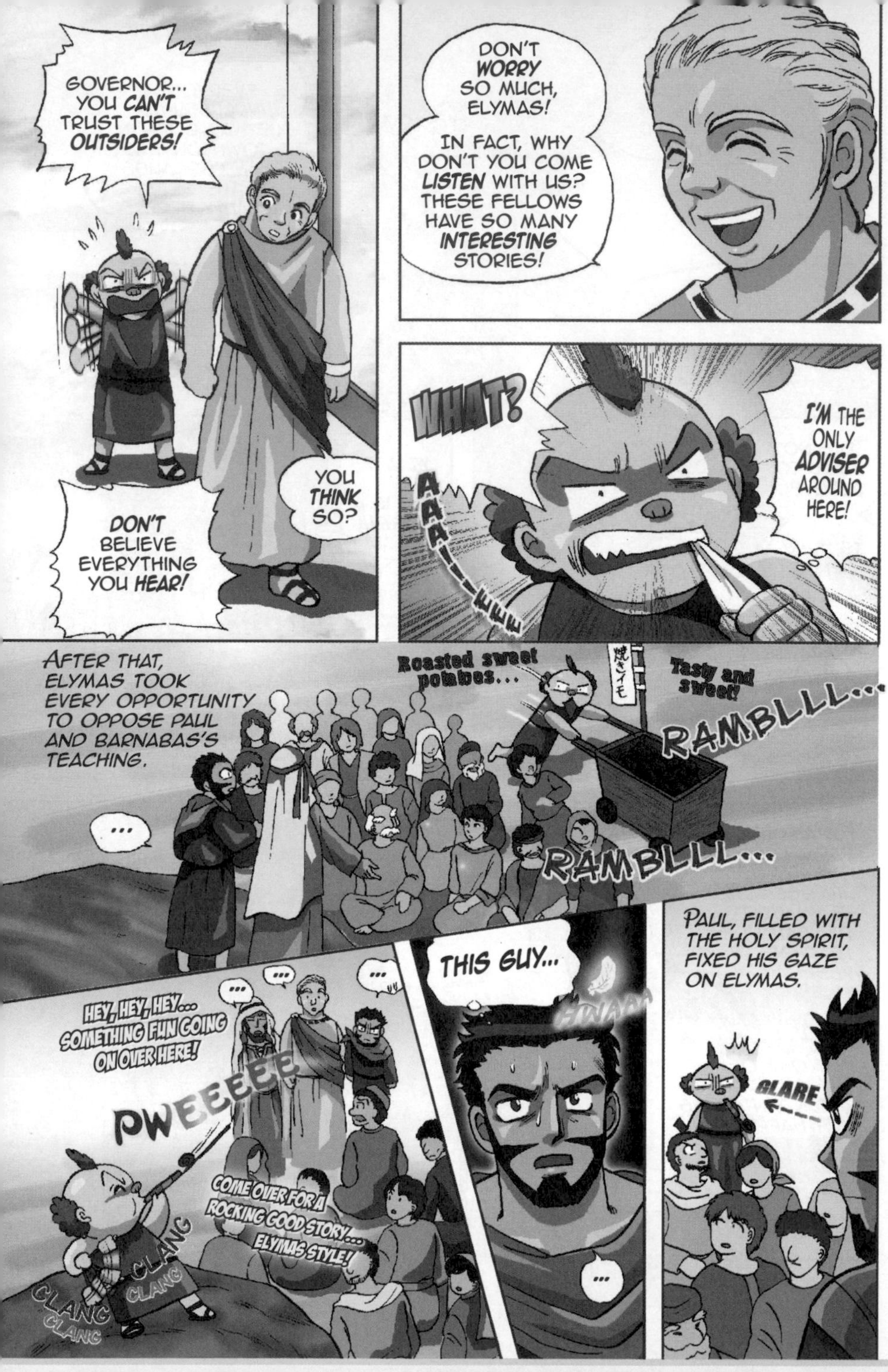
GOVERNOR... YOU CAN'T TRUST THESE OUTSIDERS!
DON'T WORRY SO MUCH, ELYMAS!
IN FACT, WHY DON'T YOU COME LISTEN WITH US? THESE FELLOWS HAVE SO MANY INTERESTING STORIES!
DON'T BELIEVE EVERYTHING YOU HEAR!
YOU THINK SO?
WHAT?
I'M THE ONLY ADVISER AROUND HERE!
AAAII...WWW
AFTER THAT, ELYMAS TOOK EVERY OPPORTUNITY TO OPPOSE PAUL AND BARNABAS'S TEACHING.
Roasted sweet potatoes...
焼きイモ
Tasty and sweet!
RAMBLLL...
RAMBLLL...
...
HEY, HEY, HEY... SOMETHING FUN GOING ON OVER HERE!
...
...
...
PWEEEEE
COME OVER FOR A ROCKING GOOD STORY... ELYMAS STYLE!
CLANG CLANG
CLANG CLANG
THIS GUY...
...
PAUL, FILLED WITH THE HOLY SPIRIT, FIXED HIS GAZE ON ELYMAS.
GLARE

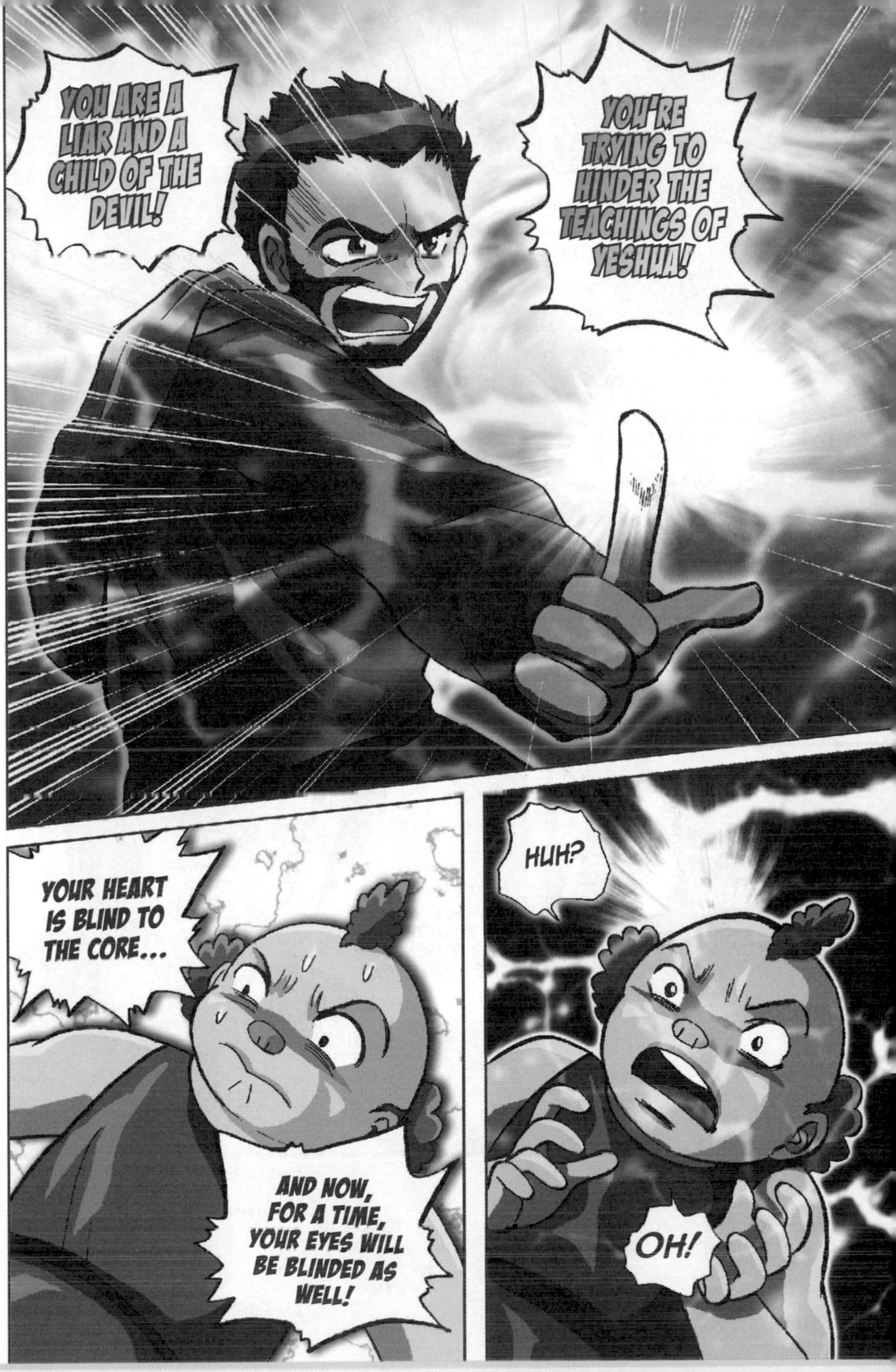
YOU ARE A LIAR AND A CHILD OF THE DEVIL!
YOU'RE TRYING TO HINDER THE TEACHINGS OF YESHUA!
YOUR HEART IS BLIND TO THE CORE...
AND NOW, FOR A TIME, YOUR EYES WILL BE BLINDED AS WELL!
HUH?
OH!

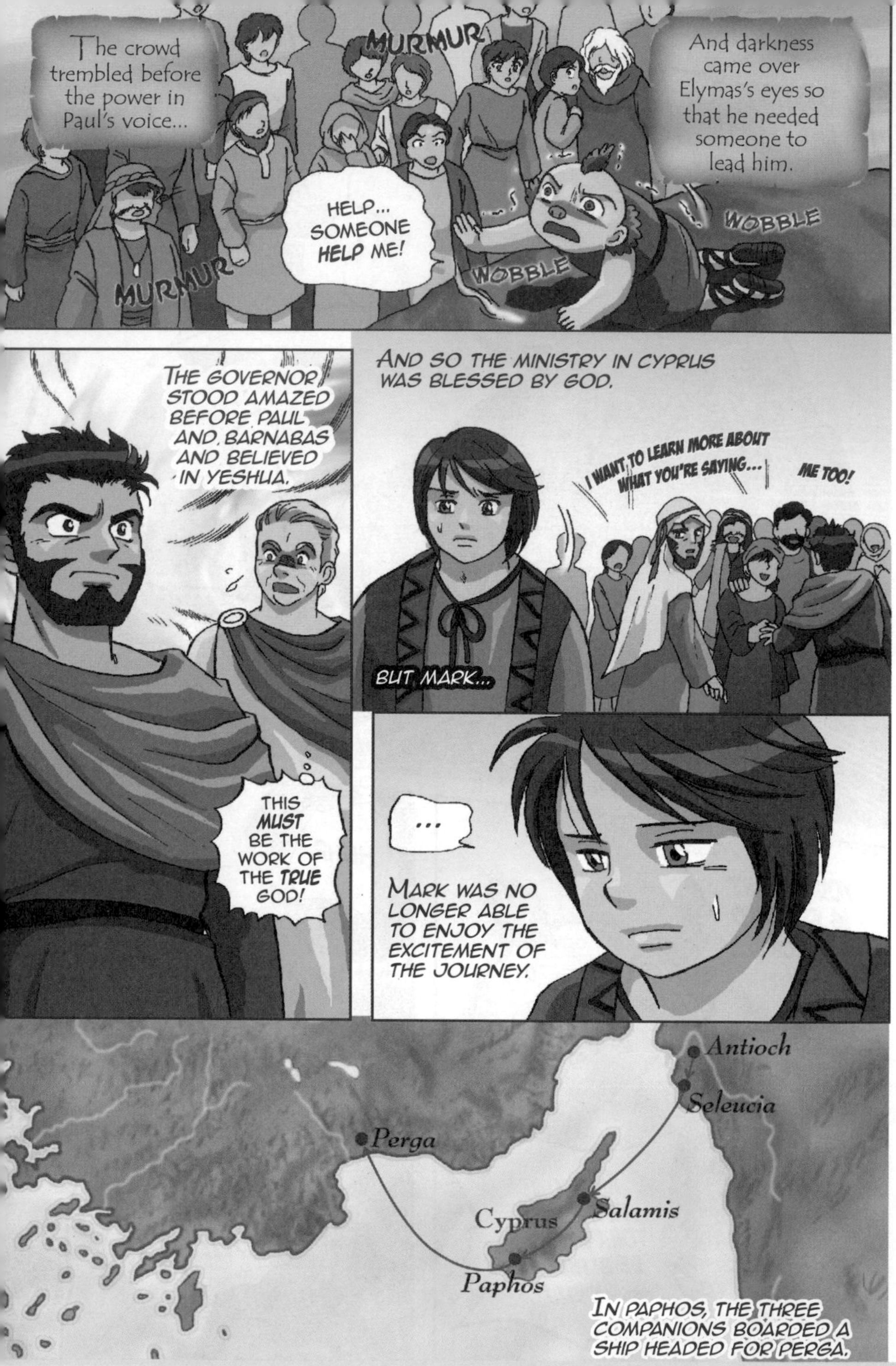

The crowd trembled before the power in Paul's voice...
MURMUR
MURMUR
HELP... SOMEONE HELP ME!
WOBBLE
WOBBLE
And darkness came over Elymas's eyes so that he needed someone to lead him.
THE GOVERNOR STOOD AMAZED BEFORE PAUL AND BARNABAS AND BELIEVED IN YESHUA.
THIS MUST BE THE WORK OF THE TRUE GOD!
AND SO THE MINISTRY IN CYPRUS WAS BLESSED BY GOD.
I WANT TO LEARN MORE ABOUT WHAT YOU'RE SAYING...
ME TOO!
BUT MARK...
...
MARK WAS NO LONGER ABLE TO ENJOY THE EXCITEMENT OF THE JOURNEY.
Antioch
Seleucia
Perga
Salamis
Cyprus
Paphos
IN PAPHOS, THE THREE COMPANIONS BOARDED A SHIP HEADED FOR PERGA.

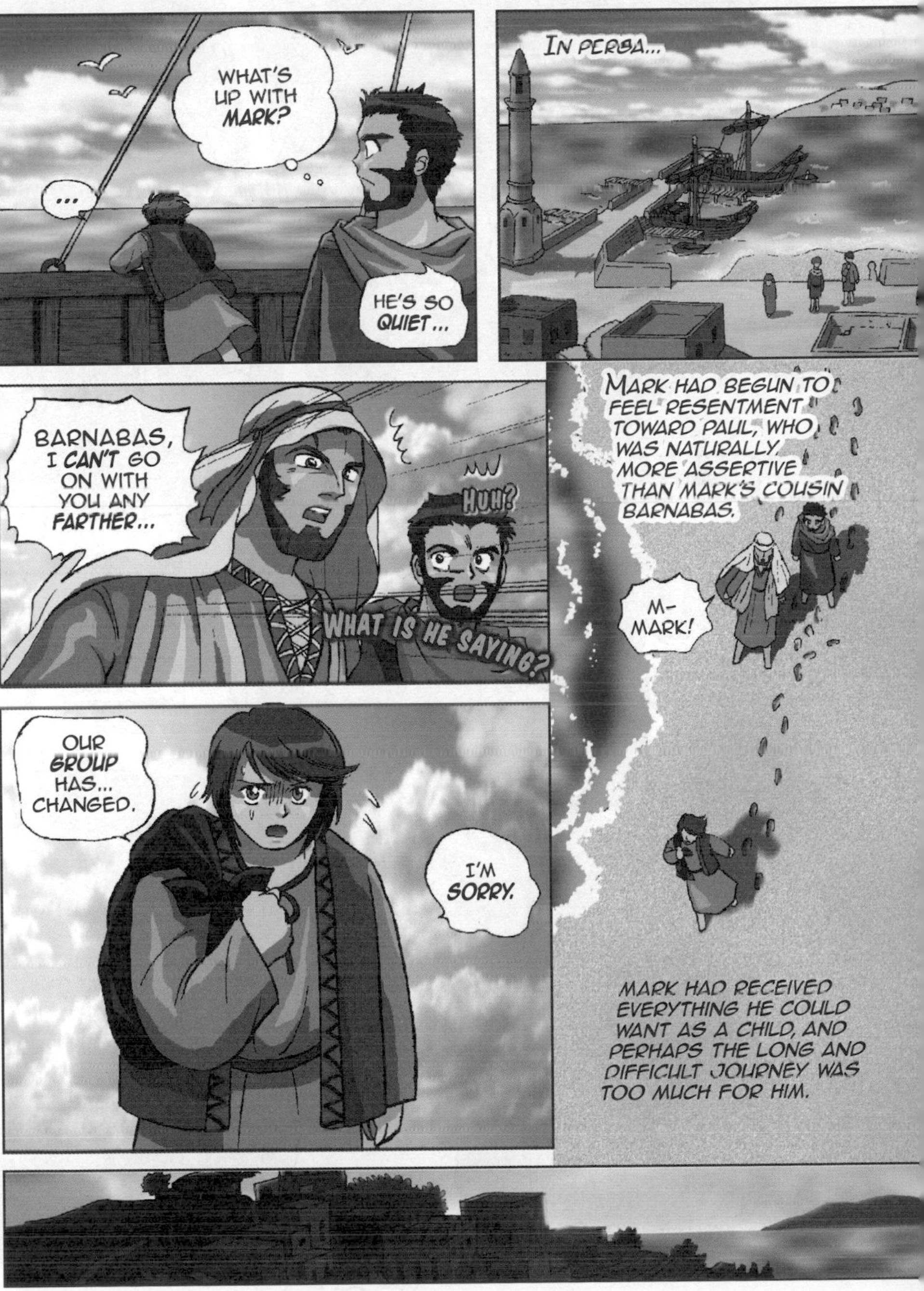

WHAT'S UP WITH MARK?
...
HE'S SO QUIET...
IN PERGA...
BARNABAS, I CAN'T GO ON WITH YOU ANY FARTHER...
HUH?
WHAT IS HE SAYING?
MARK HAD BEGUN TO FEEL RESENTMENT TOWARD PAUL, WHO WAS NATURALLY MORE ASSERTIVE THAN MARK'S COUSIN BARNABAS.
M-MARK!
OUR GROUP HAS... CHANGED.
I'M SORRY.
MARK HAD RECEIVED EVERYTHING HE COULD WANT AS A CHILD, AND PERHAPS THE LONG AND DIFFICULT JOURNEY WAS TOO MUCH FOR HIM.

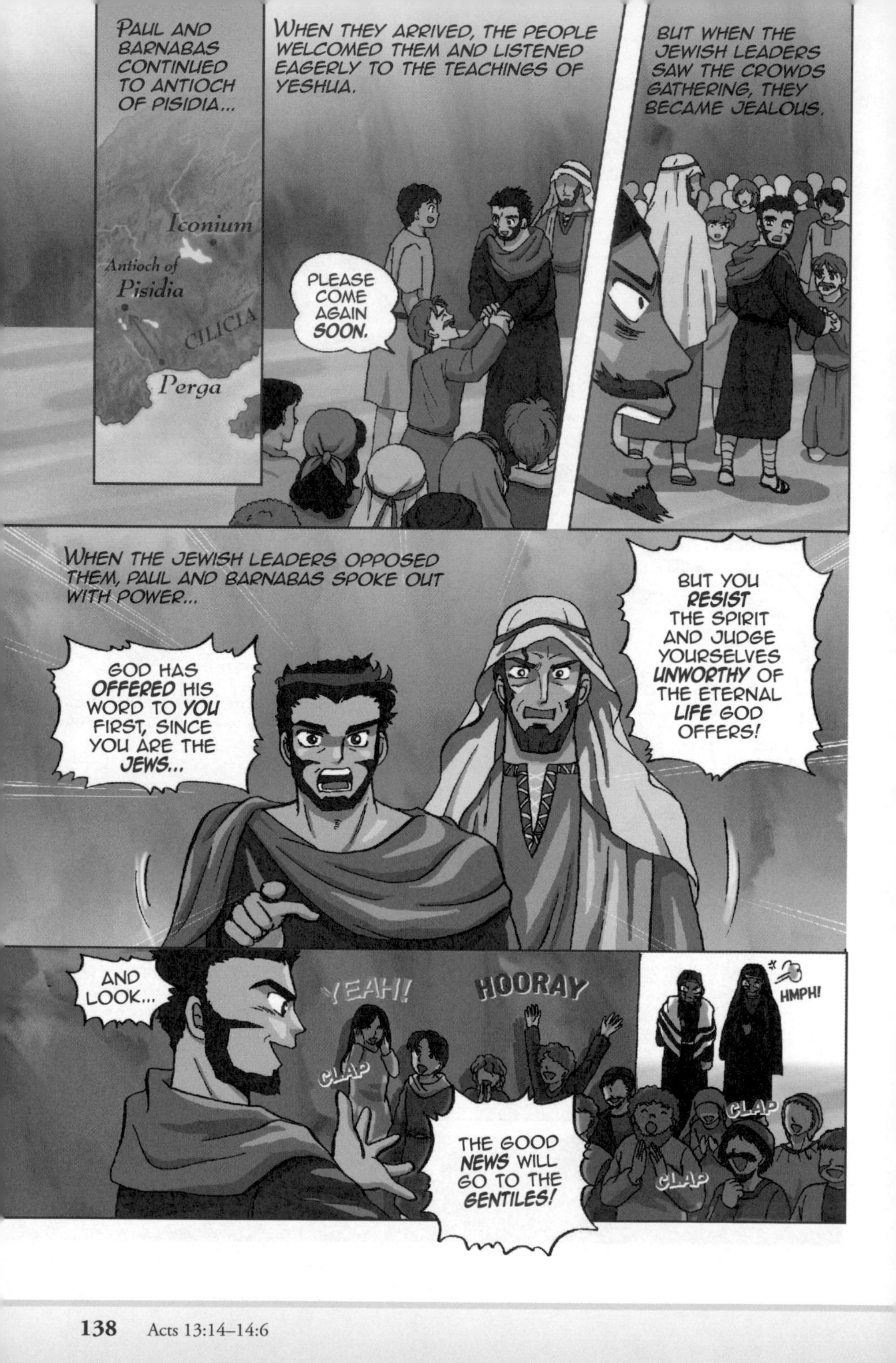

PAUL AND BARNABAS CONTINUED TO ANTIOCH OF PISIDIA...
Iconium
Antioch of Pisidia
CILICIA
Perga
WHEN THEY ARRIVED, THE PEOPLE WELCOMED THEM AND LISTENED EAGERLY TO THE TEACHINGS OF YESHUA.
PLEASE COME AGAIN SOON.
BUT WHEN THE JEWISH LEADERS SAW THE CROWDS GATHERING, THEY BECAME JEALOUS.
WHEN THE JEWISH LEADERS OPPOSED THEM, PAUL AND BARNABAS SPOKE OUT WITH POWER...
GOD HAS OFFERED HIS WORD TO YOU FIRST, SINCE YOU ARE THE JEWS...
BUT YOU RESIST THE SPIRIT AND JUDGE YOURSELVES UNWORTHY OF THE ETERNAL LIFE GOD OFFERS!
AND LOOK...
YEAH!
HOORAY
CLAP
THE GOOD NEWS WILL GO TO THE GENTILES!
CLAP
CLAP
HMPH!

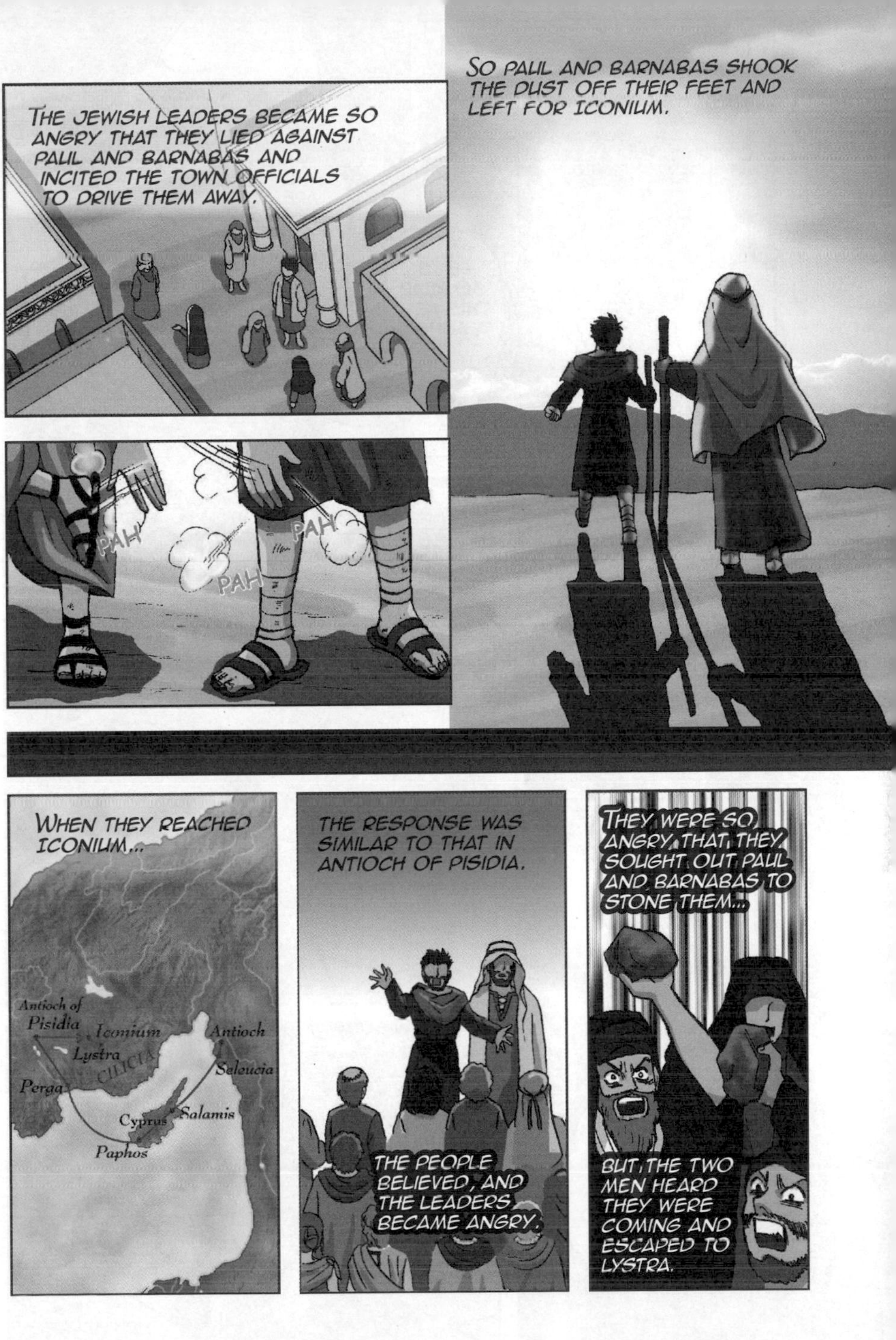
THE JEWISH LEADERS BECAME SO ANGRY THAT THEY LIED AGAINST PAUL AND BARNABAS AND INCITED THE TOWN OFFICIALS TO DRIVE THEM AWAY.
SO PAUL AND BARNABAS SHOOK THE DUST OFF THEIR FEET AND LEFT FOR ICONIUM.
PAH
PAH
PAH
WHEN THEY REACHED ICONIUM...
Antioch of Pisidia
Iconium
Antioch
Lystra
CILICIA
Seleucia
Perga
Cyprus
Salamis
Paphos
THE RESPONSE WAS SIMILAR TO THAT IN ANTIOCH OF PISIDIA.
THE PEOPLE BELIEVED, AND THE LEADERS BECAME ANGRY.
THEY WERE SO ANGRY THAT THEY SOUGHT OUT PAUL AND BARNABAS TO STONE THEM...
BUT THE TWO MEN HEARD THEY WERE COMING AND ESCAPED TO LYSTRA.

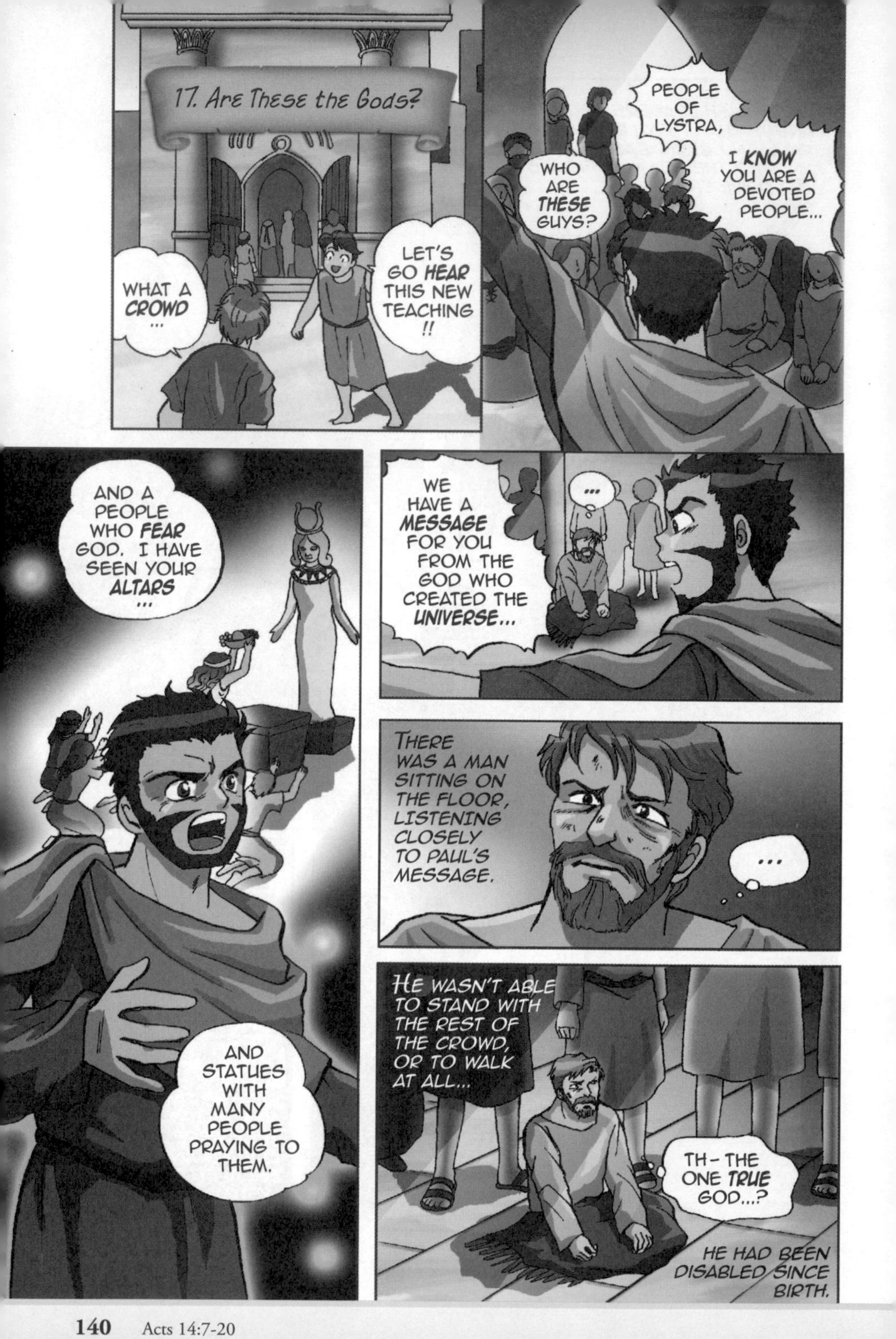
17. Are These the Gods?
WHAT A CROWD ...
LET'S GO HEAR THIS NEW TEACHING !!
PEOPLE OF LYSTRA,
WHO ARE THESE GUYS?
I KNOW YOU ARE A DEVOTED PEOPLE...
AND A PEOPLE WHO FEAR GOD. I HAVE SEEN YOUR ALTARS ...
AND STATUES WITH MANY PEOPLE PRAYING TO THEM.
WE HAVE A MESSAGE FOR YOU FROM THE GOD WHO CREATED THE UNIVERSE...
...
THERE WAS A MAN SITTING ON THE FLOOR, LISTENING CLOSELY TO PAUL'S MESSAGE.
...
HE WASN'T ABLE TO STAND WITH THE REST OF THE CROWD, OR TO WALK AT ALL...
TH- THE ONE TRUE GOD...?
HE HAD BEEN DISABLED SINCE BIRTH.

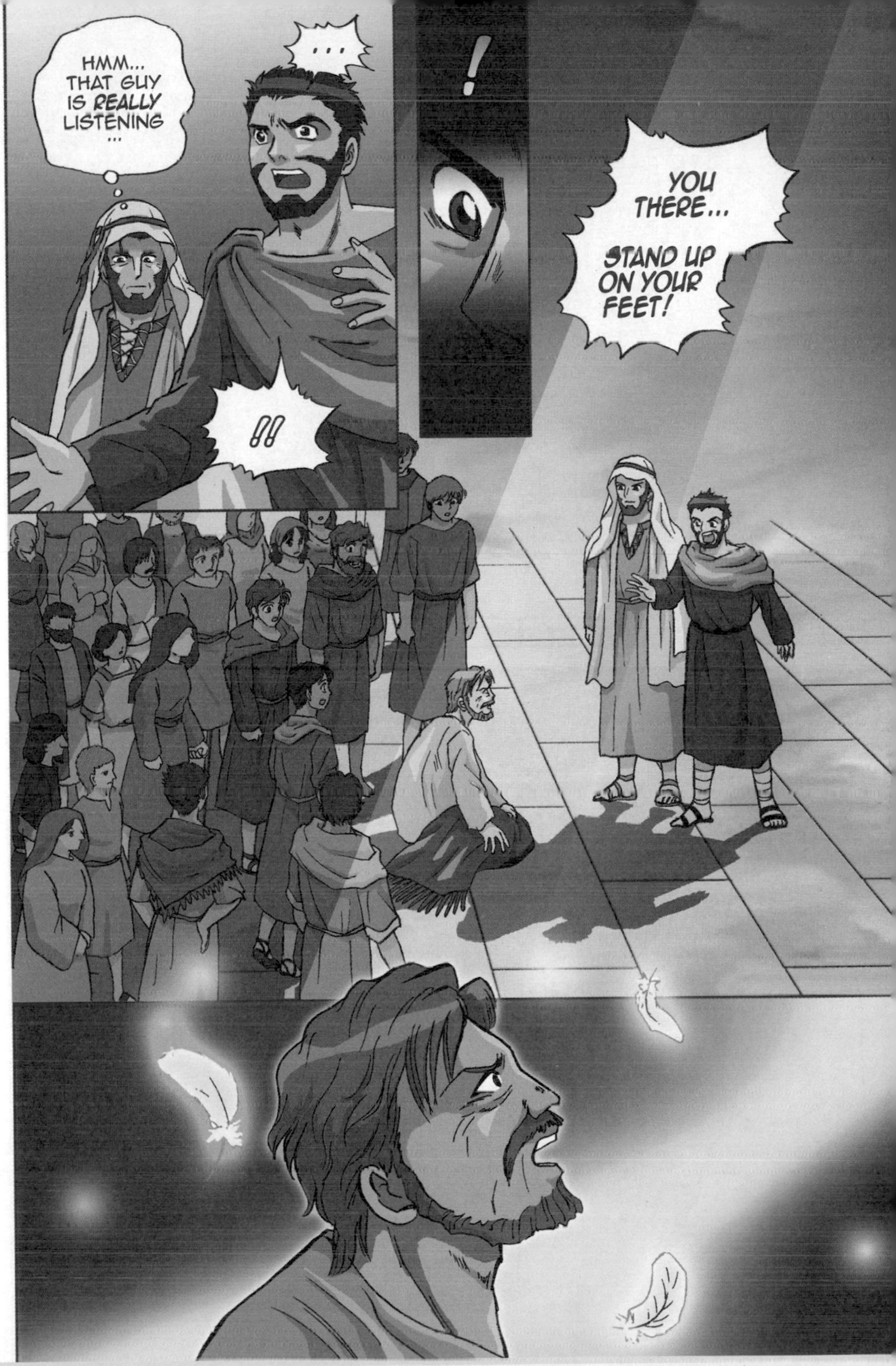
HMM... THAT GUY IS REALLY LISTENING ...
...
!
YOU THERE...
STAND UP ON YOUR FEET!
!!

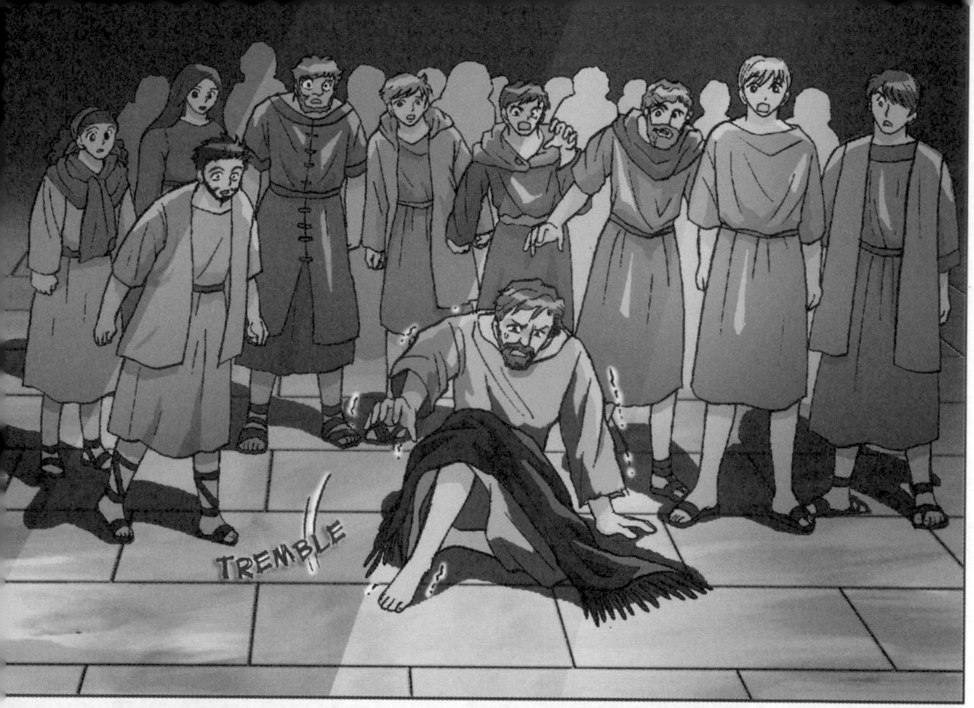
TREMBLE

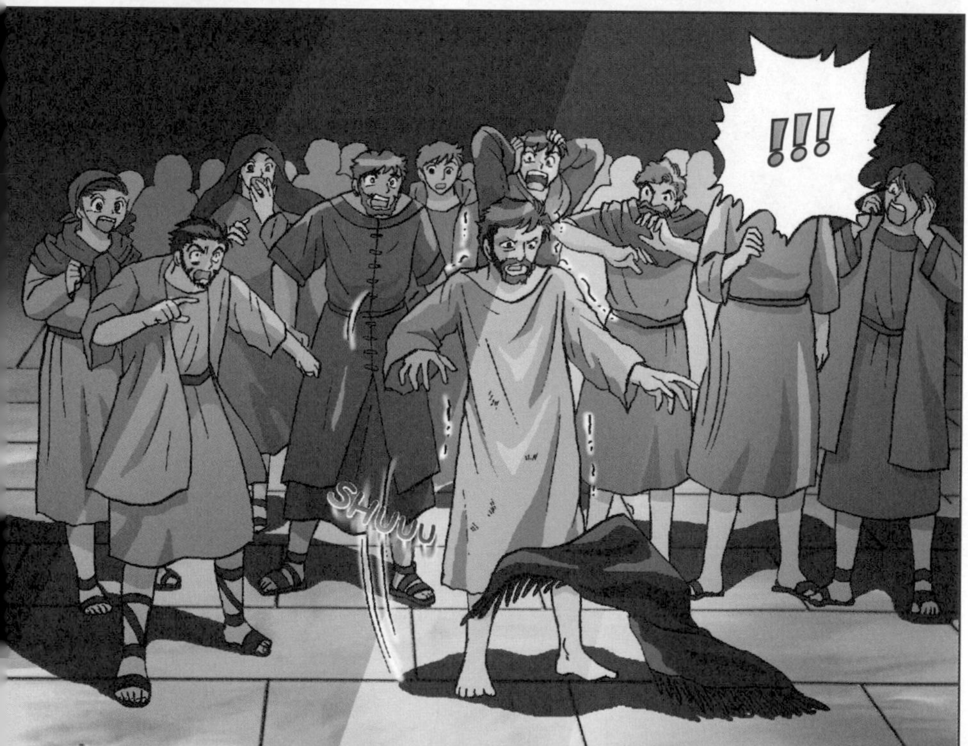
!!!
SHUUU

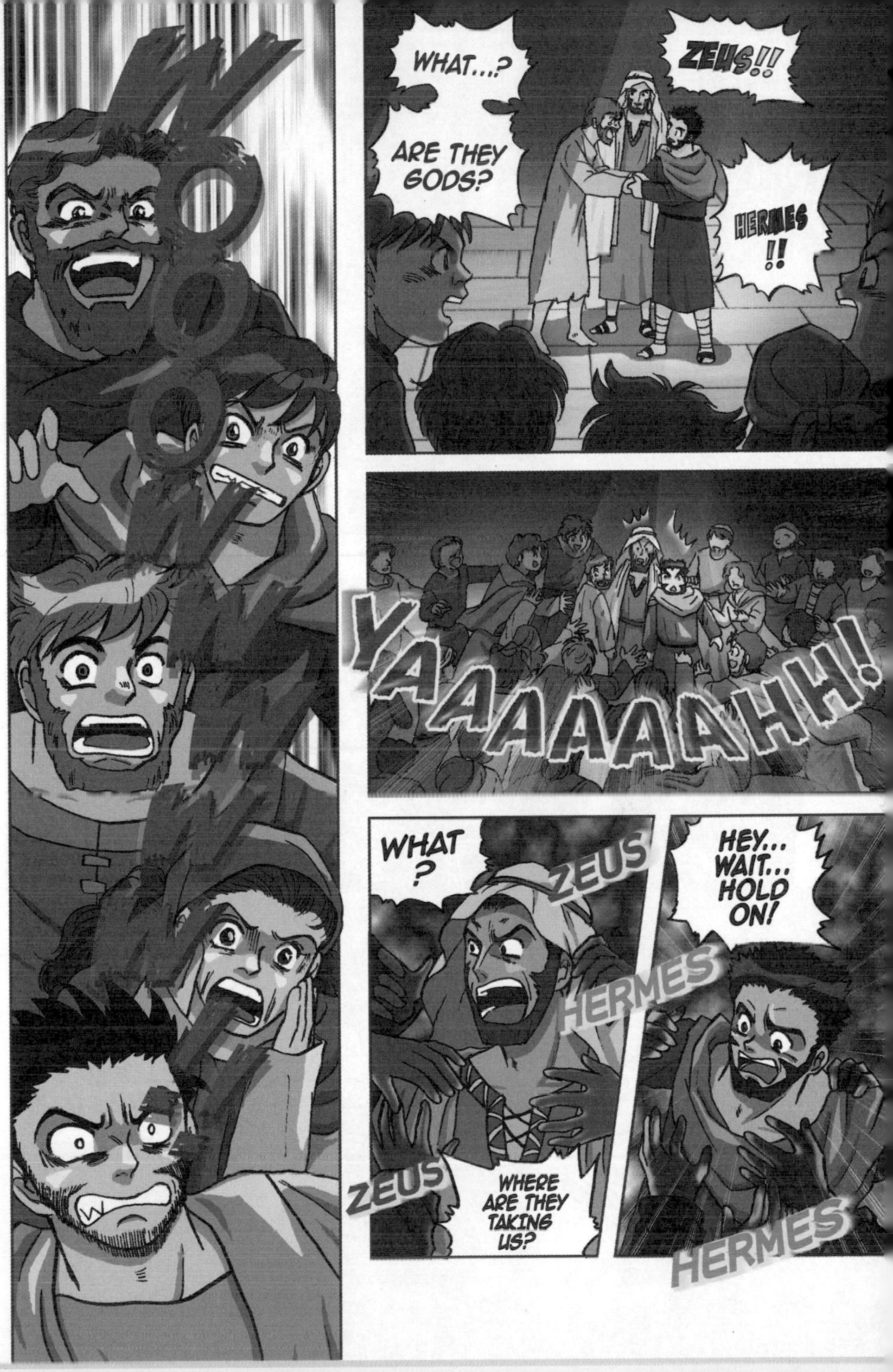
WHAT...?
ZEUS!!
ARE THEY GODS?
HERMES !!
YAAAAAAHH!
WHAT ?
ZEUS
HERMES
ZEUS
WHERE ARE THEY TAKING US?
HEY... WAIT... HOLD ON!
HERMES

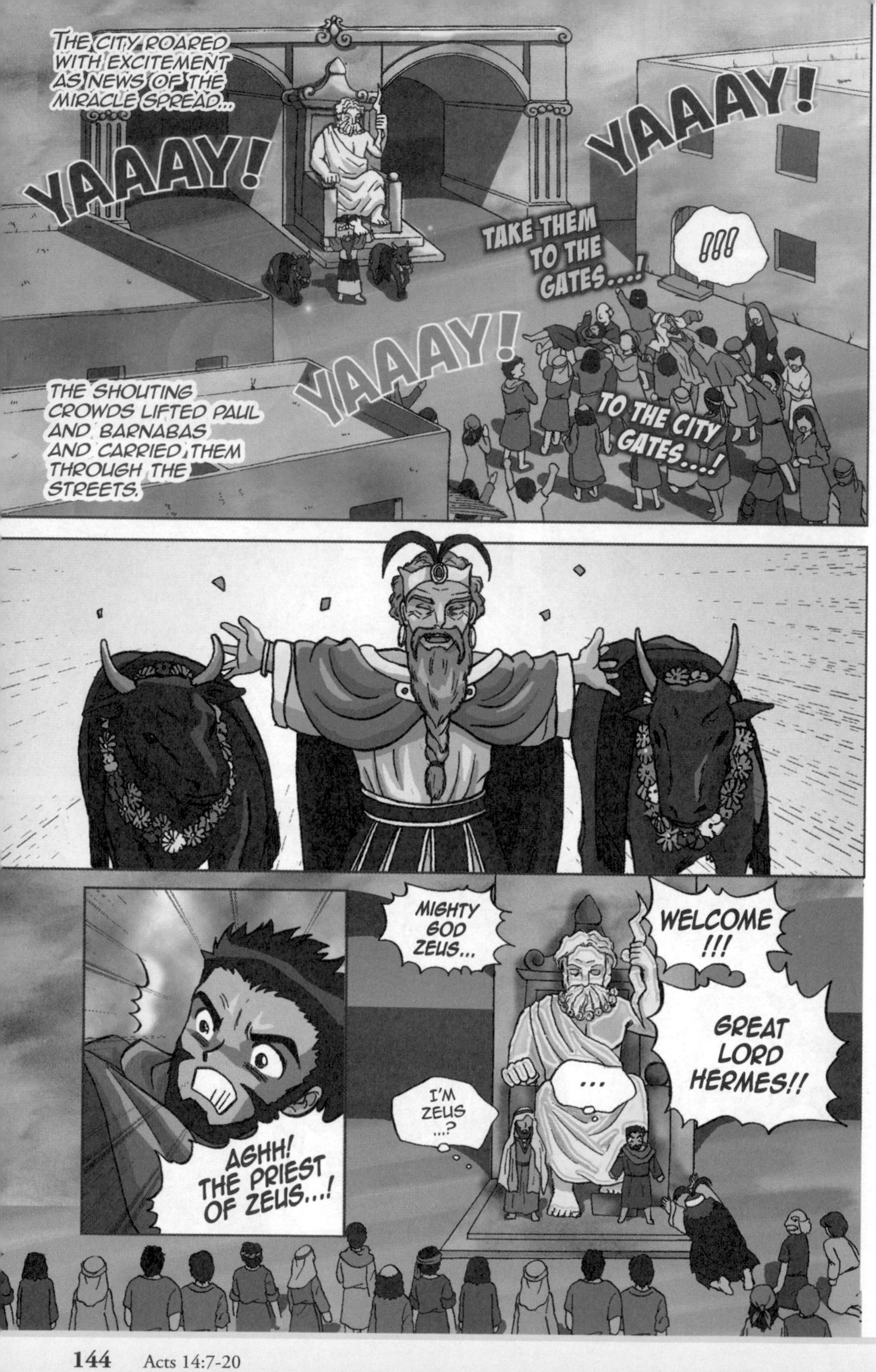
THE CITY ROARED WITH EXCITEMENT AS NEWS OF THE MIRACLE SPREAD...
YAAAY!
YAAAY!
TAKE THEM TO THE GATES...!
!!!
YAAAY!
THE SHOUTING CROWDS LIFTED PAUL AND BARNABAS AND CARRIED THEM THROUGH THE STREETS.
TO THE CITY GATES...!
AGHH! THE PRIEST OF ZEUS...!
MIGHTY GOD ZEUS...
WELCOME !!!
GREAT LORD HERMES!!
...
I'M ZEUS ...?

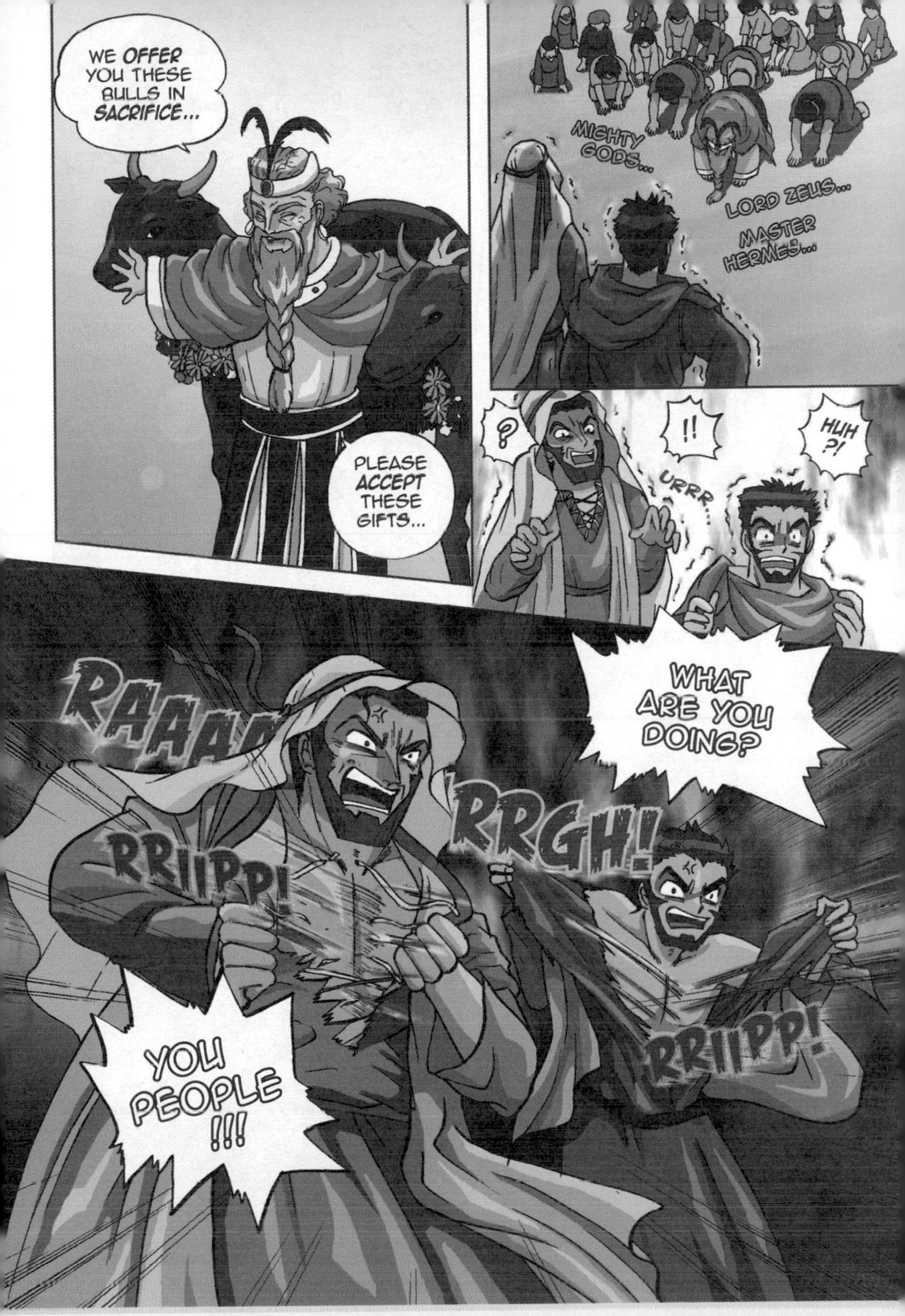
WE OFFER YOU THESE BULLS IN SACRIFICE...
MIGHTY GODS...
LORD ZEUS...
MASTER HERMES...
PLEASE ACCEPT THESE GIFTS...
?
!!
URRR...
HUH ?!
RAAAA
WHAT ARE YOU DOING?
RRGH!
RRIIPP!
RRIIPP!
YOU PEOPLE !!!

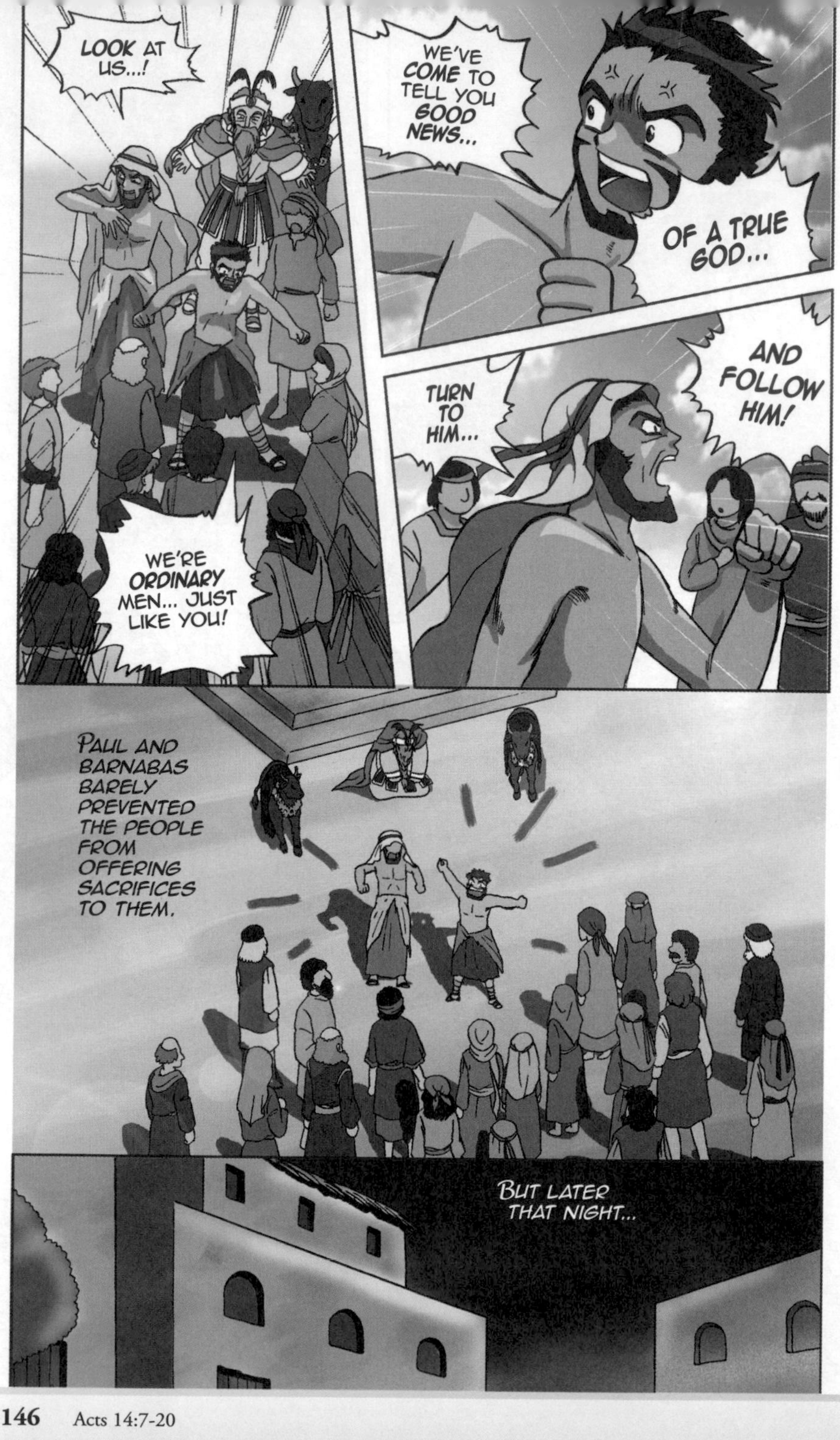
LOOK AT US...!
WE'VE COME TO TELL YOU GOOD NEWS...
OF A TRUE GOD...
WE'RE ORDINARY MEN... JUST LIKE YOU!
TURN TO HIM...
AND FOLLOW HIM!
PAUL AND BARNABAS BARELY PREVENTED THE PEOPLE FROM OFFERING SACRIFICES TO THEM.
BUT LATER THAT NIGHT...

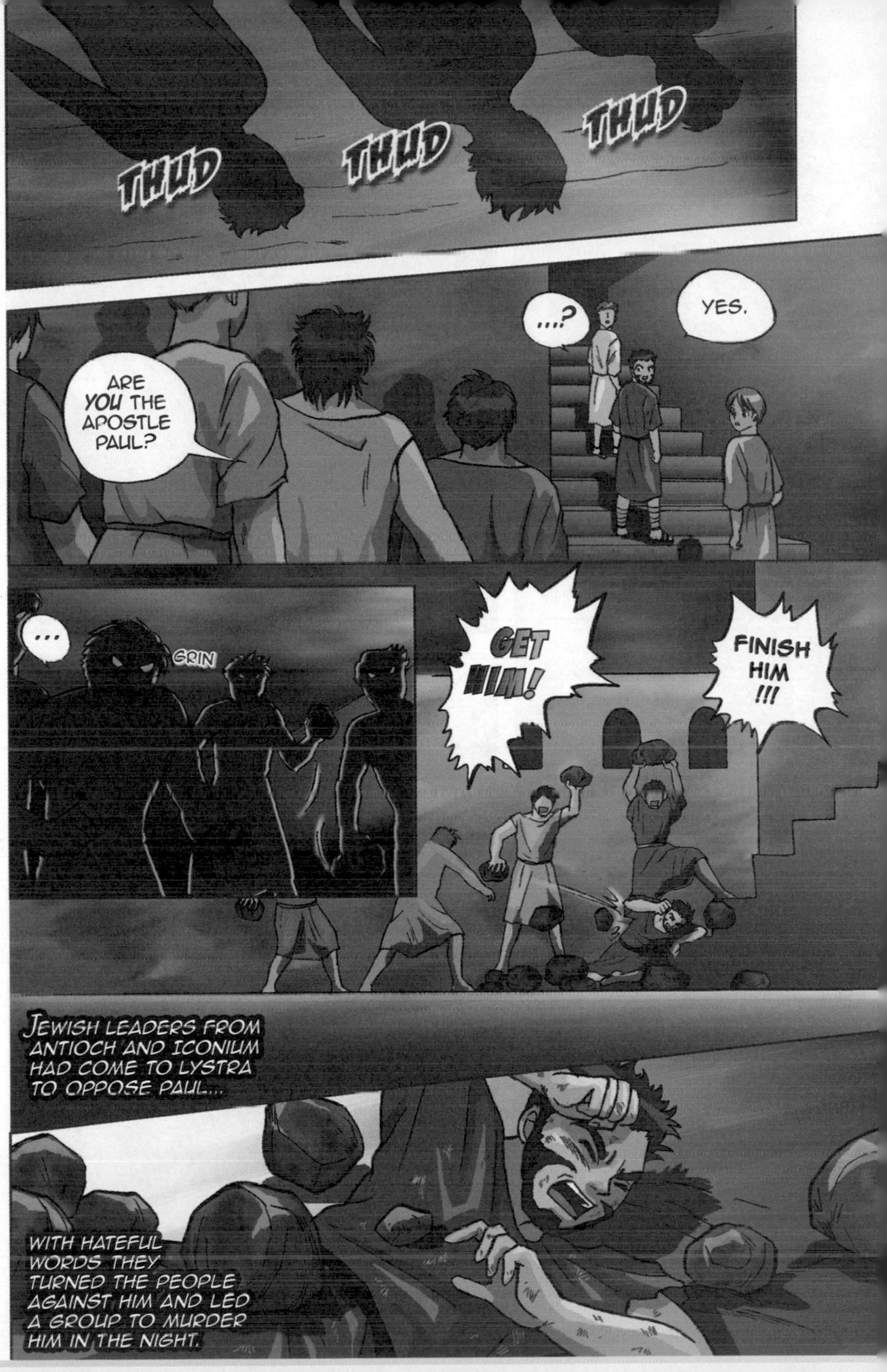
THUD
THUD
THUD
ARE YOU THE APOSTLE PAUL?
...?
YES.
...
GRIN
GET HIM!
FINISH HIM !!!
JEWISH LEADERS FROM ANTIOCH AND ICONIUM HAD COME TO LYSTRA TO OPPOSE PAUL...
WITH HATEFUL WORDS THEY TURNED THE PEOPLE AGAINST HIM AND LED A GROUP TO MURDER HIM IN THE NIGHT.

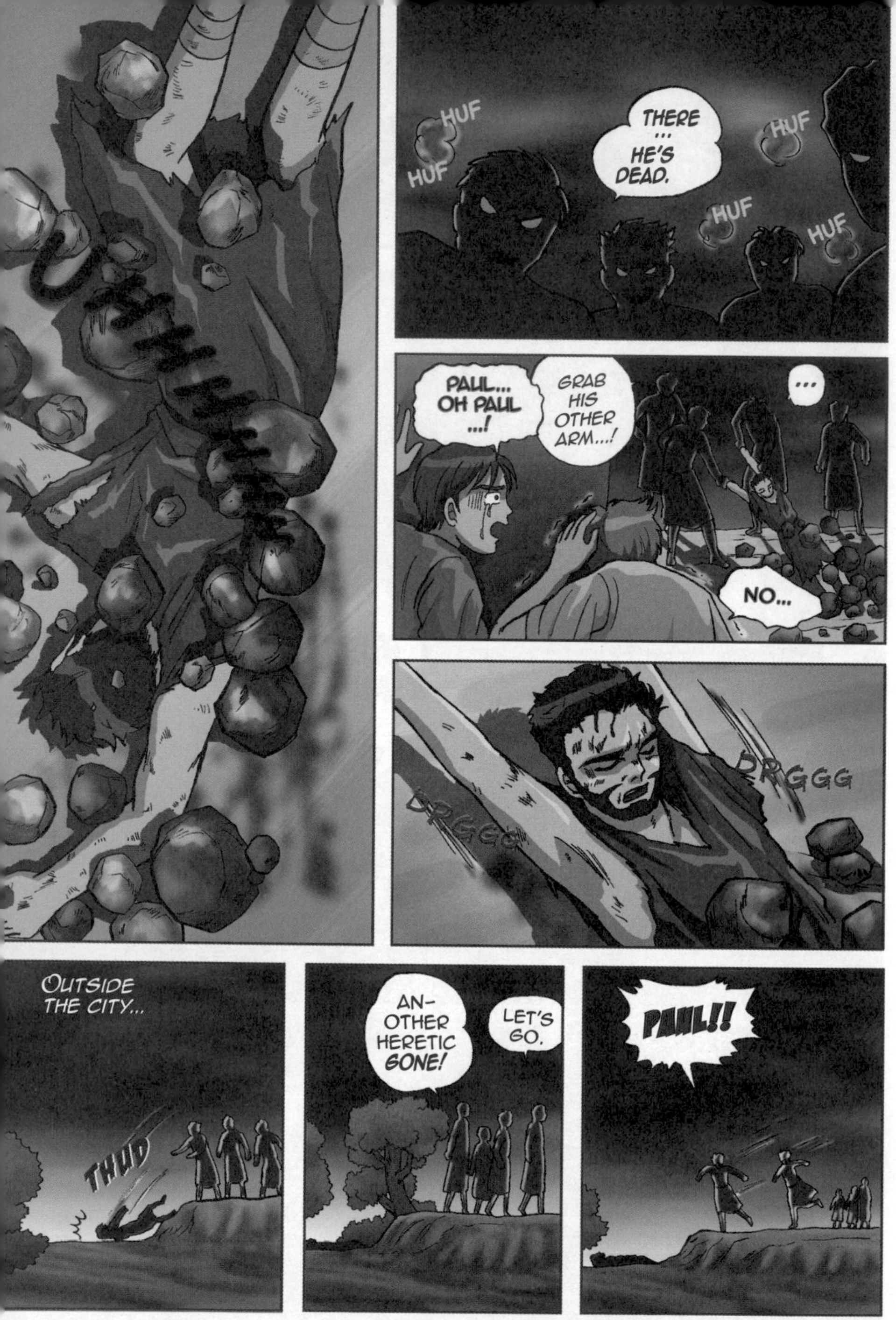
HUF
HUF
THERE ... HE'S DEAD.
HUF
HUF
HUF
PAUL... OH PAUL ...!
GRAB HIS OTHER ARM...!
...
NO...
DRGGG
DRGGG
OUTSIDE THE CITY...
THUD
AN-OTHER HERETIC GONE!
LET'S GO.
PAUL!!

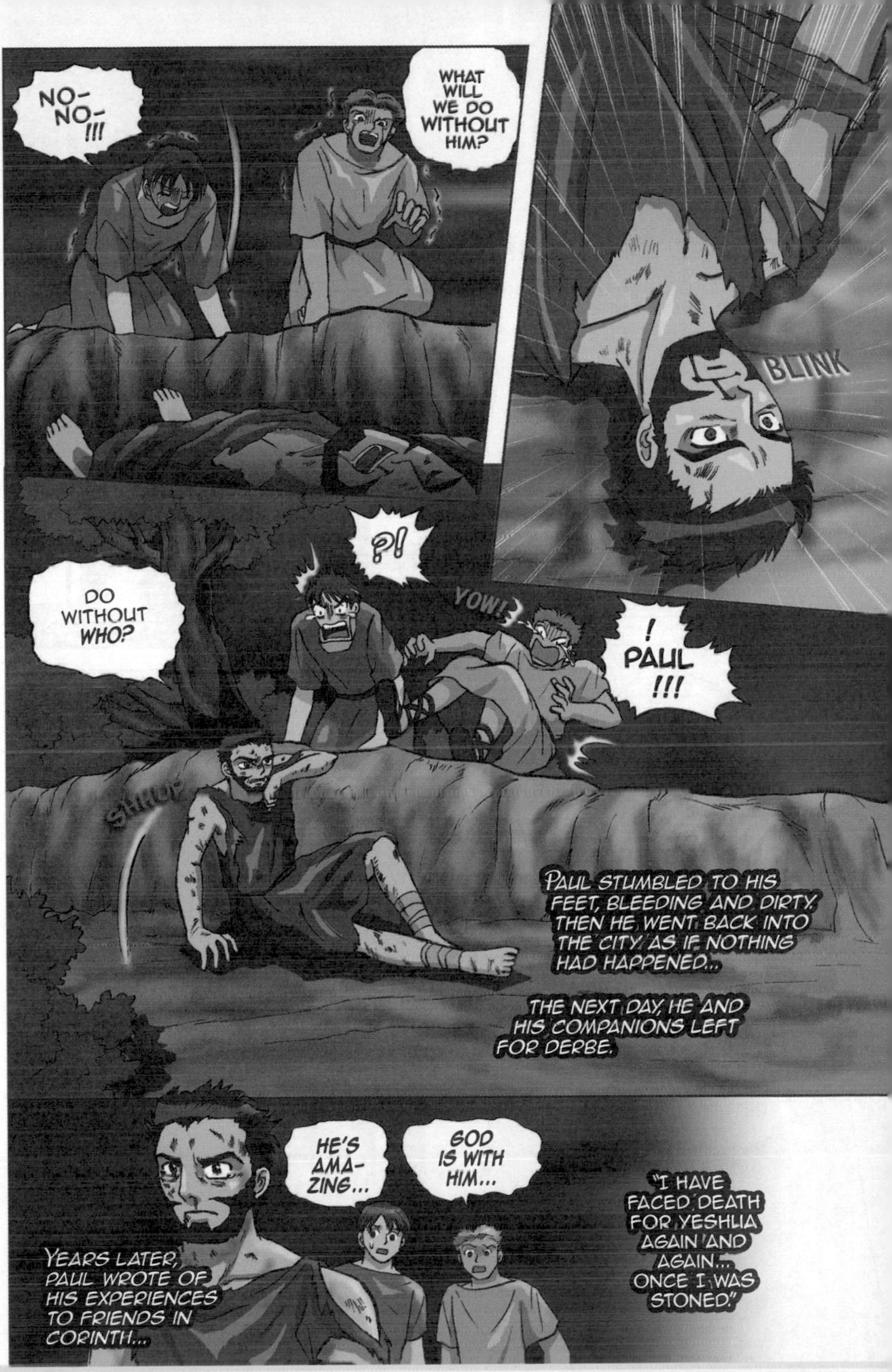
NO-
NO-
!!!
WHAT WILL WE DO WITHOUT HIM?
BLINK
?!
DO WITHOUT WHO?
YOW!
! PAUL !!!
SHHUP
PAUL STUMBLED TO HIS FEET, BLEEDING AND DIRTY. THEN HE WENT BACK INTO THE CITY AS IF NOTHING HAD HAPPENED...
THE NEXT DAY, HE AND HIS COMPANIONS LEFT FOR DERBE.
HE'S AMAZING...
GOD IS WITH HIM...
"I HAVE FACED DEATH FOR YESHUA AGAIN AND AGAIN... ONCE I WAS STONED."
YEARS LATER, PAUL WROTE OF HIS EXPERIENCES TO FRIENDS IN CORINTH...

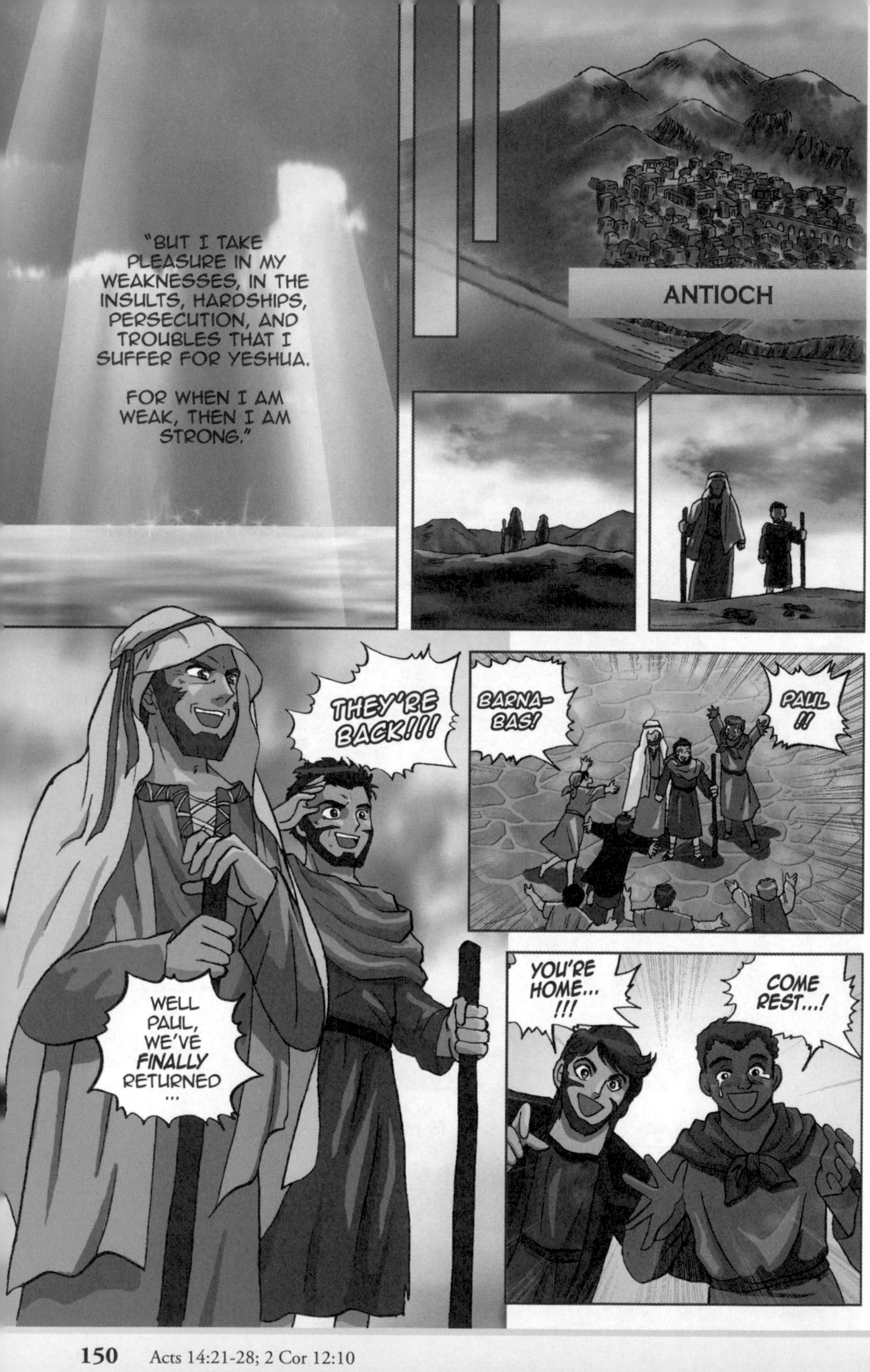
"BUT I TAKE PLEASURE IN MY WEAKNESSES, IN THE INSULTS, HARDSHIPS, PERSECUTION, AND TROUBLES THAT I SUFFER FOR YESHUA.
FOR WHEN I AM WEAK, THEN I AM STRONG."
ANTIOCH
THEY'RE BACK!!!
WELL PAUL, WE'VE FINALLY RETURNED ...
PAUL !!
BARNA-BAS!
COME REST...!
YOU'RE HOME... !!!

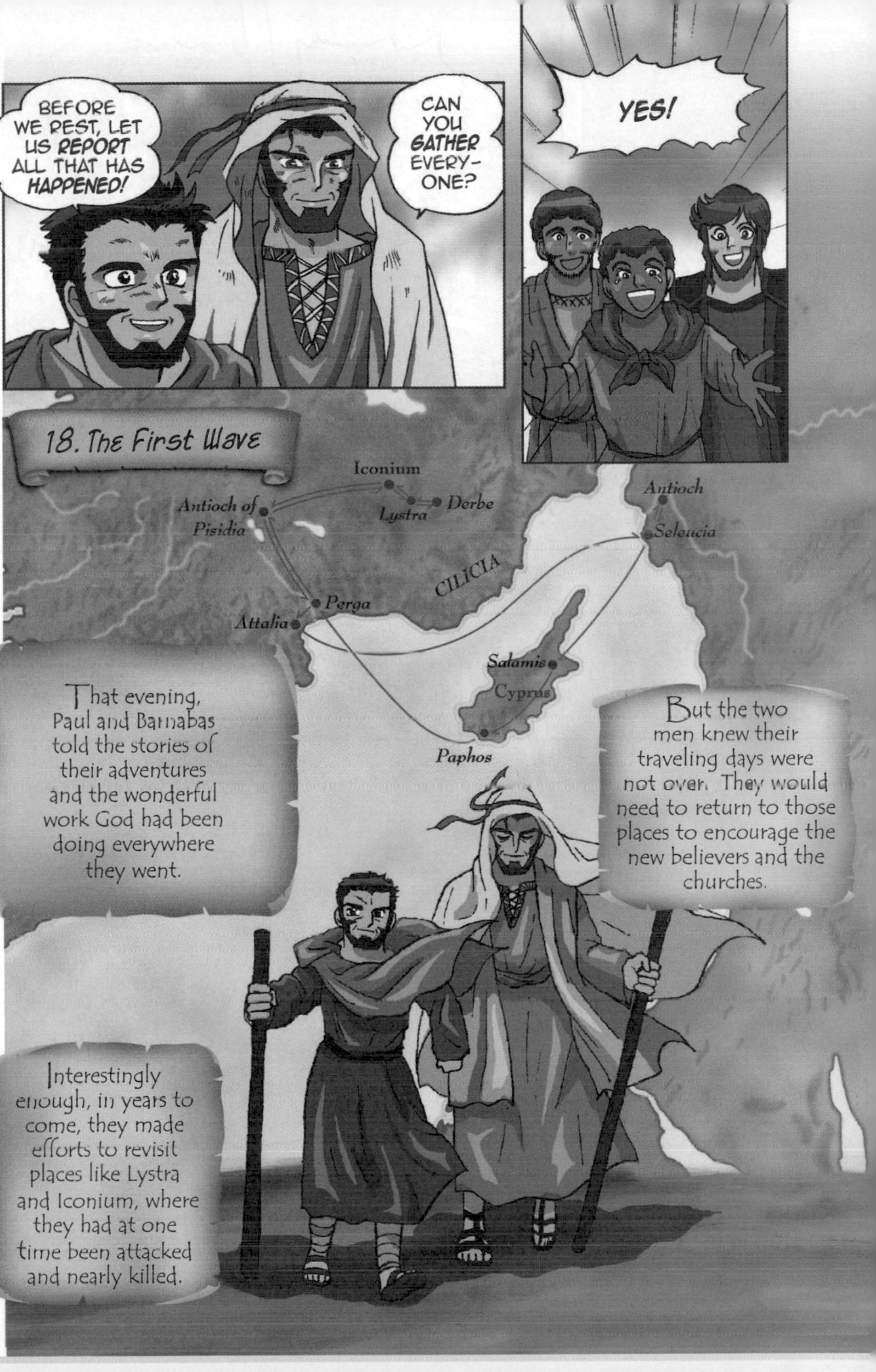

BEFORE WE REST, LET US REPORT ALL THAT HAS HAPPENED!
CAN YOU GATHER EVERY-ONE?
YES!
18. The First Wave
Iconium
Antioch of Pisidia
Lystra
Derbe
Antioch
Seleucia
CILICIA
Perga
Attalia
Salamis
Cyprus
Paphos
That evening, Paul and Barnabas told the stories of their adventures and the wonderful work God had been doing everywhere they went.
But the two men knew their traveling days were not over. They would need to return to those places to encourage the new believers and the churches.
Interestingly enough, in years to come, they made efforts to revisit places like Lystra and Iconium, where they had at one time been attacked and nearly killed.

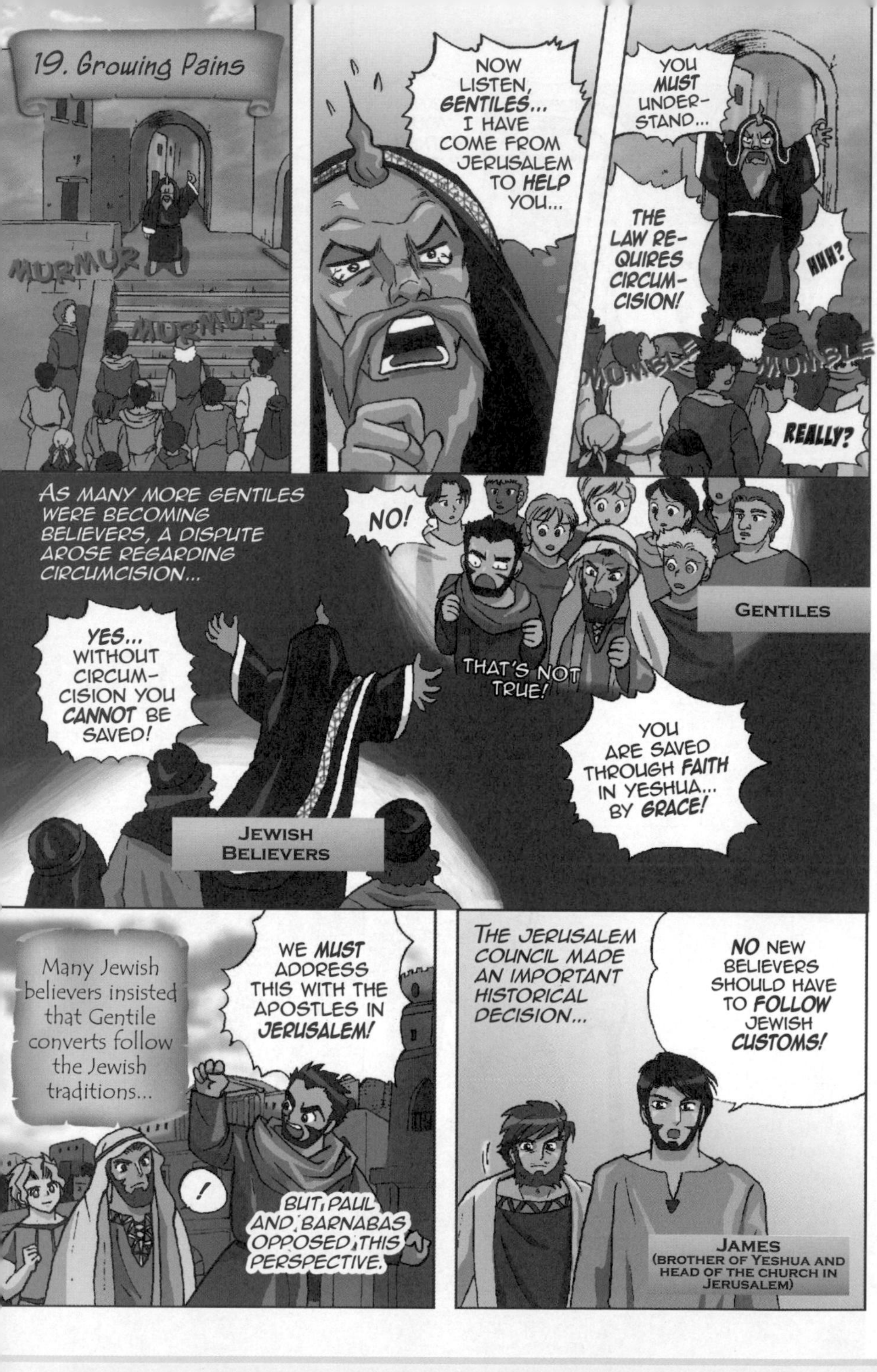
19. Growing Pains
MURMUR
MURMUR
NOW LISTEN, GENTILES... I HAVE COME FROM JERUSALEM TO HELP YOU...
YOU MUST UNDER-STAND...
THE LAW RE-QUIRES CIRCUM-CISION!
HUH?
MUMBLE
MUMBLE
REALLY?
AS MANY MORE GENTILES WERE BECOMING BELIEVERS, A DISPUTE AROSE REGARDING CIRCUMCISION...
NO!
GENTILES
YES... WITHOUT CIRCUM-CISION YOU CANNOT BE SAVED!
THAT'S NOT TRUE!
YOU ARE SAVED THROUGH FAITH IN YESHUA... BY GRACE!
JEWISH BELIEVERS
Many Jewish believers insisted that Gentile converts follow the Jewish traditions...
WE MUST ADDRESS THIS WITH THE APOSTLES IN JERUSALEM!
!
BUT PAUL AND BARNABAS OPPOSED THIS PERSPECTIVE.
THE JERUSALEM COUNCIL MADE AN IMPORTANT HISTORICAL DECISION...
NO NEW BELIEVERS SHOULD HAVE TO FOLLOW JEWISH CUSTOMS!
JAMES
(BROTHER OF YESHUA AND HEAD OF THE CHURCH IN JERUSALEM)

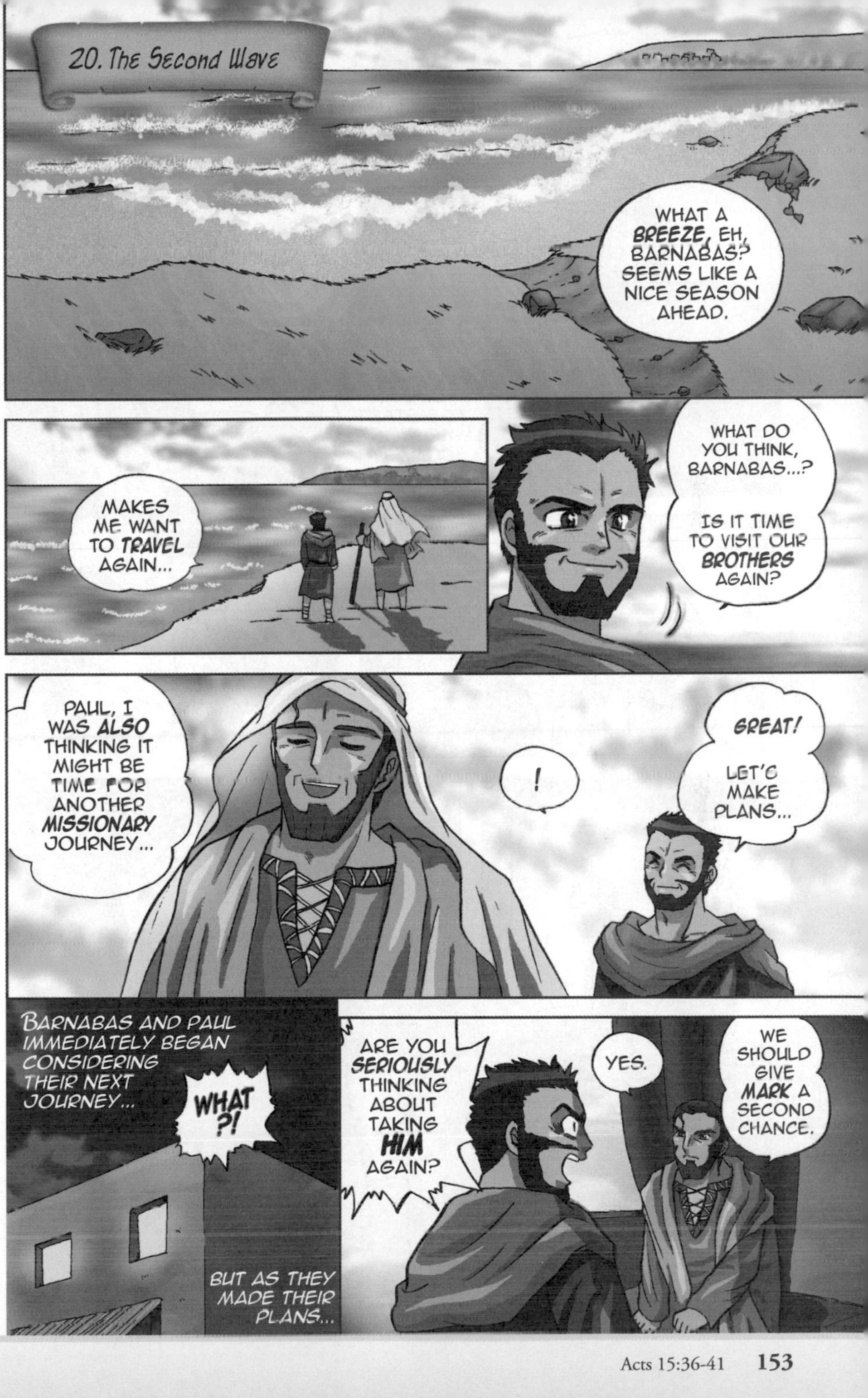

20. The Second Wave
WHAT A BREEZE, EH, BARNABAS? SEEMS LIKE A NICE SEASON AHEAD.
MAKES ME WANT TO TRAVEL AGAIN...
WHAT DO YOU THINK, BARNABAS...?
IS IT TIME TO VISIT OUR BROTHERS AGAIN?
PAUL, I WAS ALSO THINKING IT MIGHT BE TIME FOR ANOTHER MISSIONARY JOURNEY...
!
GREAT!
LET'S MAKE PLANS...
BARNABAS AND PAUL IMMEDIATELY BEGAN CONSIDERING THEIR NEXT JOURNEY...
BUT AS THEY MADE THEIR PLANS...
WHAT ?!
ARE YOU SERIOUSLY THINKING ABOUT TAKING HIM AGAIN?
YES.
WE SHOULD GIVE MARK A SECOND CHANCE.

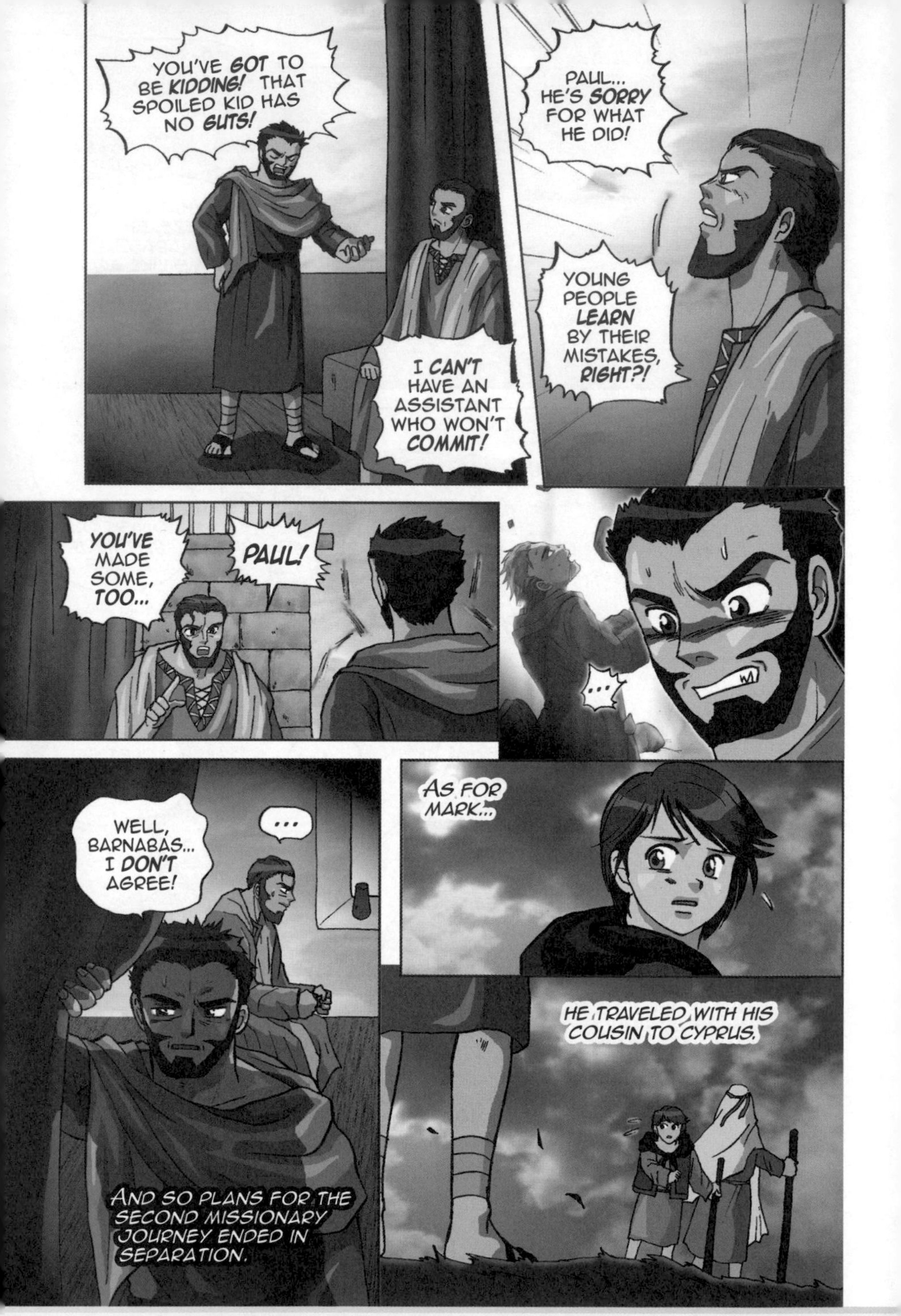
YOU'VE GOT TO BE KIDDING! THAT SPOILED KID HAS NO GUTS!
I CAN'T HAVE AN ASSISTANT WHO WON'T COMMIT!
PAUL... HE'S SORRY FOR WHAT HE DID!
YOUNG PEOPLE LEARN BY THEIR MISTAKES, RIGHT?!
YOU'VE MADE SOME, TOO...
PAUL!
...
WELL, BARNABAS... I DON'T AGREE!
...
AND SO PLANS FOR THE SECOND MISSIONARY JOURNEY ENDED IN SEPARATION.
AS FOR MARK...
HE TRAVELED WITH HIS COUSIN TO CYPRUS.

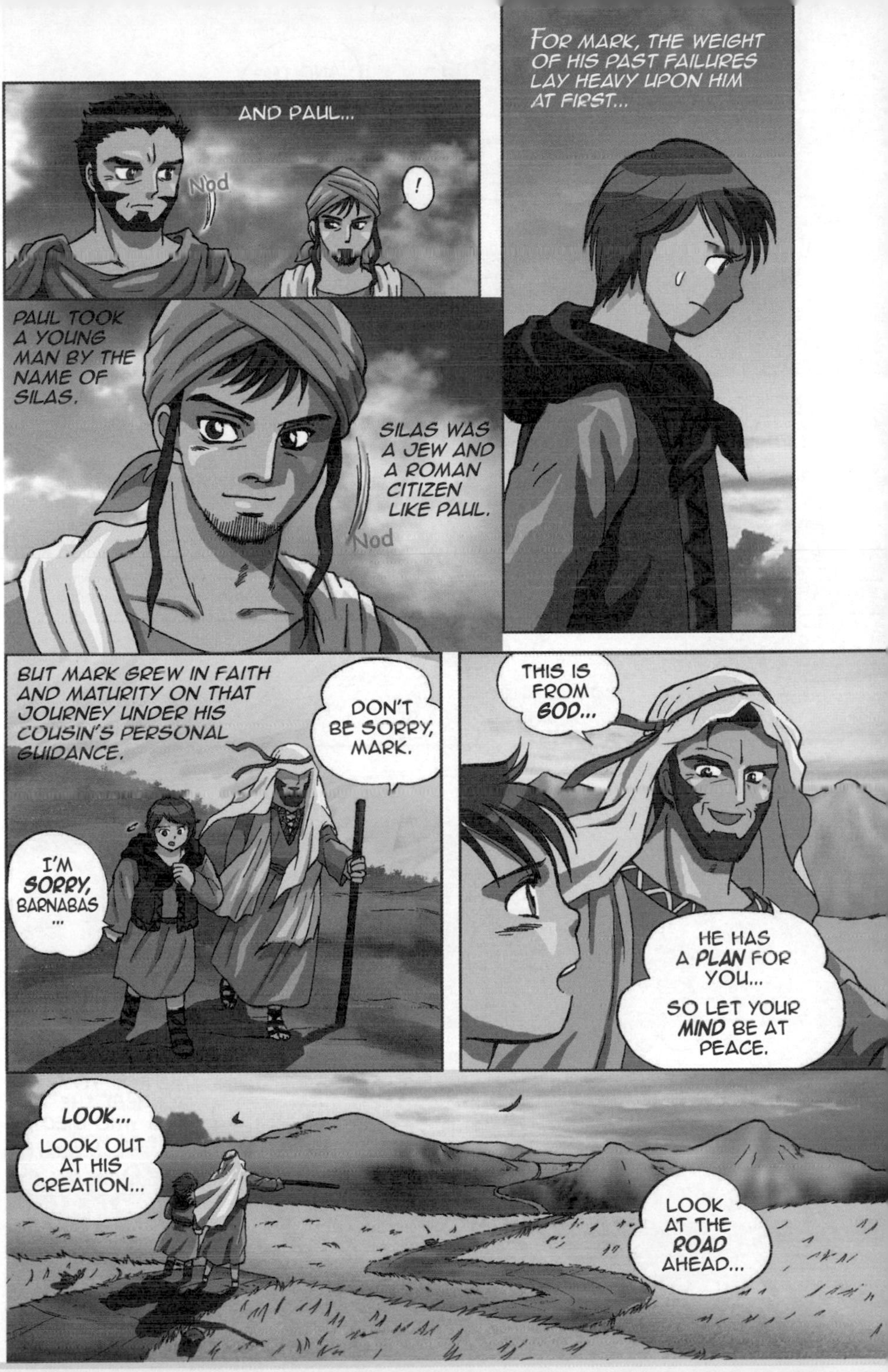
AND PAUL...
Nod
!
FOR MARK, THE WEIGHT OF HIS PAST FAILURES LAY HEAVY UPON HIM AT FIRST...
PAUL TOOK A YOUNG MAN BY THE NAME OF SILAS.
SILAS WAS A JEW AND A ROMAN CITIZEN LIKE PAUL.
Nod
BUT MARK GREW IN FAITH AND MATURITY ON THAT JOURNEY UNDER HIS COUSIN'S PERSONAL GUIDANCE.
I'M SORRY, BARNABAS ...
DON'T BE SORRY, MARK.
THIS IS FROM GOD...
HE HAS A PLAN FOR YOU...
SO LET YOUR MIND BE AT PEACE.
LOOK... LOOK OUT AT HIS CREATION...
LOOK AT THE ROAD AHEAD...

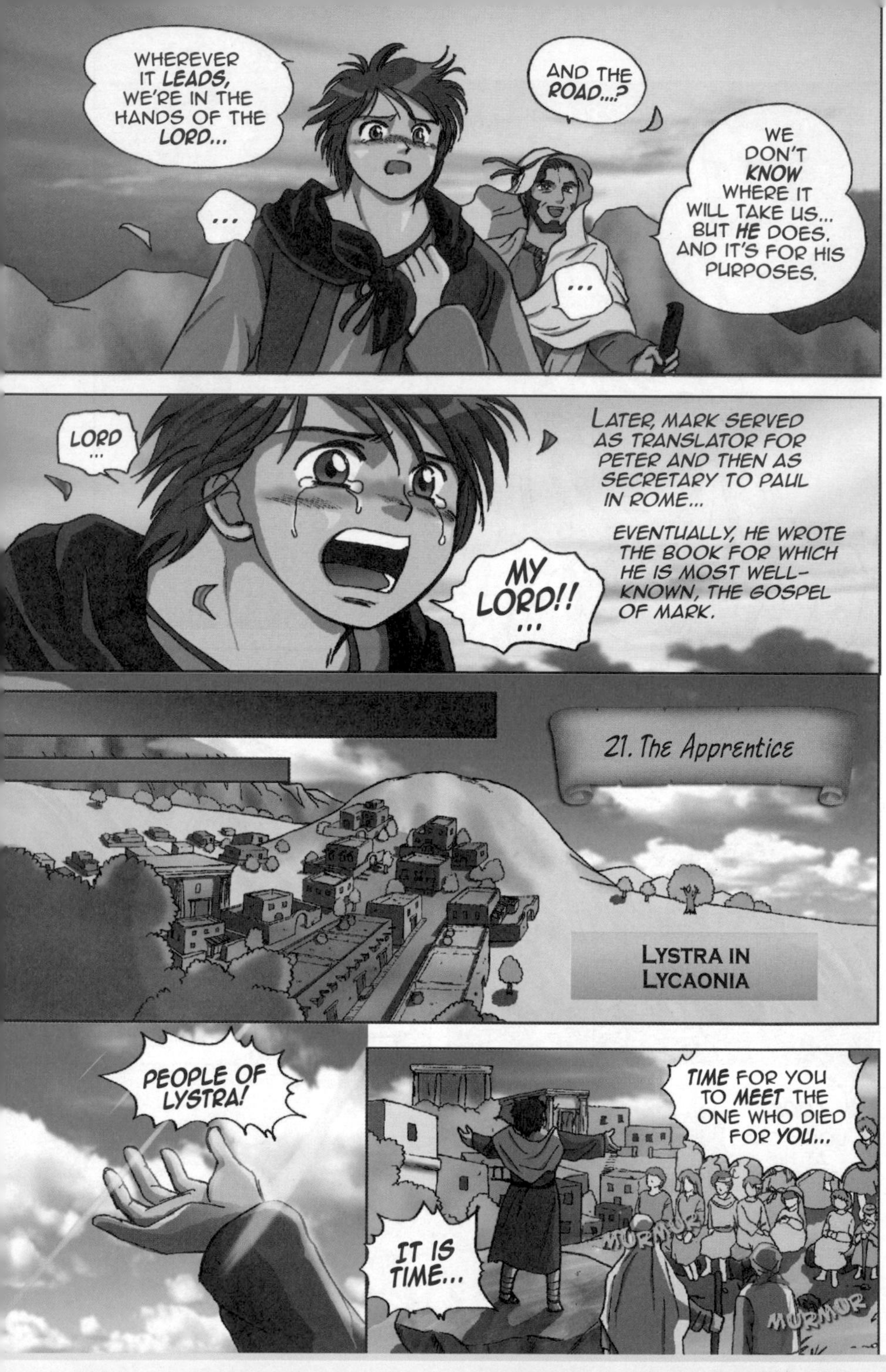
WHEREVER IT LEADS, WE'RE IN THE HANDS OF THE LORD...
AND THE ROAD...?
WE DON'T KNOW WHERE IT WILL TAKE US... BUT HE DOES. AND IT'S FOR HIS PURPOSES.
...
...
LORD ...
LATER, MARK SERVED AS TRANSLATOR FOR PETER AND THEN AS SECRETARY TO PAUL IN ROME...
EVENTUALLY, HE WROTE THE BOOK FOR WHICH HE IS MOST WELL-KNOWN, THE GOSPEL OF MARK.
MY LORD!! ...
21. The Apprentice
LYSTRA IN LYCAONIA
PEOPLE OF LYSTRA!
TIME FOR YOU TO MEET THE ONE WHO DIED FOR YOU...
IT IS TIME...
MURMUR
MURMUR

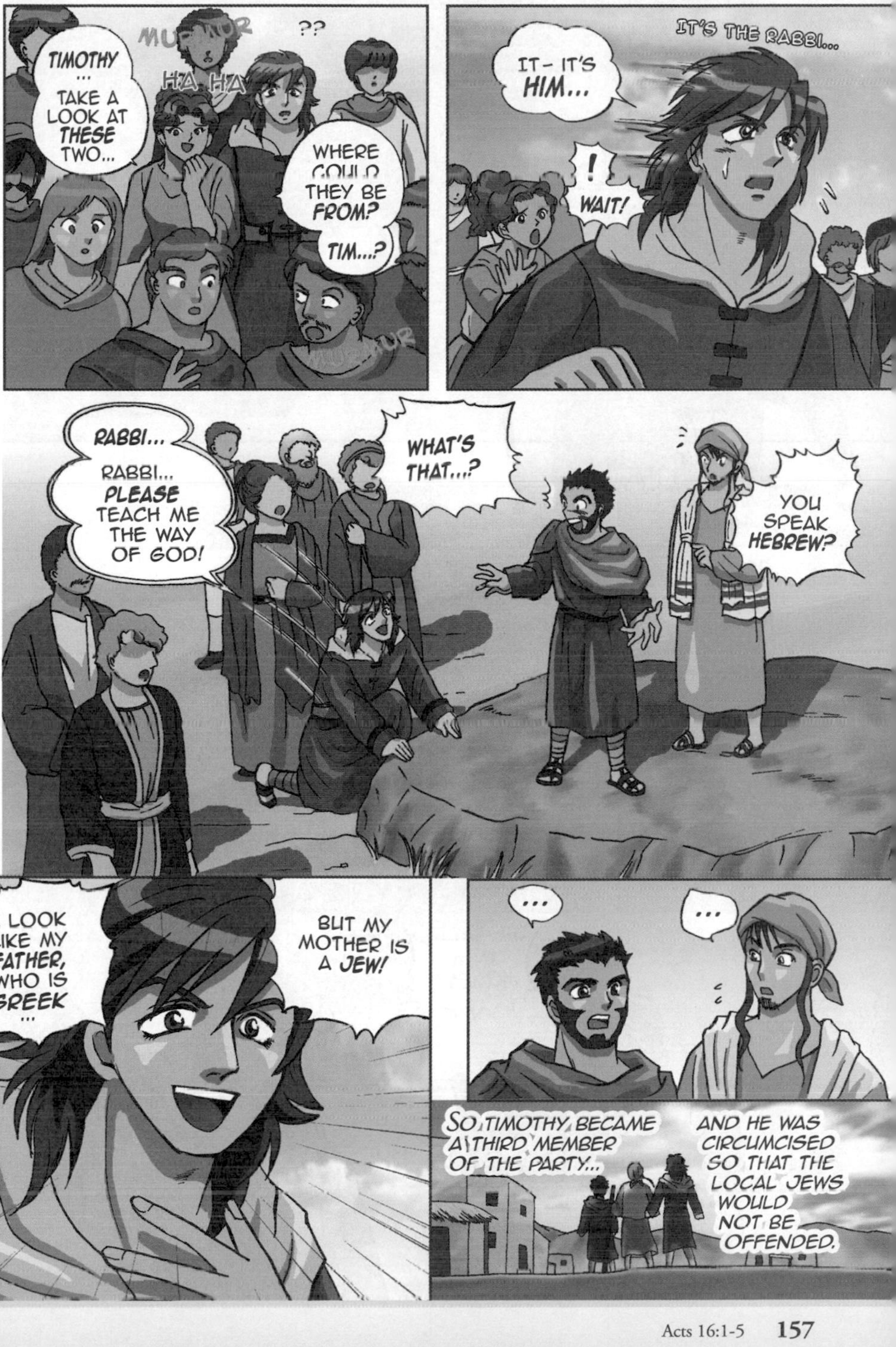
MURMUR
??
TIMOTHY ... TAKE A LOOK AT THESE TWO...
HA HA
WHERE COULD THEY BE FROM?
TIM...?
MURMUR
IT'S THE RABBI...
IT- IT'S HIM...
!
WAIT!
RABBI...
RABBI... PLEASE TEACH ME THE WAY OF GOD!
WHAT'S THAT...?
YOU SPEAK HEBREW?
I LOOK LIKE MY FATHER, WHO IS GREEK ...
BUT MY MOTHER IS A JEW!
...
...
SO TIMOTHY BECAME A THIRD MEMBER OF THE PARTY...
AND HE WAS CIRCUMCISED SO THAT THE LOCAL JEWS WOULD NOT BE OFFENDED.

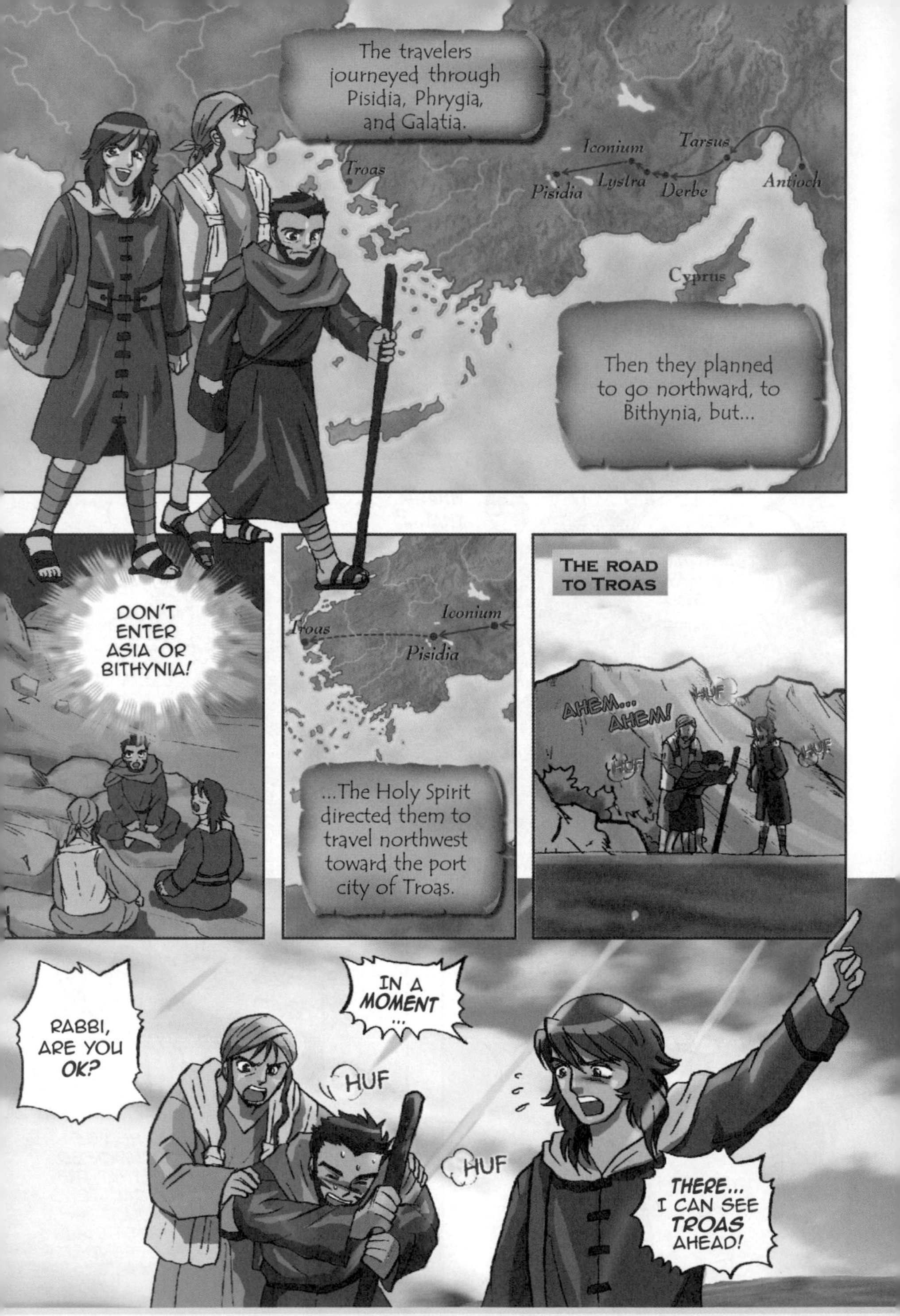

The travelers journeyed through Pisidia, Phrygia, and Galatia.
Troas
Iconium
Tarsus
Pisidia
Lystra
Derbe
Antioch
Cyprus
Then they planned to go northward, to Bithynia, but...
DON'T ENTER ASIA OR BITHYNIA!
Iconium
Troas
Pisidia
...The Holy Spirit directed them to travel northwest toward the port city of Troas.
THE ROAD TO TROAS
AHEM... AHEM!
HUF
HUF
HUF
RABBI, ARE YOU OK?
IN A MOMENT ...
HUF
HUF
THERE... I CAN SEE TROAS AHEAD!

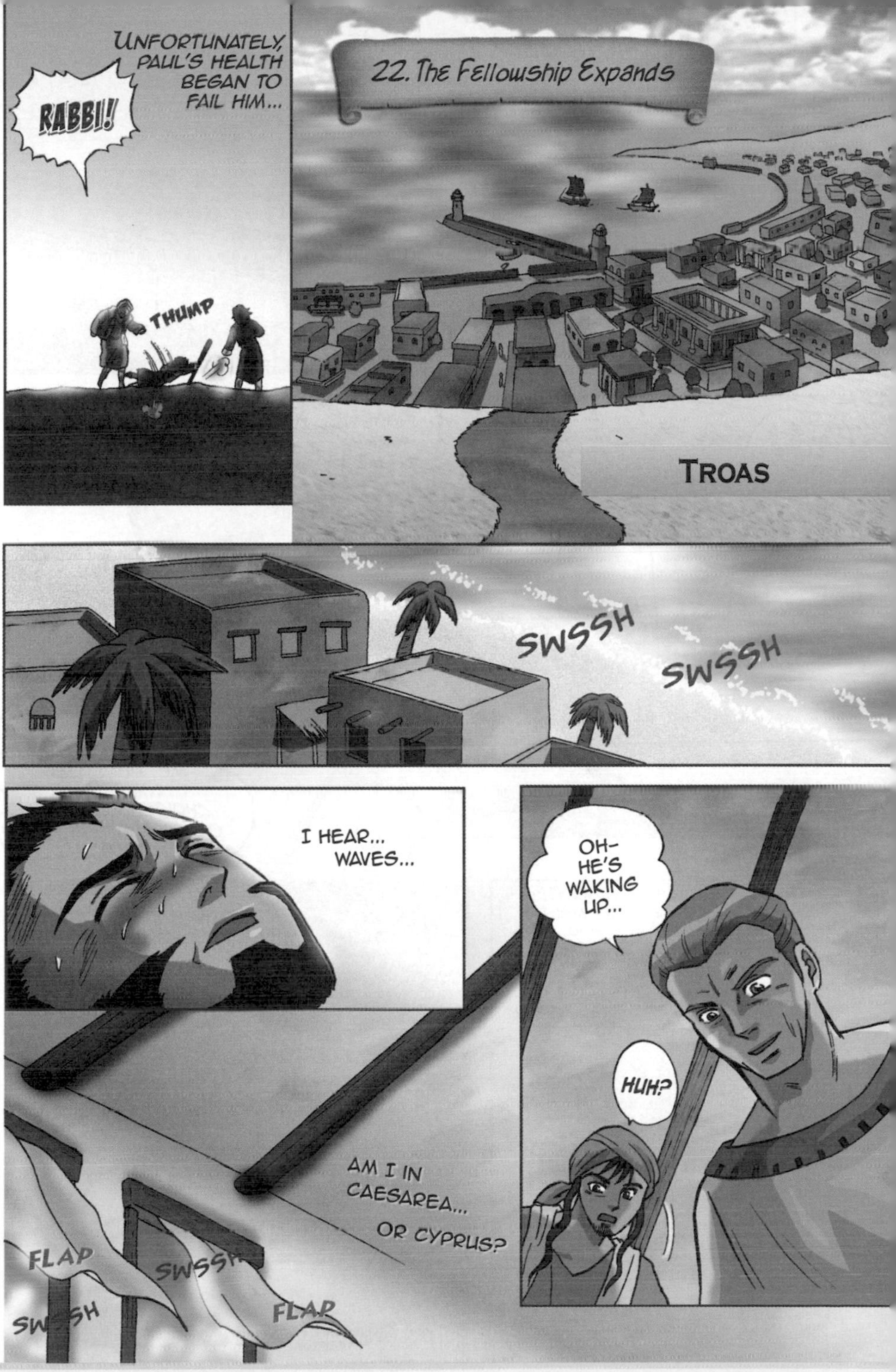

22. The Fellowship Expands
Unfortunately, Paul's health began to fail him...
RABBI!
THUMP
TROAS
SWSSH
SWSSH
I HEAR... WAVES...
AM I IN CAESAREA... OR CYPRUS?
OH- HE'S WAKING UP...
HUH?
FLAP
SWSSH
SWSSH
FLAP

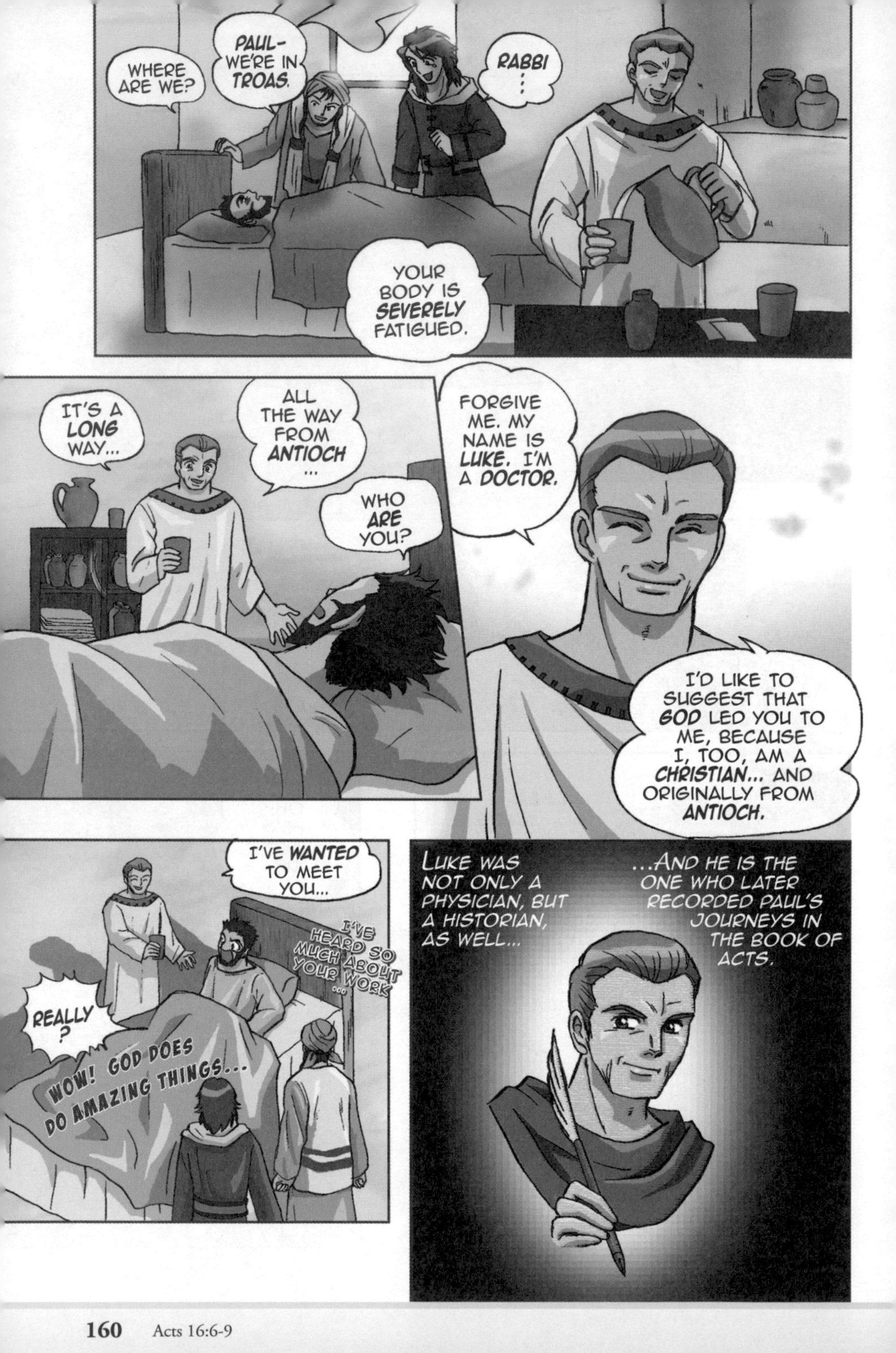
WHERE ARE WE?
PAUL- WE'RE IN TROAS.
RABBI ...
YOUR BODY IS SEVERELY FATIGUED.
IT'S A LONG WAY...
ALL THE WAY FROM ANTIOCH ...
WHO ARE YOU?
FORGIVE ME. MY NAME IS LUKE. I'M A DOCTOR.
I'D LIKE TO SUGGEST THAT GOD LED YOU TO ME, BECAUSE I, TOO, AM A CHRISTIAN... AND ORIGINALLY FROM ANTIOCH.
I'VE WANTED TO MEET YOU...
I'VE HEARD SO MUCH ABOUT YOUR WORK ...
REALLY ?
WOW! GOD DOES DO AMAZING THINGS...
LUKE WAS NOT ONLY A PHYSICIAN, BUT A HISTORIAN, AS WELL...
...AND HE IS THE ONE WHO LATER RECORDED PAUL'S JOURNEYS IN THE BOOK OF ACTS.

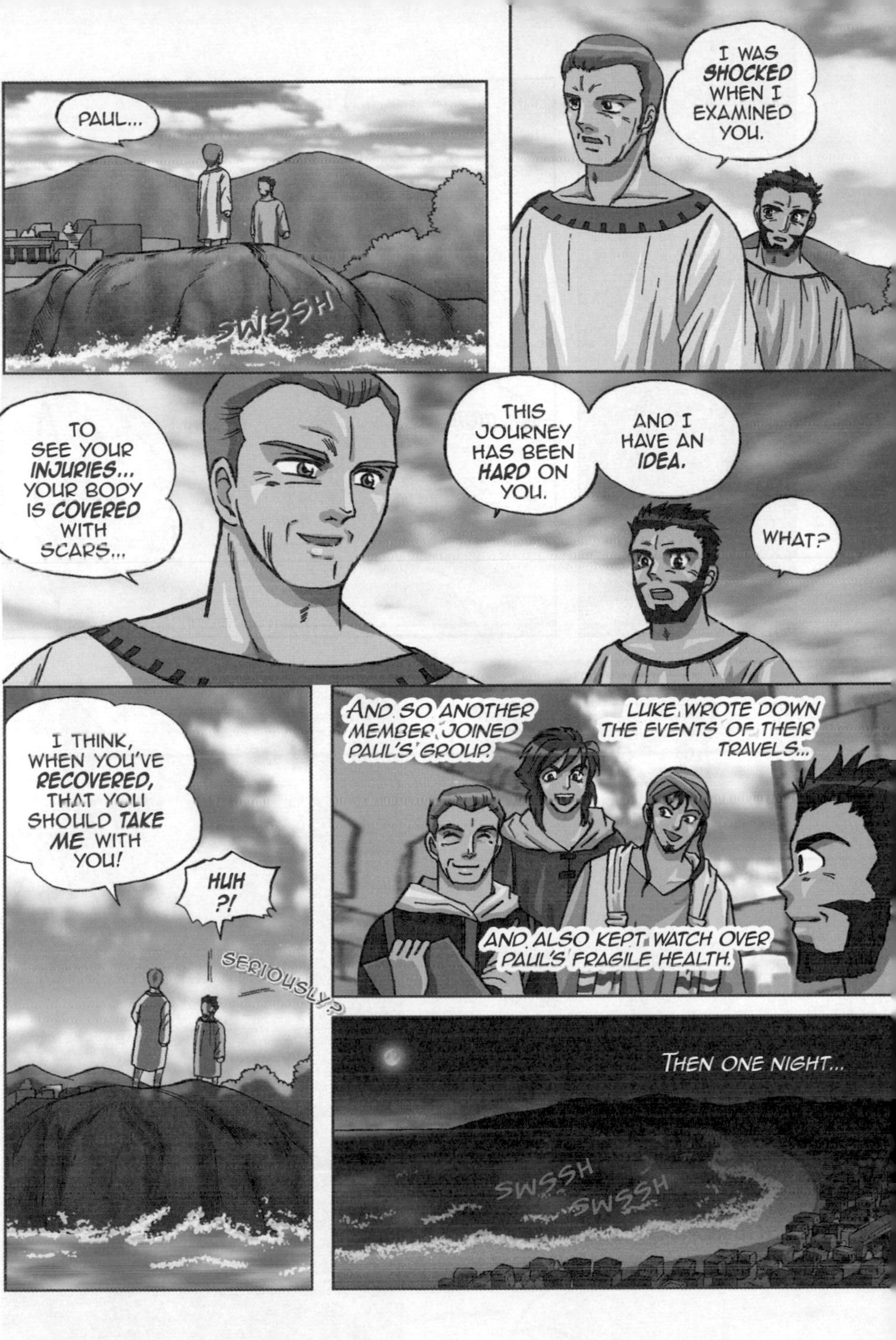
PAUL...
SWSSH
I WAS SHOCKED WHEN I EXAMINED YOU.
TO SEE YOUR INJURIES... YOUR BODY IS COVERED WITH SCARS...
THIS JOURNEY HAS BEEN HARD ON YOU.
AND I HAVE AN IDEA.
WHAT?
I THINK, WHEN YOU'VE RECOVERED, THAT YOU SHOULD TAKE ME WITH YOU!
HUH ?!
SERIOUSLY?
AND SO ANOTHER MEMBER JOINED PAUL'S GROUP.
LUKE WROTE DOWN THE EVENTS OF THEIR TRAVELS...
AND ALSO KEPT WATCH OVER PAUL'S FRAGILE HEALTH.
THEN ONE NIGHT...
SWSSH
SWSSH

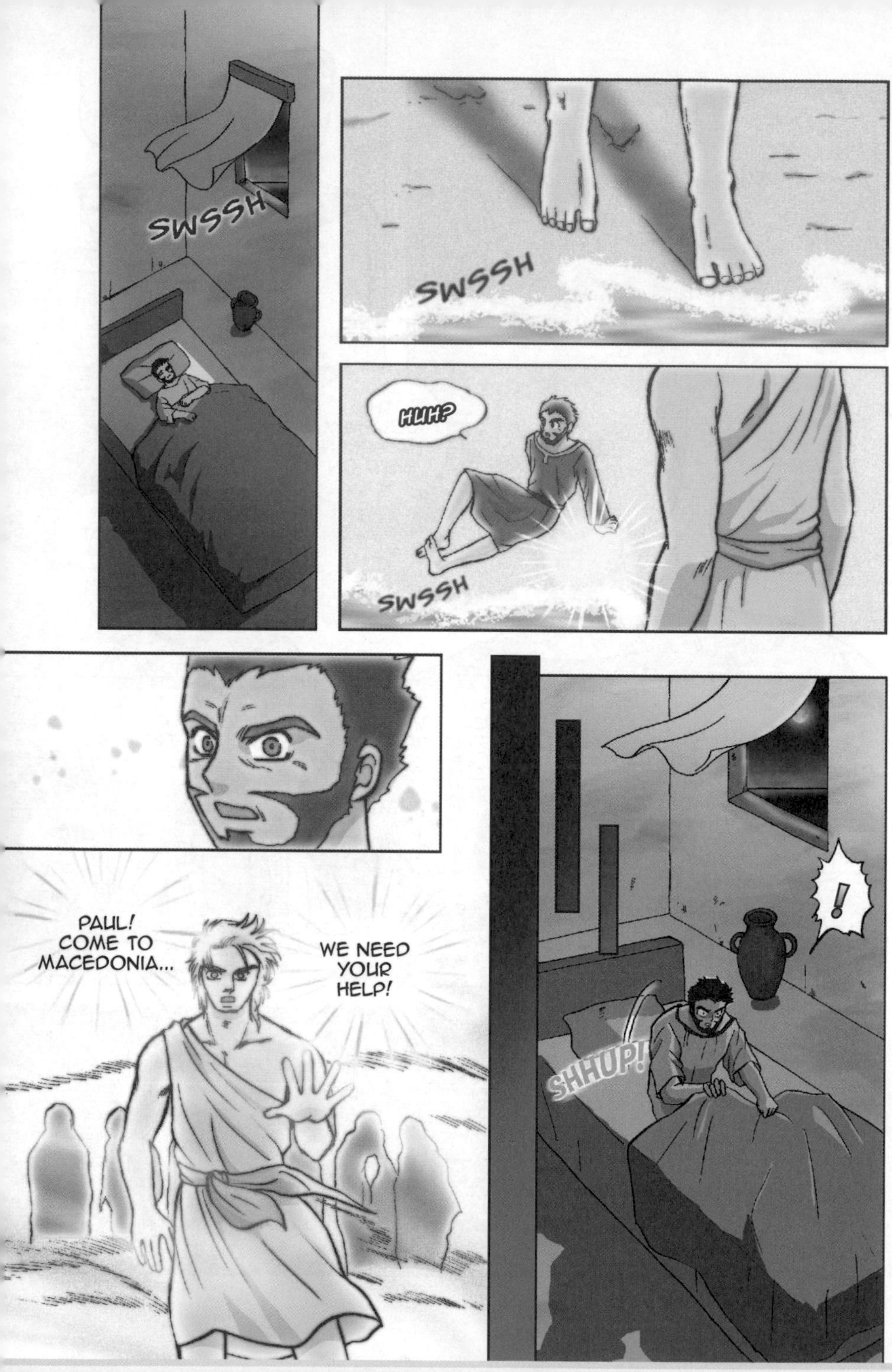
SWSSH
SWSSH
HUH?
SWSSH
PAUL! COME TO MACEDONIA...
WE NEED YOUR HELP!
!
SHHUP!

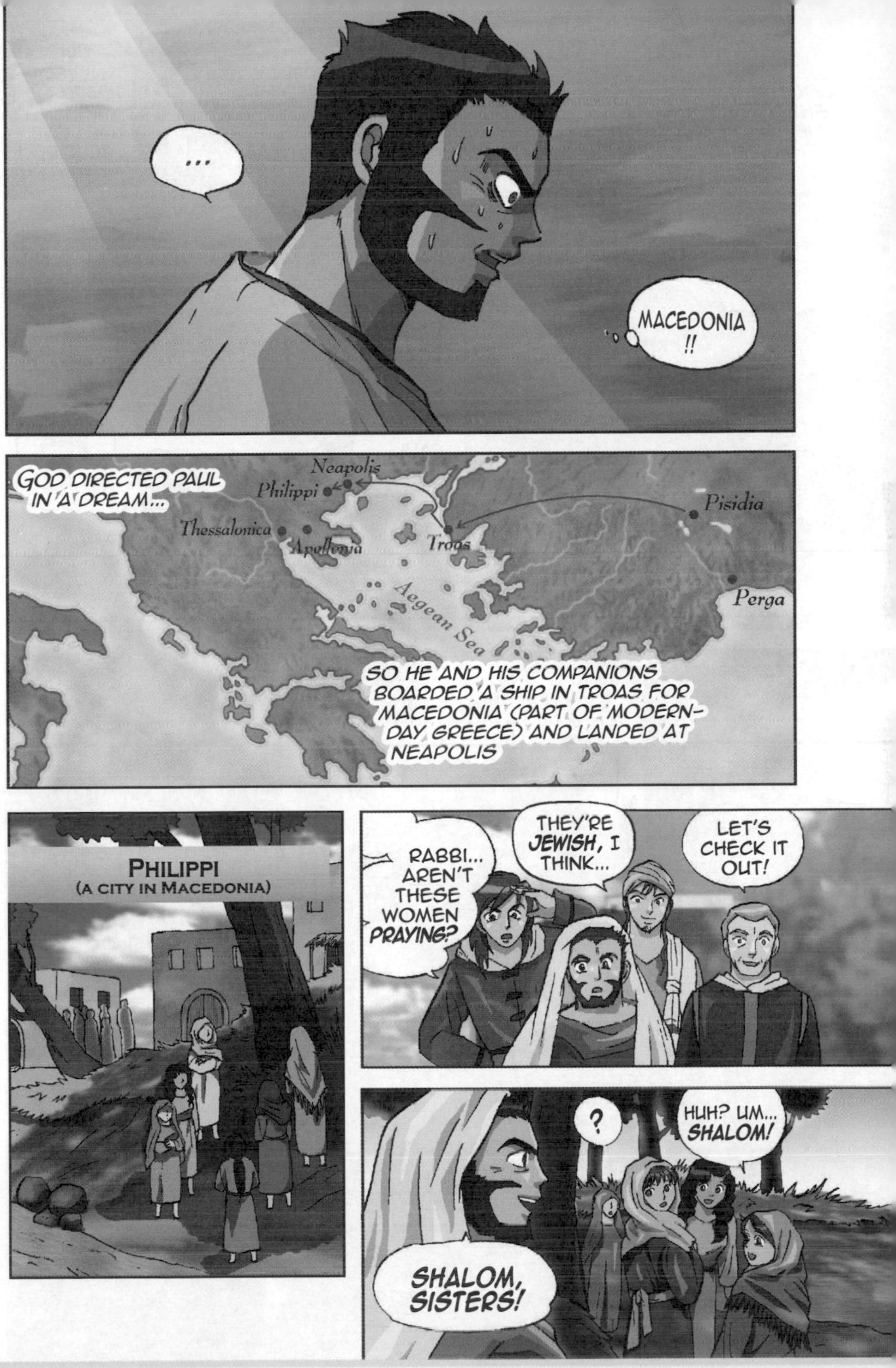
...
MACEDONIA !!
GOD DIRECTED PAUL IN A DREAM...
Neapolis
Philippi
Thessalonica
Apollonia
Troas
Pisidia
Aegean Sea
Perga
SO HE AND HIS COMPANIONS BOARDED A SHIP IN TROAS FOR MACEDONIA (PART OF MODERN-DAY GREECE) AND LANDED AT NEAPOLIS
PHILIPPI (A CITY IN MACEDONIA)
RABBI... AREN'T THESE WOMEN PRAYING?
THEY'RE JEWISH, I THINK...
LET'S CHECK IT OUT!
?
HUH? UM... SHALOM!
SHALOM, SISTERS!

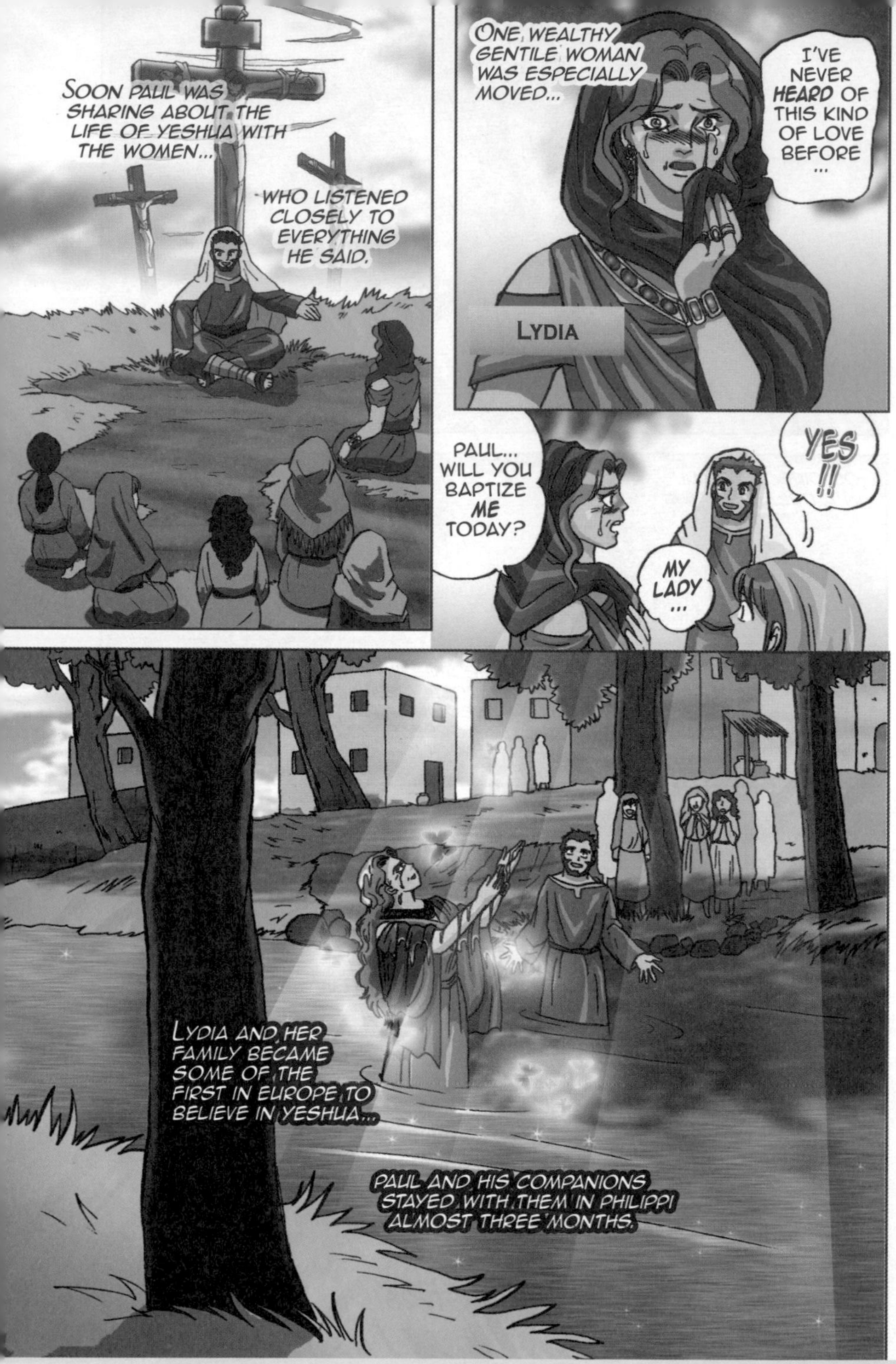
SOON PAUL WAS SHARING ABOUT THE LIFE OF YESHUA WITH THE WOMEN...
WHO LISTENED CLOSELY TO EVERYTHING HE SAID.
ONE WEALTHY GENTILE WOMAN WAS ESPECIALLY MOVED...
I'VE NEVER HEARD OF THIS KIND OF LOVE BEFORE ...
LYDIA
PAUL... WILL YOU BAPTIZE ME TODAY?
MY LADY ...
YES !!
LYDIA AND HER FAMILY BECAME SOME OF THE FIRST IN EUROPE TO BELIEVE IN YESHUA...
PAUL AND HIS COMPANIONS STAYED WITH THEM IN PHILIPPI ALMOST THREE MONTHS.

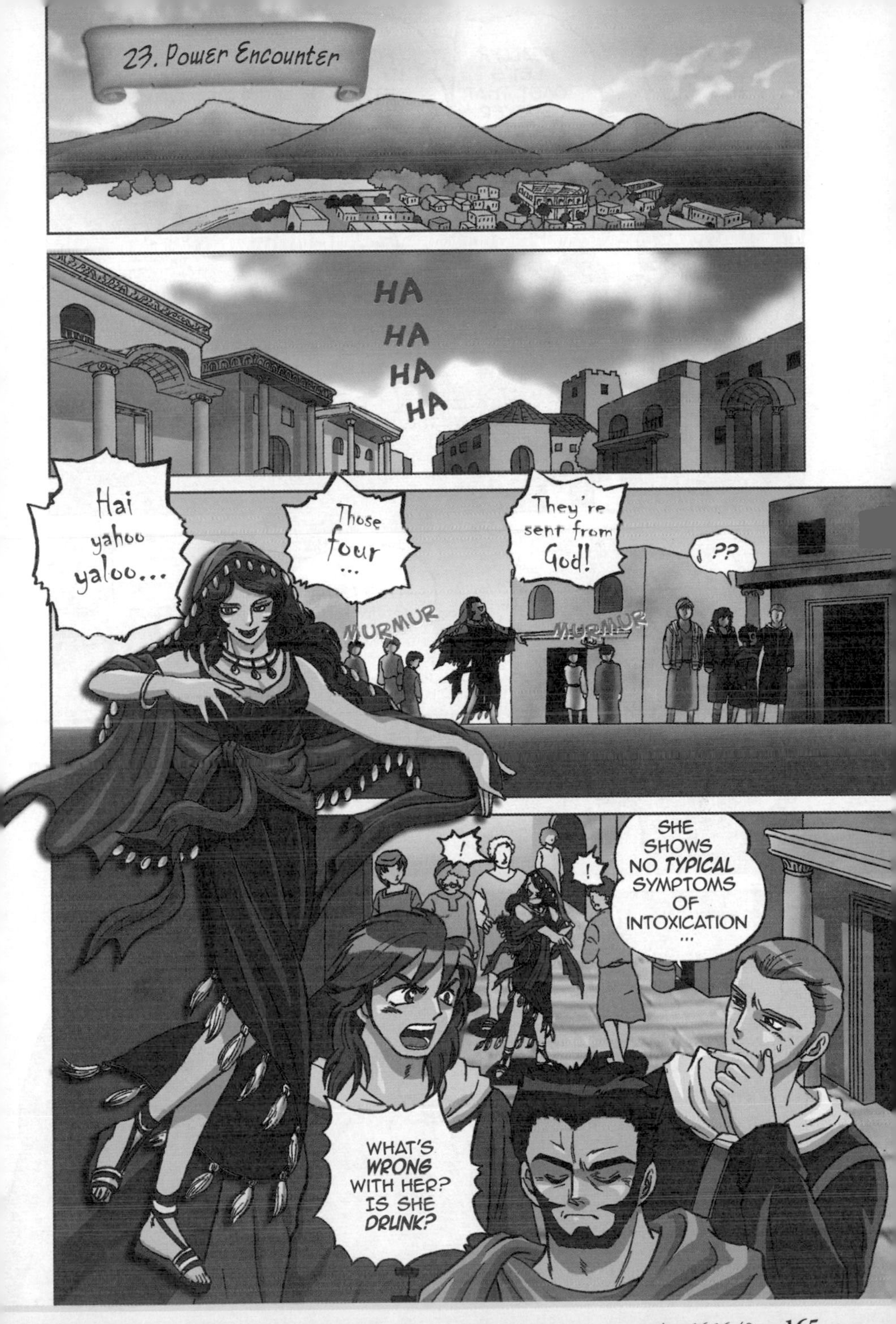
23. Power Encounter
HA HA HA HA
Hai yahoo yaloo...
Those four ...
MURMUR
They're sent from God!
MURMUR
¿ ??
!
!
SHE SHOWS NO TYPICAL SYMPTOMS OF INTOXICATION ...
WHAT'S WRONG WITH HER? IS SHE DRUNK?

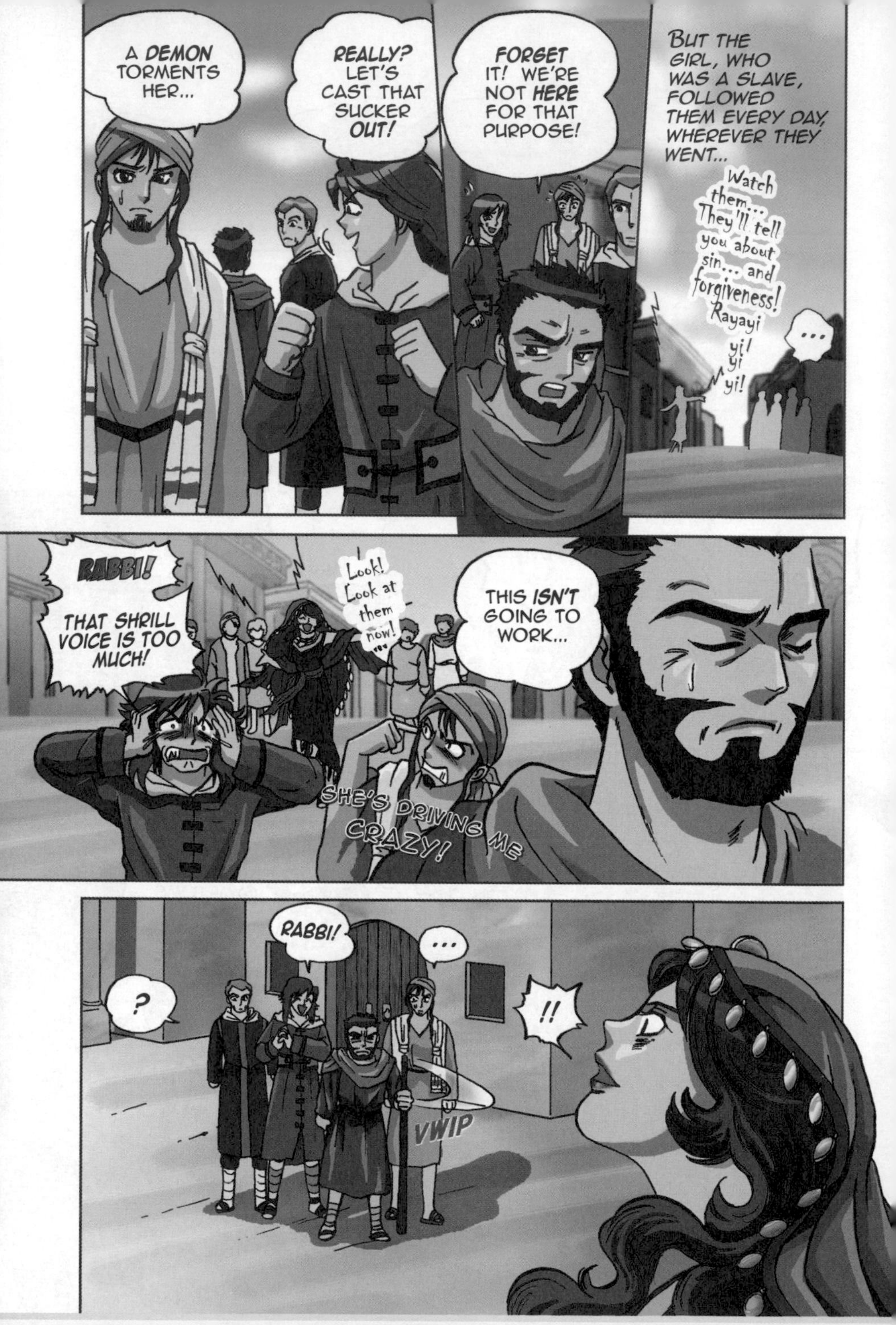
A DEMON TORMENTS HER...
REALLY? LET'S CAST THAT SUCKER OUT!
FORGET IT! WE'RE NOT HERE FOR THAT PURPOSE!
BUT THE GIRL, WHO WAS A SLAVE, FOLLOWED THEM EVERY DAY, WHEREVER THEY WENT...
Watch them... They'll tell you about sin... and forgiveness!
Rayayi yi! yi yi!
...
RABBI!
THAT SHRILL VOICE IS TOO MUCH!
Look! Look at them now!
THIS ISN'T GOING TO WORK...
SHE'S DRIVING ME CRAZY!
RABBI!
...
?
!!
VWIP

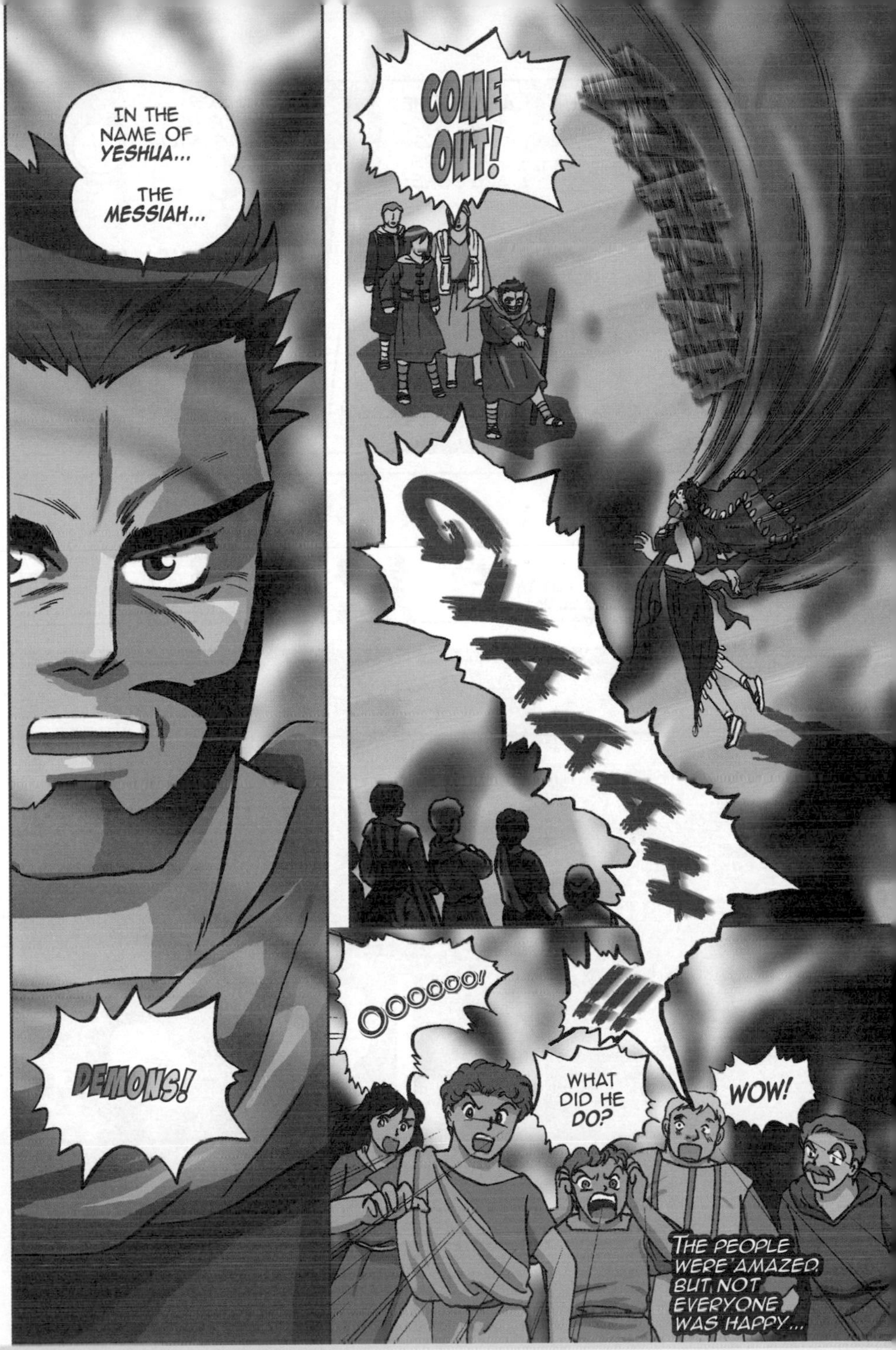

IN THE NAME OF YESHUA... THE MESSIAH...
COME OUT!
DEMONS!
GYAAAAAI!!!
OOOOOO!
WHAT DID HE DO?
WOW!
THE PEOPLE WERE AMAZED, BUT NOT EVERYONE WAS HAPPY...

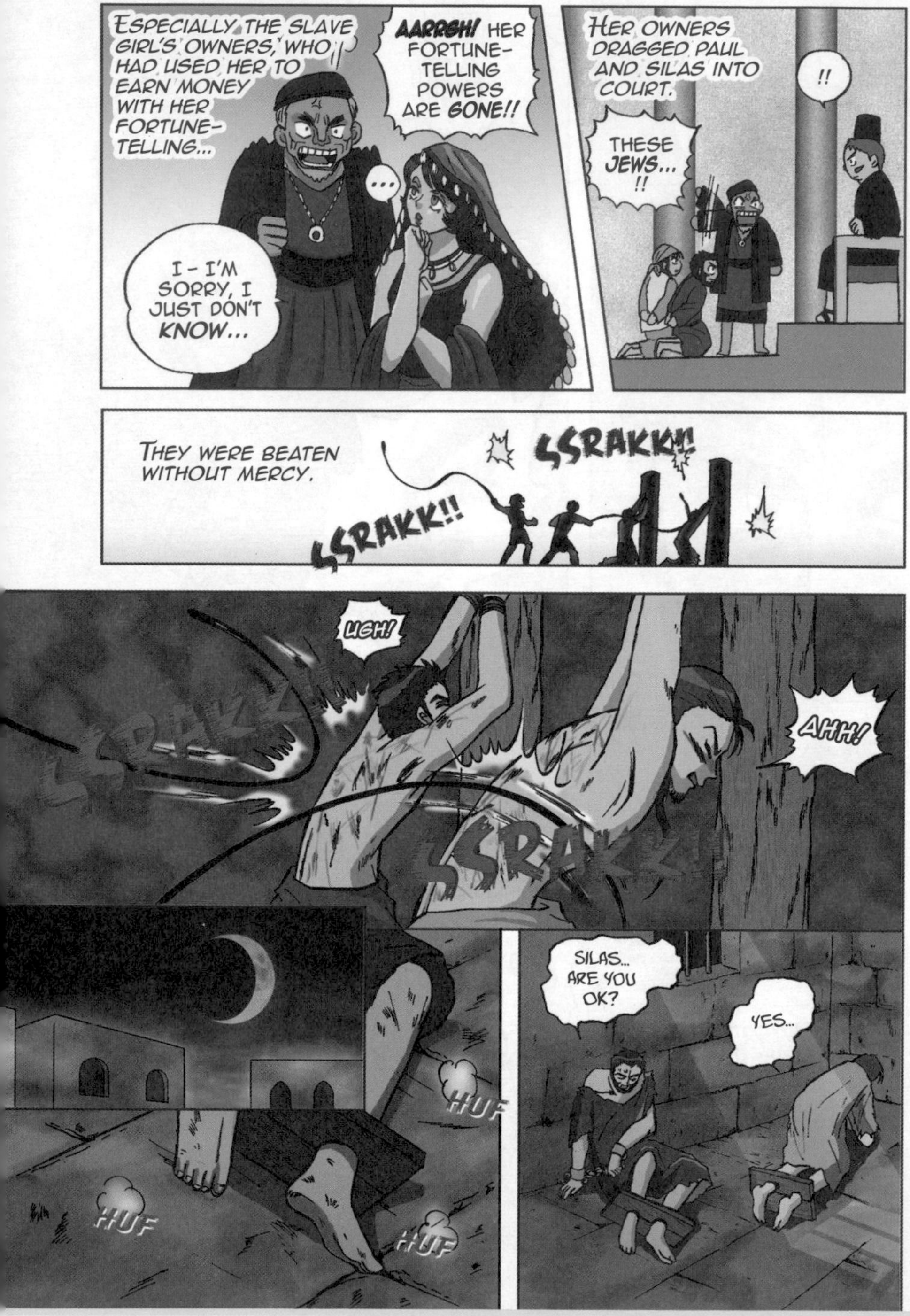
ESPECIALLY THE SLAVE GIRL'S OWNERS, WHO HAD USED HER TO EARN MONEY WITH HER FORTUNE-TELLING...
AARRGH! HER FORTUNE-TELLING POWERS ARE GONE!!
...
I - I'M SORRY, I JUST DON'T KNOW...
HER OWNERS DRAGGED PAUL AND SILAS INTO COURT.
!!
THESE JEWS... !!
THEY WERE BEATEN WITHOUT MERCY.
SSRAKK!!
SSRAKK!!
UGH!
AHH!
SSRAKK!
HUF
HUF
HUF
SILAS... ARE YOU OK?
YES...

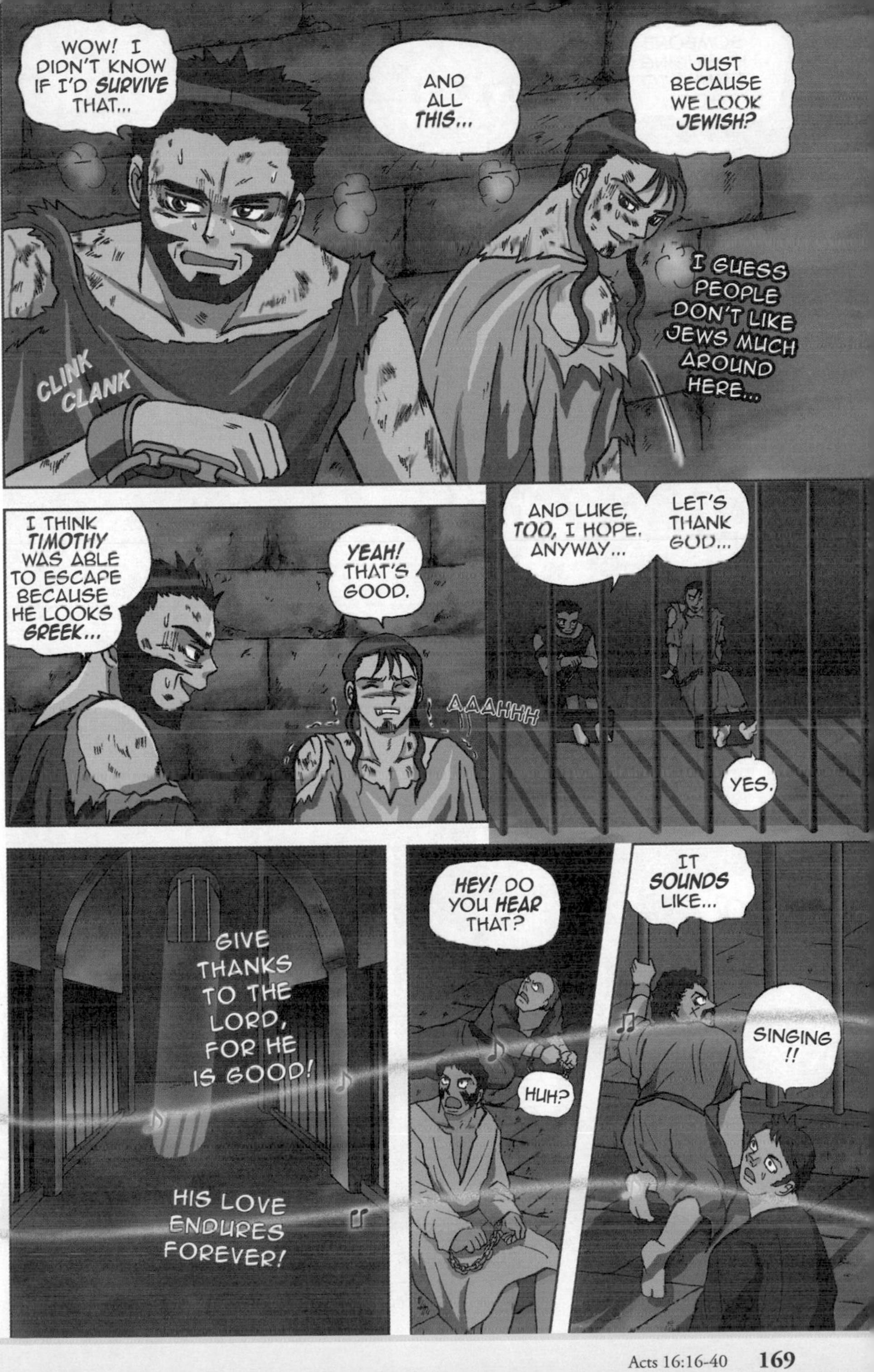
WOW! I DIDN'T KNOW IF I'D SURVIVE THAT...
AND ALL THIS...
JUST BECAUSE WE LOOK JEWISH?
I GUESS PEOPLE DON'T LIKE JEWS MUCH AROUND HERE...
CLINK CLANK
I THINK TIMOTHY WAS ABLE TO ESCAPE BECAUSE HE LOOKS GREEK...
YEAH! THAT'S GOOD.
AAAHHH
AND LUKE, TOO, I HOPE. ANYWAY...
LET'S THANK GOD...
YES.
GIVE THANKS TO THE LORD, FOR HE IS GOOD!
HIS LOVE ENDURES FOREVER!
HEY! DO YOU HEAR THAT?
HUH?
IT SOUNDS LIKE...
SINGING !!

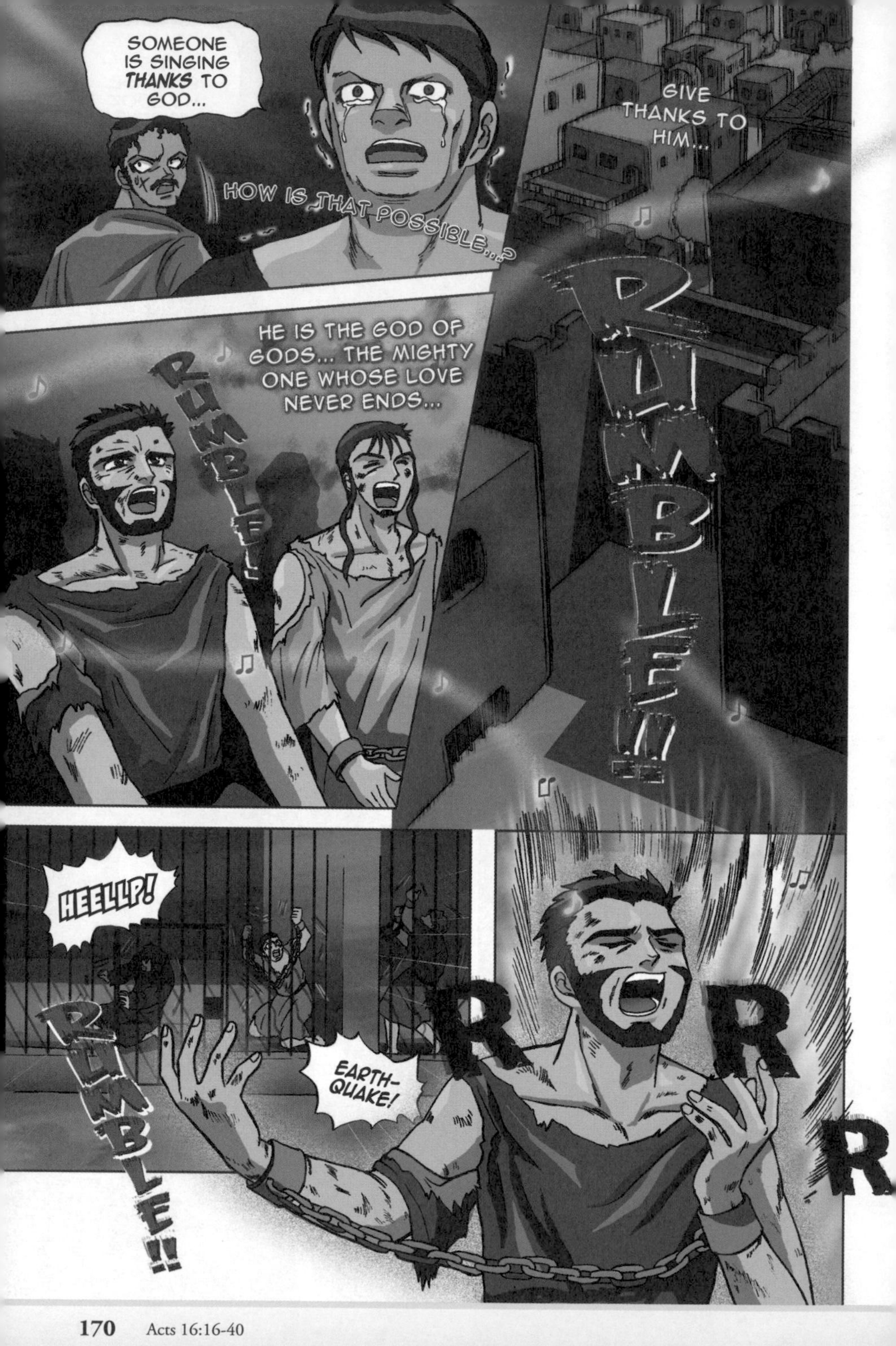
SOMEONE IS SINGING THANKS TO GOD...
HOW IS THAT POSSIBLE...?
GIVE THANKS TO HIM...
RUMBLE!!
HE IS THE GOD OF GODS... THE MIGHTY ONE WHOSE LOVE NEVER ENDS...
RUMBLE!
HEELLP!
RUMBLE!!
EARTH-QUAKE!
R R R

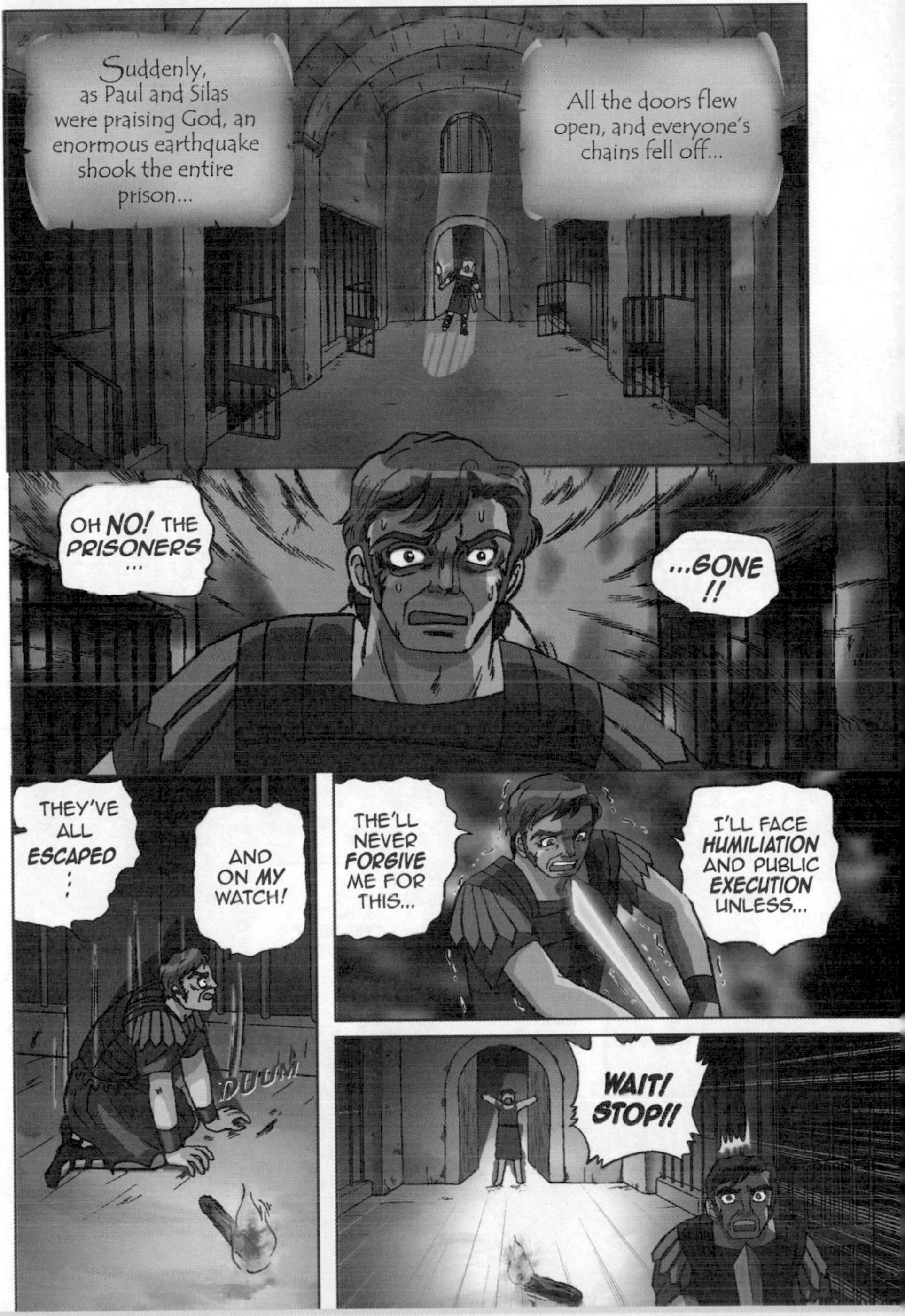
Suddenly, as Paul and Silas were praising God, an enormous earthquake shook the entire prison...
All the doors flew open, and everyone's chains fell off...
OH NO! THE PRISONERS ...
...GONE !!
THEY'VE ALL ESCAPED :
AND ON MY WATCH!
DUUM
THE'LL NEVER FORGIVE ME FOR THIS...
I'LL FACE HUMILIATION AND PUBLIC EXECUTION UNLESS...
WAIT! STOP!!

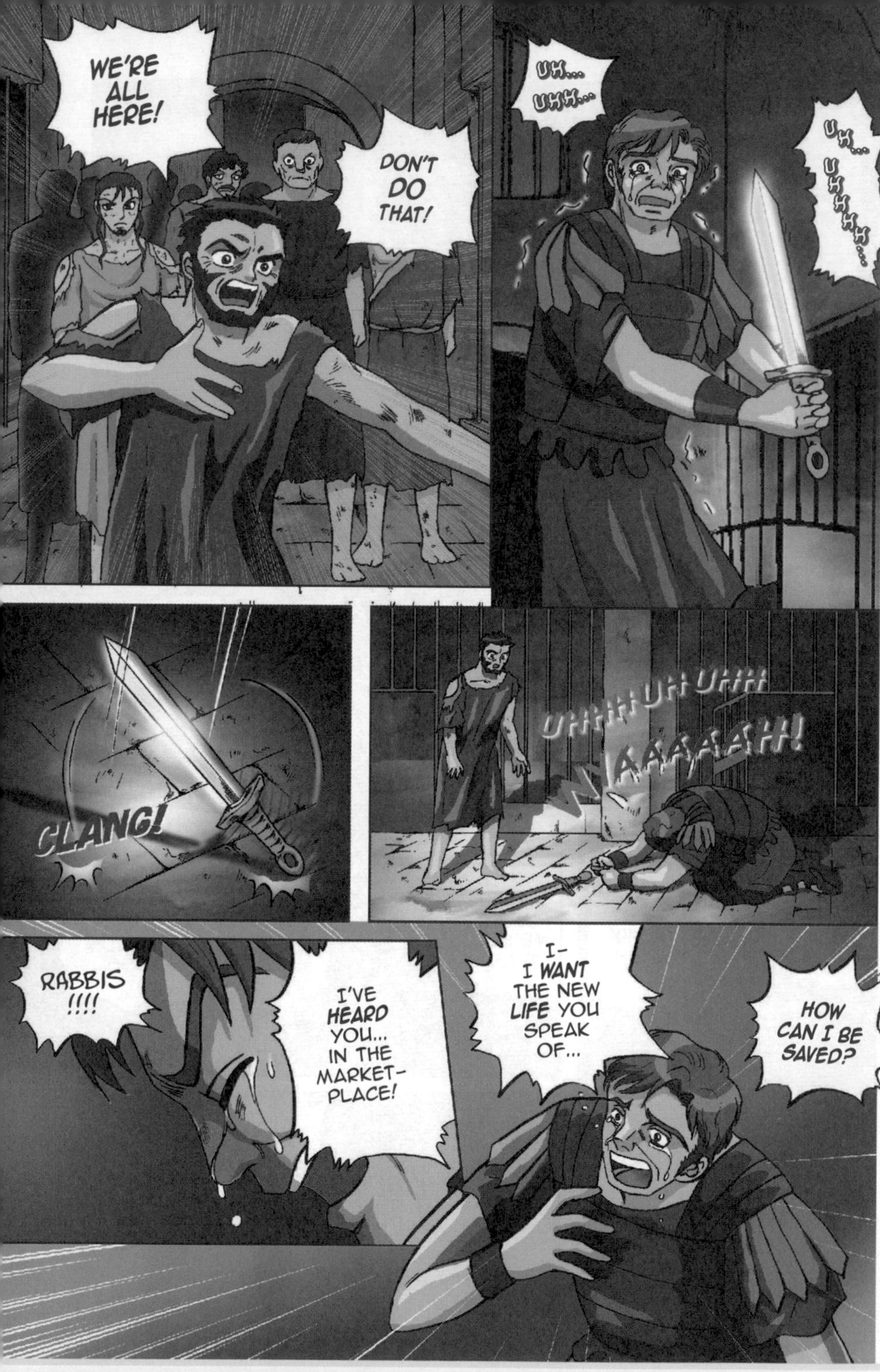
WE'RE ALL HERE!
DON'T DO THAT!
UH... UHH...
UH... UHHHH...
CLANG!
UHHH UH UHH
AAAAAAH!
RABBIS !!!!
I'VE HEARD YOU... IN THE MARKET-PLACE!
I- I WANT THE NEW LIFE YOU SPEAK OF...
HOW CAN I BE SAVED?

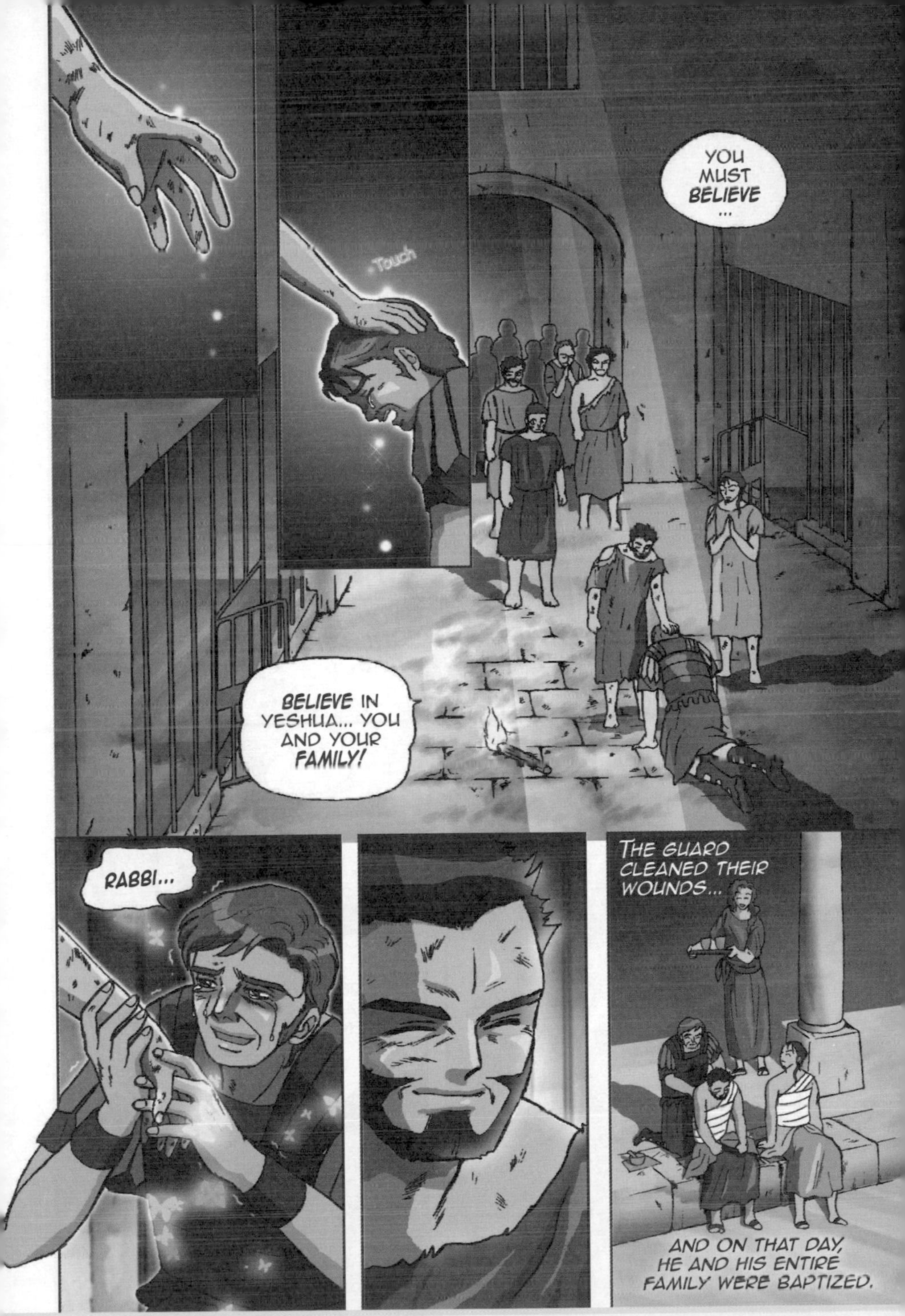
Touch
YOU MUST BELIEVE ...
BELIEVE IN YESHUA... YOU AND YOUR FAMILY!
RABBI...
THE GUARD CLEANED THEIR WOUNDS...
AND ON THAT DAY, HE AND HIS ENTIRE FAMILY WERE BAPTIZED.

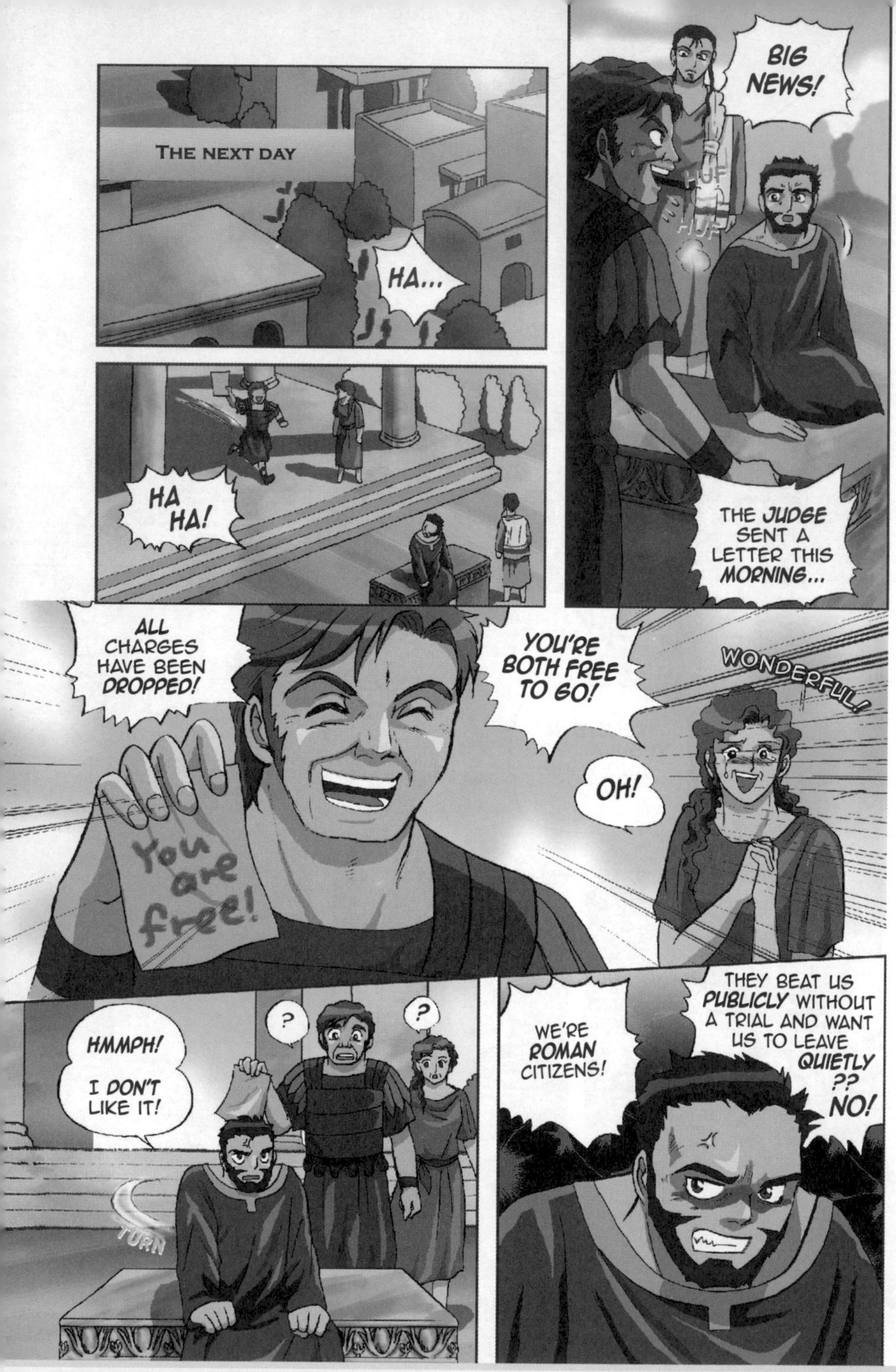

THE NEXT DAY
HA...
HA HA!
BIG NEWS!
HUF HUF
THE JUDGE SENT A LETTER THIS MORNING...
ALL CHARGES HAVE BEEN DROPPED!
You are free!
YOU'RE BOTH FREE TO GO!
WONDERFUL!
OH!
?
?
HMMPH!
I DON'T LIKE IT!
TURN
WE'RE ROMAN CITIZENS!
THEY BEAT US PUBLICLY WITHOUT A TRIAL AND WANT US TO LEAVE QUIETLY ?? NO!

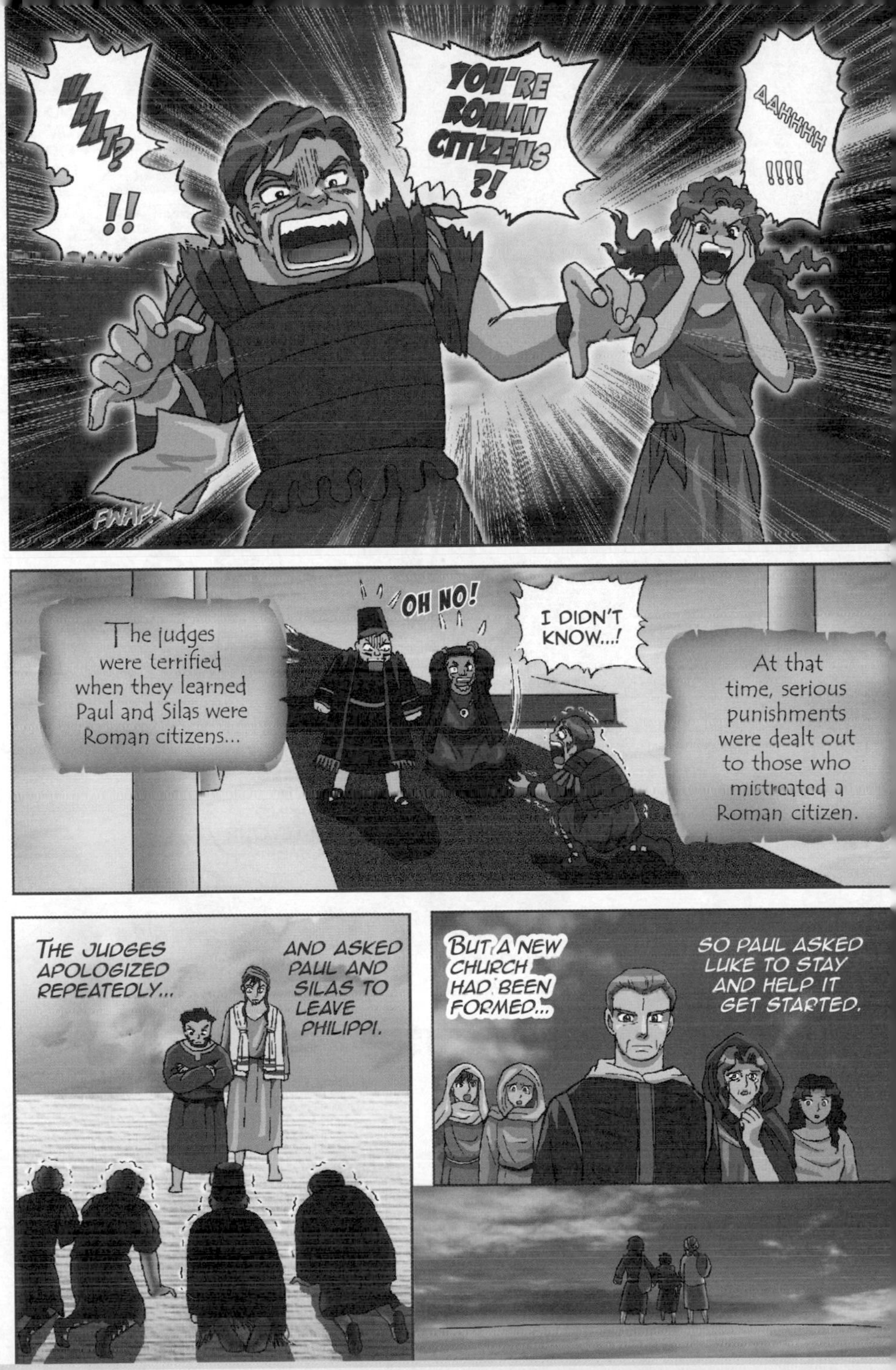
WHAT?!!
YOU'RE ROMAN CITIZENS?!
AAHHHH!!!!
FWAP!
The judges were terrified when they learned Paul and Silas were Roman citizens...
OH NO!
I DIDN'T KNOW...!
At that time, serious punishments were dealt out to those who mistreated a Roman citizen.
THE JUDGES APOLOGIZED REPEATEDLY...
AND ASKED PAUL AND SILAS TO LEAVE PHILIPPI.
BUT A NEW CHURCH HAD BEEN FORMED...
SO PAUL ASKED LUKE TO STAY AND HELP IT GET STARTED.

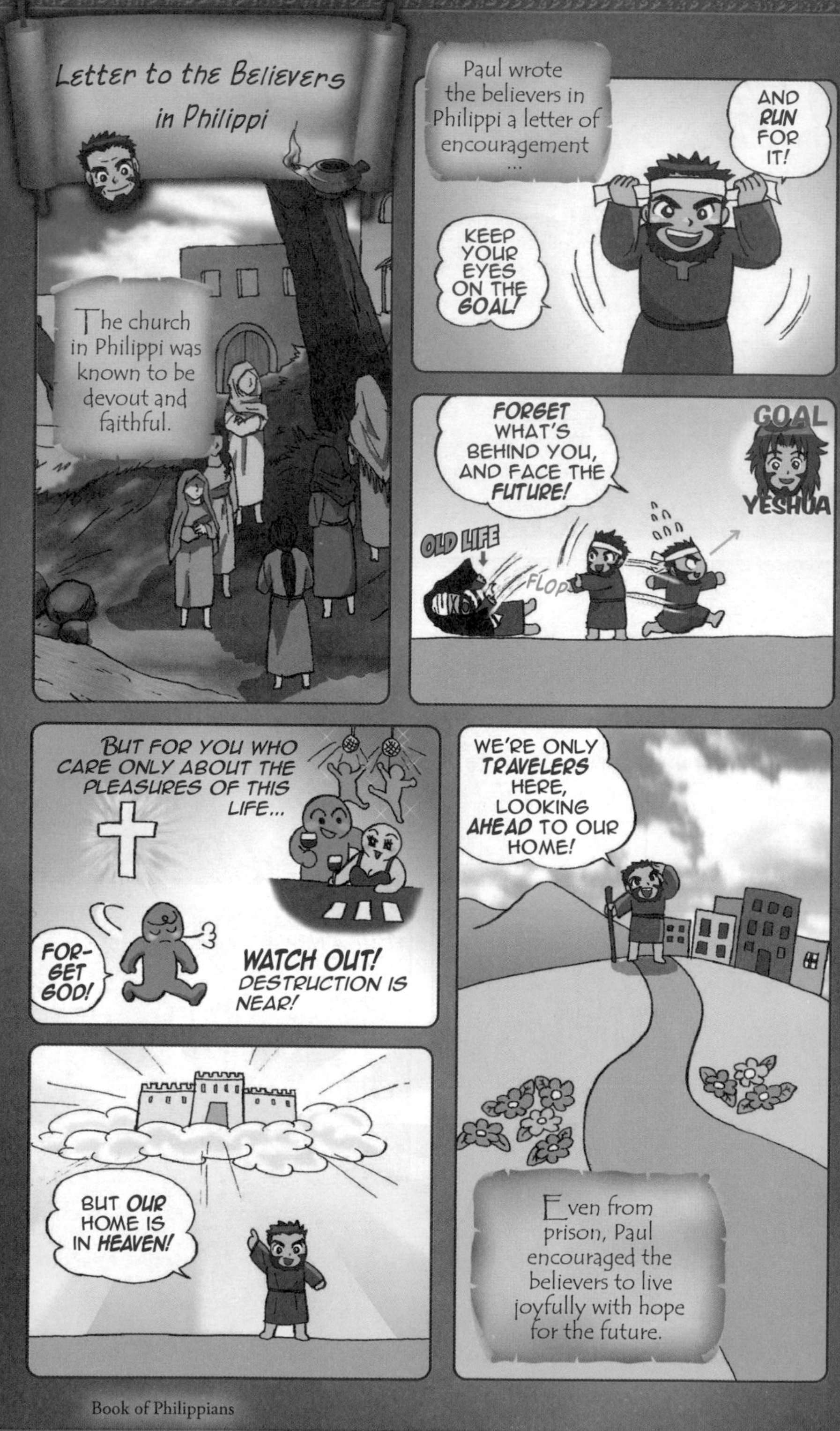

Letter to the Believers in Philippi
The church in Philippi was known to be devout and faithful.
Paul wrote the believers in Philippi a letter of encouragement ...
AND RUN FOR IT!
KEEP YOUR EYES ON THE GOAL!
FORGET WHAT'S BEHIND YOU, AND FACE THE FUTURE!
GOAL
YESHUA
OLD LIFE
FLOP
BUT FOR YOU WHO CARE ONLY ABOUT THE PLEASURES OF THIS LIFE...
FOR-GET GOD!
WATCH OUT! DESTRUCTION IS NEAR!
WE'RE ONLY TRAVELERS HERE, LOOKING AHEAD TO OUR HOME!
BUT OUR HOME IS IN HEAVEN!
Even from prison, Paul encouraged the believers to live joyfully with hope for the future.

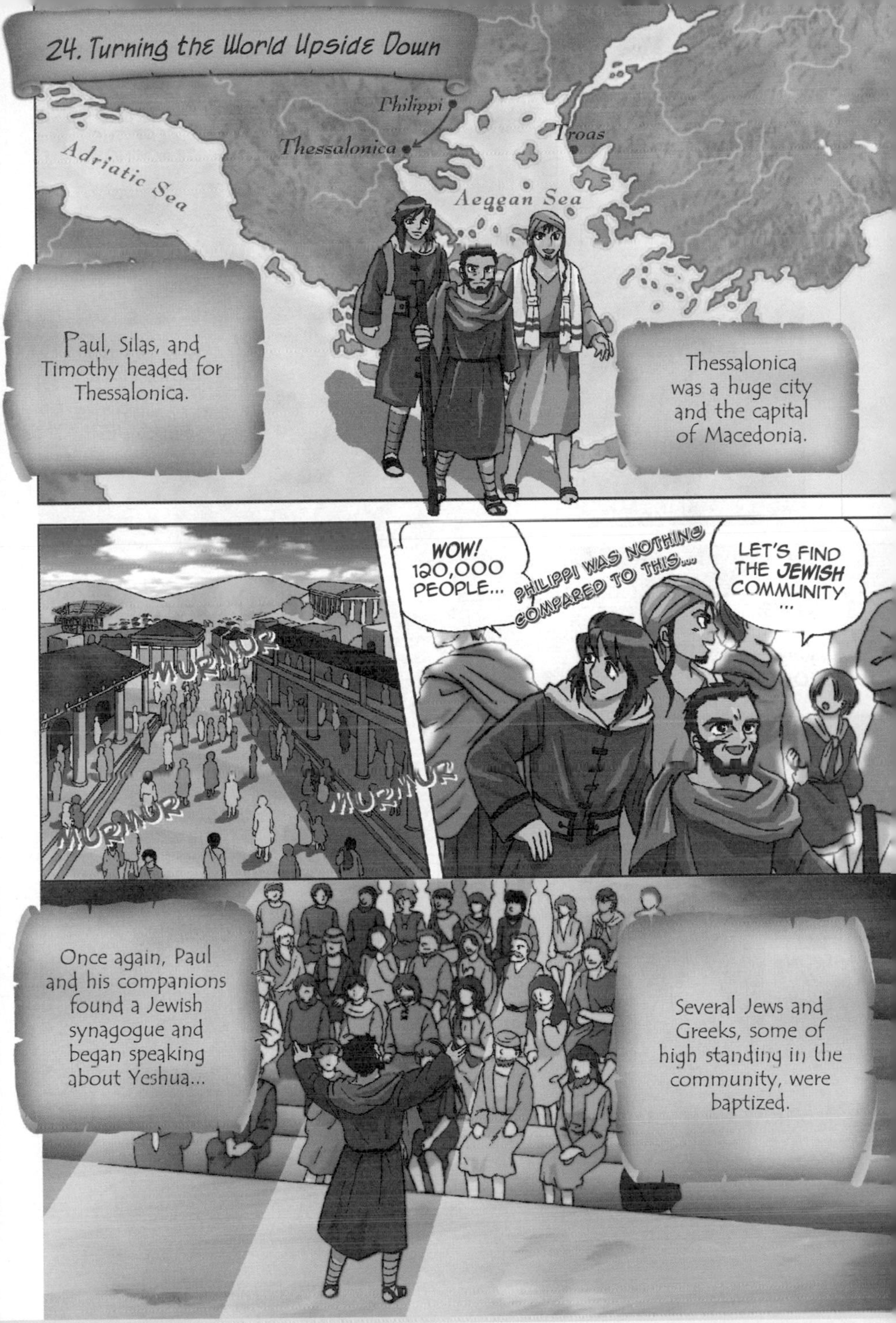
24. Turning the World Upside Down
Philippi
Thessalonica
Troas
Adriatic Sea
Aeggan Sea
Paul, Silas, and Timothy headed for Thessalonica.
Thessalonica was a huge city and the capital of Macedonia.
MURMUR
MURMUR
MURMUR
WOW! 120,000 PEOPLE...
PHILIPPI WAS NOTHING COMPARED TO THIS...
LET'S FIND THE JEWISH COMMUNITY ...
Once again, Paul and his companions found a Jewish synagogue and began speaking about Yeshua...
Several Jews and Greeks, some of high standing in the community, were baptized.

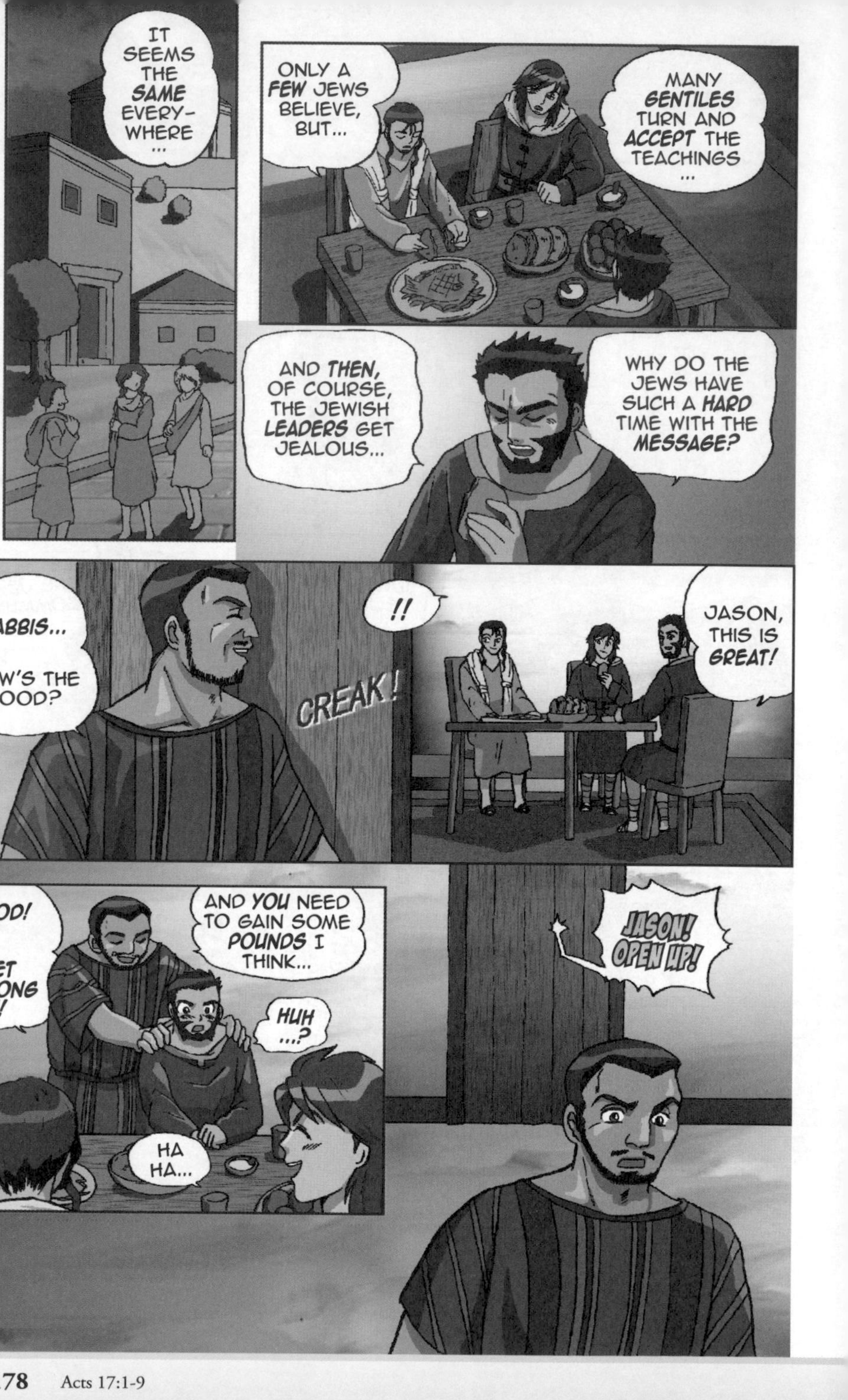
IT SEEMS THE SAME EVERYWHERE ...
ONLY A FEW JEWS BELIEVE, BUT...
MANY GENTILES TURN AND ACCEPT THE TEACHINGS ...
AND THEN, OF COURSE, THE JEWISH LEADERS GET JEALOUS...
WHY DO THE JEWS HAVE SUCH A HARD TIME WITH THE MESSAGE?
RABBIS...
HOW'S THE FOOD?
CREAK!
!!
JASON, THIS IS GREAT!
GOOD!
GET STRONG !!
AND YOU NEED TO GAIN SOME POUNDS I THINK...
HUH ...?
HA HA...
JASON! OPEN UP!

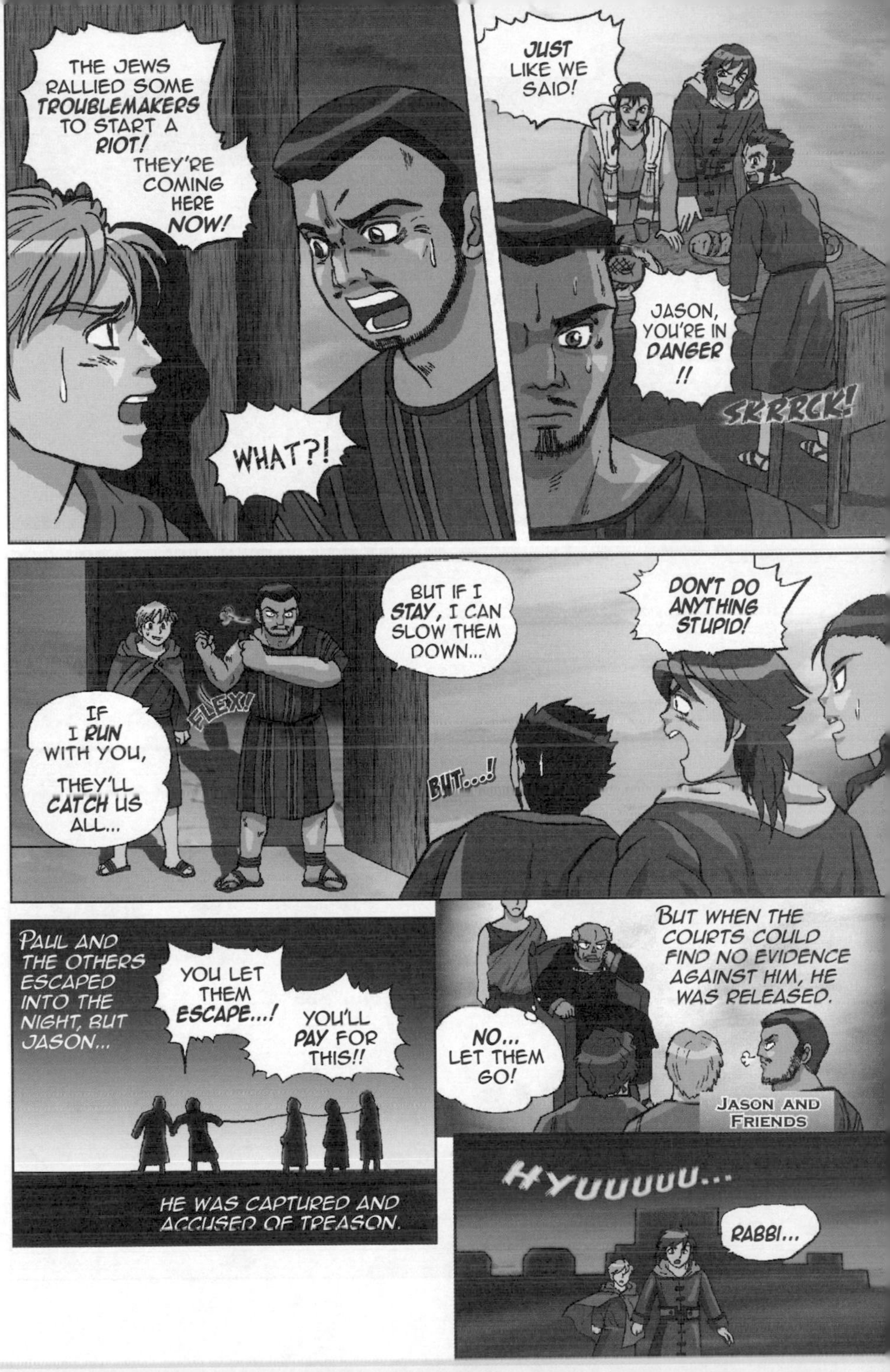
THE JEWS RALLIED SOME TROUBLEMAKERS TO START A RIOT!
THEY'RE COMING HERE NOW!
WHAT?!
JUST LIKE WE SAID!
JASON, YOU'RE IN DANGER !!
SKRRCK!
IF I RUN WITH YOU,
THEY'LL CATCH US ALL...
FLEX!
BUT IF I STAY, I CAN SLOW THEM DOWN...
DON'T DO ANYTHING STUPID!
BUT...!
PAUL AND THE OTHERS ESCAPED INTO THE NIGHT, BUT JASON...
YOU LET THEM ESCAPE...!
YOU'LL PAY FOR THIS!!
HE WAS CAPTURED AND ACCUSED OF TREASON.
BUT WHEN THE COURTS COULD FIND NO EVIDENCE AGAINST HIM, HE WAS RELEASED.
NO... LET THEM GO!
JASON AND FRIENDS
HYUUUUU...
RABBI...

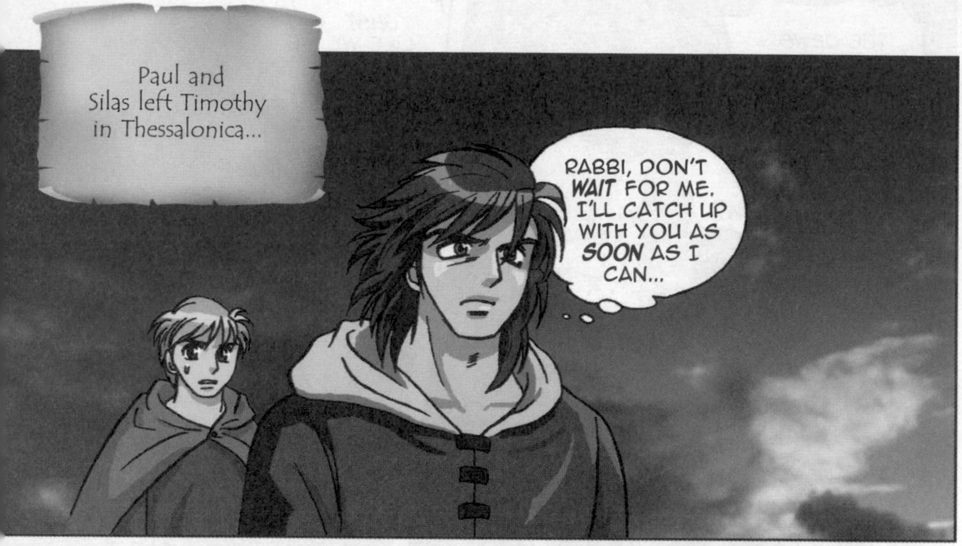
Paul and Silas left Timothy in Thessalonica...
RABBI, DON'T WAIT FOR ME. I'LL CATCH UP WITH YOU AS SOON AS I CAN...

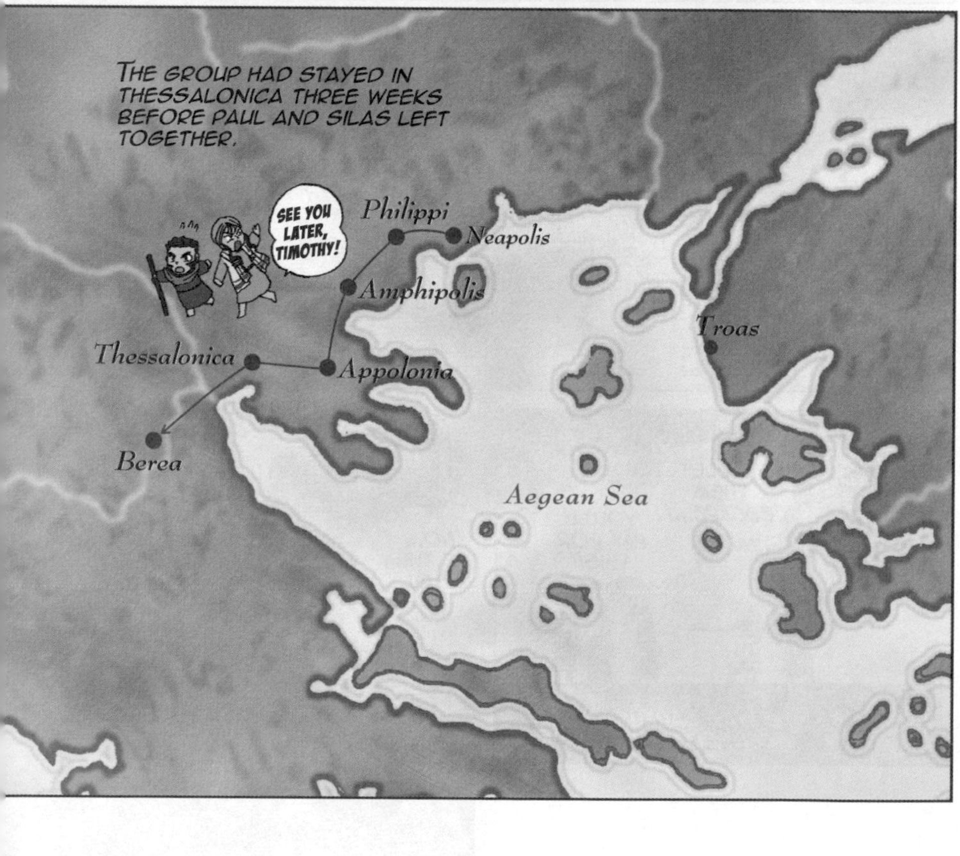
THE GROUP HAD STAYED IN THESSALONICA THREE WEEKS BEFORE PAUL AND SILAS LEFT TOGETHER.
SEE YOU LATER, TIMOTHY!
Philippi
Neapolis
Amphipolis
Troas
Thessalonica
Appolonia
Berea
Aegean Sea

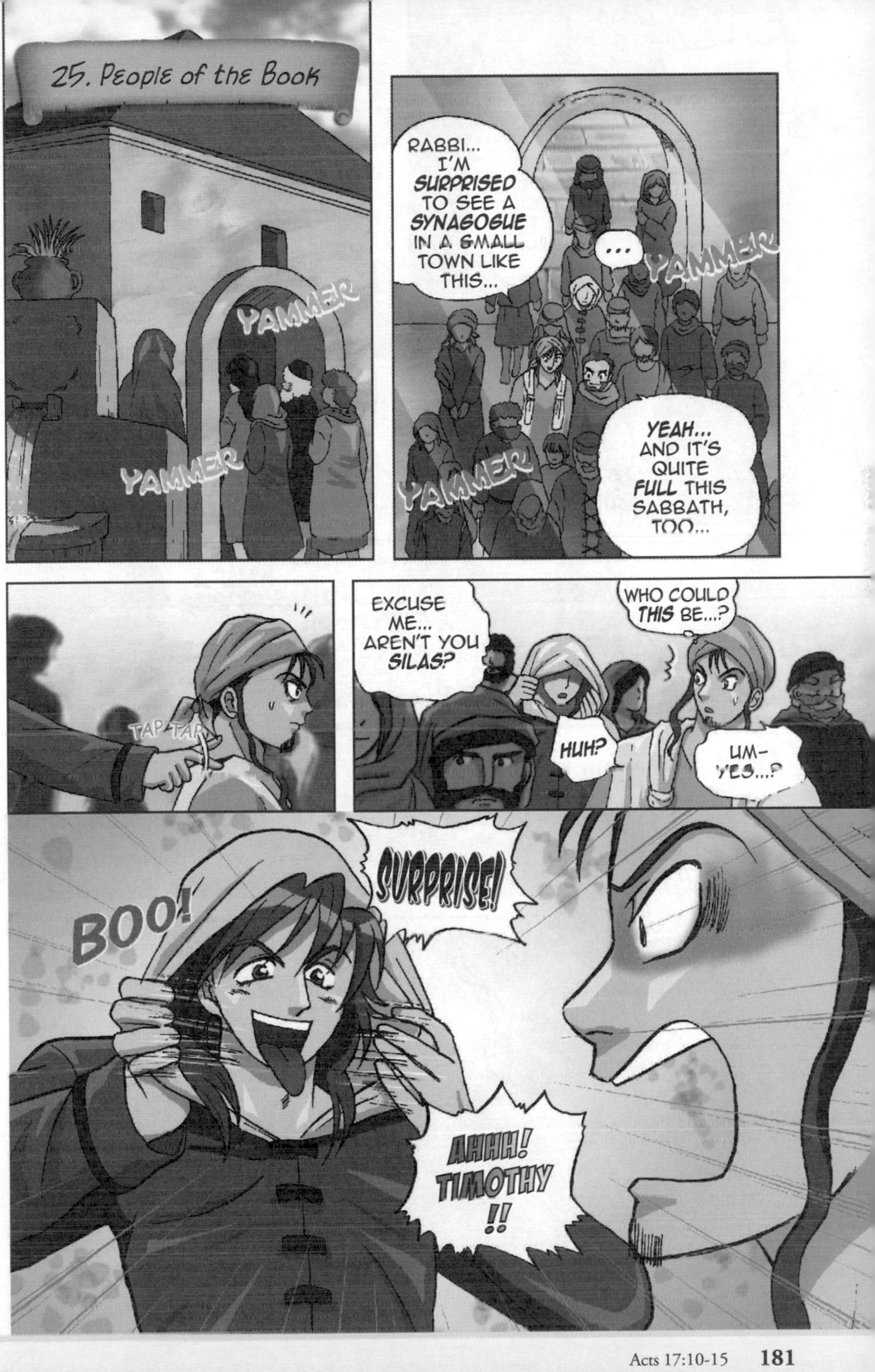
25. People of the Book
YAMMER
YAMMER
RABBI... I'M SURPRISED TO SEE A SYNAGOGUE IN A SMALL TOWN LIKE THIS...
...
YAMMER
YAMMER
YEAH... AND IT'S QUITE FULL THIS SABBATH, TOO...
TAP TAP
EXCUSE ME... AREN'T YOU SILAS?
WHO COULD THIS BE...?
HUH?
UM-YES...?
SURPRISE!
BOO!
AHHH! TIMOTHY!!

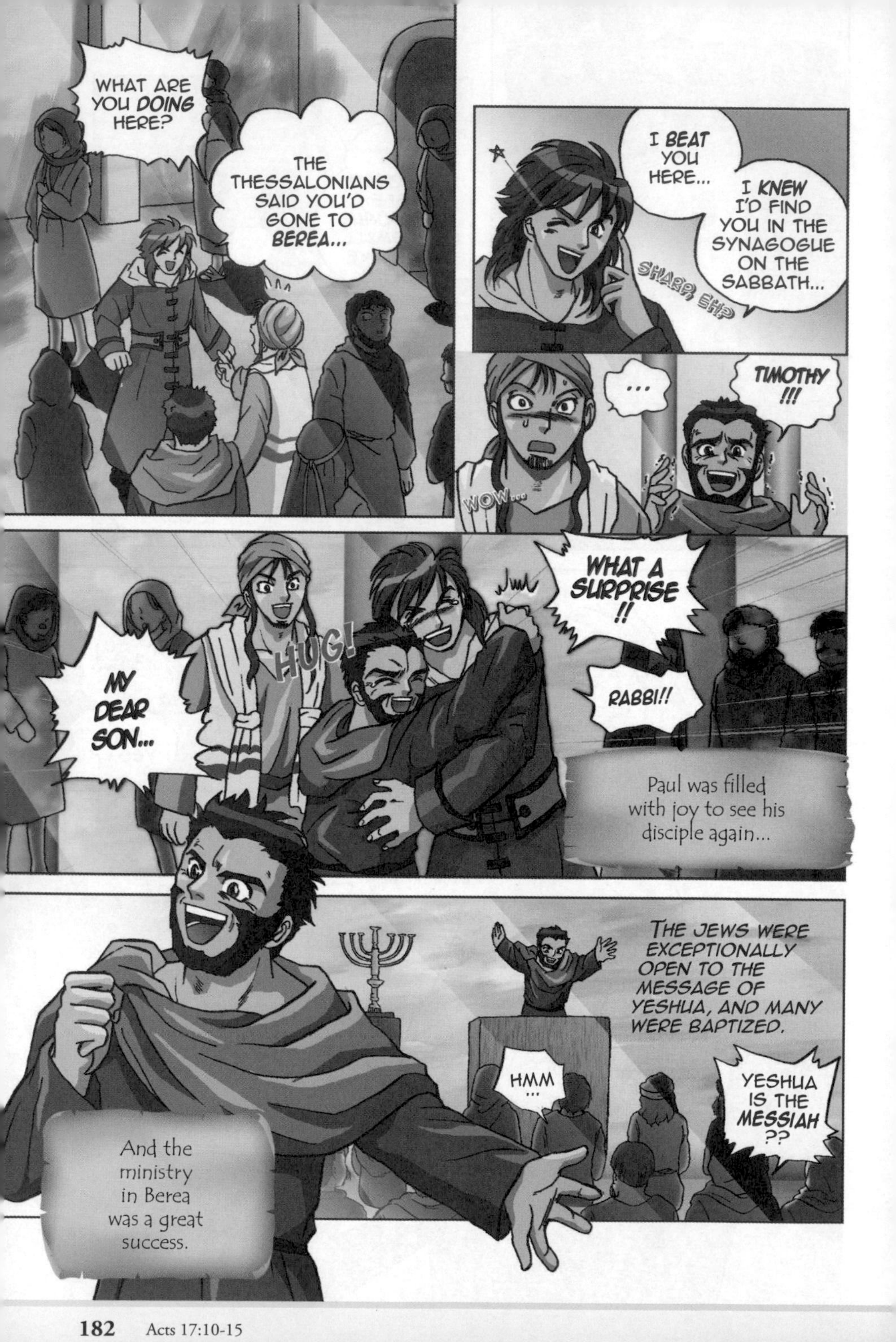
WHAT ARE YOU DOING HERE?
THE THESSALONIANS SAID YOU'D GONE TO BEREA...
I BEAT YOU HERE...
I KNEW I'D FIND YOU IN THE SYNAGOGUE ON THE SABBATH...
SHARP, EH?
...
TIMOTHY !!!
WOW...
WHAT A SURPRISE !!
HUG!
MY DEAR SON...
RABBI!!
Paul was filled with joy to see his disciple again...
THE JEWS WERE EXCEPTIONALLY OPEN TO THE MESSAGE OF YESHUA, AND MANY WERE BAPTIZED.
HMM ...
YESHUA IS THE MESSIAH ??
And the ministry in Berea was a great success.

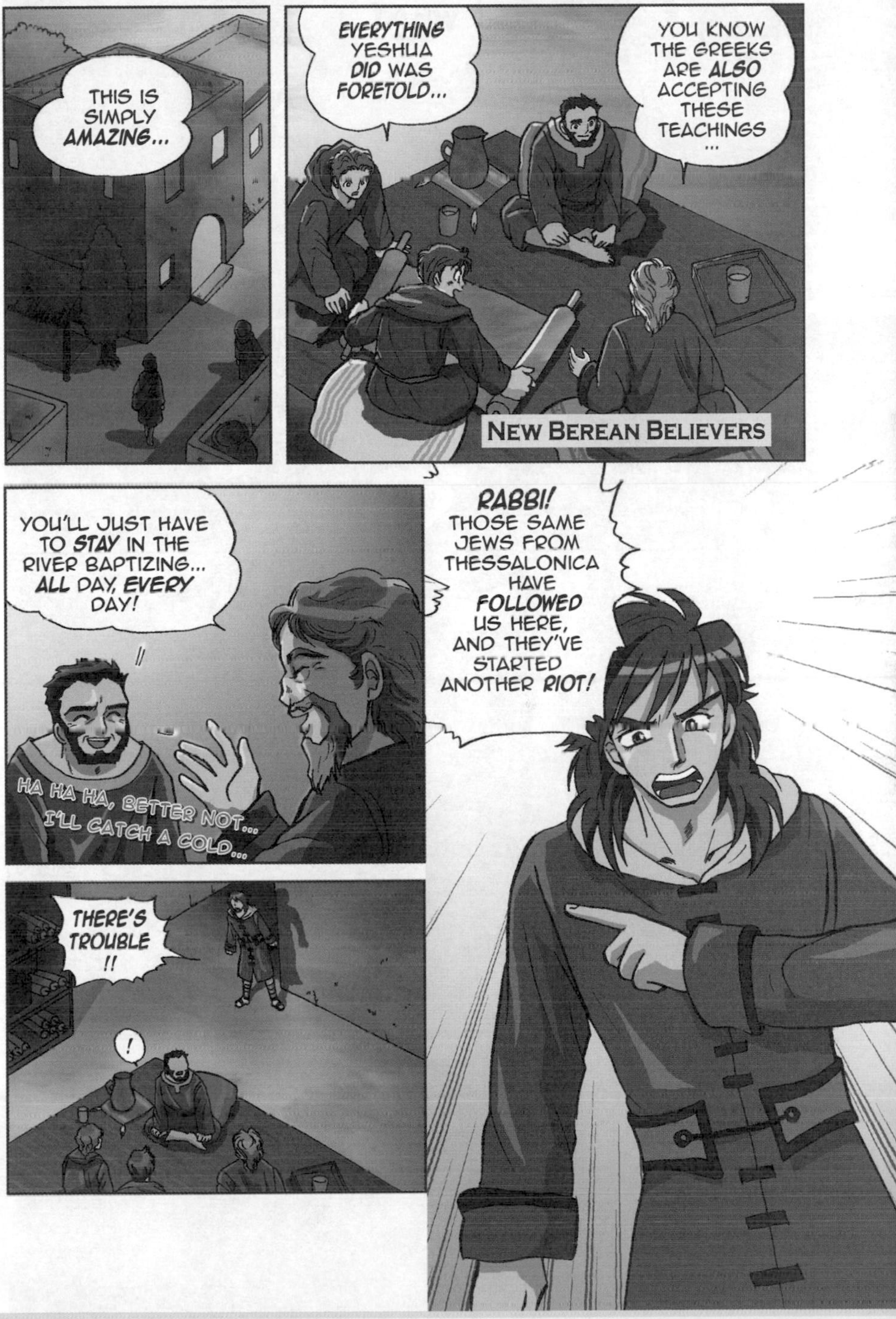
THIS IS SIMPLY AMAZING...
EVERYTHING YESHUA DID WAS FORETOLD...
YOU KNOW THE GREEKS ARE ALSO ACCEPTING THESE TEACHINGS ...
NEW BEREAN BELIEVERS
YOU'LL JUST HAVE TO STAY IN THE RIVER BAPTIZING... ALL DAY, EVERY DAY!
HA HA HA, BETTER NOT... I'LL CATCH A COLD...
THERE'S TROUBLE !!
!
RABBI! THOSE SAME JEWS FROM THESSALONICA HAVE FOLLOWED US HERE, AND THEY'VE STARTED ANOTHER RIOT!

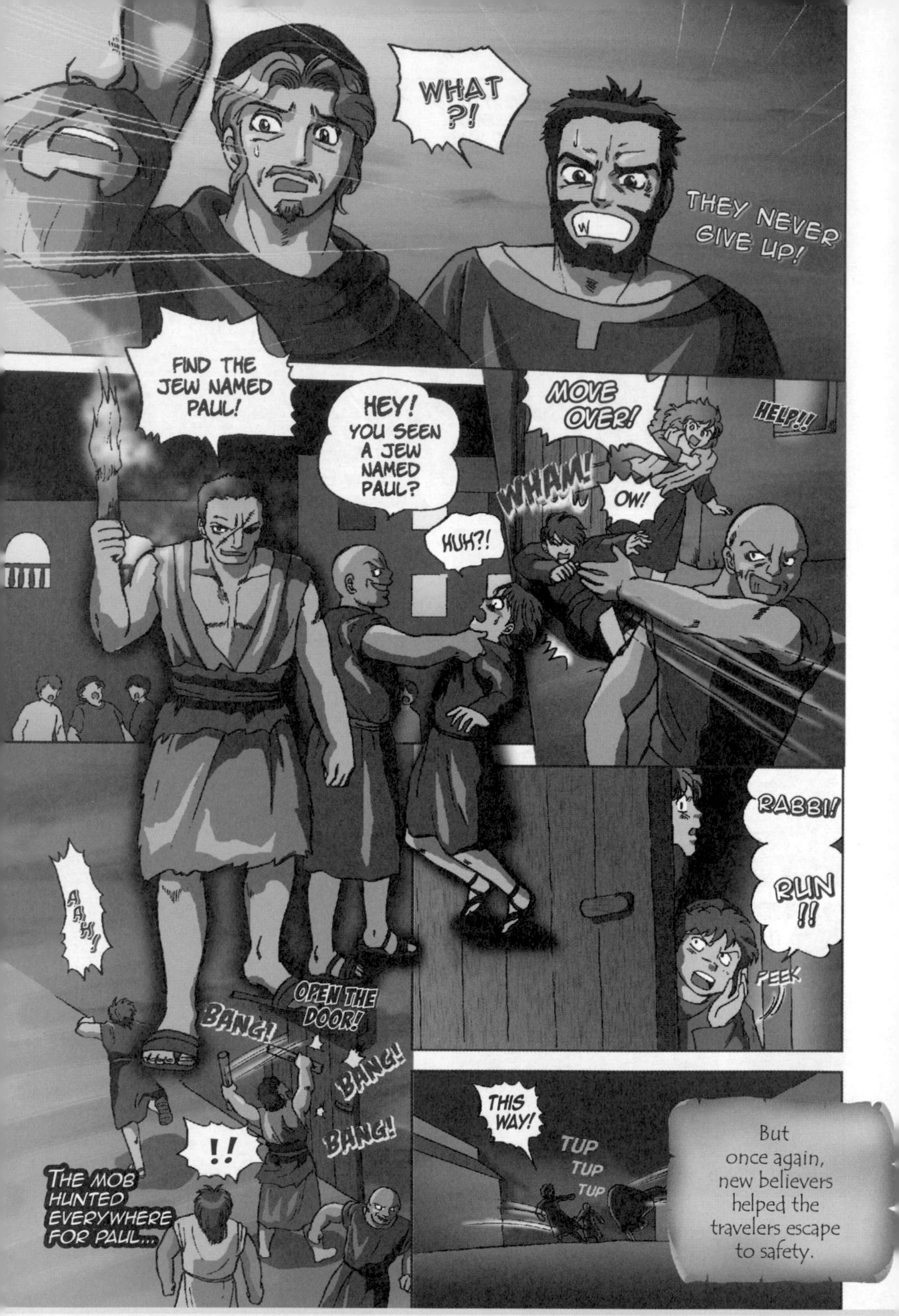
WHAT ?!
THEY NEVER GIVE UP!
FIND THE JEW NAMED PAUL!
HEY! YOU SEEN A JEW NAMED PAUL?
HUH?!
MOVE OVER!
HELP!!
WHAM!
OW!
RABBI!
RUN !!
PEEK
AAH!
OPEN THE DOOR!
BANG!
BANG!
BANG!
!!
THE MOB HUNTED EVERYWHERE FOR PAUL...
THIS WAY!
TUP
TUP
TUP
But once again, new believers helped the travelers escape to safety.

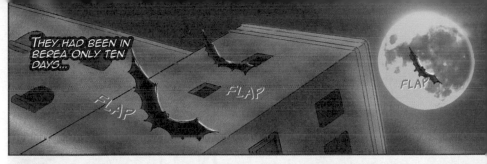

THEY HAD BEEN IN BEREA ONLY TEN DAYS...

FLAP

FLAP

FLAP

SO SILAS AND TIMOTHY REMAINED TO HELP CONTINUE THE WORK THEY HAD STARTED...

WE'LL CATCH UP WITH YOU *SOON*...

TAKE *CARE* OF YOURSELF, RABBI...

26. The Unknown God

Paul sailed to Athens without Silas and Timothy...

AHH... *ATHENS* !!

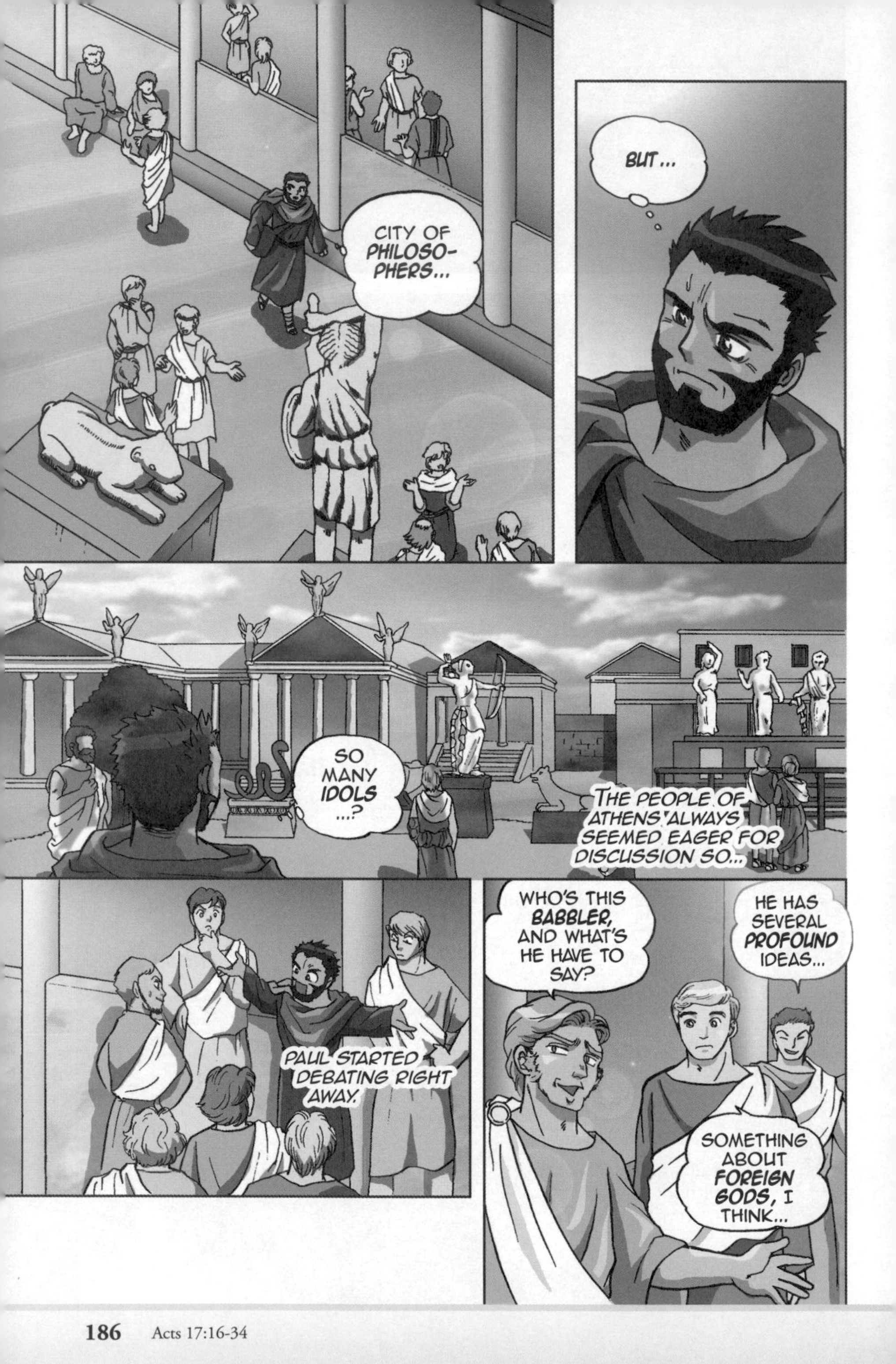
CITY OF PHILOSO-PHERS...
BUT...
SO MANY IDOLS ...?
THE PEOPLE OF ATHENS ALWAYS SEEMED EAGER FOR DISCUSSION SO...
PAUL STARTED DEBATING RIGHT AWAY.
WHO'S THIS BABBLER, AND WHAT'S HE HAVE TO SAY?
HE HAS SEVERAL PROFOUND IDEAS...
SOMETHING ABOUT FOREIGN GODS, I THINK...

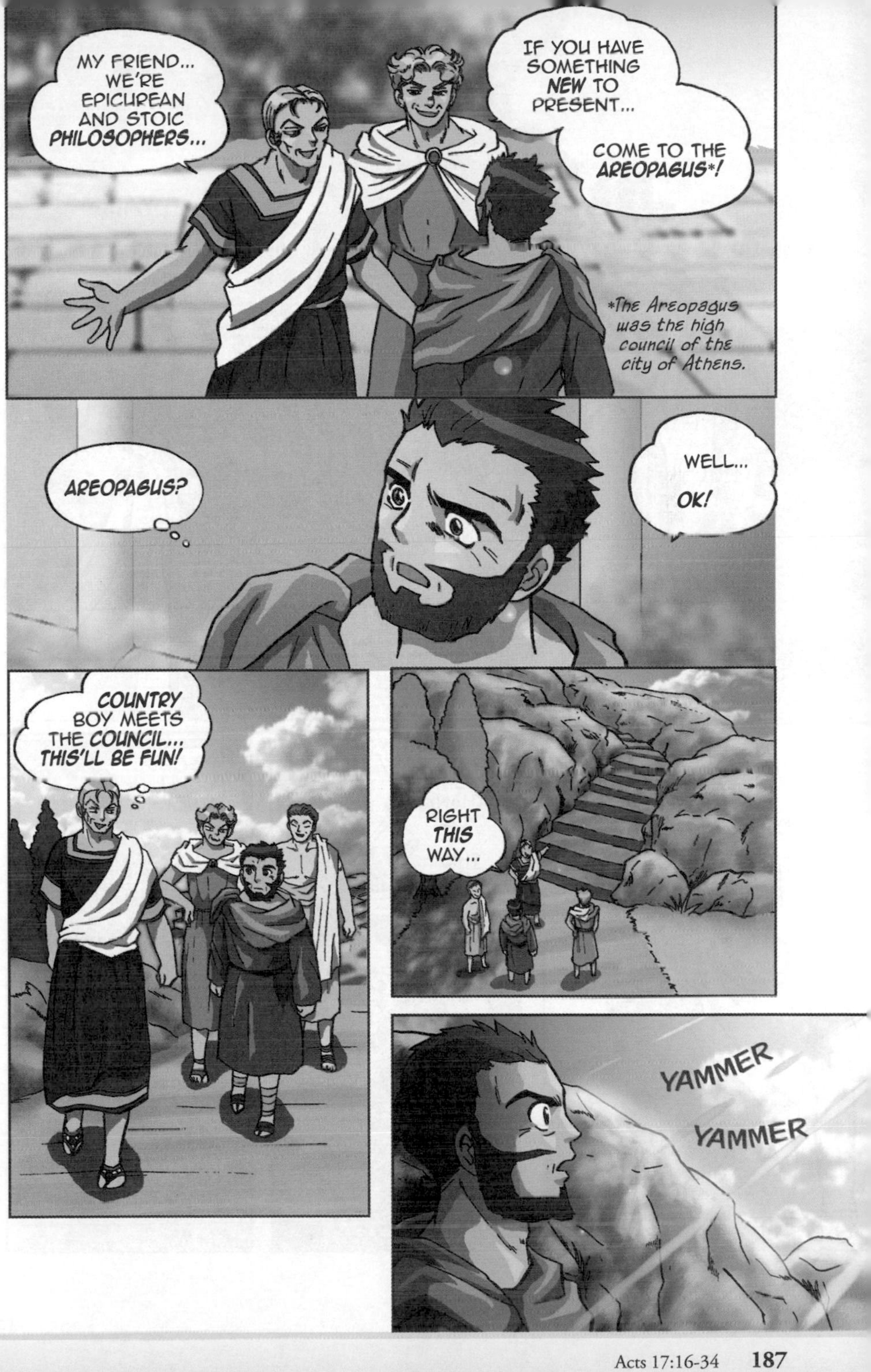
MY FRIEND... WE'RE EPICUREAN AND STOIC PHILOSOPHERS...
IF YOU HAVE SOMETHING NEW TO PRESENT...
COME TO THE AREOPAGUS*!
*The Areopagus was the high council of the city of Athens.
AREOPAGUS?
WELL...
OK!
COUNTRY BOY MEETS THE COUNCIL... THIS'LL BE FUN!
RIGHT THIS WAY...
YAMMER
YAMMER

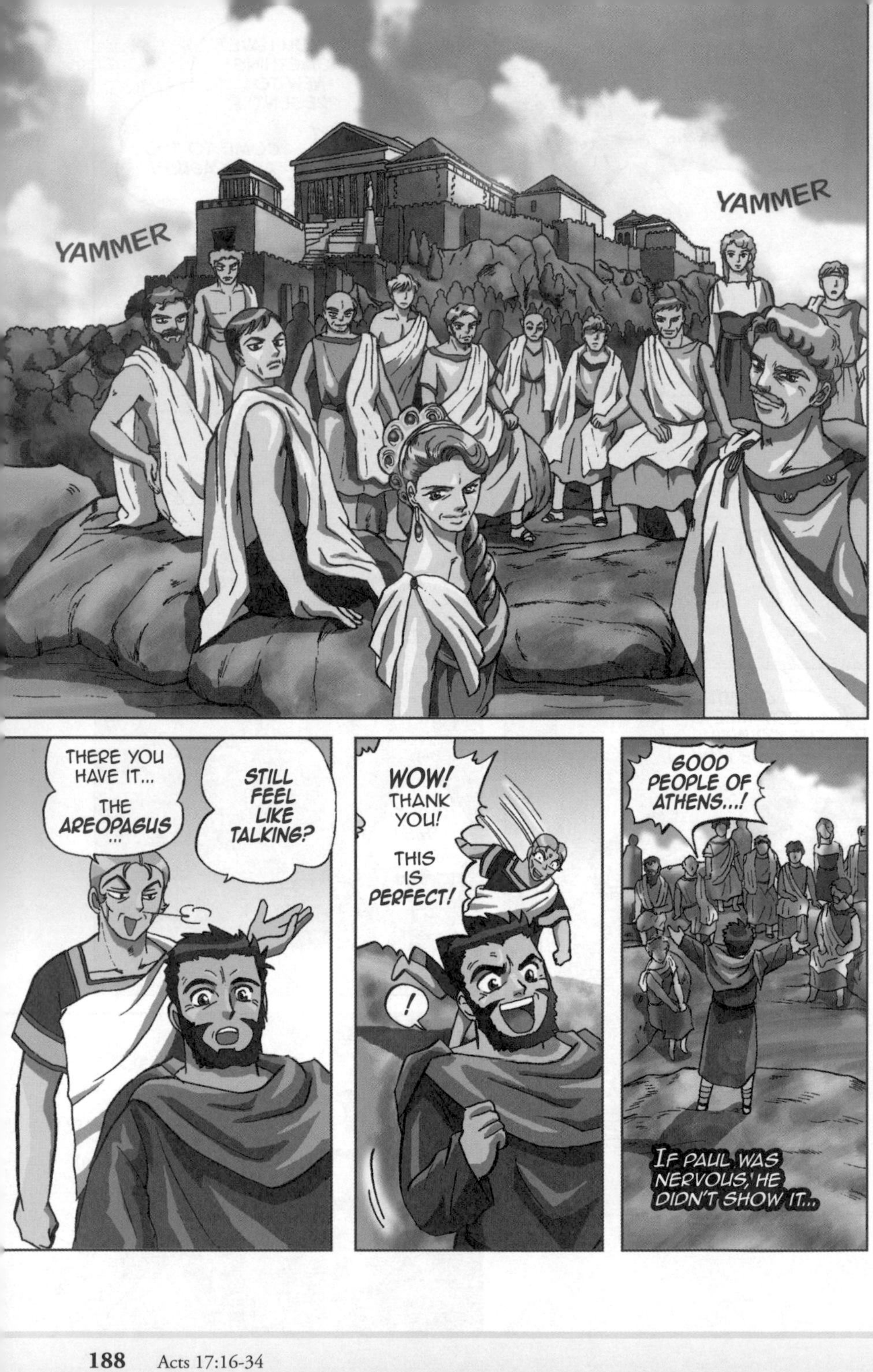

YAMMER
YAMMER
THERE YOU HAVE IT... THE AREOPAGUS ...
STILL FEEL LIKE TALKING?
WOW! THANK YOU!
THIS IS PERFECT!
!
GOOD PEOPLE OF ATHENS...!
IF PAUL WAS NERVOUS, HE DIDN'T SHOW IT...

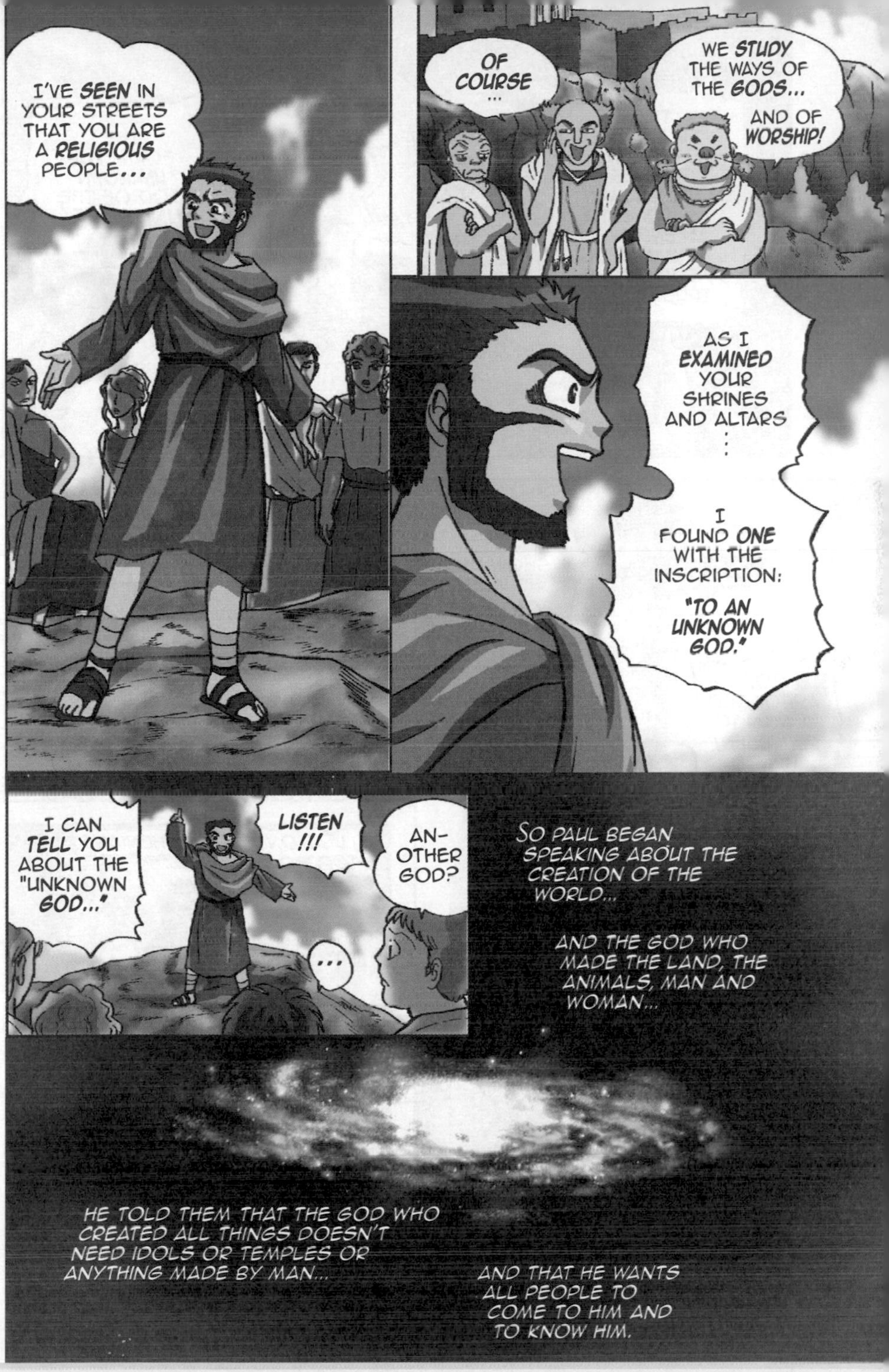

I'VE SEEN IN YOUR STREETS THAT YOU ARE A RELIGIOUS PEOPLE...
OF COURSE ...
WE STUDY THE WAYS OF THE GODS...
AND OF WORSHIP!
AS I EXAMINED YOUR SHRINES AND ALTARS ...
I FOUND ONE WITH THE INSCRIPTION:
"TO AN UNKNOWN GOD."
I CAN TELL YOU ABOUT THE "UNKNOWN GOD..."
LISTEN !!!
AN-OTHER GOD?
...
SO PAUL BEGAN SPEAKING ABOUT THE CREATION OF THE WORLD...
AND THE GOD WHO MADE THE LAND, THE ANIMALS, MAN AND WOMAN...
HE TOLD THEM THAT THE GOD WHO CREATED ALL THINGS DOESN'T NEED IDOLS OR TEMPLES OR ANYTHING MADE BY MAN...
AND THAT HE WANTS ALL PEOPLE TO COME TO HIM AND TO KNOW HIM.

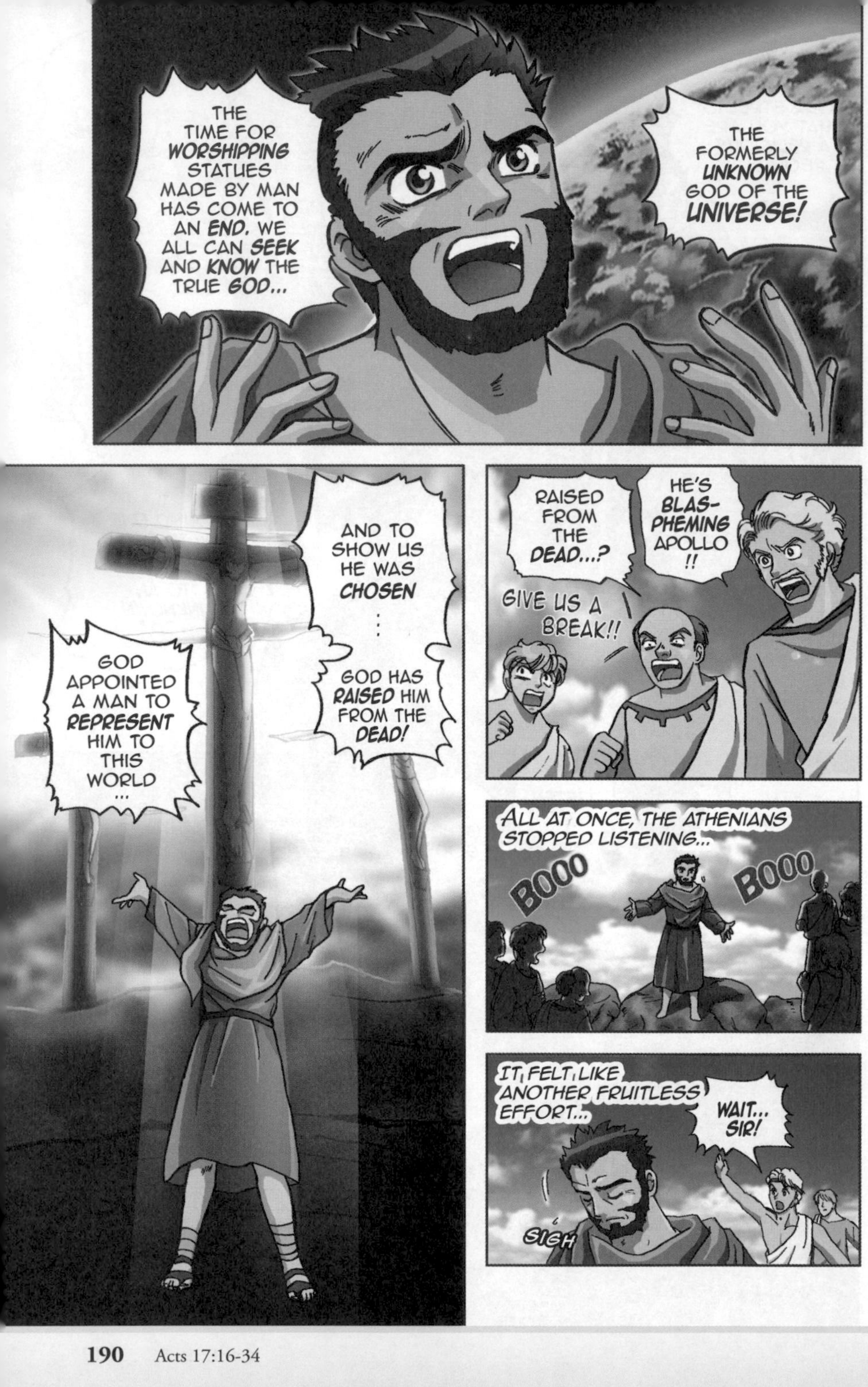
THE TIME FOR WORSHIPPING STATUES MADE BY MAN HAS COME TO AN END. WE ALL CAN SEEK AND KNOW THE TRUE GOD...
THE FORMERLY UNKNOWN GOD OF THE UNIVERSE!
GOD APPOINTED A MAN TO REPRESENT HIM TO THIS WORLD ...
AND TO SHOW US HE WAS CHOSEN ...
GOD HAS RAISED HIM FROM THE DEAD!
HE'S BLAS-PHEMING APOLLO !!
RAISED FROM THE DEAD...?
GIVE US A BREAK!!
ALL AT ONCE, THE ATHENIANS STOPPED LISTENING...
BOOO
BOOO
IT FELT LIKE ANOTHER FRUITLESS EFFORT...
WAIT... SIR!
SIGH

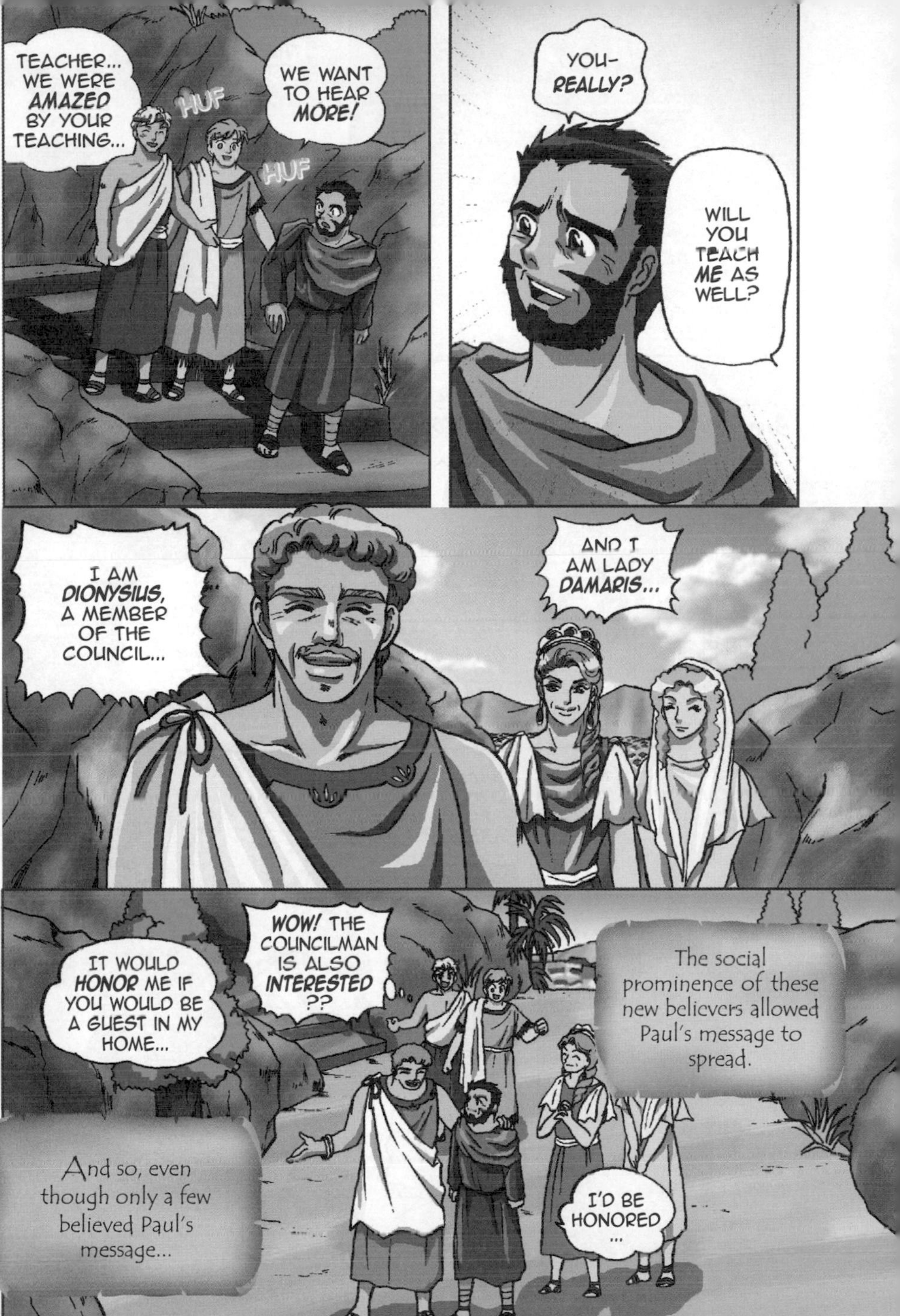
TEACHER... WE WERE AMAZED BY YOUR TEACHING...
HUF
WE WANT TO HEAR MORE!
HUF
YOU- REALLY?
WILL YOU TEACH ME AS WELL?
I AM DIONYSIUS, A MEMBER OF THE COUNCIL...
AND I AM LADY DAMARIS...
IT WOULD HONOR ME IF YOU WOULD BE A GUEST IN MY HOME...
WOW! THE COUNCILMAN IS ALSO INTERESTED ??
The social prominence of these new believers allowed Paul's message to spread.
And so, even though only a few believed Paul's message...
I'D BE HONORED ...

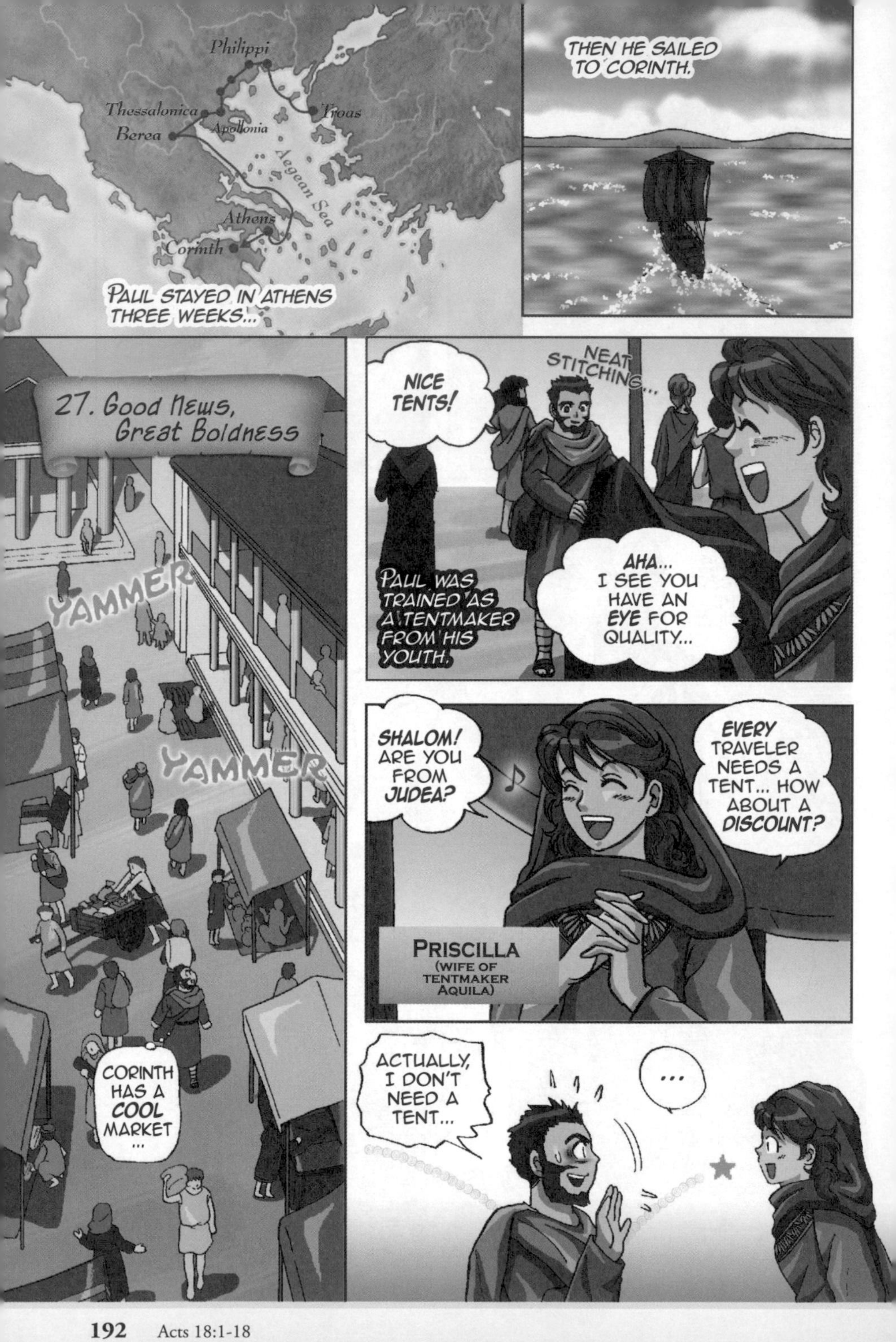
Philippi
Thessalonica
Apollonia
Berea
Troas
Aegean Sea
Athens
Corinth
PAUL STAYED IN ATHENS THREE WEEKS...
THEN HE SAILED TO CORINTH.
27. Good News, Great Boldness
YAMMER
YAMMER
CORINTH HAS A COOL MARKET ...
NICE TENTS!
NEAT STITCHING...
PAUL WAS TRAINED AS A TENTMAKER FROM HIS YOUTH.
AHA... I SEE YOU HAVE AN EYE FOR QUALITY...
SHALOM! ARE YOU FROM JUDEA?
EVERY TRAVELER NEEDS A TENT... HOW ABOUT A DISCOUNT?
PRISCILLA (WIFE OF TENTMAKER AQUILA)
ACTUALLY, I DON'T NEED A TENT...
...

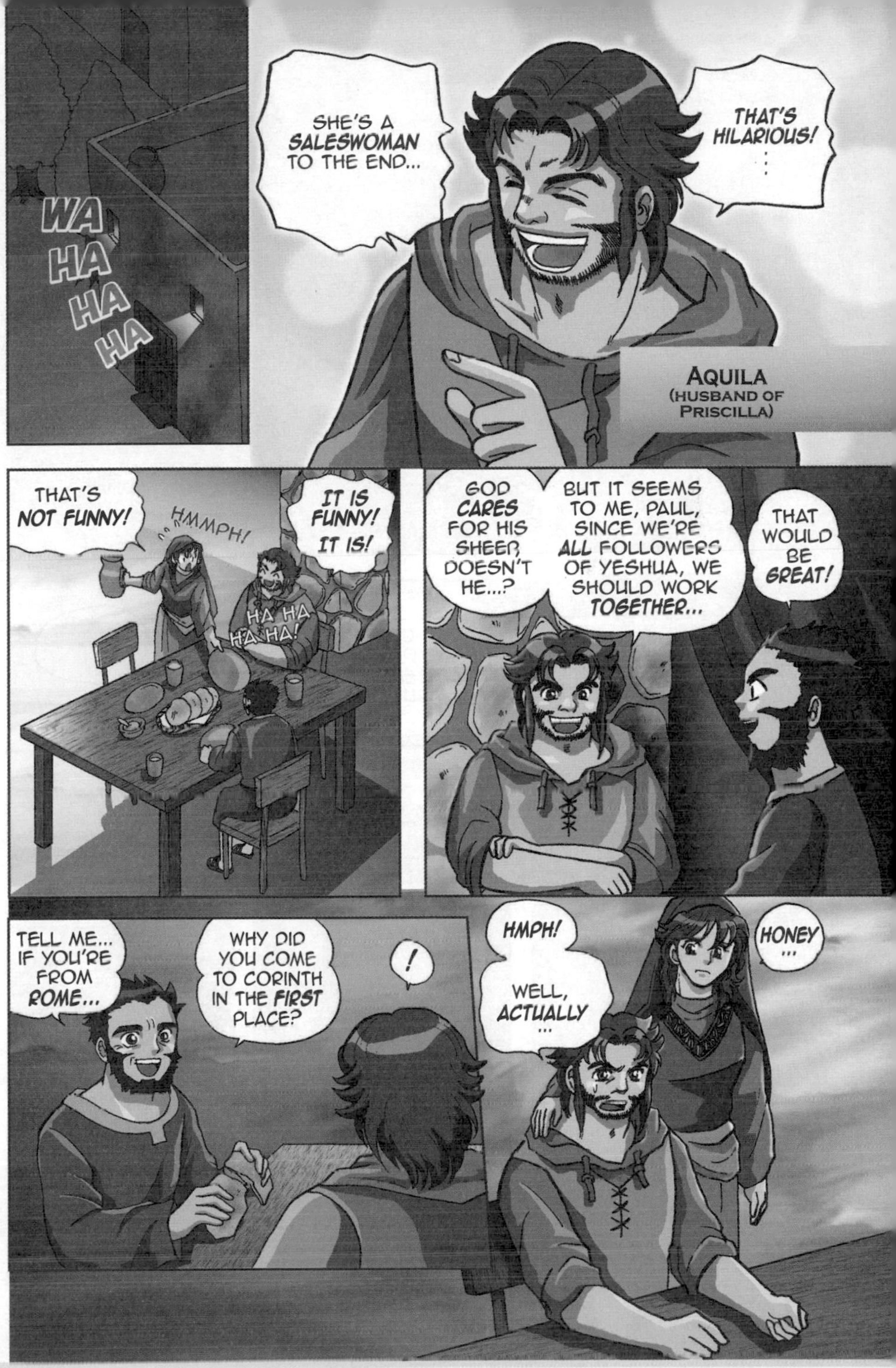
SHE'S A SALESWOMAN TO THE END...
THAT'S HILARIOUS! ...
WA HA HA HA
AQUILA (HUSBAND OF PRISCILLA)
THAT'S NOT FUNNY!
HMMPH!
IT IS FUNNY! IT IS!
HA HA HA HA!
GOD CARES FOR HIS SHEEP, DOESN'T HE...?
BUT IT SEEMS TO ME, PAUL, SINCE WE'RE ALL FOLLOWERS OF YESHUA, WE SHOULD WORK TOGETHER...
THAT WOULD BE GREAT!
TELL ME... IF YOU'RE FROM ROME...
WHY DID YOU COME TO CORINTH IN THE FIRST PLACE?
!
HMPH!
WELL, ACTUALLY ...
HONEY ...

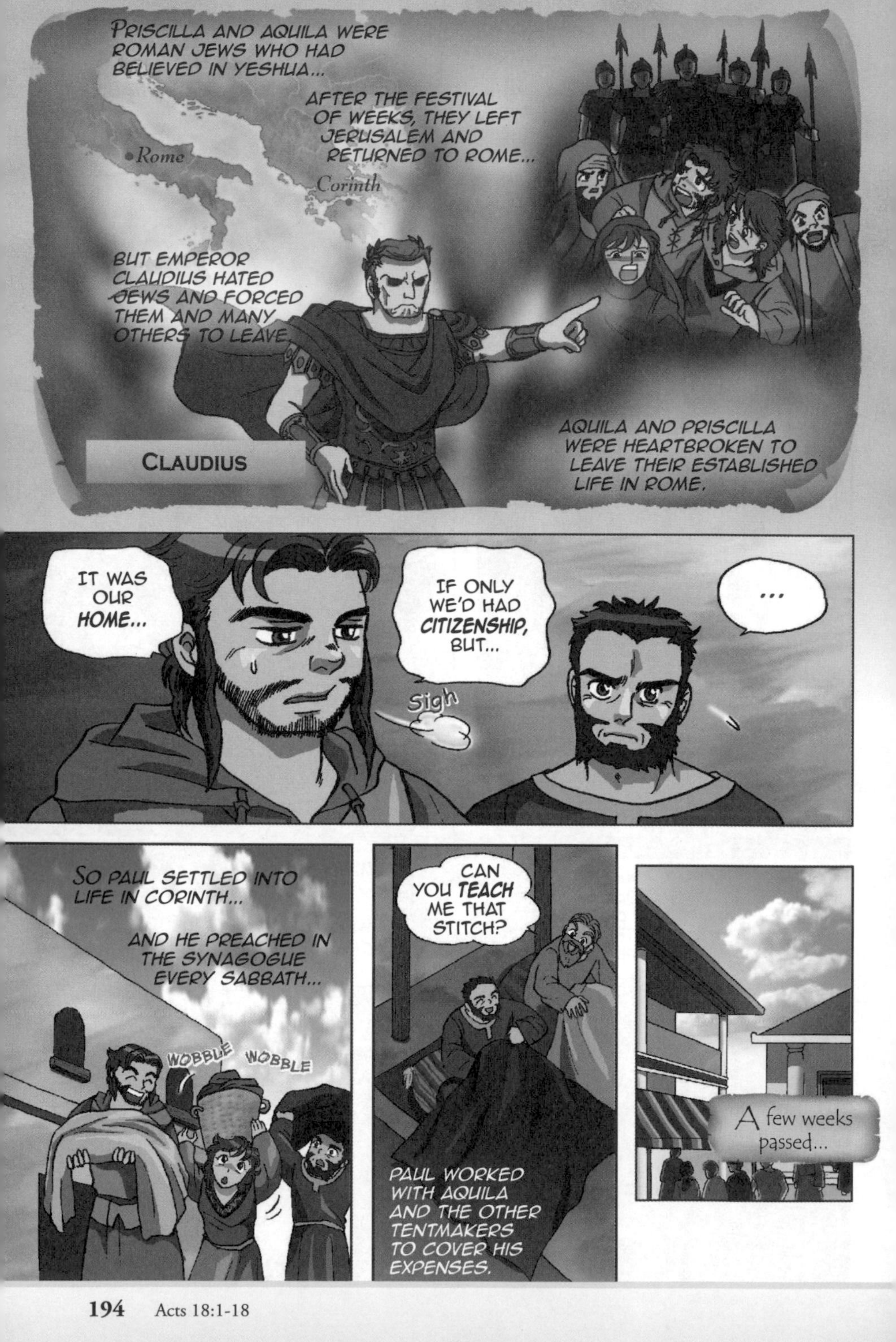
PRISCILLA AND AQUILA WERE ROMAN JEWS WHO HAD BELIEVED IN YESHUA...
AFTER THE FESTIVAL OF WEEKS, THEY LEFT JERUSALEM AND RETURNED TO ROME...
Rome
Corinth
BUT EMPEROR CLAUDIUS HATED JEWS AND FORCED THEM AND MANY OTHERS TO LEAVE.
CLAUDIUS
AQUILA AND PRISCILLA WERE HEARTBROKEN TO LEAVE THEIR ESTABLISHED LIFE IN ROME.
IT WAS OUR HOME...
IF ONLY WE'D HAD CITIZENSHIP, BUT...
Sigh
...
SO PAUL SETTLED INTO LIFE IN CORINTH...
AND HE PREACHED IN THE SYNAGOGUE EVERY SABBATH...
WOBBLE
WOBBLE
CAN YOU TEACH ME THAT STITCH?
PAUL WORKED WITH AQUILA AND THE OTHER TENTMAKERS TO COVER HIS EXPENSES.
A few weeks passed...

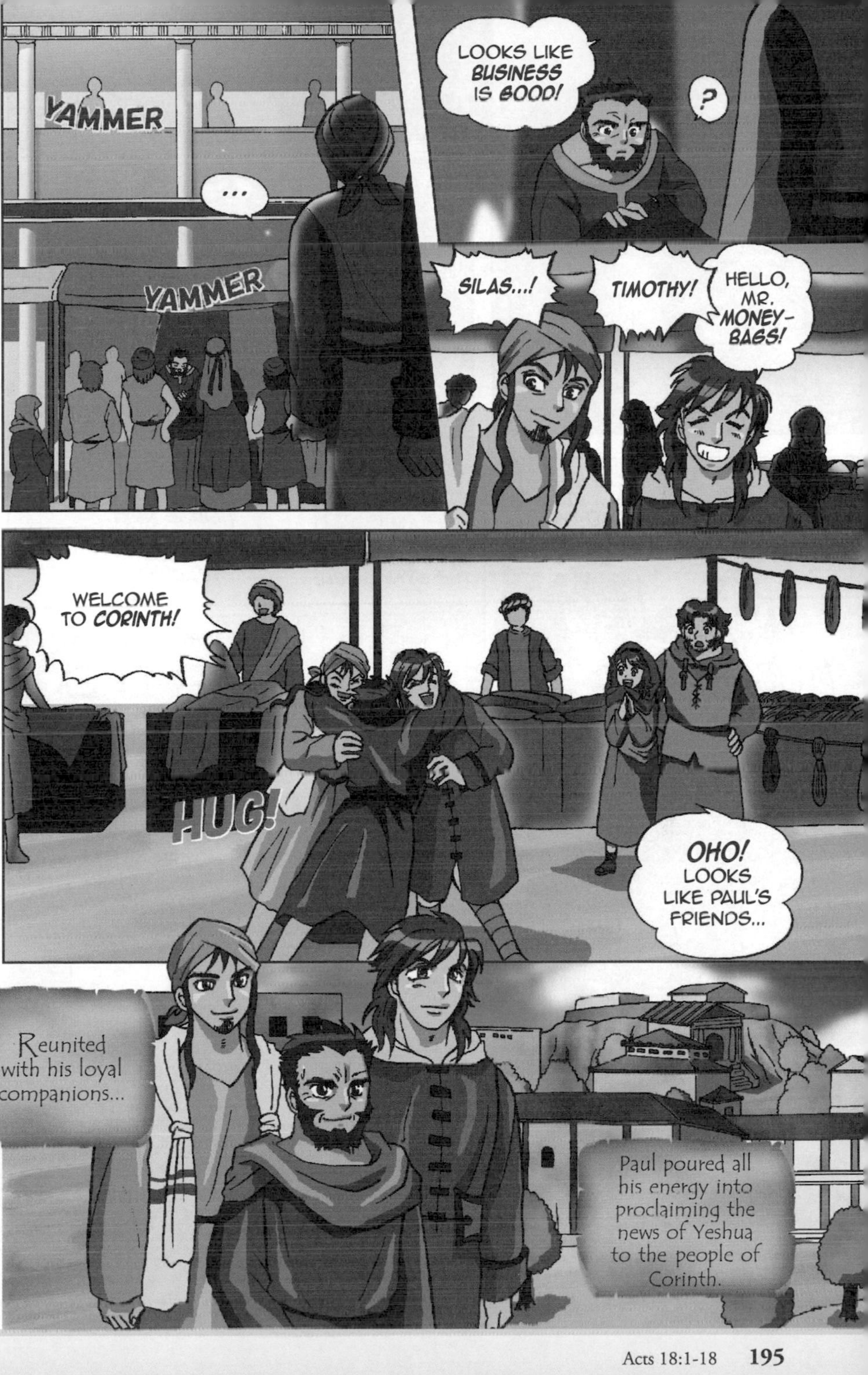
YAMMER
...
YAMMER
LOOKS LIKE BUSINESS IS GOOD!
?
SILAS...!
TIMOTHY!
HELLO, MR. MONEY-BAGS!
WELCOME TO CORINTH!
HUG!
OHO! LOOKS LIKE PAUL'S FRIENDS...
Reunited with his loyal companions...
Paul poured all his energy into proclaiming the news of Yeshua to the people of Corinth.

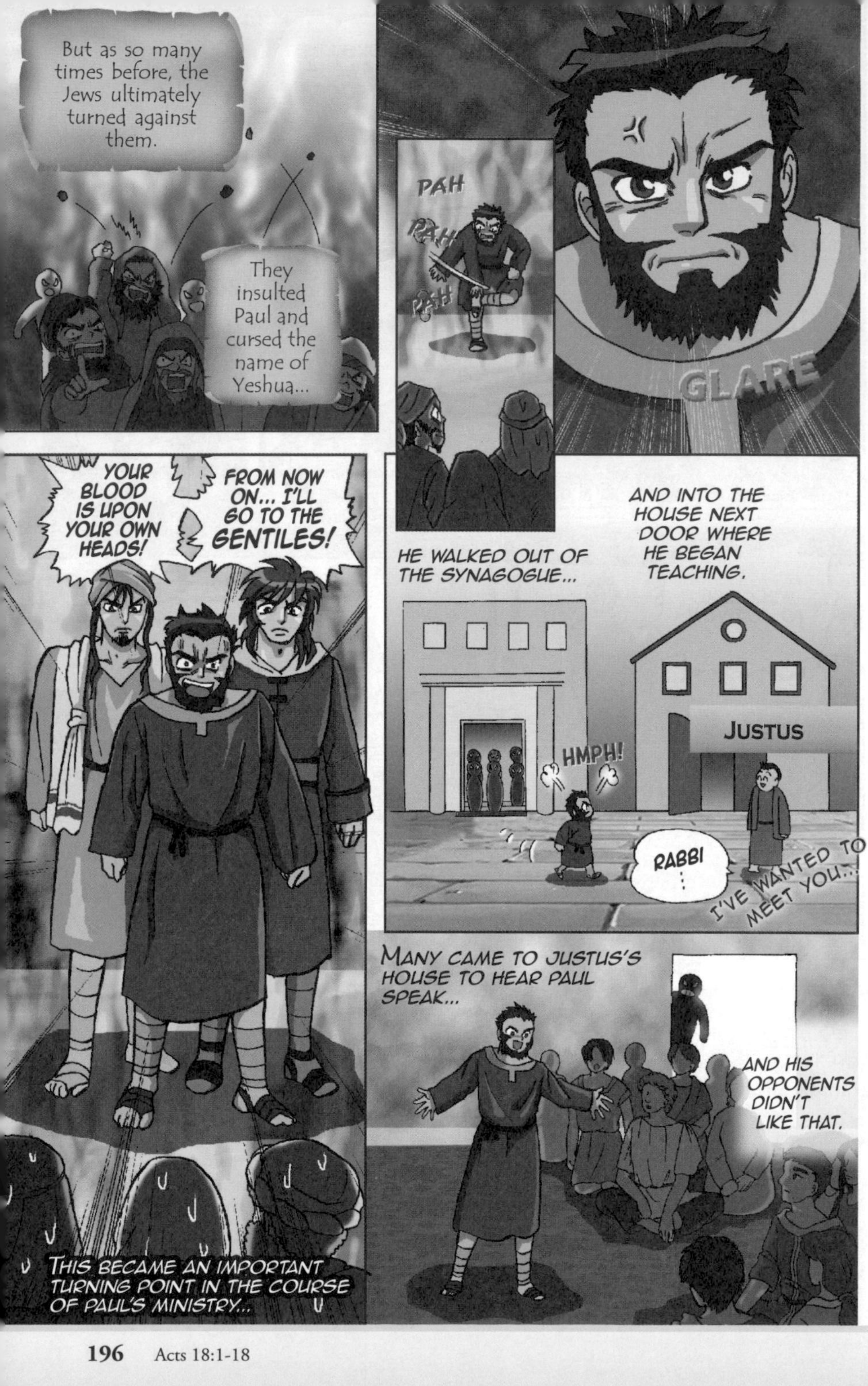
But as so many times before, the Jews ultimately turned against them.
They insulted Paul and cursed the name of Yeshua...
PAH
PAH
PAH
GLARE
YOUR BLOOD IS UPON YOUR OWN HEADS!
FROM NOW ON... I'LL GO TO THE GENTILES!
THIS BECAME AN IMPORTANT TURNING POINT IN THE COURSE OF PAUL'S MINISTRY...
HE WALKED OUT OF THE SYNAGOGUE...
AND INTO THE HOUSE NEXT DOOR WHERE HE BEGAN TEACHING.
JUSTUS
HMPH!
RABBI ...
I'VE WANTED TO MEET YOU...
MANY CAME TO JUSTUS'S HOUSE TO HEAR PAUL SPEAK...
AND HIS OPPONENTS DIDN'T LIKE THAT.

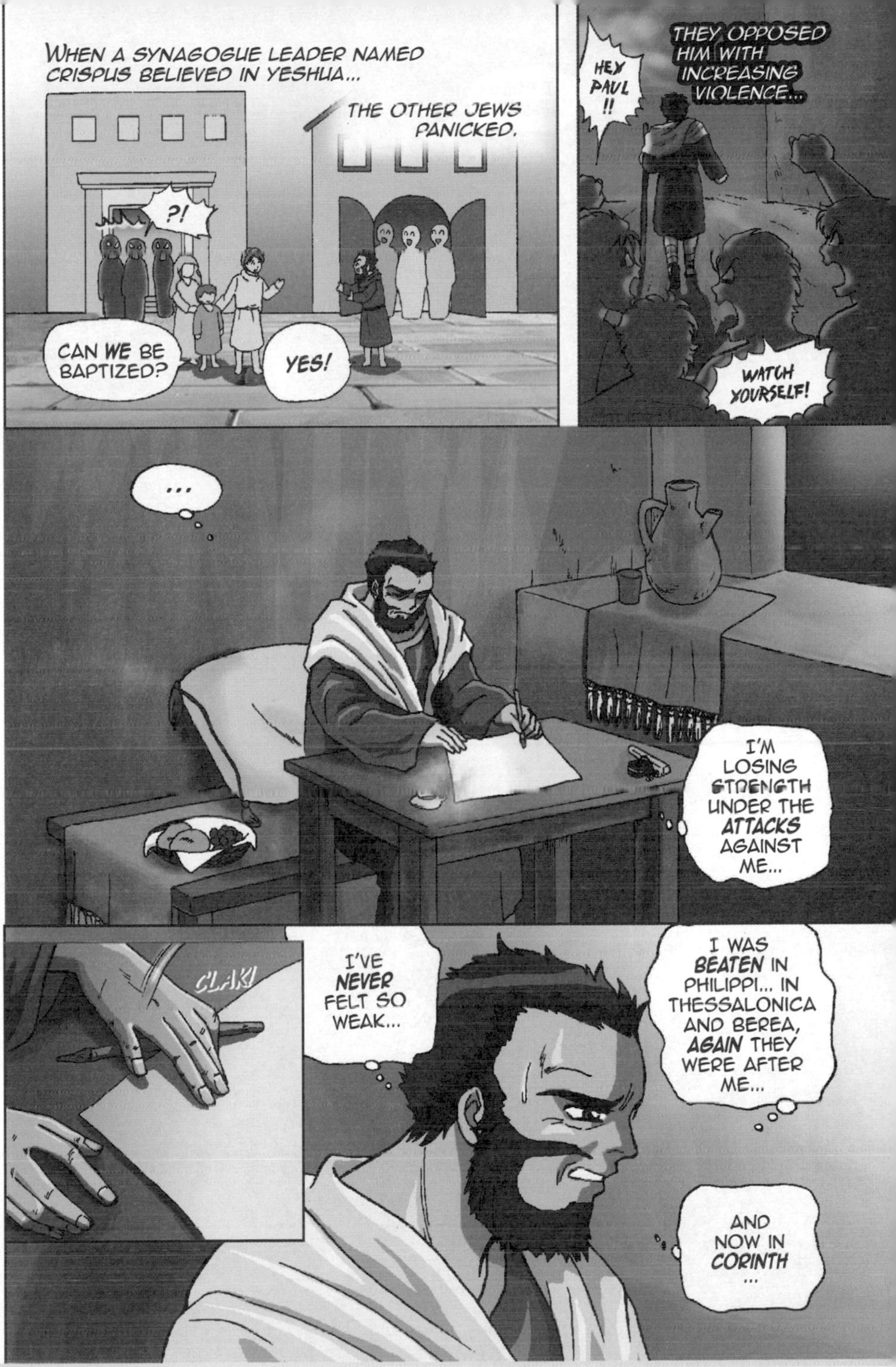
WHEN A SYNAGOGUE LEADER NAMED CRISPUS BELIEVED IN YESHUA...
THE OTHER JEWS PANICKED.
?!
CAN WE BE BAPTIZED?
YES!
THEY OPPOSED HIM WITH INCREASING VIOLENCE...
HEY PAUL !!
WATCH YOURSELF!
...
I'M LOSING STRENGTH UNDER THE ATTACKS AGAINST ME...
CLAK!
I'VE NEVER FELT SO WEAK...
I WAS BEATEN IN PHILIPPI... IN THESSALONICA AND BEREA, AGAIN THEY WERE AFTER ME...
AND NOW IN CORINTH ...

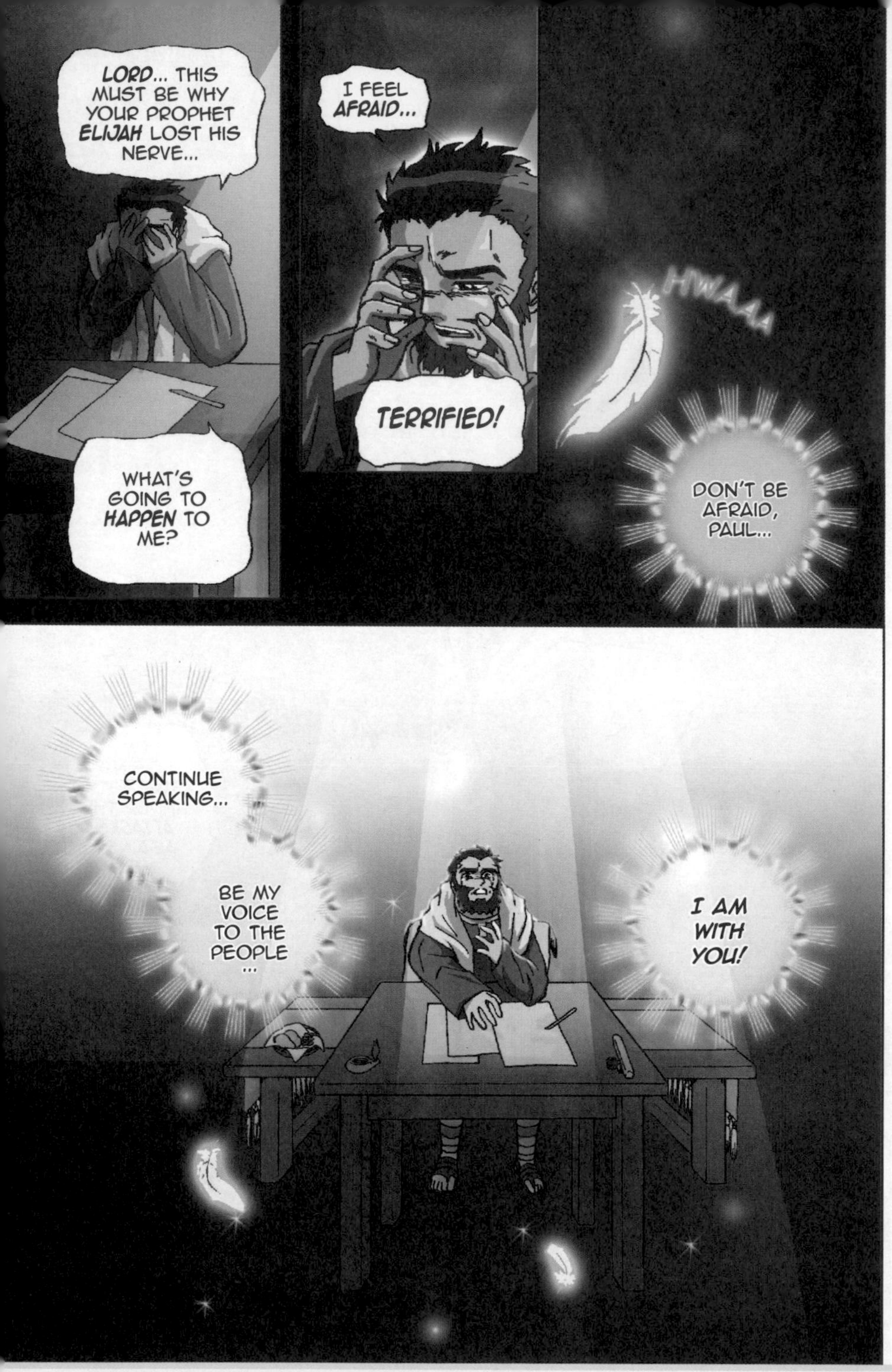
LORD... THIS MUST BE WHY YOUR PROPHET ELIJAH LOST HIS NERVE...
WHAT'S GOING TO HAPPEN TO ME?
I FEEL AFRAID...
TERRIFIED!
HWAAA
DON'T BE AFRAID, PAUL...
CONTINUE SPEAKING...
BE MY VOICE TO THE PEOPLE ...
I AM WITH YOU!

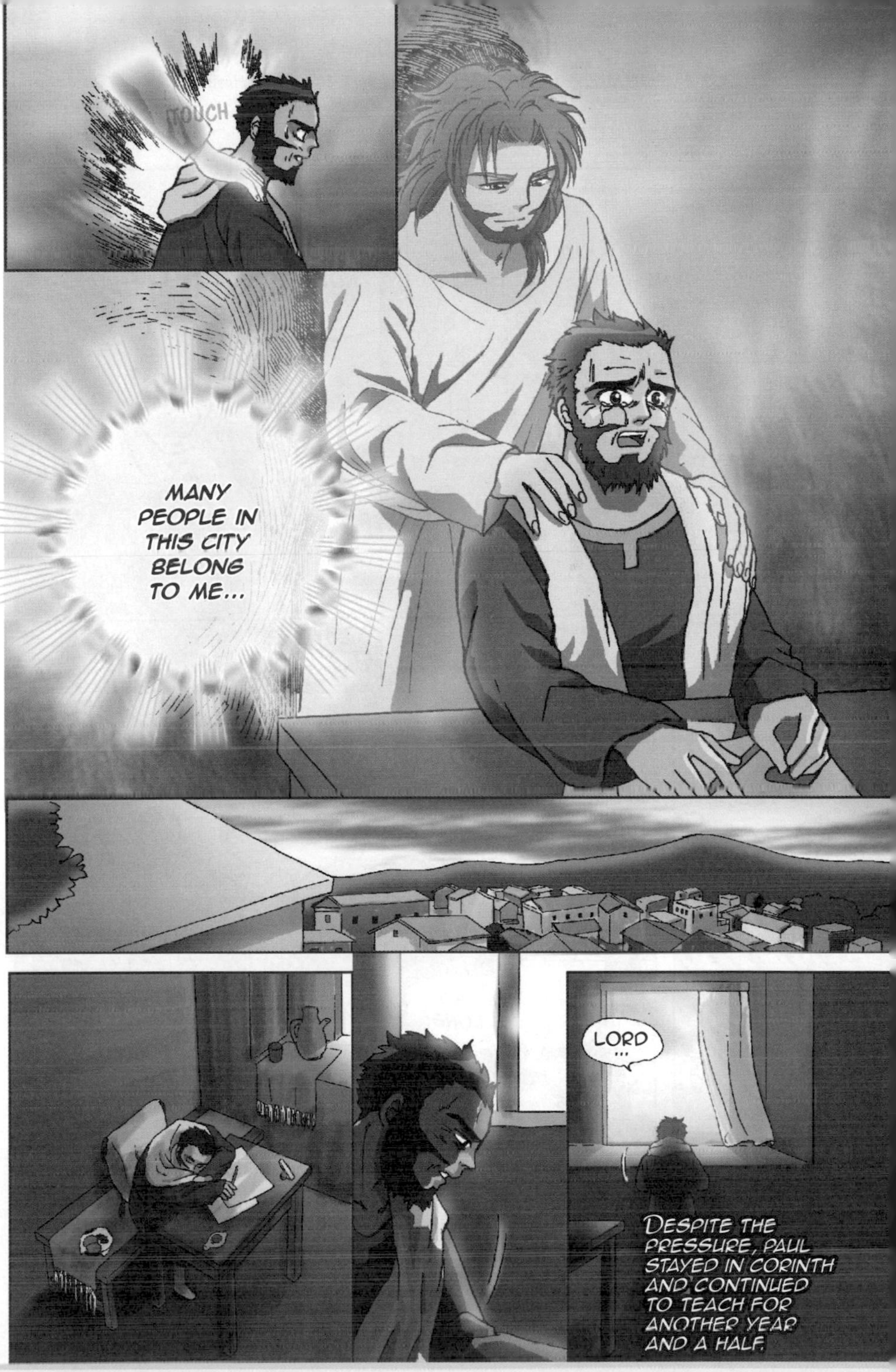
TOUCH
MANY PEOPLE IN THIS CITY BELONG TO ME...
LORD ...
DESPITE THE PRESSURE, PAUL STAYED IN CORINTH AND CONTINUED TO TEACH FOR ANOTHER YEAR AND A HALF.

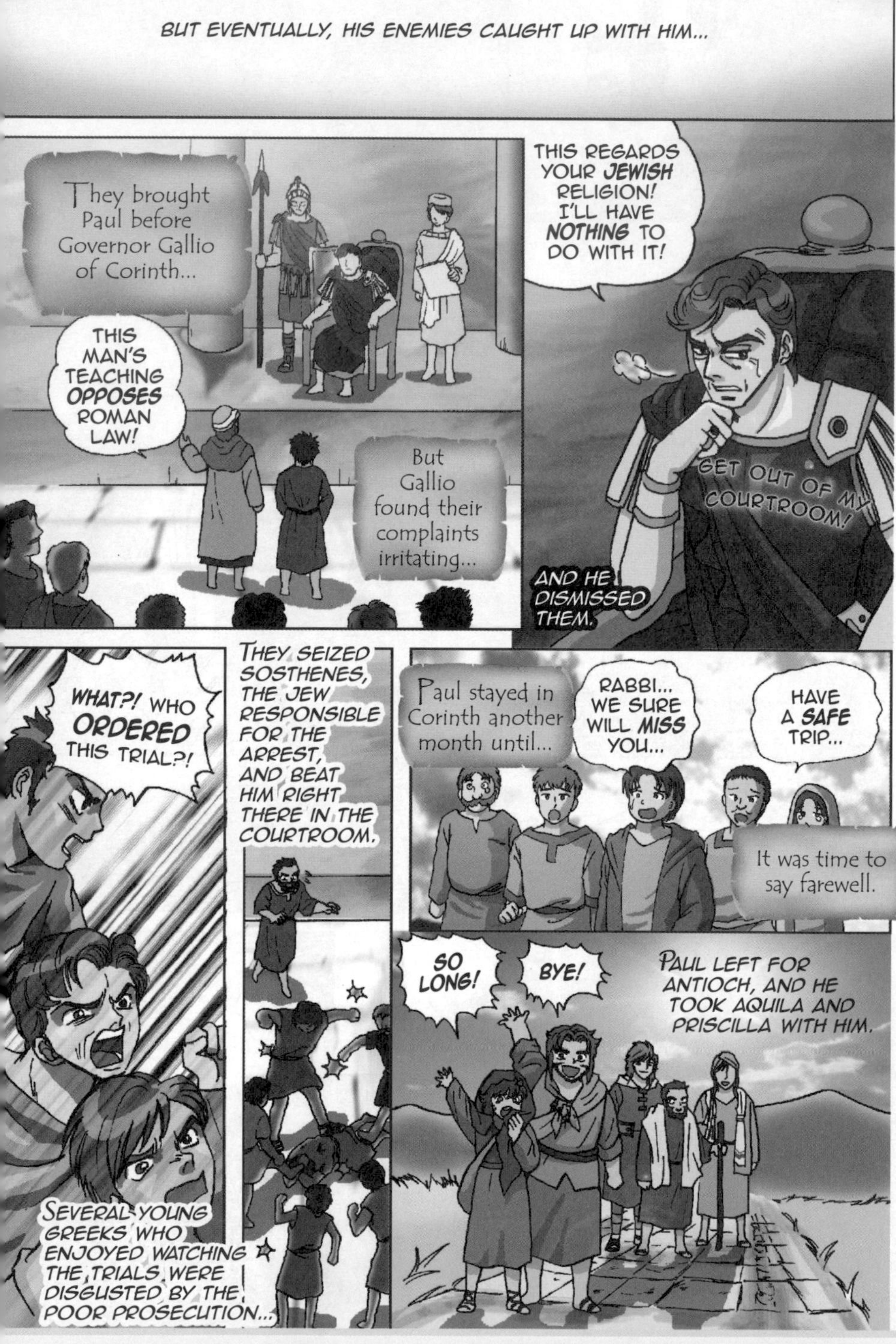
BUT EVENTUALLY, HIS ENEMIES CAUGHT UP WITH HIM...
They brought Paul before Governor Gallio of Corinth...
THIS MAN'S TEACHING OPPOSES ROMAN LAW!
But Gallio found their complaints irritating...
THIS REGARDS YOUR JEWISH RELIGION! I'LL HAVE NOTHING TO DO WITH IT!
GET OUT OF MY COURTROOM!
AND HE DISMISSED THEM.
WHAT?! WHO ORDERED THIS TRIAL?!
SEVERAL YOUNG GREEKS WHO ENJOYED WATCHING THE TRIALS WERE DISGUSTED BY THE POOR PROSECUTION...
THEY SEIZED SOSTHENES, THE JEW RESPONSIBLE FOR THE ARREST, AND BEAT HIM RIGHT THERE IN THE COURTROOM.
Paul stayed in Corinth another month until...
RABBI... WE SURE WILL MISS YOU...
HAVE A SAFE TRIP...
It was time to say farewell.
SO LONG!
BYE!
PAUL LEFT FOR ANTIOCH, AND HE TOOK AQUILA AND PRISCILLA WITH HIM.

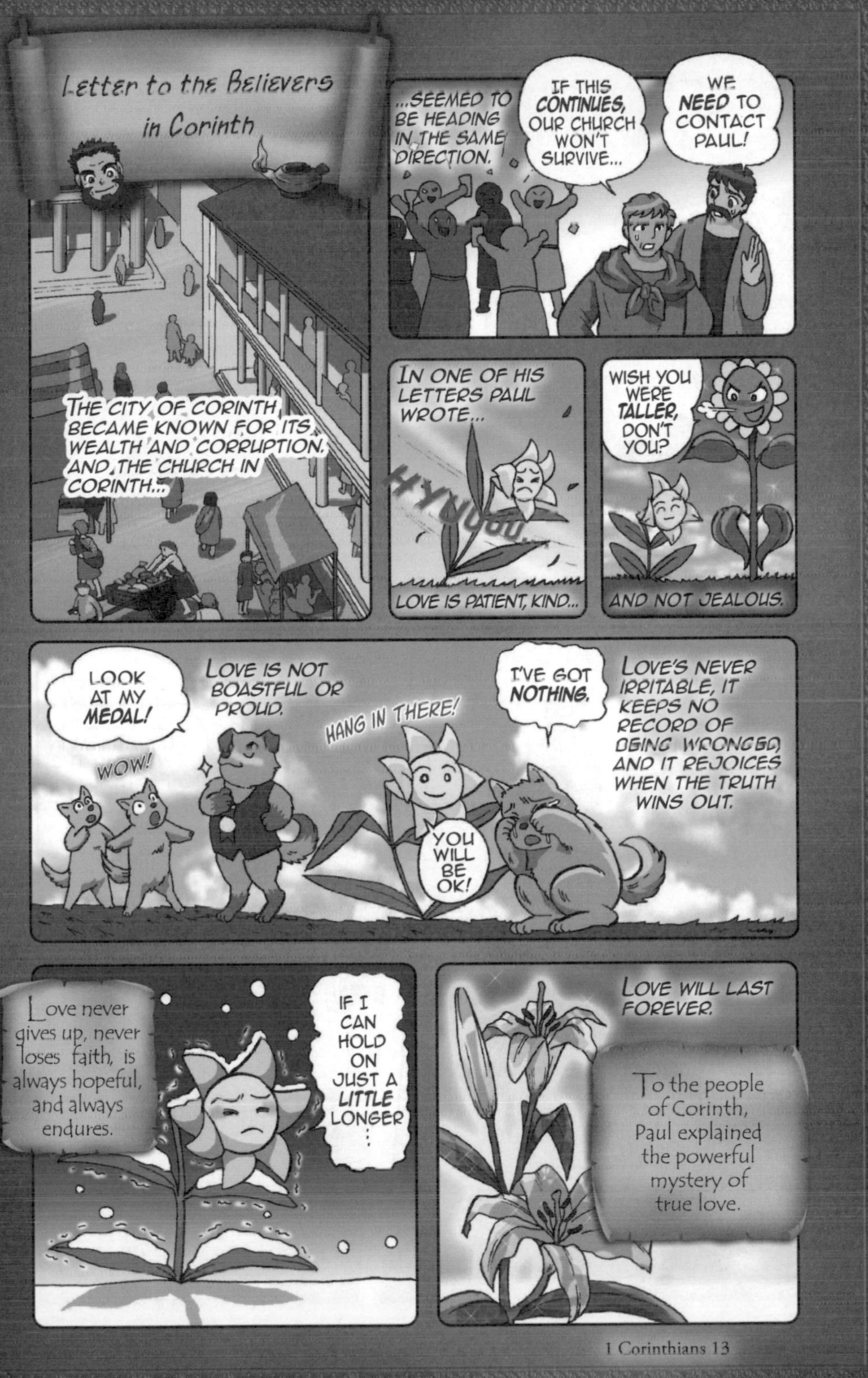
Letter to the Believers in Corinth
THE CITY OF CORINTH BECAME KNOWN FOR ITS WEALTH AND CORRUPTION. AND THE CHURCH IN CORINTH...
...SEEMED TO BE HEADING IN THE SAME DIRECTION.
IF THIS CONTINUES, OUR CHURCH WON'T SURVIVE...
WE NEED TO CONTACT PAUL!
IN ONE OF HIS LETTERS PAUL WROTE...
HYUUUU...
LOVE IS PATIENT, KIND...
WISH YOU WERE TALLER, DON'T YOU?
AND NOT JEALOUS.
LOOK AT MY MEDAL!
WOW!
LOVE IS NOT BOASTFUL OR PROUD.
HANG IN THERE!
I'VE GOT NOTHING.
YOU WILL BE OK!
LOVE'S NEVER IRRITABLE, IT KEEPS NO RECORD OF BEING WRONGED, AND IT REJOICES WHEN THE TRUTH WINS OUT.
Love never gives up, never loses faith, is always hopeful, and always endures.
IF I CAN HOLD ON JUST A LITTLE LONGER...
LOVE WILL LAST FOREVER.
To the people of Corinth, Paul explained the powerful mystery of true love.
1 Corinthians 13

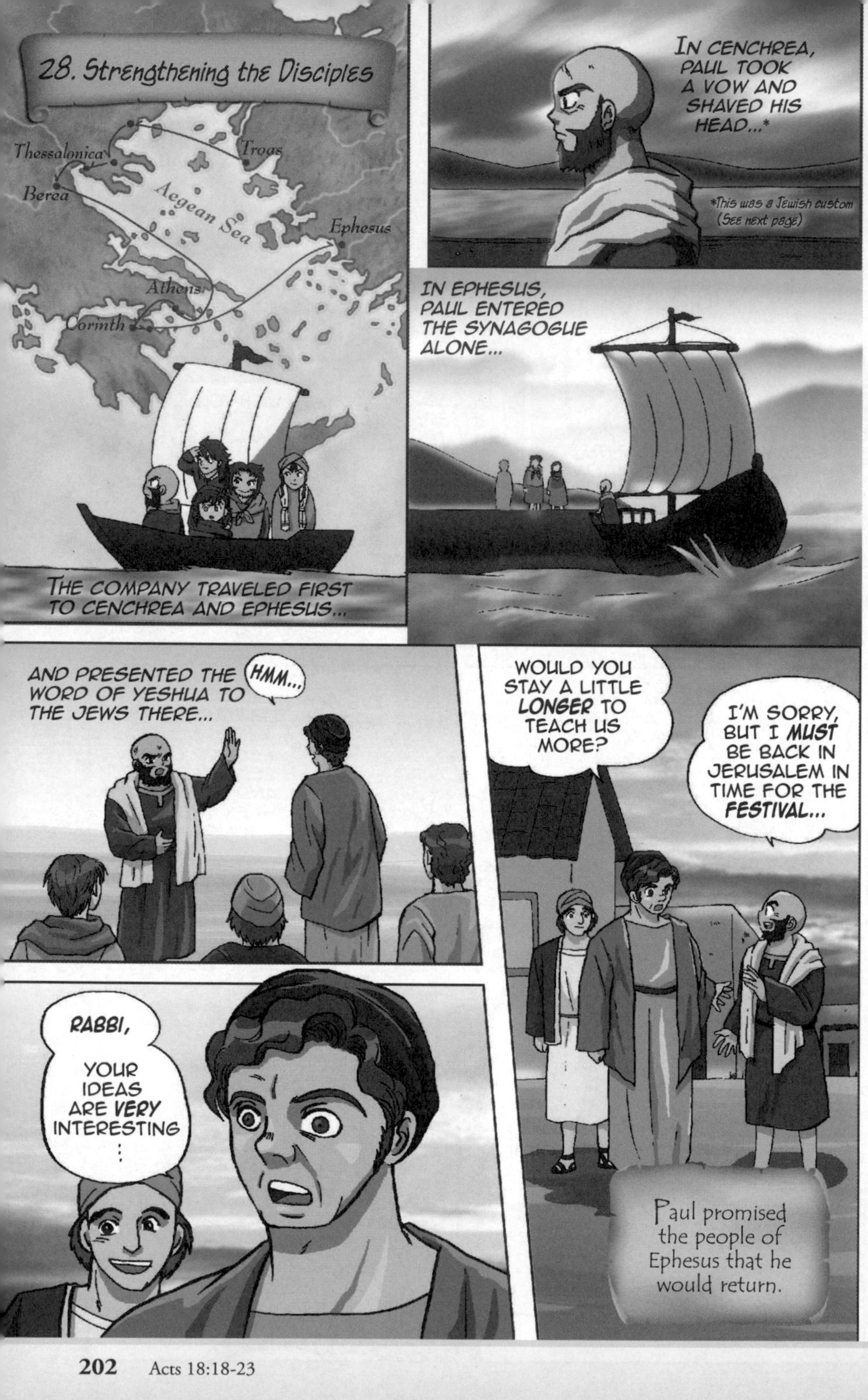
28. Strengthening the Disciples
Thessalonica
Troas
Berea
Aegean Sea
Ephesus
Athens
Corinth
THE COMPANY TRAVELED FIRST TO CENCHREA AND EPHESUS...
IN CENCHREA, PAUL TOOK A VOW AND SHAVED HIS HEAD...*
*This was a Jewish custom (See next page)
IN EPHESUS, PAUL ENTERED THE SYNAGOGUE ALONE...
AND PRESENTED THE WORD OF YESHUA TO THE JEWS THERE...
HMM...
RABBI,
YOUR IDEAS ARE VERY INTERESTING...
WOULD YOU STAY A LITTLE LONGER TO TEACH US MORE?
I'M SORRY, BUT I MUST BE BACK IN JERUSALEM IN TIME FOR THE FESTIVAL...
Paul promised the people of Ephesus that he would return.

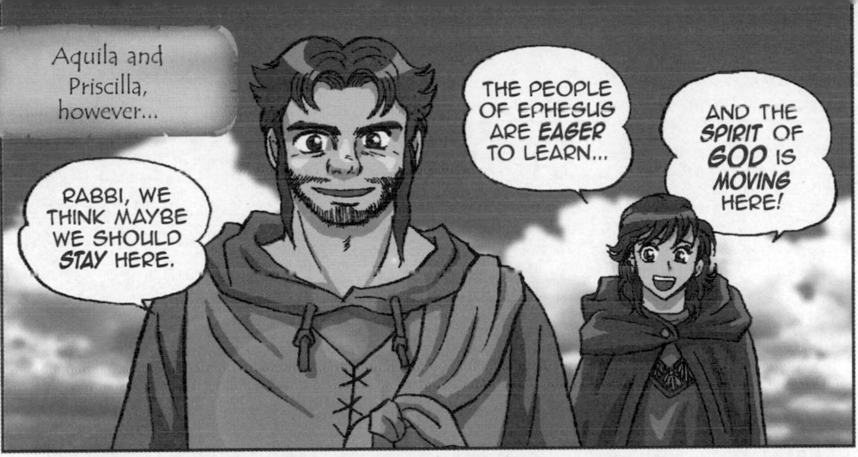
Aquila and Priscilla, however...
RABBI, WE THINK MAYBE WE SHOULD STAY HERE.
THE PEOPLE OF EPHESUS ARE EAGER TO LEARN...
AND THE SPIRIT OF GOD IS MOVING HERE!

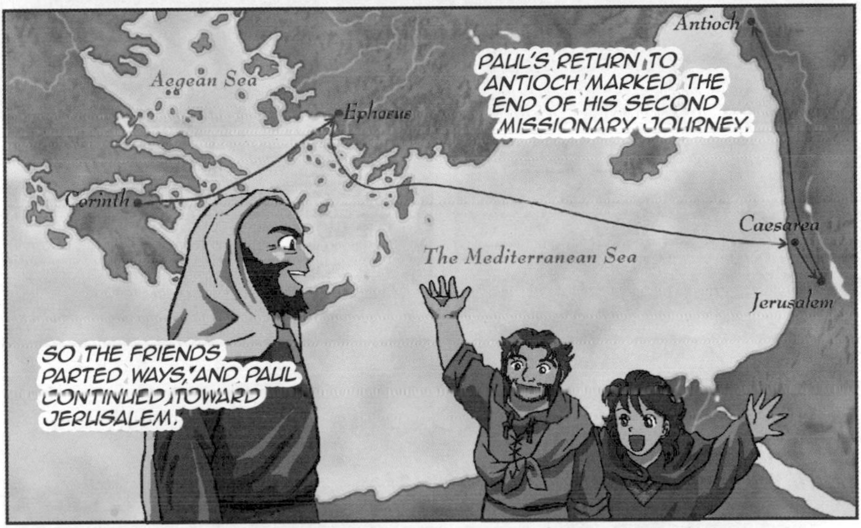
Antioch
Aegean Sea
Ephesus
Corinth
Caesarea
The Mediterranean Sea
Jerusalem
PAUL'S RETURN TO ANTIOCH MARKED THE END OF HIS SECOND MISSIONARY JOURNEY.
SO THE FRIENDS PARTED WAYS, AND PAUL CONTINUED TOWARD JERUSALEM.

THE NAZIRITE VOW

PAUL SHAVED HIS HEAD WHEN HE ARRIVED IN CENCHREA. THIS WAS A COMMON CUSTOM FOR THOSE TAKING A NAZIRITE VOW.

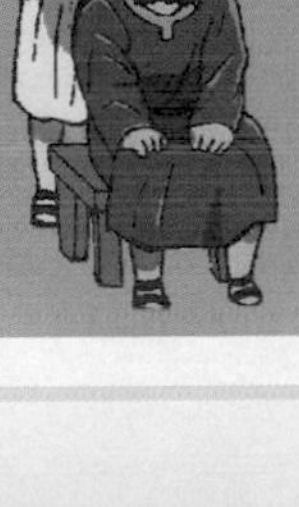

THERE ARE NO RECORDS DESCRIBING THE SPECIFIC NATURE OF PAUL'S VOW, BUT THE SHAVING OF HIS HEAD INDICATED THE VOW'S COMPLETION.

IT WAS THEN CUSTOMARY TO OFFER THE HAIR AT THE TEMPLE IN JERUSALEM, SO PAUL PROBABLY CONTINUED THERE FOR THIS PURPOSE.

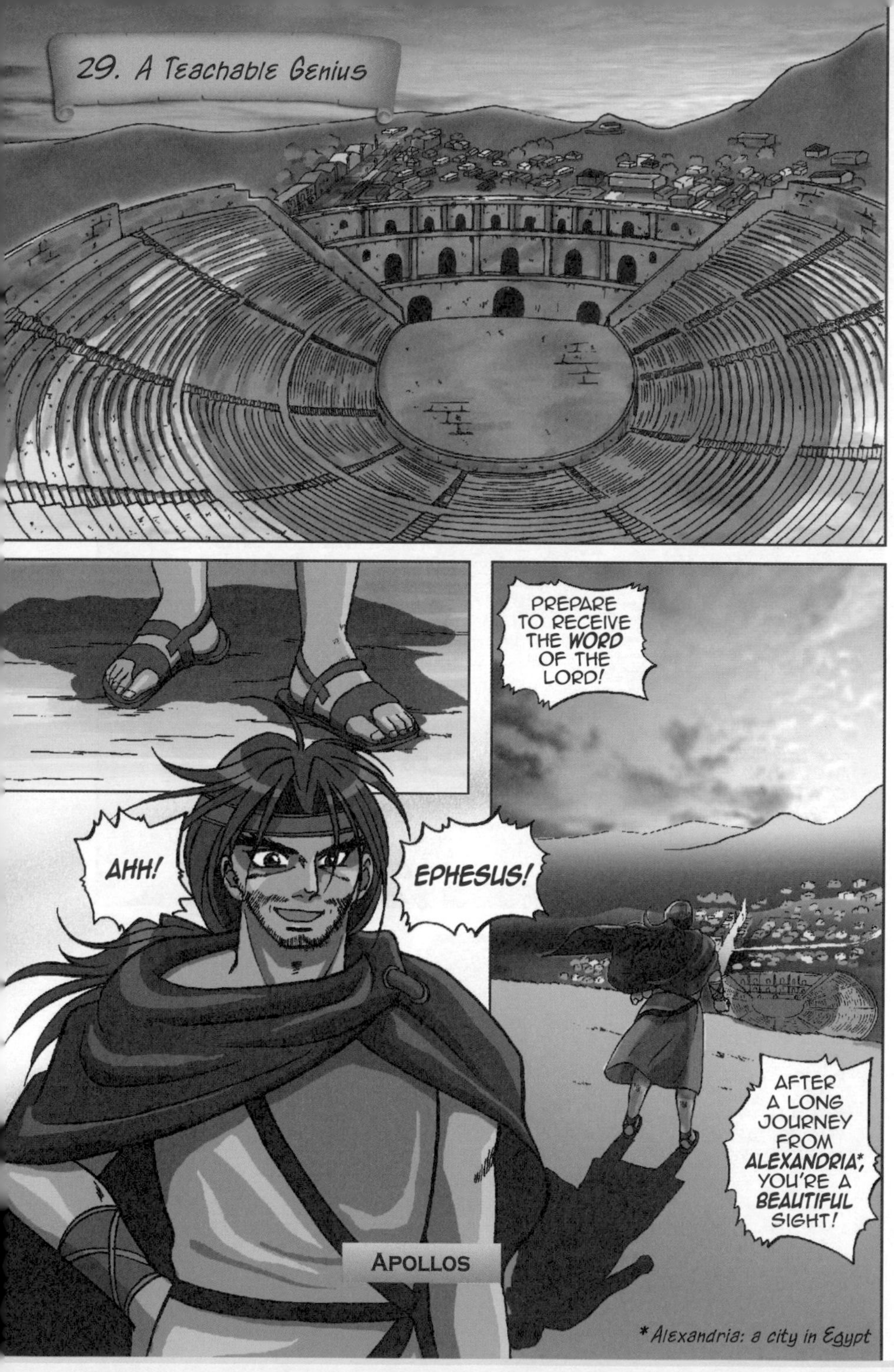
29. A Teachable Genius
PREPARE TO RECEIVE THE WORD OF THE LORD!
AHH!
EPHESUS!
AFTER A LONG JOURNEY FROM ALEXANDRIA*, YOU'RE A BEAUTIFUL SIGHT!
APOLLOS
* Alexandria: a city in Egypt

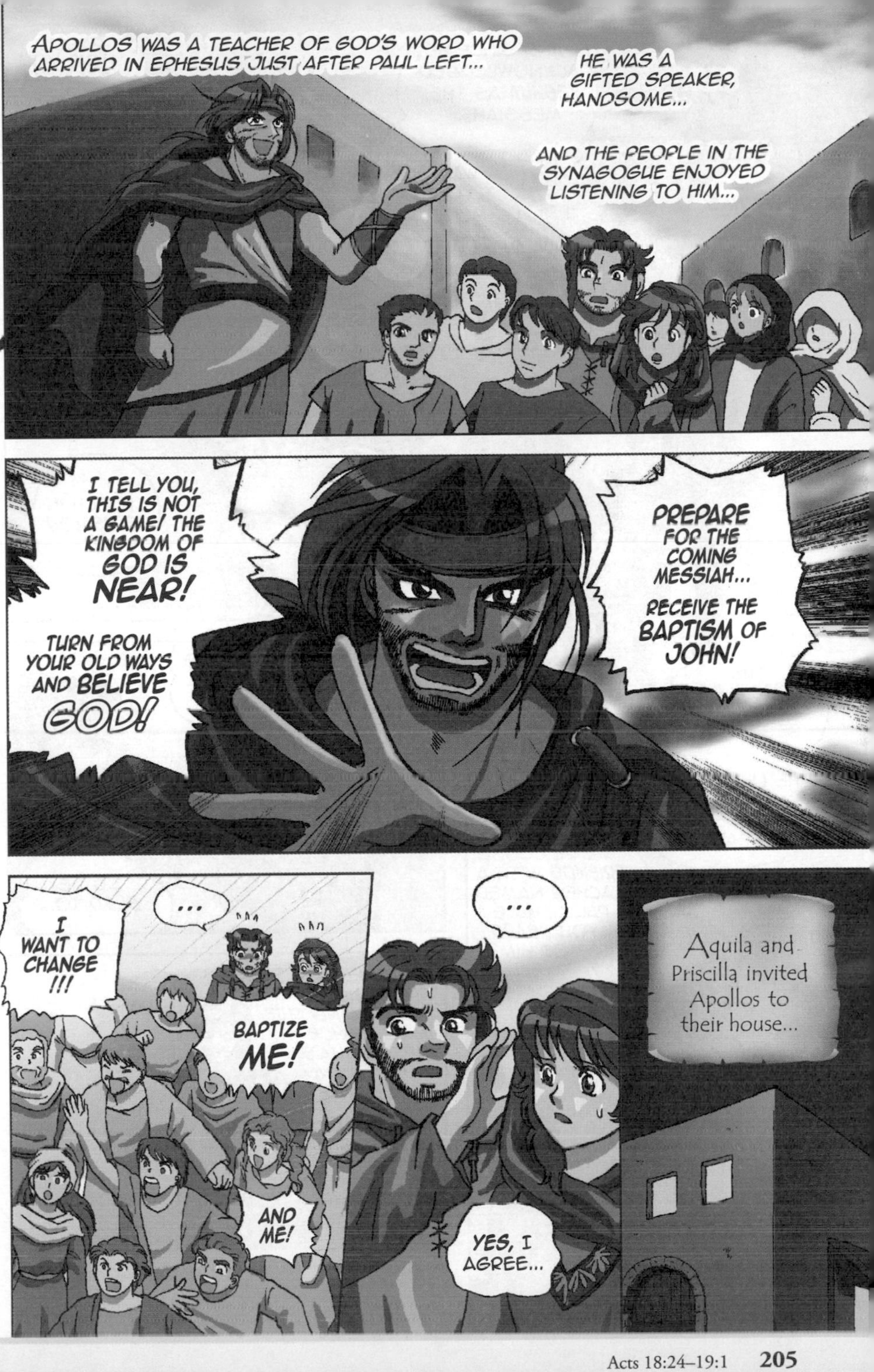
APOLLOS WAS A TEACHER OF GOD'S WORD WHO ARRIVED IN EPHESUS JUST AFTER PAUL LEFT...
HE WAS A GIFTED SPEAKER, HANDSOME...
AND THE PEOPLE IN THE SYNAGOGUE ENJOYED LISTENING TO HIM...
PREPARE FOR THE COMING MESSIAH...
RECEIVE THE BAPTISM OF JOHN!
I TELL YOU, THIS IS NOT A GAME! THE KINGDOM OF GOD IS NEAR!
TURN FROM YOUR OLD WAYS AND BELIEVE GOD!
Aquila and Priscilla invited Apollos to their house...
...
YES, I AGREE...
...
BAPTIZE ME!
I WANT TO CHANGE !!!
AND ME!

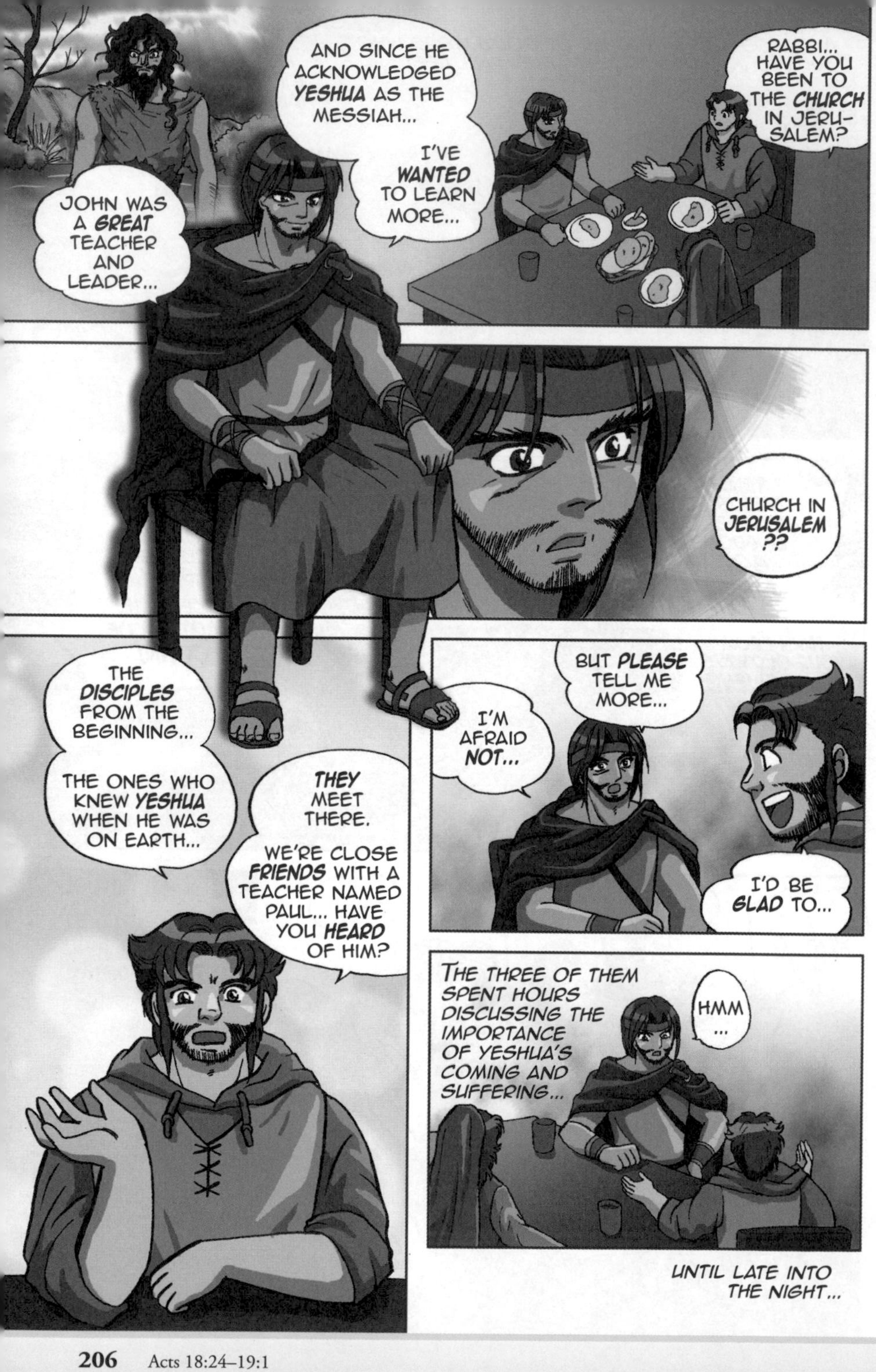

JOHN WAS A GREAT TEACHER AND LEADER...
AND SINCE HE ACKNOWLEDGED YESHUA AS THE MESSIAH...
I'VE WANTED TO LEARN MORE...
RABBI... HAVE YOU BEEN TO THE CHURCH IN JERU-SALEM?
CHURCH IN JERUSALEM??
THE DISCIPLES FROM THE BEGINNING...
THE ONES WHO KNEW YESHUA WHEN HE WAS ON EARTH...
THEY MEET THERE.
WE'RE CLOSE FRIENDS WITH A TEACHER NAMED PAUL... HAVE YOU HEARD OF HIM?
I'M AFRAID NOT...
BUT PLEASE TELL ME MORE...
I'D BE GLAD TO...
THE THREE OF THEM SPENT HOURS DISCUSSING THE IMPORTANCE OF YESHUA'S COMING AND SUFFERING...
HMM ...
UNTIL LATE INTO THE NIGHT...

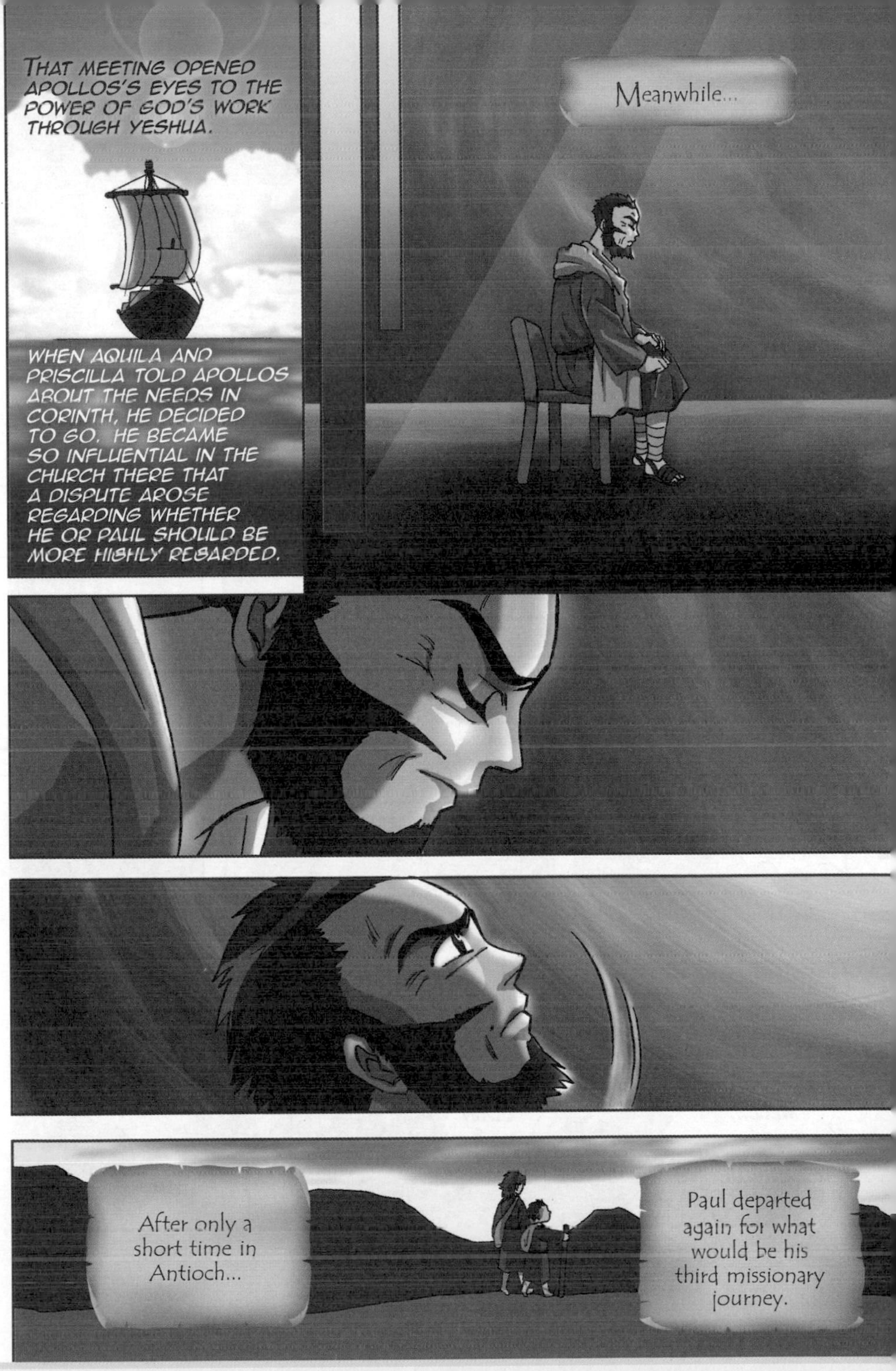
THAT MEETING OPENED APOLLOS'S EYES TO THE POWER OF GOD'S WORK THROUGH YESHUA.
WHEN AQUILA AND PRISCILLA TOLD APOLLOS ABOUT THE NEEDS IN CORINTH, HE DECIDED TO GO. HE BECAME SO INFLUENTIAL IN THE CHURCH THERE THAT A DISPUTE AROSE REGARDING WHETHER HE OR PAUL SHOULD BE MORE HIGHLY REGARDED.
Meanwhile...
After only a short time in Antioch...
Paul departed again for what would be his third missionary journey.

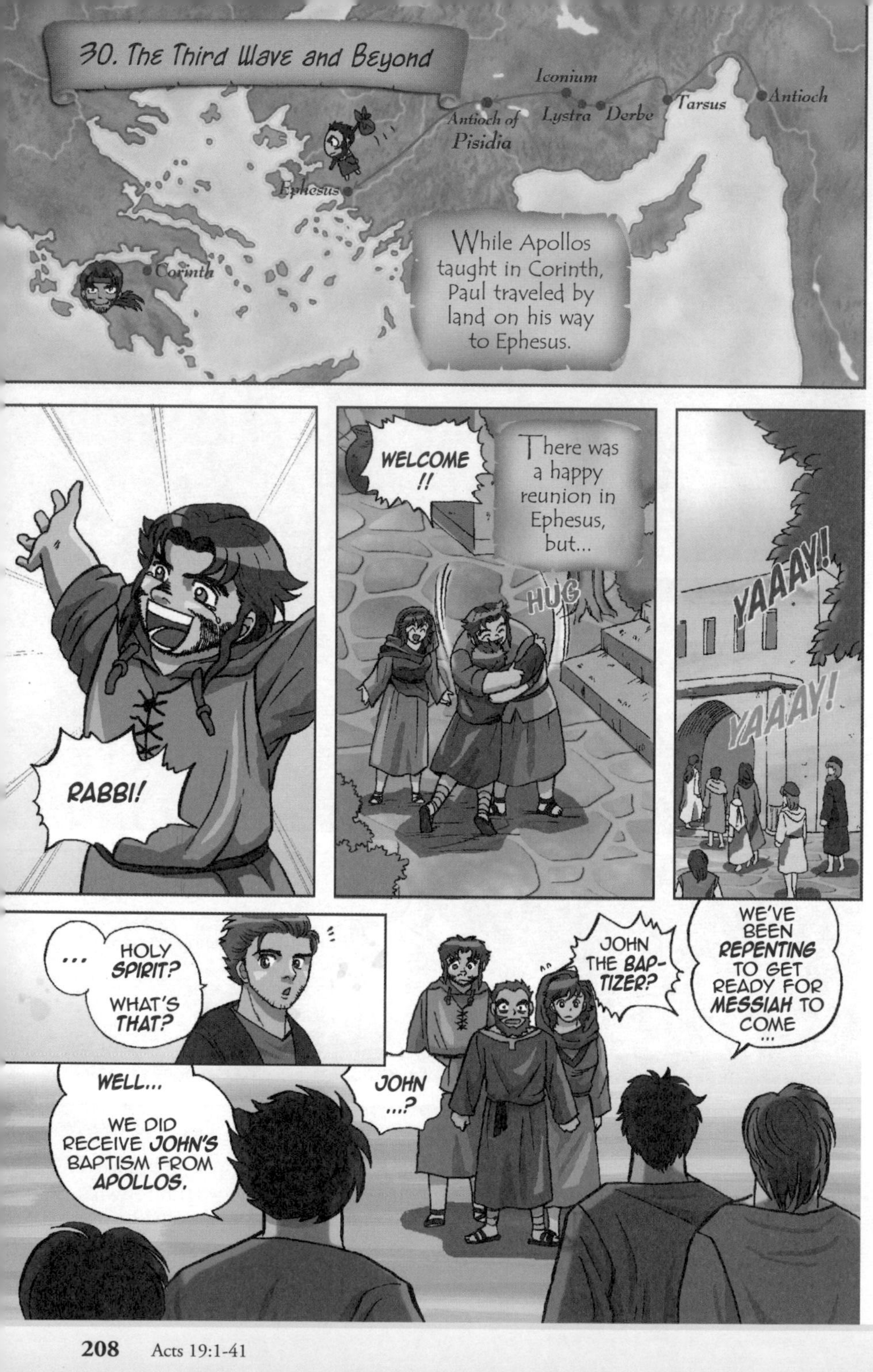
30. The Third Wave and Beyond
Iconium
Antioch of Pisidia
Lystra
Derbe
Tarsus
Antioch
Ephesus
Corinth
While Apollos taught in Corinth, Paul traveled by land on his way to Ephesus.
RABBI!
WELCOME !!
There was a happy reunion in Ephesus, but...
HUG
YAAAY!
YAAAY!
... HOLY SPIRIT? WHAT'S THAT?
JOHN THE BAPTIZER?
WE'VE BEEN REPENTING TO GET READY FOR MESSIAH TO COME ...
WELL... WE DID RECEIVE JOHN'S BAPTISM FROM APOLLOS.
JOHN ...?

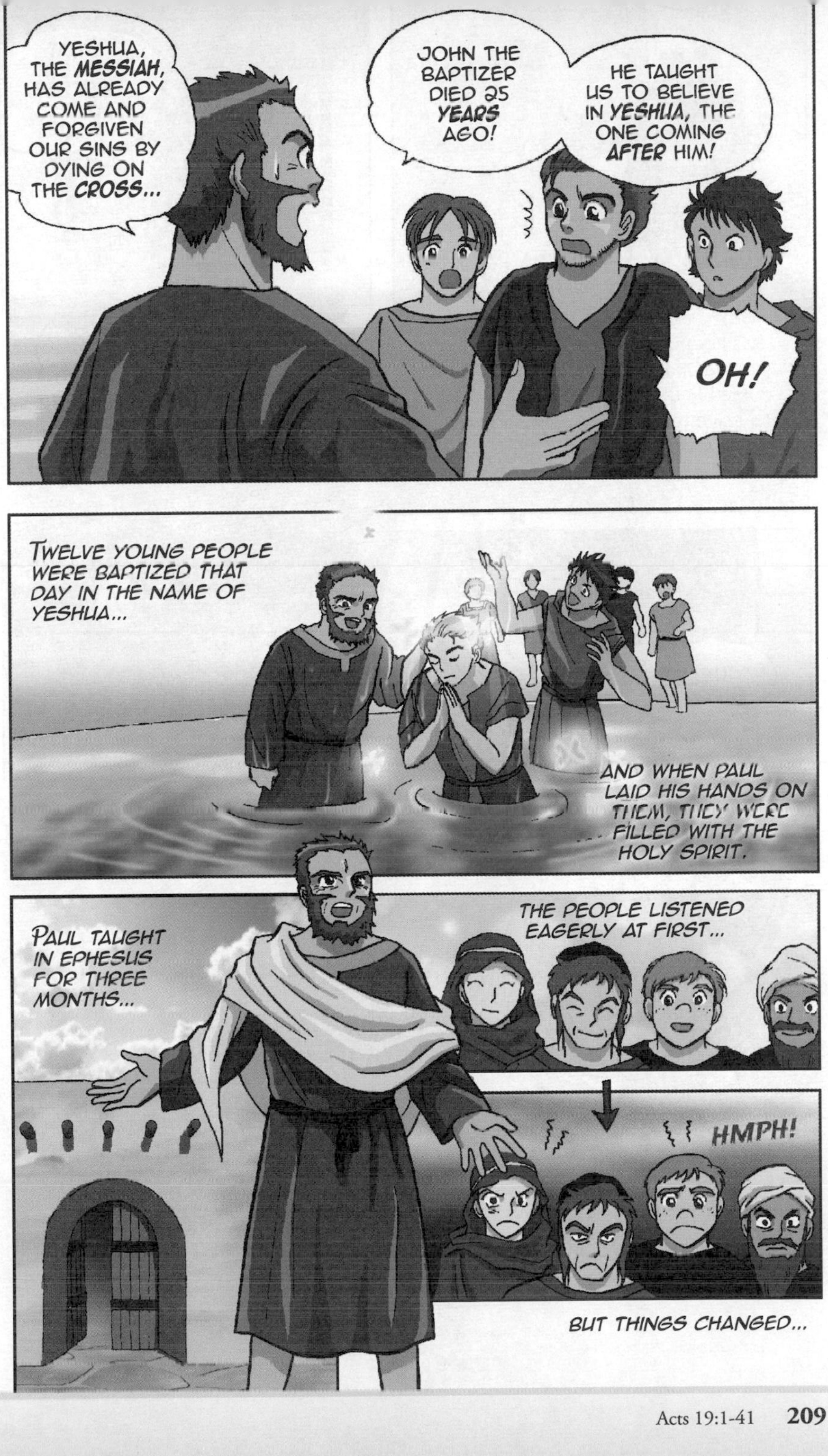
YESHUA, THE MESSIAH, HAS ALREADY COME AND FORGIVEN OUR SINS BY DYING ON THE CROSS...
JOHN THE BAPTIZER DIED 25 YEARS AGO!
HE TAUGHT US TO BELIEVE IN YESHUA, THE ONE COMING AFTER HIM!
OH!
TWELVE YOUNG PEOPLE WERE BAPTIZED THAT DAY IN THE NAME OF YESHUA...
AND WHEN PAUL LAID HIS HANDS ON THEM, THEY WERE FILLED WITH THE HOLY SPIRIT.
PAUL TAUGHT IN EPHESUS FOR THREE MONTHS...
THE PEOPLE LISTENED EAGERLY AT FIRST...
HMPH!
BUT THINGS CHANGED...

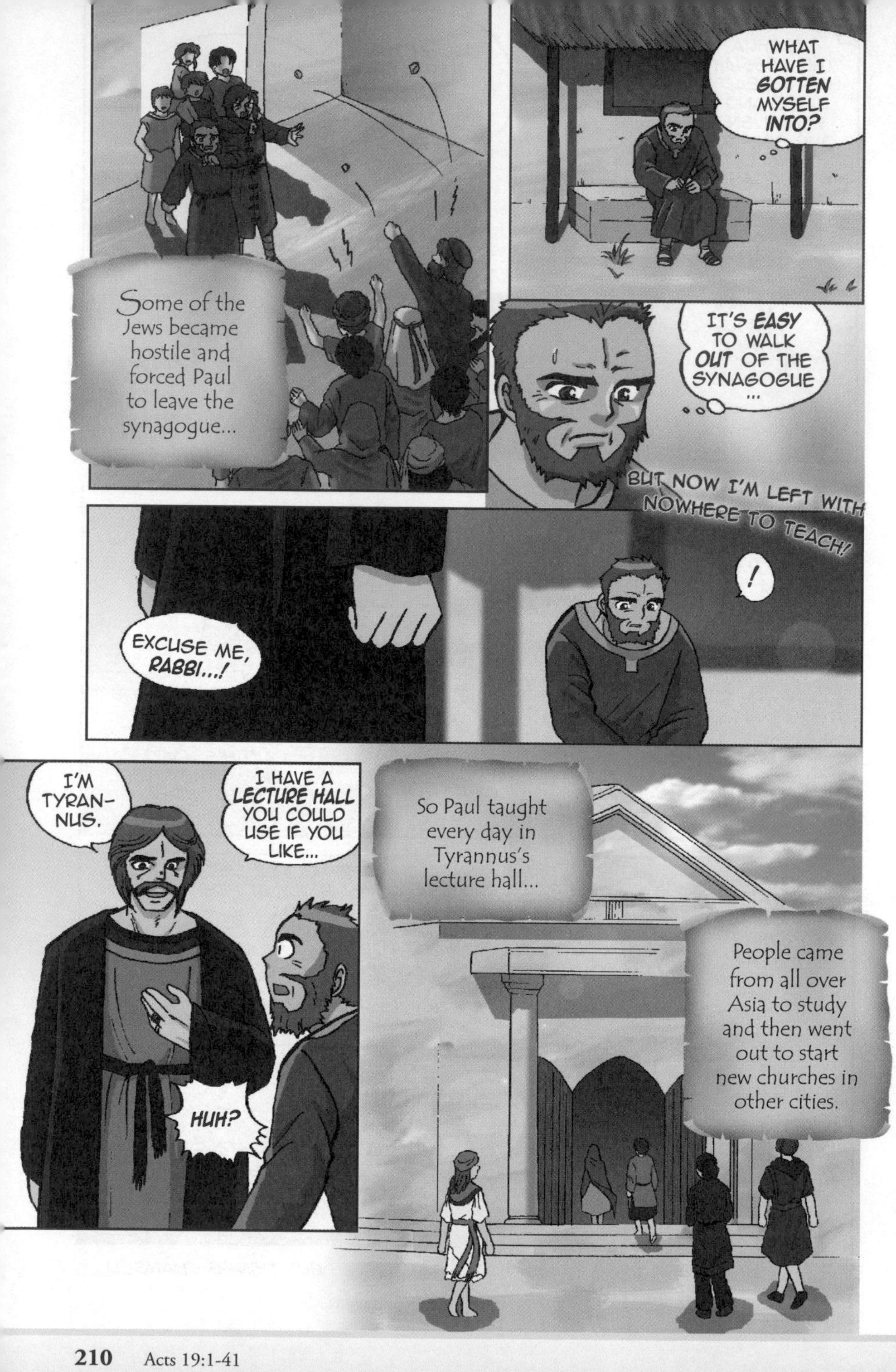
Some of the Jews became hostile and forced Paul to leave the synagogue...
WHAT HAVE I GOTTEN MYSELF INTO?
IT'S EASY TO WALK OUT OF THE SYNAGOGUE ...
BUT NOW I'M LEFT WITH NOWHERE TO TEACH!
EXCUSE ME, RABBI...!
!
I'M TYRAN- NUS.
I HAVE A LECTURE HALL YOU COULD USE IF YOU LIKE...
HUH?
So Paul taught every day in Tyrannus's lecture hall...
People came from all over Asia to study and then went out to start new churches in other cities.

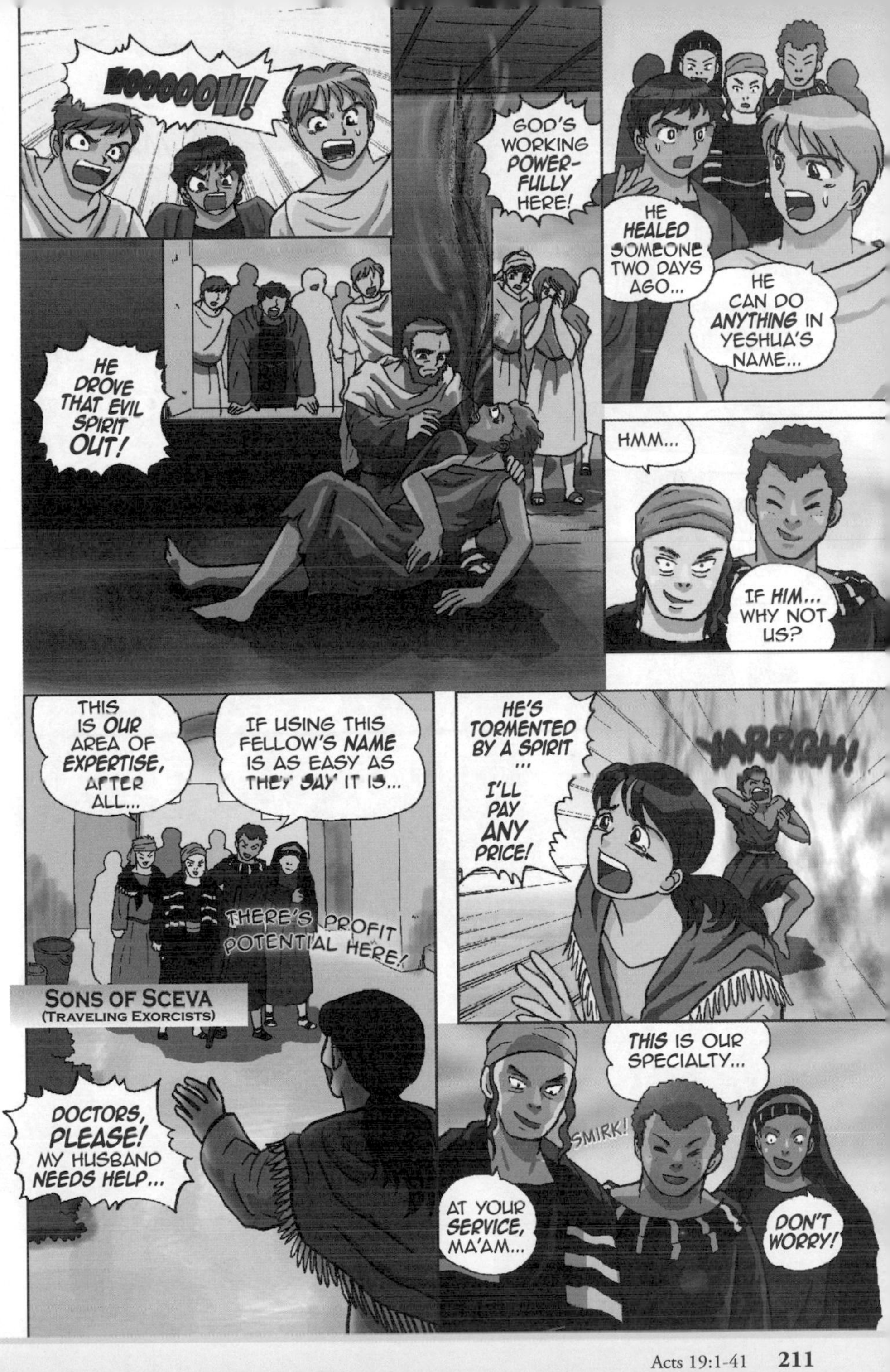
WOOOOOOW!
GOD'S WORKING POWER-FULLY HERE!
HE HEALED SOMEONE TWO DAYS AGO...
HE CAN DO ANYTHING IN YESHUA'S NAME...
HE DROVE THAT EVIL SPIRIT OUT!
HMM...
IF HIM... WHY NOT US?
THIS IS OUR AREA OF EXPERTISE, AFTER ALL...
IF USING THIS FELLOW'S NAME IS AS EASY AS THEY SAY IT IS...
THERE'S PROFIT POTENTIAL HERE!
SONS OF SCEVA
(TRAVELING EXORCISTS)
HE'S TORMENTED BY A SPIRIT ...
I'LL PAY ANY PRICE!
YARRGH!
DOCTORS, PLEASE! MY HUSBAND NEEDS HELP...
THIS IS OUR SPECIALTY...
SMIRK!
AT YOUR SERVICE, MA'AM...
DON'T WORRY!

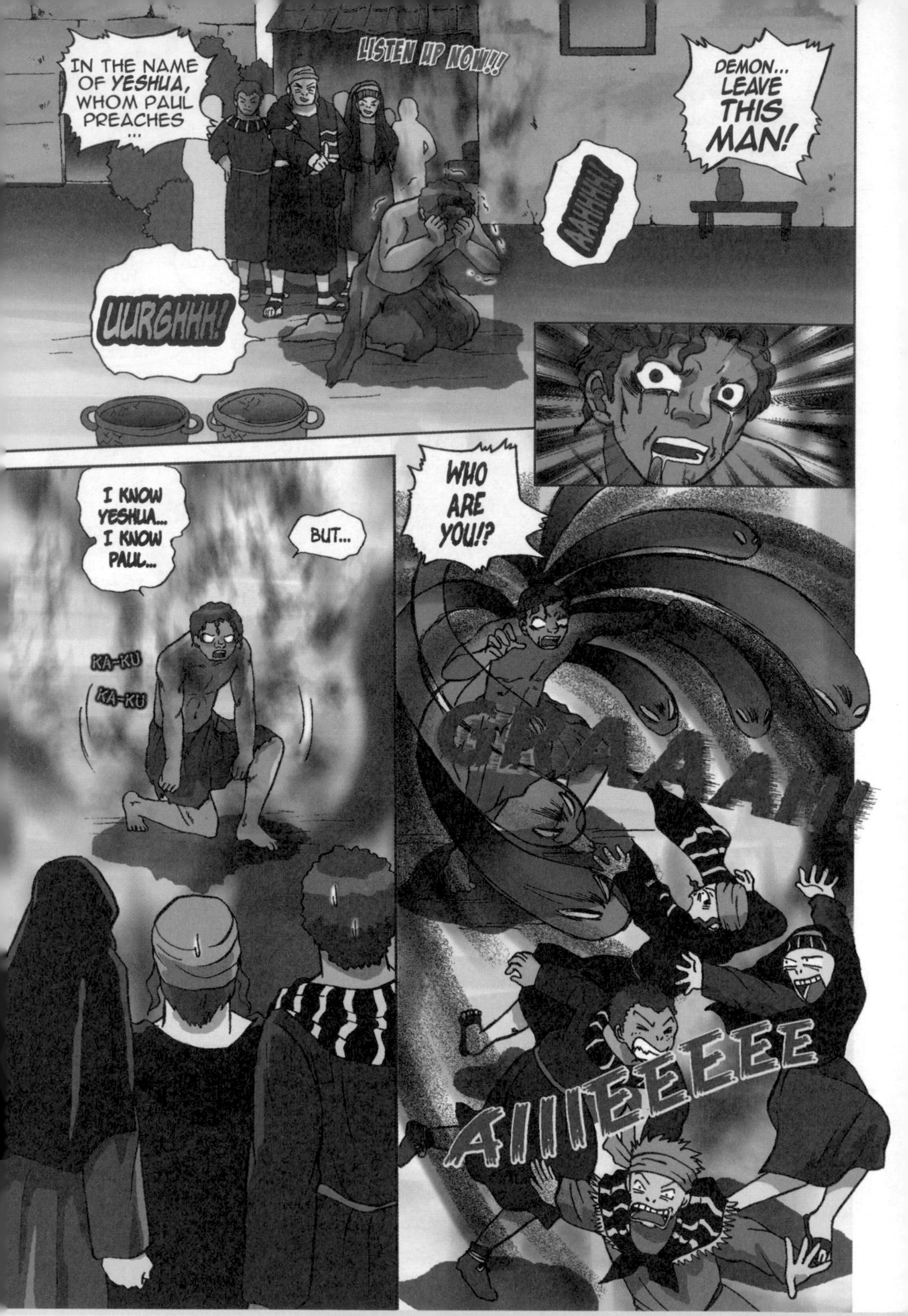

IN THE NAME OF YESHUA, WHOM PAUL PREACHES ...
LISTEN UP NOW!!
DEMON... LEAVE THIS MAN!
AAHHHH!
UURGHHH!
I KNOW YESHUA... I KNOW PAUL...
BUT...
KA-KU
KA-KU
WHO ARE YOU!?
GRAAAAH!
AIIIEEEEE

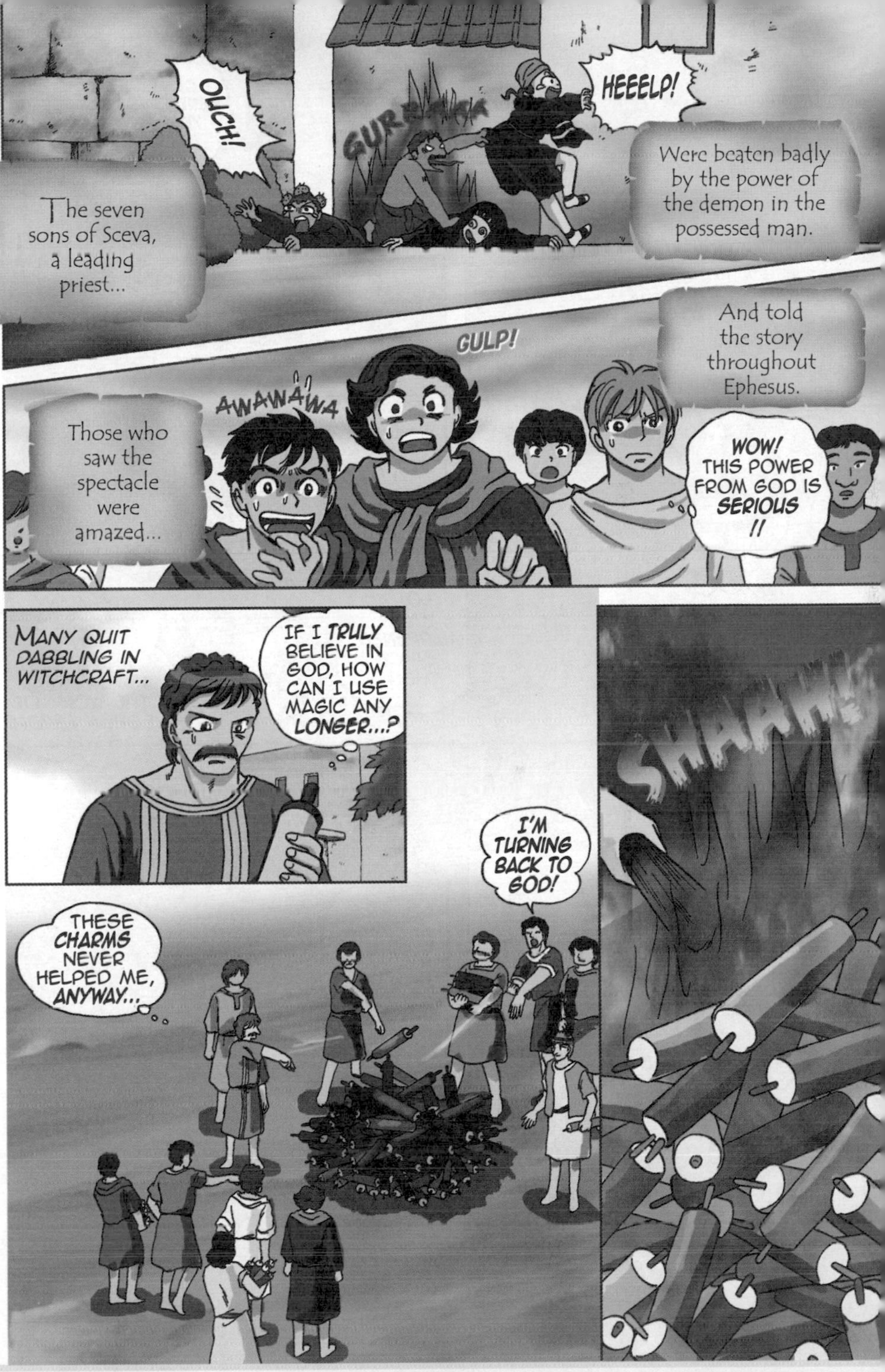

OUCH!
GURPAKKA
HEEELP!
The seven sons of Sceva, a leading priest...
Were beaten badly by the power of the demon in the possessed man.
And told the story throughout Ephesus.
GULP!
AWAWAWA
Those who saw the spectacle were amazed...
WOW! THIS POWER FROM GOD IS SERIOUS !!
MANY QUIT DABBLING IN WITCHCRAFT...
IF I TRULY BELIEVE IN GOD, HOW CAN I USE MAGIC ANY LONGER...?
I'M TURNING BACK TO GOD!
THESE CHARMS NEVER HELPED ME, ANYWAY...

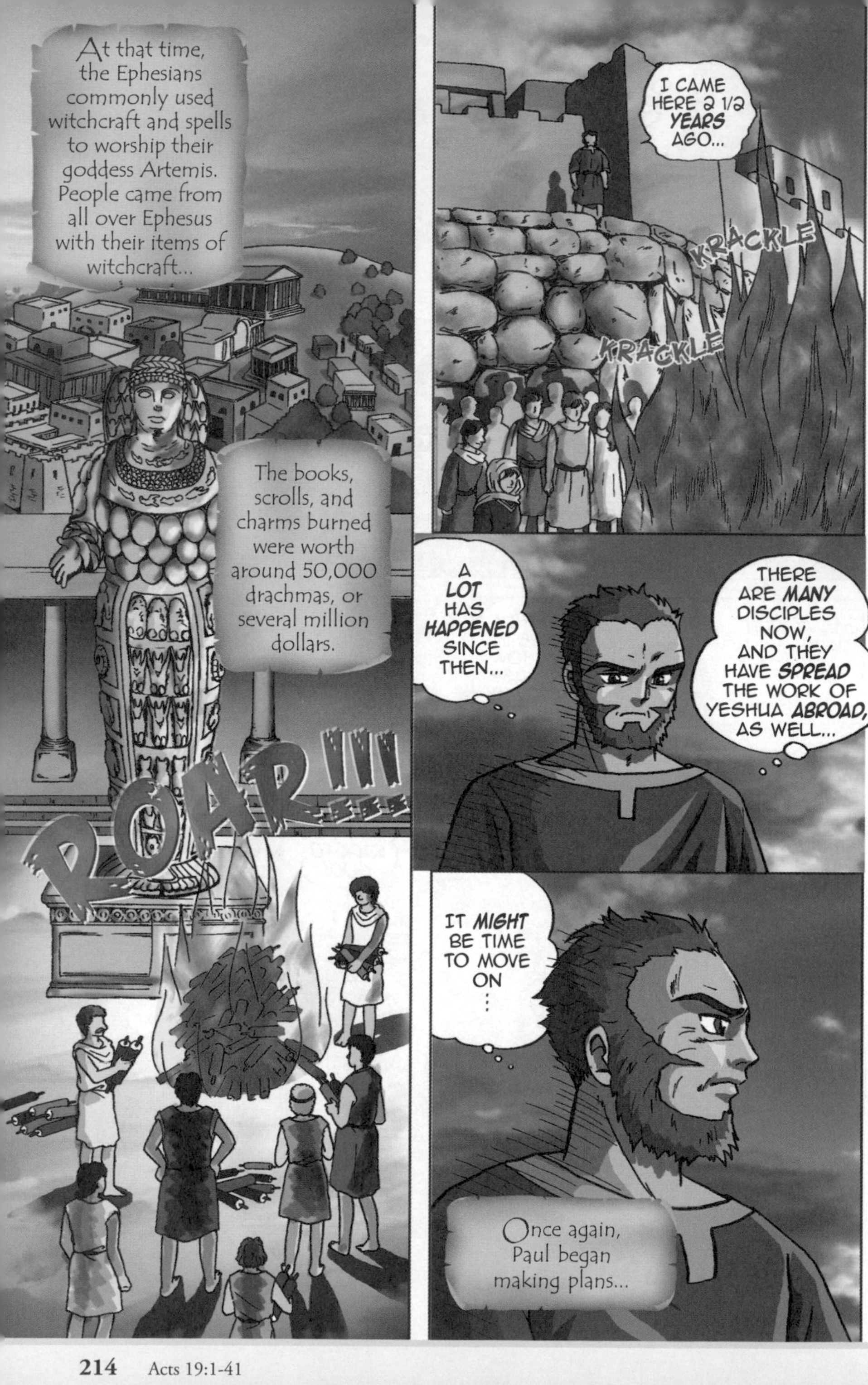
At that time, the Ephesians commonly used witchcraft and spells to worship their goddess Artemis. People came from all over Ephesus with their items of witchcraft...
The books, scrolls, and charms burned were worth around 50,000 drachmas, or several million dollars.
ROAR!!!
I CAME HERE 2 1/2 YEARS AGO...
KRACKLE
KRACKLE
A LOT HAS HAPPENED SINCE THEN...
THERE ARE MANY DISCIPLES NOW, AND THEY HAVE SPREAD THE WORK OF YESHUA ABROAD, AS WELL...
IT MIGHT BE TIME TO MOVE ON ...
Once again, Paul began making plans...

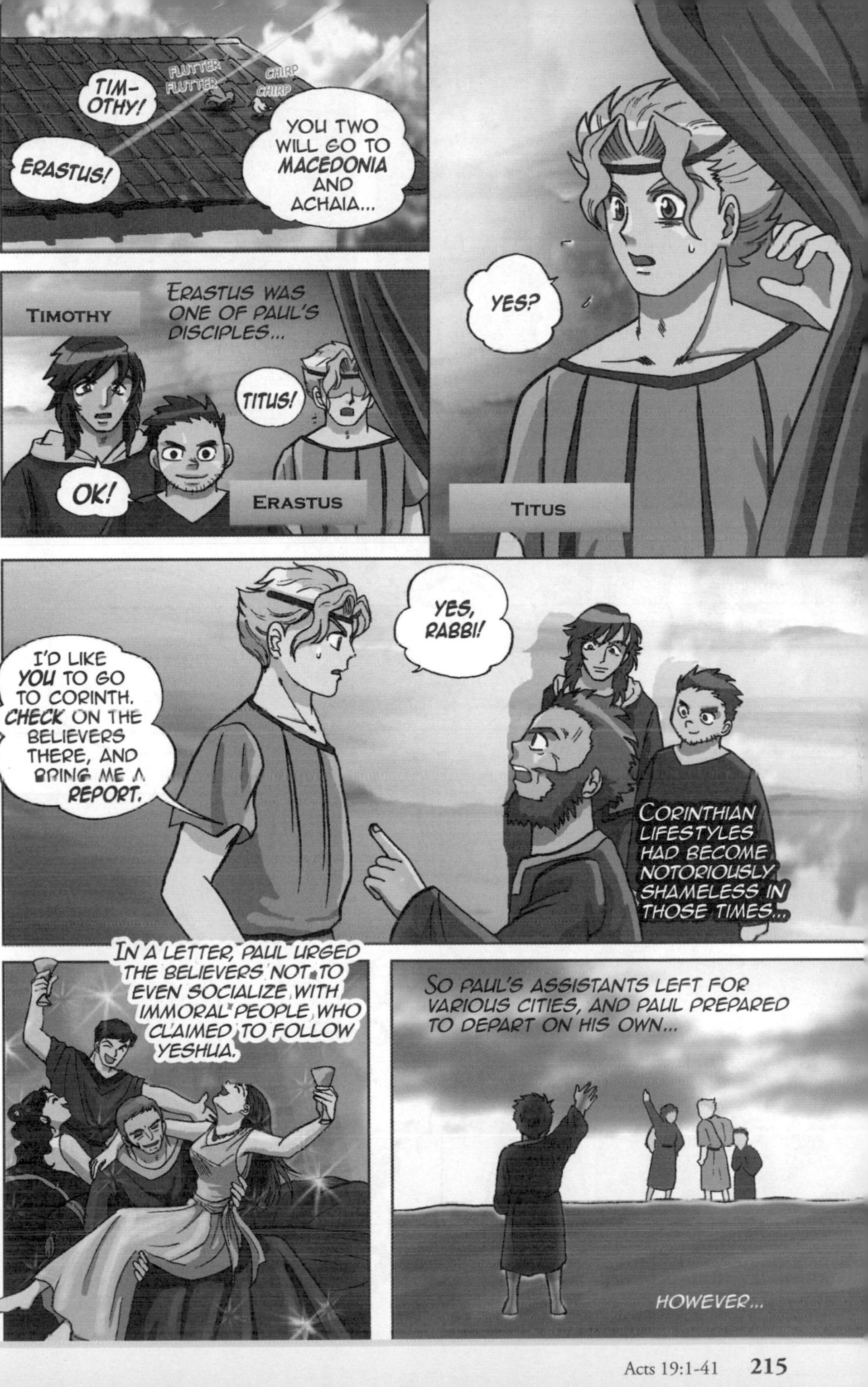
TIM-OTHY!
FLUTTER FLUTTER
CHIRP CHIRP
ERASTUS!
YOU TWO WILL GO TO MACEDONIA AND ACHAIA...
YES?
TITUS
ERASTUS WAS ONE OF PAUL'S DISCIPLES...
TIMOTHY
TITUS!
OK!
ERASTUS
I'D LIKE YOU TO GO TO CORINTH. CHECK ON THE BELIEVERS THERE, AND BRING ME A REPORT.
YES, RABBI!
CORINTHIAN LIFESTYLES HAD BECOME NOTORIOUSLY SHAMELESS IN THOSE TIMES...
IN A LETTER, PAUL URGED THE BELIEVERS NOT TO EVEN SOCIALIZE WITH IMMORAL PEOPLE WHO CLAIMED TO FOLLOW YESHUA.
SO PAUL'S ASSISTANTS LEFT FOR VARIOUS CITIES, AND PAUL PREPARED TO DEPART ON HIS OWN...
HOWEVER...

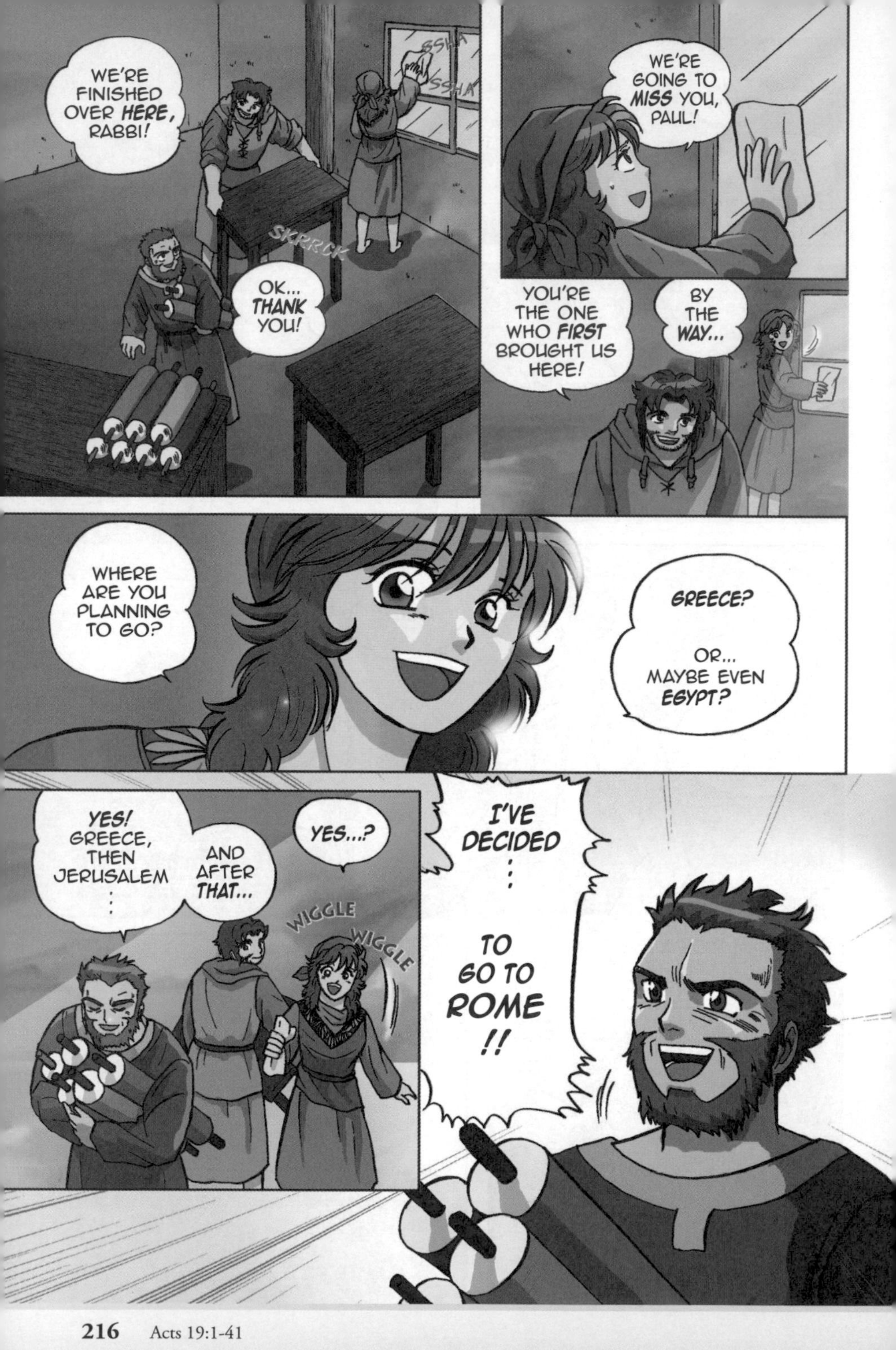
WE'RE FINISHED OVER HERE, RABBI!
SSHA
SSHA
SKRRCK
OK... THANK YOU!
WE'RE GOING TO MISS YOU, PAUL!
YOU'RE THE ONE WHO FIRST BROUGHT US HERE!
BY THE WAY...
WHERE ARE YOU PLANNING TO GO?
GREECE?
OR... MAYBE EVEN EGYPT?
YES! GREECE, THEN JERUSALEM ...
AND AFTER THAT...
YES...?
WIGGLE
WIGGLE
I'VE DECIDED ...
TO GO TO ROME !!

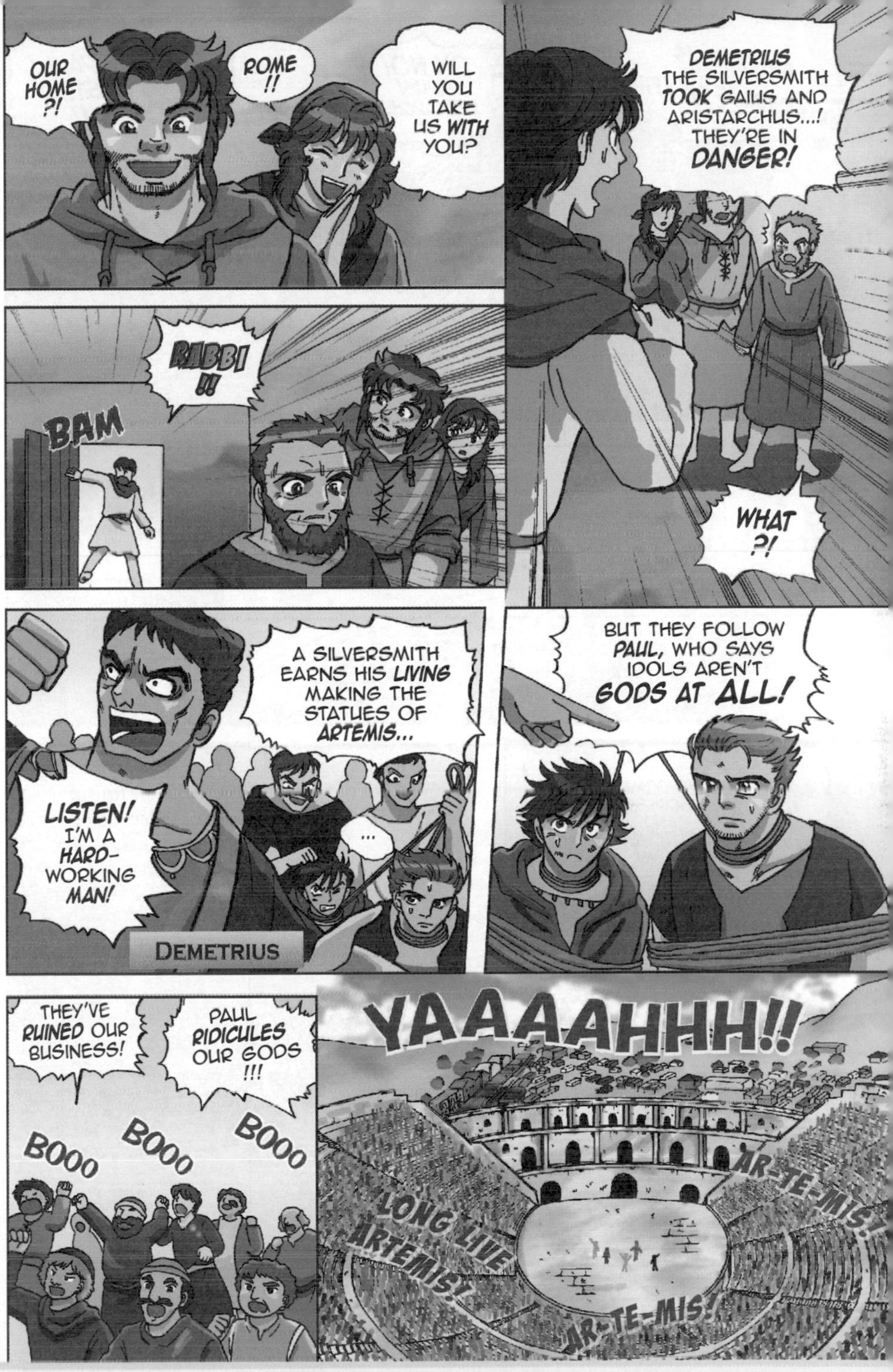
OUR HOME ?!
ROME !!
WILL YOU TAKE US WITH YOU?
DEMETRIUS THE SILVERSMITH TOOK GAIUS AND ARISTARCHUS...! THEY'RE IN DANGER!
RABBI !!
BAM
WHAT ?!
A SILVERSMITH EARNS HIS LIVING MAKING THE STATUES OF ARTEMIS...
LISTEN! I'M A HARD-WORKING MAN!
...
DEMETRIUS
BUT THEY FOLLOW PAUL, WHO SAYS IDOLS AREN'T GODS AT ALL!
THEY'VE RUINED OUR BUSINESS!
PAUL RIDICULES OUR GODS !!!
BOOO
BOOO
BOOO
YAAAAHHH!!
LONG LIVE ARTEMIS!
AR-TE-MIS!
AR-TE-MIS!

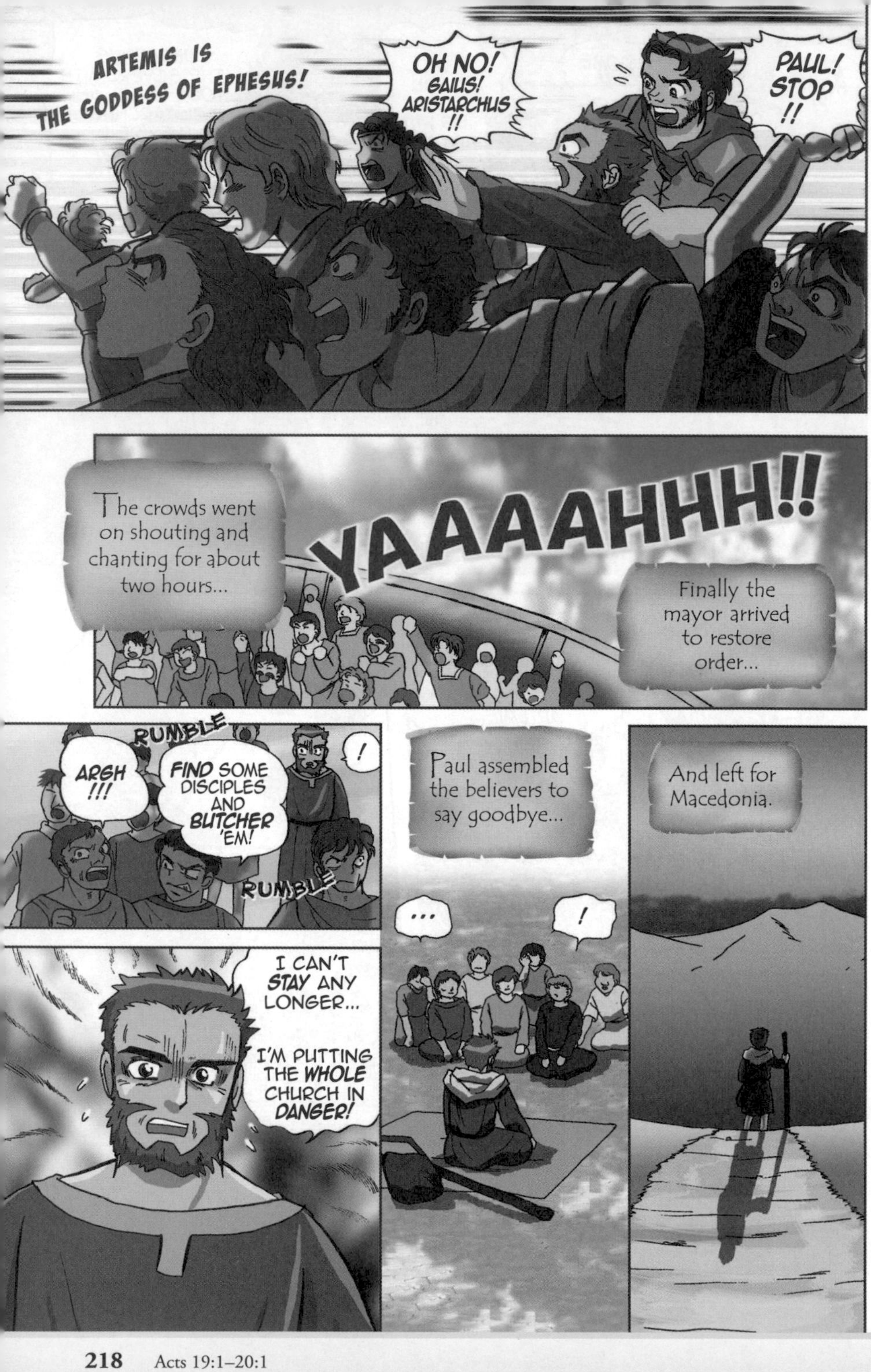
ARTEMIS IS THE GODDESS OF EPHESUS!
OH NO! GAIUS! ARISTARCHUS !!
PAUL! STOP !!
The crowds went on shouting and chanting for about two hours...
YAAAAAHHH!!
Finally the mayor arrived to restore order...
RUMBLE
ARGH !!!
FIND SOME DISCIPLES AND BUTCHER 'EM!
!
RUMBLE
I CAN'T STAY ANY LONGER...
I'M PUTTING THE WHOLE CHURCH IN DANGER!
Paul assembled the believers to say goodbye...
...
!
And left for Macedonia.

Letter to the Believers in Ephesus

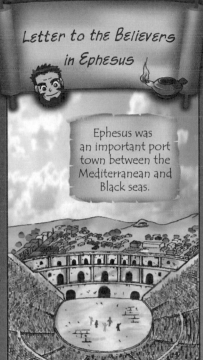

Ephesus was an important port town between the Mediterranean and Black seas.

In his letter, Paul explained how everything changed for Jews after the coming of Yeshua.

TILL NOW, YOU'VE BEEN *LIVING* LIVES...

...THAT LEAD TO *DEATH!*

DESTRUCTION

AFTER ALL MY *MISTAKES*, THERE'S NO HOPE LEFT.

BUT I *DIED* TO PAY FOR *YOUR* MISTAKES.

BUT GOD RESCUED US BY SENDING YESHUA...

IT'S *NEVER* TOO LATE TO START AGAIN, AND I WILL *LEAD* YOU.

Stand up...

A *NEW* LIFE...

I CAN HAVE A NEW *LIFE.*

So Paul encouraged the believers to speak the truth in love and to grow more and more like Yeshua, who is the head of his body, the church.

PAUL DESCRIBED THE CHURCH BY COMPARING IT TO YESHUA'S BODY.

ALL BELIEVERS ARE UNITED IN YESHUA, WORKING AND GROWING TOGETHER.

HE'S THE HEAD!

WE'RE HANDS

LEGS!

WE ARE *MANY* PARTS, AND TOGETHER WE MAKE THE *CHURCH!*

THE CHURCH

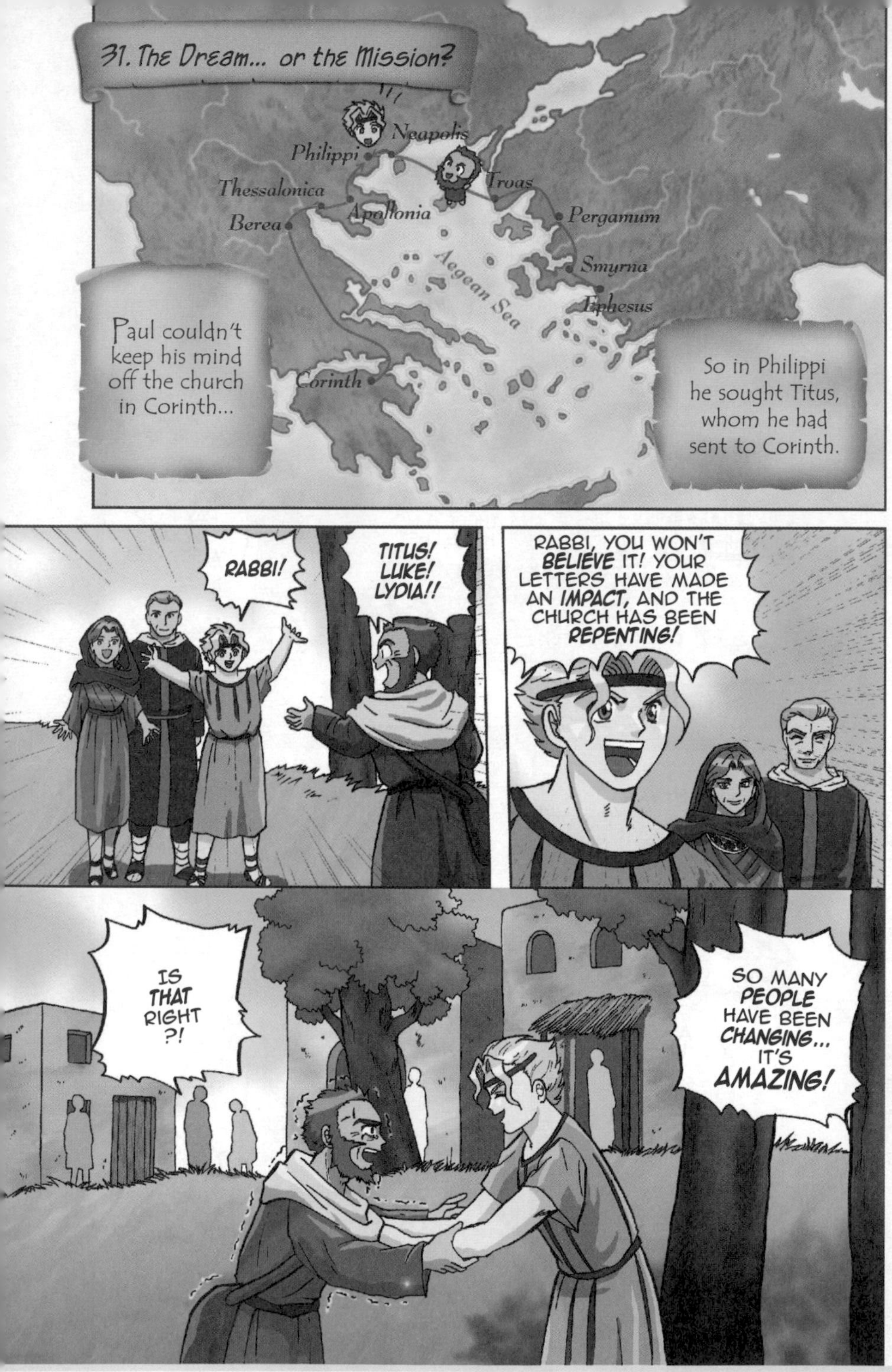
31. The Dream... or the Mission?
Neapolis
Philippi
Thessalonica
Troas
Apollonia
Berea
Pergamum
Aegean Sea
Smyrna
Ephesus
Corinth
Paul couldn't keep his mind off the church in Corinth...
So in Philippi he sought Titus, whom he had sent to Corinth.
RABBI!
TITUS! LUKE! LYDIA!!
RABBI, YOU WON'T BELIEVE IT! YOUR LETTERS HAVE MADE AN IMPACT, AND THE CHURCH HAS BEEN REPENTING!
IS THAT RIGHT ?!
SO MANY PEOPLE HAVE BEEN CHANGING... IT'S AMAZING!

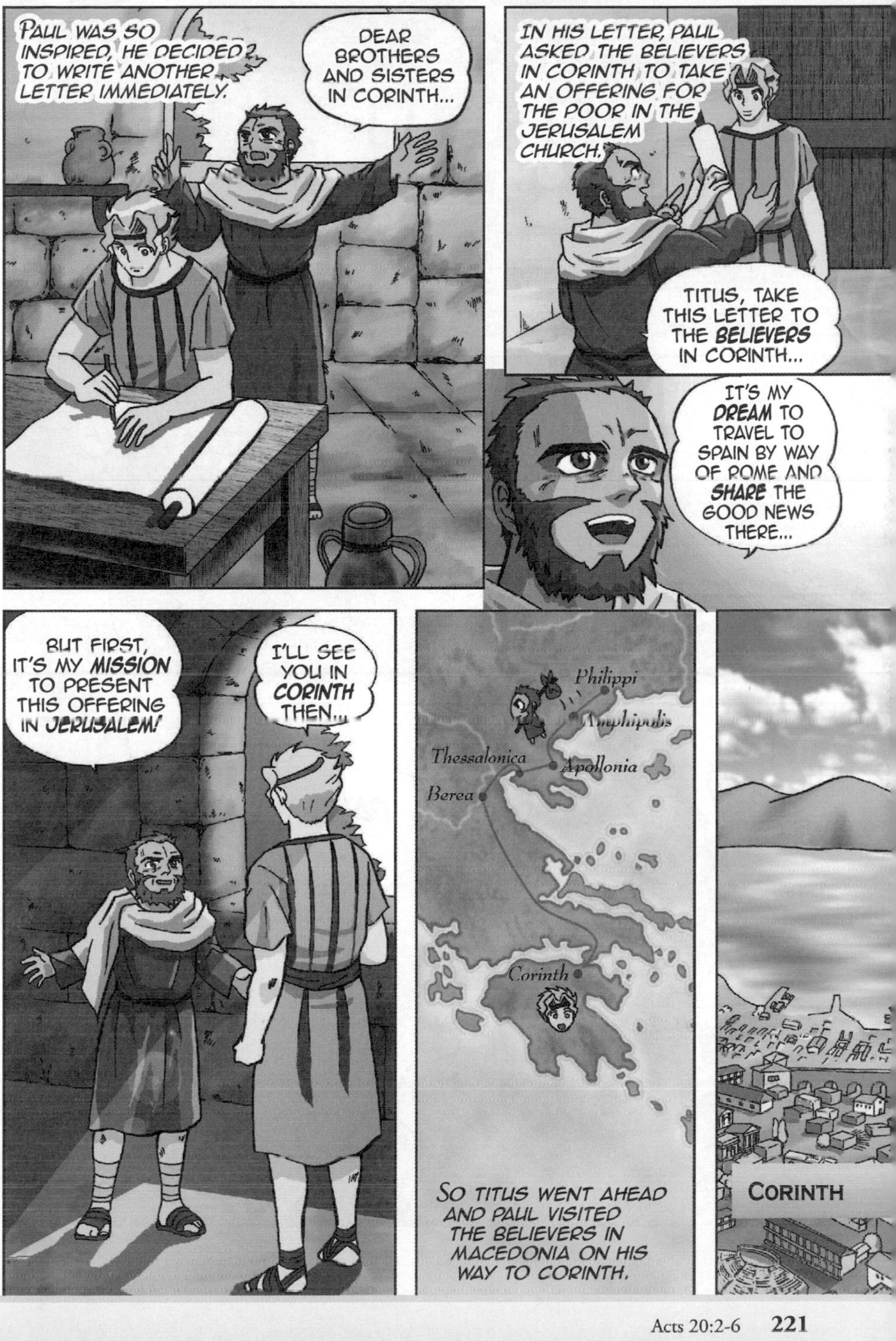

Paul was so inspired, he decided to write another letter immediately.
Dear brothers and sisters in Corinth...
In his letter, Paul asked the believers in Corinth to take an offering for the poor in the Jerusalem church.
Titus, take this letter to the believers in Corinth...
It's my dream to travel to Spain by way of Rome and share the good news there...
But first, it's my mission to present this offering in Jerusalem!
I'll see you in Corinth then...
Philippi
Amphipolis
Thessalonica
Apollonia
Berea
Corinth
So Titus went ahead and Paul visited the believers in Macedonia on his way to Corinth.
Corinth

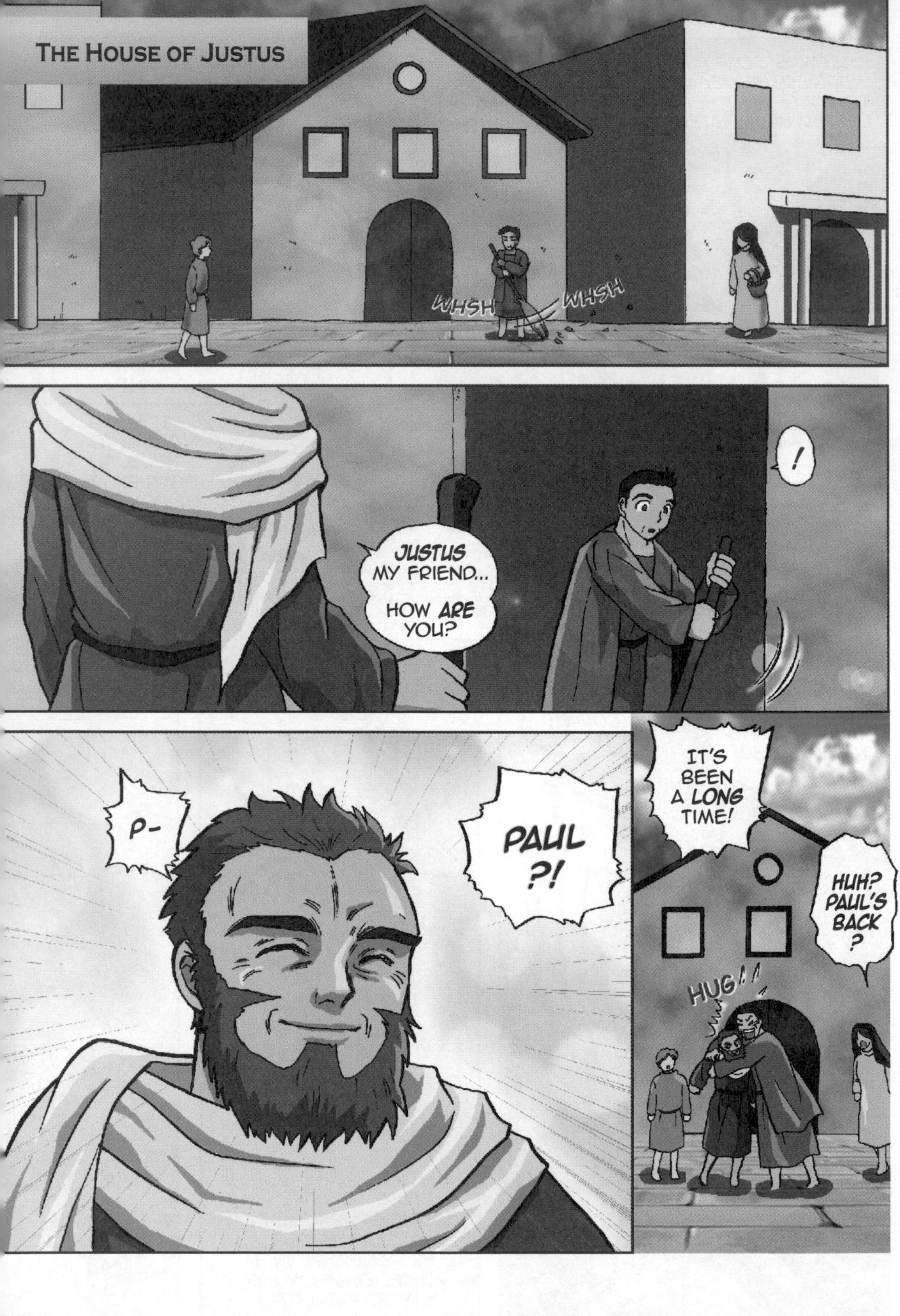
The House of Justus
WHSH
WHSH
JUSTUS MY FRIEND...
HOW ARE YOU?
!
P-
PAUL ?!
IT'S BEEN A LONG TIME!
HUH? PAUL'S BACK ?
HUG!!

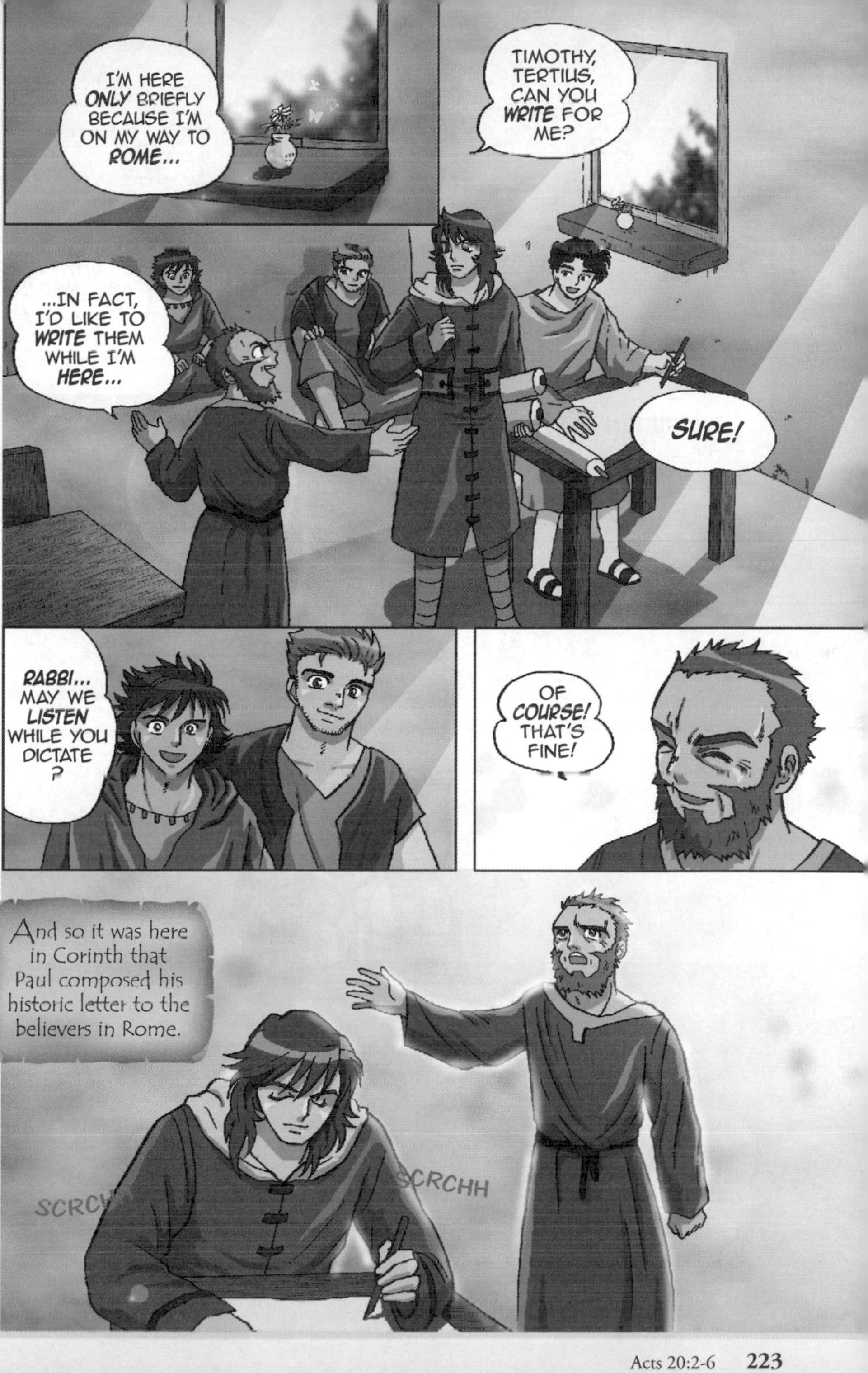
I'M HERE ONLY BRIEFLY BECAUSE I'M ON MY WAY TO ROME...
TIMOTHY, TERTIUS, CAN YOU WRITE FOR ME?
...IN FACT, I'D LIKE TO WRITE THEM WHILE I'M HERE...
SURE!
RABBI... MAY WE LISTEN WHILE YOU DICTATE ?
OF COURSE! THAT'S FINE!
And so it was here in Corinth that Paul composed his historic letter to the believers in Rome.
SCRCH
SCRCHH

Letter to the Believers in Rome

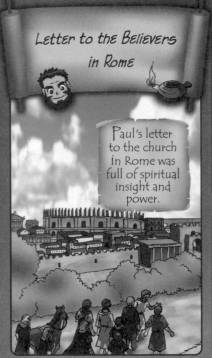

Paul's letter to the church in Rome was full of spiritual insight and power.

One of the first themes of this letter was the importance of a believer's faith...

I'M **NOT** ASHAMED OF THIS GOOD NEWS!

IT'S THE **POWER OF GOD** ...

FIRST FOR THE JEWS, BUT NOW FOR **EVERYONE** WHO BELIEVES!

Paul showed how Yeshua's work and teachings fulfilled the prophecies of the Ancient Texts.

LOOKS LIKE WE'RE THE ONLY ONES WHO'LL BE GOING TO HEAVEN!

In those days, it was understood that only the most honorable Jews would be saved...

But Paul explained that no one can be saved by being good...

EVEN THOUGH WE'RE **NOT** JEWS, WE CAN BELIEVE AND BE **SAVED?**

God chose to save the world through the Jews, and now that Yeshua has come, all people can be saved through belief in him.

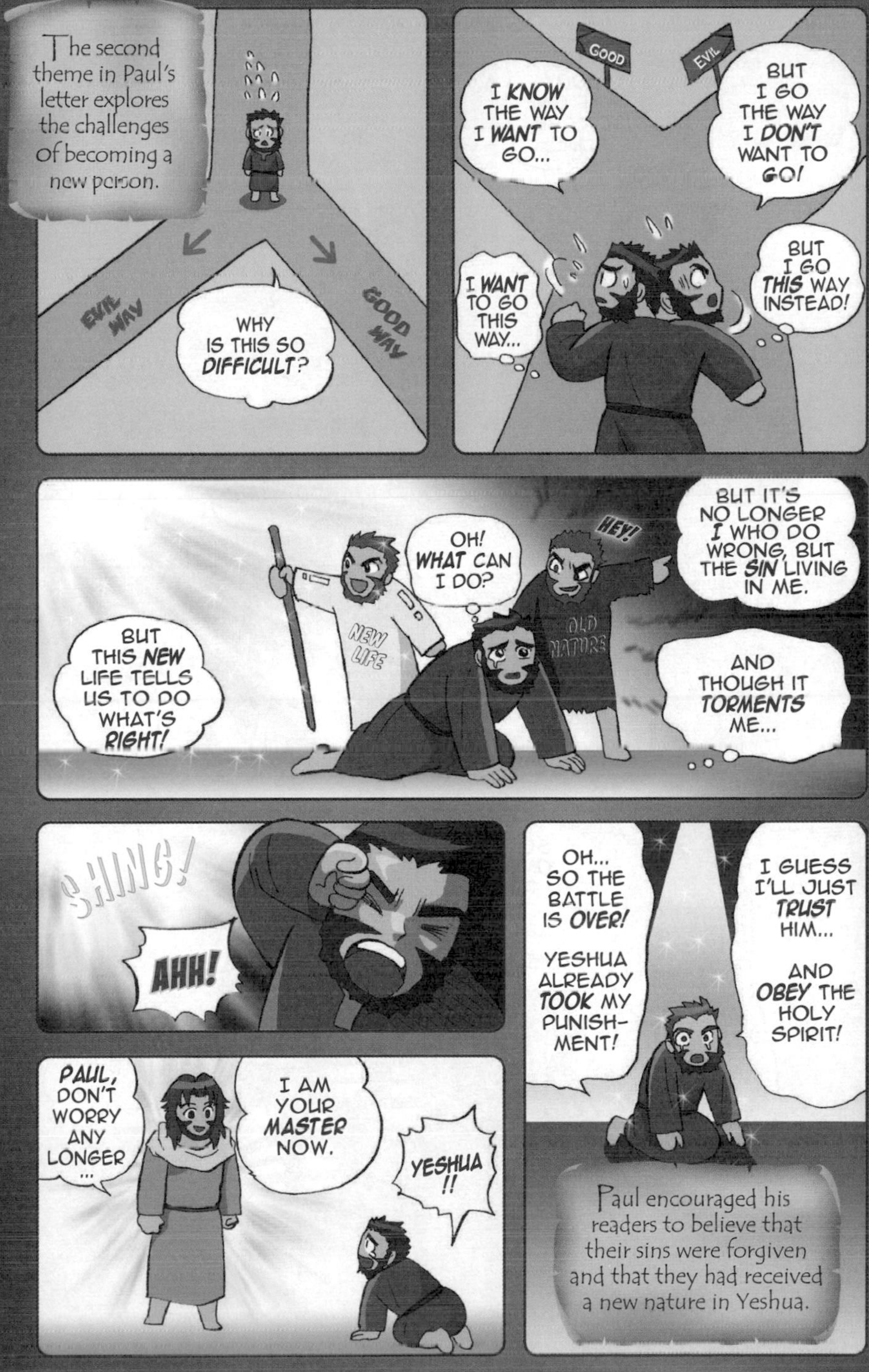
The second theme in Paul's letter explores the challenges of becoming a new person.
EVIL WAY
GOOD WAY
WHY IS THIS SO DIFFICULT?
GOOD
EVIL
I KNOW THE WAY I WANT TO GO...
BUT I GO THE WAY I DON'T WANT TO GO!
I WANT TO GO THIS WAY...
BUT I GO THIS WAY INSTEAD!
NEW LIFE
OH! WHAT CAN I DO?
HEY!
OLD NATURE
BUT IT'S NO LONGER I WHO DO WRONG, BUT THE SIN LIVING IN ME.
BUT THIS NEW LIFE TELLS US TO DO WHAT'S RIGHT!
AND THOUGH IT TORMENTS ME...
SHING!
AHH!
PAUL, DON'T WORRY ANY LONGER ...
I AM YOUR MASTER NOW.
YESHUA !!
OH... SO THE BATTLE IS OVER!
YESHUA ALREADY TOOK MY PUNISH-MENT!
I GUESS I'LL JUST TRUST HIM...
AND OBEY THE HOLY SPIRIT!
Paul encouraged his readers to believe that their sins were forgiven and that they had received a new nature in Yeshua.

Finally, Paul wrote of the future glory believers can look forward to.
THIS BODY WILL ONE DAY BE GONE...
AND THIS EARTH AS WELL...
ALL THAT WE SEE AND TOUCH WILL ONE DAY BE DESTROYED...
AND EVERYTHING WILL BE MADE NEW.
I'M NOT DEAD?
MY DAUGHTER !!
!!
!!
GRANDPA ?!
The children of God will be raised again.
SO I DON'T NEED TO BE AFRAID OF DEATH... YESHUA!
These things will happen when Jerusalem is reconciled...
I WILL LIVE BY LISTENING TO YOU, GOD.
So offer your bodies to God, as living sacrifices, holy and pleasing to him.

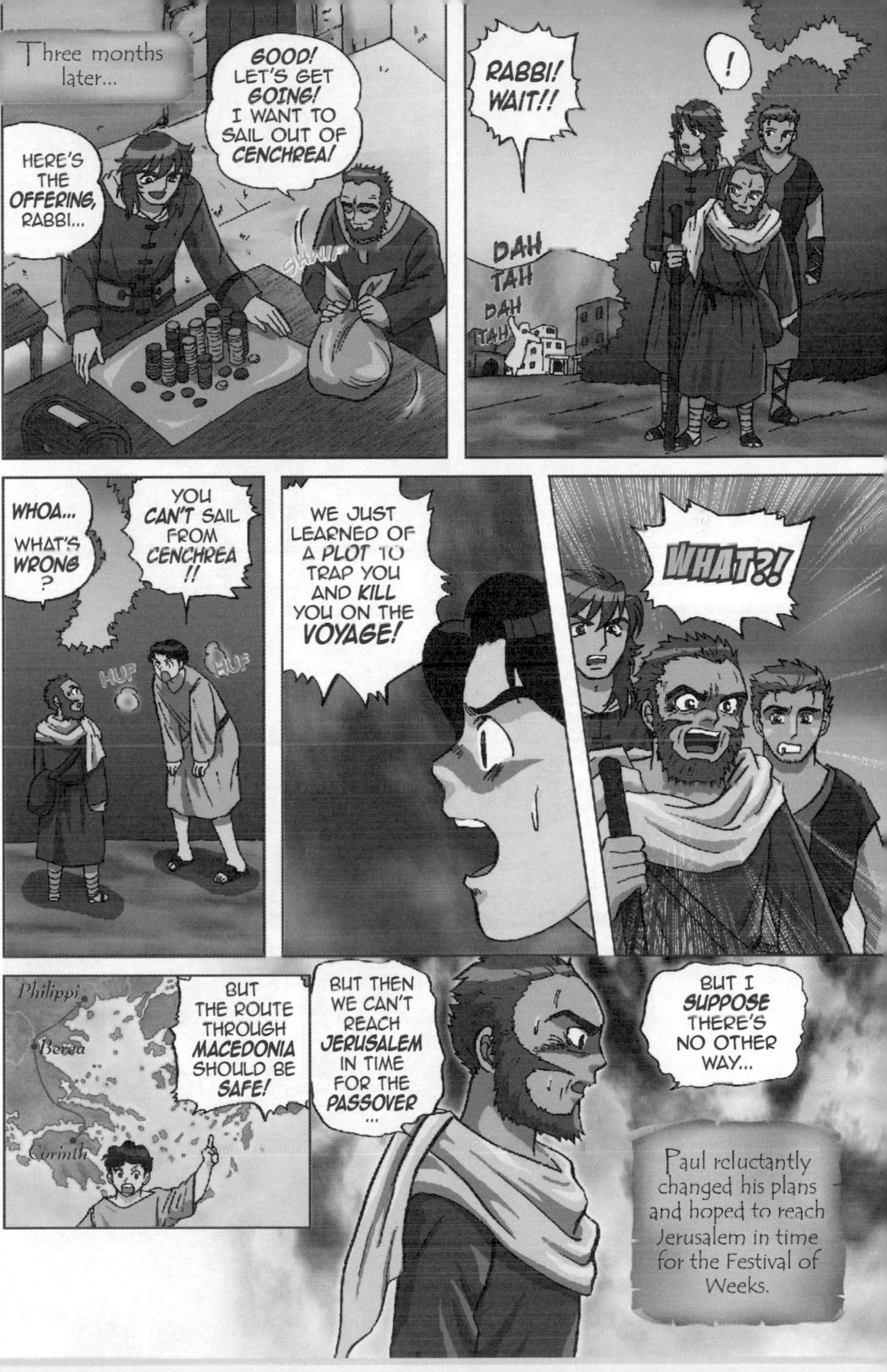
Three months later...
HERE'S THE OFFERING, RABBI...
GOOD! LET'S GET GOING! I WANT TO SAIL OUT OF CENCHREA!
RABBI! WAIT!!
!
DAH TAH DAH TAH
WHOA... WHAT'S WRONG ?
YOU CAN'T SAIL FROM CENCHREA !!
HUF HUF
WE JUST LEARNED OF A PLOT TO TRAP YOU AND KILL YOU ON THE VOYAGE!
WHAT?!
Philippi
Berea
Corinth
BUT THE ROUTE THROUGH MACEDONIA SHOULD BE SAFE!
BUT THEN WE CAN'T REACH JERUSALEM IN TIME FOR THE PASSOVER ...
BUT I SUPPOSE THERE'S NO OTHER WAY...
Paul reluctantly changed his plans and hoped to reach Jerusalem in time for the Festival of Weeks.

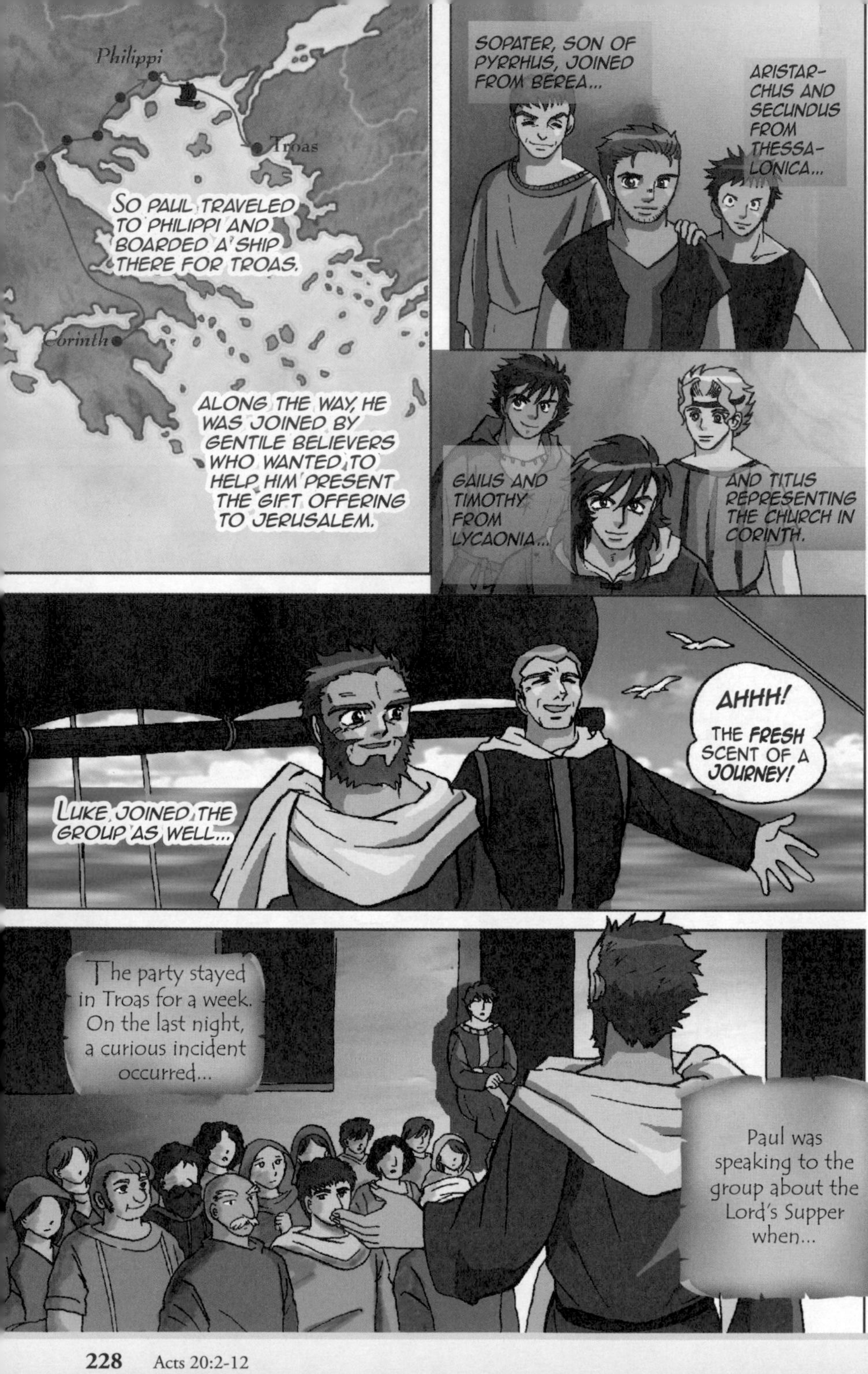
Philippi
Troas
Corinth
So Paul traveled to Philippi and boarded a ship there for Troas.
Along the way, he was joined by Gentile believers who wanted to help him present the gift offering to Jerusalem.
Sopater, son of Pyrrhus, joined from Berea...
Aristarchus and Secundus from Thessalonica...
Gaius and Timothy from Lycaonia...
And Titus representing the church in Corinth.
Luke joined the group as well...
AHHH!
The fresh scent of a journey!
The party stayed in Troas for a week. On the last night, a curious incident occurred...
Paul was speaking to the group about the Lord's Supper when...

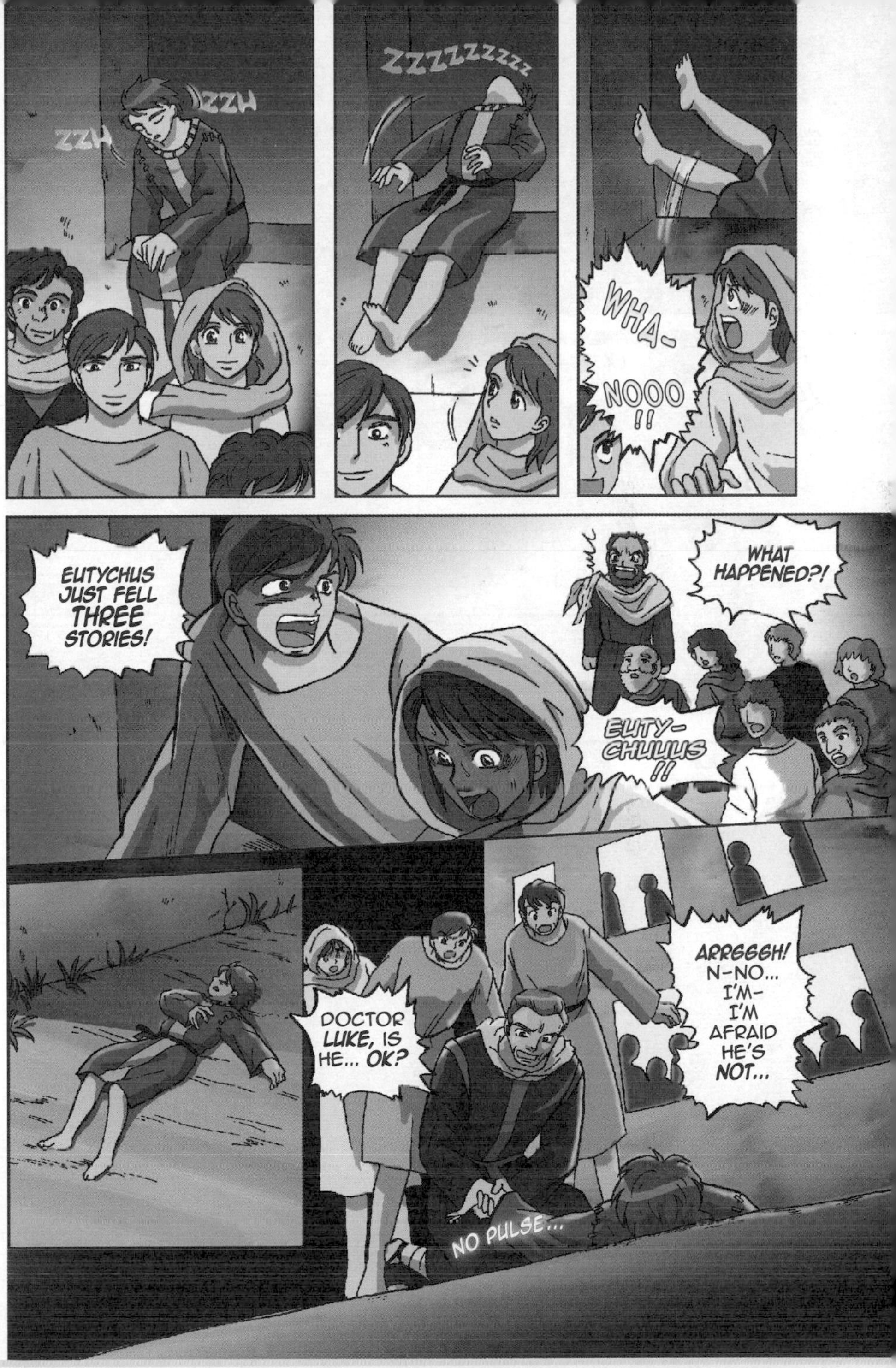
ZZH
ZZH
ZZZZZZZZZ
WHA-
NOOO!!
EUTYCHUS JUST FELL THREE STORIES!
WHAT HAPPENED?!
EUTY-CHUUUS!!
DOCTOR LUKE, IS HE... OK?
NO PULSE...
ARRGGGH! N-NO... I'M- I'M AFRAID HE'S NOT...

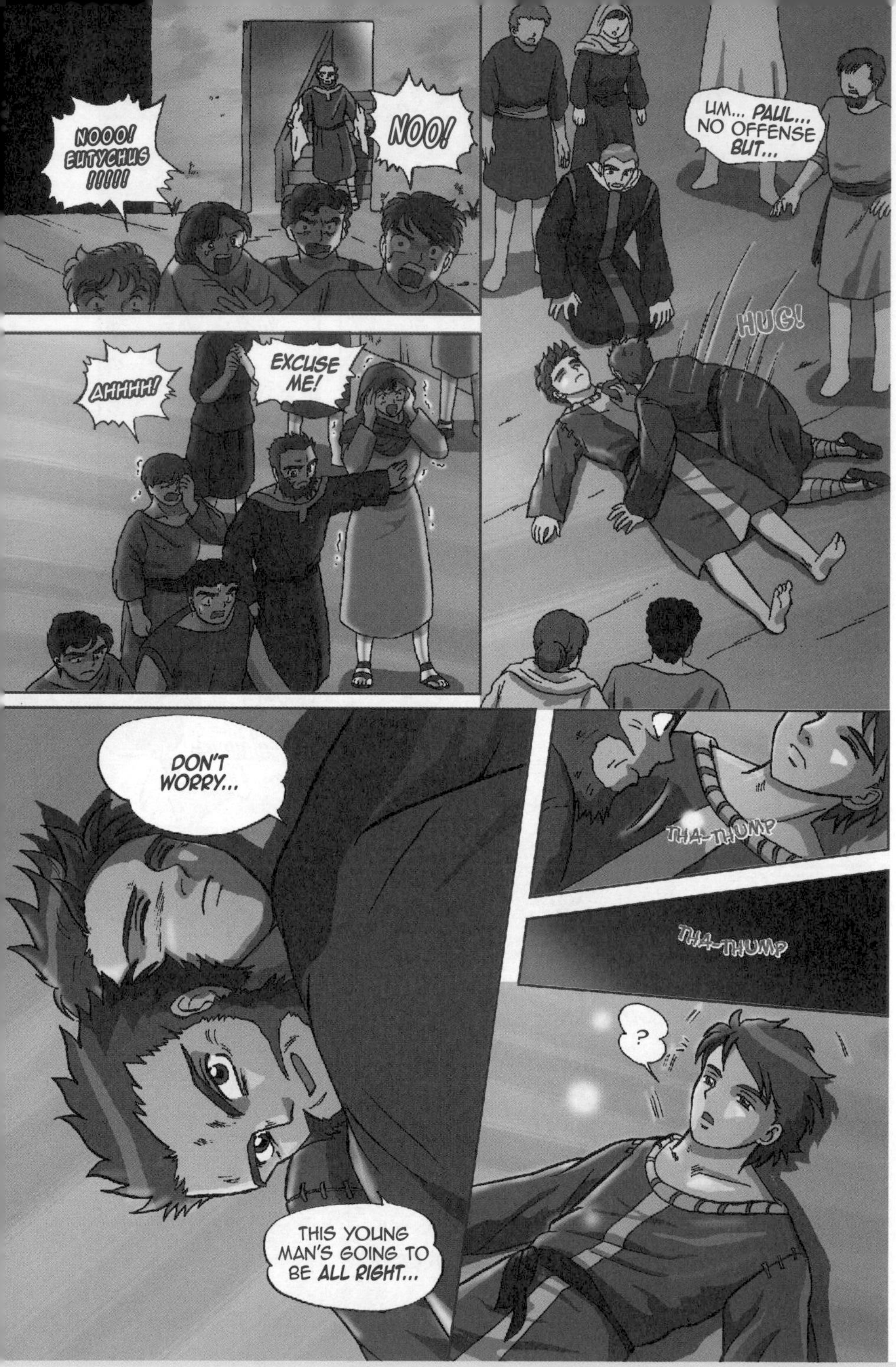
NOOO! EUTYCHUS !!!!!
NOO!
UM... PAUL... NO OFFENSE BUT...
AHHHH!
EXCUSE ME!
HUG!
DON'T WORRY...
THA-THUMP
THA-THUMP
?
THIS YOUNG MAN'S GOING TO BE ALL RIGHT...

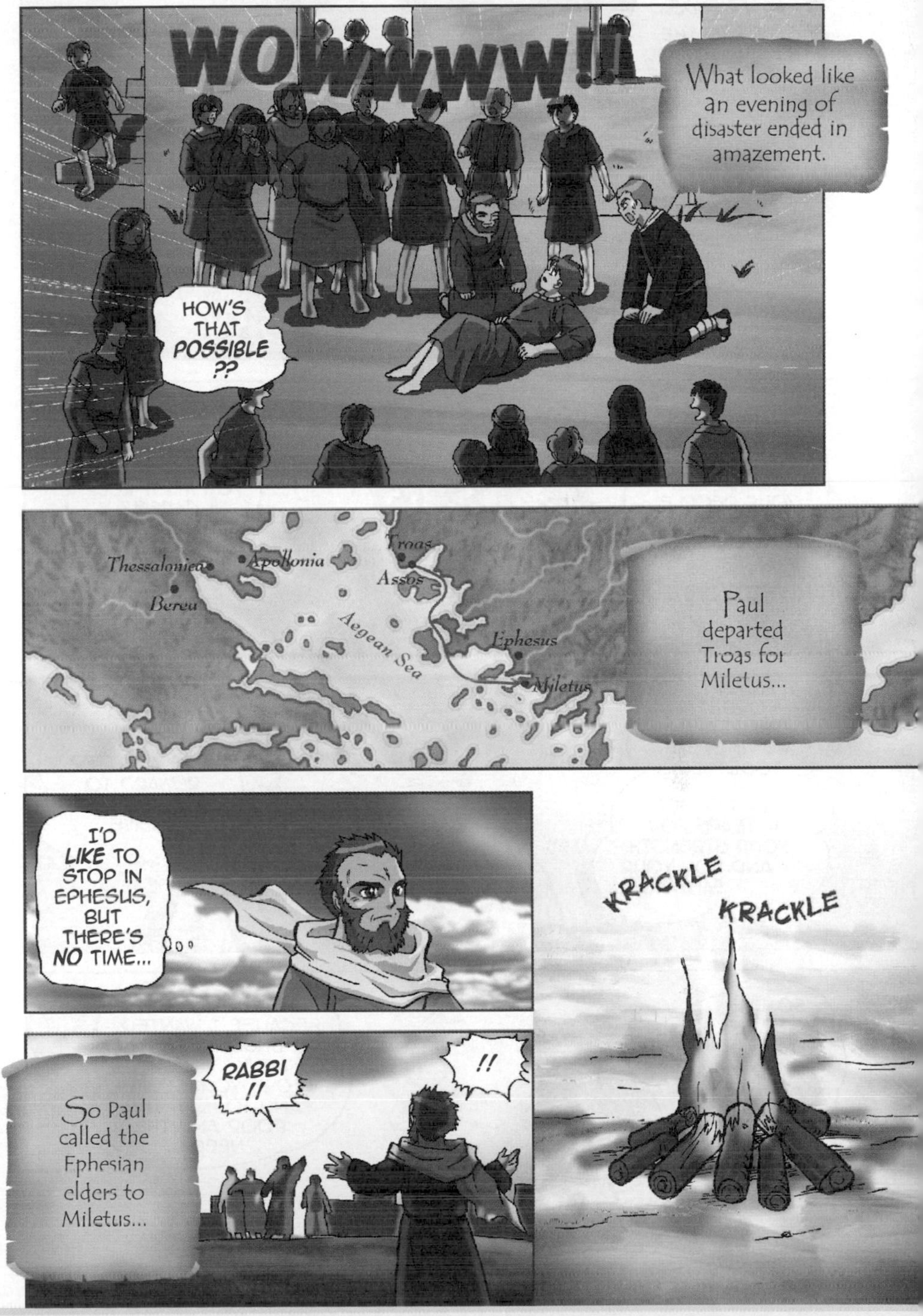
WOWWWWW!!
What looked like an evening of disaster ended in amazement.
HOW'S THAT POSSIBLE ??
Thessalonica
Apollonia
Berea
Troas
Assos
Aegean Sea
Ephesus
Miletus
Paul departed Troas for Miletus...
I'D LIKE TO STOP IN EPHESUS, BUT THERE'S NO TIME...
KRACKLE
KRACKLE
So Paul called the Ephesian elders to Miletus...
RABBI !!
!!

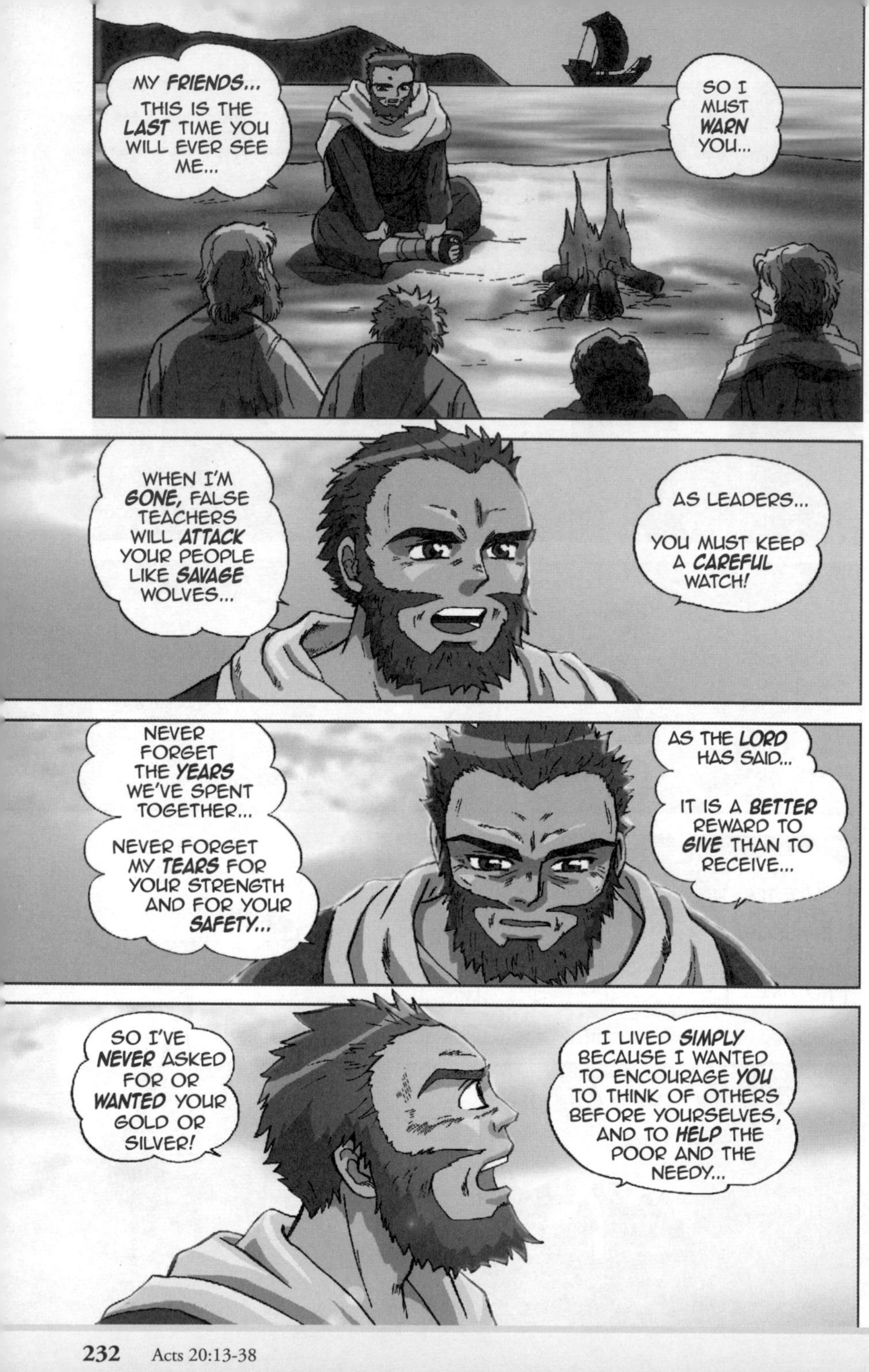
MY FRIENDS... THIS IS THE LAST TIME YOU WILL EVER SEE ME...
SO I MUST WARN YOU...
WHEN I'M GONE, FALSE TEACHERS WILL ATTACK YOUR PEOPLE LIKE SAVAGE WOLVES...
AS LEADERS... YOU MUST KEEP A CAREFUL WATCH!
NEVER FORGET THE YEARS WE'VE SPENT TOGETHER...
NEVER FORGET MY TEARS FOR YOUR STRENGTH AND FOR YOUR SAFETY...
AS THE LORD HAS SAID... IT IS A BETTER REWARD TO GIVE THAN TO RECEIVE...
SO I'VE NEVER ASKED FOR OR WANTED YOUR GOLD OR SILVER!
I LIVED SIMPLY BECAUSE I WANTED TO ENCOURAGE YOU TO THINK OF OTHERS BEFORE YOURSELVES, AND TO HELP THE POOR AND THE NEEDY...

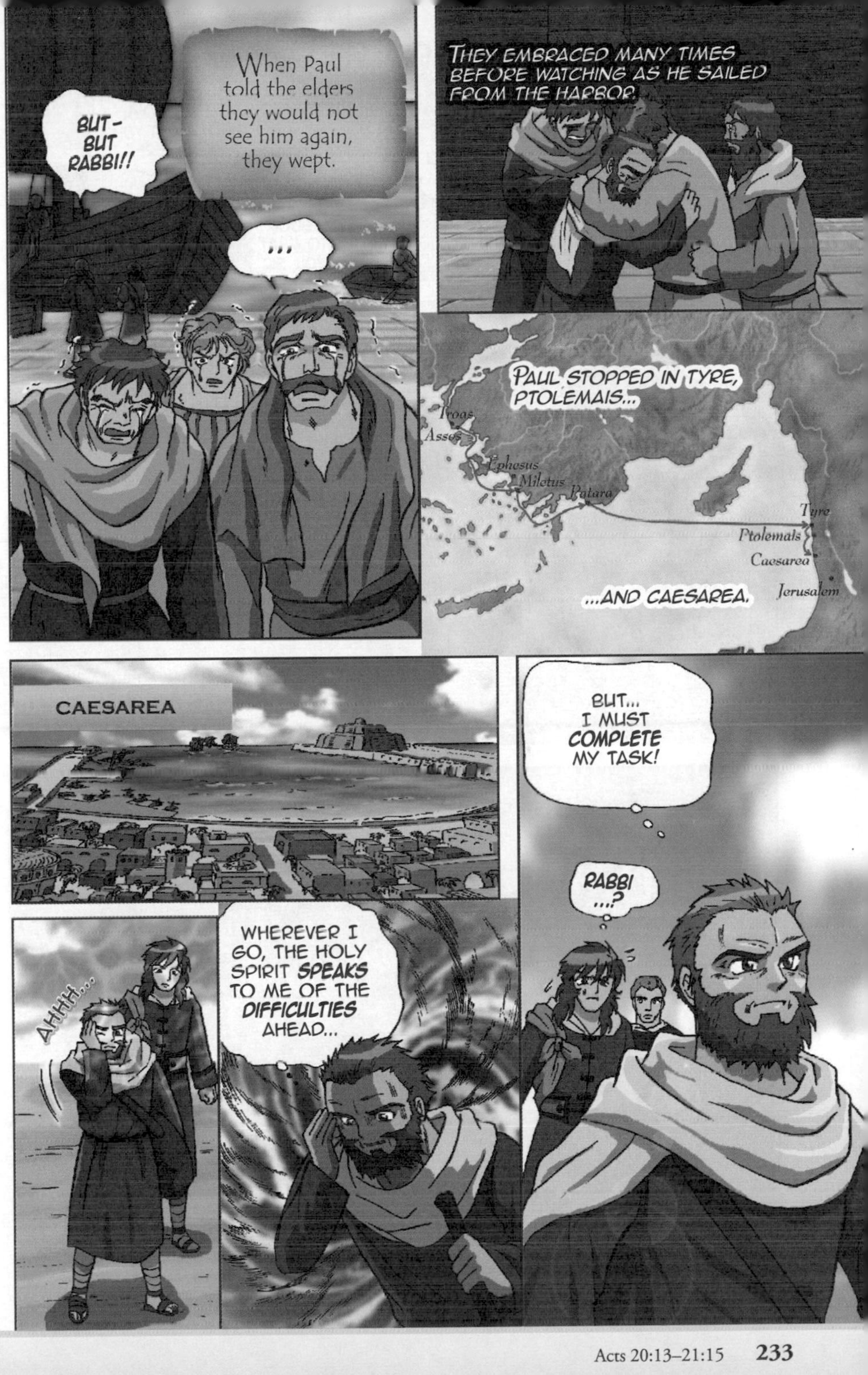
When Paul told the elders they would not see him again, they wept.
BUT-BUT RABBI!!
...
THEY EMBRACED MANY TIMES BEFORE WATCHING AS HE SAILED FROM THE HARBOR.
PAUL STOPPED IN TYRE, PTOLEMAIS...
Troas
Assos
Ephesus
Miletus
Patara
Tyre
Ptolemais
Caesarea
Jerusalem
...AND CAESAREA.
CAESAREA
AHHH...
WHEREVER I GO, THE HOLY SPIRIT SPEAKS TO ME OF THE DIFFICULTIES AHEAD...
BUT... I MUST COMPLETE MY TASK!
RABBI ...?

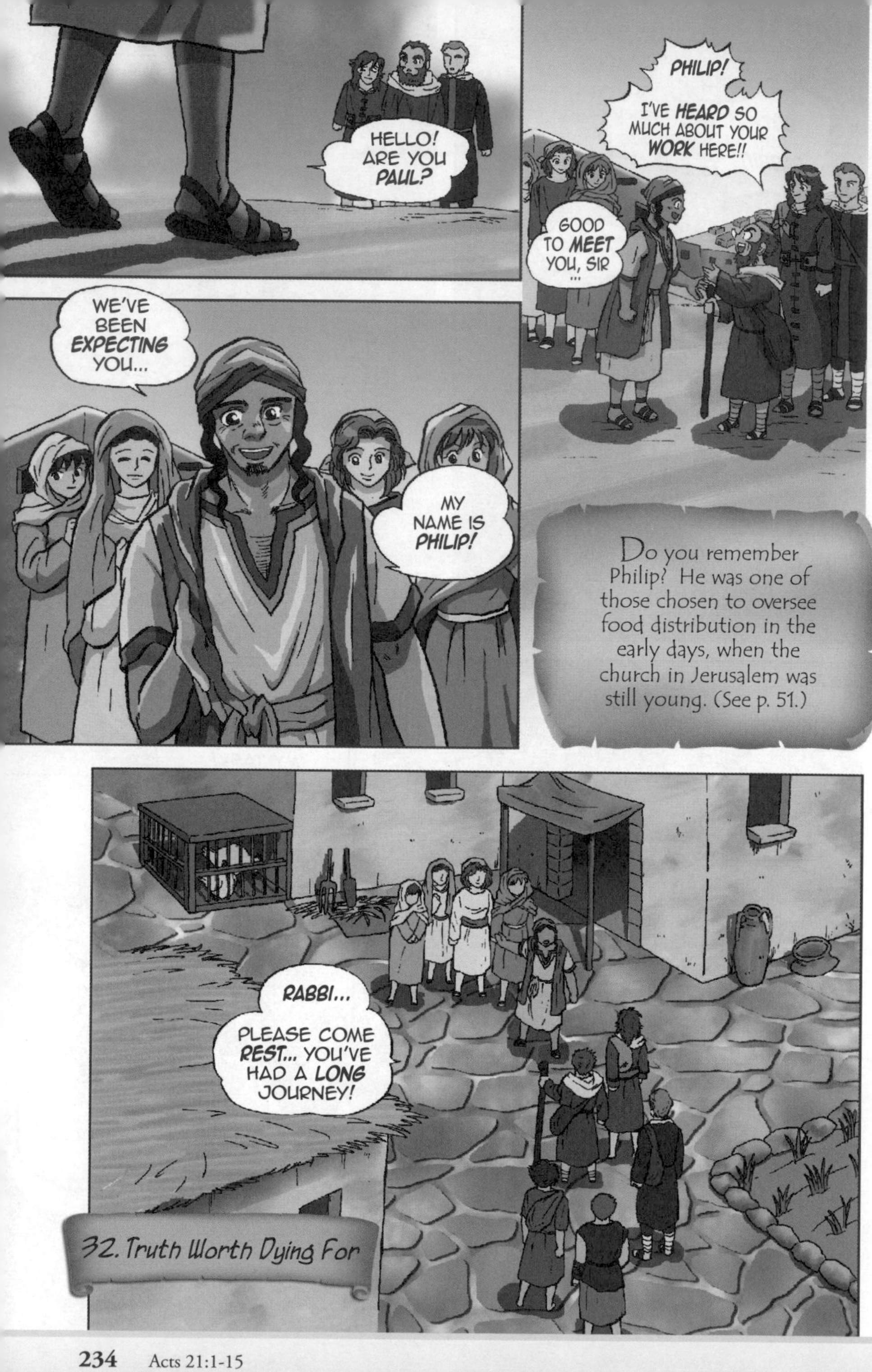
HELLO! ARE YOU PAUL?
PHILIP!
I'VE HEARD SO MUCH ABOUT YOUR WORK HERE!!
GOOD TO MEET YOU, SIR ...
WE'VE BEEN EXPECTING YOU...
MY NAME IS PHILIP!
Do you remember Philip? He was one of those chosen to oversee food distribution in the early days, when the church in Jerusalem was still young. (See p. 51.)
RABBI...
PLEASE COME REST... YOU'VE HAD A LONG JOURNEY!
32. Truth Worth Dying For

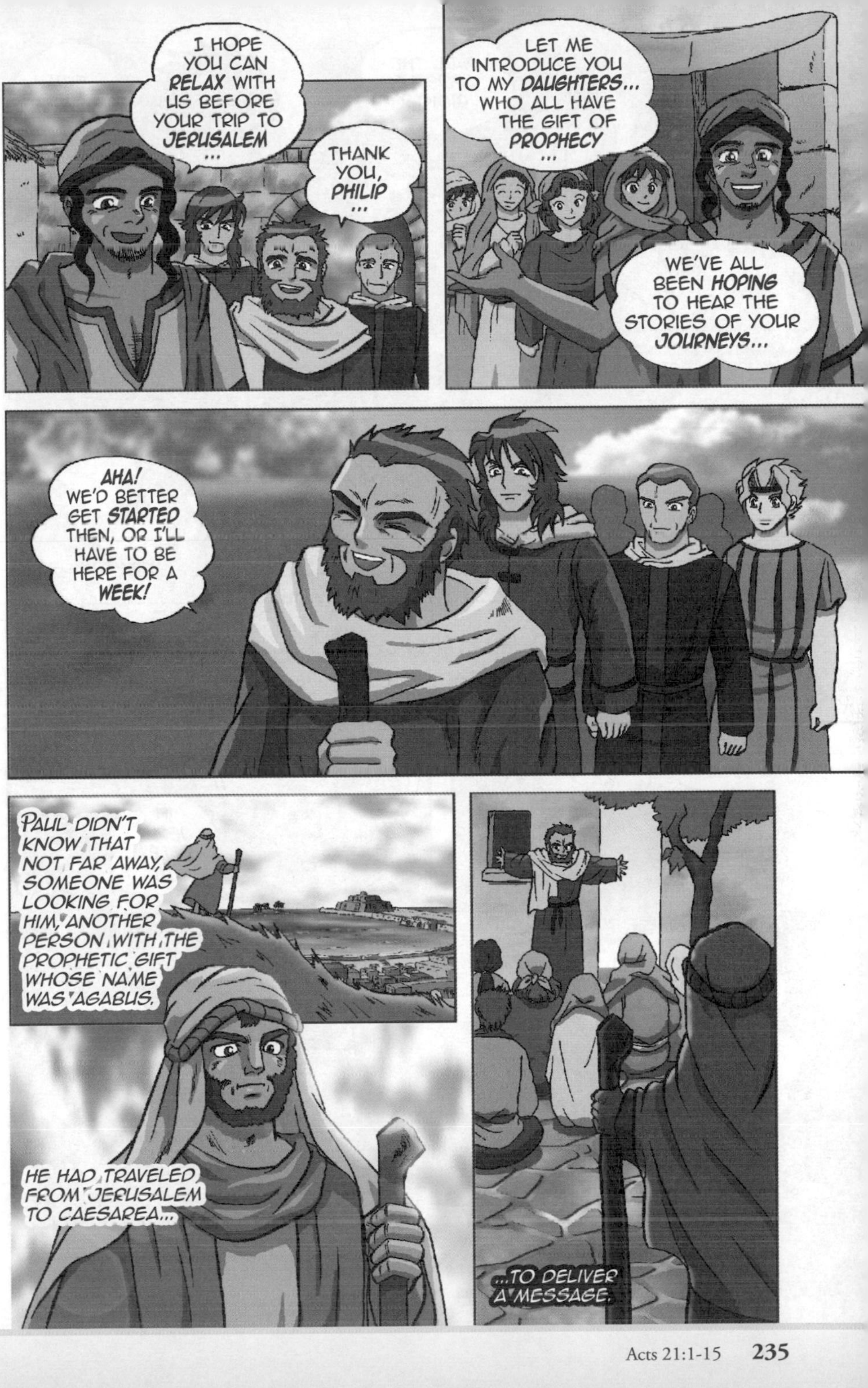
I HOPE YOU CAN RELAX WITH US BEFORE YOUR TRIP TO JERUSALEM...
THANK YOU, PHILIP...
LET ME INTRODUCE YOU TO MY DAUGHTERS... WHO ALL HAVE THE GIFT OF PROPHECY...
WE'VE ALL BEEN HOPING TO HEAR THE STORIES OF YOUR JOURNEYS...
AHA! WE'D BETTER GET STARTED THEN, OR I'LL HAVE TO BE HERE FOR A WEEK!
PAUL DIDN'T KNOW THAT NOT FAR AWAY, SOMEONE WAS LOOKING FOR HIM, ANOTHER PERSON WITH THE PROPHETIC GIFT WHOSE NAME WAS AGABUS.
HE HAD TRAVELED FROM JERUSALEM TO CAESAREA...
...TO DELIVER A MESSAGE.

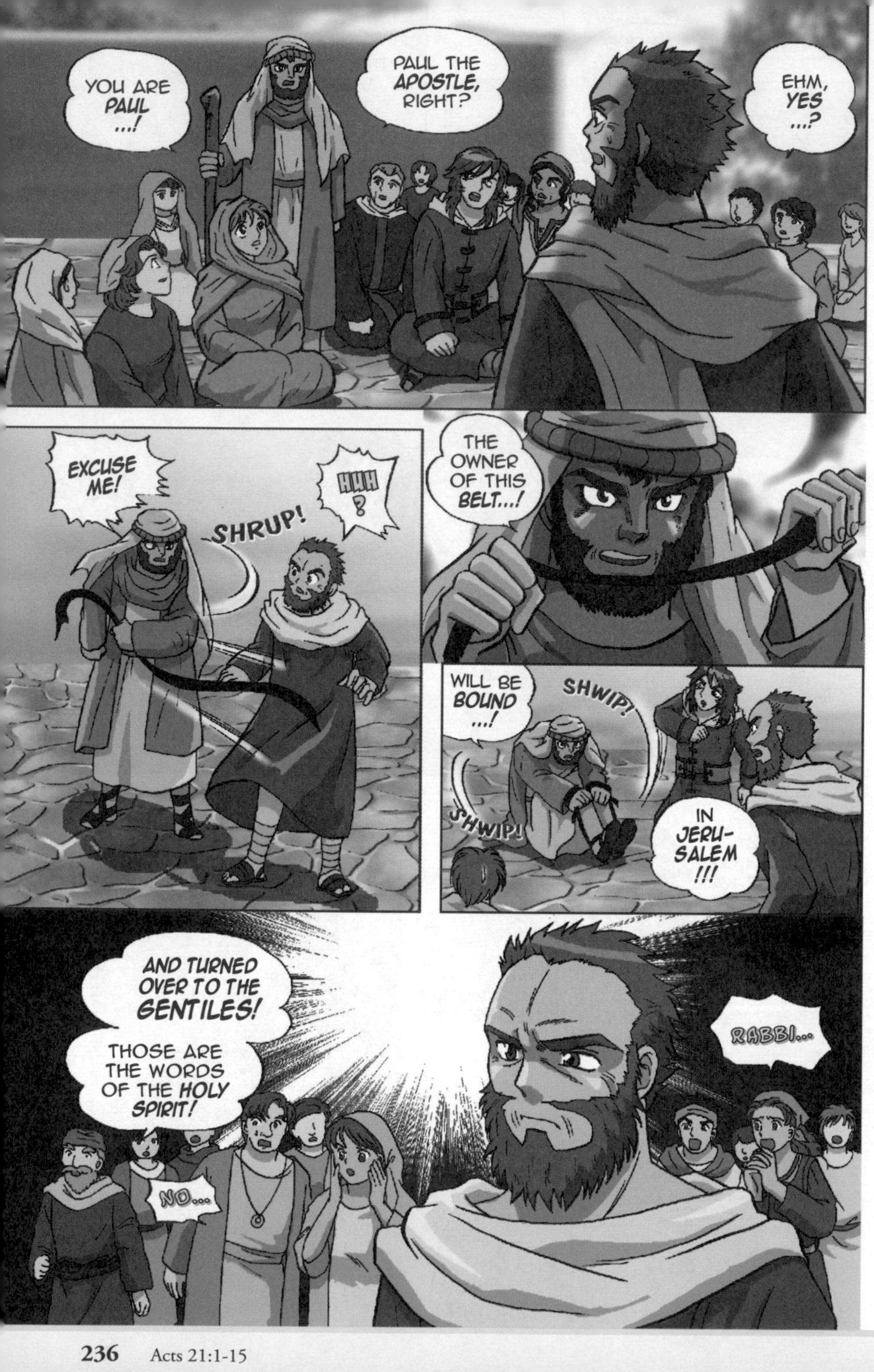
YOU ARE PAUL ...!
PAUL THE APOSTLE, RIGHT?
EHM, YES ...?
EXCUSE ME!
SHRUP!
HUH ?
THE OWNER OF THIS BELT...!
WILL BE BOUND ...!
SHWIP!
SHWIP!
IN JERU-SALEM !!!
AND TURNED OVER TO THE GENTILES!
THOSE ARE THE WORDS OF THE HOLY SPIRIT!
RABBI...
NO...

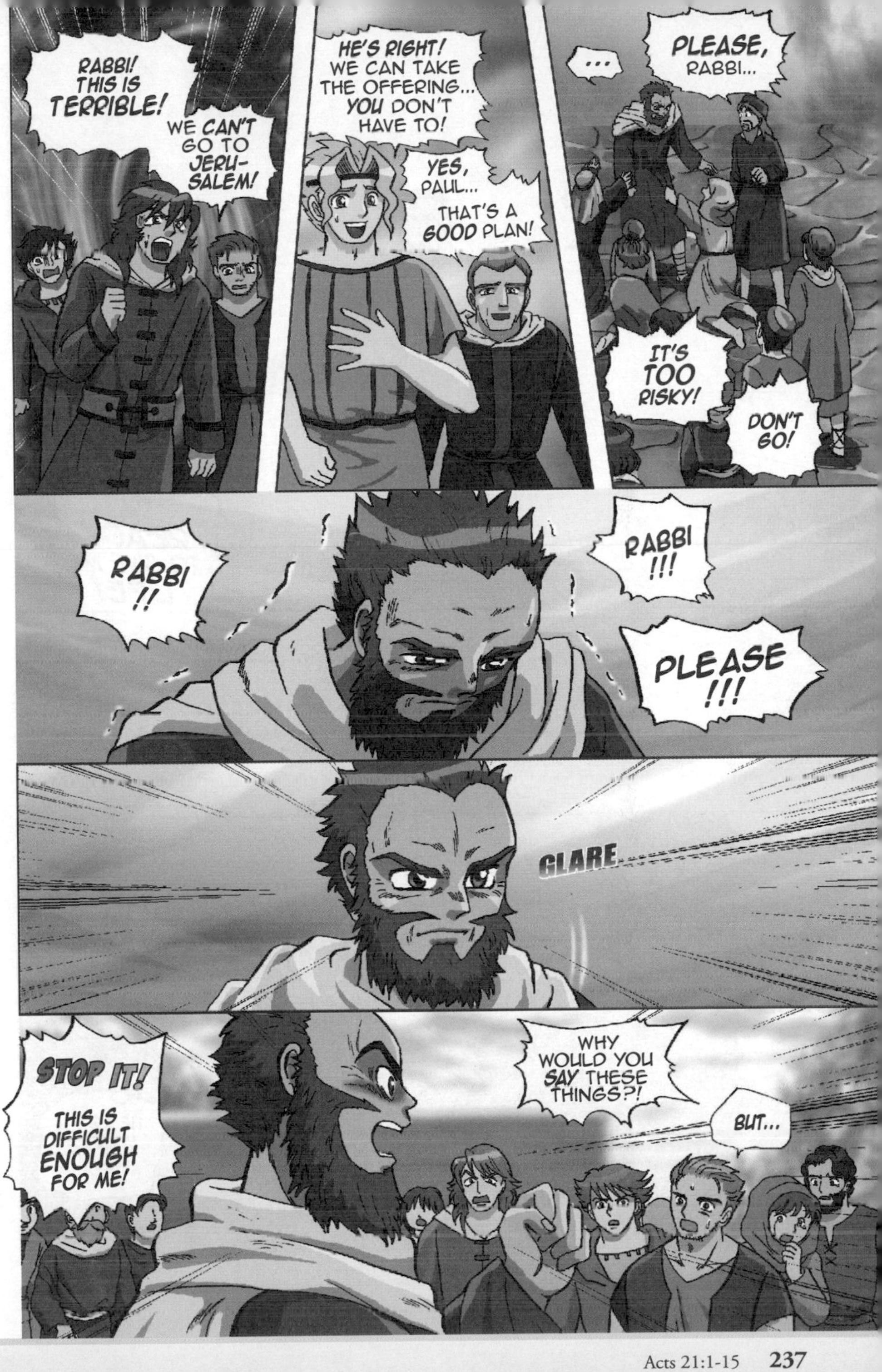
RABBI! THIS IS TERRIBLE!
WE CAN'T GO TO JERU-SALEM!
HE'S RIGHT! WE CAN TAKE THE OFFERING... YOU DON'T HAVE TO!
YES, PAUL...
THAT'S A GOOD PLAN!
...
PLEASE, RABBI...
IT'S TOO RISKY!
DON'T GO!
RABBI !!
RABBI !!!
PLEASE !!!
GLARE
STOP IT!
THIS IS DIFFICULT ENOUGH FOR ME!
WHY WOULD YOU SAY THESE THINGS?!
BUT...

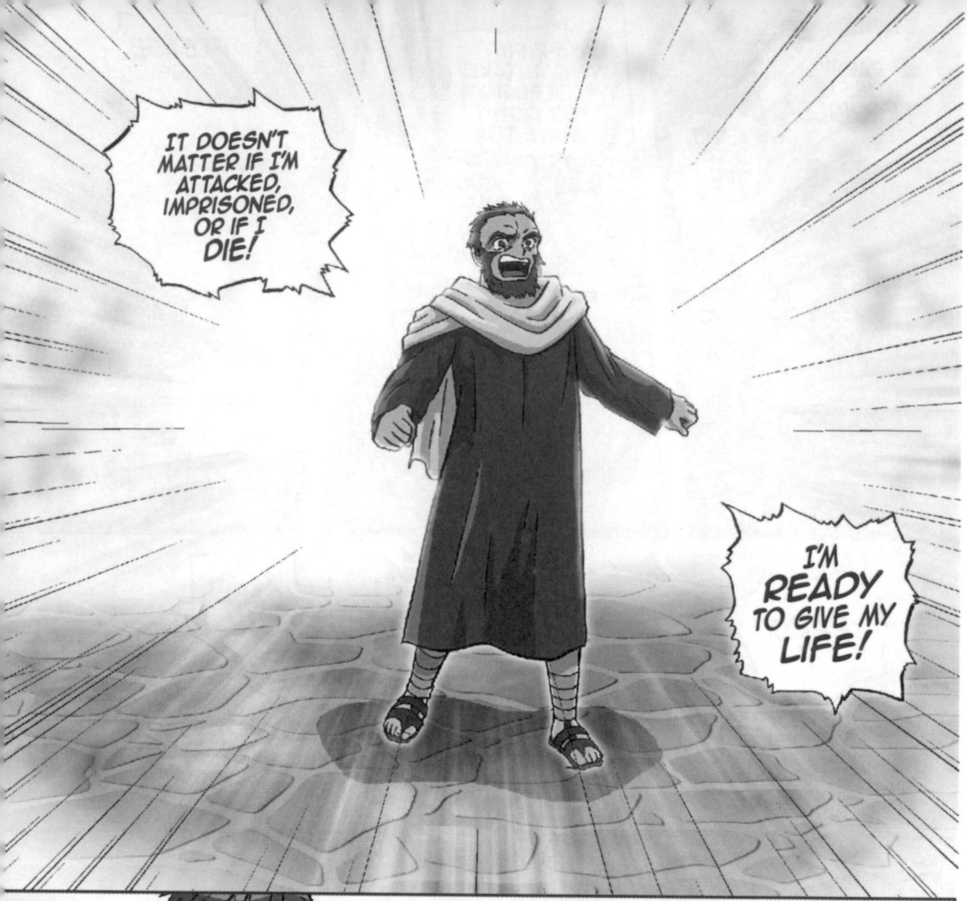
IT DOESN'T MATTER IF I'M ATTACKED, IMPRISONED, OR IF I DIE!
I'M READY TO GIVE MY LIFE!

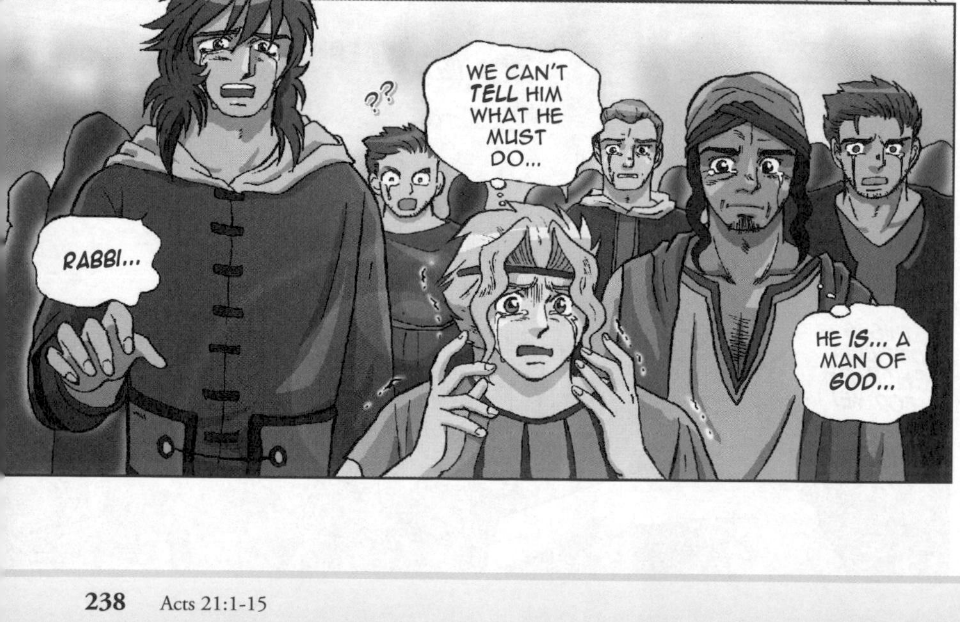
RABBI...
??
WE CAN'T TELL HIM WHAT HE MUST DO...
HE IS... A MAN OF GOD...

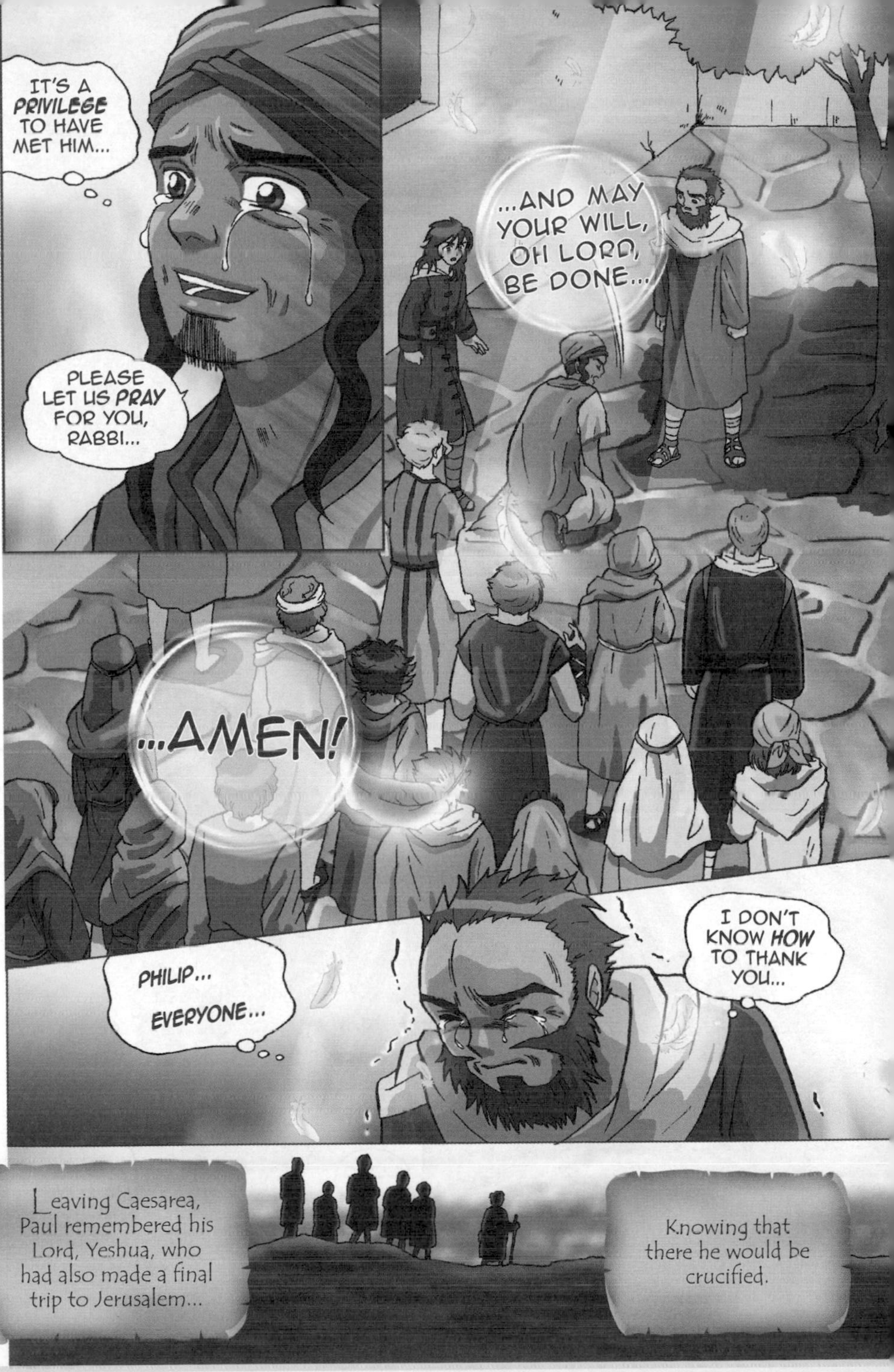
IT'S A PRIVILEGE TO HAVE MET HIM...
PLEASE LET US PRAY FOR YOU, RABBI...
...AND MAY YOUR WILL, OH LORD, BE DONE...
...AMEN!
PHILIP...
EVERYONE...
I DON'T KNOW HOW TO THANK YOU...
Leaving Caesarea, Paul remembered his Lord, Yeshua, who had also made a final trip to Jerusalem...
Knowing that there he would be crucified.

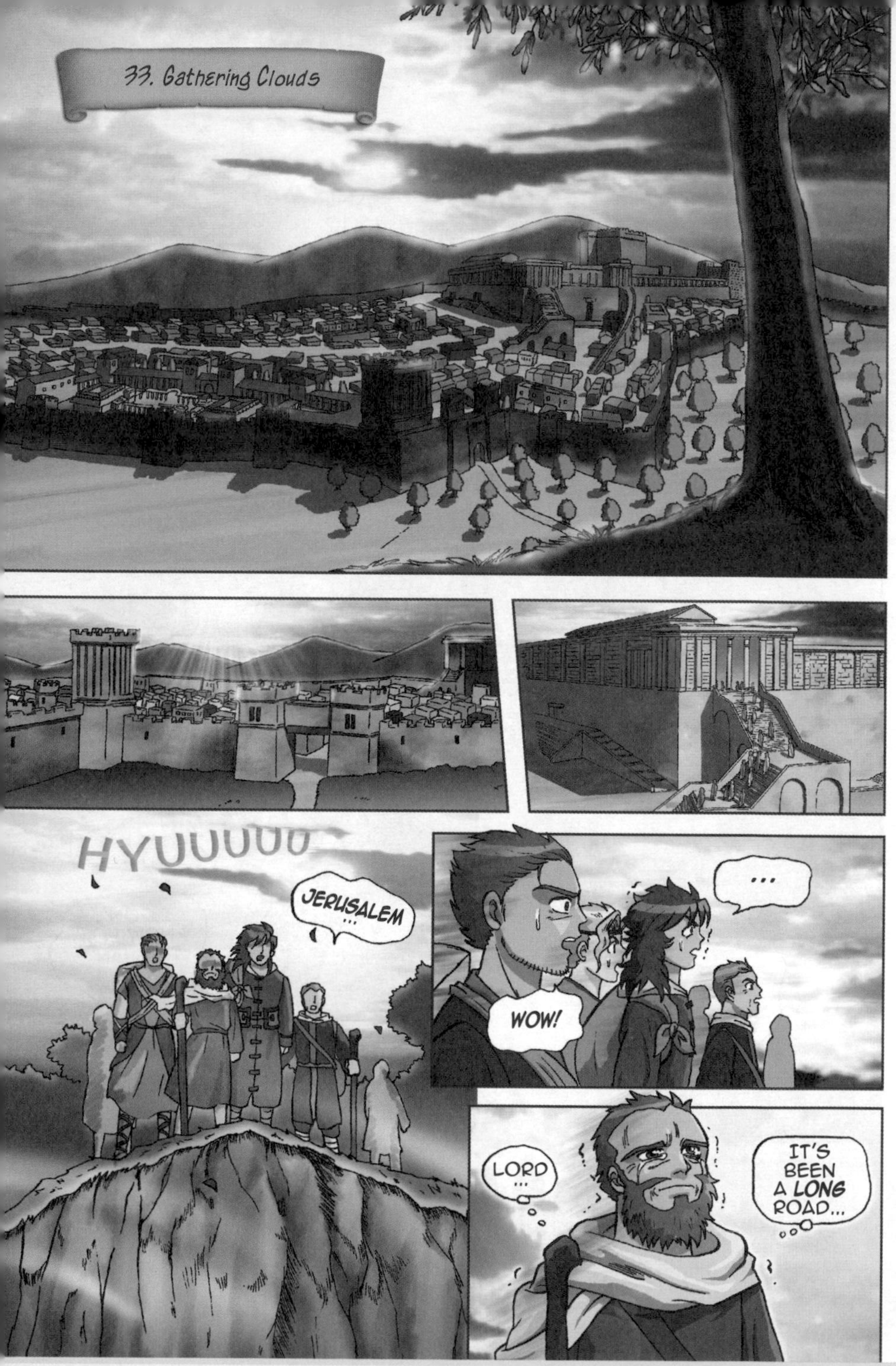
33. Gathering Clouds
HYUUUUU
JERUSALEM ...
...
WOW!
LORD ...
IT'S BEEN A LONG ROAD...

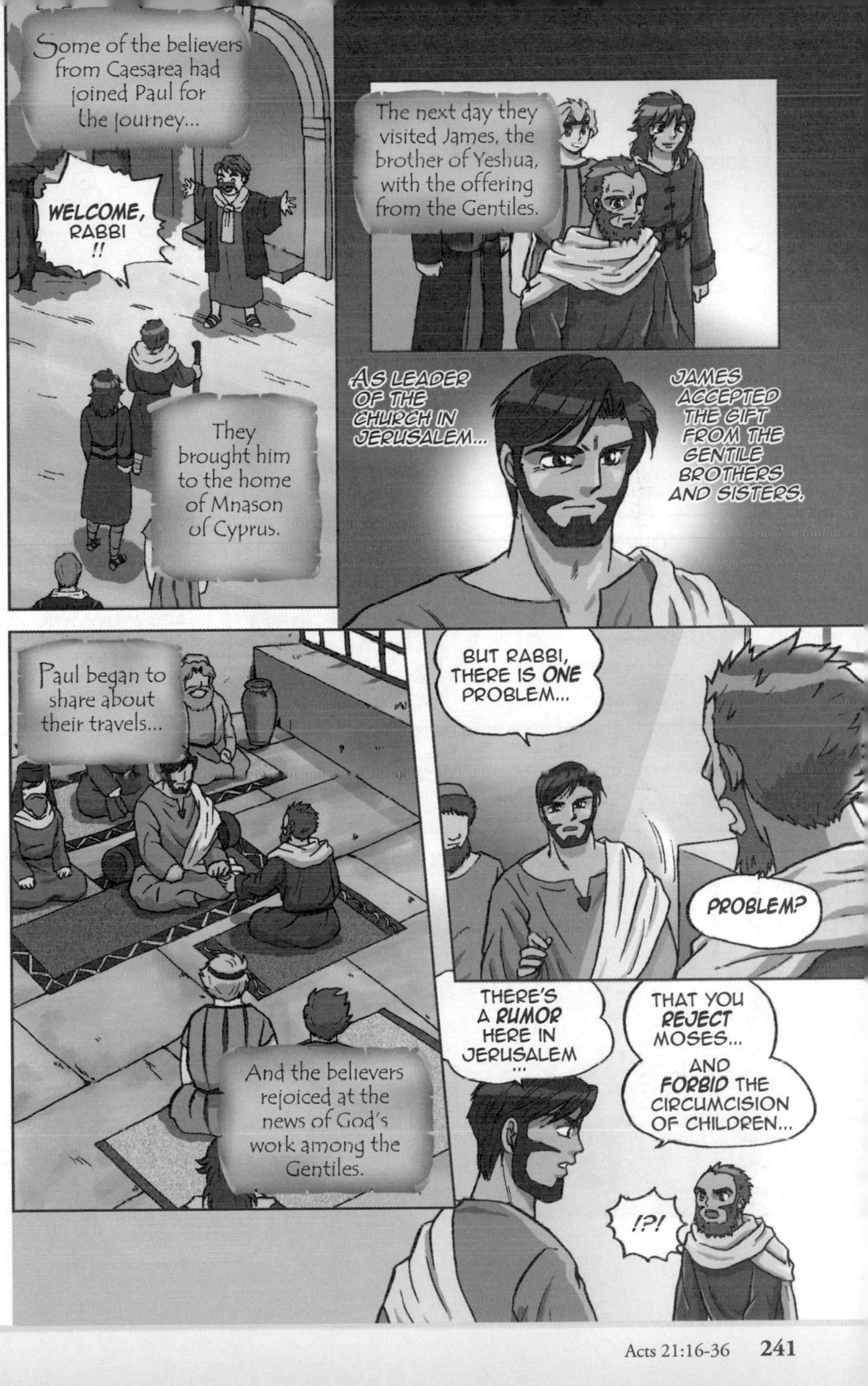
Some of the believers from Caesarea had joined Paul for the journey...
WELCOME, RABBI !!
They brought him to the home of Mnason of Cyprus.
The next day they visited James, the brother of Yeshua, with the offering from the Gentiles.
AS LEADER OF THE CHURCH IN JERUSALEM...
JAMES ACCEPTED THE GIFT FROM THE GENTILE BROTHERS AND SISTERS.
Paul began to share about their travels...
And the believers rejoiced at the news of God's work among the Gentiles.
BUT RABBI, THERE IS ONE PROBLEM...
PROBLEM?
THERE'S A RUMOR HERE IN JERUSALEM ...
THAT YOU REJECT MOSES... AND FORBID THE CIRCUMCISION OF CHILDREN...
!?!

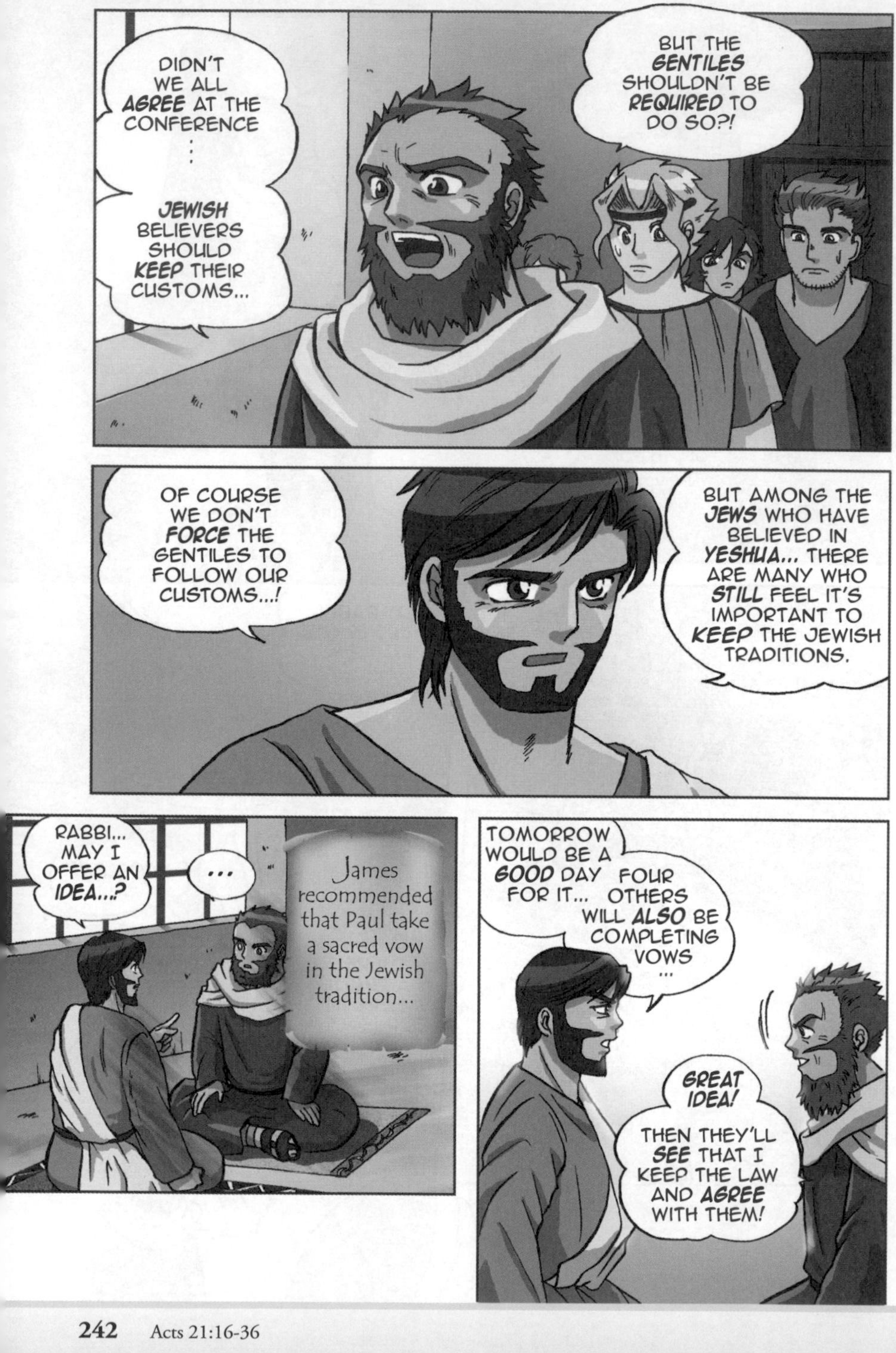
DIDN'T WE ALL AGREE AT THE CONFERENCE . . . JEWISH BELIEVERS SHOULD KEEP THEIR CUSTOMS...
BUT THE GENTILES SHOULDN'T BE REQUIRED TO DO SO?!
OF COURSE WE DON'T FORCE THE GENTILES TO FOLLOW OUR CUSTOMS...!
BUT AMONG THE JEWS WHO HAVE BELIEVED IN YESHUA... THERE ARE MANY WHO STILL FEEL IT'S IMPORTANT TO KEEP THE JEWISH TRADITIONS.
RABBI... MAY I OFFER AN IDEA...?
...
James recommended that Paul take a sacred vow in the Jewish tradition...
TOMORROW WOULD BE A GOOD DAY FOR IT... FOUR OTHERS WILL ALSO BE COMPLETING VOWS ...
GREAT IDEA!
THEN THEY'LL SEE THAT I KEEP THE LAW AND AGREE WITH THEM!

AND THE **REST** OF YOU...

DON'T WORRY!

BUT FOR THE SAKE OF THE **JEWISH** BELIEVERS ...

...

PLEASE DON'T EAT **BLOOD**, OR FOOD SACRIFICED TO **IDOLS** ...

NO MEAT OF STRANGLED **ANIMALS**,

NO SEXUAL **IMMORALITY**...

AND YOU'LL BE **FINE!**

Phew!

Ugh!

?

YOU **DON'T** WANT TO BE CIRCUMCISED AS AN ADULT! **TRUST ME!**

VICTIM

THE NEXT DAY, PAUL WENT TO THE TEMPLE, AS PLANNED.

THE CEREMONY LASTED SEVEN DAYS...

ON THE LAST DAY, PARTICIPANTS HAD THEIR HEADS SHAVED AT THE TEMPLE...

EVERYONE FELT THIS WAS AN EXCELLENT WAY TO DEFUSE ANY POTENTIAL HOSTILITY. HOWEVER...

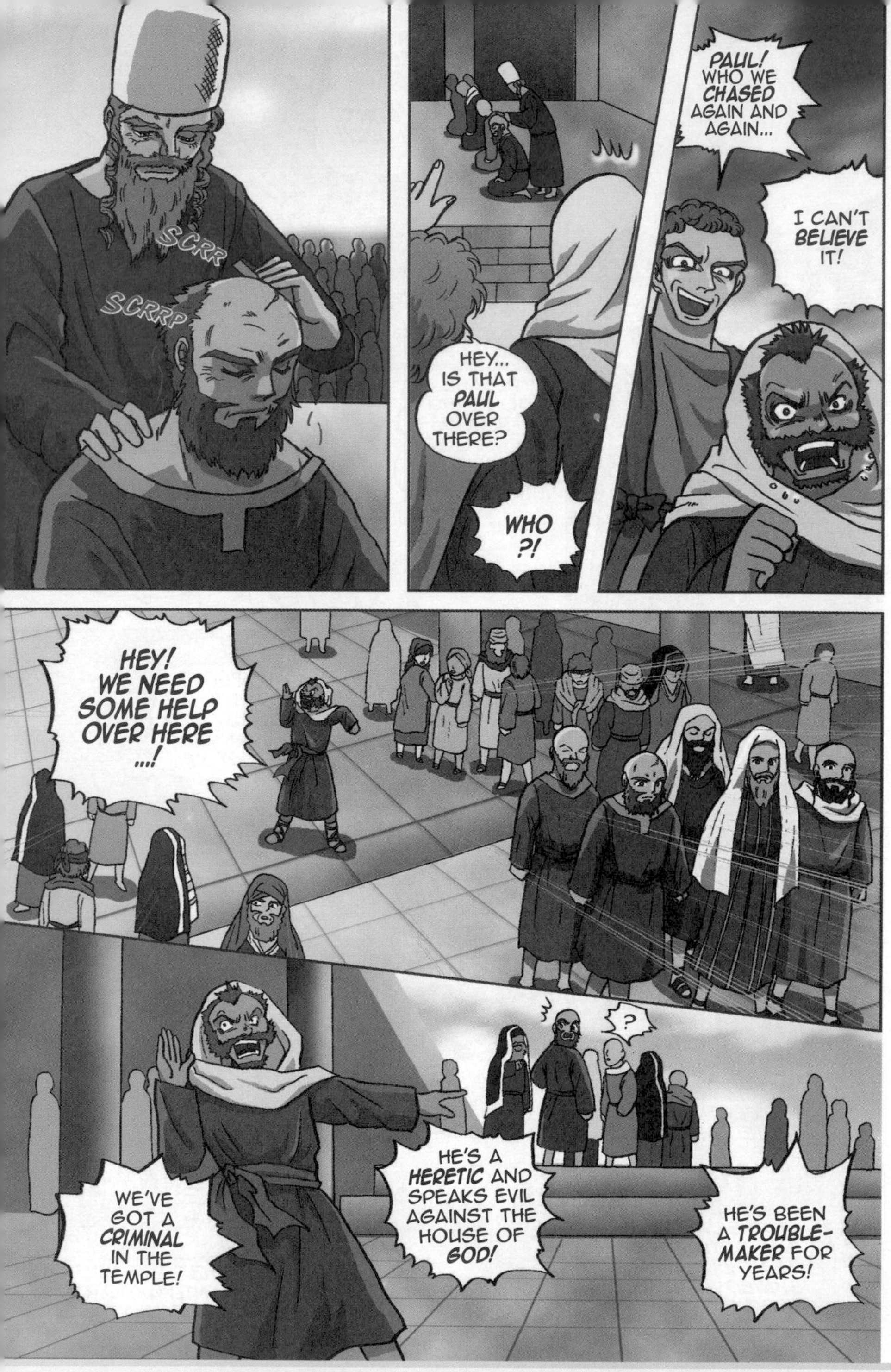
SCRR
SCRRP
HEY... IS THAT PAUL OVER THERE?
WHO ?!
PAUL! WHO WE CHASED AGAIN AND AGAIN...
I CAN'T BELIEVE IT!
HEY! WE NEED SOME HELP OVER HERE ...!
?
WE'VE GOT A CRIMINAL IN THE TEMPLE!
HE'S A HERETIC AND SPEAKS EVIL AGAINST THE HOUSE OF GOD!
HE'S BEEN A TROUBLE-MAKER FOR YEARS!

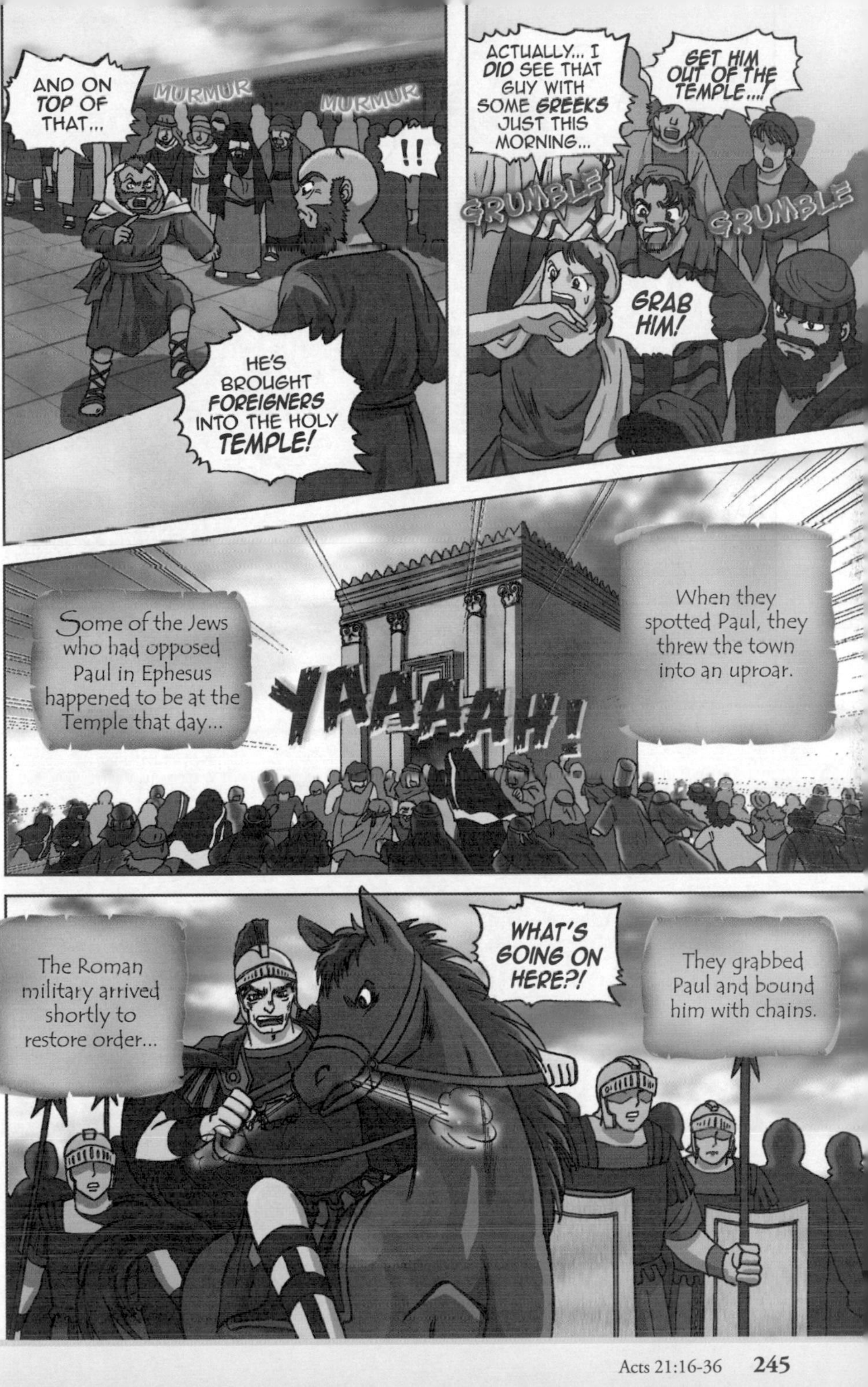

AND ON TOP OF THAT...
MURMUR
MURMUR
!!
HE'S BROUGHT FOREIGNERS INTO THE HOLY TEMPLE!
ACTUALLY... I DID SEE THAT GUY WITH SOME GREEKS JUST THIS MORNING...
GET HIM OUT OF THE TEMPLE...!
GRUMBLE
GRUMBLE
GRAB HIM!
Some of the Jews who had opposed Paul in Ephesus happened to be at the Temple that day...
YAAAAH!
When they spotted Paul, they threw the town into an uproar.
The Roman military arrived shortly to restore order...
WHAT'S GOING ON HERE?!
They grabbed Paul and bound him with chains.

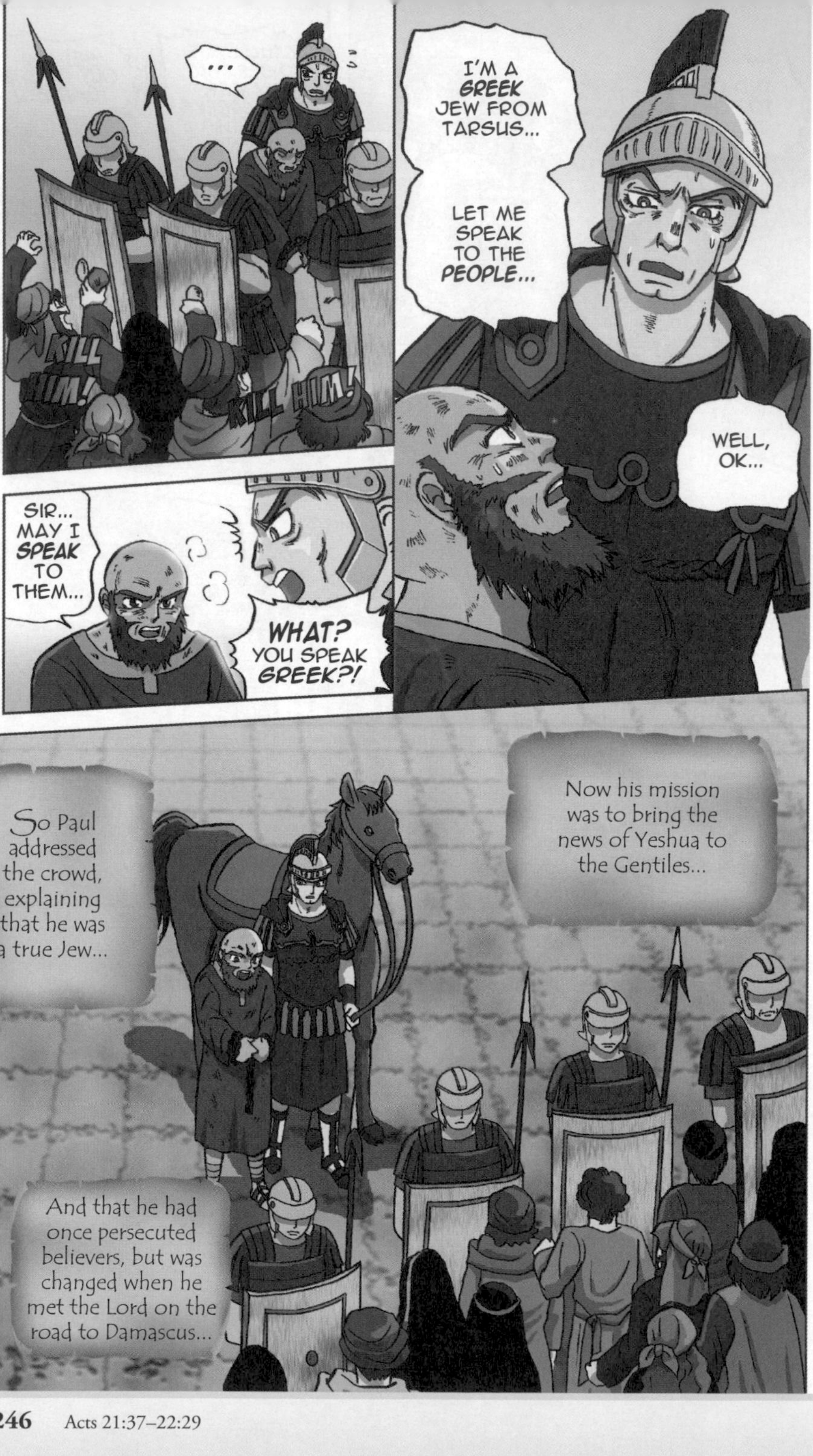
...
KILL HIM!
KILL HIM!
I'M A GREEK JEW FROM TARSUS...
LET ME SPEAK TO THE PEOPLE...
SIR... MAY I SPEAK TO THEM...
WHAT? YOU SPEAK GREEK?!
WELL, OK...
So Paul addressed the crowd, explaining that he was a true Jew...
Now his mission was to bring the news of Yeshua to the Gentiles...
And that he had once persecuted believers, but was changed when he met the Lord on the road to Damascus...

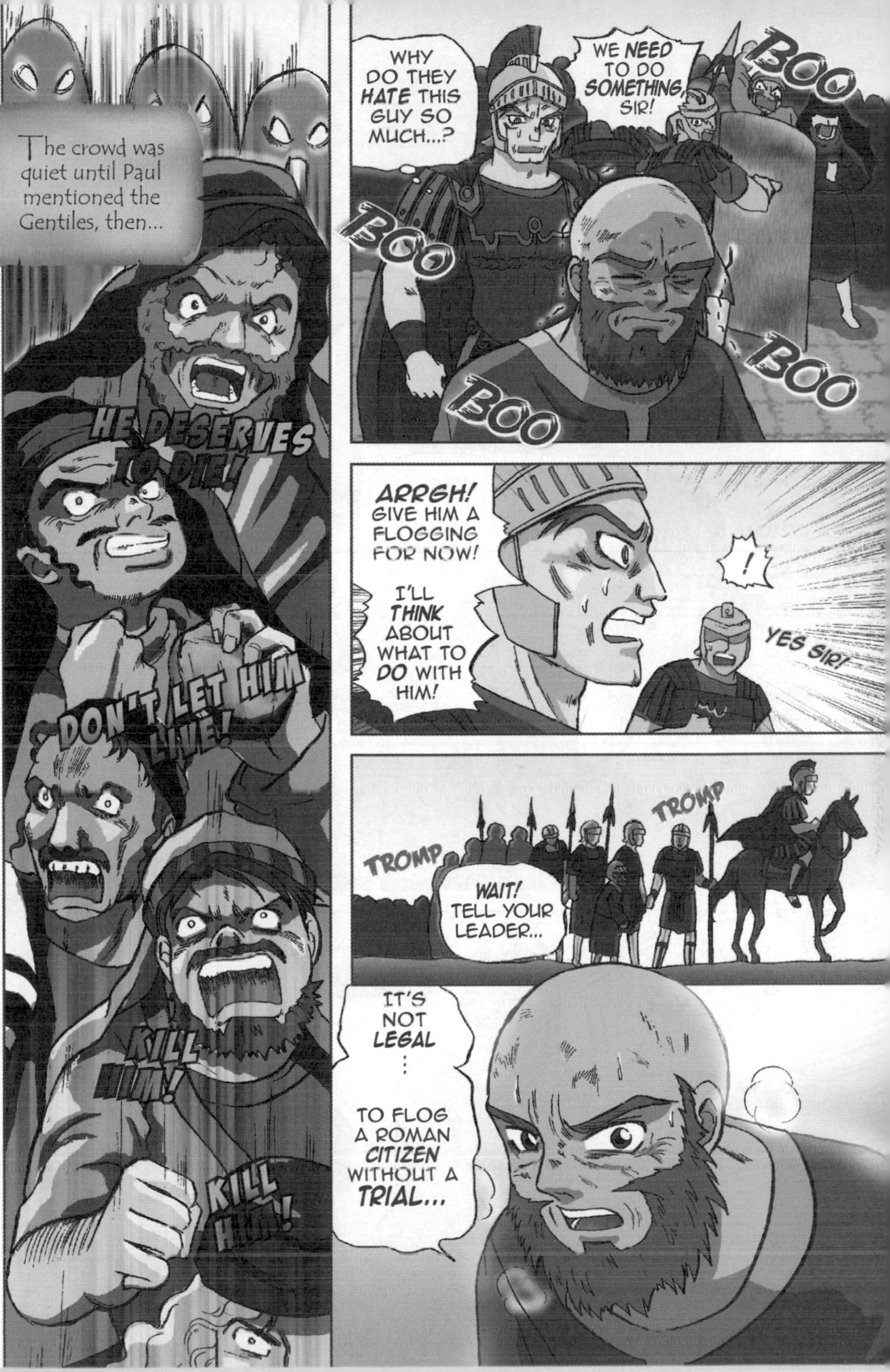
The crowd was quiet until Paul mentioned the Gentiles, then...
HE DESERVES TO DIE!
DON'T LET HIM LIVE!
KILL HIM!
KILL HIM!
WHY DO THEY HATE THIS GUY SO MUCH...?
WE NEED TO DO SOMETHING, SIR!
BOO
BOO
BOO
BOO
ARRGH! GIVE HIM A FLOGGING FOR NOW!
I'LL THINK ABOUT WHAT TO DO WITH HIM!
!
YES SIR!
TROMP
TROMP
WAIT! TELL YOUR LEADER...
IT'S NOT LEGAL ...
TO FLOG A ROMAN CITIZEN WITHOUT A TRIAL...

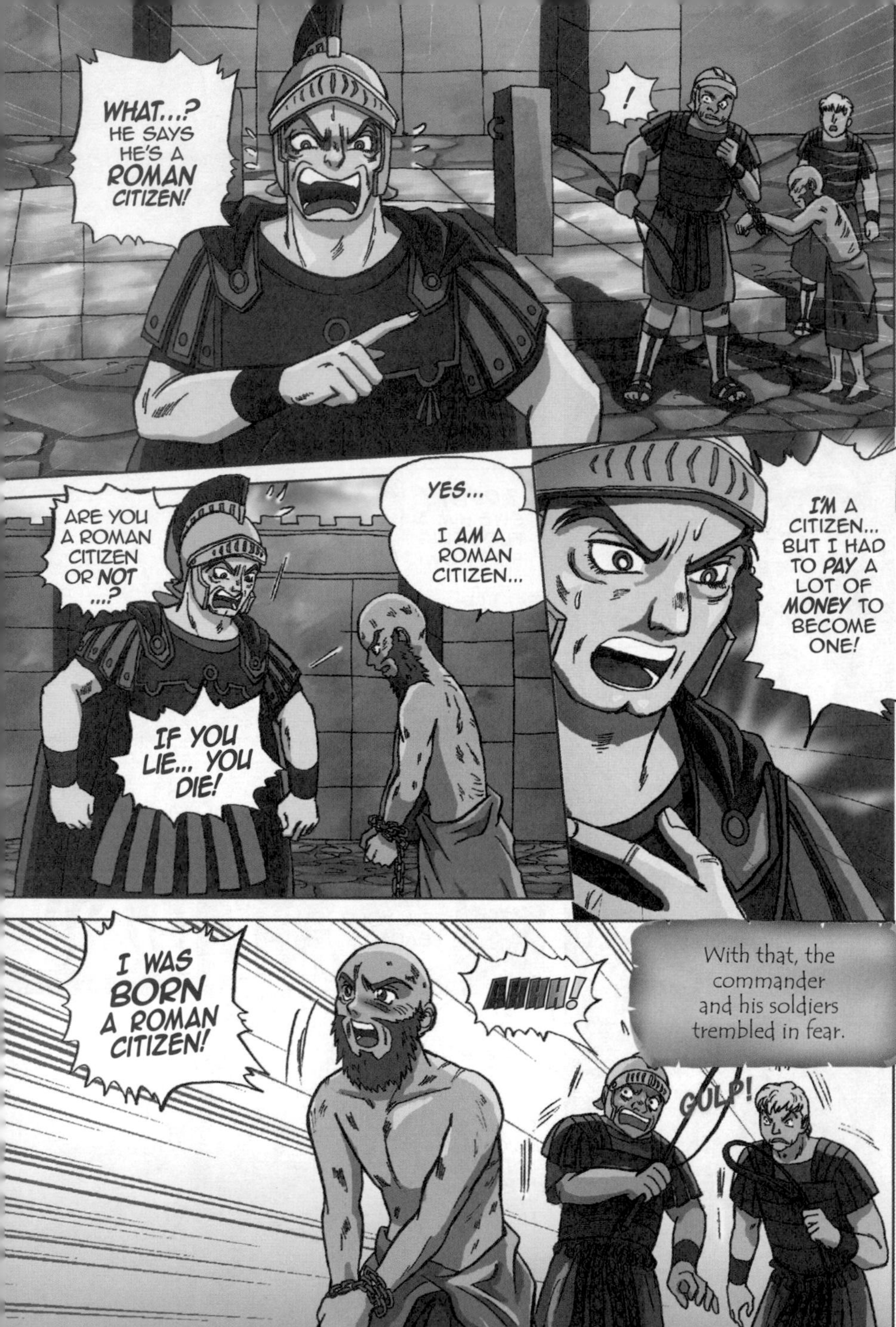
WHAT...? HE SAYS HE'S A ROMAN CITIZEN!
!
ARE YOU A ROMAN CITIZEN OR NOT ...?
IF YOU LIE... YOU DIE!
YES...
I AM A ROMAN CITIZEN...
I'M A CITIZEN... BUT I HAD TO PAY A LOT OF MONEY TO BECOME ONE!
I WAS BORN A ROMAN CITIZEN!
AHHH!
With that, the commander and his soldiers trembled in fear.
GULP!

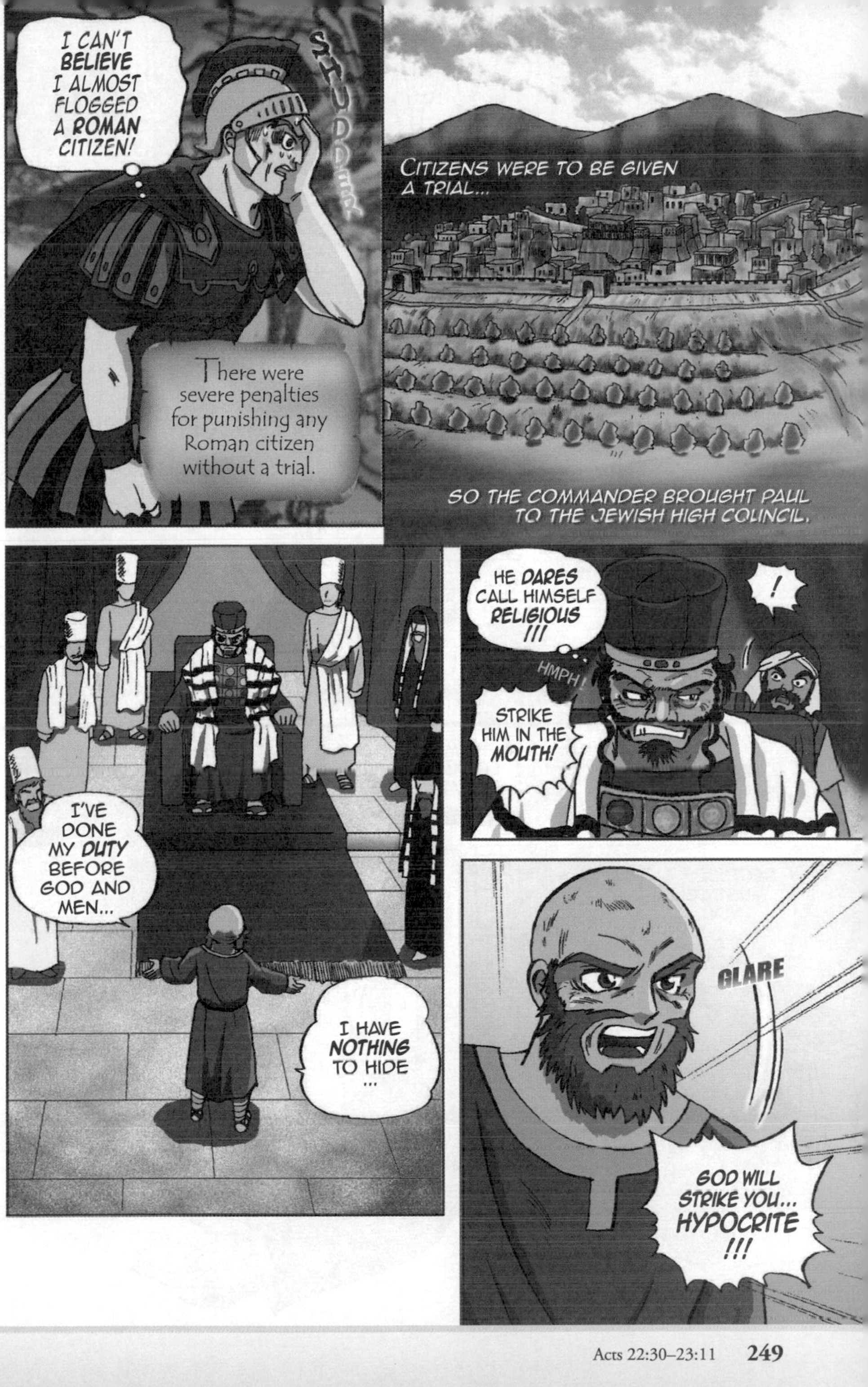
I CAN'T BELIEVE I ALMOST FLOGGED A ROMAN CITIZEN!
SHUDDER
There were severe penalties for punishing any Roman citizen without a trial.
CITIZENS WERE TO BE GIVEN A TRIAL...
SO THE COMMANDER BROUGHT PAUL TO THE JEWISH HIGH COUNCIL.
I'VE DONE MY DUTY BEFORE GOD AND MEN...
I HAVE NOTHING TO HIDE ...
HE DARES CALL HIMSELF RELIGIOUS !!!
HMPH!
STRIKE HIM IN THE MOUTH!
!
GLARE
GOD WILL STRIKE YOU... HYPOCRITE !!!

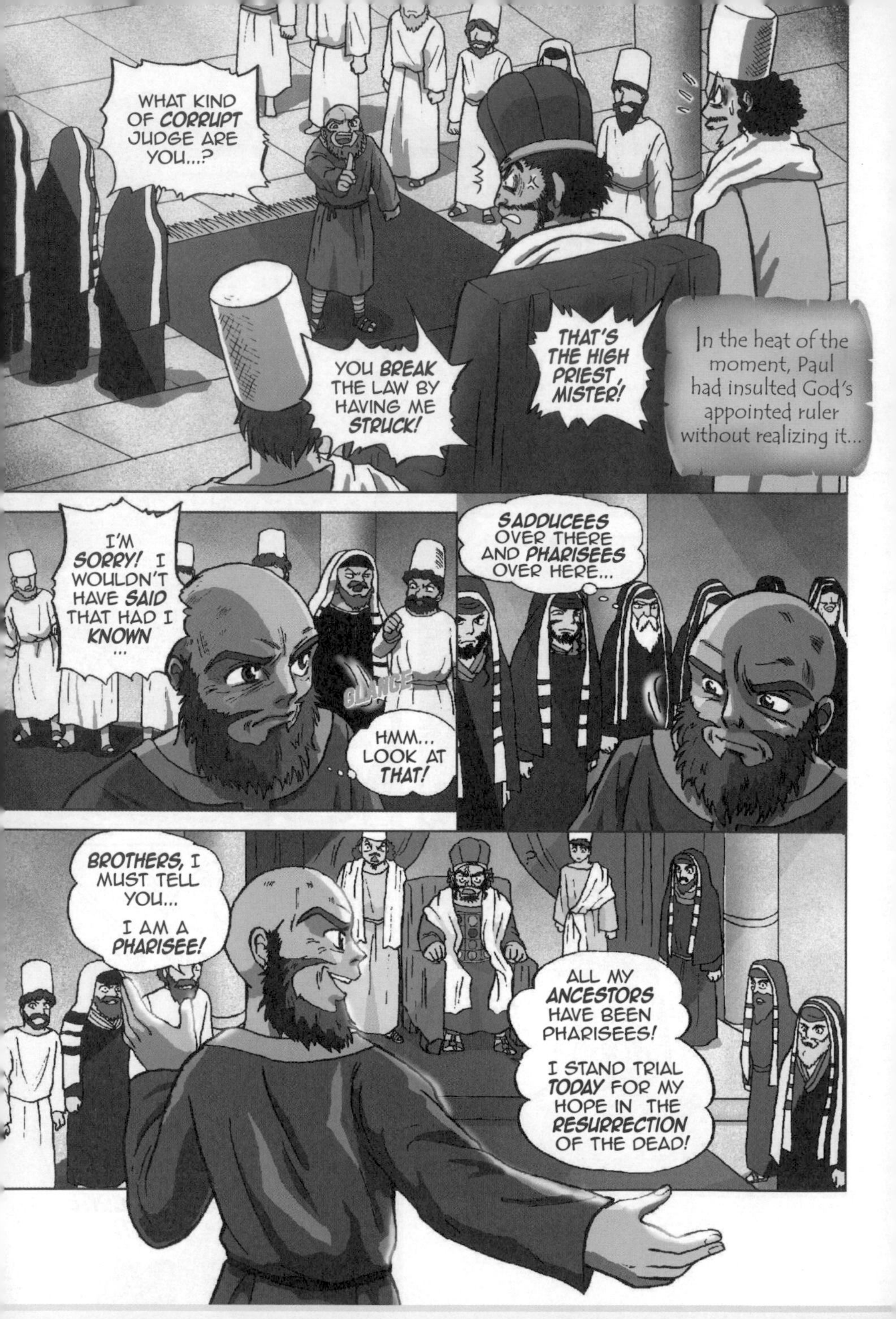
WHAT KIND OF CORRUPT JUDGE ARE YOU...?
YOU BREAK THE LAW BY HAVING ME STRUCK!
THAT'S THE HIGH PRIEST, MISTER!
In the heat of the moment, Paul had insulted God's appointed ruler without realizing it...
I'M SORRY! I WOULDN'T HAVE SAID THAT HAD I KNOWN ...
GLANCE
HMM... LOOK AT THAT!
SADDUCEES OVER THERE AND PHARISEES OVER HERE...
BROTHERS, I MUST TELL YOU...
I AM A PHARISEE!
ALL MY ANCESTORS HAVE BEEN PHARISEES!
I STAND TRIAL TODAY FOR MY HOPE IN THE RESURRECTION OF THE DEAD!

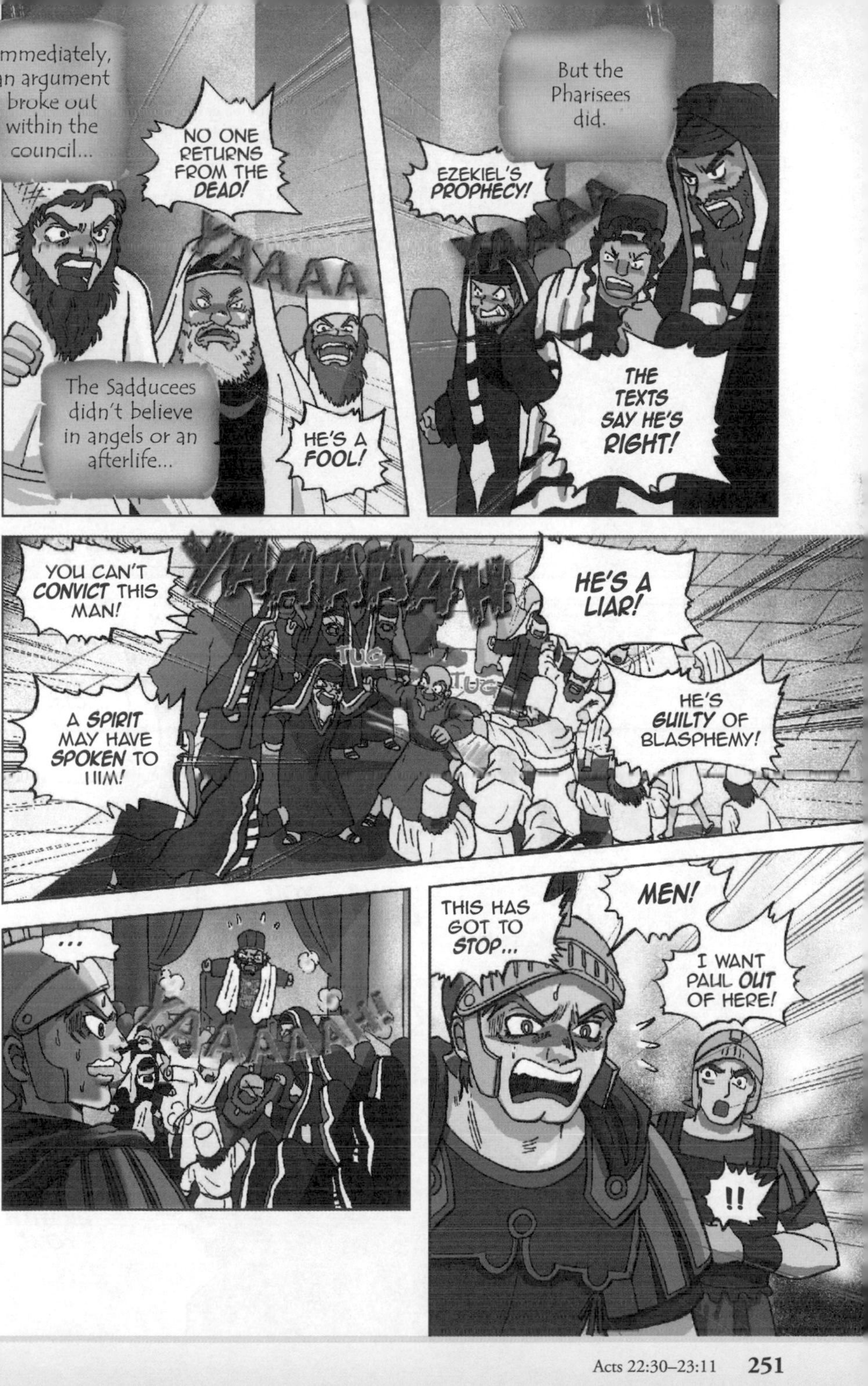
Immediately, an argument broke out within the council...
NO ONE RETURNS FROM THE DEAD!
The Sadducees didn't believe in angels or an afterlife...
HE'S A FOOL!
But the Pharisees did.
EZEKIEL'S PROPHECY!
THE TEXTS SAY HE'S RIGHT!
YOU CAN'T CONVICT THIS MAN!
YAAAAAH!
A SPIRIT MAY HAVE SPOKEN TO HIM!
TUG
TUG
HE'S A LIAR!
HE'S GUILTY OF BLASPHEMY!
...
THIS HAS GOT TO STOP...
MEN!
I WANT PAUL OUT OF HERE!
!!

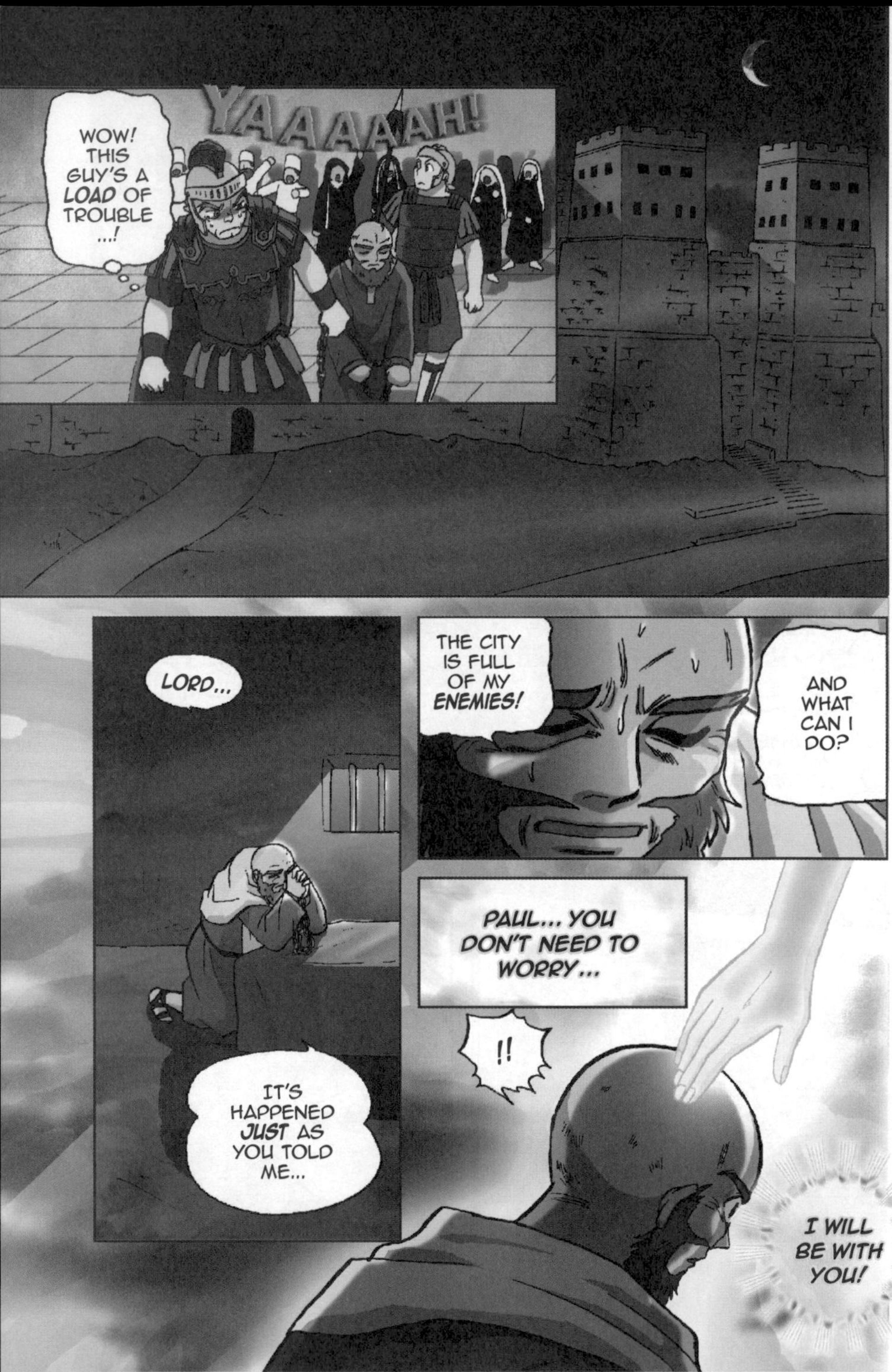
YAAAAAH!
WOW! THIS GUY'S A LOAD OF TROUBLE ...!
LORD...
IT'S HAPPENED JUST AS YOU TOLD ME...
THE CITY IS FULL OF MY ENEMIES!
AND WHAT CAN I DO?
PAUL... YOU DON'T NEED TO WORRY...
!!
I WILL BE WITH YOU!

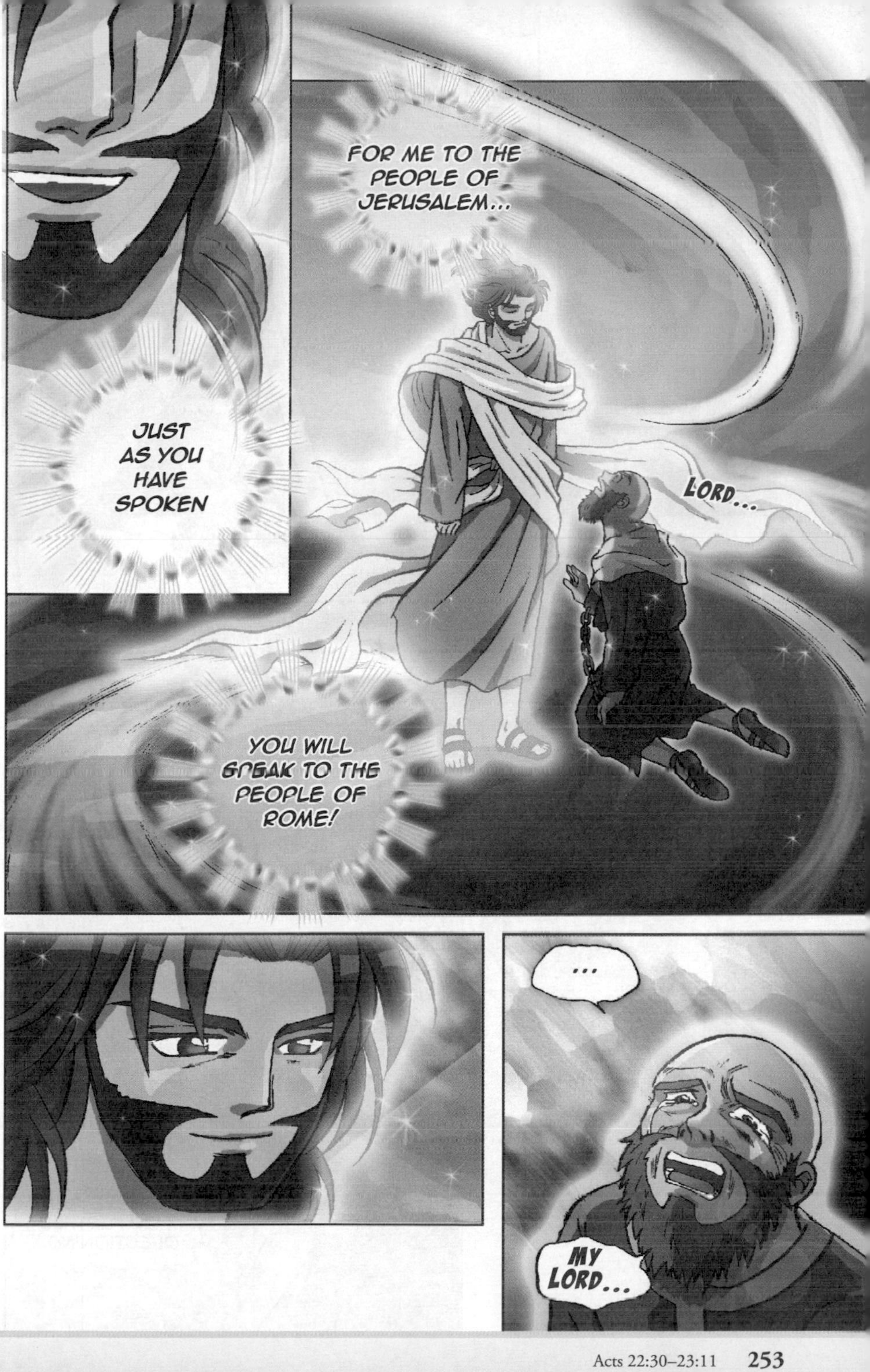
JUST AS YOU HAVE SPOKEN
FOR ME TO THE PEOPLE OF JERUSALEM...
YOU WILL SPEAK TO THE PEOPLE OF ROME!
LORD...
...
MY LORD...

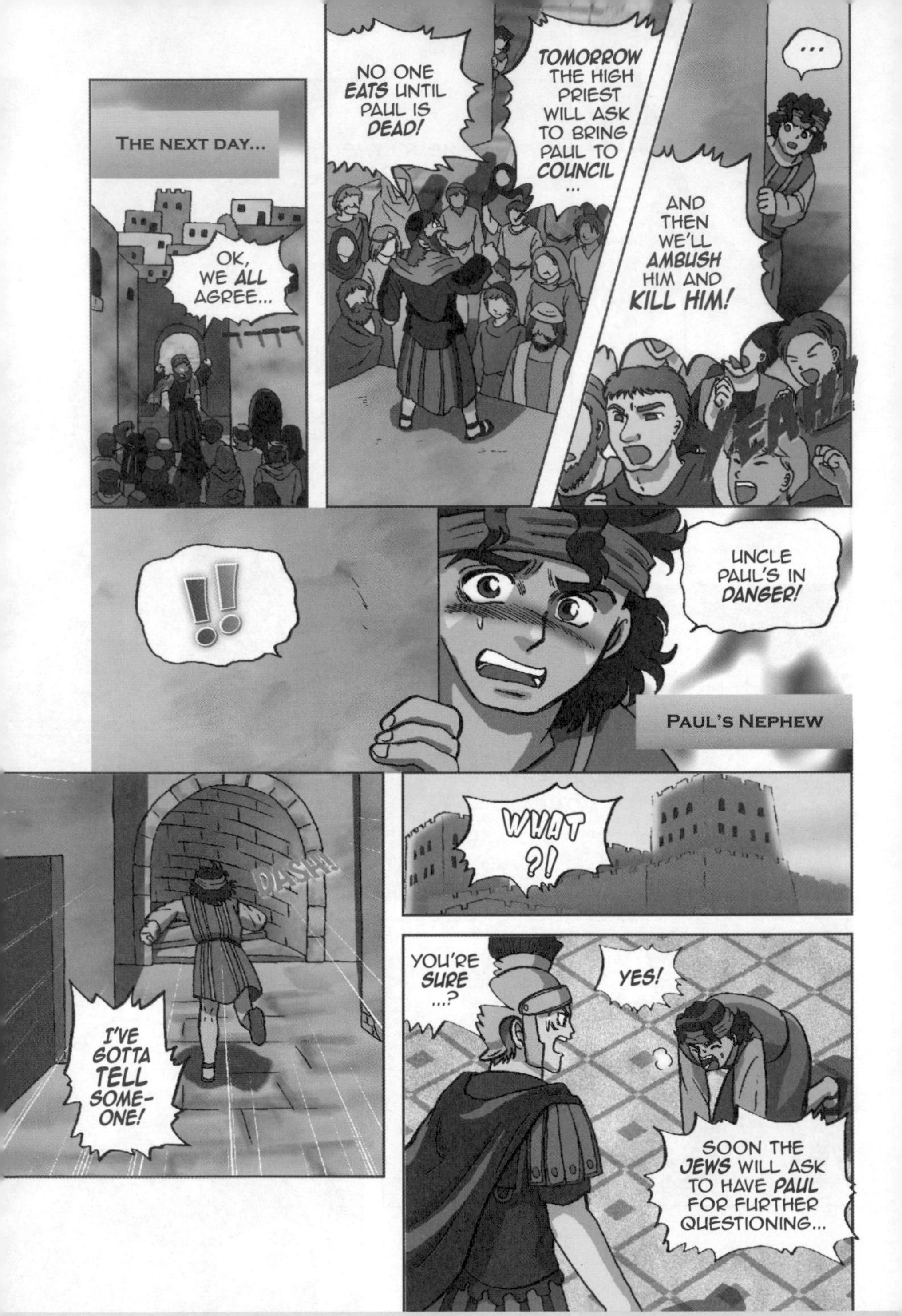
THE NEXT DAY...
OK, WE ALL AGREE...
NO ONE EATS UNTIL PAUL IS DEAD!
TOMORROW THE HIGH PRIEST WILL ASK TO BRING PAUL TO COUNCIL ...
...
AND THEN WE'LL AMBUSH HIM AND KILL HIM!
YEAH!
!!
UNCLE PAUL'S IN DANGER!
PAUL'S NEPHEW
DASH!
I'VE GOTTA TELL SOME-ONE!
WHAT ?!
YOU'RE SURE ...?
YES!
SOON THE JEWS WILL ASK TO HAVE PAUL FOR FURTHER QUESTIONING...

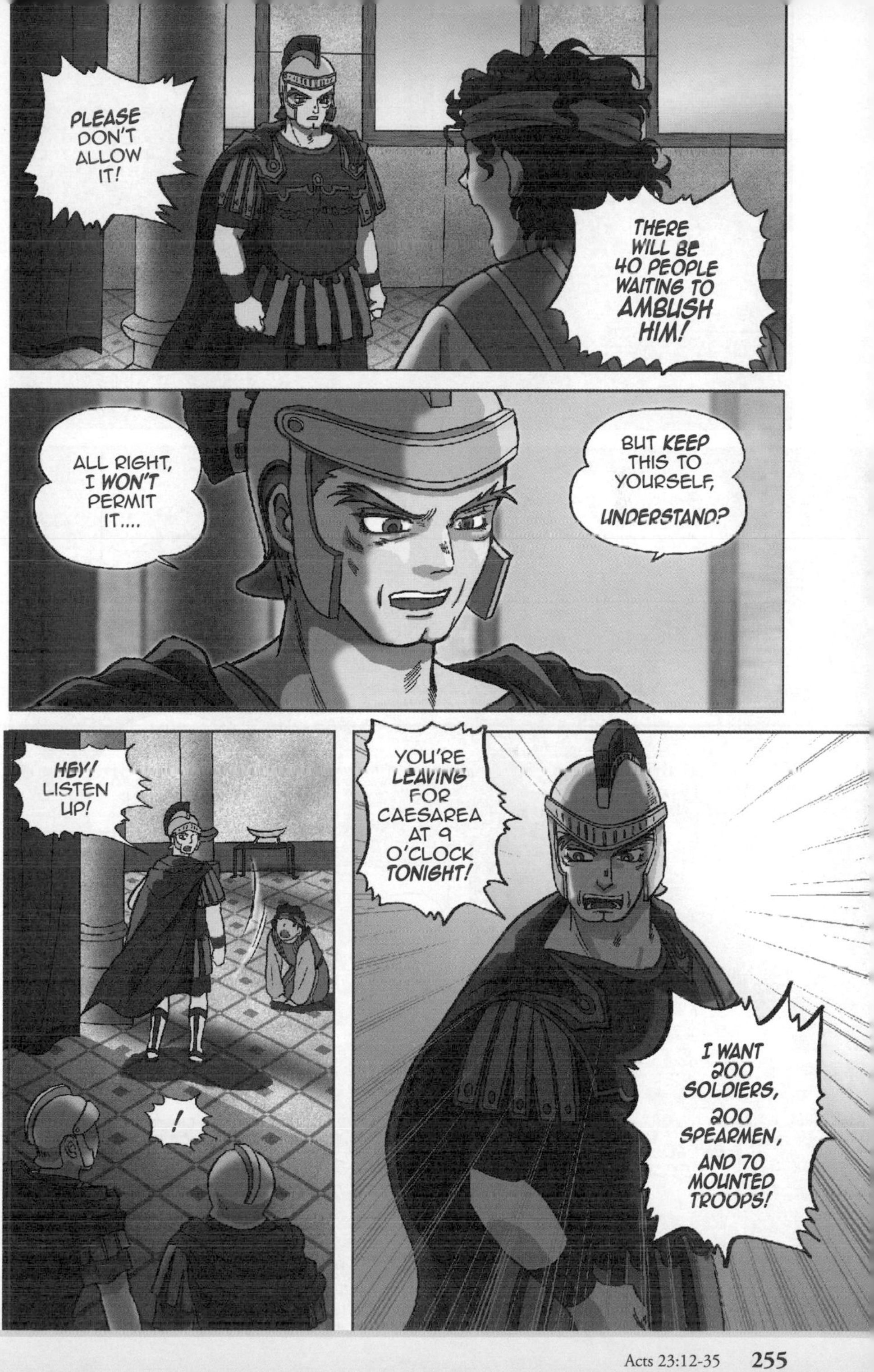
PLEASE DON'T ALLOW IT!
THERE WILL BE 40 PEOPLE WAITING TO AMBUSH HIM!
ALL RIGHT, I WON'T PERMIT IT....
BUT KEEP THIS TO YOURSELF,
UNDERSTAND?
HEY! LISTEN UP!
!
YOU'RE LEAVING FOR CAESAREA AT 9 O'CLOCK TONIGHT!
I WANT 200 SOLDIERS,
200 SPEARMEN,
AND 70 MOUNTED TROOPS!

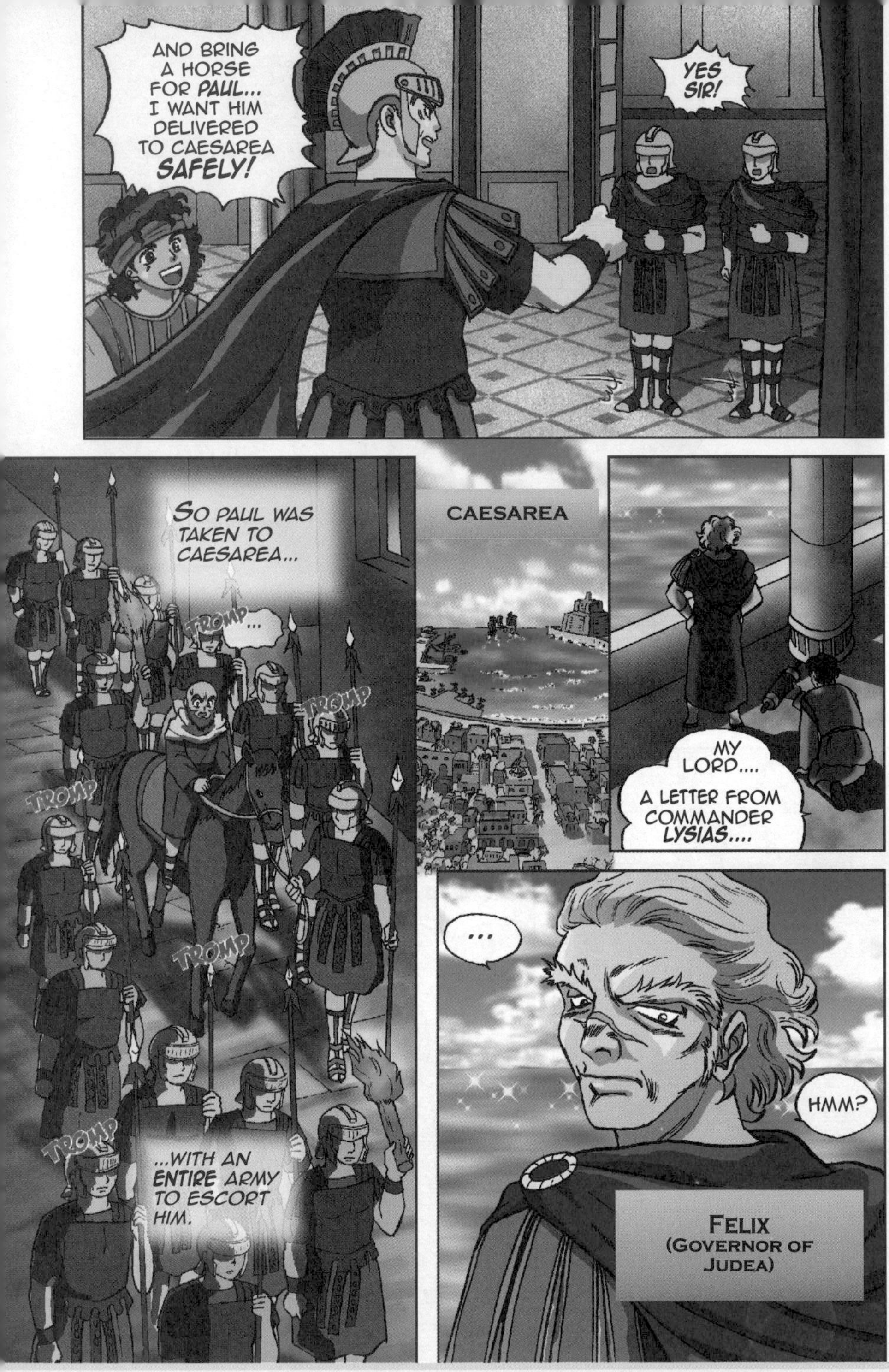
AND BRING A HORSE FOR PAUL... I WANT HIM DELIVERED TO CAESAREA SAFELY!
YES SIR!
SO PAUL WAS TAKEN TO CAESAREA...
TROMP...
TROMP
TROMP
TROMP
TROMP
...WITH AN ENTIRE ARMY TO ESCORT HIM.
CAESAREA
MY LORD....
A LETTER FROM COMMANDER LYSIAS....
...
HMM?
FELIX (GOVERNOR OF JUDEA)

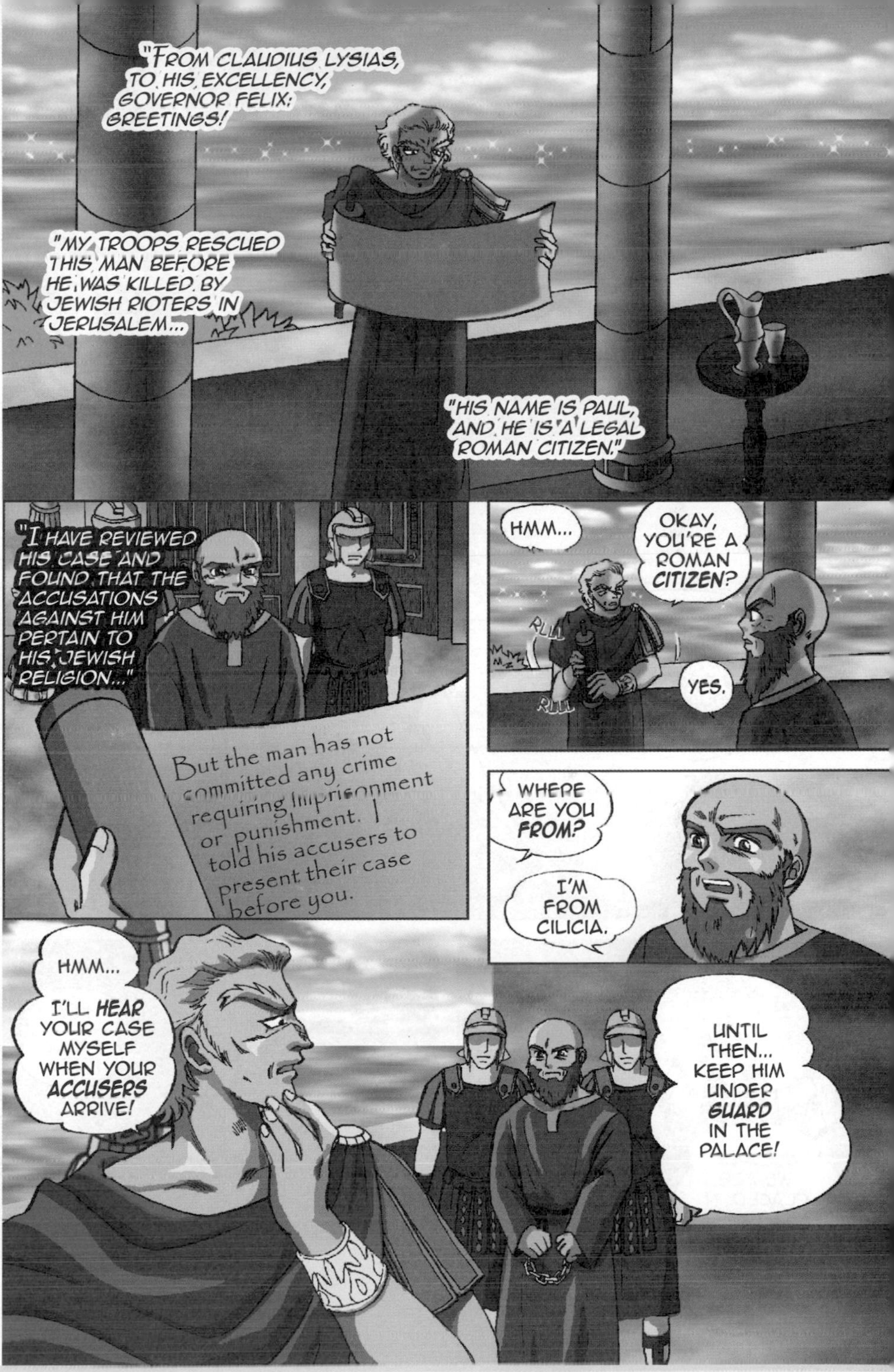
"FROM CLAUDIUS LYSIAS, TO HIS EXCELLENCY, GOVERNOR FELIX: GREETINGS!
"MY TROOPS RESCUED THIS MAN BEFORE HE WAS KILLED BY JEWISH RIOTERS IN JERUSALEM...
"HIS NAME IS PAUL, AND HE IS A LEGAL ROMAN CITIZEN."
"I HAVE REVIEWED HIS CASE AND FOUND THAT THE ACCUSATIONS AGAINST HIM PERTAIN TO HIS JEWISH RELIGION..."
But the man has not committed any crime requiring imprisonment or punishment. I told his accusers to present their case before you.
HMM...
OKAY, YOU'RE A ROMAN CITIZEN?
YES.
WHERE ARE YOU FROM?
I'M FROM CILICIA.
HMM...
I'LL HEAR YOUR CASE MYSELF WHEN YOUR ACCUSERS ARRIVE!
UNTIL THEN... KEEP HIM UNDER GUARD IN THE PALACE!

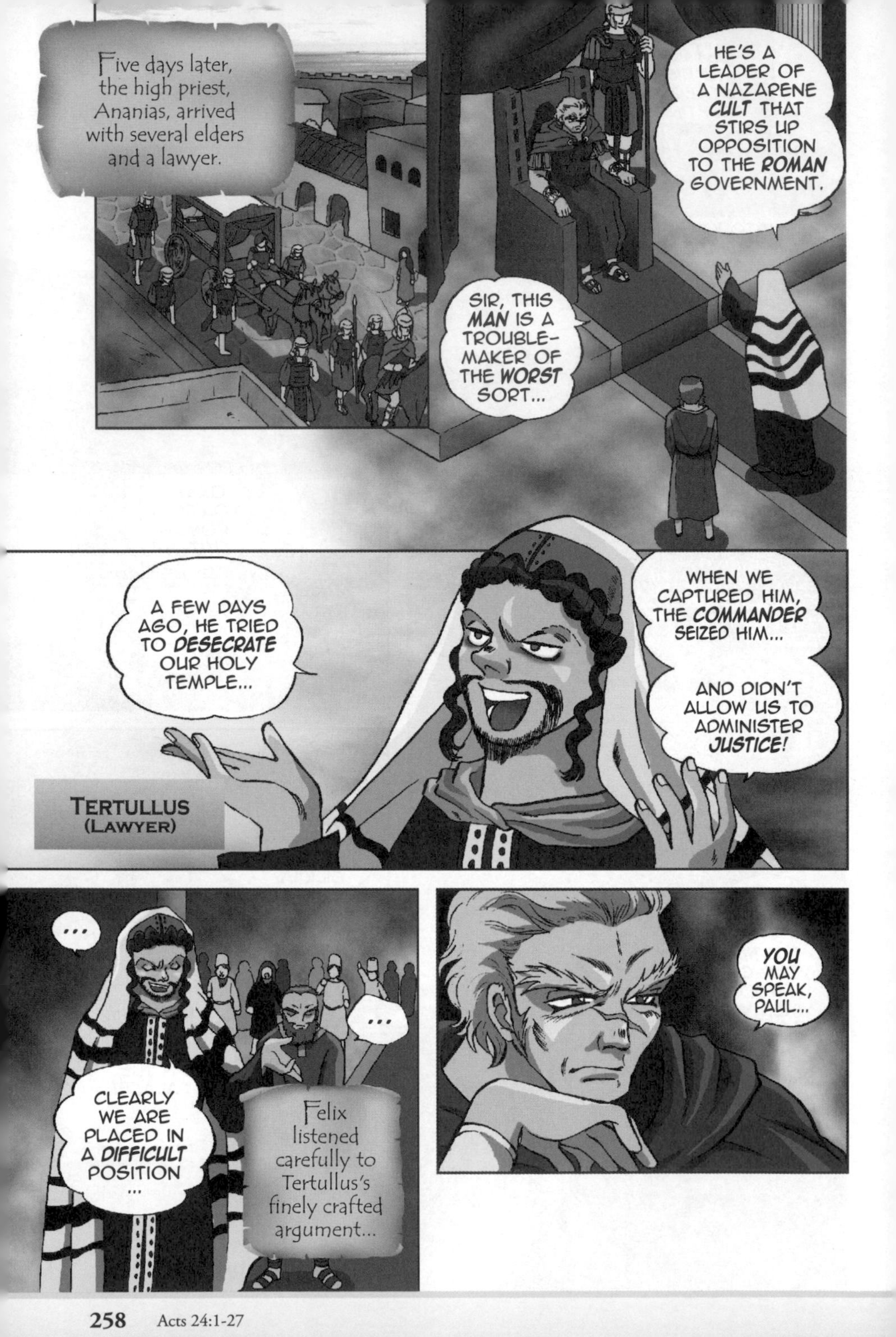
Five days later, the high priest, Ananias, arrived with several elders and a lawyer.
HE'S A LEADER OF A NAZARENE CULT THAT STIRS UP OPPOSITION TO THE ROMAN GOVERNMENT.
SIR, THIS MAN IS A TROUBLE-MAKER OF THE WORST SORT...
A FEW DAYS AGO, HE TRIED TO DESECRATE OUR HOLY TEMPLE...
WHEN WE CAPTURED HIM, THE COMMANDER SEIZED HIM...
AND DIDN'T ALLOW US TO ADMINISTER JUSTICE!
TERTULLUS (LAWYER)
...
...
CLEARLY WE ARE PLACED IN A DIFFICULT POSITION ...
Felix listened carefully to Tertullus's finely crafted argument...
YOU MAY SPEAK, PAUL...

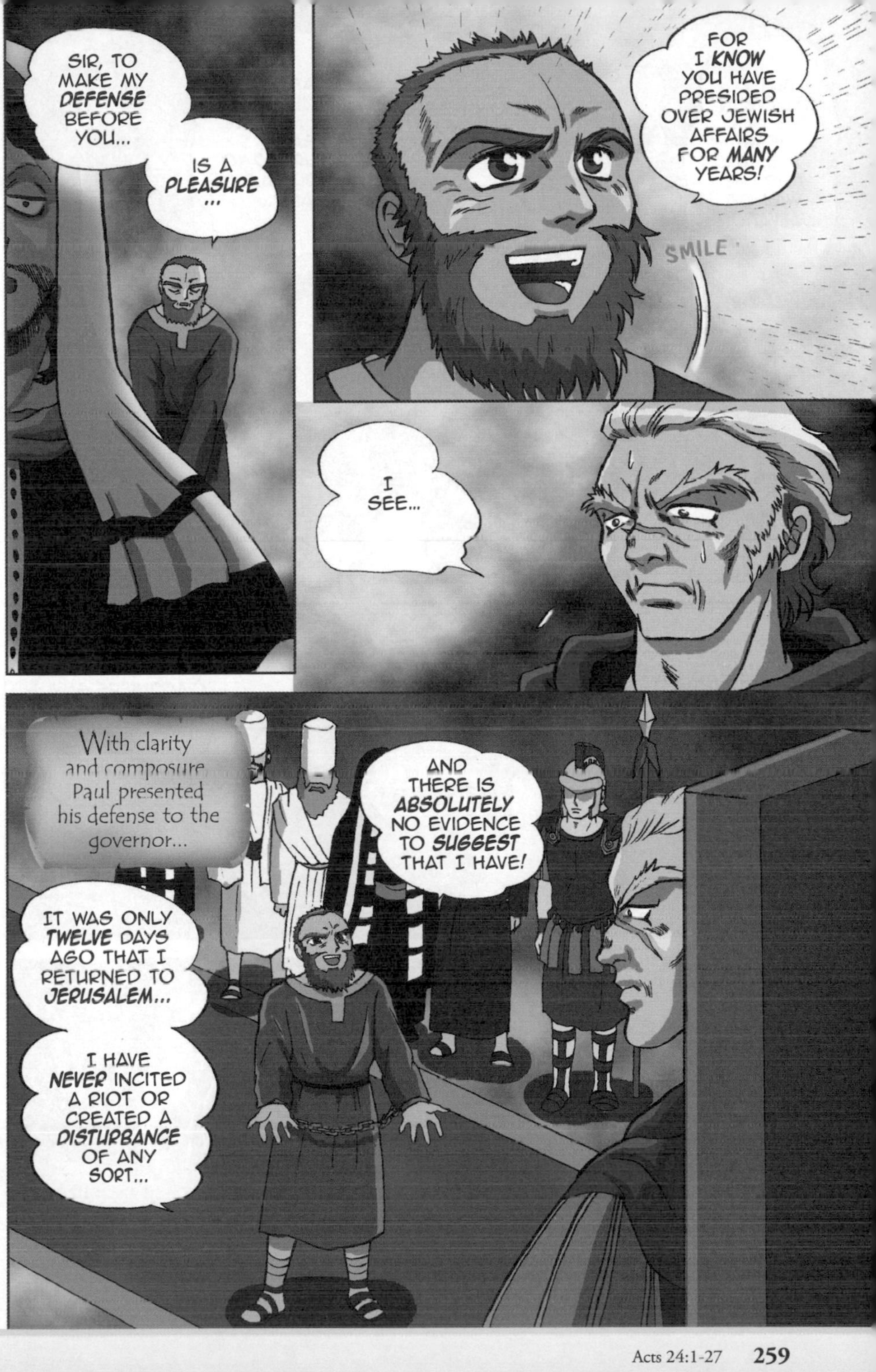
SIR, TO MAKE MY DEFENSE BEFORE YOU...
IS A PLEASURE ...
FOR I KNOW YOU HAVE PRESIDED OVER JEWISH AFFAIRS FOR MANY YEARS!
SMILE
I SEE...
With clarity and composure Paul presented his defense to the governor...
IT WAS ONLY TWELVE DAYS AGO THAT I RETURNED TO JERUSALEM...
I HAVE NEVER INCITED A RIOT OR CREATED A DISTURBANCE OF ANY SORT...
AND THERE IS ABSOLUTELY NO EVIDENCE TO SUGGEST THAT I HAVE!

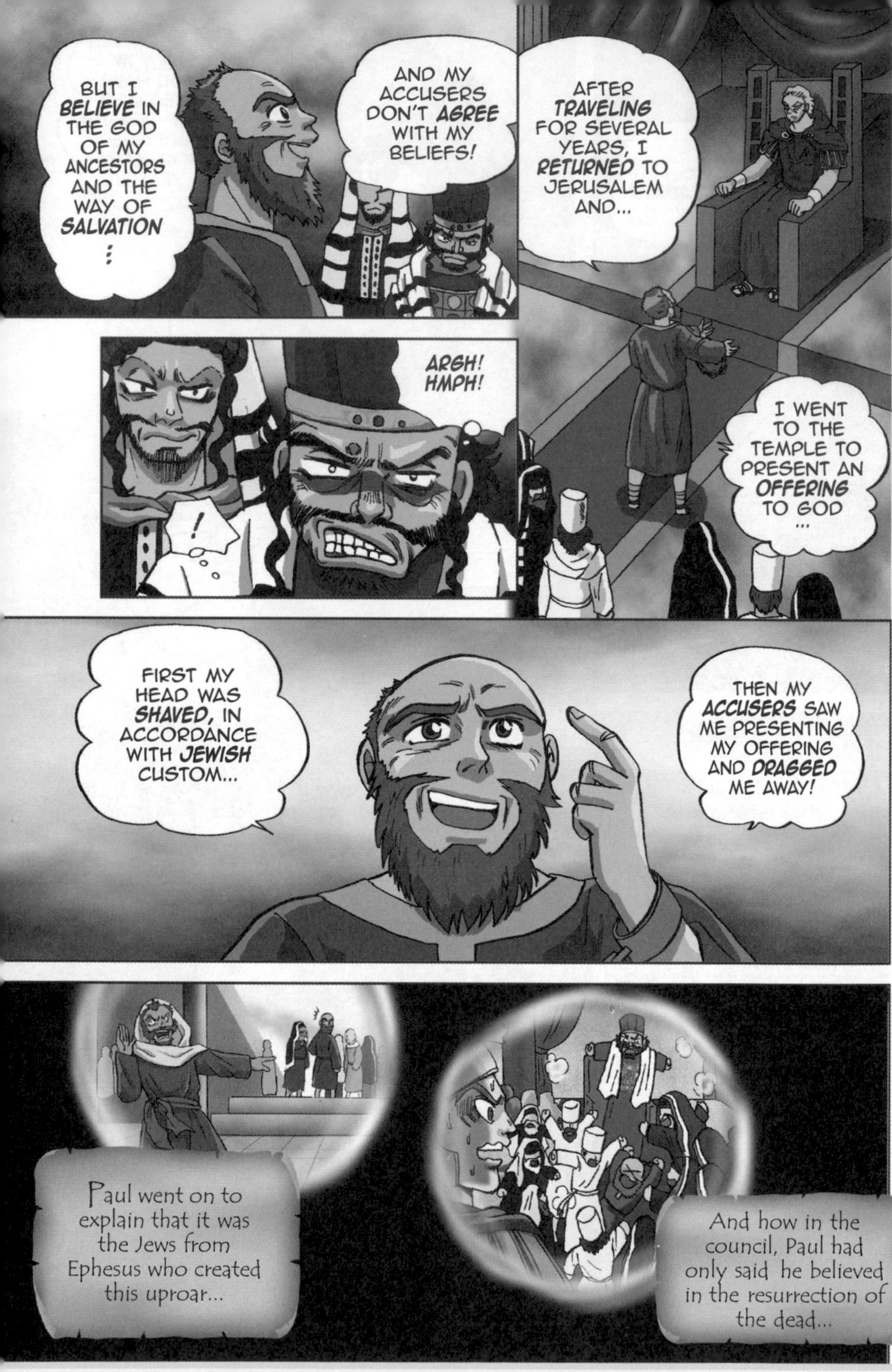
BUT I BELIEVE IN THE GOD OF MY ANCESTORS AND THE WAY OF SALVATION ...
AND MY ACCUSERS DON'T AGREE WITH MY BELIEFS!
AFTER TRAVELING FOR SEVERAL YEARS, I RETURNED TO JERUSALEM AND...
ARGH! HMPH!
!
I WENT TO THE TEMPLE TO PRESENT AN OFFERING TO GOD ...
FIRST MY HEAD WAS SHAVED, IN ACCORDANCE WITH JEWISH CUSTOM...
THEN MY ACCUSERS SAW ME PRESENTING MY OFFERING AND DRAGGED ME AWAY!
Paul went on to explain that it was the Jews from Ephesus who created this uproar...
And how in the council, Paul had only said he believed in the resurrection of the dead...

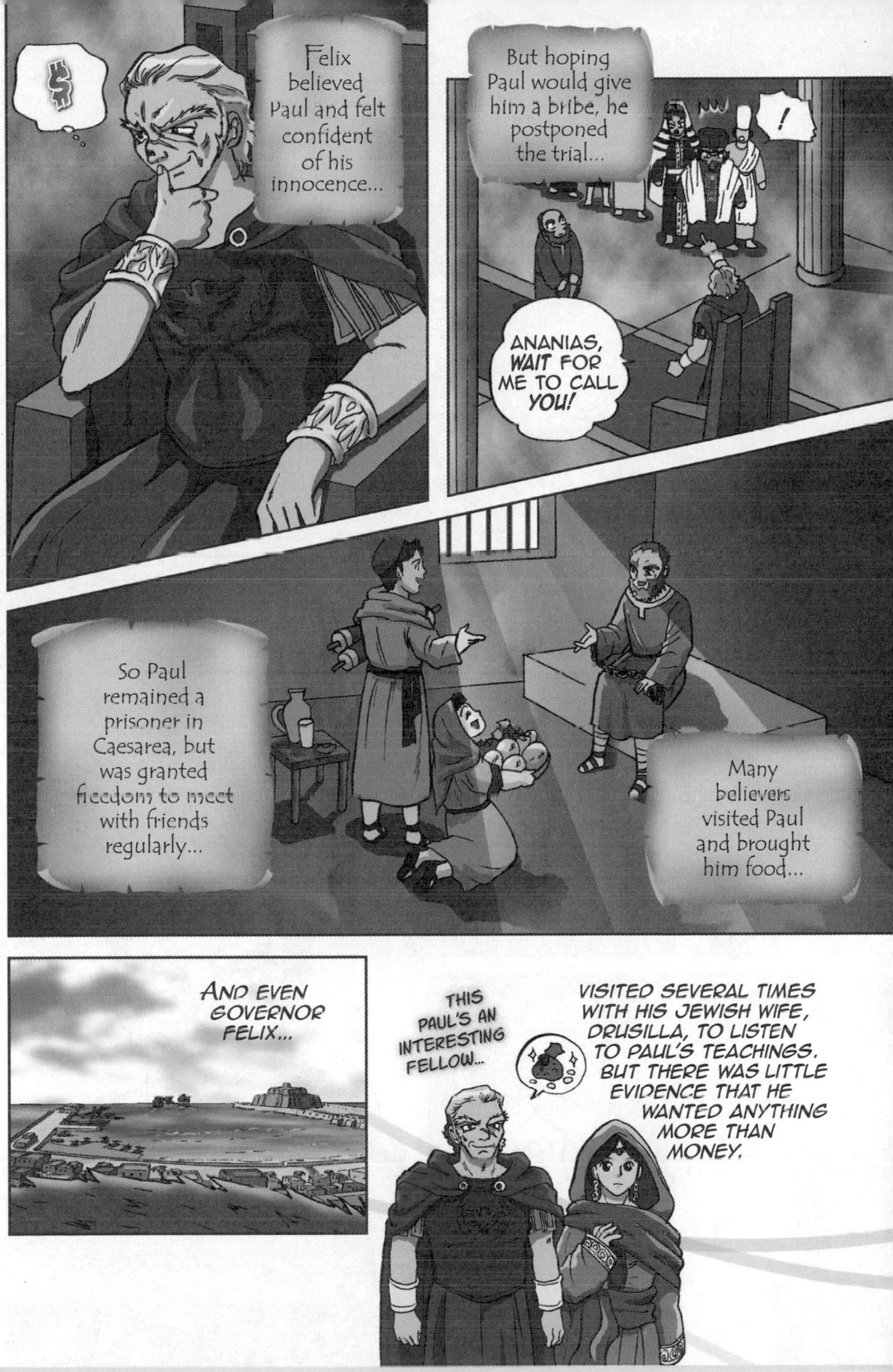
$
Felix believed Paul and felt confident of his innocence...
But hoping Paul would give him a bribe, he postponed the trial...
!
ANANIAS, WAIT FOR ME TO CALL YOU!
So Paul remained a prisoner in Caesarea, but was granted freedom to meet with friends regularly...
Many believers visited Paul and brought him food...
AND EVEN GOVERNOR FELIX...
THIS PAUL'S AN INTERESTING FELLOW...
VISITED SEVERAL TIMES WITH HIS JEWISH WIFE, DRUSILLA, TO LISTEN TO PAUL'S TEACHINGS. BUT THERE WAS LITTLE EVIDENCE THAT HE WANTED ANYTHING MORE THAN MONEY.

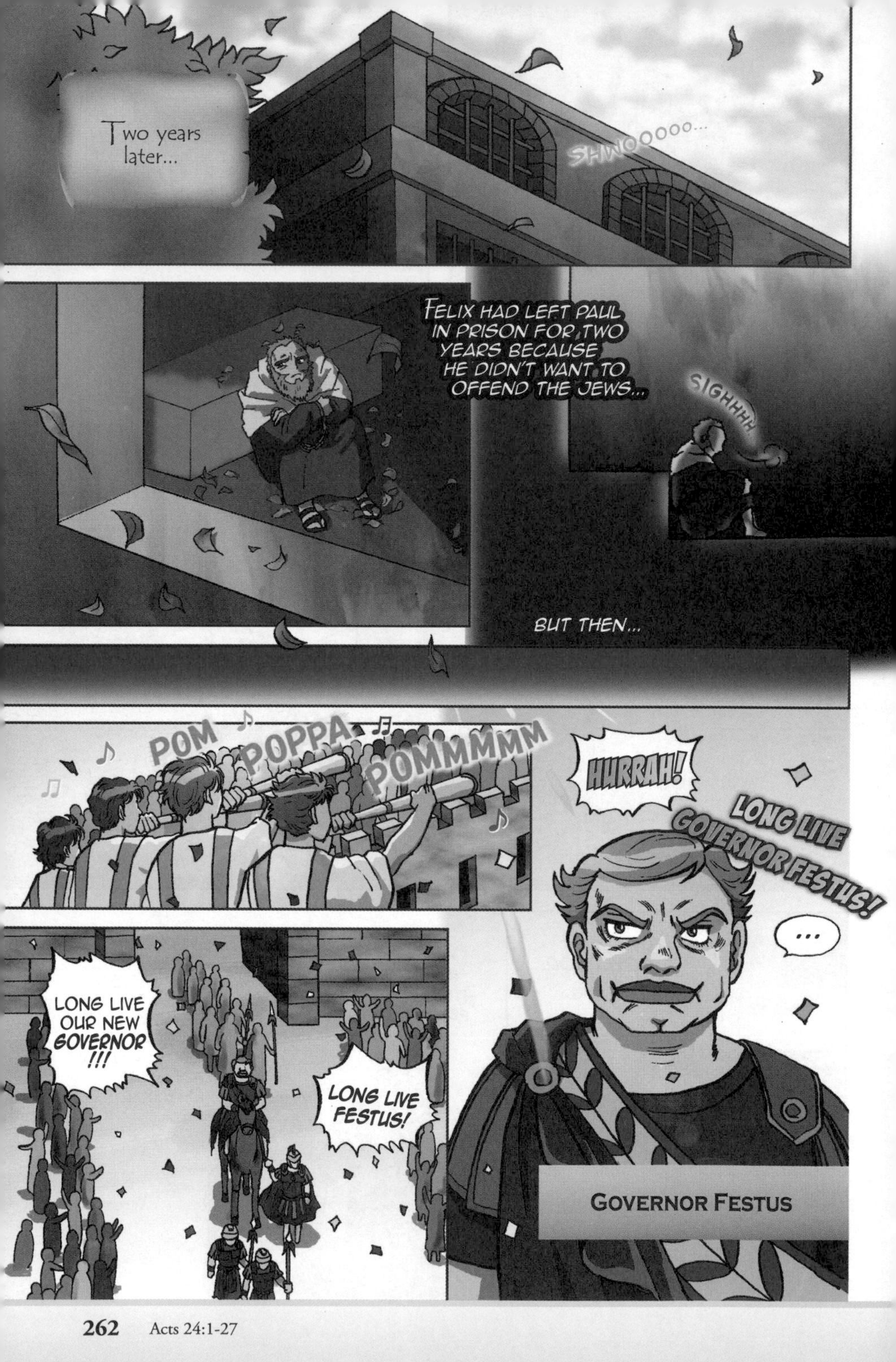
Two years later...
SHWOOOOO...
FELIX HAD LEFT PAUL IN PRISON FOR TWO YEARS BECAUSE HE DIDN'T WANT TO OFFEND THE JEWS...
SIGHHHH
BUT THEN...
POM POPPA POMMMMM
HURRAH!
LONG LIVE GOVERNOR FESTUS!
...
LONG LIVE OUR NEW GOVERNOR !!!
LONG LIVE FESTUS!
GOVERNOR FESTUS

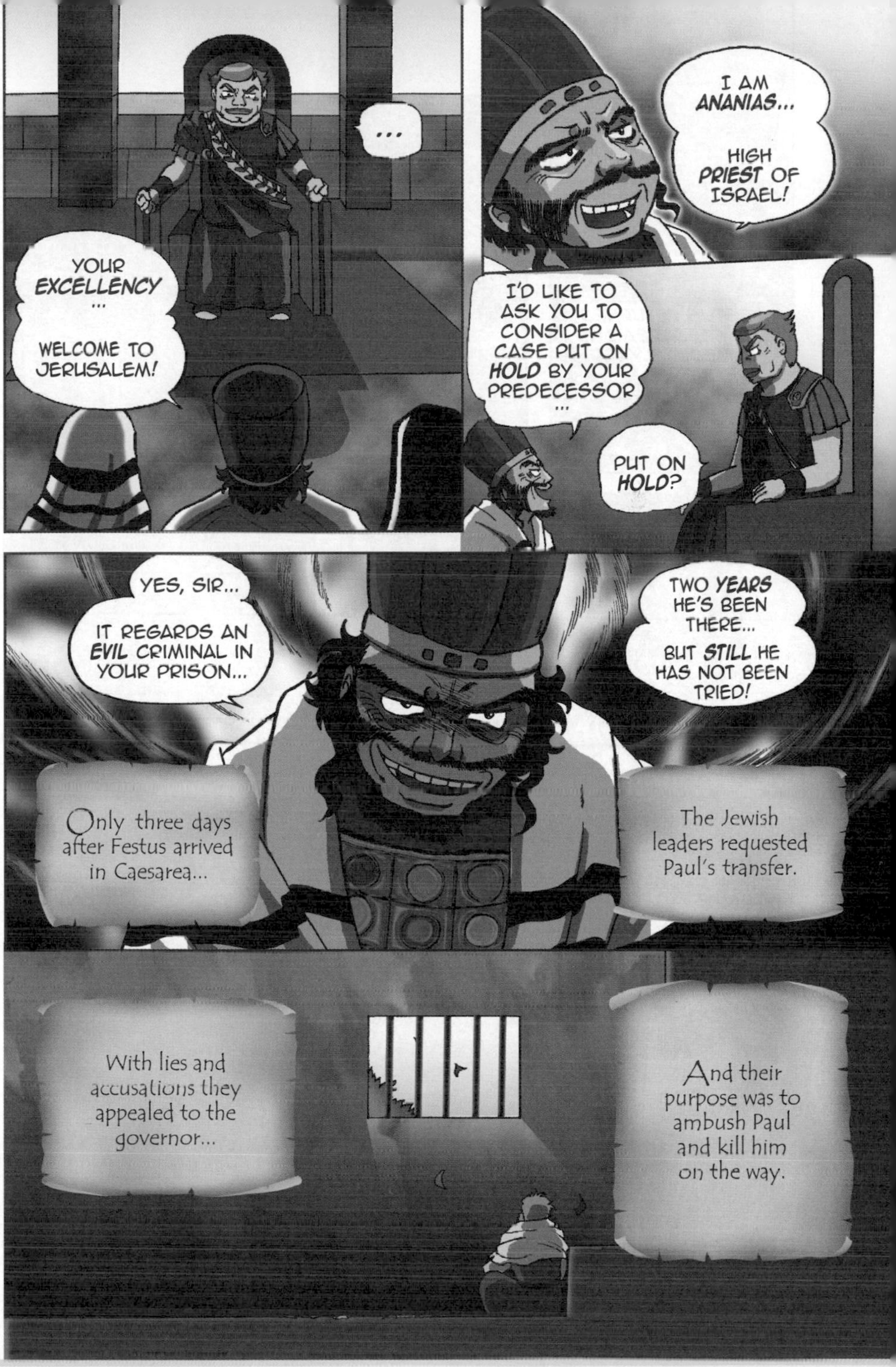
...
I AM ANANIAS...
HIGH PRIEST OF ISRAEL!
YOUR EXCELLENCY ...
WELCOME TO JERUSALEM!
I'D LIKE TO ASK YOU TO CONSIDER A CASE PUT ON HOLD BY YOUR PREDECESSOR ...
PUT ON HOLD?
YES, SIR...
IT REGARDS AN EVIL CRIMINAL IN YOUR PRISON...
TWO YEARS HE'S BEEN THERE...
BUT STILL HE HAS NOT BEEN TRIED!
Only three days after Festus arrived in Caesarea...
The Jewish leaders requested Paul's transfer.
With lies and accusations they appealed to the governor...
And their purpose was to ambush Paul and kill him on the way.

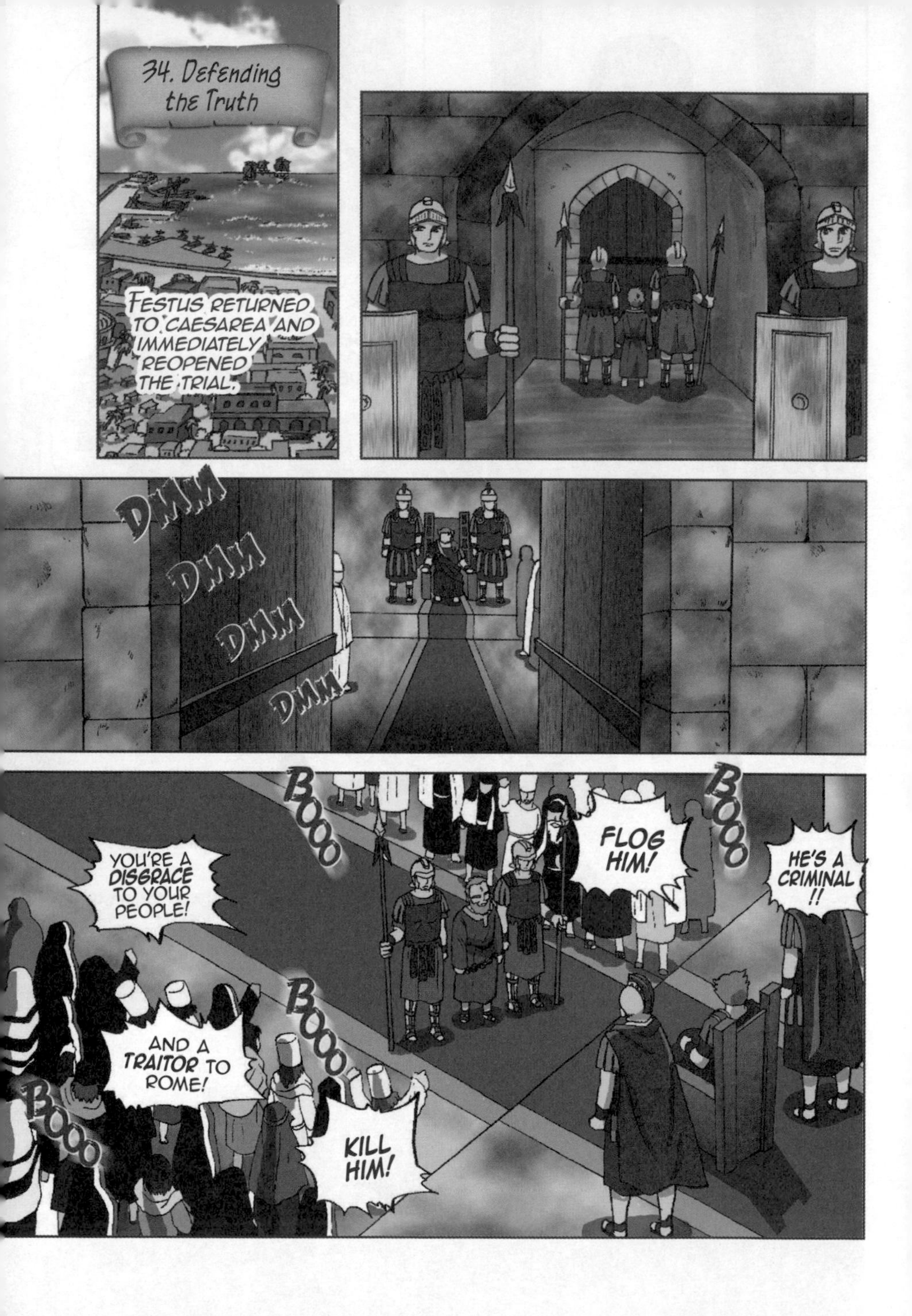
34. Defending the Truth
Festus returned to Caesarea and immediately reopened the trial.
DMM
DMM
DMM
DMM
BOOO
YOU'RE A DISGRACE TO YOUR PEOPLE!
FLOG HIM!
BOOO
HE'S A CRIMINAL !!
BOOO
AND A TRAITOR TO ROME!
BOOO
KILL HIM!

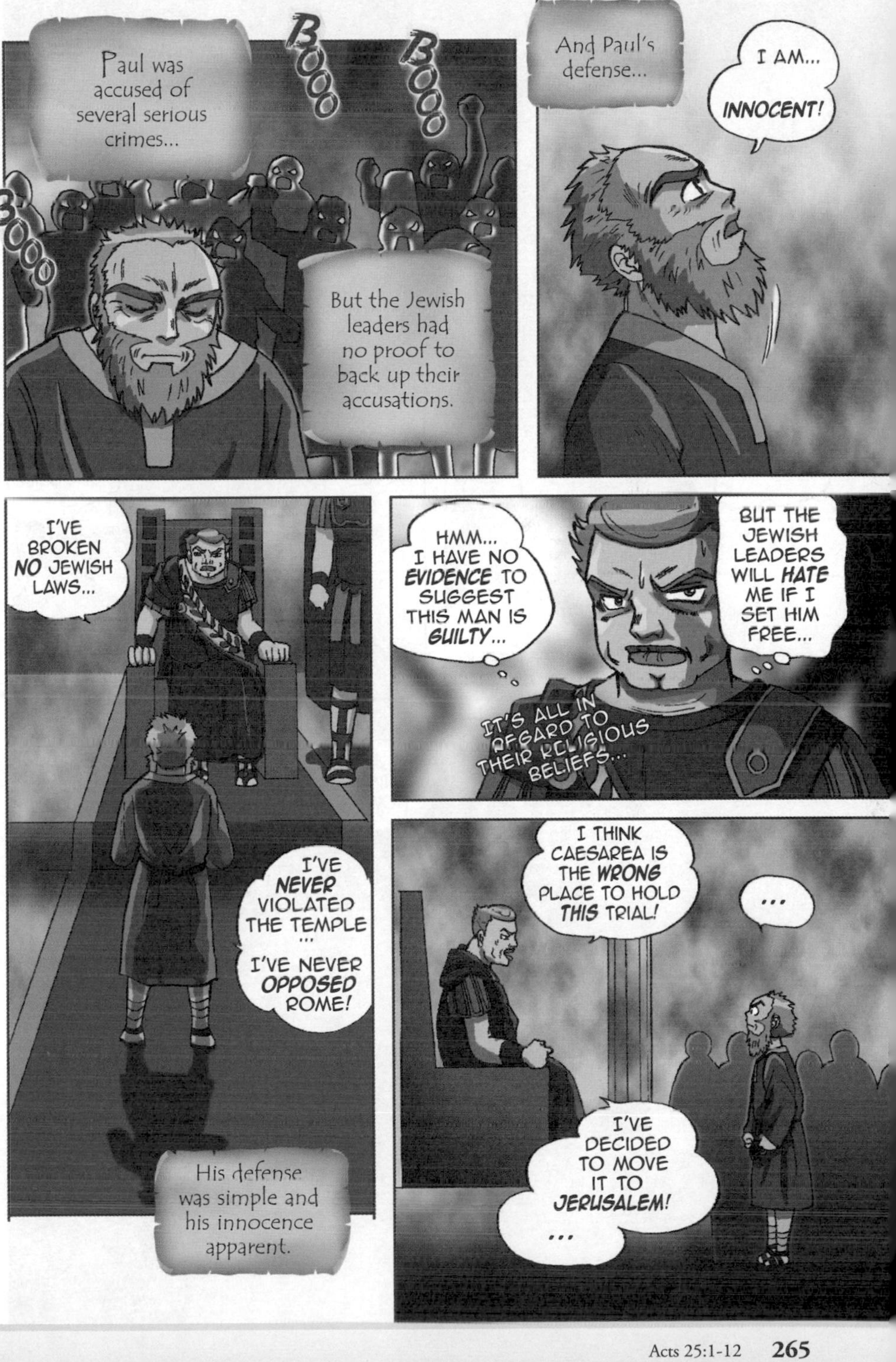
Paul was accused of several serious crimes...
BOOO
BOOO
BOOO
But the Jewish leaders had no proof to back up their accusations.
And Paul's defense...
I AM... INNOCENT!
I'VE BROKEN NO JEWISH LAWS...
I'VE NEVER VIOLATED THE TEMPLE ...
I'VE NEVER OPPOSED ROME!
His defense was simple and his innocence apparent.
HMM... I HAVE NO EVIDENCE TO SUGGEST THIS MAN IS GUILTY...
IT'S ALL IN REGARD TO THEIR RELIGIOUS BELIEFS...
BUT THE JEWISH LEADERS WILL HATE ME IF I SET HIM FREE...
I THINK CAESAREA IS THE WRONG PLACE TO HOLD THIS TRIAL!
...
I'VE DECIDED TO MOVE IT TO JERUSALEM!
...

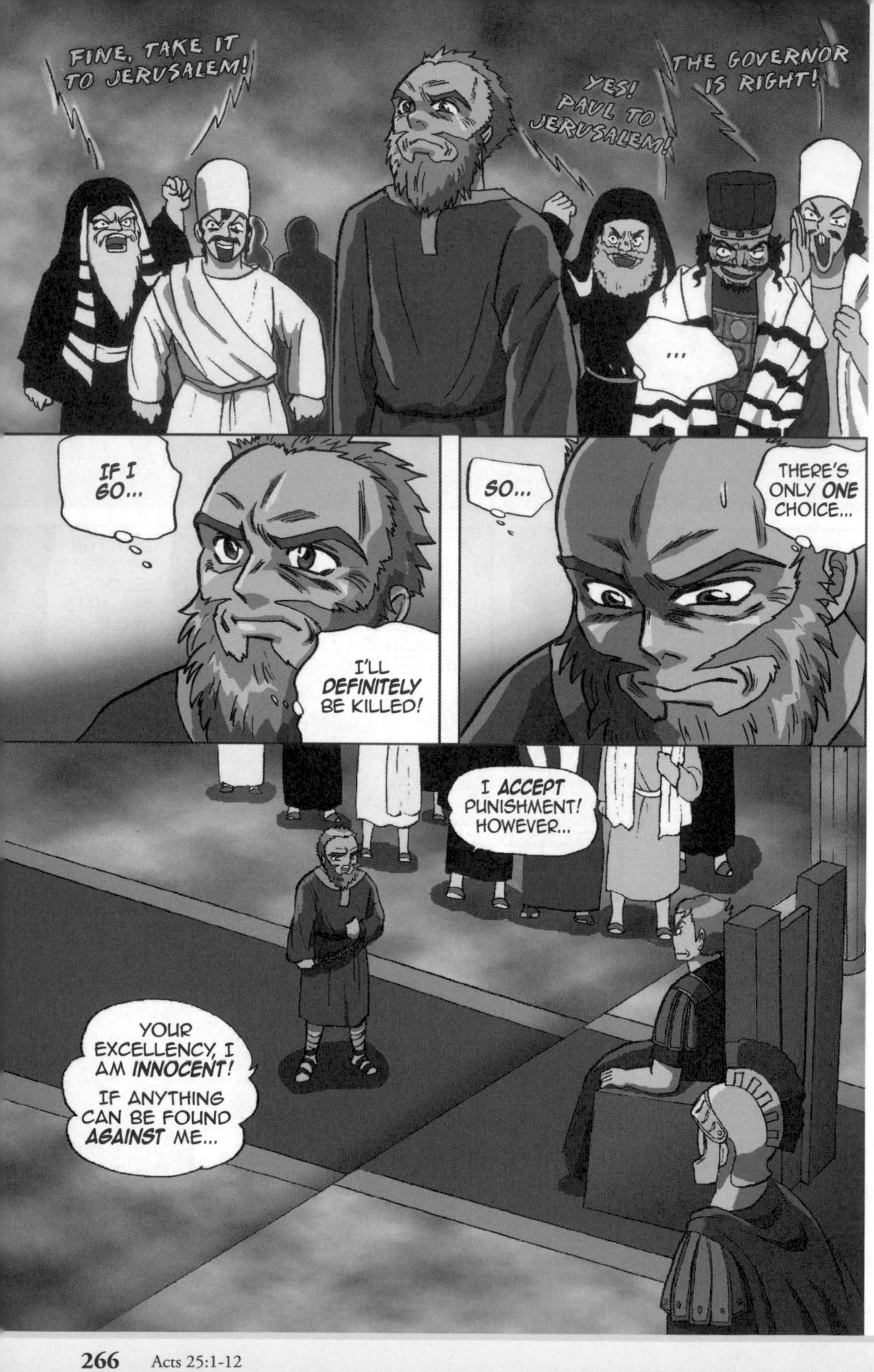
FINE, TAKE IT TO JERUSALEM!
YES! PAUL TO JERUSALEM!
THE GOVERNOR IS RIGHT!
...
IF I GO...
I'LL DEFINITELY BE KILLED!
SO...
THERE'S ONLY ONE CHOICE...
I ACCEPT PUNISHMENT! HOWEVER...
YOUR EXCELLENCY, I AM INNOCENT!
IF ANYTHING CAN BE FOUND AGAINST ME...

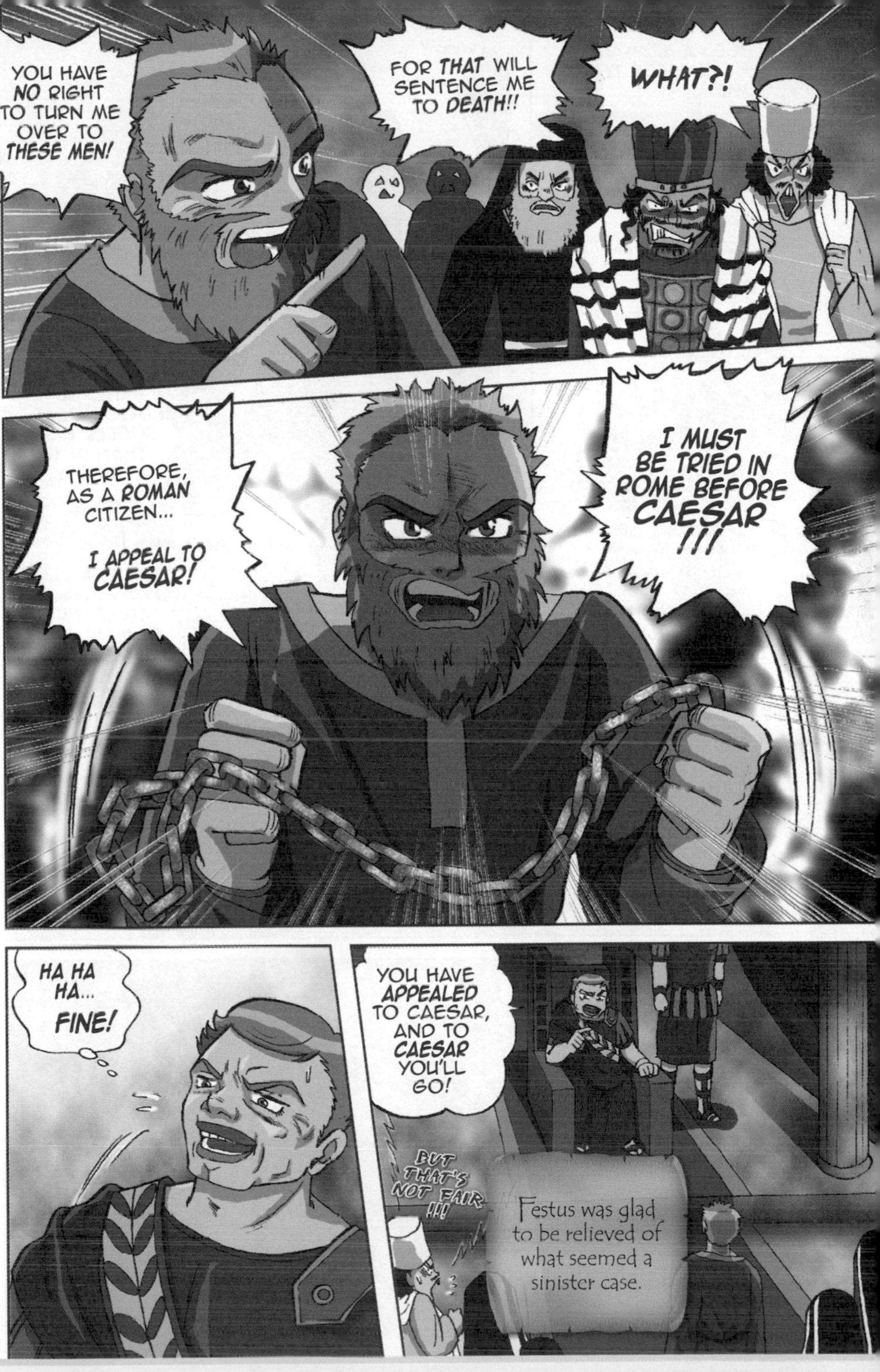
YOU HAVE NO RIGHT TO TURN ME OVER TO THESE MEN!
FOR THAT WILL SENTENCE ME TO DEATH!!
WHAT?!
THEREFORE, AS A ROMAN CITIZEN...
I APPEAL TO CAESAR!
I MUST BE TRIED IN ROME BEFORE CAESAR !!!
HA HA HA... FINE!
YOU HAVE APPEALED TO CAESAR, AND TO CAESAR YOU'LL GO!
BUT THAT'S NOT FAIR !!!
Festus was glad to be relieved of what seemed a sinister case.

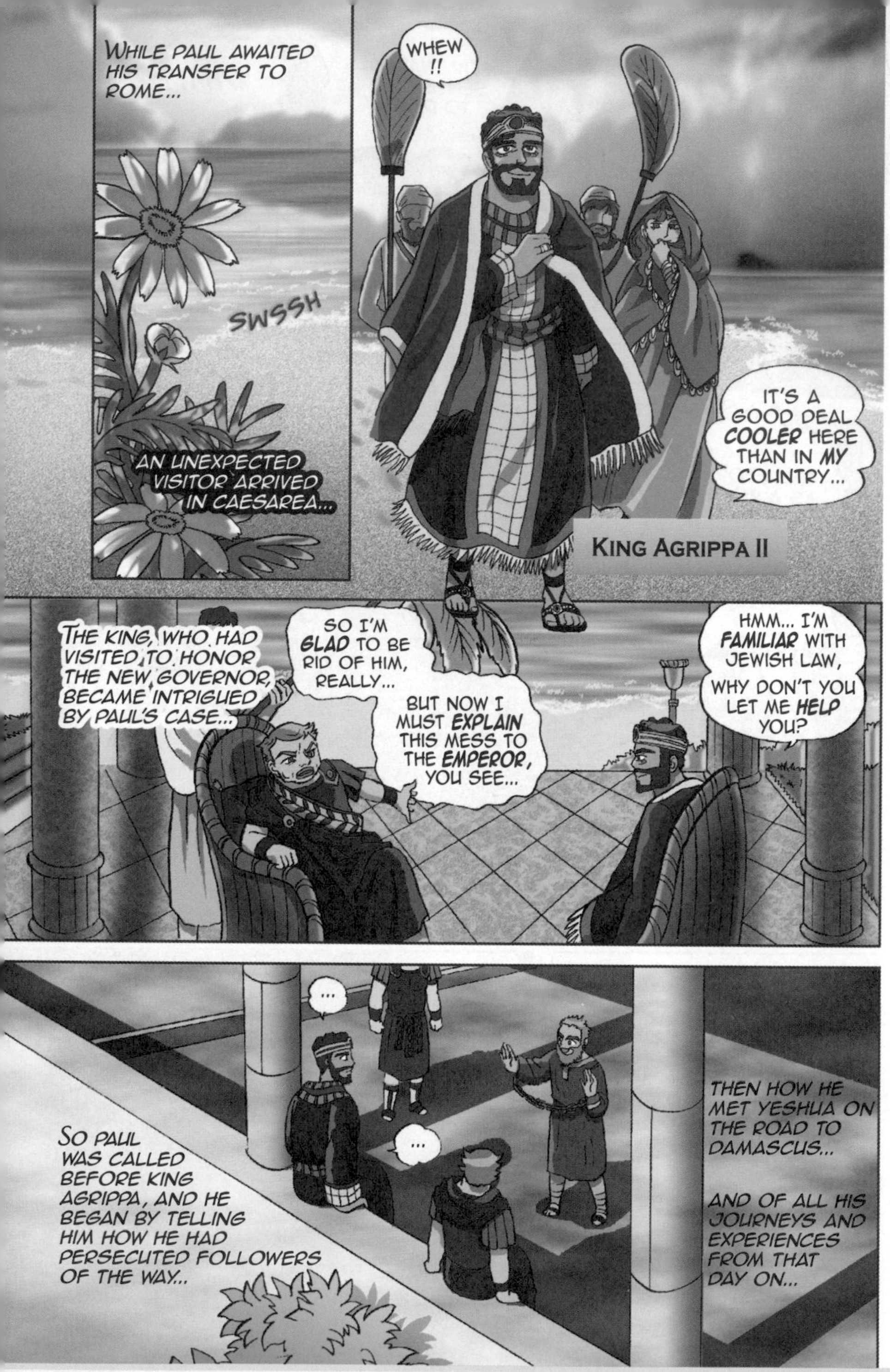

WHILE PAUL AWAITED HIS TRANSFER TO ROME...
WHEW !!
SWSSH
AN UNEXPECTED VISITOR ARRIVED IN CAESAREA...
IT'S A GOOD DEAL COOLER HERE THAN IN MY COUNTRY...
KING AGRIPPA II
THE KING, WHO HAD VISITED TO HONOR THE NEW GOVERNOR, BECAME INTRIGUED BY PAUL'S CASE...
SO I'M GLAD TO BE RID OF HIM, REALLY...
BUT NOW I MUST EXPLAIN THIS MESS TO THE EMPEROR, YOU SEE...
HMM... I'M FAMILIAR WITH JEWISH LAW, WHY DON'T YOU LET ME HELP YOU?
...
...
SO PAUL WAS CALLED BEFORE KING AGRIPPA, AND HE BEGAN BY TELLING HIM HOW HE HAD PERSECUTED FOLLOWERS OF THE WAY...
THEN HOW HE MET YESHUA ON THE ROAD TO DAMASCUS...
AND OF ALL HIS JOURNEYS AND EXPERIENCES FROM THAT DAY ON...

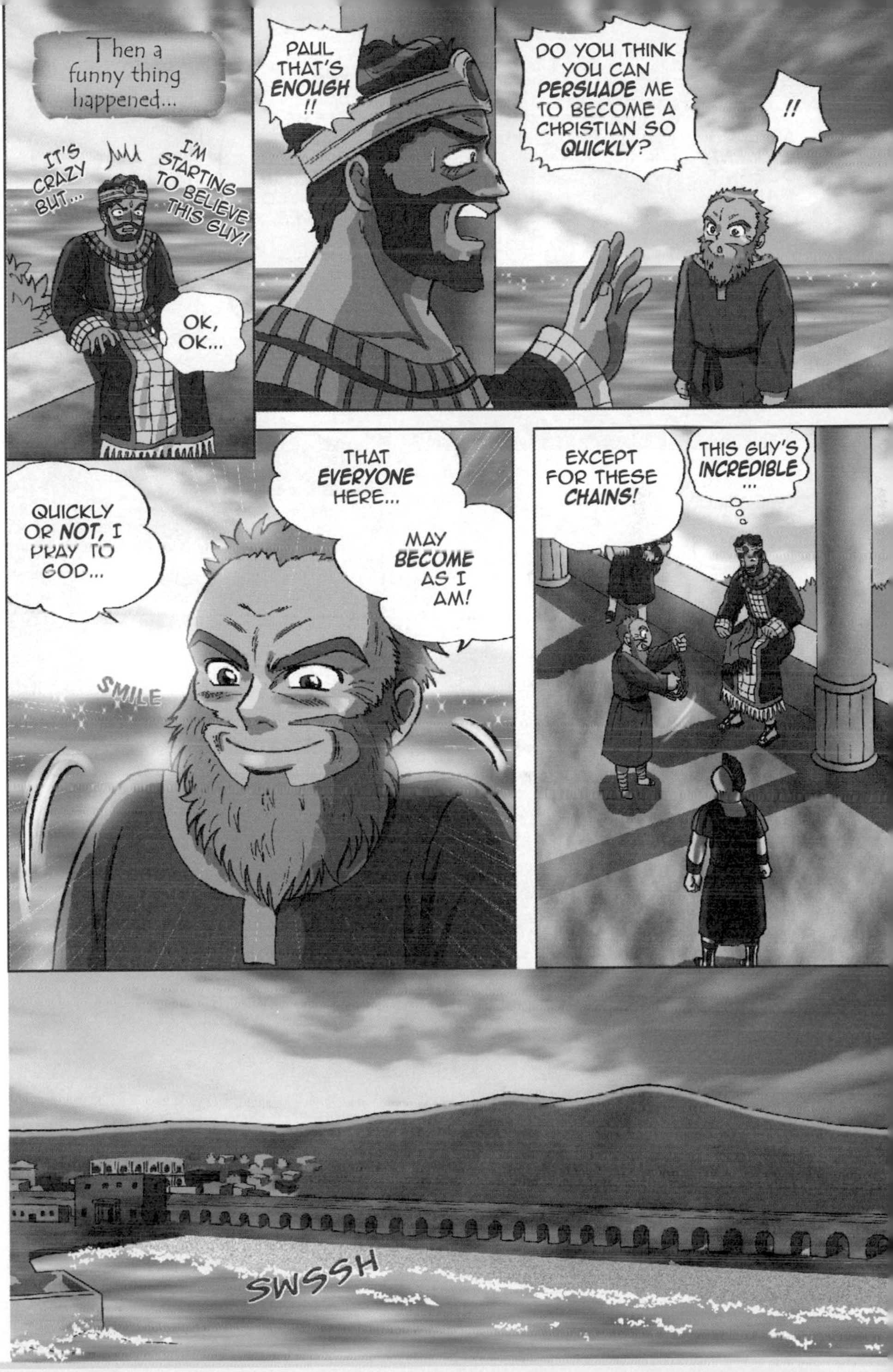
Then a funny thing happened...
IT'S CRAZY BUT...
I'M STARTING TO BELIEVE THIS GUY!
OK, OK...
PAUL THAT'S ENOUGH !!
DO YOU THINK YOU CAN PERSUADE ME TO BECOME A CHRISTIAN SO QUICKLY?
!!
QUICKLY OR NOT, I PRAY TO GOD...
THAT EVERYONE HERE...
MAY BECOME AS I AM!
SMILE
EXCEPT FOR THESE CHAINS!
THIS GUY'S INCREDIBLE ...
SWSSH

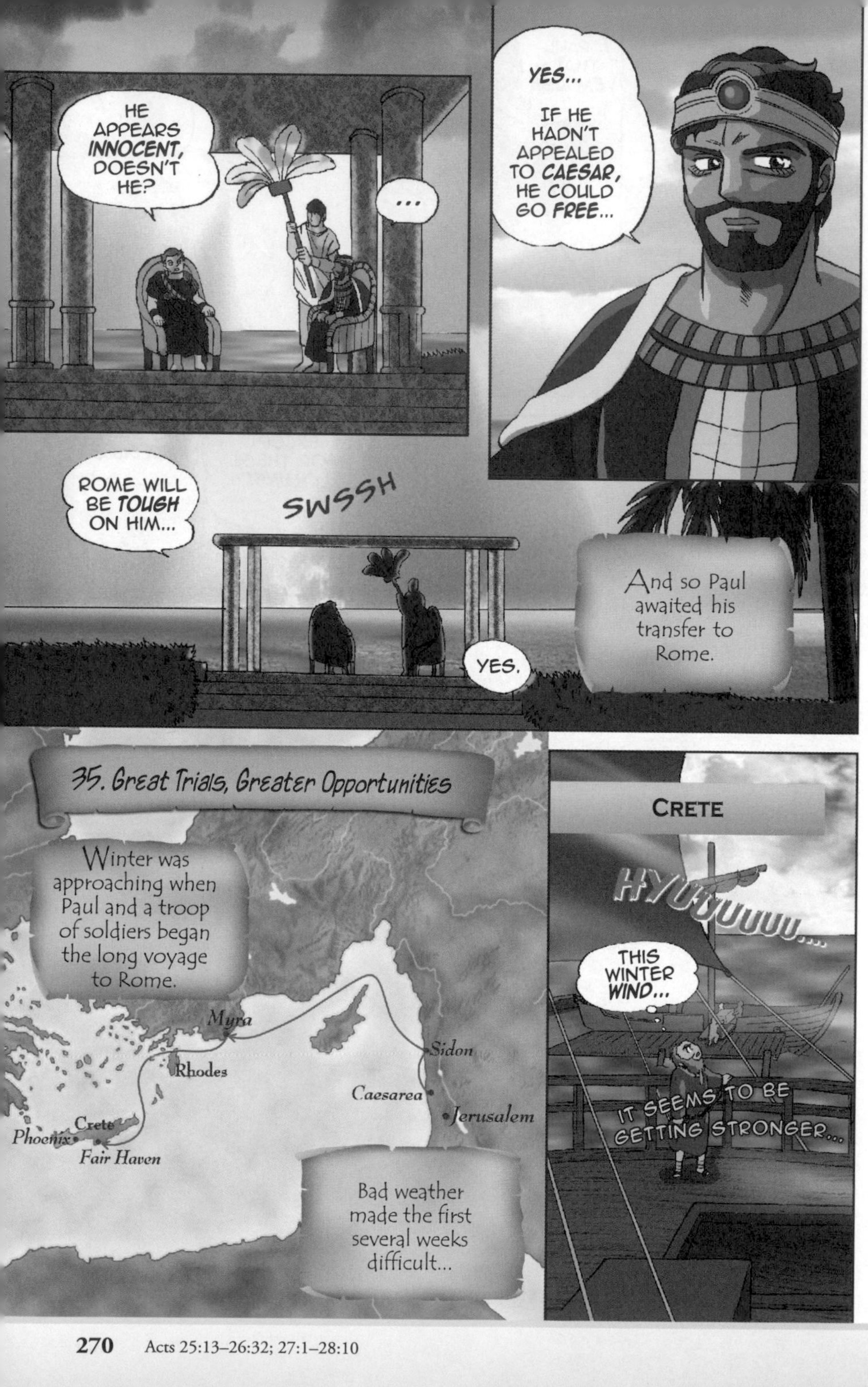
HE APPEARS INNOCENT, DOESN'T HE?
...
YES...
IF HE HADN'T APPEALED TO CAESAR, HE COULD GO FREE...
ROME WILL BE TOUGH ON HIM...
SWSSH
YES.
And so Paul awaited his transfer to Rome.
35. Great Trials, Greater Opportunities
Winter was approaching when Paul and a troop of soldiers began the long voyage to Rome.
Myra
Sidon
Rhodes
Caesarea
Jerusalem
Crete
Phoenix
Fair Haven
Bad weather made the first several weeks difficult...
CRETE
HYUUUUUU....
THIS WINTER WIND...
IT SEEMS TO BE GETTING STRONGER...

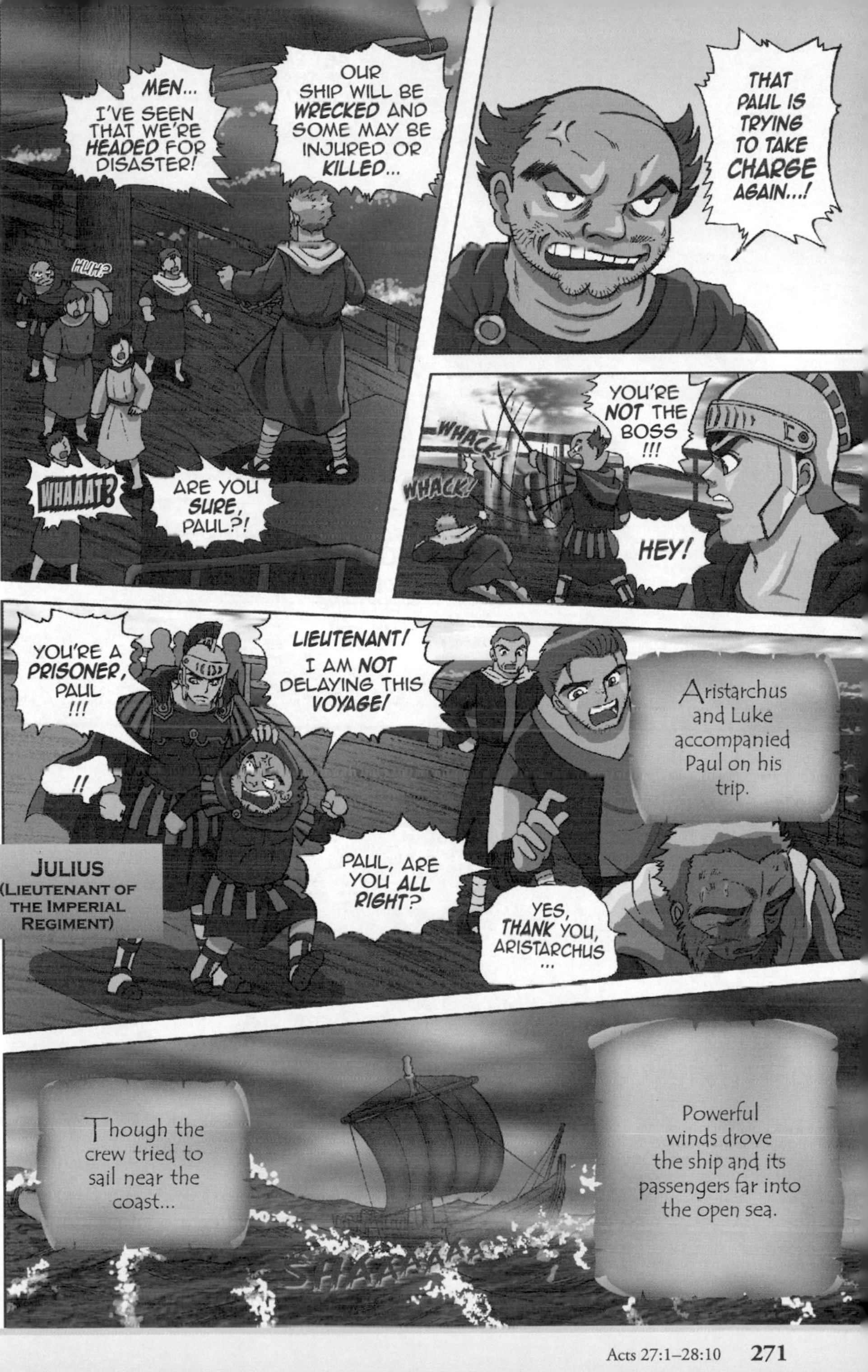
MEN... I'VE SEEN THAT WE'RE HEADED FOR DISASTER!
OUR SHIP WILL BE WRECKED AND SOME MAY BE INJURED OR KILLED...
HUH?
WHAAAT?
ARE YOU SURE, PAUL?!
THAT PAUL IS TRYING TO TAKE CHARGE AGAIN...!
YOU'RE NOT THE BOSS !!!
WHACK
WHACK!
HEY!
YOU'RE A PRISONER, PAUL !!!
!!
LIEUTENANT! I AM NOT DELAYING THIS VOYAGE!
Aristarchus and Luke accompanied Paul on his trip.
JULIUS (LIEUTENANT OF THE IMPERIAL REGIMENT)
PAUL, ARE YOU ALL RIGHT?
YES, THANK YOU, ARISTARCHUS ...
Though the crew tried to sail near the coast...
Powerful winds drove the ship and its passengers far into the open sea.

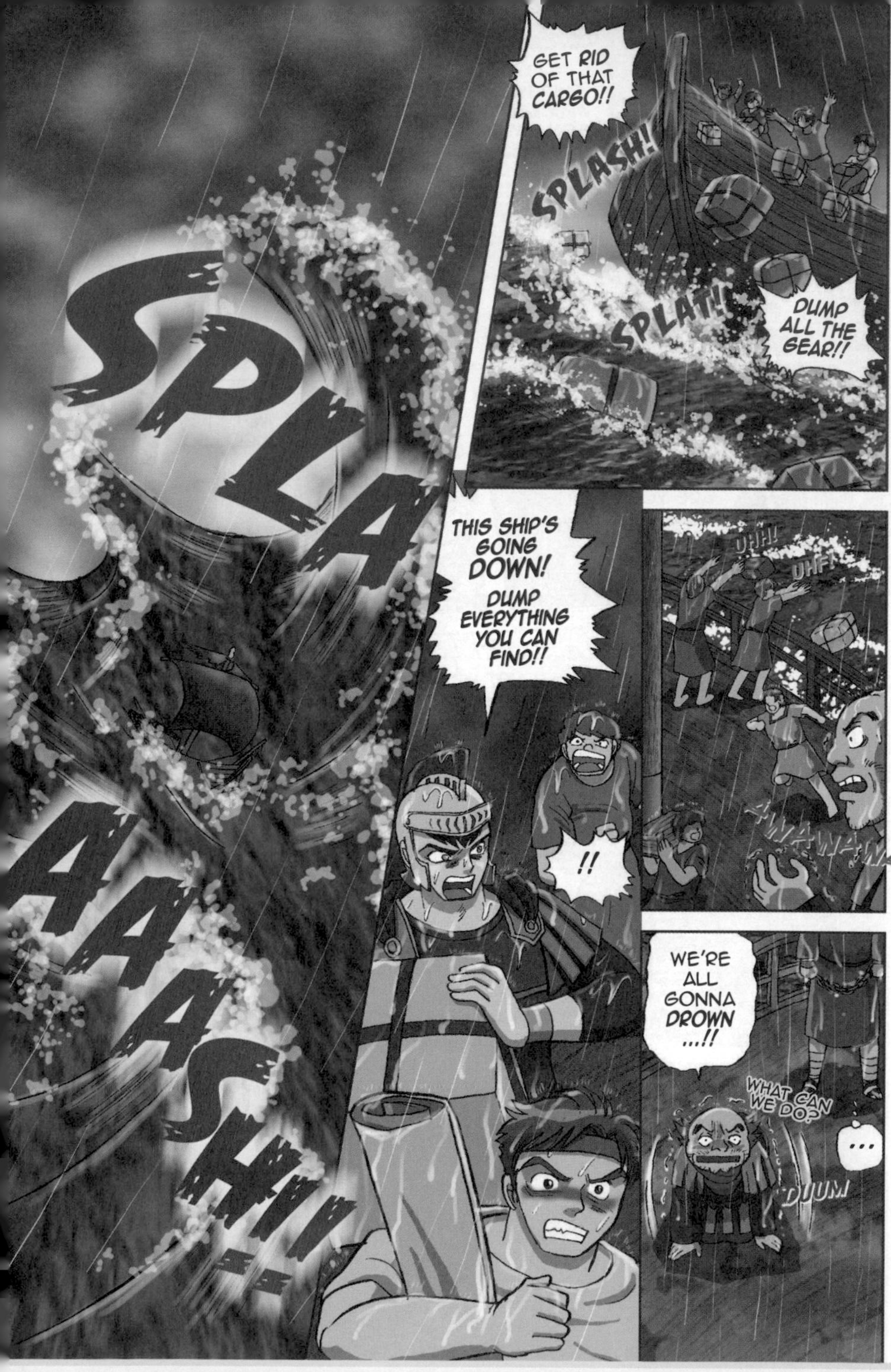
SPLAAAASHH
GET RID OF THAT CARGO!!
SPLASH!
SPLAT!!
DUMP ALL THE GEAR!!
THIS SHIP'S GOING DOWN! DUMP EVERYTHING YOU CAN FIND!!
!!
UHH!
UHF
WE'RE ALL GONNA DROWN ...!!
WHAT CAN WE DO?
...
DUUM

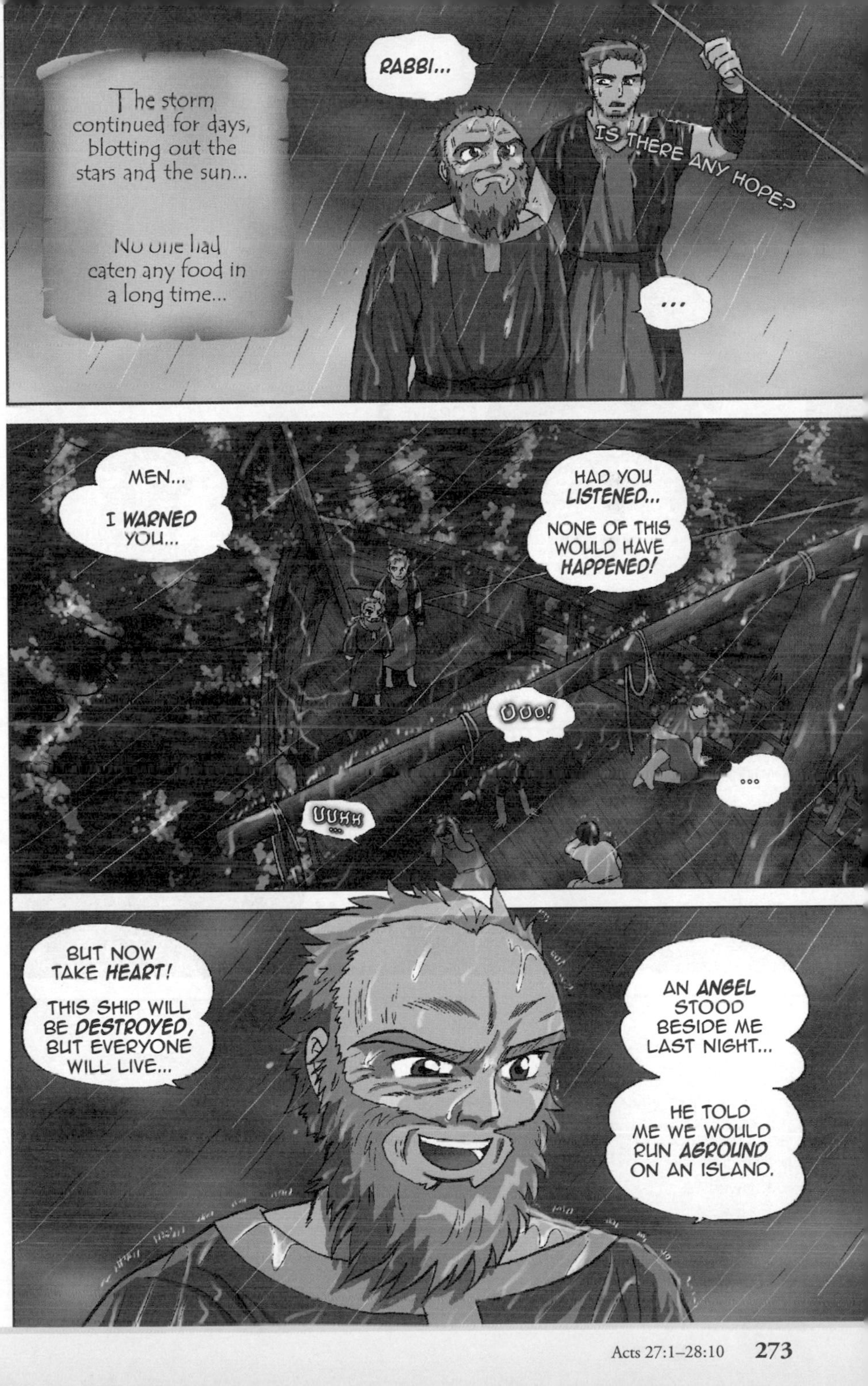
The storm continued for days, blotting out the stars and the sun...
No one had eaten any food in a long time...
RABBI...
IS THERE ANY HOPE?
...
MEN...
I WARNED YOU...
HAD YOU LISTENED...
NONE OF THIS WOULD HAVE HAPPENED!
OOO!
...
UUHH...
BUT NOW TAKE HEART!
THIS SHIP WILL BE DESTROYED, BUT EVERYONE WILL LIVE...
AN ANGEL STOOD BESIDE ME LAST NIGHT...
HE TOLD ME WE WOULD RUN AGROUND ON AN ISLAND.

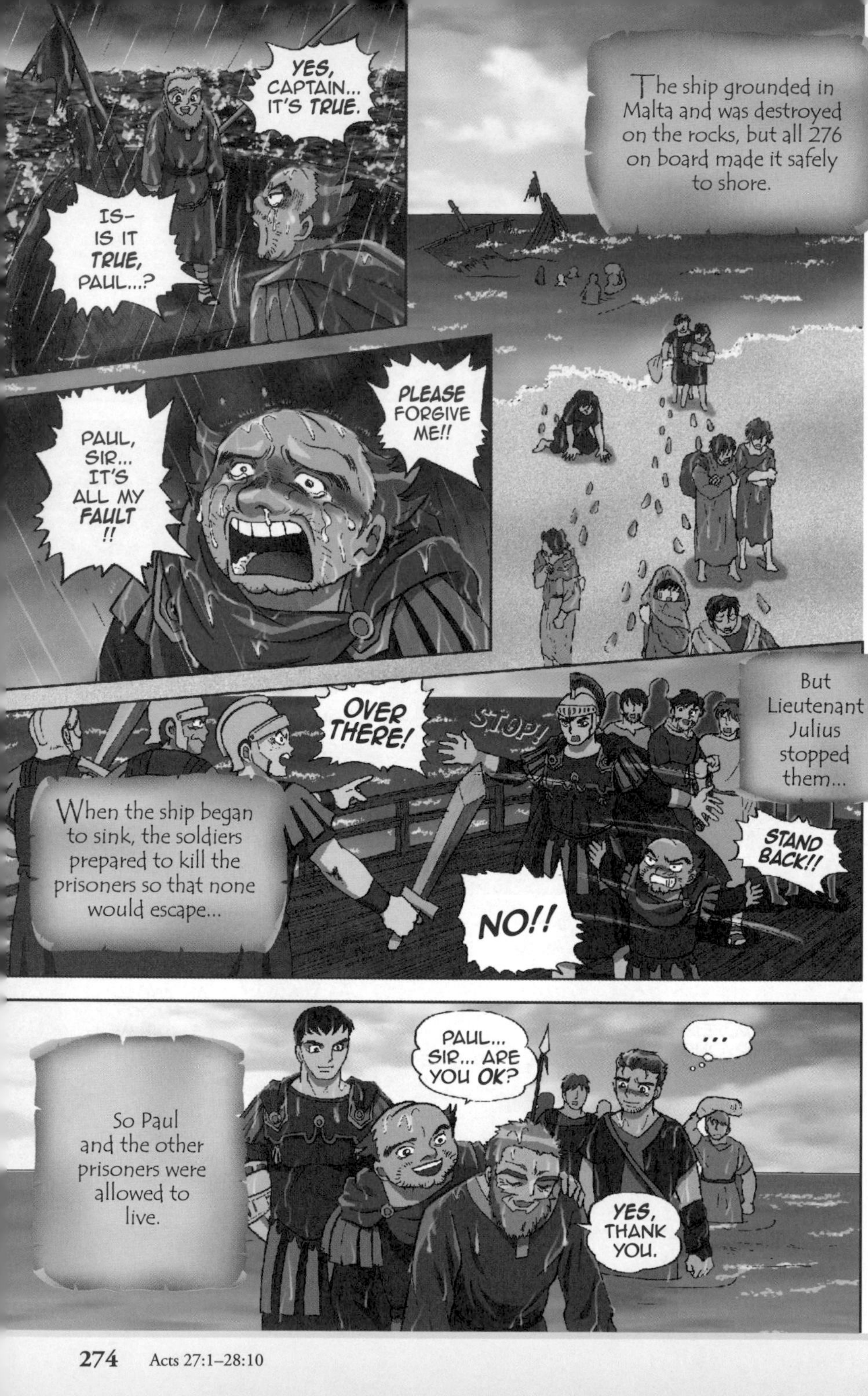
IS-
IS IT
TRUE,
PAUL...?
YES,
CAPTAIN...
IT'S TRUE.
The ship grounded in Malta and was destroyed on the rocks, but all 276 on board made it safely to shore.
PAUL,
SIR...
IT'S
ALL MY
FAULT
!!
PLEASE
FORGIVE
ME!!
When the ship began to sink, the soldiers prepared to kill the prisoners so that none would escape...
OVER
THERE!
STOP!
But Lieutenant Julius stopped them...
STAND
BACK!!
NO!!
So Paul and the other prisoners were allowed to live.
PAUL...
SIR... ARE
YOU OK?
...
YES,
THANK
YOU.

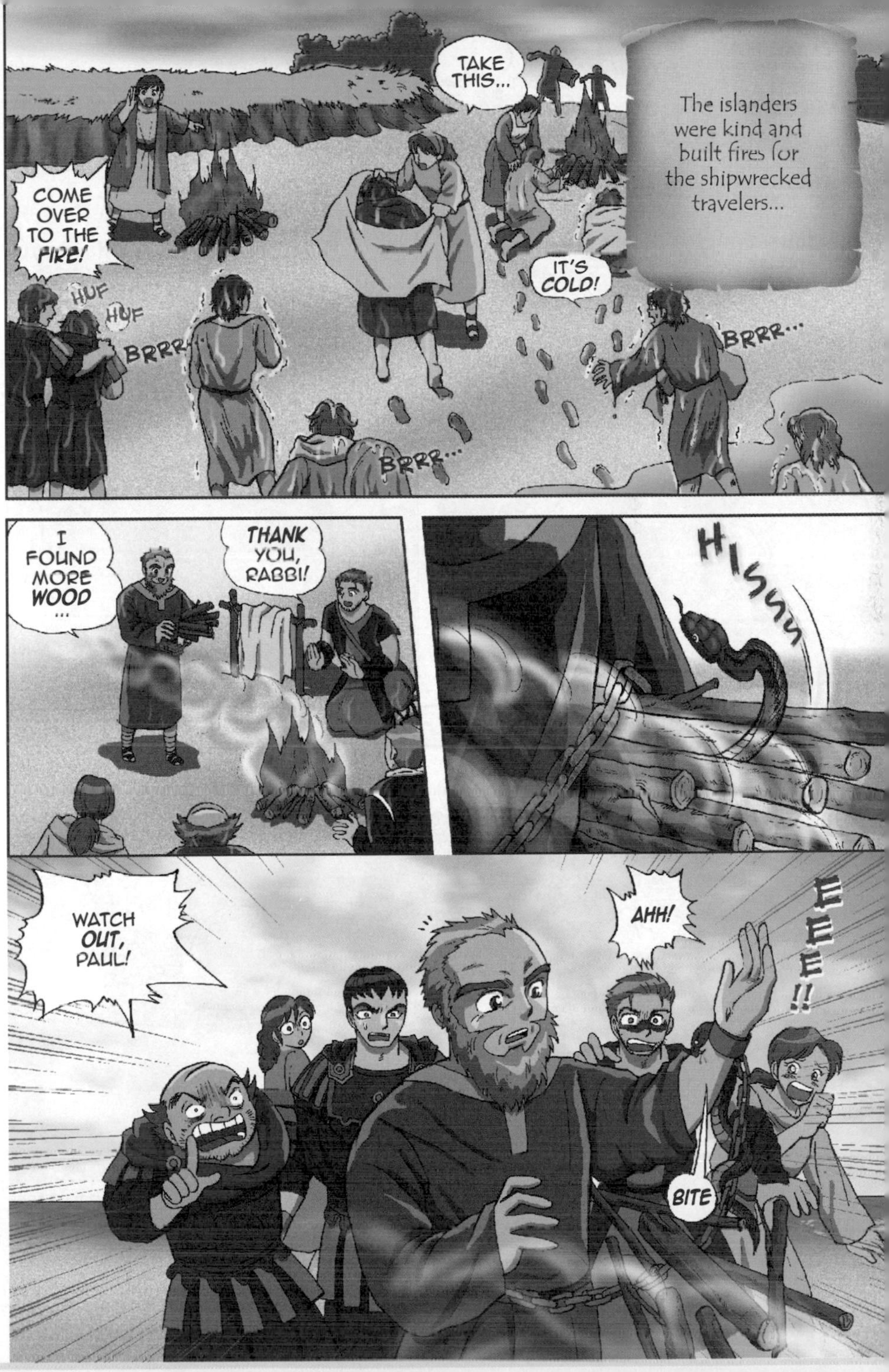

The islanders were kind and built fires for the shipwrecked travelers...
TAKE THIS...
COME OVER TO THE FIRE!
IT'S COLD!
HUF
HUF
BRRR
BRRR...
BRRR...
I FOUND MORE WOOD ...
THANK YOU, RABBI!
HISSSS
WATCH OUT, PAUL!
AHH!
EEE!!
BITE

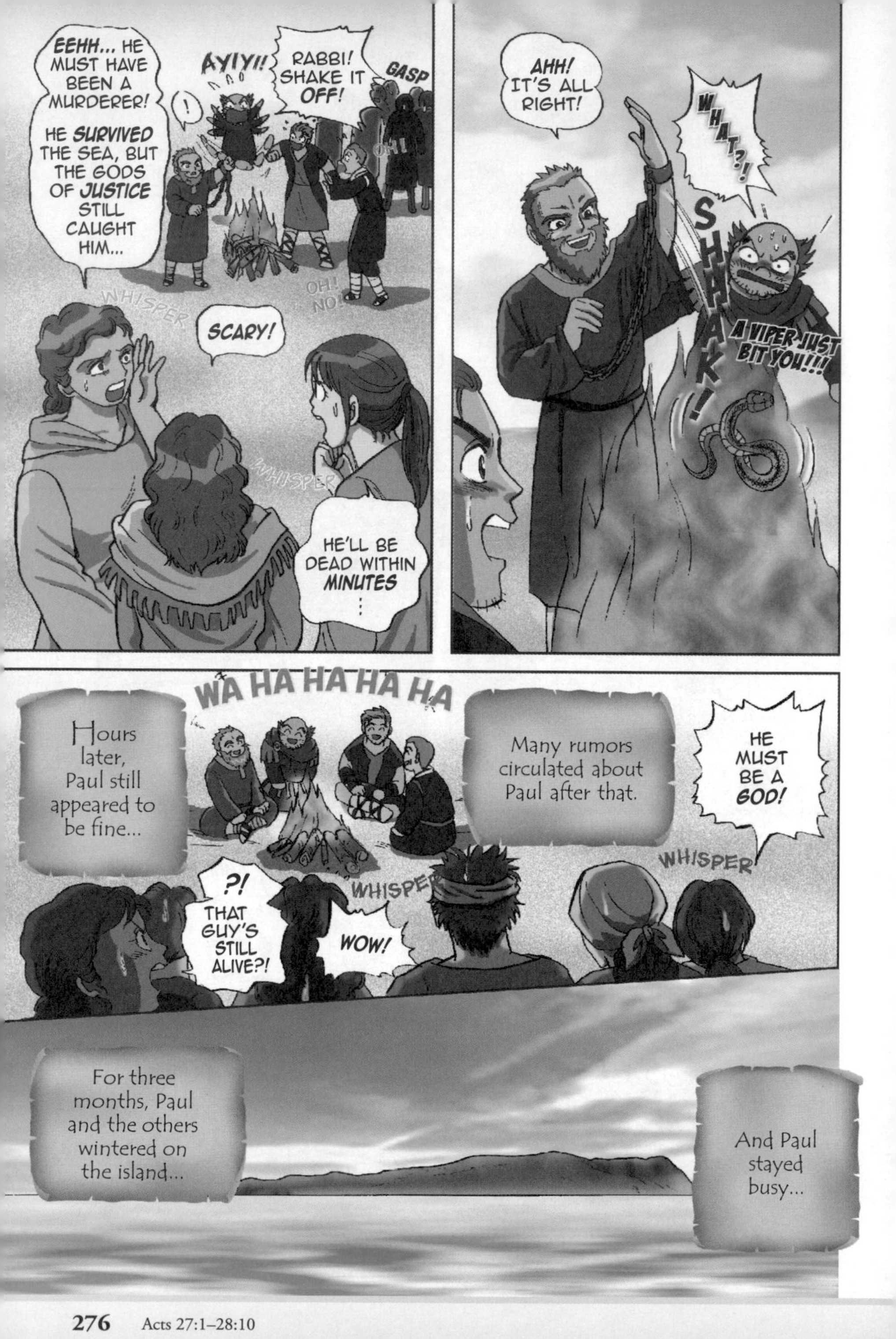
EEHH... HE MUST HAVE BEEN A MURDERER!
HE SURVIVED THE SEA, BUT THE GODS OF JUSTICE STILL CAUGHT HIM...
AYIYI!!
!
RABBI! SHAKE IT OFF!
GASP
OH!
OH! NO!
WHISPER
SCARY!
WHISPER
HE'LL BE DEAD WITHIN MINUTES
...
AHH! IT'S ALL RIGHT!
WHAT?!
SHHAAK!
A VIPER JUST BIT YOU!!!
WA HA HA HA HA
Hours later, Paul still appeared to be fine...
Many rumors circulated about Paul after that.
HE MUST BE A GOD!
WHISPER
?!
THAT GUY'S STILL ALIVE?!
WHISPER
WOW!
For three months, Paul and the others wintered on the island...
And Paul stayed busy...

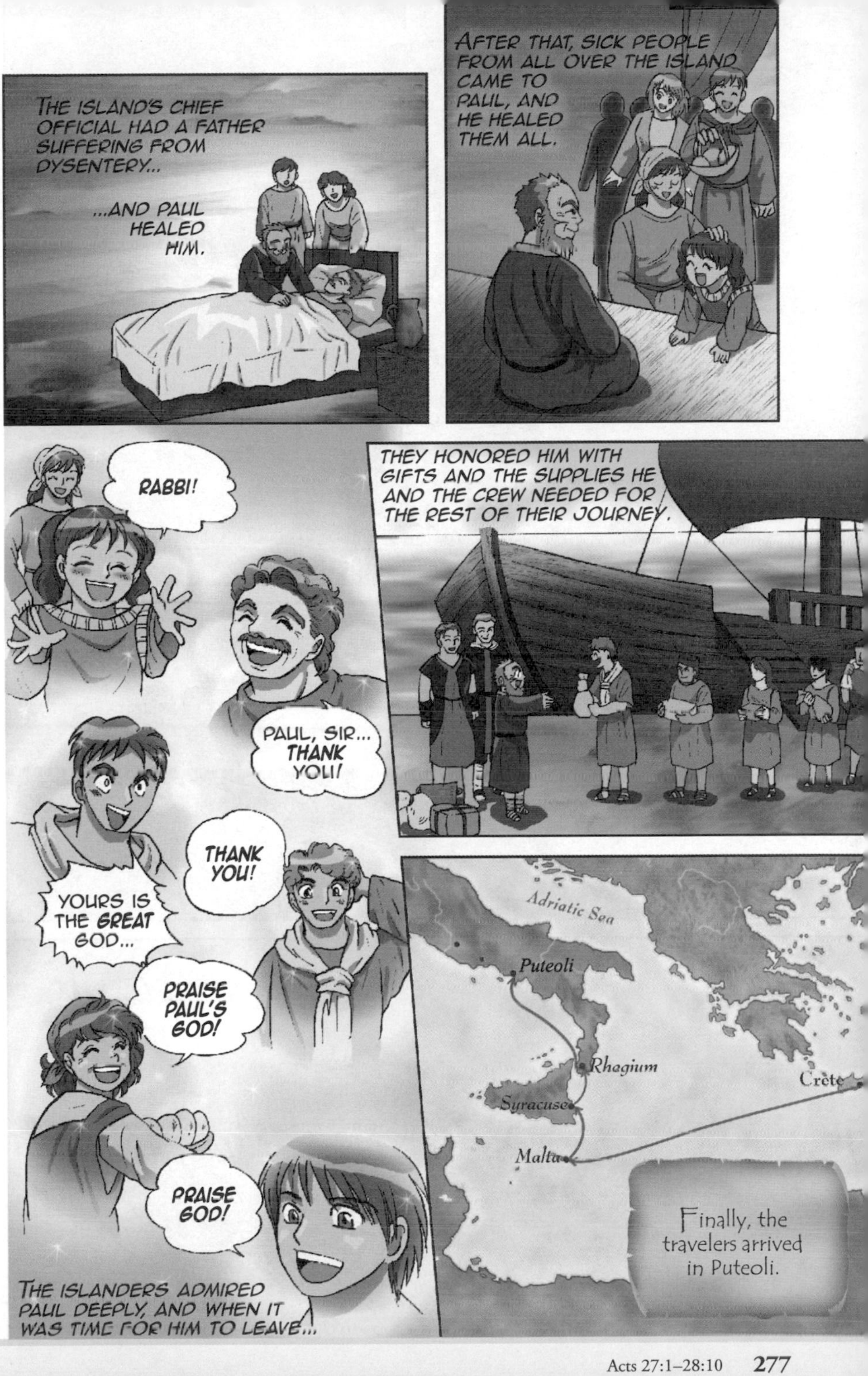
THE ISLAND'S CHIEF OFFICIAL HAD A FATHER SUFFERING FROM DYSENTERY...
...AND PAUL HEALED HIM.
AFTER THAT, SICK PEOPLE FROM ALL OVER THE ISLAND CAME TO PAUL, AND HE HEALED THEM ALL.
RABBI!
PAUL, SIR... THANK YOU!
THANK YOU!
YOURS IS THE GREAT GOD...
PRAISE PAUL'S GOD!
PRAISE GOD!
THE ISLANDERS ADMIRED PAUL DEEPLY, AND WHEN IT WAS TIME FOR HIM TO LEAVE...
THEY HONORED HIM WITH GIFTS AND THE SUPPLIES HE AND THE CREW NEEDED FOR THE REST OF THEIR JOURNEY.
Adriatic Sea
Puteoli
Rhegium
Crete
Syracuse
Malta
Finally, the travelers arrived in Puteoli.

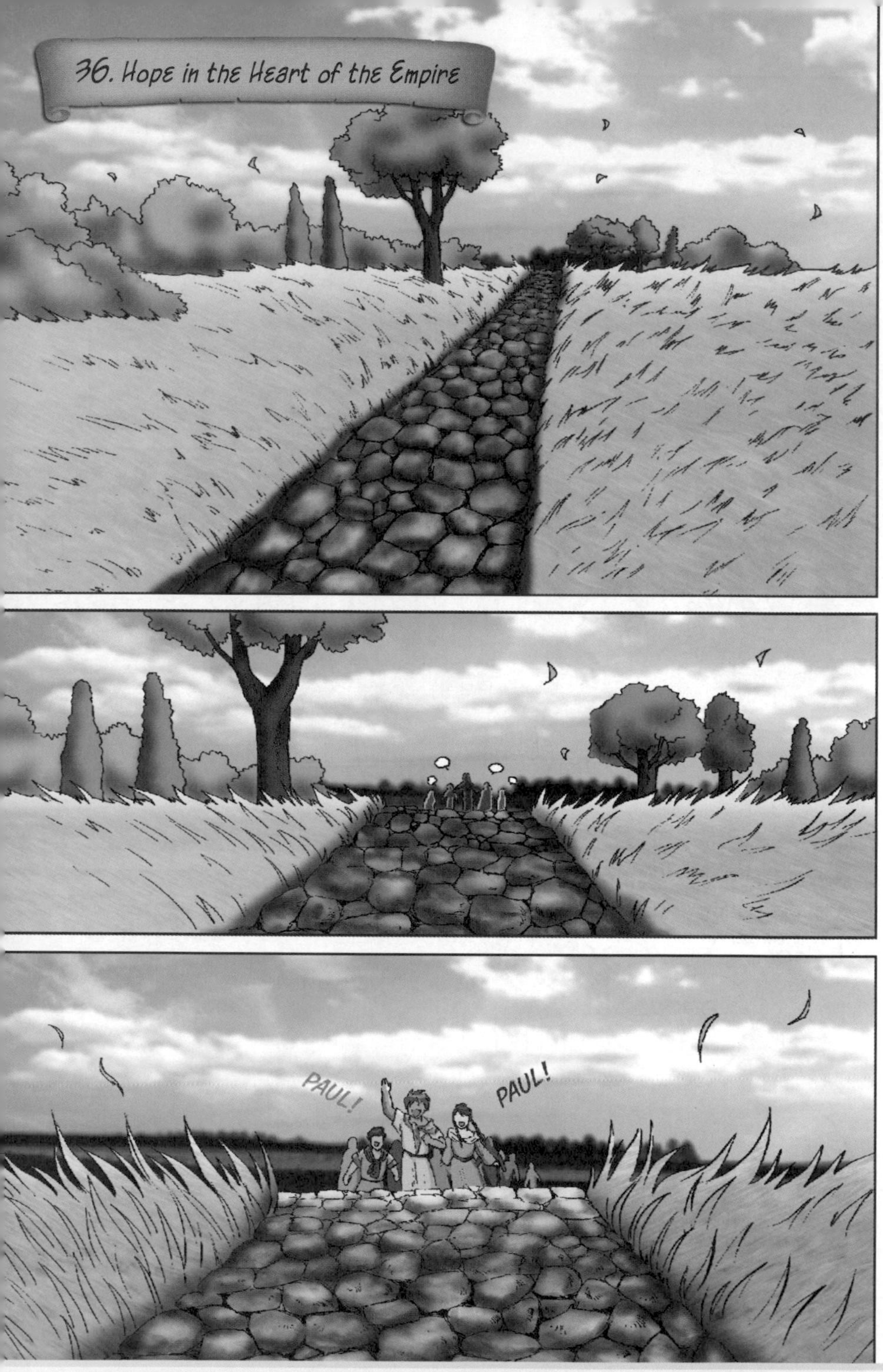
36. Hope in the Heart of the Empire
PAUL!
PAUL!

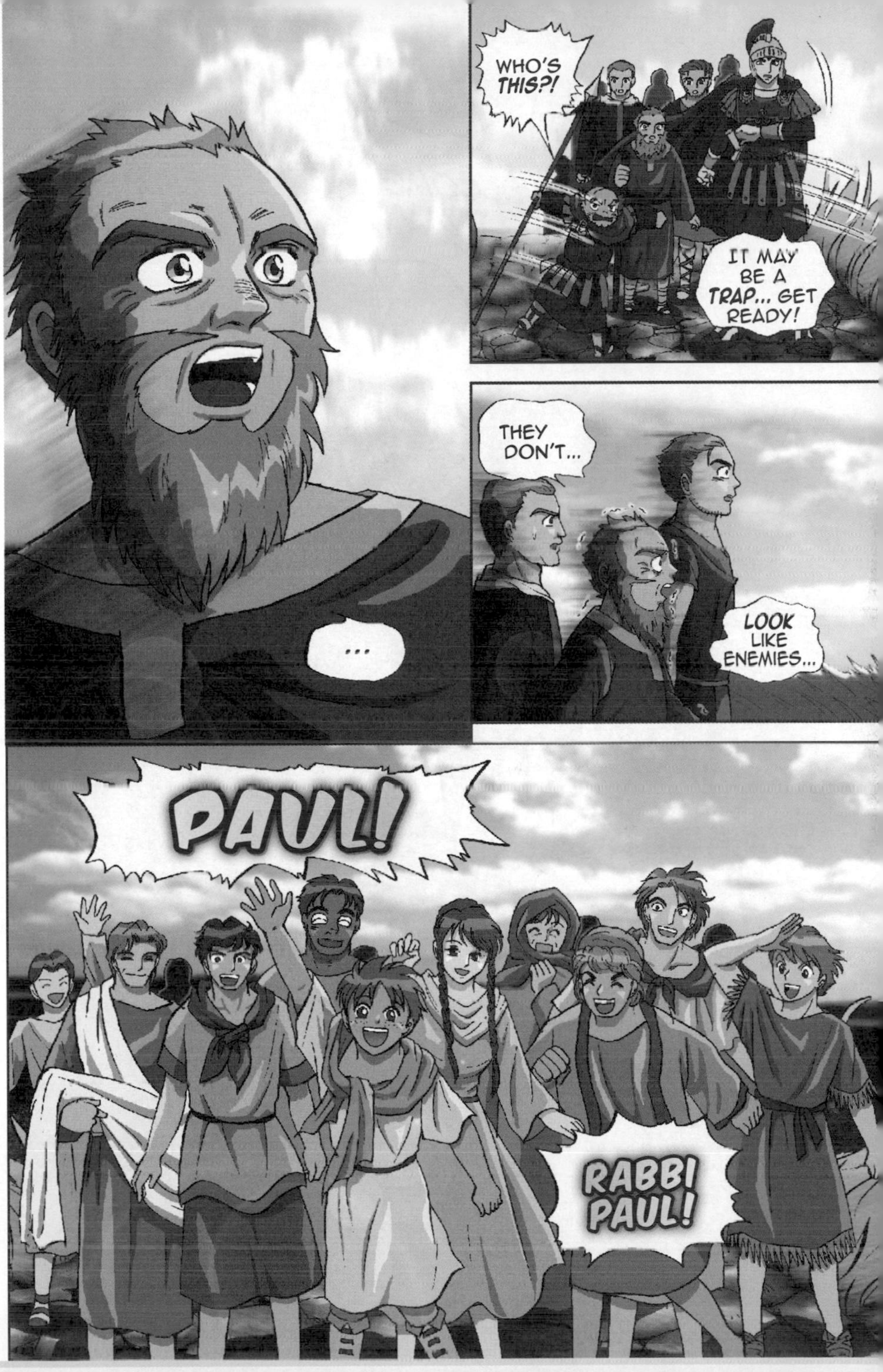
...
WHO'S THIS?!
IT MAY BE A TRAP... GET READY!
THEY DON'T...
LOOK LIKE ENEMIES...
PAUL!
RABBI PAUL!

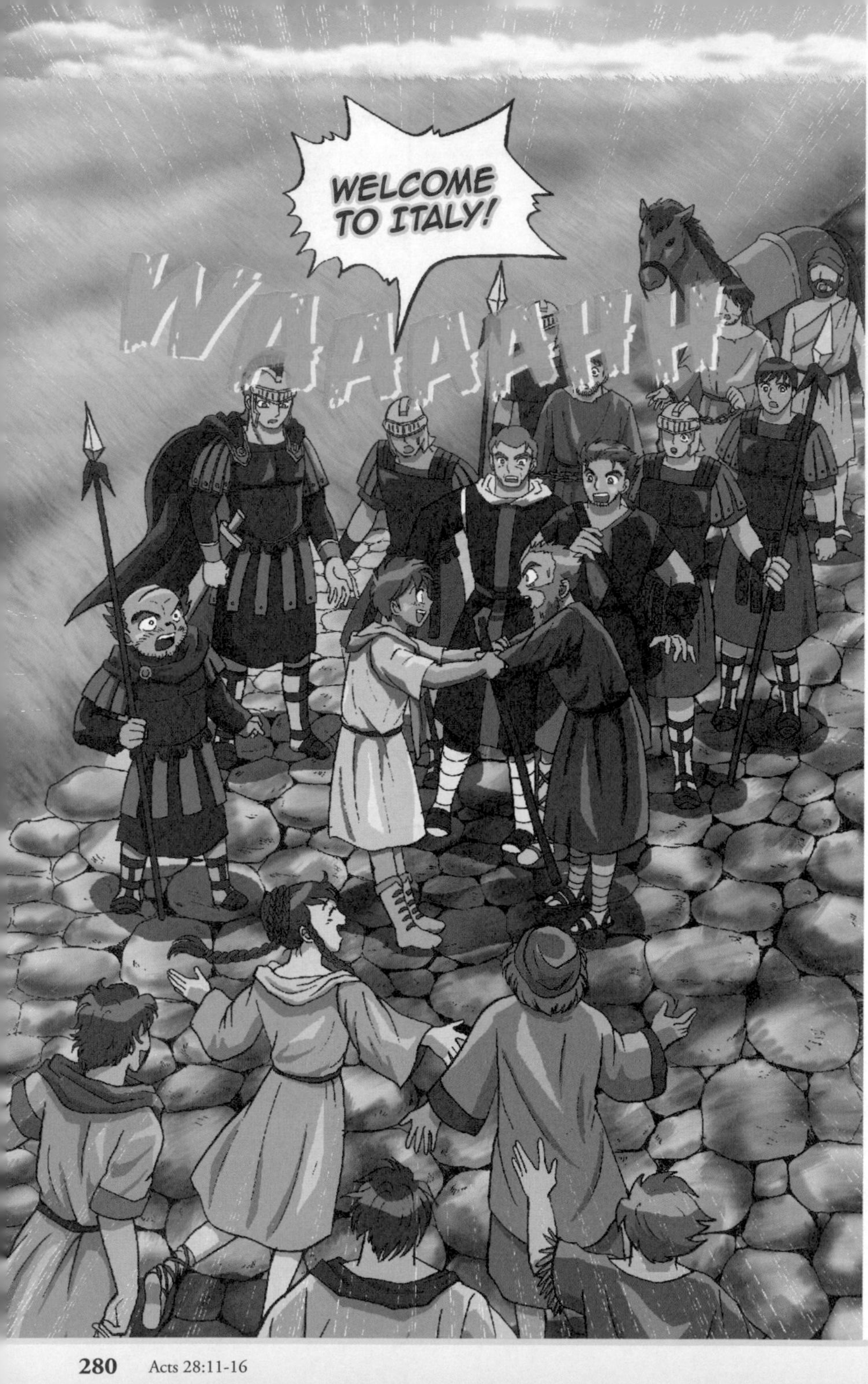
WELCOME TO ITALY!
WAAAHH

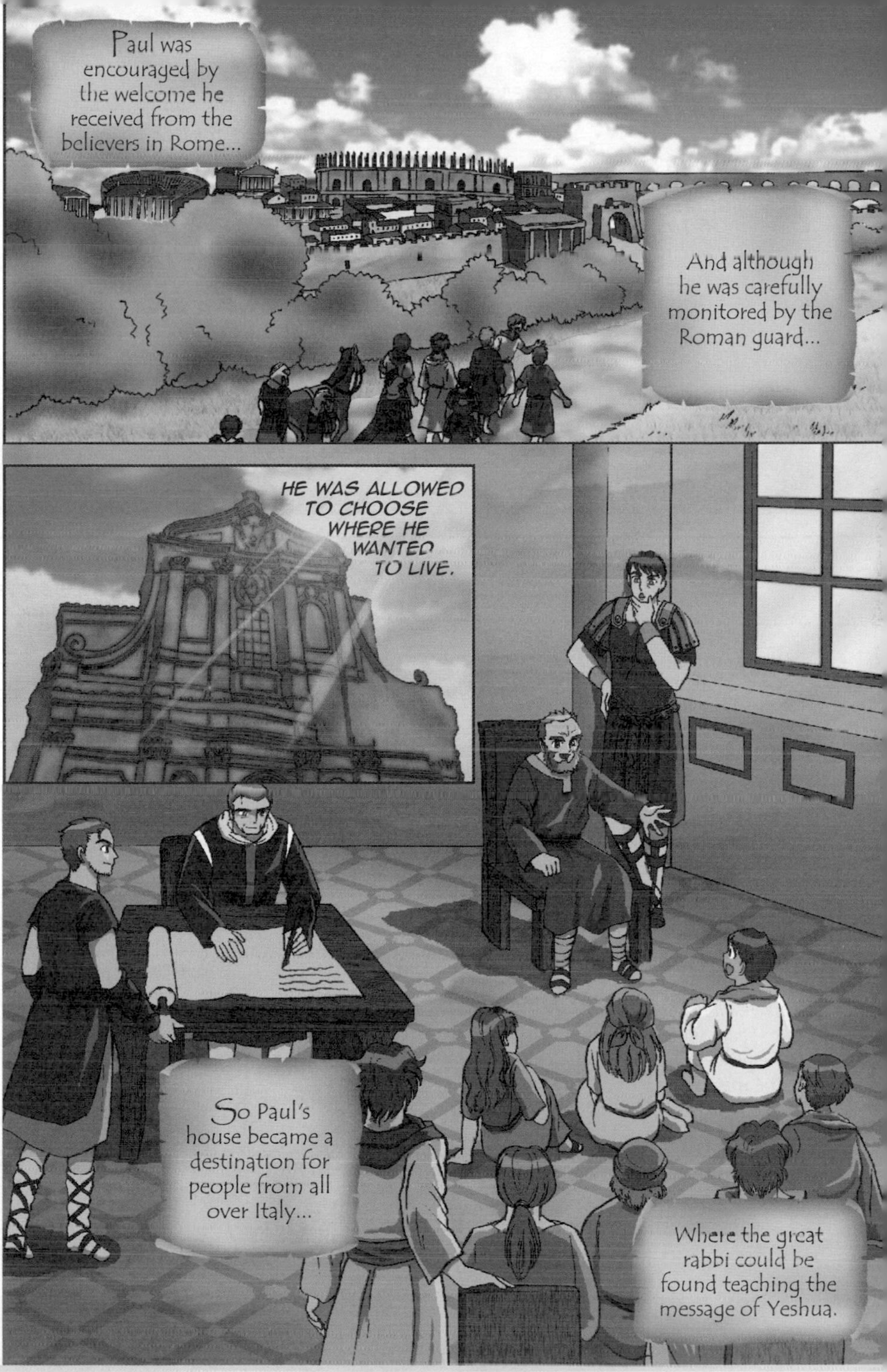
Paul was encouraged by the welcome he received from the believers in Rome...
And although he was carefully monitored by the Roman guard...
HE WAS ALLOWED TO CHOOSE WHERE HE WANTED TO LIVE.
So Paul's house became a destination for people from all over Italy...
Where the great rabbi could be found teaching the message of Yeshua.

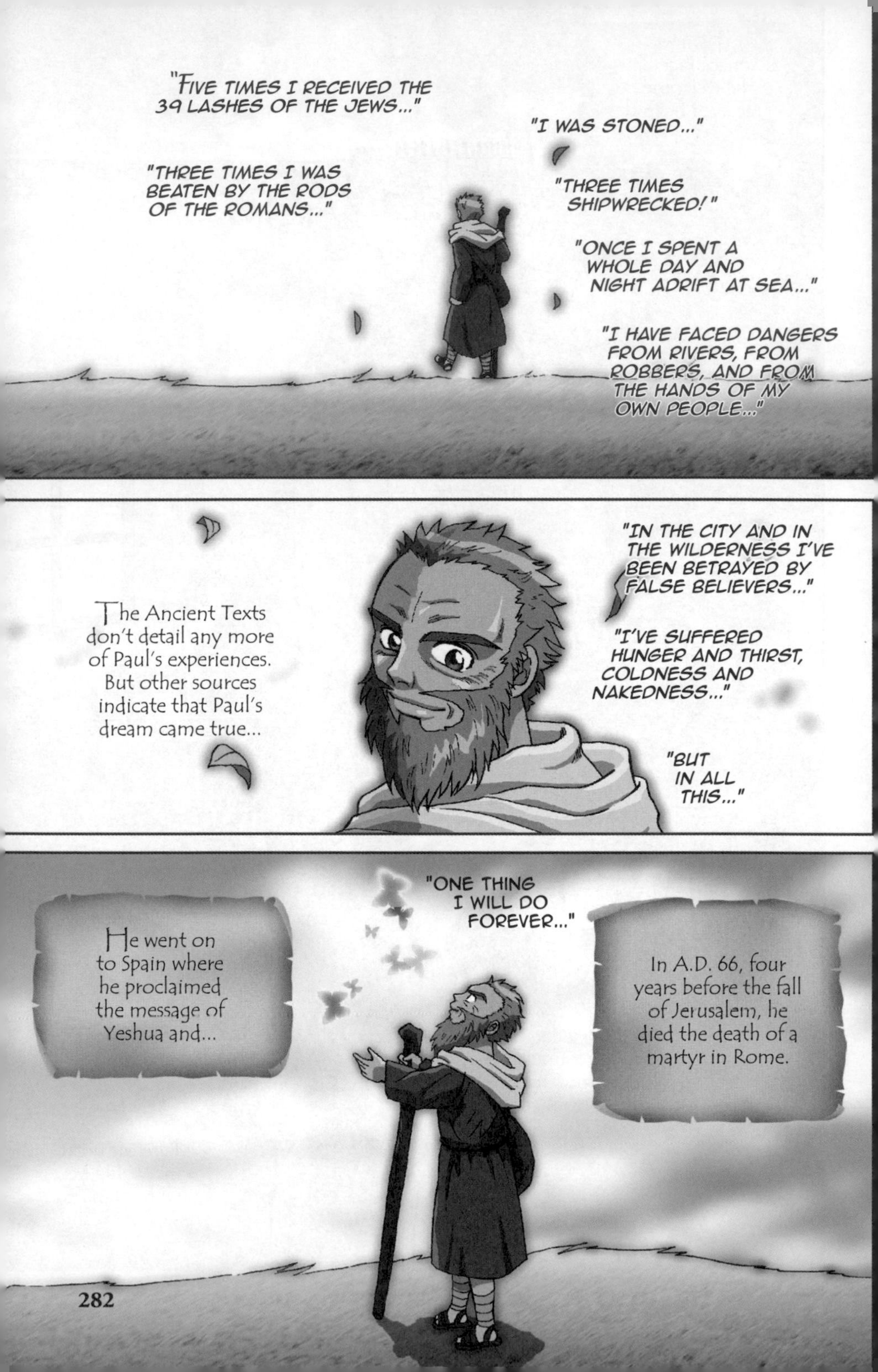
"FIVE TIMES I RECEIVED THE 39 LASHES OF THE JEWS..."
"THREE TIMES I WAS BEATEN BY THE RODS OF THE ROMANS..."
"I WAS STONED..."
"THREE TIMES SHIPWRECKED!"
"ONCE I SPENT A WHOLE DAY AND NIGHT ADRIFT AT SEA..."
"I HAVE FACED DANGERS FROM RIVERS, FROM ROBBERS, AND FROM THE HANDS OF MY OWN PEOPLE..."
The Ancient Texts don't detail any more of Paul's experiences. But other sources indicate that Paul's dream came true...
"IN THE CITY AND IN THE WILDERNESS I'VE BEEN BETRAYED BY FALSE BELIEVERS..."
"I'VE SUFFERED HUNGER AND THIRST, COLDNESS AND NAKEDNESS..."
"BUT IN ALL THIS..."
He went on to Spain where he proclaimed the message of Yeshua and...
"ONE THING I WILL DO FOREVER..."
In A.D. 66, four years before the fall of Jerusalem, he died the death of a martyr in Rome.

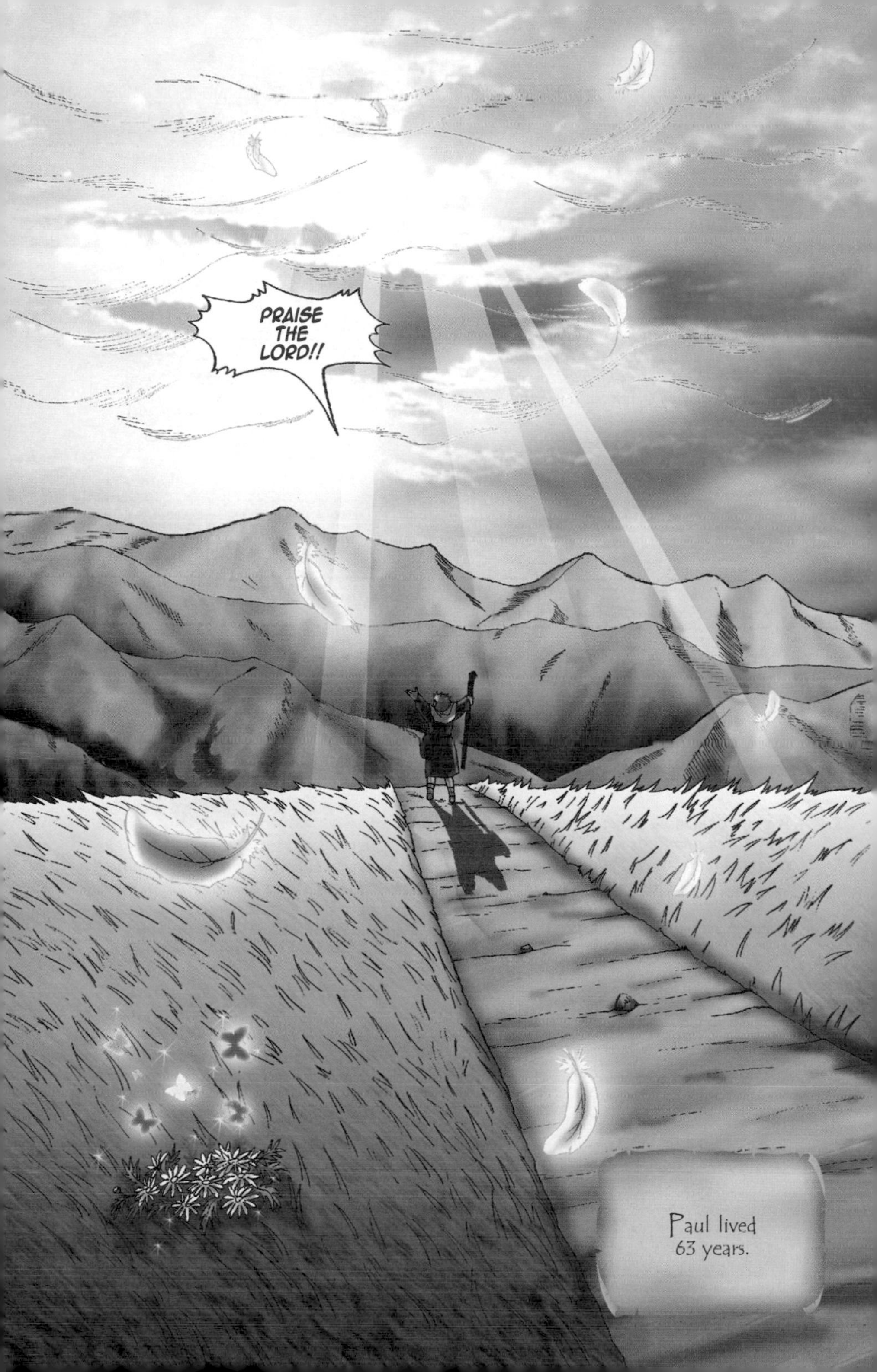
PRAISE THE LORD!!
Paul lived 63 years.

CHARACTER PROFILES

Messiah Yeshua

The Savior, who overcame crucifixion and death through his resurrection power. He appeared to many afterward in various places. People placed their hope in him, and all who met him after he was raised from the dead experienced a great change of heart.

Peter

When Yeshua said, "I will build my Church upon this rock," he was referring to Peter. In Yeshua's name, Peter performed many miracles, and the foundation of the church was laid. It was exactly as Yeshua said.

Paul

His former name was Saul, and he was a born-and-bred Jew. Although he started out as a belligerent persecutor who was determined to wipe out the name of Yeshua, he encountered Yeshua on the road to Damascus and changed his heart. After that, he became a bold preacher of Yeshua's name and resurrection. Although he caused a ruckus everywhere he went, it didn't faze him. He was determined to live the rest of his life to preach his Savior, Yeshua.

Stephen

Stephen was a man filled with the Spirit and wisdom. In accordance with his duty, he daily rationed out food to all who gathered. Although he was loved by the townspeople, others were jealous and had him stoned to death. He became the first martyr for the faith, but before taking his last breath, he witnessed Yeshua standing at the right hand of God the Father.

Mark

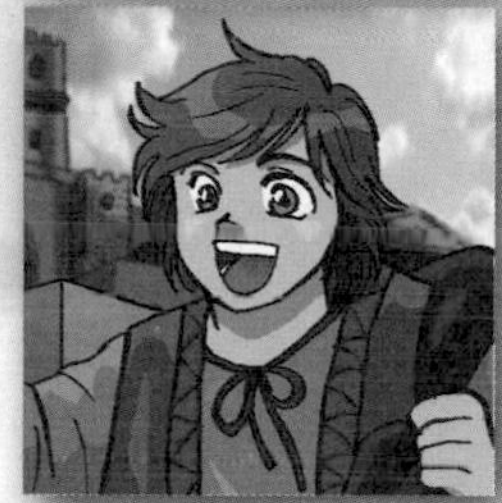

Mark was born in Jerusalem. He accompanied his cousin Barnabas on Paul's first missionary journey, but he left them along the way. Eventually maturing under Barnabas's guidance, he became an interpreter and secretary, actively participating in the work of the faith alongside Paul and Peter. Later he wrote the Gospel of Mark.

Barnabas

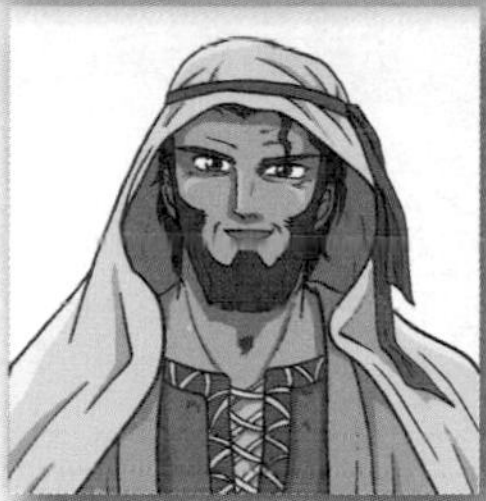

Barnabas was a citizen of Cyprus and a pioneer evangelist. Although fearing post-conversion Paul, he arranged a meeting between Paul and Peter, which eventually led to Paul's being accepted among the apostles. He recognized Paul's gift as an evangelist and accompanied him on his first missionary journey.

Cornelius

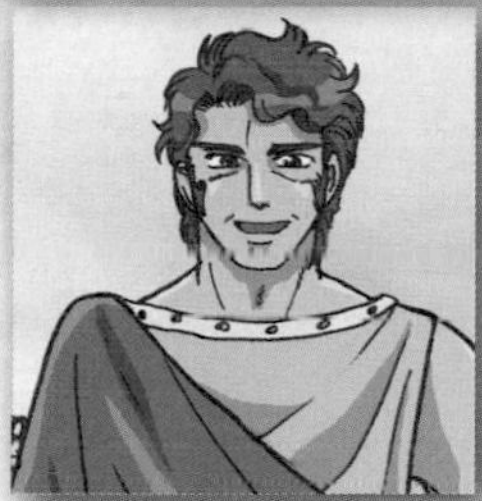

A Roman centurion and God-fearing man, Cornelius obeyed the angel of God and invited Peter to his home. There he believed in Yeshua and was baptized. He was the first Gentile to become a Christian.

Timothy

A young man whose father was Greek and mother was Jewish, he went along as an assistant on Paul's second and third missionary journeys.

Silas

As a helper replacing Barnabas, he accompanied Paul on his trip to Asia Minor. He was also known as a prophet.

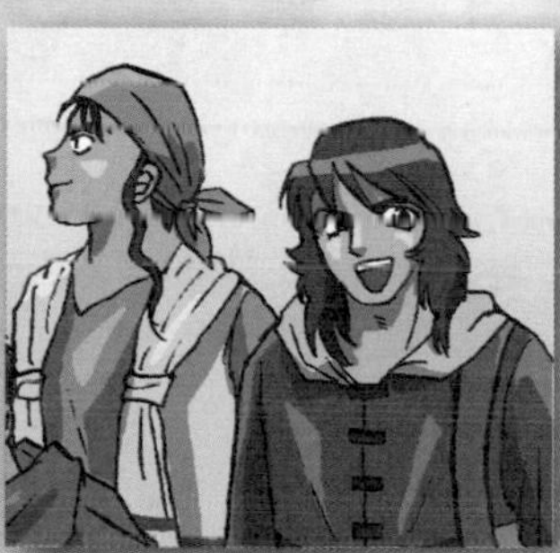

Priscilla & Aquila

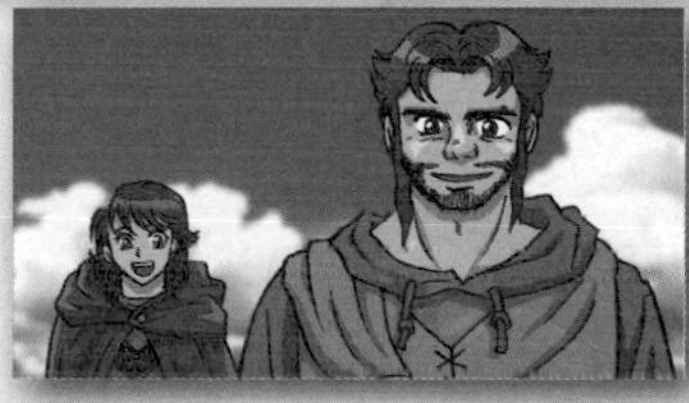

A Jewish couple whose occupation was tent-making, they met Paul in Corinth after Emperor Claudius ordered them to leave Rome, providing Paul with physical and spiritual care.

Luke

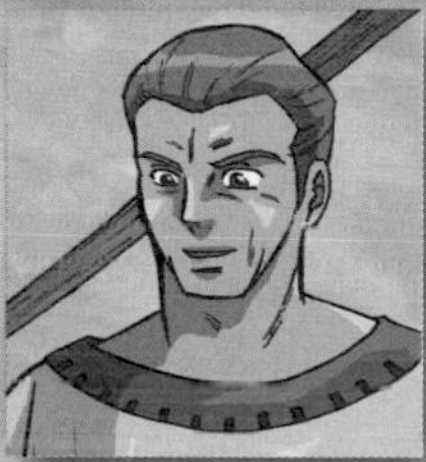

A physician who cared for Paul when he became ill at Troas, he accompanied Paul on his second and third missionary journeys and eventually chronicled these events in the Acts of the Apostles. He also wrote the Gospel of Luke.

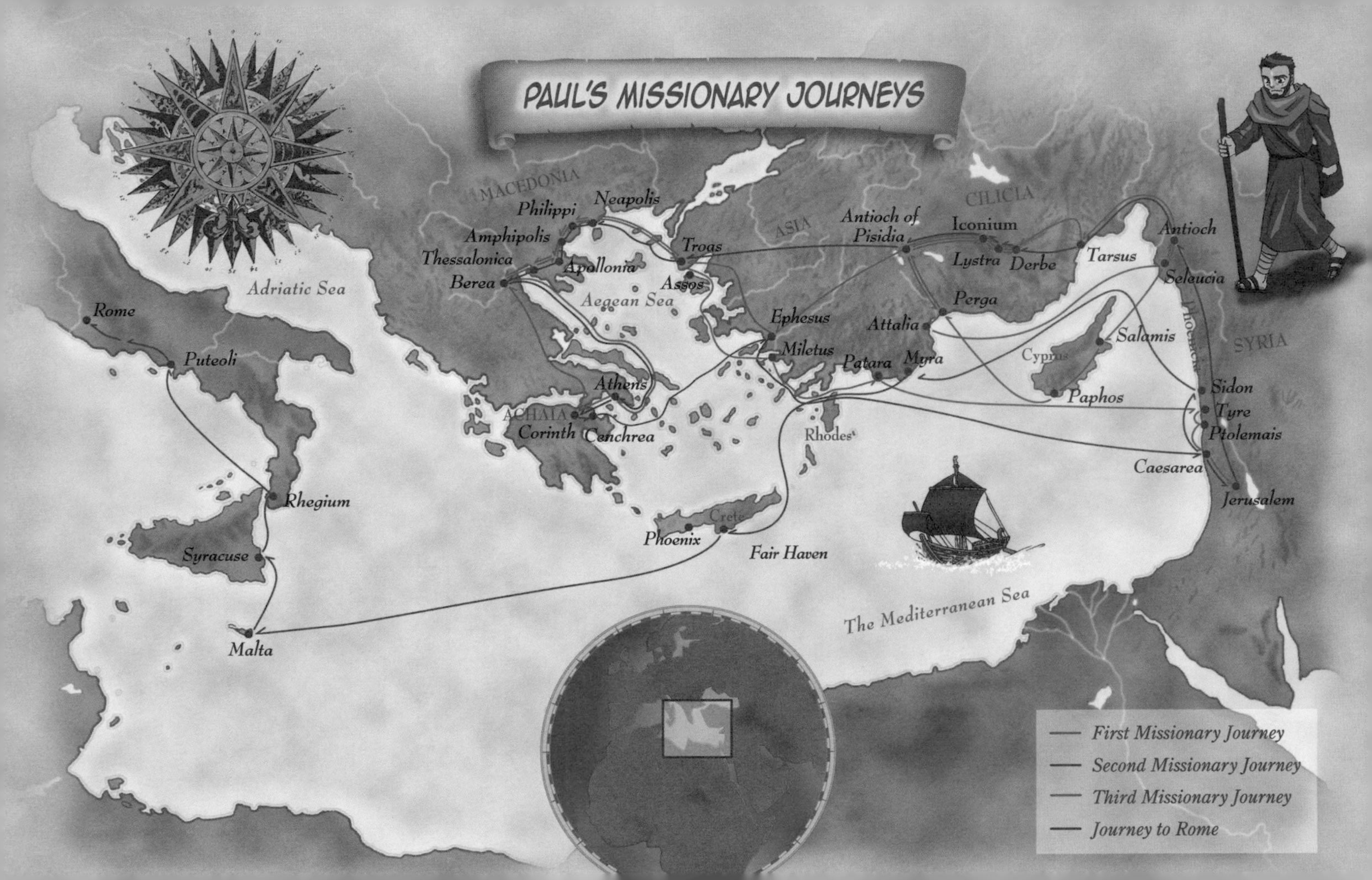
PAUL'S MISSIONARY JOURNEYS
MACEDONIA
Philippi
Neapolis
Amphipolis
Thessalonica
Apollonia
Berea
Troas
Assos
Aegean Sea
Adriatic Sea
Rome
Puteoli
ASIA
Antioch of Pisidia
Iconium
Lystra
Derbe
CILICIA
Tarsus
Antioch
Seleucia
Ephesus
Miletus
Attalia
Perga
Patara
Myra
Athens
ACHAIA
Corinth
Cenchrea
Rhodes
Cyprus
Salamis
Paphos
SYRIA
Sidon
Tyre
Ptolemais
Caesarea
Jerusalem
Rhegium
Syracuse
Malta
Crete
Phoenix
Fair Haven
The Mediterranean Sea
First Missionary Journey
Second Missionary Journey
Third Missionary Journey
Journey to Rome

CHRONOLOGY (A.D.)

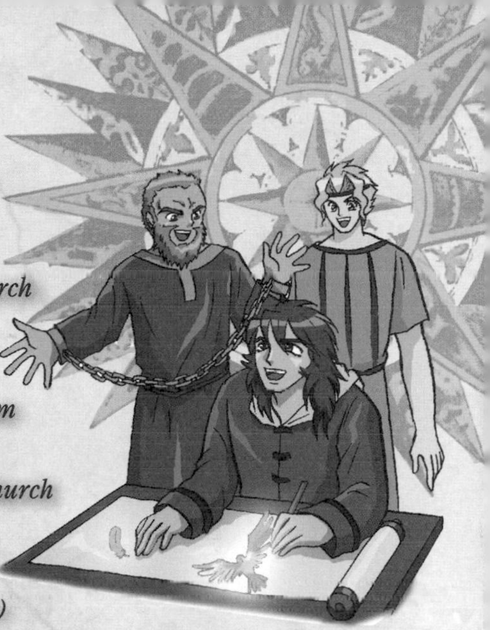

About Year 30	*Yeshua's crucifixion*	
.	*The birth of Jerusalem church*	
About Year 32	*Stephen's martyrdom*	
	Paul's conversion	
About Year 34	*Paul's first visit to Jerusalem*	
	Cornelius's conversion	
About Year 42	*The birth of the Antioch church (the first Gentile church)*	
About Year 47–48	*Paul's first mission (to Galatia in Asia Minor)*	
About Year 48	*Apostles' council at Jerusalem*	
Year 49–52	*Paul's second mission (to Macedonia and Greece)*	Letters to the Thessalonians 1 & 2
	Churches birthed at Philippi, Corinth, and Thessalonica	
Year 54–57	*Paul's third mission (to Greece and west Asia Minor)*	Letters to the Corinthians 1 & 2 Letter to the Galatians Letter to the Philippians Letter to Philemon Letter to the Ephesians Letter to the Colossians Letter to the Romans
Year 57	*Paul to Macedonia*	
Year 57–58	*Paul to Corinth*	
Year 58–60	*Paul's stay at Caesarea*	
Year 60–61	*Paul to Rome*	
Year 61–63	*Paul's imprisonment in Rome*	
	Peter and Paul martyred in Rome	Letters of Peter 1 & 2 Letter of James Letter to the Hebrews
Year 64	*Persecution by Nero*	
Year 66–70	*Coming Jewish war*	
Year 70	*Destruction of the Jewish Temple*	Letters to Timothy 1 & 2 Letter to Titus Letter of Jude
Year 95	*Persecution by Emperor Domitian*	Revelation of John
Year 313	*Recognition of the Christian church*	
Year 392	*Christianity made state religion in Roman Empire*